SECOND EDITION
Service Management and Operations

Cengiz Haksever
Rider University

Barry Render
Rollins College

Roberta S. Russell
Virginia Polytechnic Institute and State University

Robert G. Murdick
Florida Atlantic University

Prentice Hall, Upper Saddle River, New Jersey 07458

Senior Editor: Tom Tucker
Editorial Assistant: Kerri Limpert
Editor-in-Chief: Natalie Anderson
Assistant Editor: Kristen Imperatore
Marketing Manager: Debbie Clare
Director of Production: Michael Weinstein
Production Manager: Gail Steier de Acevedo
Production Coordinator: Maureen Wilson
Permissions Coordinator: Monica Stipanov
Manufacturing Buyer: Natacha St. Hill Moore
Senior Manufacturing Manager: Vincent Scelta
Cover Design: Cheryl Asherman
Cover Photos: Michael Busselle/Tony Stone Images
Full Service Composition: Rainbow Graphics, LLC

Library of Congress Cataloging-in-Publication Data
Service management and operations / Cengiz Haksever ... [et al].—2nd ed.
    p.   cm.
    Includes bibliographical references and index.
    ISBN 0-13-081338-9
    1. Service industries—Management.   I. Haksever, Cengiz.

   HD9980.5 .S42517   2000
   658 21—dc21

                       99-045709

Prentice-Hall International (UK) Limited, London
Prentice-Hall of Australia Pty. Limited, Sydney
Prentice-Hall Canada, Inc., Toronto
Prentice-Hall Hispanoamericana, S.A., Mexico
Prentice-Hall of India Private Limited, New Delhi
Prentice-Hall of Japan, Inc., Tokyo
Prentice-Hall (Singapore) Pte Ltd.
Editora Prentice-Hall do Brasil, Ltda., Rio de Janeiro

Printed in the United States of America

10 9 8 7 6 5 4 3 2

This book is dedicated to
Ozan—CH
and to
Donna, Charlie, and Jesse—BR

Brief Contents

Contents

Preface

This second edition of *Service Management and Operations* includes significant changes from our first edition, written one decade ago. Seven entirely new chapters have been added, and major revisions have been made in seven chapters. The text is now reorganized into four parts with extensive new cases.

Service Encounters, Globalization of Services, Service Design and Development, and Service Productivity are new to this edition. These have emerged as important topics to service managers and scholars and we believe they deserve more attention. Three other new chapters are Customers as the Focus of Service Management, Service Strategy and Competitiveness, and Management of Public and Private Nonprofit Organizations.

Part I consists of chapters 1 through 6 and focuses on *understanding services*. It introduces students to the service concept and provides background material in several important areas. Chapter 1 addresses the role of services in our society. Chapter 2 discusses characteristics of services and examines the importance of the service encounter. Chapter 3 focuses on the customer as a consumer of services and his or her needs and motives as they impact service purchase decisions. Chapter 4 provides an international perspective on services and discusses the challenges of globalization. Chapter 5 prepares the groundwork for the three themes of quality, customer satisfaction, and value creation, and focuses on the impact of strategy on competitiveness. Chapter 6 explores the relationship between the marketing and operations functions in a service organization.

The emphasis of Part II is on *building the system to create customer value and satisfaction* with superior quality services. Chapter 7 focuses on the role technology plays in service management. Chapter 8 lays out the principles of service design and discusses the application of techniques that have been successfully used in manufacturing to build quality and value into services. Chapter 9 focuses on human resource development issues for the creation of customer value and satisfaction. A special topic related to this chapter, Work Measurement, is presented in a supplement. Chapter 10 discusses two other important topics in building the system: facility location and layout design.

Part III is concerned with issues related to *operating the service system* and challenges managers of service organizations face. One of the major challenges, managing the demand for and supply of services, is the topic of Chapter 11. A supplement to this chapter covers two important topics: queuing and simulation. Chapter 12 provides the basic concepts of quality in general and service quality in particular. Technical aspects of quality assurance are presented in a supplement. One of the biggest challenges service managers face is increasing the productivity of service employees. This important topic and approaches to increasing productivity in service organizations are discussed in chapter 13. We also present a brief discussion of data envelopment analysis as a powerful tool in measuring the efficiency of service organizations. Part III concludes with a discussion of a very important segment of the service industry: public and nonprofit service organizations. We discuss the nature of these organizations as well as the challenges their managers face.

Part IV presents the *tools and techniques for managing service operations*. Forecasting, Vehicle Routing and Scheduling, Project Management, Linear and Goal Programming, and Inventory Systems for Service Operations are included in this section. Instructors preferring a quantitative approach in their course can use Part IV extensively.

This text has been written from a multidisciplinary perspective. Discussions of topics blend concepts, theory, and practice from fields such as operations, marketing, international management, economics, strategy, psychology, human resources, and management science. This text is suitable for a service management course with or without quantitative orientation. It is also suitable for a traditional operations management course with special emphasis on services.

The text contains more material than one could normally cover in a one-semester course. Chapters are written independently of each other. Consequently, instructors have flexibility in selecting the chapters they want to cover and the order in which they are covered to tailor their course to suit their objectives.

Some professors put a lot of emphasis on, and allocate considerable time to, case discussion in their teaching. Consequently, they choose textbooks that have a large number of good cases, preferably comprehensive ones. Others may also use cases but allocate less class time to them; hence, they may prefer shorter cases. We have tried to accommodate both approaches by including one short and one long case at the end of most nonquantitative chapters. As in the first edition, we have included discussion questions at the end of each chapter and problems at the end of quantitative chapters.

ACKNOWLEDGMENTS

The authors wish to thank the following reviewers of the second edition for their contribution: Leland Nicholls, University of Wisconsin–Stout; Paul Mulligan, Babson College; Sidhartha Das, George Mason University; Sal Agnihothri, Binghamton University; Abdel Aziz Mohamed, California State University–Northridge; Hugh Williamson, University of Wisconsin–Stout.

We also acknowledge the contributions of the following reviewers to the first edition: James L. Heskett, David A. Collier, Vincent A. Mabert, Aleda V. Roth, Tim Davis, Ted Helmer, Scott Shafer, John Larsen, Asoo Vahkaria, Peter Mills, Pradeep Korgaonkar, Sid Das, and Joanna Baker.

We appreciate the support and continual encouragement of our editor Tom Tucker and his assistant Kerri Limpert. We are also thankful for the competent and professional work of Maureen Wilson, Debbie Claire, Karen Goldsmith, Monica Stipanov, and Kristen Imperatore of Prentice Hall. Last but not the least, we thank Melissa Steffens for her tireless efforts in providing important material to the first author in preparing this second edition.

CHAPTER 1

Services in Our Society

1.1   INTRODUCTION

There has been a surge of interest in all aspects of service management in recent times. Many books, articles, and research papers on services and service management have appeared in the popular as well as academic business literature during the 1980s and 1990s. The impetus for this phenomenon can be traced back to two major developments in our recent history. First, the quality movement that started in the 1980s had brought most consumers, news media, and academicians to the realization that the overall quality of services in the United States was not ideal, acceptable, or competitive in the international markets. Second, the fact that services no longer formed the least important (e.g., "tertiary") sector of the economy became obvious. Contrary to the once widely held view among economists, services in the second half of the twentieth century had increasingly played a significant role in the economic life in the United States as well as in all industrialized countries.

Growing attention paid to service quality and customer satisfaction had stirred managers of many service organizations into action. Even the executives and managers of one service conglomerate almost everyone loved to criticize, the federal government, were not immune to the mounting pressure.[1] A lot has been done to improve quality and customer satisfaction in most service industries during the 1980s and 1990s. As a result, there have been marked improvements in the quality of many services. Nevertheless, mediocre service quality is still a fact of life in the United States and around the world. A look at Exhibit 1-1 will confirm this fact.

Exhibit 1-1 presents a summary of American Customer Satisfaction Index (ACSI) numbers for 1994 to 1997. The ACSI is designed to measure the quality of goods and services as evaluated by customers. The index is based on surveys of the customers of over 200 organizations in more than 40 industries in seven major con-

---

[1] For improvements made in the federal government and its services, see Al Gore, Vice President of the United States, *The Best Kept Secrets in Government: A Report to President Clinton* (Washington, DC, National Performance Review, September 1997).

EXHIBIT 1-1   American Customer Satisfaction Index (ACSI) Results by Economic Sector Final 1997 Scores (0–100 Scale)

	1994	*1995*	*1996*	*1997*	*% Difference 1996–1997*
ACSI National Index	**74.5**	**73.7**	**72.2**	**71.1**	**–1.5**
SECTORS:					
Manufacturing					
Nondurables	81.6	81.2	79.0	78.5	–0.6
Durables	79.2	79.8	78.8	78.4	–0.5
Services					
Transportation, communications, and utilities	75.5	75.1	75.5	71.6	–5.2
Retail	75.7	73.6	74.6	73.2	–1.9
Finance and insurance	75.4	74.8	74.1	74.5	0.5
Miscellaneous services	74.4	74.2	71.2	67.7	–4.9
Public administration/ government	64.3	61.9	59.2	62.4	5.4

Source: American Customer Satisfaction Index 1994–1997, University of Michigan Business School, ASQ (American Society for Quality), Arthur Andersen. Copyright 1998, The Regents of the University of Michigan.

sumption areas.[2] It measures satisfaction by asking consumers to compare their expectations of a good or service with their actual experience with it. It is clear from this data that overall customer satisfaction with goods and services has declined since 1994. Exhibit 1-1 shows that customer satisfaction with three services declined from 1994 to 1997. Finance and insurance showed a slight improvement. A surprising outcome is the significant rise in satisfaction with government services. However, satisfaction with government services is still the lowest of all services.

Perhaps the most important revelation of the ACSI data is that no service in the recent past has had a customer satisfaction index equal to those for goods. It is not certain if an index of 100 percent satisfaction will ever be achieved, or if that is even possible, in any industry. However, it is clear that both private and public service organizations have a long way to go, and managers of these organizations face a tremendous challenge. Will they rise to the challenge and raise customer satisfaction with services to the same levels attained by manufacturers, or possibly surpass them? We certainly hope so! This book is written with the hope that it will help managers of service organizations develop strategies and practices to do so. We begin here in chapter 1 by defining services and exploring the role of services in our society.

1.2   WHAT ARE SERVICES?

The material gains of a society are achieved by adding value to natural resources. In advanced societies, there are many organizations that extract raw materials, add value through processing them, and transform intermediate materials and components into finished products. There are, however, other organizations that facilitate the production and

[2] Claes Fornell, Michael D. Johnson, Eugene W. Anderson, Jaesung Cha, and Barbara E. Bryant, "The American Customer Satisfaction Index: Nature, Purpose, and Findings," *Journal of Marketing*, vol. 60 (October 1996), pp. 7–18.

distribution of goods, and organizations that add value to our personal lives through a variety of intangibles they provide. Outputs of this latter group are called **services.**

Services can be defined as economic activities that produce time, place, form, or psychological utilities. Services are acts, deeds, or performances; they are intangible. A maid service saves the consumer's **time** from doing household chores himself. Department stores and grocery stores provide many commodities for sale in one convenient **place.** A database service puts together information in a **form** more usable for the manager. A night out at a restaurant or movie provides **psychological** refreshment in the middle of a busy workweek.

Services also can be defined in contrast to goods. A **good** is a tangible object that can be created and sold or used later. A service is intangible and perishable. It is created and consumed simultaneously (or nearly simultaneously). Although these definitions may seem straightforward, the distinction between goods and services is not always clear-cut. For example, when we purchase a car, are we purchasing a good or the service of transportation? A television set is a manufactured good, but what use is it without the service of television broadcasting? When we go to a fast-food restaurant, are we buying the service of having our food prepared for us or are we buying goods that happen to be ready-to-eat food items?

In reality, almost all purchases of goods are accompanied by **facilitating services,** and almost every service purchase is accompanied by **facilitating goods.** Thus, the key to understanding the difference between goods and services lies in the realization that these items are not completely distinct, but rather are two poles on a continuum. Exhibit 1-2 shows such a continuum.

Referring to Exhibit 1-2, the first three items would probably be classified as "goods" because of their high material content. There is little service in purchasing self-service gasoline; an automobile is mostly a physical item; and while its lease does require some service, a leased car is a good. Take-out food can be considered half good and half service. The remaining items would probably be classified as "services"

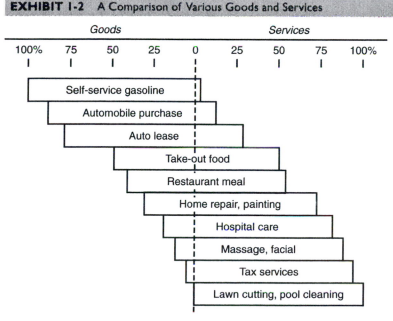

EXHIBIT 1-2   A Comparison of Various Goods and Services

Based on: Earl W. Sasser, Jr., R. P. Olsen, and D. Daryl Wyckoff, *Management of Service Operations* (Boston, Allyn and Bacon, 1978), p. 11.

because of their high service content, although some physical materials may be received. For instance, restaurants not only give the customer a meal of physical food and drink, but also a place to eat it, chefs to prepare it, waiters to serve it, and an atmosphere in which to dine. Tax preparation is almost pure service, with very little material goods (perhaps a finished tax return) received by the consumer. Can you identify the goods and services content of the other examples in Exhibit 1-2?

1.3   THE SERVICE SECTOR OF OUR ECONOMY

From a macro viewpoint, our economy may be divided into three different sectors for study: the extractive sector, which includes mining and agriculture, the goods-producing sector, which includes manufacturing and construction, and the service sector. The service sector has a tremendous impact on the U.S. economy. We discuss this impact under five headings: employment, gross domestic product, number of business starts, international trade, and contributions to manufacturing.

Employment   The role services play in terms of employment is the easiest to illustrate. The U.S. economy today is characterized as a *service economy*. This is because the majority of the working population is employed in the service sector. Trend analyst John Naisbitt made the following observation: "In 1956, for the first time in American history, white-collar workers in technical, managerial, and clerical positions outnumbered blue-collar workers. Industrial America was giving way to a new society, where, for the first time in history, most of us worked with information rather than producing goods."[3] The share of the service jobs grew steadily to 75 percent by the mid-1990s, and as indicated in Exhibit 1-3, it is expected to reach 80 percent by the

EXHIBIT 1-3   Employment Prospects for the Year 2005 (in millions)

Industry	1970		1980		1990		2005[a]	
Extraction	**4.08**	**5%**	**4.34**	**5%**	**3.93**	**4%**	**3.84**	**3%**
Agriculture	3.46		3.36		3.22		3.40	
Mining	0.62		1.03		0.71		0.44	
Goods Producing	**22.96**	**31%**	**24.64**	**26%**	**24.20**	**21%**	**22.49**	**17%**
Construction	3.59		4.35		5.12		5.50	
Manufacturing	19.37		20.29		19.08		16.99	
Service Producing	**47.31**	**64%**	**64.75**	**69%**	**84.50**	**75%**	**107.25**	**80%**
Transportation, communication, and utilities	4.52		5.15		5.79		6.43	
Wholesale trade	4.01		5.29		6.17		6.56	
Retail trade	11.03		15.02		19.60		23.09	
Finance, insurance, and real estate	3.65		5.16		6.71		7.37	
Miscellaneous services	11.55		17.89		27.93		42.81	
Government (federal, state, and local)	12.55		16.24		18.30		20.99	
Total Employed	**74.35**	**100%**	**93.73**	**100%**	**112.63**	**100%**	**133.58**	**100%**

[a]Projection.

Source: U.S. Bureau of the Census, *Statistical Abstract of the United States*, 1997 (Washington, DC, 1997).

[3] John Naisbitt, *Megatrends: Ten New Directions Transforming Our Lives* (New York, Warner Books, 1982), p. 12.

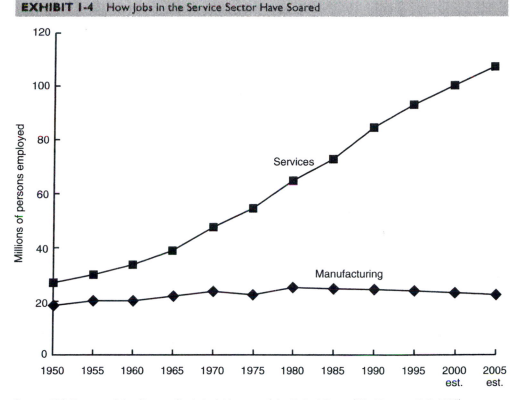

EXHIBIT I-4   How Jobs in the Service Sector Have Soared

Source: U.S. Bureau of the Census, *Statistical Abstract of the United States* (Washington, DC, 1997).

year 2005. In other words, anyone who is planning to enter the workforce today has about an 80 percent chance that she'll be working in a service organization. Exhibit 1-4 illustrates the dramatic increase in service jobs since 1950.

Gross Domestic Product   Gross domestic product (GDP) is the total output of goods and services produced in the United States, valued at market prices. In other words, GDP represents the total value of goods and services attributable to labor and resources located in the United States. Services will be producing more than 75 percent of GDP in the years ahead. Exhibit 1-5 presents data on the breakdown of GDP and change in its composition since 1970. It is clear from this exhibit that the service sector produces most of the value in our economy. This does not imply that manufacturing will eventually disappear or become unimportant, but does indicate that more of the economic activity will be in the service sector. As can be seen in Exhibit 1-6, the share of extraction industries has stabilized at about 3 percent of GDP since 1986. The share of goods production is expected to stabilize at about 20 percent, and services at about 77 percent, during the first few years of the twenty-first century.

Number of Business Starts   Some of the new jobs are created in the existing organizations as they grow, but others are created when new companies are established. The data in Exhibit 1-7 indicate that the service sector is where most new companies are formed. About 70 percent of all new private businesses are service companies. In other words, the service sector is "where the action is" and where entrepreneurial spirit is most vigorous.

EXHIBIT 1-5 Gross Domestic Product by Industry (in billions of dollars)

Industry	1970		1980		1990		2000[a]		2005[a]	
Extraction	**48.5**	**5%**	**179.4**	**7%**	**221.0**	**4%**	**246.3**	**3%**	**270.3**	**3%**
Agriculture	29.8		66.7		108.7		136.4		153.8	
Mining	18.7		112.7		112.3		109.9		116.5	
Goods Producing	**300.7**	**30%**	**713.0**	**16%**	**1,276.6**	**22%**	**1,814.3**	**21%**	**2,091.8**	**20%**
Construction	51.1		128.6		245.2		339.0		392.5	
Manufacturing	249.6		584.4		1031.4		1475.3		1699.3	
Service Producing	**684.5**	**66%**	**1,864.3**	**67%**	**4,228.8**	**74%**	**6,704.1**	**76%**	**7,940.5**	**77%**
Transportation, communications, and utilities	88.1		242.1		482.1		736.6		858.6	
Wholesale trade	72.1		195.2		367.2		573.5		671.6	
Retail trade	100.2		245.9		503.5		764.1		892.7	
Finance, insurance, and real estate	146.0		418.3		1,024.1		1,669.7		1,991.2	
Miscellaneous services	120.5		377.3		1,059.4		1,787.3		2,156.0	
Government (federal, state, and local)	157.6		385.5		792.5		1,172.9		1,370.4	
Statistical discrepancy	1.9	[b]	27.5	[b]	17.4	[b]				
Total	**1,035.6**	**100%**	**2,784.2**	**100%**	**5,743.8**	**100%**	**8,764.7**	**100%**	**10,302.6**	**100%**

[a]Estimated by the authors.

[b]Less than 1%.

Source: Department of Commerce, Bureau of Economic Analysis, in *The Economic Report of the President* (Washington, DC, U.S. Government Printing Office, 1998).

International Trade   Services also play an important role in the U.S. international trade. During the 1960s and 1970s, service exports constituted about 22 percent of the U.S. exports. However, in the 1980s and 1990s our service exports reached almost 30 percent of our total exports. We also import services from abroad; currently, about 20 percent of our imports are services. The most important fact, however, is that our service exports consistently exceeded service imports since 1971. In other words, services we export bring more revenue than what we pay other nations for their services. The United States has had a negative trade balance every year since 1976. That is, what we paid to other countries for goods and services that we bought from them exceeded what we received from them for the goods and services we sold to them. Exhibit 1-8 provides international trade balance data from the recent past. As can be seen from this exhibit, the trade deficit would have been much bigger had it not been for surplus in service trade.

Contributions to Manufacturing   Although we customarily divide the economy into three sectors, these sectors are not wholly independent of each other. The relationship between manufacturing and services is the strongest; one cannot exist without the other. Some services would not exist if not for goods. For example, automobile repair service would not exist without cars. Similarly, some goods would not exist without the existence of services. For example, stadiums would not be built if there were no football, baseball, or soccer to be played in them; or there would be no drugs to cure illnesses without research and development services.

EXHIBIT 1-6   Gross Domestic Product by Industry

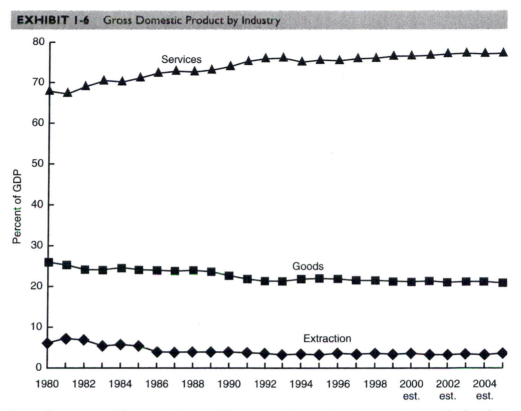

Source: Department of Commerce, Bureau of Economic Analysis, in *The Economic Report of the President* (Washington, DC, U.S. Government Printing Office, 1998).

The relationship between manufacturing and services goes much beyond this simple relationship in which one uses the output of the other. Most manufacturing companies would not be able to produce goods without the support of numerous services. Exhibit 1-9 illustrates the dependency of manufacturing activities on support services. Some of these services are commonly provided internally, such as accounting, design, advertising, and legal services. Other services are provided by outside vendors in areas such as banking, telecommunications, transportation, and police and fire protection.

EXHIBIT 1-7   Number of Business Starts

Industry	1985		1990		1995	
Extraction	6,063	2%	3,349	2%	2,763	2%
Goods producing	56,398	23%	36,116	23%	29,152	17%
Service producing	184,487	74%	115,581	73%	113,446	67%
Unclassifiable establishments	2,282	1%	3,884	2%	22,797	14%
Total	249,770	100%	158,930	100%	168,158	100%

Source: Dun & Bradstreet Corporation, "A Decade of Business Starts," in *Statistical Abstract of the United States*, 1997, p. 547.

EXHIBIT 1-8 U.S. Trade Balance (in billions of dollars)

Year	Total	Goods	Services
1993	−72.04	−132.61	60.57
1994	−104.38	−166.12	61.74
1995	−105.06	−173.42	68.36
1996	−111.04	−191.17	80.13
1997	−113.68	−198.97	85.29

Sources: 1993–1995: U.S. Bureau of the Census, U.S. International Trade in Goods and Services, Series FT-900(95), *Statistical Abstract of the United States*, 1997.

1996–1997: U.S. Department of Commerce, Bureau of Economic Analysis and Bureau of the Census, *Survey of Current Business* (May 1998).

1.4 THEORIES EXPLAINING THE GROWTH OF SERVICES

Economists have been studying the reasons for the growth of services for many years. An early contribution to this line of inquiry was by A. G. B. Fisher, who introduced the concept of primary, secondary, and tertiary industries.[4] Primary production was defined as agriculture, pastoral production, fishing, forestry, hunting, and mining. Secondary production consisted of manufacturing and construction. Some authors in-

EXHIBIT 1-9 Interactions among Manufacturing and Service Activities

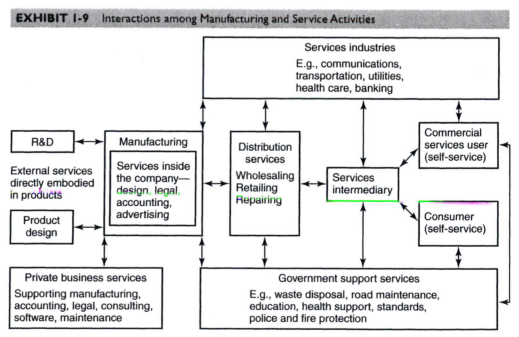

Source: J. B. Quinn and T. L. Doorley, "Key Policy Issues Posed by Services," in B. R. Guile and J. B. Quinn (eds.), *Technology in Services: Policies for Growth, Trade, and Employment* (Washington, DC, National Academy Press, 1988), pp. 211–234.

---

[4] A. G. B. Fisher, "Economic Implications of Material Progress," *International Labour Review* (July 1935), pp. 5–18; and "Primary, Secondary and Tertiary Production," *Economic Record* (June 1939), pp. 24–38.

cluded mining this in category. Finally, tertiary production comprised transportation, communications, trade, government, and personal services. Fisher suggested that an economy can be characterized with respect to the proportion of its labor force employed in these sectors. He also argued that as income rises, demand shifts from the primary to secondary and then to tertiary sectors.

Sociologist Daniel Bell described the development of human societies in three general stages.[5]

Preindustrial Society   The dominant characteristic of economic activity in preindustrial society is extractive (i.e., agriculture, fishing, forestry, and mining). Life is primarily a game against nature. Level of technology is low or nonexistent; people are dependent on raw muscle power to survive, and therefore the productivity is low. Their success is largely dependent on the elements—the seasons, rain, the nature of the soil. The social life is organized around the family and extended household. Because of low productivity and large population, there is significant underemployment in both the agricultural and domestic-service sectors. Because most people in this society struggle not to starve, they often seek only enough to feed themselves. Thus, there are a large number of people employed or available to be employed in personal or household services (see Exhibit 1-10).

Industrial Society   The dominant characteristic of economic activity in industrial society is goods production. Life is a game against fabricated nature. Economic and social life have become mechanized and more efficient. Machines and the energy that powers them dominate production; they have replaced muscle power. Productivity has increased tremendously; the art of making more with less is valued. The economic watchwords are maximization and optimization. Division of labor is further extended. Technological advancements lead to new, faster, and more specialized machines that constantly improve productivity and replace more workers. The workplace is where men, materials, machines, and markets are organized for efficient production and distribution of goods. It is a world of planning and scheduling in which components for production are brought together at the right time and in the right proportions to speed the flow of goods. The workplace is also a world of organization based on bureaucracy and hierarchy. People are treated as "things" because it is easier to coordinate things than people. The unit of social life is the individual in a free market society. Quantity of goods possessed by an individual is an indicator of his standard of living.

Postindustrial Society   The dominant characteristic of economic activity in postindustrial society is service production. Life is now a game between persons. What matters now is not muscle or machine power or energy, but information and knowledge. The central character of economic life is the professional. She possesses the kinds of skills and knowledge increasingly demanded in this society. This demand for increased technical knowledge and skills in the workplace makes higher education a prerequisite to entry into postindustrial society and good life. The quantity and quality of services such as health, education, and recreation that an individual can afford are indicators of his standard of living. Citizens' demand for more services such as health care, education, arts, and so forth, and the inadequacy of the market mechanism in meeting these demands, lead to the growth of government, especially at the state and local level.

---

[5] The discussion of preindustrial, industrial, and postindustrial societies has been adapted from Daniel Bell, *The Coming of Post-Industrial Society: A Venture in Social Forecasting* (New York, Basic Books, 1973), pp. 123–129.

EXHIBIT 1-10	General Schema of Social Change			
	Preindustrial	*Industrial*	*Postindustrial*	
Economic sector:	Primary	Secondary	Tertiary	Quaternary
	Extractive:	Goods producing:	Transport	Trade
	Agriculture	Manufacturing	Recreation	Finance
	Mining	Processing		Insurance
	Fishing			Real estate
	Timber			
				Quinary
				Health
				Education
				Research
				Government
Occupational scope:	Farmer	Semiskilled worker	Professional and technical	
	Miner	Engineer	Scientists	
	Fisherman			
	Unskilled worker			
Technology:	Raw materials	Energy	Information	
Design:	Game against nature	Game against fabricated nature	Game between persons	
Methodology:	Common sense experience	Empiricism Experimentation	Abstract theory: models, simulation, decision theory, systems analysis	
Time perspective:	Orientation to the past	Ad hoc adaptiveness	Future orientation	
	Ad hoc responses	Projections	Forecasting	
Axial principle:	Traditionalism: Land/resource limitation	Economic growth: State or private control of investment decisions	Centrality of and codification of theoretical knowledge	

Source: Daniel Bell, *The Coming of Post-Industrial Society: A Venture in Social Forecasting* (New York, Basic Books, 1973), p. 117.

Several substages are involved in the transition from an industrial to a postindustrial society. First, an expansion of services such as transportation and public utilities is needed for the development of industry and distribution of goods. Second, mass consumption of goods and population growth require an expansion of wholesale and retail services, as well as services such as finance, real estate, and insurance. Finally, as personal incomes rise, the percentage of money devoted to food declines. Increments in income are first spent for durable consumer goods, such as housing, automobiles, and appliances. Further increases in income are spent on services such as education, health care, vacations, travel, restaurants, entertainment, and sports. This tendency in consumption behavior leads to the growth of the personal services sector.

There are many other reasons given to explain the growth of services—some inspired by the theories discussed above, and some independently developed by various researchers. We summarize some of these as follows[6]:

[6] For a more detailed discussion of the various theories explaining the growth of services, see P. W. Daniels, *Service Industries in the World Economy* (Oxford, UK, Blackwell Publishers, 1993), chapter 1, pp. 1–24; Steven M. Shugan, "Explanations for the Growth of Services," in Roland T. Rust and Richard L. Oliver (eds.), *Service Quality: New Directions in Theory and Practice* (Thousand Oaks, London, Sage Publications, 1994), pp. 223–240; and J. N. Marshall and P. A. Wood, *Services and Space: Key Aspects of Urban and Regional Development* (Essex, England, Longman Scientific and Technical, 1995), chapter 2, pp. 9–37.

- The increase in efficiency of agriculture and manufacturing that releases labor to services
- The flow of workers from agriculture and other extraction to manufacturing and then to services
- The application of comparative advantage in international trade
- A decrease in investment as a percentage of GDP in high-income industrialized countries or an increase in the percentage of the GDP in low-income countries
- A rise in per capita income
- An increase in urbanization
- Deregulation
- Demographic shifts
- An increase in international trade
- Joint symbiotic growth of services with manufacturing

1.5   OVERVIEW OF THE BOOK

This book covers a wide range of issues in managing service organizations and their operations. It focuses on creating value and customer satisfaction. Therefore, the book is designed to provide a comprehensive coverage of topics relevant to that end. Its content is quite different from traditional operations management textbooks, although we have also included some of the topics covered in those books. Our discussions draw upon the knowledge and experience of various areas of business as well as on disciplines other than business. For example, discussions frequently rely on the theory and practice of strategy, marketing, international management, human resources, management science, economics, psychology, and sociology. We hope that this multi-disciplinary and cross-functional approach helps managers and future managers develop a well-rounded and solid understanding of the complexities of services and their management.

The book is organized in four parts. Part One, chapters 1 through 6, begins with this introduction and focuses on developing an in-depth understanding of services. Chapter 2 discusses the nature of services and service encounters. Chapter 3 examines customers and their needs, and factors that influence their decisions in services purchasing. Chapter 4 discusses the globalization of services and forms of globalization. Chapter 5 deals with the issues concerning value creation and service strategy. Finally, chapter 6 contains a discussion of how services should be positioned and marketed for competitiveness and profitability.

Part Two covers topics relevant to developing service systems. Building a competitive service system that creates value and customer satisfaction requires the effective use of certain inputs. These inputs include technology (chapter 7), service design and development (chapter 8), human resources (chapter 9), the selection of an appropriate site for a service facility, and the design of its layout (chapter 10).

Part Three is devoted to topics that are crucial to managers for operating a service system effectively and efficiently. Topics covered in this part include managing demand and supply (chapter 11), service quality and continuous improvement (chapter 12), and service productivity and measurement of performance (chapter 13). Chapter 14 includes a brief study of the management of public and nonprofit service organizations, because these organizations are coming to play an increasingly important role in our economic and social life.

Part Four presents various quantitative tools and techniques for managing service operations. This part contains chapters discussing some of the most powerful and widely used techniques in managing operations of both manufacturing and service organizations. Chapter 15 discusses forecasting. Chapter 16 focuses on techniques to optimize decisions in routing vehicles. Project management is discussed in chapter 17, and linear and goal programming in chapter 18. Chapter 19, the final chapter, covers inventory systems for service operations.

1.6 SUMMARY

This chapter has examined the concept of services from a macro viewpoint. Definitions of service and service economies were presented, as well as the importance of services in our society. The important role services play in the U.S. economy was discussed with respect to employment, gross domestic product, number of business starts, international trade, and contributions to manufacturing. The theories explaining why services grew so much in the economies of industrial nations in the second half of the twentieth century were then considered. Theories concerning the three types of production—primary, secondary, and tertiary—and how societies may migrate from one dominant form of production to the next were also discussed.

Discussion Questions

1. Why is it difficult to define a service? What is meant by the term *facilitating good*?
2. Discuss why the service sector is important to the U.S. economy.
3. What are the primary, secondary, and tertiary industries?
4. What are the characteristics of a preindustrial society?
5. What are the characteristics of an industrial society?
6. What are the characteristics of a postindustrial society?
7. Why do service economies necessarily follow industrial economies?
8. What things indicate that the United States has become a service economy?
9. What is happening in other countries? Is Japan, for example, also becoming a primarily service economy?
10. "There are no such things as service industries . . . only industries whose service components are greater or less than those of other industries."[7] Explain this statement. Do you agree or disagree?

References

Bell, Daniel, *The Coming of Post-Industrial Society: A Venture in Social Forecasting* (New York, Basic Books, 1973).

Bureau of the Census, *Statistical Abstract of the United States* (Washington DC, 1997).

Clark, Colin, *The Conditions of Economic Progress*, 3rd ed. (London, Macmillan, 1957).

Daniels, P. W., *Service Industries in the World Economy* (Oxford, UK, Blackwell Publishers, 1993).

The Economic Report of the President (Washington, DC, U.S. Government Printing Office, 1998).

Fisher, A. G. B., "Economic Implications of Material Progress," *International Labour Review* (July 1935), pp. 5–18.

Fisher, A. G. B., "Primary, Secondary and Tertiary Production," *Economic Record* (June 1939), pp. 24–38.

Foot, Nelson N., and Paul K. Hatt, "Social Mobility and Economic Advancement," *American Economic Review*, vol. 43 (1953), pp. 364–378.

Fornell, Claes, Michael D. Johnson, Eugene W. Anderson, Jaesung Cha, and Barbara E. Bryant, "The American Customer Satisfaction Index: Nature, Purpose, and Findings," *Journal of Marketing*, vol. 60 (October 1996), pp. 7–18.

---

[7] Theodore Levitt, "Production-line Approach to Service," *Harvard Business Review* (September–October 1972), pp. 41–52.

Gore, Al, Vice President of the United States, *The Best Kept Secrets in Government: A Report to President Clinton* (Washington, DC, National Performance Review, September, 1997).

Levitt, Theodore, "Production-line Approach to Service," *Harvard Business Review* (September–October 1972), pp. 41–52.

Marshall, J. N., and P. A. Wood, *Services and Space: Key Aspects of Urban and Regional Development* (Essex, England, Longman Scientific and Technical, 1995).

Naisbitt, John, *Megatrends: Ten New Directions Transforming Our Lives* (New York, Warner Books, 1982).

Shugan, Steven M., "Explanations for the Growth of Services," in Roland T. Rust and Richard L. Oliver (eds.), *Service Quality: New Directions in Theory and Practice* (Thousand Oaks, London, Sage Publications, 1994), pp. 223–240.

CHAPTER 2

The Nature of Services and Service Encounters

2.1   INTRODUCTION

The definition of a service business or service organization has been a continuing problem for students of productive systems. Manufacturing is often taken as the point of departure, and service firms are distinguished in terms of differences from manufacturing organizations. This approach tries to identify services by some criteria for the output, the process, or the consumption of the output that contrasts with manufacturing organizations.

This chapter examines the general concepts of a productive system and the characteristics that make services unique. Also discussed are service encounters, which play a crucial role in the relationship between a customer and a service organization and significantly impact perceptions of service quality, customer satisfaction, and repeat purchase decisions.

2.2   GENERAL CONCEPT OF A PRODUCTIVE SYSTEM

A **system** is, simply, a set of elements that works toward a common goal by acting on inputs to produce outputs. A productive system is one that adds value, economic or otherwise, in the conversion of inputs to outputs. A general representation of a productive system is shown in Exhibit 2-1.

A productive system consists of physical elements related to each other. There are five types of productive systems:

1. Extraction of materials or energy from the environment
2. Biological growth and change
3. Tangible-output conversion systems
4. Intangible-output conversion systems
5. Hybrid conversion systems

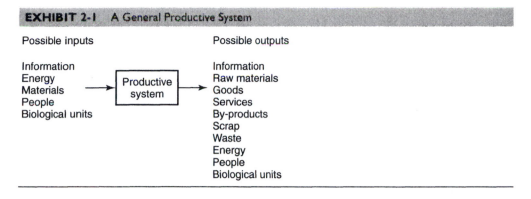

EXHIBIT 2-1   A General Productive System

Possible inputs

Information
Energy
Materials
People
Biological units

Productive system

Possible outputs

Information
Raw materials
Goods
Services
By-products
Scrap
Waste
Energy
People
Biological units

Examples of each of these are shown in Exhibit 2-2. We may note that **services,** as usually defined, fall into either of the last two groups. For example, a restaurant is generally considered to be a service, but its output consists of both tangible and intangible components. For example, while the food consumed by the customer is tangible, the pleasant dining experience is an intangible component of the service. Manufacturing organizations also fall within two groups, the third and the fifth. The sole output of a manufacturing organization cannot be intangible (the fourth group). However most "manufacturing" firms provide a *combination* of tangible and intangible outputs. Consider a custom automobile "manufacturer" that works in contact with a customer throughout the process. Is this firm really a manufacturer or is it primarily a "service" firm?

From the preceding, we see that the dichotomy of "service" versus "manufacturing" is not easily maintained. Rather, there is a continuous spectrum of organizations with varying amounts of tangible and intangible outputs (see Exhibit 2-3). Intangibility is an important characteristic of services. The next section presents a discussion of intangibility and some other important characteristics that distinguish services.

EXHIBIT 2-2   Types of Productive Systems

Extraction
Mining the earth (or moon) surface
Mining under the ocean
Processing oceans or other bodies of water
  (such as salt lakes)
Extracting gases from the atmosphere

Biological
Agriculture
Animal and fish husbandry
Biological growth and genetic changing of
  microorganisms

Tangible-Output Conversion Systems
Unit, or custom
Batch
Continuous (long runs of identifiable units)
Process (identity of individual units is lost as
  in chemical, textile, rubber, and electrical
  power production)

Intangible-Output Conversion System
Consulting
Movies
Radio broadcasting
Physical examinations
Day-care centers
Public administration

Hybrid Conversion Systems
Restaurants
Book publishing
Barber shop
Automobile repair
Surgery

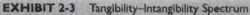

EXHIBIT 2-3 Tangibility–Intangibility Spectrum

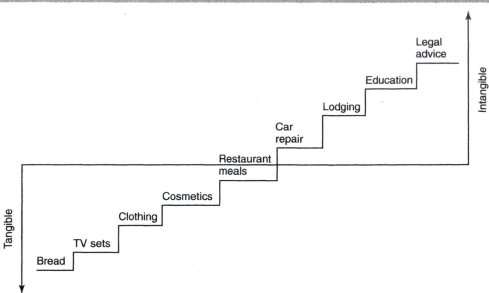

Source: Adapted from G. Lynn Shostack, "Breaking Free from Product Marketing," *Journal of Marketing* (April 1987).

2.3 CHARACTERISTICS OF SERVICES

Through the years, researchers and analysts have used one or more criteria to characterize services. They have identified various characteristics that are common to most services. The following four are the most often mentioned characteristics[1] that differentiate them from manufactured goods—the primary characteristics of services:

1. Intangibility
2. Inseparability
3. Perishability
4. Variability

Although not all services possess all of these characteristics, they do exhibit most of them and some others that are the consequences of them. These characteristics will now be discussed in more detail. The discussion will also provide hints of some of the unique problems managers of service operations encounter.

Intangibility

Most services are intangible. This characteristic can be understood most easily when one thinks about the tangible nature of goods. A good is a physical object; it can be touched, felt, sometimes smelled, and if it is a food item, can be tasted. Services are not physical objects. They may utilize physical objects or be embodied in physical objects but they themselves are not physical. For example, software consists of instructions for a computer to perform. It is written in a computer language and its instructions can be exe-

---

[1] See, for example, W. Earl Sasser, Jr., R. Paul Olsen, and D. Daryl Wyckoff, *Management of Service Operations: Text, Cases, and Readings* (Boston, Allyn and Bacon, 1978), pp. 15–18; and Roland T. Rust, Anthony J. Zahorik, and Timothy L. Keiningham, *Service Marketing* (New York, HarperCollins, 1996), pp. 7–10.

cuted only by a computer. These instructions are usually recorded on a CD or floppy disk, or can be downloaded to a hard disk from the Internet. Consequently, the service provided by a software developer is embodied in a physical object (CD, floppy, or hard disk) and cannot be used without the aid of another physical object (computer).

Most services are performances. A service such as legal advising usually involves the act of giving advice and representation of a client in a courtroom. Such services usually have no tangible output. When there is a tangible output, it is not the service itself but a medium through which the service output is delivered to the customer. For example, a report that proposes solutions to a client's business problem is not the real output of a consulting service; the real output is the ideas expressed in the report to solve the problem. Other services combine an intangible output with a physical output, as in the case of restaurants, gasoline stations, or interior decorating. Although it is true that manufacturing output also can include intangibles (such as warranties, technical information, and prestige of ownership), the primary output of manufacturing is always a physical product. Intangibility describes the uniqueness of services more succinctly than any other characteristic.

An important consequence of intangibility is that for most services, purchasing the service does not result in ownership. Purchasing a good implies ownership. For example, a customer who buys a stereo system becomes the owner of the system and can do a number of things with it: enjoy music, give it to someone as a gift, trade it for a TV set, or sell it. Purchasers of most services do not have such options. For example, if you buy a ticket to a Broadway show, you obtain the right to be in the audience at a particular date and time. If you watch the show, you have exercised that right and it is gone; you cannot claim a right to watch the show again unless you buy another ticket. In other words, you do not have the ownership of anything. An exception to this limitation is when the service is embedded in a physical product. For example, if you buy the video of the Broadway show, you will have the same options a good provides.

Inseparability

Provision and consumption of most services are inseparable: They can be consumed only when they are produced. For most goods, these two processes can be and usually are separate. A TV set can be produced in a factory in one geographic location and shipped to wholesalers and retailers all over the world and consumed in many different places. Someone who buys a TV set does not have to use it right away; it can stay in its box indefinitely. A physician's advice to a patient, however, is consumed as it is given.

A second form of inseparability is the inseparability of the customer from the service delivery process. In other words, most services cannot be stored for future use; the customer must be present when the service is created. A customer's presence is not required when a TV set is produced, but a physical examination in a doctor's office cannot be performed unless the patient is there. A lecture in a classroom, a football game, a rock concert, and a train ride are just a few additional examples in which both forms of inseparability can be seen; the performance and consumption of these services are simultaneous and inseparable, and customers must be present to enjoy the benefits of these services.

Joint consumption of some services is a third form of inseparability. Some services are provided for a large group of customers. For example, a theatrical production, a concert, and a cruise ship vacation are services produced for and experienced by a group of people. Although each person's experience may be different in these services, the entire group may suffer from the behavior of an intoxicated and unruly patron. Consequently, in some services, what one customer experiences cannot be separated from the entire group's experience.

Perishability

Most services, because they are simultaneously produced and consumed, are considered perishable, noninventoriable commodities. The person who phones in to a time service to find the correct time uses up the service at the time it is provided. Hotel rooms, seats on an airplane or in a theater, and an hour of a lawyer's day cannot be stored and retrieved for later use.

However, perishability may be different from a consumer's point of view. Although a customer cannot carry home a service after it is produced, she can enjoy the "effects" of the service long after it has been purchased. For example, the surgeon who performs a heart transplant is providing not just a single operation, but rather a benefit that is enjoyed over the patient's life. Even a movie may be enjoyed in retrospect or provide educational benefits that extend beyond the time that the movie is presented.

The perishability of services, coupled with the highly varying demand patterns that most services experience, requires that managers allocate service capacity carefully and attempt to actively manage service demand.

Variability

Most services are provided by humans for other humans. A service provider may be performing a service on a customer's body, mind, or property. In any case, however, the customer and service provider(s) must interact. The outcome of the service depends on the outcome of this interaction and on the customer's perception of it. When humans interact, results usually exhibit great variability and are not easily predictable. The beauty shop, the custom dress design firm, and the executive recruiting firm provide services that vary with the individual client.

On one level, this means that even if the same person provides a service to several customers in exactly the same way, different customers may have different perceptions of what they have received and therefore experience different levels of satisfaction. On another level, the same person performing the same service may not deliver the exact same service at every performance. His physical and psychological condition play an important role in service delivery, and these conditions may not always be the same every day.

The variability in the performance of service providers and in the perception of customers creates significant challenges for managers in services. An important consequence of this is that most services defy attempts at standardization. It is difficult, if not impossible, to standardize the output because each client varies in terms of desires before and during the performance of the service. In many services, the design of the service is determined by the person who actually provides the service, such as the consultant, the real estate agent, or the physician. The individual service provider must match the service to the client's needs and desires. Variability in service outcomes also makes control and assurance of quality very difficult. Finally, variability makes measurement of productivity a challenging task for managers of service organizations.

2.4   THE SERVICE ORGANIZATION AS A SYSTEM

This chapter began with a description of the general concept of a productive system. That concept will now be applied to service organizations in more detail. In chapter 1, services were defined as "economic activities that produce time, place, form, and psychological utilities." In other words, services are deeds, acts, or performances that are created through one or more processes. For many services, the process and the output of the system are the same or closely related. These processes are designed and applied as a result of a concerted effort by various components of the service organization. For our purposes, the most important components of this system are represented in Exhibit 2-4. Let's take a closer look at a service organization as a system.

The service organization exists to provide a service (or set of services) to its customers. It is defined and shaped by its mission, strategies, and policies. The **operations** system designs the service package and the delivery system in cooperation with marketing, finance, and human resources. Other functions of the operations system include day-to-day running of the system, deploying the resources to produce the service(s) and providing input for personnel training. The **marketing system** manages the organization's contact with customers, including advertising, sales, promotion, distribution, and market research. Operations and marketing functions overlap in many cases. For example, in some cases, operations personnel, while providing a service, may also sell other services of the company and act as marketers. In general, these two functions have to work closely and cooperate for success. Probably the most important area of cooperation is the design of the **service** and the **delivery system.**

The marketing system collects data and provides information to operations concerning the customer needs and requirements. This is the main input to the design process. Service design should also consider the organization's mission, strategies, competencies, and resources. Other inputs to service design include environmental factors, such as laws and government regulations, customs, and norms. The objective of the design process is to determine what benefits to provide to the customer. Design of the delivery system aims at determining where, when, and how these benefits should be provided. A service delivery system consists of equipment and physical facilities, processes, and personnel. Service personnel play a crucial role in service delivery and success of the organization. Selection, hiring, and training of service providers are fa-

EXHIBIT 2-4   The Service System

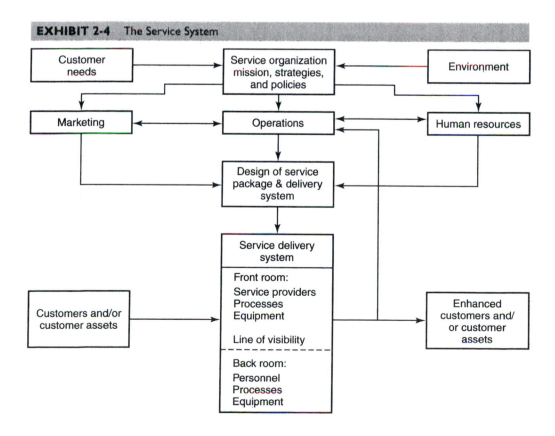

cilitated by the **human resources** function. Chapter 8 discusses design of services and delivery systems in more detail.

The service delivery system can be considered into two parts—front room and back room. The front room, also known as front stage, is part of the delivery system that is visible to the customer. This is where the customer interacts with service providers and comes into contact with facilities and processes. The back room, or backstage, is invisible to the customer and consists of all the personnel, facilities, equipment, and processes that support the front-line personnel and processes. An imaginary "line of visibility" separates the two parts of the delivery system. What goes on below this line is usually of no concern to the customer; however, failures in the back room may seriously affect the front room activities and customer satisfaction. J. W. "Bill" Marriott, Jr., the chairman and chief executive officer (CEO) of Marriott International Inc., describes the back room in a large hotel as follows:

> In every large hotel—hidden from the eyes and ears of guests—exists an invisible city. Behind doors, below ground, a maze of corridors connects kitchens to loading docks, housekeeping to the laundry, accounting to the communications center. An around-the-clock army of cooks, housekeepers, engineers, waiters, dishwashers, electricians, and other specialists bustles along these hallways, each member responsible for making his or her part of hotel operations run smoothly. The lodging industry has a special term to describe this hidden world. We call it the "heart of the house."[2]

Finally, in the model in Exhibit 2-4, customers and/or their assets enter into the service process as inputs. The service may consist of tangible actions applied to customers' bodies (such as dental services), tangible actions applied to their goods or physical possessions (such as car repair), intangible actions directed at their minds (such as entertainment programs), or intangible actions directed at their intangible assets (such as investment banking). Examples of these are shown in Exhibit 2-5 and discussed in more detail below.[3]

1. *People processing: tangible actions directed at the customer's body.* These services require the physical presence of the customer during the service process. Services such as a heart transplant operation or air travel require the presence of the customer. In these cases, the customer will have close contact with the service organization and its employees and facilities, usually for a significant length of time.
2. *Possession processing: tangible actions directed at goods and other physical possessions of the customer.* These services require the presence of the object but not necessarily the customer himself. In many cases, the customer drops off the object, or the service provider comes to it; he gives the necessary information and instructions for the service; and is no longer needed until the service is completed. Car repair and landscaping/lawncare are two examples. In both cases, the length of the encounter is usually very short, unless the customer chooses to be present during the service.
3. *Mental stimulus processing: intangible actions directed at the customer's mind.* When these services are delivered, the customer must be mentally but not necessarily physically present. For some of these services, such as TV or radio broadcast, the message is the only contact the customer has with the service organiza-

[2] J. W. Marriott, Jr. and Kathi Ann Brown, *The Spirit to Serve: Marriott's Way* (New York, Harper Business, 1997), pp. xvii–xviii.
[3] Christopher H. Lovelock, *Services Marketing*, 3rd ed. (Upper Saddle River, NJ, Prentice Hall, 1996).

EXHIBIT 2-5   Services and Service Processes

INPUTS	TANGIBLE	INTANGIBLE
CUSTOMER	PEOPLE PROCESSING Passenger transportation Heart transplant Immunization Physical therapy Criminal justice system	MENTAL STIMULUS PROCESSING Entertainment Education Art exhibit Concerts TV programs
ASSETS	POSSESSION PROCESSING Repair and maintenance Dry cleaning Housecleaning services Landscaping Package delivery	INFORMATION PROCESSING Internet services Banking Financial services Insurance Software development

Source: Adapted from Christopher H. Lovelock, *Services Marketing*, 3rd ed. (Upper Saddle River, NJ, Prentice Hall, 1996), p. 29.

tion. In others, such as traditional educational institutions, concerts, and counseling, the customer's presence is required. Therefore, in the latter case, a service provider's performance as well her behavior determine the customer's perception of the service he has received. In addition, physical environment, policies of the organization, and other customers may play an important role in forming this perception if the customer is in the facility.

4. *Information processing: intangible actions directed at the customer's intangible assets.* These are services that process the customer's money, records, data, and the like. After the customer contacts the service organization and requests the service, her presence or involvement is not necessary. The nature of these services and the current level of technology make physical contact with the service organization almost unnecessary. Many banking services, for example, can be obtained over the phone, by mail, or through automated teller machines. However, there are still some services many people prefer to receive in person, such as opening a savings account or applying for a home mortgage loan.

The outputs of the service system are enhanced customers, or assets that have increased in value. The role of the service operations manager is to monitor and control the service process based on feedback from the system to ensure that the needs of the customers and service personnel are being met. In other words, feedback from the customers and employees make quality assurance possible.

2.5   SERVICE ENCOUNTERS

Professor Leonard L. Berry describes a service as "a deed, a performance, an effort."[4] Although some services may result in physical goods, such as a consultant's report, what is invariably important in all services is the transformation of the customer's

---

[4] Leonard L. Berry, "Services Marketing Is Different," *Business* (May–June 1980).

body, mind, assets, or information. These transformations are achieved by a series of purposeful acts, that is, through a **process.** A customer comes into contact with the service organization when her body, mind, assets, or information is processed. This is generally known as a service encounter. Whether or not the customer is satisfied with the service experience depends on the outcome of the service encounter. A service encounter involves not only the customer and service employees, but also other customers, the service delivery system, and physical evidence.

A **service encounter,** also known as a "moment of truth," can be defined as:

Any episode in which the customer comes into contact with any aspect of the organization and gets an impression of the quality of its service.[5]

The term *moment of truth* comes from the language of bullfighting and refers to the moment when the matador faces the bull before he takes his final action that ends the fight. The term was introduced to service management literature by Richard Normann[6] to dramatize the importance of the encounter of a customer with a service organization. Jan Carlzon, the former president of Scandinavian Airlines System (SAS), popularized the term in his effort to turn the money-losing company into one of the best-run airlines. He expressed the importance of service encounters as follows:

> Last year, each of our 10 million customers came in contact with approximately five SAS employees, and this contact lasted an average of 15 seconds each time. Thus SAS is "created" in the minds of our customers 50 million times a year, 15 seconds at a time. These 50 million "moments of truth" are the moments that ultimately determine whether SAS will succeed or fail as a company. They are the moments when we must prove to our customers that SAS is their best alternative.[7]

It must be emphasized that a service encounter may occur practically at any time and any place. Some obvious service encounters are as follows: A customer enters a service facility, asks directions from a service employee, is given forms to fill out, or is in contact with the service provider during the service performance. A customer also experiences a service encounter when he sees a billboard advertisement or a TV commercial by the service organization or a vehicle in the street that belongs to the organization, reads a news item in a newspaper or hears someone talk about the service or the organization, and when he receives a bill for the service. Probably the most important thing for managers to remember is that for a customer in a service encounter, whatever or whomever she is in contact with, she perceives it/him as the organization. In other words, when a customer is treated badly by an employee, the customer does not think that he came into contact with a rude person working for the company, but he thinks he is dealing with a rude company. When a customer sits in a waiting area that is not kept clean, she sees a dirty company, not failed custodial services. When a technician fails to show up for a scheduled cable service, the customer concludes that the cable company is unreliable. In short, most customers equate service failures or quality problems with the organization that is responsible for the service. Therefore, Carlzon was right when he said his company is "created" in the minds of customers during service encounters.

Most customers do not think about a service or the organization outside the encounters, and when they do, it is usually for a limited length of time. A service organi-

---

[5] Karl Albrecht, *At America's Service* (New York, Warner Books, 1988), p. 26.

[6] Richard Normann, *Service Management* (Chichester, John Wiley & Sons, 1984).

[7] Jan Carlzon, *Moments of Truth* (Cambridge, MA, Ballinger, 1987).

zation, therefore, has a few brief opportunities to make a good impression on the customer. There are, however, many opportunities to make mistakes and lose customers. It is clear that a service organization cannot leave these service encounters to chance if it wants to keep its customers satisfied and keep them coming back. Therefore, service encounters must be carefully designed and managed. Naturally, we need to understand these events well before we can discuss their design and management.

The Nature of Service Encounters

Service encounters may be very simple or very complex processes. Usually, they consist not of a single episode but a series of episodes, with multiple facets of an organization. For instance, consider the hypothetical example of a music lover going to a rock concert (Exhibit 2-6). Obviously, this example may have included many more encounters, but our rock music fan had 14 service encounters. Most of these encounters were with the rock group, but there were other organizations associated with the concert. For example, the arena where the concert was held most likely is not owned but rented by the group or the organizer. In addition to providing a place for the concert, the arena's management may have also provided ticket, parking, and security services. Similarly, the vendor who sells the group's T-shirts is probably a different organization that paid royalties to the group for the use of its name. The concession stand is probably run by still another organization. Clearly, performances of other service organizations may have an effect on the overall experience of the customer. If the customer experiences a problem with any of them, she may not be able to distinguish it from the rock group's organizational performance and hence may conclude that "the concert was good, but organization terrible." However, if everything goes well, she probably would not even be aware of most of these encounters.

The encounters in the above example are fairly simple. More complex encounters include a lawyer interacting with a client, or a physician trying to diagnose a patient's

---

EXHIBIT 2-6   Service Encounters: Going to a Rock Concert

1. A music lover has seen in a newspaper an advertisement of an upcoming concert by a popular rock group at the local arena.
2. She calls the arena for schedule, prices, and directions, getting the information she needs from a recording.
3. She calls another number to reserve her ticket with her credit card.
4. On a local TV news program, she views a report about the rock group's arrival in town.
5. On the day of the concert, she drives to the arena; at the entrance, she sees banners of the group.
6. Security personnel direct her to the entrance of the parking lot.
7. She pays for parking and parks her car.
8. She arrives at the ticket window, gives her name, and receives her ticket.
9. She approaches the entrance and sees the crowd and security personnel.
10. She presents her ticket to an attendant and goes in.
11. She buys a T-shirt commemorating the concert.
12. She goes to a concession stand and buys a soda.
13. She receives help from an usher to locate her seat.
14. She enjoys the concert.

illness. The complexity originates from the knowledge and skills needed for these services as well as the presence of risk and customer emotions.

For most organizations, the "make-or-break" service encounters are those between customers and service providers. We can view these encounters as human interactions with the following characteristics[8]:

1. *Service encounters are purposeful.* Regardless of who initiates it, all service encounters are goal oriented. A sick patient walks into a hospital to get a diagnosis and medical treatment for his ailment. A commercial on TV is aimed at current or potential customers. The UPS symbol on a brown delivery truck has a purpose—to advertise and tell everyone that United Parcel Service is making a delivery.

2. *Service providers are not altruistic.* Most service encounters are part of daily work life, at least for the service provider. The primary purpose of the service provider is to perform duties for which she is paid. Therefore, for her, a service encounter is "work." It is possible that the customer is also at work during the service encounter. For example, a secretary may call a service technician to have the copy machine in her office repaired. In this case, both are at work when they interact in an encounter. There are, of course, many exceptions, such as a lawyer doing pro bono work or a volunteer working in a soup kitchen.

3. *Prior acquaintance is not required.* In most cases, the customer and the service provider are strangers who would not normally interact outside the service setting. However, they usually feel comfortable interacting, in many cases, even without introducing themselves to each other. Examples include buying a ticket at a theater box office, a passenger asking directions from a bus driver on a public transit system, or buying a sandwich at a fast-food restaurant. These encounters usually have no long-term consequences. However, others not only require formal introduction, they also require a lot more information to be given, usually by the customer. For example, a patient visiting a dentist for the first time has to be known not only by name, but also by other important data such as address, telephone number, age, allergies, insurance company, records of previous dental work, and so on. Consequently, the patient and the dentist are no longer strangers.

4. *Service encounters are limited in scope.* Although greetings, courtesies, and small talk may be part of some service encounters, the time spent on nontask issues is usually very short. The scope of interaction between the customer and the service employee is limited by the nature of the service task. A physician normally would not discuss with a patient how he can repair his car, and a car mechanic normally would not offer medical advice during a service encounter.

5. *Task-related information exchange dominates.* Most service encounters with a service provider require information exchange. Although some informal settings may involve non-task-related information exchange, task-related information is indispensable and has the priority. For example, in a beauty salon, most of the conversation between a customer and a beautician may be on the weather and the latest fashion. However, task-related information, such as how short the customer wants her hair, what style she wants, and whether she needs a shampoo, must be provided first. At the other extreme, a telephone encounter between a

---

[8] J. A. Czepiel, M. R. Solomon, C. F. Surprenant, and E. G. Gutman, "Service Encounters: An Overview," in J. A. Czepiel, M. R. Solomon, and C. F. Surprenant (eds.), *The Service Encounter: Managing Employee/Customer Interaction in Service Businesses* (Lexington, MA, Lexington Books, 1985), pp. 3–15.

financial advisor and his client, for example, will probably move to the point and focus entirely on the requirements of the customer. In some cases, it may be difficult to separate the two. Consider, for example, a travel agent scheduling a vacation package for a couple. In addition to the relevant information about the vacation package, the agent may recount her own vacation at some of the locations the couple is going to visit. Such conversation may be considered "small talk," but it may also provide useful information to the customers.

6. *Client and provider roles are well defined.* The interaction between a customer and a service provider in an encounter requires rules of behavior for effective and efficient service performance. The relevant rules are usually learned from experience; otherwise, a service provider may guide the customer to conform with the rules. For a landscaping project, the customer tells the contractor how he wants his lawn and garden to look, what types of flowers to plant, and the like, and the contractor is expected to follow these instructions. In an encounter between a physician and a patient, however, roles are different; in this case, the patient answers questions and is expected to follow the doctor's instructions.

7. *A temporary status differential may occur.* An important characteristic of some service encounters is that they involve a temporary suspension of "normal" social status enjoyed by each party. For example, a lawyer, who is considered to have a high social status, may work for a criminal, whose status is much lower. A judge who is stopped by a police officer for a traffic violation has to follow the instructions of the officer.

Service Encounters from Various Perspectives

Service encounters may be depicted in various ways, depending on one's orientation during the exchange. Obviously, an encounter involving human interactions has a social component, but it can also be viewed from economic, productive, contractual, and employment perspectives.[9]

- *Social encounter.* Service encounters may be seen as social encounters in which customers come into contact with service providers and interact as human beings. Participants in the encounter are expected to follow certain rules of the society that apply to similar interactions between people. A proper greeting, courtesy, and treatment as a human being are minimum standards expected of both sides in many countries. Some encounters may involve small talk, such as weather and recent sporting events, but most exchanges between the parties are task related. Another understanding is that customers will be treated equally, and the same or equal level of service will be provided to all customers.

- *Economic exchange.* Some service encounters may also be characterized as economic exchanges in which resources are exchanged between a customer and a service organization. More specifically, a service organization gives up its resources in the form of labor, skill, technology, or information to satisfy some need of a customer or provide a benefit. In return, the customer sacrifices some of her resources, such as money, time, and labor.

- *Production process.* Customers come to a service organization to satisfy some need, such as food, or to obtain a benefit, such as education. The service organization has to deploy its resources for this purpose. Resources may include labor,

---

[9] P. K. Mills, *Managing Service Industries: Organizational Practices in a Postindustrial Economy* (Cambridge, MA, Ballinger, 1986), pp. 22–24.

technology, information, and facilities; their proper use will create the desired result. Therefore, a service encounter is a production process in which resources are converted to satisfactions and benefits for the customer. Although most resources will be supplied by the organization, sometimes the customer's resources will also be used.

- *Contract.*   Another way to view a service encounter is as a contractual relationship between a service organization and a customer. The customer hires the service organization to perform a service on his behalf. Through this contract, the customer delegates some authority to the organization or the service provider to make decisions about himself or his property. Therefore, both sides operate within the implicit contractual agreement. A surgeon, for example operates on a patient with the patient's permission. During the surgery, the patient is likely to be unconscious, but the surgeon has to make many decisions. She makes all the necessary decisions due to the authority delegated to her by the patient and is expected to keep the patient's best interests in mind.

- *Partial employment.*   Some services require active participation of the customer in the creation of the service, such as a patron preparing a salad at the salad bar in a restaurant. In these cases, the customer provides the necessary labor, and hence, in a sense, is employed by the service organization. Clearly, this is not employment in the regular sense; nevertheless, it is usually beneficial to both sides; the restaurant saves money on labor and passes part of the savings on to the customer in the form of lower cost of meals. Therefore, we may say, the customer is "paid" by the restaurant for his labor.

Elements of a Service Encounter

A service encounter is made up of four elements: (1) the customer, (2) the service provider, (3) the delivery system, and (4) the physical evidence.

Customer

The customer is the most important element of a service encounter. The ultimate objective of an encounter must be the satisfaction of the customer. The customer's perception of service quality, her overall satisfaction with the service, and repeat purchase decision all depend to a large extent on her perception of the service encounter. Therefore, the service and its delivery system must be designed to meet the customer's needs in the most effective and efficient manner. Various characterizations of a service encounter given earlier remind us that first of all a customer is a human being and expects to be treated with courtesy and respect. She also expects to be treated equally as other customers and given the same or equal service. These are the basic, minimum requirements for a service encounter regardless of the nature of the service.

However, in many cases the organization has to go beyond that minimum for successful encounters, especially if the service consists of tangible actions directed at a customer's body. Encounters in "people-processing services" need to be designed and managed with utmost care. The major reason for this is that the customer is physically present in the service facility, probably for an extended period of time. This gives the customer an opportunity to observe the service performance and make a judgment about its quality. Consequently, a customer's comfort, safety, and overall well-being should be a major concern for the service organization. If it is the customer's possession that is being processed, and he is not required to be present during the service, the focus of the service organization will be on efficient operations that will optimize convenience for the customer, as well as minimize the time and effort he needs to spend for the service.

When a customer is expected to supply her labor for the service, she would probably like to have some benefit from her contribution to the service production. In these cases, the service organization must provide clear instructions as to what is expected from the customer and make sure that the equipment she has to use is in working order and easy to operate. Failure to educate customers in proper procedures may lead to inefficient operations and unsatisfactory encounters. On the other hand, a customer may also have a significant impact on the outcome of a service encounter by her behavior. If a customer fails to provide the necessary information, follow instructions, or conform to her expected role, or in general, if she is a difficult person, she may make the service provider's job very difficult and the experience unsatisfactory for both parties and even for other customers.

Service Provider

The service provider or employee is the other crucial human element in service encounters. As a human being, he expects courtesy from customers and fellow employees and would like to be appreciated by customers and management. He has to have the requisite knowledge and proper training to perform his tasks. However, this is usually not sufficient for successful encounters.

A service employee represents the organization and is the force that keeps the delivery system going. Her words and actions are seen by the customer as those of the organization. As indicated earlier, she is expected to act on behalf of the customer and in his best interest, because the customer has entrusted himself or his property to her care. This dual role may sometimes be problematic for the service employee, especially when the customer's best interests conflict with company policies or when she is bound by strict rules as to what she can and cannot do. There may be many other stressful situations for the employee as well as the customer. For example, when the service involves some risk to the customer, as in surgery, or to his property, as in dry cleaning, the employee has to demonstrate more than technical competence—she has to have the skills and ability to ease customer's concerns about the process. This means that she must have interpersonal skills.

Another important thing to remember is that a service encounter may be a first, or one of very few, for a customer, but for the provider it is one of hundreds of encounters during a workday or week. Years of performing the same tasks may condition employees to look at the encounter only in terms of its efficiency and effectiveness rather than the entire process experienced by the customer. Understanding the customer's inexperience, anxiety, or concerns about the service, and at times showing empathy go a long way in making the encounter a satisfactory one for the customer. It is largely management's responsibility to help a service employee to develop interpersonal skills such as friendliness, warmth, concern, and empathy. Sometimes, they have to suppress their own feelings and interact with customers with the organization's goals and customers' interests in mind. In short, service providers must be able to look at service encounters and processes from the customer's viewpoint. Therefore, the employee must be trained to develop these behavior patterns. Obviously, these are not easy traits to acquire, and training alone does not guarantee the desired result. Management must also exercise great care in selecting employees who will be interacting with customers.

Simultaneous production and consumption of some services and the intangible nature of most services make quality control very difficult. Unlike manufacturing goods, services cannot be inspected before they are produced or delivered. Even after delivery, most services present a challenge in quality assessment. "Did your lawyer present your case in the most effective way?" "Did your tax preparer find all the tax deductions you are entitled to?" "Did your doctor diagnose your illness correctly or did your symptoms disappear by themselves?" These and similar questions may never be answered. A common way for managers to assure quality in service delivery is to control inputs, that is, choose who to serve, and carefully select the right people for the job, check their competency and credentials, give them a proper training, and provide them with clear guidelines as to what is expected of them.

While satisfying customers may be the most important issue for a service organization, a related and very important matter is to satisfy service providers. Some companies go even further. Herb Kelleher, CEO of Southwest Airlines, one of the most successful airlines in the United States, explains:

> It used to be a business conundrum: "Who comes first?: The employees, customers, or shareholders?" . . . That's never been an issue to me. The employees come first. If they're happy, satisfied, dedicated, and energetic, they'll take real good care of the customers. When the customers are happy, they come back. And that makes the shareholders happy.[10]

Delivery System

A delivery system consists of equipment, supplies, processes, programs, and procedures, as well as the rules, regulations, and organizational culture. Many service organizations assume that if their departments or functions are organized to operate in the most effective and efficient way according to well-established principles of the relevant field, this will also assure customer satisfaction. For example, a service organization may believe that if its processes are designed to collect and keep the most accurate accounting records, the customers will be best served by such a system. Or, a hospital administration may assume that if its facilities and procedures are designed and followed carefully so that a test lab can operate in the most efficient manner, this will assure that patients will receive the best possible medical care. Unfortunately, this approach usually ends up frustrating customers and may lead them to competitors.

We are, of course, referring to the part of the system that is above the line of visibility, the part with which customers come into direct contact (see Exhibit 2-4). This part has to be designed and operated with the customer and his needs in mind. The backroom, or backstage, operations should be designed to support the operations above the line of visibility. Once these premises have been established, there is no harm in focusing on the efficiency of backstage operations.

Another important issue in delivery system design is the core service. As Lovelock[11] points out, many services consist of a core service and several supplementary services. A prerequisite for customer satisfaction is flawless delivery of the core service. Excellence in supplementary services will not mean much to the customer if the organization fails in the core service. Therefore, it is critical that the delivery system is designed and managed for perfection in the delivery of the core service. Supplementary services may then be added to support and enhance the core service. These issues will be covered in more detail in chapter 8.

Physical Evidence

Physical evidence includes all the tangible aspects of a service or service organization a customer experiences. Backstage facilities, or facilities below the line of visibil-

---

[10] Kristin Dunlap Godsey, "Slow Climb to New Heights," *Success* (October 20, 1996).

[11] Christopher H. Lovelock, "Competing on Service: Technology and Teamwork in Supplementary Services," *Planning Review* (July/August 1995), pp. 32–47.

ity, are not considered part of physical evidence because they are not directly experienced by the customer. A subset of physical evidence, called *servicescape*,[12] is the physical facility in which the service is delivered and consumed. For example, the exterior design of the building where the service organization is located, parking, landscape, as well as all the furniture and fixtures in the building, equipment, signage, lighting, temperature and noise level within the facility, and tidiness and cleanliness of the facility constitute the servicescape. Other tangibles, such as forms and supplies used in service processes, brochures, and employee dresses and uniforms, make the rest of the physical evidence.

Physical evidence is important for the success of service encounters, especially in "people-processing" services. First of all, because most services are produced and consumed at the same time, in general, customer satisfaction may be enhanced or diminished by the servicescape. If the customer's body is the recipient of tangible actions, then customer comfort and safety must be the primary focus in the design of physical evidence. In general, the longer the customer is in the facility, the greater the importance of the physical evidence.

In addition, physical evidence may affect the behavior of both customers and employees; consumer research has shown that servicescape can influence customer behavior and purchase decisions. For example, Barnes & Noble, which owns and operates a chain of bookstores, has adopted a revolutionary concept in store design. Their superstores have sofas, lounge chairs, and tables for customers to sit and read books, as well as a cafe within the store where customers can have gourmet coffee and pastries. An executive of the bookstore industry made the following observation on this approach: "Barnes & Noble understood the social implications of a bookstore. They understood the role of coffee, high ceiling heights, the sofas, the chairs. They understood the stores could be an extension of my living room."[13]

Service providers spend most of their working hours within the service facility, hence their job satisfaction as well as motivation and performance may also be affected by the physical evidence. Servicescape should be designed to help employees perform their tasks with minimum hindrance and facilitate flow of customers and work through the system. For example, proper signage in large facilities, such as a full-service hospital, a metropolitan airport, a subway system, or an amusement park, will help reduce the number of disoriented people, avoid congestion, and relieve service employees from the time-consuming task of giving directions.

Role of Other Customers in Service Encounters

Many services are produced for and consumed by a large group of people. Some of these can be enjoyed by the customer in the privacy of her home without any contact with other consumers, such as Internet services, recorded music, and radio and TV broadcasts. However, some others, such as air and rail travel, vacation on a cruise ship, live entertainment, sporting events, and traditional education, require the physical presence of the customer and proximity to other customers. In these cases, behavior of one customer or a group of customers may have an impact on the outcome of service encounter for others. A drunk passenger on an airliner may make the trip an unpleasant experience for other passengers and service providers. On the other hand, a group of cruise ship vacationers with similar interests and social background may

[12] Mary Jo Bitner, "Servicescapes: The Impact of Physical Surroundings on Customers and Employees," *Journal of Marketing*, vol. 56 (April 1992), pp. 57–71.

[13] Patrick M. Reilly, "Street Fighters: Where Borders Group and Barnes & Noble Compete, It's a War," *Wall Street Journal* (September 3, 1996).

have a very enjoyable experience because of the mix of the group. It is largely management's responsibility to make sure that the encounter is a pleasant one for everyone. This can be accomplished by[14]:

1. *Selecting the right customers.* A service organization may use formal and informal rules to limit the service offering only to those who would enhance each other's positive experience. Formal criteria may include age limits, such as the "adults only" resorts, dress codes, such as the "formal attire" requirement at some restaurants, or membership requirement at some clubs. Informal criteria include limited targeted advertising, pricing, and design of servicescape. For example, for many years suburban malls have been a favorite hangout place for teenagers, but the congregation of teenagers sometimes leads to unsavory incidents, which adult shoppers do not appreciate, such as loud talk, food-court fights, and even shooting. As a result, mall developers and management companies are trying to control their customer mix by selecting more exclusive stores that do not attract teenagers, offering few places for them to congregate and creating opulent interiors meant to evoke a luxury hotel.[15]

2. *Establishing rules of behavior expected from customers.* Management can establish and communicate clear rules of behavior in service facilities to ensure a satisfactory encounter for all customers. "No smoking" signs on public transportation and "no running, no diving, no horse play" signs at swimming pools are examples that may prevent undesirable behavior before it happens.

3. *Facilitating positive customer–customer interaction.* Interaction with others may increase the enjoyment of some services, such as a vacation at a resort or on a cruise ship. Management can organize gatherings or activities for customers to mix and socialize and create shared enjoyment. In a completely different environment, such as a hospital, interaction among patients who suffer from the same ailment may help reduce their anxiety and risk perception. Toronto's Shouldice Hospital performs only external-type abdominal hernia operations on healthy patients. From the moment patients arrive, Shouldice creates many opportunities and organizes activities for patients to meet, socialize, and share their experiences. One of these activities is an evening tea-and-cookies gathering, where preoperative patients talk to patients whose operations have been completed earlier that same day.

2.6 SUMMARY

A productive system is defined as a set of elements that works together toward the common goal of creating value through conversion of inputs into outputs. There are five kinds of productive systems: extraction, biological growth, tangible-output conversion, intangible-output conversion, and hybrid conversion systems. Services fall into the last two categories. Services exhibit some important characteristics that differentiate them from goods: Services are intangible and perishable. Service output exhibits much variability due to the involvement of humans and their varied needs, perceptions, and expectations. Service production and consumption are inseparable for most services. Another distinguishing characteristic of services is customer involvement, and sometimes participation, in service delivery. Due to these characteristics,

---

[14] Adrian Palmer and Catherine Cole, *Services Marketing, Principles and Practice* (Upper Saddle River, NJ, Prentice Hall, 1995), pp. 110–111.

[15] Louise Lee, "To Keep Teens Away, Malls Turn Snooty," *Wall Street Journal* (October 17, 1996).

service quality and productivity are difficult to measure, and measures of effectiveness are usually subjective.

The service organization as a system consists of three main subsystems: operations, marketing, and human resources. The operations system, which produces and delivers the service, consists of a front room and a back room, with an imaginary line of visibility separating the two. Services and their delivery systems can be classified into four categories: (1) people processing: tangible actions directed at the customer's body; (2) possession processing: tangible actions directed at goods and other physical possessions of the customer; (3) mental stimulus processing: intangible actions directed at the customer's mind; and (4) information processing: intangible actions directed at customer's intangible assets.

A service encounter is defined as "any episode in which the customer comes into contact with any aspect of the organization and gets an impression of the quality of its service." These encounters are events of utmost importance to a service organization because they have a significant influence on customer satisfaction. That is why they are also called *moments of truth*. It is important that service managers understand the nature and dynamics of service encounters. Most service encounters are purposeful interactions between a customer and service provider. In these interactions, service providers are not necessarily altruistic. Interactions are also "work" to service employees. Prior acquaintance is not required for service encounters and they are limited in scope. Task-related information exchange dominates most encounters. Client and provider roles are well defined, and sometimes a temporary status differential occurs between a customer and a service provider.

A service encounter may be perceived in different ways, depending on the interest of the observer. It can be seen as a social encounter or an economic exchange. It is also possible to view a service encounter as a production process, or as a contract between the service organization and a customer. Finally, because some services require customers to perform some of the tasks of service production, service encounters can be seen as partial employment for the customer.

Service encounters have four basic elements: (1) the customer, (2) the service provider, (3) the delivery system, and (4) the physical evidence. "Other customers" in the service system can be added as a fifth element because they sometimes influence a customer's service experience. These elements and their interrelationships must be kept in mind when designing effective service systems that create value for the customer.

Discussion Questions

1. How would you define a service?
2. How would you characterize the output of services? Is it possible to identify units of service output?
3. Describe how the following characteristics are used to describe services:
   a. Decentralization
   b. Customer contact
   c. Customer participation
4. How do the following differ for service firms versus manufacturing firms?
   a. Measures of effectiveness
   b. Measures of productivity
   c. Quality control
5. Can services be mass produced? Why or why not?
6. Why are services more labor intensive than most manufacturing firms? What management problems does this pose?

7. Discuss the role of the service provider. What impact does the individual performance of service employees have on company performance?
8. Discuss the concept of "service as a system." How do the components of a service system impact the outcome of a service encounter?
9. What is meant by "front room" and "back room" operations? How can you distinguish between the two? Why is it important to separate the two?
10. Describe the nature of service encounters.
11. Discuss the role of the customer in service encounters. How would the customer's behavior effect the "moment of truth"?
12. Discuss the role of the service provider in "people-processing" service encounters. What types of behavior and skills are needed in these encounters?
13. Discuss the role of the service provider in "information-processing" service encounters. What types of behavior and skills are needed in these encounters?
14. What is a service delivery system? Describe a delivery system of a service with which you are familiar.
15. What are the implications of characterizing service encounters as "human interactions"?
16. Discuss the role of physical evidence in "people-processing" service encounters.
17. Discuss the role of physical evidence in "possession-processing" service encounters.
18. What role may other customers play in service encounters? Discuss measures that management can take to ensure desirable outcomes when many customers are present in service performance.

CASES

CASE 2–1   Walt Disney Makes Everyone a Star

The Walt Disney Company is a diversified international entertainment organization whose operations include filmed entertainment, consumer products, and theme parks and resorts.

It is in the area of theme parks and resorts that the company has acquired a reputation for providing a consistently high level of consumer satisfaction. A major reason for this success lies in the careful analysis of just what visitors to its theme parks expect from their visit and detailed specification of the service standards to be provided. In delivering high-quality services, particular attention is paid to the roles played by the employees of the organization who are responsible for front-line service encounters.

The company's business mission involves making guests happy, and this mission has embedded itself in the cultural values shared by all employees. Once employed, all new employees learn about the history of the Disney Company and gain an understanding of the original philosophy of Walt Disney himself and the whole corporate culture. One approach used by Walt Disney to achieve its mission is to treat its theme parks as giant entertainment stages in which a series of satisfying service encounters take place. People paying to come into the park are considered not as customers but as guests. Similarly, employees are considered as cast members in this encounter and wear costumes appropriate to their tasks, rather than uniforms.

After being introduced to the basic cultural values of the organization, each cast member is given clear written instructions about his or her role expectations, where to report, what to wear, and how to handle typical encounters with guests. Role playing prepares cast members for a wide range of guest requests, for example, meeting their requests for directions or guidance on the best places to eat.

New employees are assigned particular roles, whose titles indicate the strength of the entertainment culture:

Role	Function
Custodial hosts	Street cleaners
Food and beverage hosts	Restaurant workers
Transportation hosts	Drivers
Security hosts	Police

Walt Disney's role scripting is based on careful analysis of what guests particularly value in the actions of cast members, and the interactions between cast members and guests are manipulated in such a positive way that the guests' expectations are exceeded. In order for roles to be performed effectively, Disney provides extensive training, including several days of training for each employee before he or she comes into contact with guests. Regular training sessions and newsletters are used to keep employees informed of new developments. Should training have failed to prepare an employee to cope with a guest's problem on the spot, the employee can contact backup support by telephone in order to satisfy the guest's request promptly.

In order to ensure that management is aware of the experiences of front-line staff, each member of the management team spends a week each year as a front-line member of the workforce. In addition, each member of management is also expected to bring his or her family for one day to experience the resort as a guest and thereby perceive the experience from the guest's perspective.

Finally, employees themselves are used to monitor the quality of service encounters. Peer review by current cast members is used in the selection of new recruits, the primary criterion for selection being service. All employees are expected to complete a questionnaire on their own perceptions of working for the organization. The results are then analyzed, and from the results, employee satisfaction is measured. The Disney philosophy is that if employees are satisfied with their encounters, then so ultimately will be the customer. ■

SOURCE: Adrian Palmer and Catherine Cole, *Services Marketing, Principles and Practice* (Upper Saddle River, NJ, Prentice Hall, 1995), pp. 105–107.

CASE QUESTIONS

1. Within the context of Disney World, what is meant by *scripting*?

2. A critical incident can be defined as an encounter between a customer and a service provider that is especially satisfying or dissatisfying. How can Walt Disney identify what constitutes a critical incident and measure whether it has achieved customer satisfaction?

3. Choose any encounter that is likely to occur with Disney's theme parks and either identify the steps of the encounter or construct a flow-chart to describe and analyze the encounter. Identify functions that may be below the line of visibility supporting the service provider in this encounter.

CASE 2–2   Sullivan's Auto World

Viewed from Wilson Avenue, the dealership presented a festive sight. Strings of triangular pennants in red, white, and blue fluttered gaily in the late afternoon breeze. Rows of new model cars gleamed and winked in the sunlight. Geraniums graced the flowerbeds outside the showroom entrance. A huge rotating sign at the corner of Wilson Avenue and Victoria Street sported the Ford logo and identified the business as Sullivan's Auto World. Banners below urged "Let's Make a Deal!"

Inside the handsome, high ceilinged showroom, three of the new Fords were on display—a dark-blue minivan, a red convertible, and a white Taurus. Each car was polished to a high sheen. Two groups of customers were chatting with salespeople, and a middle-aged man sat in the driver's seat of the convertible, studying the controls.

Upstairs in the comfortably furnished general manager's office, Carol Sullivan-Diaz finished running another spreadsheet analysis on her laptop computer. She felt tired and depressed. Her father, Walter Sullivan, had died four weeks earlier at the age of 56 of a sudden heart attack. As executor of his estate, the bank had asked her to temporarily assume the position of general manager of the dealership. The only visible changes that she had made to her father's office were installing a fax machine and laser printer, but she had been very busy analyzing the current position of the business.

Sullivan-Diaz did not like the look of the numbers on the printout. Auto World's financial situation had been deteriorating for 18 months, and it had been running in the red for the first half of the current year. New car sales had declined, reflecting a turndown in the regional economy. Margins had been squeezed by promotions and other efforts to move new cars off the lot. Industry forecasts of future sales were discouraging, and so were her own financial projections for Auto World's sales department. Service revenues, which were below average for a dealership of this size, had also declined, although the service department still made a small surplus.

Had she had made a mistake last week, Carol wondered, in turning down Bill Froelich's offer to buy the business? It was true that the price offered had been substantially below the offer from Froelich that her father had rejected two years earlier, but the business had been more profitable then.

THE SULLIVAN FAMILY

Walter Sullivan had purchased a small Ford dealership in 1977, renaming it Sullivan Auto, and had built it up to become one of the best known in the metropolitan area. Six years back, he had borrowed heavily to purchase the current site at a major suburban highway intersection, in an area of town with many new housing developments.

There had been a dealership on the site, but the buildings were 30 years old. Sullivan had retained the service and repair bays, but torn down the showroom in front of them, and replaced it by an attractive modern facility. On moving to the new location, which was substantially larger than the old one, he had renamed his business Sullivan's Auto World.

Everbody had seemed to know Walt Sullivan. He had been a consummate showman and entrepreneur, appearing in his own radio and television commercials and active in community affairs. His approach to car sales had emphasized promotions, discounts, and deals in order to maintain volume. He was never happier than when making a sale.

Carol Sullivan-Diaz, aged 28, was the eldest of Walter and Carmen Sullivan's three daughters. After obtaining a bachelor's degree in economics, she had gone on to take an MBA degree and had then embarked on a career in health care management. She was married to Dr. Roberto Diaz, a surgeon at St. Luke's Hospital. Her 20-year-old twin sisters, Gail and Joanne, who were students at the local university, lived with their mother.

In her own student days, Sullivan-Diaz had worked part-time in her father's business on secretarial and bookkeeping tasks, and also as a service writer in the service department: so she was quite familiar with the operations of the dealership. At business school, she had decided on a career in health care management. After graduation, she had worked as an executive assistant to the president of St. Luke's, a large teaching hospital. Two years later, she joined Metropolitan Health Plan as assistant director of marketing, a position she had now held for almost three years. Her responsibilities included attracting new members, complaint handling, market research, and member retention programs.

Carol's employer had given her a six-week leave of absence to put her father's affairs in order. She doubted that she could extend that leave much beyond the two weeks still remaining. Neither she nor other family members were interested in making a career of running the dealership. However, she was prepared to take time out from her health care career to work on a turnaround if that seemed a viable proposition. She had been successful in her present job and believed it would not be difficult to find another health management position in the future.

THE DEALERSHIP

Like other car dealerships, Sullivan's Auto World operated both sales and service departments, often referred to in the trade as "front end" and "back end," respectively. However, Auto World did not have a body shop for repairing damaged bodywork. Both new and used vehicles were sold, since a high proportion of new car and van purchases involved trading in the purchaser's existing vehicle. Auto World would also buy well maintained used cars at auction for resale. Purchasers who decided that they could not afford a new car would often buy a "preowned" vehicle instead, while shoppers who came in looking for a used car could sometimes be persuaded to buy a new one.

The front end of the dealership employed a sales manager, seven salespeople, an office manager, and a secretary. One of the salespeople had given notice and would be leaving at the end of the following week. The service department, when fully staffed, consisted of a service manager, a parts supervisor, nine mechanics, and two service writers. The Sullivan twins often worked part-time as service writers, filling in at busy periods, when one of the other writers was sick or on vacation, or when—as currently—there was an unfilled vacancy. The job entailed scheduling appointments for repairs and maintenance, writing up each work order, calling customers with repair estimates, and assisting customers when they returned to pick up the cars and pay for the work that had been done.

Sullivan-Diaz knew from her own experience as a service writer that it could be a stressful job. Few people liked to be without their car, even for a day. When a car broke down or was having problems, the owner was often nervous about how long it would take to get it fixed and, if the warranty had expired, how much the labor and parts would cost. Customers were quite unforgiving when a problem was not fixed completely on the first attempt and they had to return their vehicle for further work.

Major mechanical failures were not usually difficult to repair, although the parts replacement costs might be expensive. It was often the "little" things like water leaks and wiring problems that were the hardest to diagnose and correct, and it might be necessary for the customer to return two or three times before such a problem was resolved. In these situations, parts and materials costs were relatively low, but labor costs mounted up quickly, being charged out at $45 an hour. Customers could often be quite abusive, yelling at service writers over the phone or arguing with service writers, mechanics, and the service manager in person.

Turnover in the service writer job was high, which was one reason why Carol—and more recently her sisters—had often been pressed into service by their father to "hold the fort" as he described it. More than once, she had seen an exasperated service writer respond sharply to a complaining customer or hang up on one who was being abusive over the telephone. Gail and Joanne were currently taking turns to cover the vacant position, but there were times when both of them had classes and the dealership had only one service writer on duty.

By national standards, Sullivan's Auto World was a medium-sized dealership, selling around 1,100 cars a year, equally divided between new and used vehicles. In the most recent year, its revenues totaled $26.6 million from new and used car sales and $2.9 million from service and parts—down from $30.5 million and $3.6 million, respectively, in the previous year. Although the unit value of car sales was high, the margins were quite low. The reverse was true for service. Industry guidelines suggested that the contribution margin (known as the departmental selling gross) from car sales should be about 5.5 percent of sales revenues, and from service, around 25 percent of revenues. In a typical dealership, 60 percent of the selling gross came from sales and 40 percent from service. The selling gross was then applied to fixed expenses, such as administrative salaries, rent or mortgage payments, and utilities.

For the most recent 12 months at Auto World, Sullivan-Diaz had determined that the selling gross figures were 4.6 percent and 24 percent, respectively, both of them lower than in the previous year and insufficient to cover the dealership's fixed expenses. Her father had made no mention of financial difficulties and she had been shocked to learn from the bank after his death that Auto World had been two months behind in mortgage payments on the property. Further analysis also showed that accounts payable had also risen sharply in the previous six months. Fortunately, the dealership held a large insurance policy on Sullivan's life, and the proceeds from this had been more than sufficient to bring mortgage payments up to date, pay down all overdue accounts, and leave some funds for future contingencies.

The opportunities for expanding new car sales did not appear promising, given the state of the economy. However, recent promotional incentives had reduced the inventory to manageable levels. From discussions with Larry Winters, Auto World's sales manager, Sullivan-Diaz had concluded that costs could be reduced by not replacing the departing sales rep, maintaining inventory at somewhat lower levels, and trying to make more efficient use of advertising and promotion. Although Winters did not have Walter's exuberant personality, he had been Auto World's leading sales rep before being promoted, and had shown strong managerial capabilities in his current position.

As she reviewed the figures for the service department, Sullivan-Diaz wondered what potential might exist for improving its sales volume and selling gross. Her father had never been very interested in the parts and service business, seeing it simply as a necessary adjunct of the dealership. "Customers always seem to be miserable back there," he had once remarked to her. "But here in the front end, everybody's happy when someone buys a new car." The service facility was not easily visible from the main highway, being hidden behind the showroom. The building was old and greasy, although the equipment was modern and well maintained.

Customers were required to bring cars in for servicing before 8:30 A.M. After parking their cars, customers entered the service building by a side door and waited their turn to see the service writers, who occupied a cramped room with peeling paint and an interior window overlooking the service bays. Customers stood while work orders for their cars were written up by hand on large sheets. Ringing telephones frequently interrupted the process. Filing cabinets containing customer records and other documents lined the far wall of the room.

If the work were of a routine nature, such as an oil change or tune up, the customer was given an estimate immediately. For more complex jobs, they would be called with an estimate later in the morning once the car had been examined. Customers were required to pick up their cars by 6:00 P.M. on the day the work was completed. On several occasions, Carol had urged her father to computerize the service work order process, but he had never acted on her suggestions.

The service manager, Rick Obert, who was in his late forties, had held the position since Auto World opened at its current location. The Sullivan family considered him to be technically skilled, and he managed the mechanics effectively. However, his manner with customers could be gruff and argumentative.

Customer Survey Results

Another set of data that Sullivan-Diaz had studied carefully were the results of the customer satisfaction surveys that were mailed to the dealership monthly by a research firm retained by the Ford Motor Company.

Purchasers of all new Ford cars were sent a questionnaire by mail within 30 days of making the purchase and asked to use a five-point scale to rate their satifaction with the dealership sales department, vehicle preparation, and the characteristics of the vehicle itself. The questionnaire asked how likely the purchaser would be to recommend the dealership, the salesperson, and the manufacturer to someone else. Other questions asked if the customers had been introduced to the dealer's service department and been given explanations on what to do if their cars needed service. Finally, there were some classification questions relating to customer demographics.

A second survey was sent to new car purchasers nine months after they had bought their cars. This questionnaire began by asking about satisfaction with the vehicle and then asked customers if they had taken their vehicles to the selling dealer for service of any kind. If so, respondents were then asked to rate the service department on 14 different attributes—ranging from the attitudes of service personnel to the quality of the work performed—and then to rate their overall satisfaction with service from the dealer.

Customers were also asked about where they would go in the future for maintenance service, minor mechanical and electrical repairs, major repairs in those same categories, and bodywork. The options listed for service were selling dealer, another Ford dealer, "some other place," or "do-it-yourself." Finally, there were questions about overall satisfaction with the dealer sales department and the dealership in general, as well as the likelihood of their purchasing another Ford Motor Company product and buying it from the same dealership.

Dealers received monthly reports summarizing customer ratings of their dealership for the most recent month and for several previous months. To provide a comparison with how other Ford dealerships performed, the reports also included regional and national rating averages. After analysis, completed questionnaires were returned to the dealership; since these included each customer's name, a dealer could see which customers were satisfied and which were not.

In the 30-day survey of new purchasers, Auto World achieved better than average ratings on most dimensions. One finding which puzzled Carol was that almost 90 percent of respondents answered "yes" when asked if someone from Auto World had explained what to do if they needed service, but less than a third said that they had been introduced to someone in the service department. She resolved to ask Larry Winters about this discrepancy.

The nine-month survey findings disturbed her. Although vehicle ratings were in line with national averages, the overall level of satisfaction with service at Auto World was consistently low, placing it in the bottom 25 percent of all Ford dealerships.

The worst ratings for service concerned promptness of writing up orders, convenience of scheduling the work, convenience of service hours, and appearance of the service department. On length of time to complete the work, availability of needed parts, and quality of work done ("was it fixed right?"), Auto World's rating was close to the average. For interpersonal variables such as attitude of service department personnel, politeness, understanding of customer problems, and explanation of work performed, its ratings were relatively poor.

When Sullivan-Diaz reviewed the individual questionnaires, she found that there was a wide degree of variation between customers' responses on these interpersonal variables, ranging all the way across a 5-point scale from "completely satisfied" to "very dissatisfied." Curious, she had gone to the service files and examined the records for several dozen customers who had recently completed the nine-month surveys. At least part of the ratings could be explained by which service writers the customer had dealt with. Those who had been served two or more times by her sisters, for instance, gave much better ratings than those who had dealt primarily with Jim Fiskell, the service writer who had recently quit.

Perhaps the most worrying responses were those relating to customers' likely use of Auto World's service department in the future. More than half indicated that they would use another Ford dealer or "some other place" for maintenance service (such as oil change, lubrication, or tune-up) or for minor mechanical and electrical repairs. About 30 percent would use another source for major repairs. The rating for overall satisfaction with the selling dealer after nine months was below average and the customer's likelihood of purchasing from the same dealership again was a full point below that of buying another Ford product.

An Unwelcome Disturbance

Sullivan-Diaz pushed aside the spreadsheets she had printed out and shut down her laptop. It was time to go home for dinner. She saw the options for the dealership as basically twofold: either prepare the business for an early sale at what would amount to a distress price, or take a year or two to try to turn it around financially. In the latter instance, if the turnaround succeeded, the business could subsequently be sold at a higher price than it presently commanded, or the family could install a general manager to run the dealership for them.

Bill Froelich, owner of another nearby dealership, had offered to buy Auto World for a price that represented a fair valuation of the net assets, according to Auto World's accountants, plus $150,000 in goodwill. However, the rule of thumb when the auto industry was enjoying good times was that goodwill should be valued at $1,000 per vehicle sold each year.

As Carol left her office, she spotted the sales manager coming up the stairs leading from the showroom floor. "Larry," she said, "I've got a question for you."

"Fire away!" replied the sales manager.

"I've been looking at the customer satisfaction surveys. Why aren't our sales reps introducing new customers to the folks in the Service Department? It's supposedly part of our sales protocol, but it only seems to be happening about one-third of the time!"

Larry Winters shuffled his feet. "Well, Carol, basically I leave it to their discretion. We tell them about service, of course, but some of the guys on the floor feel a bit uncomfortable taking folks over to the service bays after they've been in here. It's quite a contrast, if you know what I mean."

Suddenly, the sound of shouting arose from the floor below. A man of about 40, wearing a windbreaker and jeans, was standing in the doorway yelling at one of the salespeople. The two managers could catch snatches of what he was saying, in between various obscenities: ". . . three visits . . . still not fixed right . . . service stinks . . . who's in charge here?" Everybody else in the showroom had stopped what they were doing and had turned to look at the newcomer.

Winters looked at his young employer and rolled his eyes. "If there was something your dad couldn't stand, it was guys like that, yelling and screaming in the showroom and asking for the boss. Walt would go hide out in his office! Don't worry, Tom'll take care of that fellow and get him out of here. What a jerk!"

"No," said Sullivan-Diaz, "I'll deal with him! One thing I learned when I worked at St. Luke's was that you don't let people yell about their problems in front of everybody else. You take them off somewhere, calm them down, and find out what's bugging them."

She stepped quickly down the stairs, wondering to herself, "What else have I learned in health care that I can apply to this business.?" ■

SOURCE: Christopher H. Lovelock, *Services Marketing*, 3rd ed. (Upper Saddle River, NJ, Prentice Hall, 1996), pp. 122–126. Copyright © 1996 by Christopher H. Lovelock.

CASE QUESTIONS

1. How does marketing cars differ from marketing service for those same vehicles?
2. Compare the sales and service departments at Auto World.
3. Sales and service departments are referred to as the "front end" and "back end," respectively, of the car dealership business. Are these terms equivalent to "front room" and "back room," in the service management literature? If not, describe front and back rooms in Auto World.
4. Describe a typical service encounter for a customer who comes to the dealership to (a) buy a new car and (b) have his or her car repaired. What should Auto World do to make sure that these are satisfactory encounters for customers?
5. What useful parallels do you see between running a car dealership and health care services?
6. Flowchart the servicing of a car (bring your flowchart to class; be prepared to present it).
7. How should Sullivan-Diaz handle the angry customer in the showroom?
8. What advice would you give to Carol Sullivan-Diaz regarding:
   - Improving service quality
   - Marketing the service department
   - Marketing the dealership
   - Selling Auto World now versus attempting a turnaround

References

Albrecht, Karl, and Ron Zemke, *Service America!* (Homewood, IL, Dow Jones-Irwin, 1985).

Albrecht, K., *At America's Service* (New York, Warner Books, 1988).

Bateson, J. E., "Perceived Control and the Service Encounter," in J. A. Czepiel, M. R. Solomon, and C. F. Surprenant (eds.), *The Service Encounter: Managing Employee/ Customer Interaction in Service Businesses* (Lexington, MA, Lexington Books, 1985), pp. 67–82.

Berry, Leonard L., "Services Marketing is Different," *Business* (May–June 1980).

Berry, L. L., *On Great Service: A Framework for Action* (New York, Free Press, 1996).

Bitner, Mary Jo, "Servicescapes: The Impact of Physical Surroundings on Customers and Employees," *Journal of Marketing*, vol. 56 (April 1992), pp. 57–71.

Carlzon, J., *Moments of Truth* (Cambridge, MA, Ballinger, 1987).

Chase, R. B., "Where Does the Customer Fit in a Service Operation?" *Harvard Business Review*, vol. 56, no. 6 (November–December 1978), pp. 138–139.

Collier, David A., *Service Management: The Automation of Services* (Reston, VA, Reston Publishing Co., 1985).

Czepiel, J. A., M. R. Solomon, C. F. Surpranant, and E. G. Gutman, "Service Encounters: An Overview," in J. A. Czepiel, M. R. Solomon, and C. F. Surpranant, (eds.), *The Service Encounter: Managing Employee/Customer Interaction in Service Businesses* (Lexington, MA, Lexington Books, 1985), pp. 3–15.

George, W. R., M. G. Weinberger, and J. P. Kelly, "Consumer Risk Perceptions: Managerial Tool for the Service Encounter," in J. A. Czepiel, M. R. Solomon, and C. F. Surprenant (eds.), *The Service Encounter: Managing Employee/ Customer Interaction in Service Businesses* (Lexington, MA, Lexington Books, 1985), pp. 83–100.

Godsey, Kristin Dunlap, "Slow Climb to New Heights," *Success* (October 20, 1996).

Grove, S. J., R. P. Fisk, and M. J. Bitner, "Dramatizing the Service Experience: A Managerial Approach," in T. A. Swartz, D. E. Bowen, and S. W. Brown (eds.), *Advances in Services Marketing and Management: Research and Practice*, vol. 1 (Greenwich, CT, JAI Press Inc., 1992), pp. 91–121.

Grönroos, C., *Service Management and Marketing* (Lexington, MA, Lexington Books, 1990).

Heskett, James L., *Managing in the Service Economy* (Boston, Harvard Business School Press, 1986).

Heskett, J. L., W. E. Sasser, Jr., and C. W. L. Hart, *Service Breakthroughs: Changing the Rules of the Game* (New York, Free Press, 1990).

Lee, Louise, "To Keep Teens Away, Malls Turn Snooty," *Wall Street Journal* (October 17, 1996).

Lovelock, Christopher H., "Classifying Services to Gain Strategic Marketing Insights," *Journal of Marketing*, vol. 47, no. 3 (summer 1983), pp. 9–20.

Lovelock, Christopher H., "Competing on Service: Technology and Teamwork in Supplementary Services," *Planning Review* (July/August 1995), pp. 32–47.

Lovelock, Christopher H., *Services Marketing*, 3rd ed. (Upper Saddle River, NJ, Prentice Hall, 1996).

Marriott, J. W., Jr., and Kathi Ann Brown, *The Spirit to Serve: Marriott's Way* (New York, NY, Harper Business, 1997).

Mills, P. K., *Managing Service Industries: Organizational Practices in a Postindustrial Economy* (Cambridge, MA, Ballinger, 1986).

Mills, Peter K., and Newton Margulies, "Toward a Core Typology of Service Organizations," *Academy of Management Review*, vol. 5, no. 2 (April 1980), pp. 255–266.

Mills, Peter K., and Dennis J. Moberg, "Perspectives on the Technology of Service Operations," *Academy of Management Review*, vol. 7, no. 3 (July 1982), pp. 467–478.

Mills, P. K., and D. J. Moberg, "Strategic Implications of Service Technologies," in D. E. Bowen, R. B. Chase, and T. G. Cummings (eds.), *Service Management Effectiveness* (San Francisco, Jossey-Bass, 1990), pp. 97–125.

Normann, Richard, *Service Management: Strategy and Leadership in Service Businesses*, 2nd ed. (Chichester, England, John Wiley, 1991).

Nyquist, J. D., M. J. Bitner, and B. H. Booms, "Identifying Communication Difficulties in the Service Encounter: A Critical Incident Approach," in J. A. Czepiel, M. R. Solomon, and C. F. Surprenant (eds.), *The Service Encounter: Managing Employee/Customer Interaction in Service Businesses* (Lexington, MA, Lexington Books, 1985), pp. 195–212.

Palmer, A., and C. Cole, *Services Marketing, Principles and Practice* (Upper Saddle River, NJ, Prentice Hall, 1995).

Reilly, Patrick M., "Street Fighters: Where Borders Group and Barnes & Noble Compete, It's a War," *Wall Street Journal* (September 3, 1996).

Riddle, D. I., *Service-Led Growth: The Role of the Service Sector in World Development* (New York, Praeger Publishers, 1986).

Rust, Roland T., Anthony J. Zahorik, and Timothy L. Keiningham, *Service Marketing* (New York, HarperCollins, 1996).

Sasser, W. Earl, Jr., R. Paul Olsen, and D. Daryl Wyckoff, *Management of Service Operations* (Boston, Allyn and Bacon, 1978).

Schmenner, Roger W., "How Can Service Businesses Survive and Prosper?" *Sloan Management Review*, vol. 27, no. 3 (Spring 1986), pp. 24–35.

Shostack, L. G., "Planning the Service Encounter," in J. A. Czepiel, M. R. Solomon, and C. F. Surprenant (eds.), *The Service Encounter: Managing Employee/ Customer Interaction in Service Businesses* (Lexington, MA, Lexington Books, 1985), pp. 243–253.

Zeithaml, Valarie A., and Mary Jo Bitner, *Services Marketing* (New York, McGraw-Hill, 1996).

CHAPTER 3

Customers: The Focus of Service Management

3.1   INTRODUCTION

There is a keen awareness today among the successful manufacturing and service companies that customers are the most valuable assets a company has. Several years ago, this fact was expressed most convincingly by an executive who achieved one of the most amazing turnarounds in Europe, former CEO of Scandinavian Airlines System (SAS) Jan Carlzon:

> Look at our balance sheet. On the asset side, you can still see so-and-so many aircraft worth so-and-so many billions. But it's wrong; we are fooling ourselves. What we should put on the asset side is, last year SAS carried so-and-so many happy passengers. Because that is the only asset we've got—people who are happy with our service and are willing to come back and pay for it once again.[1]

Karl Albrecht, the co-author of the best-selling book *Service America*, takes this assertion a step further and characterizes customers as an *appreciating asset*. "An appreciating asset is one that grows over time, and that is exactly what happens if customer satisfaction and customer loyalty are increasing over time."[2] There is also research evidence to support these claims. Frederick F. Reichheld and W. Earl Sasser, Jr.,[3] estimated that service companies can increase profits by almost 100 percent by retaining just 5 percent more of their customers. They also estimated the value of loyal customers for specific services. For example, if a credit card company reduces the defection rate of its customers from 20 percent to 10 percent, the average life of a

---

[1] Jan Carlzon, *Moments of Truth* (Cambridge, MA, Ballinger, 1987).

[2] Karl Albrecht, *At America's Service* (New York, Warner Books, 1988), p. 24.

[3] Frederick F. Reichheld and W. Earl Sasser, Jr., "Zero Defections: Quality Comes to Services," *Harvard Business Review* (September–October 1990), pp. 105–111.

customer account doubles from five to ten years and the value of that customer increases from $130 to $300. Another 5 percent reduction in defection rate boosts profits to $500, a 75 percent increase. Exhibit 3-1 shows how L. L. Bean, a legendary service company, defines its customers.

The importance of the customer cannot be more evident in any management theory than in the quality and continuous improvement movement that started in the 1980s in the United States. This movement indisputably has the "customer" as its focus. The quality and continuous improvement movement had achieved a significant level of development when the Malcolm Baldrige National Quality Award (MBNQA) was established in 1987 as a result of a collaborative effort between the federal government and the private sector. *Customer-driven quality* is one of the core values of the MBNQA. Customer satisfaction is a major criterion by which companies that apply for the award are evaluated.

Whether they are manufacturers or service providers, excellent companies know their customers; they know customers' needs and requirements. Each company may have a different way of knowing or discovering its customers' needs, but usually they go to great lengths to gather this information. It is true that sometimes customers cannot articulate their needs and requirements, but this does not mean an organization should not pursue this goal. Chapter 2 discussed service encounters, or "moments of truth." Recall that many service encounters involve face-to-face interaction with a customer. This is very different from manufacturing a good, say a TV set, in a plant, and shipping it to a retailer, who will then sell it to a nameless, faceless customer in a faraway place. Almost all service providers are in contact with customers—either verbal or physical contact is necessary. Consequently, service customers are neither nameless nor faceless. They may show emotions; they may be happy or they may be angry. Whatever the situation, they cannot and should not be easily ignored. Hence, knowing your customer takes on a very different meaning in services. Creating a successful service encounter every time is not the only reason for understanding customers and their needs. Service providers need this information to be able to design effective and efficient services and delivery systems that satisfy customers, to position and market services effectively, and to forecast and manage demand.

EXHIBIT 3-1   L. L. Bean's Notion of a Customer

What Is a Customer?

- A customer is the most important person ever in this office . . . in person or by mail.
- A customer is not dependent on us . . . we are dependent on him.
- A customer is not an interruption of our work . . . he is the purpose of it. We are not doing him a favor by serving him . . . he is doing us a favor by giving the opportunity to do so.
- A customer is not someone to argue or match wits with. Nobody ever won an argument with a customer.
- A customer is a person who brings us his wants. It is our job to handle them profitably to him and to ourselves.

(A poster that is prominently displayed all around L. L. Bean, in Freeport, Maine)

Source: Tom Peters and Nancy Austin, *A Passion for Excellence* (New York, Random House, 1985), p. 95.

Learning about customers, their needs and requirements may take many forms, such as surveys, interviews, focus groups, and test marketing. Discussion of these instruments is beyond the scope of this book, however. This chapter provides a general framework for understanding customers and their needs and requirements based on consumer behavior theories and demographics. Although organizations constitute an important segment of customers for services, the main focus in this chapter will be on individuals (single individuals or a group of individuals, such as a family) as service customers.

3.2   CUSTOMERS AND THEIR NEEDS

Customers purchase goods and services to satisfy their needs. Dr. Abraham Maslow, a clinical psychologist, developed a theory of hierarchy of human needs to help explain human motivation.[4] Maslow identified five categories of needs that he ranked in decreasing order of priority: physiological, safety, social, egoistic, and self-actualization needs. Humans try to satisfy the lower-level needs before attempting to satisfy needs that are at a higher level. This does not imply that a lower need must be completely satisfied before a higher need comes into play. For most people, no need is 100 percent satisfied; rather, they are satisfied at decreasing percentages as one goes up the hierarchy. Theory suggests that human behavior is influenced by these needs; unsatisfied needs motivate behavior. It must be pointed out, however, that human behavior is not usually determined entirely by a single need, and not all behavior is motivated by the basic needs. The hierarchy of needs is represented in Exhibit 3-2. Although these needs are represented in the exhibit as mutually exclusive categories for convenience, Maslow's theory does make it clear that there is some overlap between levels; satisfaction of some needs may serve as a channel for the satisfaction of other needs. For example, a person who thinks he is hungry may actually be seeking comfort or companionship rather than nutrients.

Physiological needs are those that are essential to maintain human life, such as food, air, water, sex, clothing, and shelter. These constitute the most basic category of needs; they dominate other needs when they are chronically unsatisfied. If the physiological needs are relatively satisfied, **safety needs** emerge and dominate other needs until they are fairly satisfied. These needs include personal physical safety and secu-

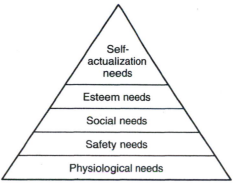

EXHIBIT 3-2   Maslow's Hierarchy of Needs

---

[4] Abraham H. Maslow, "A Theory of Human Motivation," *Psychological Review*, vol. 50 (1943), pp. 370–396.

rity from wild animals, criminals, extremes of temperatures, and natural forces. Also included are desire for health, order, stability, routine, and familiar surroundings and people. Maslow labeled the third category as **love needs.** However, **social needs** is probably a more appropriate title because it includes not only the need for love, but also needs such as affection, belongingness, friendship, and affiliation. Most human beings have a desire for "high evaluation of themselves, for self-respect, or self-esteem, and for the esteem of others."[5] These needs are called **esteem needs** and include desire for strength, achievement, adequacy, confidence, independence, and freedom as well as desires for esteem from other people, such as desire for a good reputation or prestige, recognition, attention, importance, and appreciation. The need to be what one *can* be is called the **self-actualization need.** The need to achieve self-fulfillment, to achieve one's potential to become everything one is capable of becoming, emerges only after the physiological, safety, social, and esteem needs are satisfied. According to Maslow, most people are not able to satisfy the first four levels to reach the fifth level.

Maslow's theory provides a useful framework for managers for understanding human behavior in general, and consumption behavior in particular. Many services exist to satisfy various needs at every level of the hierarchy. For example, a fitness center may appeal to the human desire for a long and healthy life; health or homeowner's insurance helps consumers meet their safety needs; a dating service, as well as a fitness center, may help a single person achieve his social needs by creating opportunities for meeting other singles; learning a skill or getting a college education may help one achieve esteem, as well as self-actualization needs.

3.3 CONSUMER BEHAVIOR AND A CONSUMER DECISION MODEL

Despite its usefulness and wide acceptance, Maslow's theory is not nearly sufficient to explain the purchase behavior of contemporary consumers. Modern consumers differ in their lifestyles, tastes, expectations, and requirements. It is not possible to categorize them in a few well-defined groups; they may have some common characteristics, but they also exhibit a great deal of variety. Furthermore, consumer characteristics change through time; consumers' lifestyles, tastes, expectations, and requirements change constantly and diversify. These challenges, together with other factors that emerged mostly after World War II, such as the fast pace of product introduction, shorter product life cycles, environmental concerns, increased interest in consumer protection, public policy concerns, growth of services, and nonprofit organizations and international markets, created a need for the development of consumer behavior as a separate field of study.[6]

Consumer behaviorists study how individuals make purchasing decisions. They also investigate what consumers buy, why they buy it, how often, and where and when they buy it. The field of consumer behavior borrows from concepts and theory developed in other fields of study, such as psychology, sociology, social psychology, cultural anthropology, and economics.

Marketing scholars who study consumer behavior have developed various models of consumer decision making. This section reviews one of these models by Hawkins, Best, and Coney[7] based on a generic consumer decision model. It is a descriptive

[5] Abraham H. Maslow, "A Theory of Human Motivation."
[6] Leon G. Schiffman and Leslie L. Kanuk, *Consumer Behavior*, 4th ed. (Upper Saddle River, NJ, Prentice Hall, 1991), pp. 9–10.
[7] Del I. Hawkins, Roger J. Best, and Kenneth A. Coney, *Consumer Behavior*, 5th ed. (Homewood, IL, Irwin, 1992), pp. 16–23.

model that portrays consumer decision making as a process to satisfy various needs that emanate from consumers' lifestyles.

Consumer lifestyle plays a central role in the formation of needs and attitudes. Lifestyle is how a person lives. It includes goods and services a consumer buys, how she views them, as well as how she views herself. A person's, or a family's, lifestyle is the result of many influences as shown in Exhibit 3-3. These influences may be organized into two subgroups: external and internal influences.

External Influences

External influences are forces outside an individual's sphere of influence that nevertheless form the environment in which he operates. Consequently, these forces influence the way the individual lives, perceives the world around him, thinks, and makes decisions—including purchase decisions.

Culture is the personality of a society and for that reason influences almost anything we do or how we think. Culture is learned and is not static; it changes over time, usually very slowly. However, culture is not a set of prescriptions for behavior; rather, it defines the boundaries within which most people think and act. Clearly, culture provides guidance and direction in our thinking and behavior and therefore has a significant influence on our consumption decisions.

Values are part of our culture learned from parents, family, religious organizations, school, and from the environment in which we live. Cultural values are widely held beliefs that identify what is desirable or right. Values may be self-oriented, other oriented, or environment oriented. Self-oriented values concern the individual—they

EXHIBIT 3-3   A Consumer Behavior Model

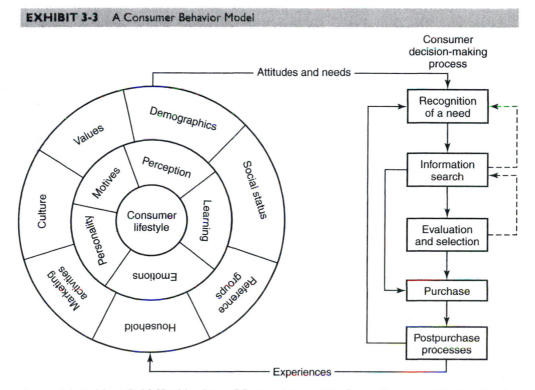

Source: Adapted from Del I. Hawkins, Roger J. Best, and Kenneth A. Coney, *Consumer Behavior*, 5th ed. (Homewood, IL, Irwin, 1992), p. 22.

reflect his objectives and approach to life in general. Other-oriented values reflect the society's desires concerning the relationships between individuals and groups. Environment-oriented values represent a society's view of the desired relationship with its economic and natural environment.

Statistical characteristics, such as age, sex, education, income, occupation, and distribution and density of population, make the **demographics** of a society. Demographic information is widely used by marketing professionals and managers to provide objective assessment of potential customers and reveal trends in important characteristics of the population such as age and income distribution, and geographic shifts of population.

Social status is the position of an individual relative to the rest of the population in terms of some measurable demographic characteristics, such as education, occupation, and income. Individuals with the same or very similar position are identified as a social class. It is generally assumed that people in the same social class have similar values, beliefs, lifestyles, preferences, and buying habits. Identifying and understanding the differences between social classes help companies develop different services to meet differing needs of people in each group. For example, banks offer different levels of service to different customers depending on their wealth.

A group is a collection of two or more people. Groups are formed because people with similar interests, objectives, values, or beliefs want to relate to each other, exchange information, or work toward common goals. Most people belong to a large number of groups. Groups that influence consumers' purchase decisions are called consumer **reference groups.** Family, friendship groups, formal social groups, and work groups are some of the reference groups. Companies that advertise their goods and services by appealing to a certain group hope to induce members to buy as a requirement for conformance to group norms and values.

Households with two or more people are important both as reference groups and as consumption units. They influence the purchase behavior of its members, and as a unit, they buy and consume many goods and services. Services such as telephone, cable TV, electricity, trash collection, security, and police and fire protection are provided to households; therefore, changes in household demographics and consumption patterns are usually more important than changes in general population characteristics for the provision of these services.

Marketing activities focus on building and maintaining relationships with customers that will benefit both sides. They interact with both external and internal factors. Marketers must also have a good understanding of internal factors that play a significant role in consumers' purchase decisions. This is especially important because of the intangibility of services. Service organizations appeal to some or all of the internal elements by making an intangible product tangible through promotions such as "Reach out and touch someone."(These issues will be discussed further in chapter 6.)

Internal Influences

Influences that originate within an individual's body or mind are called internal influences. Clearly, they may be in response to the external environment, but they are unique to the individual; that is, the same events will elicit different responses from different individuals.

Emotions are strong and uncontrollable feelings that are generally triggered by outside events. Fear, anger, joy, sadness, acceptance, disgust, expectancy, and surprise are considered basic emotions.[8] Physiological changes such as increased heart rate, in-

---

[8] R. Plutchik, *Emotion: A Psychoevolutionary Synthesis* (New York, Harper & Row, 1980).

creased perspiration, and rapid breathing are believed to *precede* emotion. Emotions may be positive or negative. Most often, consumers seek products and services that lead to the arousal of positive emotions. However, a movie or a book that makes us sad is not necessarily considered a bad consumption experience. Adventure travel packages, movies, books, music, and in general all types of entertainment services appeal to the emotions.

Personality is the whole set of psychological characteristics that distinguishes an individual. It is believed that personality plays an important role in an individual's purchase decisions and the way he responds to advertising messages. This influence, however, is believed to be operational only in broad product categories, not in brand preferences.

A **motive** is an inner force, created by a need or desire, that stimulates and compels a person to act. This inner force usually emerges as a result of an unsatisfied need. Consequently, the individual engages in behavior to reduce the tension created by the unfulfilled need. Recalling Maslow's hierarchy of needs, some motives are physiological in origin, whereas others are created by social and psychological needs. It is important for managers to understand the motives their goods and services encourage. For example, an increase in burglaries in a neighborhood may appeal to an individual's safety need, which motivates the purchase of a house security system and service.

Humans learn many things to maintain their lives and function in a society. **Learning** can be defined as the process through which humans acquire knowledge, which leads to a change in the long-term **memory.** We learn when acquired information becomes part of the long-term memory. Most of our values, attitudes, preferences, tastes, and behavior are learned. Knowledge of goods and services that can satisfy our needs must also be acquired. Consumers have to know something about existing alternatives, prices, product characteristics, quality, and the like before they can make a purchase decision. Sources of information for consumption purposes are many and include family, friends, mass media, advertising, institutions, and personal experiences.

Perception is how we see the world around us. It is a process through which we select, organize, and make sense of stimuli from our environment. Stimuli are inputs, such as sound, light, image, odor, and so forth, that affect our sense organs—the eyes, ears, nose, mouth, and skin. Perception is subjective and very personal; a set of stimuli may lead to very different perceptions in different individuals. Because consumers make purchase decisions based on their perceptions, marketers try very hard to create positive perceptions of their goods and services in consumer minds.

Attitudes and Needs

Attitudes represent our orientation, favorably or unfavorably, toward an object in our environment, such as a good, service, retail outlet, or an advertisement. Attitudes are learned from the environment and formed as a result of the internal and external factors previously discussed. On the other hand, some needs are learned, and some are innate, such as food and water. Attitudes and needs are both influenced by an individual's lifestyle and a reflection of lifestyle.

Consumer Decision-Making Process

The Hawkins, Best, and Coney model portrays **consumer lifestyle** as a function of internal and external influences. Consumer lifestyle, in turn, influences attitudes and needs, which trigger the decision-making process shown in Exhibit 3-3. It must be emphasized that the influence is usually indirect and subtle. The need to understand this relationship and operationalize it for marketing purposes led to the development of a strand of research known as psychographics. Psychographics attempts to describe and segment consumers based on psychological dimensions. Originally, it focused on activities, interests, and opinions, but more recently, psychographic studies also include attitudes, values, demographics, media patterns, and usage rates.[9]

Need Recognition and Information Search   When a consumer realizes that a need exists, the satisfaction of that need becomes the consumer's problem. If the problem can be solved with the purchase of a good and/or service, the consumer decision process begins. First, the consumer searches for relevant information. Two types of information are needed; information for developing criteria for an effective decision and information on the existing brands. The time spent by the consumer in this stage varies and depends on the nature of the need. For example, high school seniors spend a considerable amount of time in choosing a college or university. However, a consumer who needs his suits cleaned would not spend nearly as much time in choosing a dry cleaner.

Evaluation and Selection   Consumers need criteria to select the good or service that will satisfy their needs. They also need to narrow the choices down to a manageable size. This is necessary because most consumers have limited time, energy, and capacity to process information. The resulting set of alternatives, or brands, is known as the **evoked set.** The criteria developed to select a good or service are called **evaluative criteria.** Consumers may actually start working on both of these during the information search and will probably continue after sufficient information has been collected. The nature, number, and importance of criteria depend on the consumer and the nature of the need. Some examples of criteria that are commonly used in selecting services include price, quality, convenience, ease of access, friendliness of servers, and reputation of the company.

Choice of Service Outlet and Purchase   In many cases, selection of the service and the service organization are concurrent decisions. In other cases, the consumer has to select where to buy the selected brand. Clearly, service dimensions such as availability of sales personnel to help with the purchase, their attitude, size and layout of the store, and its atmosphere all play a role in this decision.

Postpurchase Processes   After the purchase and use of the good or service, one of the following possible outcomes will occur: (1) the performance confirms the expectations of the consumer, leading to a neutral feeling of satisfaction; (2) the performance exceeds expectations and the customer is delighted, which is known as *positive disconfirmation*; or (3) the performance is below the expectations and the customer is not satisfied, which is known as *negative disconfirmation*. Repeat purchase is most likely when positive disconfirmation or a neutral feeling is the result. Consumers engage in more postpurchase evaluation and information seeking with services than with goods. They also engage in more postpurchase evaluation than prepurchase evaluation when selecting and consuming services. This is because many qualities of a service cannot be evaluated until after the service is experienced. Consumer experience with a good or service becomes an input to lifestyle and future decisions, as indicated in Exhibit 3-3. Information on the use and postpurchase evaluation is very important to operations and marketing managers because this information influences product strategies and design decisions.

[9] Hawkins, Best, and Coney, pp. 327–328.

3.4   UNIQUE ASPECTS OF SERVICE PURCHASES

The model we have just reviewed is a fairly general model that is applicable to most goods and services. However, consumer decision-making process in purchasing services exhibit some important differences that are worth considering.

Different Criteria

Consumers evaluate services differently from goods. This difference originates from the intangibility of services and the human involvement which lead to variability in results and can be understood with reference to the following three properties (Exhibit 3-4) consumers use in evaluation[10]:

1. *Search qualities.* These attributes can be determined before a purchase decision is made. Most goods are high in search qualities and therefore are relatively easy to evaluate. Search qualities that are frequently used as evaluative criteria for goods include price, style, color, available sizes, fit, feel, and smell. For services, this list is usually short, and may include price, location, options and levels of service, and availability (e.g., hours of operation).

2. *Experience qualities.* Experience qualities are those attributes that can only be judged during or after consumption, such as taste, wearability, and satisfaction with the performance of a service provider.

3. *Credence qualities.* Attributes that the consumer may be unaware of or lack the technical knowledge to evaluate, even during or after consumption, are known as credence qualities. Services that are performed by professionals, such as med-

EXHIBIT 3-4   Continuum of Consumer Evaluation of Goods and Services

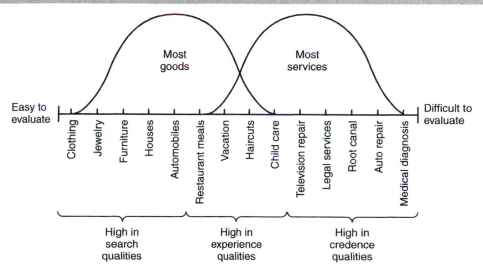

Source: Valarie A. Zeithaml, "How Consumer Evaluation Processes Differ Between Goods and Services," in N. H. Donnelly and W. R. George (eds.), *Marketing of Services,* Proceedings of the 1981 Conference on Services Marketing (Chicago: American Marketing Association, 1981), p. 186. Used with permission.

---

[10] Valarie A. Zeithaml, "How Consumer Evaluation Processes Differ Between Goods and Services?" in J. H. Donnelly and W. R. George (eds.), *Marketing of Services,* Proceedings of the 1981 Conference on Services Marketing (Chicago: American Marketing Association, 1981), pp. 186–190.

ical and legal services, and services that require special technical knowledge and skills, such as auto repair, are high in credence qualities. Typical consumers of these services have neither the technical expertise nor all the relevant information for evaluation, and frequently will not be able to assess the quality or the necessity of the service even after the service is performed.

Exhibit 3-4 views consumer evaluation of goods and services on a continuum from high in search qualities to high in credence qualities.

Different Sources of Information

There are five basic sources of information[11]: *memory* (personal experiences), *personal sources* (friends and family), *independent sources* (consumer groups), *marketing sources* (sales personnel and advertising), and *experiential sources* (inspection or trial use). When buying services, consumers rely mostly on memory and personal sources. This is true because mass media sources provide information about search qualities but very little about experience qualities. Friends and experts who are familiar with the service can provide reliable information on experience qualities. Also, nonpersonal sources may not be available because some service organizations are small local companies that do not have the funds or expertise to advertise.[12]

A Smaller Evoked Set

As stated earlier, the limited number of alternatives a consumer considers for purchase is called an evoked set. This set tends to be smaller for services than for goods. The major reason for this is that a certain brand of good can be purchased at many different retail outlets, but service companies almost always sell only one "brand"—theirs. Consequently, for most services, once a brand decision has been made, there is only one place to buy the selected brand. Some service companies, such as banks, may have branches at various locations. In such a case, once the bank has been selected, the problem may simply be determining the branch that has the most convenient location. Another reason for the limited evoked set is that demand in a given geographic location can support only a small number of service companies, and therefore a consumer is not likely to find an extensive set of alternative companies offering the desired service.

Brand Switching and Repeat Purchase Behavior

Brand switching in services is less frequent. Consumers make some service purchase decisions very few times in their lives, and do not consider them again until a major event or a problem occurs. For example, after a consumer selects a bank for his checking and/or savings accounts, he tends to stay with it until he moves to another town or becomes unhappy with the bank's service. For some services, the decision is whether or not to buy it, because the company offering the service is the only alternative. This is the case for most utilities, such as gas, electric, water, and telephone services. Another reason for infrequent brand-switching behavior in services is the switching costs and perceived risk. The costs involved in switching brands may be greater in services than in goods. Switching costs many be monetary, such as installation and membership fees, or nonmonetary, such as the disruption it may cause in one's lifestyle, and time spent in information gathering, evaluation of alternatives, decision making, and learning the new system and its requirements.

[11] Hawkins, Best, and Coney, p. 471.
[12] Valarie A. Zeithaml and Mary Jo Bitner, *Services Marketing* (New York, McGraw-Hill, 1996), p. 61.

Risk Perception

Research indicates that consumers usually perceive greater risk in service consumption than purchase and use of goods.[13] Perceived risks that consumers find to be higher in services than in goods include time, performance, financial, social, and psychological. Also, some research indicates that consumers perceive no difference between goods and services in terms of physical risk. The major reason for this is the intangibility of services and their simultaneous production and consumption. If the customer is unfamiliar with the service or not a frequent user, she faces many unknowns, and unknowns usually imply risk. Another reason for risk perception is the nonstandardized nature of many services. Even if the same company and the same server provide the service, there may be variations in the performance and the outcome. A third reason for the perceived risk is that some services do not come with guarantees or warranties, or they are not meaningful; a money-back guarantee is not much use if your dentist pulls the wrong tooth. For these reasons, some service purchases are "habitual" (same barber for a haircut) or automatic (telephone service).

3.5   A CULTURAL PROFILE OF AMERICAN CUSTOMERS

The previous section focused on consumers at a micro level, that is, examined the individual customer and how he is influenced by internal and external factors in shaping a lifestyle, which in turn influences his purchase decisions. This, of course, is essential for understanding customers and designing appropriate service systems. However, we also need to understand consumers as a group, how they behave as a group, and how they change their consumption behavior. This section reviews cultural characteristics of the residents of the United States (Americans, for short).

The United States is usually characterized as a country built by immigrants who came from many countries of the world; hence, Americans have a rich and varied cultural and ethnic background. This leads to the obvious question: "Can the character of such a large population of people with a mosaic of ethnic origins be accurately described with a few cultural traits?" The answer seems to be "yes," according to two recent studies. Following are five cultural forces that define Americans.[14]

1. *Individualism and an insistence on choice.* Americans insist on freedom of choice. It is in our constitution. Individualism and choice are the dominant forces in our pursuit of happiness. Choice is the force that brought the Pilgrims to Plymouth Rock, and it is the force that brought all that followed them to America's shores. Freedom of choice prompts customers to demand a wide range of alternative goods and services to satisfy individual needs.
2. *The impossible dream.* America has institutionalized the dream process and created a national environment where anything is possible. Americans tend to sympathize with the "underdog." Advertisers appeal to this trait with ads such as Avis's "We try harder" campaign because "we're number 2" (i.e., the underdog to Hertz).
3. *Obsession with big and more.* We like things big—very big—the bigger the better. If we cannot have something bigger, we will settle for more. That way, we eventually

---

[13] For a review of research findings, see, for example, William R. George, Marc G. Weinberger, and J. Patrick Kelly, "Consumer Risk Perceptions: Managerial Tool for the Service Encounter," in J. A. Czepiel, M. R. Solomon, and C. F. Surprenant (eds.), *The Service Encounter: Managing Employee/Customer Interaction in Service Businesses* (Lexington, MA, Lexington Books, 1985), pp. 83–100.

[14] Adapted from Josh Hammond and James Morrison, *The Stuff Americans Are Made Of* (New York, Macmillan, 1996); and Leon G. Schiffman and Leslie L. Kanuk, *Consumer Behavior*, 4th ed. (Upper Saddle River, NJ, Prentice Hall, 1991), pp. 410–424.

get bigger by having more. Increased consumption is fueled by a need for achievement and success. More goods and services are symbols of accomplishment.

4. *Impatience with time.* America is the most time-obsessed country in the world. We are uniquely impatient with time and live in the present/future (now) with little or no regard for the past (yesterday is history). Americans believe that "time is money," and "time waits for no man." Therefore, goods and services that save time and make daily chores easier or completely eliminate them are a big part of our culture.

5. *Fixation on "watsnew."* As individuals, we are in a perpetual search for new identities, new ideas, new strategies, new consumer goods, and new services. Progress is a favorite word with Americans. We make progress through improvising. Once the situation is fixed, we are free to move on to something else, and moving on is a major occupation in America. Advertisers' claims such as "new," "all new," "improved," and "longer lasting," appeal to our positive view of change and progress. Americans are also preoccupied with looking and acting young. Being "young at heart," "young in spirit," and "looking young," are among our favorite expressions and are frequently used in ads promoting various goods and services. This is closely related to, and a reinforcing effect on, the recent concern with staying fit and healthy.

3.6 A LOOK INTO THE FUTURE

As we look into the early part of the twenty-first century, there are several trends relevant to the consumption of goods and services.[15]

Age Distribution

Probably the most important trend is the "graying" or "maturing" of American population. The size of the age group "65 and over" was less than 20 million in 1970, but this group is expected to quadruple to almost 80 million by 2050. By that time, one in five Americans will be 65 or over. This change in the age distribution is expected to have a significant impact on social, economic, and political life.

In addition to health care, the elderly will demand many other services. It must be pointed out that the 65 and over age group is not homogenous; depending on the status of their health, their needs will be quite different.[16] They will be experienced, mature, and well-educated consumers. Many people in this group will think younger and lead active lifestyles—they will travel, eat out, and vacation a lot. This will create growth opportunities in the entertainment, air travel, hospitality, resort, and cruise industries. The elderly will also be purchasing many other services they once performed themselves, such as lawn care, cooking, home maintenance, snow removal, and repairs of all types. As they age further and become less mobile, their demand for some of these services as well as health-related services will increase, and some additional services will be demanded, such as transportation services for shopping and doctor visits, home delivery of groceries, and home shopping for all types of goods. They will also have an increased demand for physical and psychological security.

[15] Unless otherwise stated, all demographic data in this section are from *Statistical Abstract of the United States*, 116th ed. (Washington, DC, U.S. Department of Commerce, 1996).

[16] W. Lazer, P. LaBarbera, J. M. MacLachlan, and A. E. Smith, *Marketing 2000 and Beyond* (Chicago, American Marketing Association, 1990), pp. 81–82.

Households

The household is an important consumption unit. Demand for some goods and services depends on the nature and size of the household and the ages of the members. According to Census Bureau projections, the number of households will be 103.2 million in the year 2000, 108.8 million in 2005, and 114.8 million in 2010. An increase in households will create more demand for household-related goods and services. Some of the services that are affected by these increases include lawn mowing, snow removal, landscaping, telephone, water, waste removal, electricity, cable and satellite broadcast, and package and newspaper delivery services. Related to these, demand for services that are provided by governments at different levels, such as mail, police and fire protection, and parks and recreational services, will also increase.

Education, Occupation, and Income

American consumers will be more educated and better informed. As our economy becomes more and more knowledge based, the best-paying and most exciting jobs will go to those with advanced education and skills. It is also clear that current and future technologies will change the delivery and perhaps the nature of education. Distance learning, Internet, videos, and satellite link-ups are some examples of technology used at all levels of our educational system. Learning and education will become a lifelong effort as knowledge and skills become obsolete faster. These trends will lead to an increase in demand for new, more efficient and effective tools and methods of learning and updating and upgrading skills and knowledge.

Income individuals receive is an important factor in their consumption decisions and lifestyles. There is a trend of increasing disparity in income distribution in the United States that is very disturbing to many people.[17] According to the Bureau of the Census figures, between 1973 and 1992 real wages of males declined for all but the top quintile of the workforce. One result of the income disparity is in the new reality called *two-tier marketing*. "Companies are tailoring their products and pitches to two different Americas. . . . today, in industry after industry, the market is bifurcating— between private banking services and check-cashing outfits, high-speed data lines linked to the Internet and prepaid phone cards, leather-upholstered sport-utility vehicles and spiffed-up used cars."[18]

Some More Predictions about the Future

This chapter will close with some more and general predictions about the future by insightful futurists, business executives, and academicians, compiled by the American Marketing Association[19]:

- Emphasis will shift from the flow of materials and goods to the flow of information; data banks, artificial intelligence systems, advanced communications, and knowledge will gain prominence.
- Conservation rather than consumption will be the focus with its emphasis on efficient utilization of resources, preserving environments, abating pollution, downsizing, recycling, and securing the world of tomorrow.

---

[17] See, for example, Lester C. Thurow, *The Future of Capitalism: How Today's Economic Forces Shape Tomorrow's World* (New York, William Morrow, 1996), and Tom Morganthau, "The Face of the Future," *Newsweek*, January 27, 1997.

[18] David Leonhart, "Two-Tier Marketing," *Business Week*, March 17, 1997.

[19] Adapted from Lazer et al., *Marketing 2000 and Beyond*, p. 36.

- A global perspective will dominate the approach of many businesses rather than a national or regional perspective.
- Smokestack industries will give way to high-tech industries that are information driven, focused on creation of new knowledge.
- The nature of many businesses will shift from labor driven to education driven, featuring highly educated labor/management inputs, research, software, advanced communication systems, and computers.
- Standardization and homogeneity of products will give way to individualization, customization, and differentiation.

3.7 SUMMARY

This chapter provided basic concepts of consumer behavior and a cultural and demographic profile of American consumers. Maslow's hierarchy of needs has been presented to explain some of the consumer needs. Maslow's theory asserts that human needs have a hierarchy: physiological needs or innate needs such as hunger and thirst have the first priority. Safety needs, social needs, esteem needs, and self-actualization needs have decreasing degrees of priority. Humans try to satisfy these needs in the given order of priority; however, a higher-level need may emerge even if lower-level needs have not been completely satisfied.

The Hawkins, Best, and Coney consumer behavior model explains how consumers' lifestyles are formed by a set of external and internal influences. External influences include values, demographics, social status, reference groups, and household and marketing activities. Internal influences are emotions, personality, motives, learning and memory, and perception. The model depicts lifestyle as a determining factor for consumer attitudes and needs and then explains what steps are usually taken by consumers before a purchase decision is made to satisfy those needs. The decision process begins with need recognition, followed by information search and evaluation and selection of a brand and purchase outlet. The final step is postpurchase evaluation to assess the value of the product and satisfaction level.

The purchase decision for services is significantly different from the purchase decision for goods. Consumers tend to reduce the alternatives to a small set of choices, called the evoked set. The evoked set is usually smaller for services than for goods. Services are high in experience and credence qualities; goods are high on search qualities. Consumers perceive higher risks with service purchases and do not switch brands as readily.

This chapter also presented a cultural profile of Americans and developing trends. The most important demographic change in the future is the aging of the American population.

Discussion Questions

1. Explain what types of services will help a consumer satisfy each level of needs in Maslow's hierarchy of needs.
2. Explain what "lifestyle" means and how it influences a consumer's decisions in buying services.
3. Explain how external factors influence the emergence of our needs for services.
4. Explain how internal factors influence the emergence of our needs for services.
5. What are the similarities and differences between goods and services in the consumer decision-making process?

6. Refer to Maslow's hierarchy of needs and the decision-making process of the consumer behavior model presented in this chapter. From which level(s) would the need for the following services emerge and how the process applies in purchasing them?
   a. College education
   b. Entertainment for an evening (e.g., movie, concert, sports event)
   c. Dental services
   d. Renting a place (e.g., restaurant, hotel ballroom) for a special occasion, such as a birthday, wedding reception, or bar mitzvah
   e. Air travel
7. Identify the search qualities, experience qualities, and credence qualities of the following services. Also refer to Exhibit 3-4 and determine approximately where each service will fall along the continuum.
   a. Pizza parlor
   b. Fire department or other emergency services
   c. Management seminar
   d. Car rental
   e. Master of business administration (MBA) program
8. Recall the five possible sources of information for buying goods and services: *memory*, *personal sources*, *independent sources*, *marketing sources*, and *experiential sources*. What are examples of services for which each of these sources would be most relevant in purchase decisions?
9. What are some strategies service organizations can use to reduce the consumer's perceived risk of their services?
10. What are some strategies for consumers to reduce the perceived risks in services?
11. Which services do you think will be helpful to consumers in maintaining and/or enhancing each of the five common American characteristics given in Section 3.5?
12. Refer to the predictions given in Section 3.6 about American consumers in the future. Which of the existing services do you think will enjoy a higher demand than currently? What new services do you think will be needed in the early part of the twenty-first century?

CASES

CASE 3–1   Oasis Laundries, Inc.*

With 30 percent of U.S. households without washers and dryers, there is considerable market for laundries. More than 20 million Americans frequent some 45,000 laundries each week. Eighty percent of these laundries have machines that are over 10 years old, and most are neglected by absentee owners. So who wants to hang out at a laundromat? There are all those machines that don't work, those horrid plastic chairs, and the dreaded crusty linoleum floor. All this, combined with the warm smell of lint and a task most people disdain, makes the laundromat one of the least desirable places to spend time.

A bad situation in many ways is nothing more than an untapped market opportunity. Oasis Laundries, Inc., management saw a large market for a clean, comfortable laundromat in a desirable environment. There was virtually no competition.

LARGE MARKET STRATEGY

Oasis Laundries, Inc., of San Jose, California, launched its upscale laundromat in spring 1987. While Oasis attracts all kinds of users, its primary target market is 18 to 34 years old with above-average income. These are the type of consumers who are more likely to buy a VCR and a CD player than their own washer or dryer.

The first Oasis laundries featured big-screen TVs, video games, snack bars, attendants, lounges, and lots of tables for fluffing and folding. And, because there are many consumers who do not want to bother with laundry, they also offered drop-off laundry and dry-cleaning services. While the first Oasis laundries were very pleasant, they did not make a profit. The first Oasis laundry was one third laundry equipment and two thirds devoted to entertainment, including a tanning salon. It looked more like a discotheque than a laundry. It was nice, but it wasn't serving the consumers' needs; once 8 to 10 people came into the laundry, it was full. The revised format can accommodate 30 to 40 customers and still maintain a comfortable flow.

POSITIONING

Oasis also learned that no matter how nice the laundry, people still want to get away from it. This was further verified with focus group interviews. In general, consumers viewed laundries as "dirty, things don't work, and there are strange people with raincoats lurking around." Oasis decided to promote its laundries as a place to confront and conquer one's fear of the laundry. Rather than promote all the benefits, the company decided on a Freudian approach.

Because laundries tend to be used by a mobile population, Oasis and its ad agency decided to use billboards to position and advertise Oasis Laundries. Ideas for three of four billboards came directly from the focus group interviews. One billboard showed a hamper overflowing with dirty laundry and the burning question:

Are you buying underwear to avoid using your laundromat?

(One of the focus group participants admitted to this practice.)

Another billboard shows a prison cellblock with:

Most people would rather spend time here than in a laundromat.

A third billboard features a hospital operating room with the headline:

It's almost as clean as our laundromats.

Since Oasis began in 1987, competitors have entered the market. However, Oasis management views this as good, because it helps promote awareness and a new attitude toward laundromats. By the end of 1990, Oasis planned to have doubled the number of locations to 40. To expand the reach

---

* Derived from "An Oasis for Hip Consumers," *Marketing News*, February 19, 1990, p. 2.

of their business, they considered adding franchisees committed to adding five to eight stores in a market area. Other marketing activities include such specials as senior-citizen nights and events catering to young adults, to bring them in during off hours. ■

SOURCE: Del I. Hawkins, Roger J. Best, and Kenneth A. Coney, *Consumer Behavior*, 5th ed. (Homewood, IL, Irwin, 1992), pp. 582–584.

CASE QUESTIONS

1. Describe the potential customers of a laundry with respect to age, income, social status, values, reference groups, and household characteristics.

2. What is the market potential for laundries such as Oasis? Is the future demand likely to increase, stay the same, or decline? Justify your answer in terms of demographics.

3. Do you believe that a Freudian approach to advertising is better than an ad promoting the differential benefits of an Oasis laundry?

4. Discuss the risks customers of a laundry may perceive in using this service. What measures can the management take to reduce the perceived risks?

5. What additional services and promotions could Oasis add to appeal to potential users of the Oasis laundry?

CASE 3–2   Merrill Lynch Financial Services

Though the financial holdings of female investors are enormous, it was not until recently that financial services companies such as Merrill Lynch recognized the unique needs of different female investors. Some facts were well known. The financial wealth controlled by females was in the billions of dollars and larger than that held by males. In addition to financial assets controlled throughout the life cycle, women outlive men and acquire a large quantity of stocks, bonds, mutual funds, certificates of deposit, and so on in the latter stages of the household life cycle.

However, until recently the female investor market was largely ignored and was not targeted as an important market opportunity. Consumer analysis of the female investor market uncovered a variety of differences with respect to needs, demographics, lifestyles, income, and awareness and knowledge of investment alternatives. Other differences such as media habits pointed out the fact that there is tremendous diversity among this group of investors. A quantitative analysis of this information uncovered the existence of three market segments, each unique in terms of needs for financial services, demographics, consumer lifestyle, awareness and knowledge of financial services, and media habits.

Each of these female investor segments represents a unique market opportunity. In order to design an effective marketing strategy for any or all of these segments, it is first necessary to understand the unique aspects of each female investor segment.

THE CAREER WOMAN

This segment of the female investor market is the smallest but is growing rapidly. These investors are younger (30 to 40 years old), college educated, and actively pursuing a career. Their incomes are high relative to other working women and growing as they progress in their careers. This group includes single and married females, but the majority did not have children living in their households.

While their demographics are unique, equally important differences exist in their needs for financial services. Women in this segment have higher incomes and pay considerable taxes because they are single or, if married, have two sources of income. As a result, their needs focus on ways to increase their financial holdings without incurring additional tax obligations. Also, because they do not need current income, they have a greater need for long-term capital appreciation rather than current interest or dividend income.

THE SINGLE PARENT

This segment is the second largest in size and also growing. These female investors are middle aged (35 to 45 years old), unmarried, but have children living at home. Their single-parent status could be the result of divorce or death of a spouse. Because these events tend to happen more often at middle age, this particular female investor is often thrust into managing money without much experience. Current income is generally under pressure and money affairs have to be carefully budgeted.

For this segment, security is first. With parental responsibility and limited income they want to make sure their money will be there in the future. As a result, they prefer investments that offer secure growth. This investment will be a source of income later in life and/or used for their children's education. In either case these consumers do not want to risk their futures.

THE OLDER INVESTOR

This segment is the largest of the female market for financial services. These female investors are older (55 and up) and typically single. Unlike the "Single Parent," these female investors do not have children at home and often have more discretionary income. Also, many of these investors have considerable knowledge and experience with the many financial alternatives that exist.

A need for current income makes this segment of female investors different from the other two segments. In many instances, these women support themselves from interest and dividends on their investments. Because investments are often their sole source of income, they seek safety and minimum risk in the investments they hold. Thus, their ideal investment portfolio would include a variety of secure investments that yield good current income.

While many differences exist among the many female investors, these three female investor segments capture important differences in basic needs, demographics, and lifestyle as summarized in Exhibit 3-5. Based on these differences, individualized marketing strategies could be developed for each segment. The degree to which such strategies will succeed will depend on how well each strategy satisfies the specific needs of each segment in terms of both product offerings and market communications. ■

EXHIBIT 3-5 Summary of Female Investor Segmentation

Segment	Basic Needs	Experience	Key Demographics
Career woman	Tax avoidance, long-term growth	Limited to average	Educated, working at career, between 25 and 40
Single parent	Security, future income	None to limited	Unmarried with children, between 35 and 55
Older investor	Current income, security	Limited to extensive	Typically single, 55 and older

SOURCE: Del I. Hawkins, Roger J. Best, and Kenneth A. Coney, *Consumer Behavior*, 5th ed. (Homewood, IL, Irwin, 1992), pp. 210–212.

CASE QUESTIONS

1. Discuss how different demographic situations (e.g., age, income, marital status) contribute to different financial needs among female investors.

2. How might each of these segments be further segmented demographically? What would be the advantages and disadvantages of further segmentation of this market?

3. Which internal and external factors influence each segment in its needs and decision in purchasing financial services?

4. Which advertising media (e.g., TV, magazines, newspapers, radio, direct mail) do you think will be most appropriate to communicate the information about the financial services to the three segments of female investors? Explain your reasons for making this recommendation.

References

Albrecht, Karl, *At America's Service* (New York, Warner Books, 1988).

Bateson, John E. G., "Understanding Services Consumer Behavior," in Carole A. Congram and L. Margaret (eds.), *Handbook of Marketing for the Service Industries* (New York, American Management Association, 1991), pp. 135–149.

Booms, B. H., and M. J. Bitner, "Marketing Strategies and Organization Structures for Service Firms," in J. H. Donnelly and W. R. George (eds.), *Marketing of Services* (Chicago, American Marketing Association, 1981), pp. 47–52.

Carlzon, Jan, *Moments of Truth* (Cambridge, MA, Ballinger, 1987).

Day, Jennifer Cheeseman, *Population Projections of the United States by Age, Sex, Race, and Hispanic Origin: 1995 to 2050*, U.S. Bureau of the Census, Current Population Reports, P25–1130 (Washington, DC, U.S. Government Printing Office, 1996).

George, William R., Marc G. Weinberger, and Patrick J. Kelly, "Consumer Risk Perceptions: Managerial Tool for the Service Encounter," in J. A. Czepiel, M. R. Solomon, and C. F. Surprenant (eds.), *The Service Encounter: Managing Employee/Customer Interaction in Service Businesses* (Lexington, MA, Lexington Books, 1985), pp. 83–100.

Grönroos, Christian, *Service Management and Marketing* (Lexington, MA, Lexington Books, 1990).

Hammond, Josh, and James Morrison, *The Stuff Americans Are Made Of* (New York, Macmillan, 1996).

Hawkins, Del I., Roger J. Best, and Kenneth A. Coney, *Consumer Behavior*, 5th ed. (Homewood, IL, Irwin, 1992).

Lazer, William, Priscilla LaBarbera, James M. MacLachlan, and Allen E. Smith, *Marketing 2000 and Beyond* (Chicago, American Marketing Association, 1990).

Leonhart, David, "Two-Tier Marketing," *Business Week* (March 17, 1997).

Maslow, Abraham H., "A Theory of Human Motivation," *Psychological Review*, vol. 50 (1943), pp. 370–396.

Morganthau, Tom, "The Face of the Future," *Newsweek* (January 27, 1997).

Plutchik, R., *Emotion: A Psychoevolutionary Synthesis* (New York, Harper & Row, 1980).

Reichheld, Frederick F., and W. Earl Sasser, Jr., "Zero Defections: Quality Comes to Services," *Harvard Business Review* (September–October 1990), pp. 105–111.

Schiffman, Leon G., and Leslie L. Kanuk, *Consumer Behavior*, 4th ed. (Upper Saddle River, NJ, Prentice Hall, 1991).

Statistical Abstract of the United States, 116th ed. (Washington, DC, U.S. Department of Commerce, 1996).

Thurow, Lester C., *The Future of Capitalism: How Today's Economic Forces Shape Tomorrow's World* (New York, William Morrow, 1996).

Zeithaml, Valarie A., "How Consumer Evaluation Processes Differ Between Goods and Services?" in J. H. Donnelly and W. R. George (eds.), *Marketing of Services*, Proceedings of the 1981 Conference on Services Marketing (Chicago: American Marketing Association, 1981), pp. 186–190.

Zeithaml, Valarie A., and Mary Jo Bitner, *Services Marketing* (New York, McGraw-Hill, 1996).

CHAPTER 4

Globalization of Services: Service Management in the International Arena

4.1   INTRODUCTION

Foreign trade has been in existence since states, cities, and even villages identified themselves as separate entities from others and traded with them. As early as 4,000 years ago, there was active trade in the Middle East and Asia Minor (current Turkey). Egyptians were trading with peoples of this region, and the Sumerians, who inhabited the region of present-day Iraq, traded with Asia Minor and Syria.[1] Today, international trade is alive and well and growing stronger every year. International trade in services existed alongside the trade in goods for all these years, for without services, international trade in goods would not be possible.

This chapter focuses on the globalization of services, which includes not only international trade but also investments made in other countries to produce and sell services to the residents of those countries. Unlike international trade, foreign direct investment in services has only recently become a significant phenomenon in the world economy.[2]

Globalization of services plays a very important role in the U.S. economy as well. In 1960, the United States exported $19.7 billion worth of goods and $6.3 billion of services, while importing $14.8 billion worth of goods and $7.7 billion of services.[3] By the end of 1997, these numbers had grown tremendously (see Exhibit 4-1): exports of

---

[1] R. Vernon, L. T. Wells, and S. Rangan, *The Manager in the International Economy*, 7th ed. (Upper Saddle River, NJ, Prentice Hall, 1996), pp. 3–4.

[2] K. P. Sauvant, "The Tradability of Services," in P. A. Messerlin and K. P. Sauvant (eds.), *The Uruguay Round, Services in the World Economy* (Washington, DC, The World Bank, 1990), pp. 114–122.

[3] The data in this section are from Economic Report of the President, 1997 (Washington, DC, United States Government Printing Office, 1997); and U.S. Department of Commerce, Bureau of Economic Analysis and Bureau of the Census, *Survey of Current Business* (May 1998).

EXHIBIT 4-1   Growth of the U.S. International Trade in Goods and Services

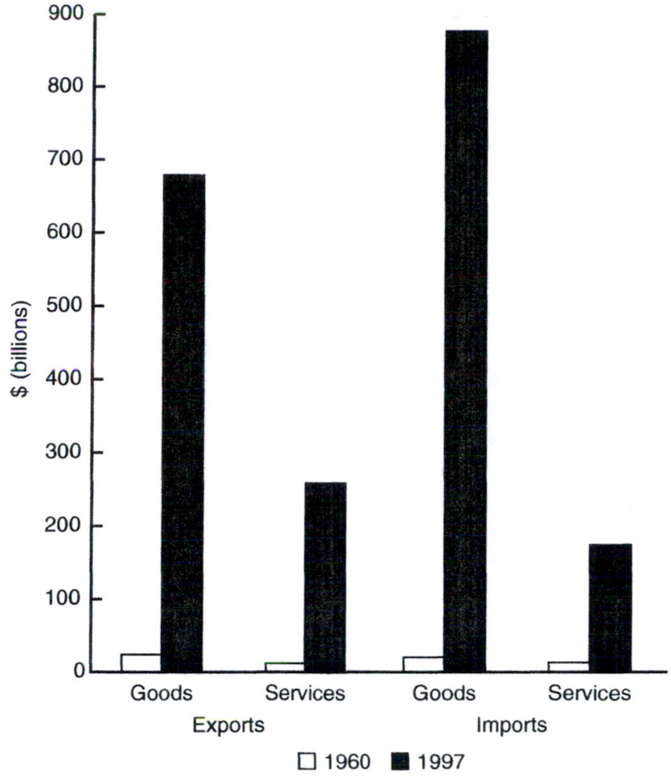

Source: *Economic Report of the President, 1997* (Washington, DC, United States Government Printing Office, 1997); and U.S. Department of Commerce, Bureau of Economic Analysis and Bureau of the Census, *Survey of Current Business* (May 1998).

goods to $678.2 billion and services to $253.2 billion. Similarly, imports of goods grew to $877.1 billion and services to $167.9 billion. From these numbers, we can see that in 1997 we had a trade deficit of about $199 billion in goods, but a surplus of $85.3 billion in services. As a matter of fact, the U.S. international trade balance was negative between 1971 and 1997 (except in 1973 and 1975), but the service trade has been consistently positive during this period. In other words, the trade deficit many people have been concerned about would have been much larger had it not been for services. Consequently, in addition to constituting more than 75 percent of gross domestic product (GDP), services also play a significant role in foreign trade, and hence in the overall U.S. economy.

This chapter explores international trade and foreign direct investment in services, the environment in which global service companies operate, different forms of going global, and recent trends in service globalization.

4.2   INTERNATIONAL TRADE IN SERVICES

International trade would not be possible without services. This is true for services provided both domestically and in the international arena. Some of the essential services for international exchange of goods and services include transportation, telecommunication, insurance, legal, and banking. When these services are used by a domestic company in exporting goods or services to another country, or by a foreign company importing goods or services to the United States, they are being traded internationally. For example, if an American shipping company transports machine tools sold to Russia by an American manufacturer, it is exporting transportation services to Russia. Or if a Russian shipping company transports these machine tools, then the Russian company is exporting shipping services to the United States. Similarly, companies that insure the shipment, provide credit for the purchase, transfer funds, and carry communications between the trading companies are all involved in international trade. Clearly, then, international trade would not exist without these and other services.

In these examples, services are involved in international trade indirectly. It is, of course, possible for services to be exported or imported directly. For example, an American movie producer who sells the European rights of her movie to a movie distributor in England is exporting a service. An American automobile manufacturer who hires an Italian designer for his next model is importing a service from Italy. In short, when services are bought from or sold to foreigners, a service is being traded internationally.

The dollar volume of international trade in services has been increasing for the past several decades. There are two basic reasons for this increase: a general increase in the demand for services in many countries and increase in world merchandise trade.

General Increase in Demand for Services

The economic role services play has been increasing steadily for decades in many countries. In industrialized countries, the share of services in the GDP reached or exceeded 65 percent in the early 1990s, and it has been significant in other countries. Households and firms have been demanding more and better-quality services. This increase in demand can be explained by four developments[4]: a growing underlying need for service functions, deintegration of service activities formerly performed in-house to specialized outside service vendors, the privatization of public services, and advances in computer and telecommunications technologies.

A Growing Need for Services   Many countries around the world are enjoying a higher standard of living, which leads to many changes in lifestyles, such as urbanization, a higher demand for travel, vacation, entertainment, demand for higher quality health care services, and a higher demand for domestic services. Businesses are also demanding more of a variety of services. As competition intensifies, the demand for advertising, consulting, legal, and investment services increases, creating new opportunities for American companies in those countries. For example, countries of the former Soviet bloc have little experience and few well-established organizations in advertising, accounting/consulting, or investment banking. Consequently, experienced international service organizations may find an untapped market in these countries. Also, as the complexity and technological sophistication of goods increase, the demand for design, training, and maintenance services increases. Regulatory changes and advances in technology also lead to the creation of new services, such as hazardous waste disposal and testing services.

Deintegration of Service Activities   Many households in developed as well as developing countries are dual career households. This, together with increased prosperity, creates both the necessity and ability to purchase some services previously performed by household members. For example, these households may use more of take

---

[4] The first three of these developments have been suggested by Michael E. Porter, *Competitive Advantage of Nations* (New York, The Free Press, 1990), p. 242.

out or delivered food services. This is one of the reasons for the expansion of American fast food outlets in many countries. For example, Domino's Pizza had 1,744 stores in 62 countries in 1999. Similarly, many businesses are outsourcing some of the non-critical services previously performed internally, such as payroll processing, security, custodial and maintenance services for their office buildings. In many cases the main reason for the deintegration is the cost savings offered by the specialized service companies which are able to achieve economies of scale in some aspects of their service operations through standardization of equipment, procedures, and methods, and in purchasing equipment and supplies because of larger volume of business they are able to obtain. When large companies outsource, foreign companies specializing in these services find an attractive market.

Privatization of Public Services   A third reason for the increased demand for services is the privatization of some government services in both industrialized and developing countries. For example, many developing as well as former Soviet bloc countries are privatizing telecommunications, health care, and education services.

Advances in Computer and Telecommunication Technologies   Advances in computers and voice and data transmission capabilities of telecommunications networks amazes many people daily. They also have a significant impact on the service trade; these developments have made the trade easier for many services, increased the speed of information exchange, and created opportunities for new services. The impact is most visible in services that rely on data and information exchange and processing, such as collection and dissemination of the news and financial data, and distribution of databases and software.

These developments lead not only to an increase in trade, but also to an increase in foreign direct investments in services. Whether through changes in incomes and lifestyles or through deintegration, as the demand for various services in each country increases, these markets become more attractive to international service companies. Before privatization, many service markets, such as telecommunications, education, and health care, were not open to competition—they were mainly government monopolies. Now that these monopolies are disappearing, their markets are not only becoming more competitive, but they are also opening up for international firms.

Increase in International Trade of Goods

As the international trade volume increases, so does the demand for certain services. Transportation, communication, insurance, banking, and legal services are the most essential services needed for international trade. Internationally traded goods must be transported by ship, train, truck, or planes between countries. Sometimes, it is necessary for people involved in the trade to travel to other countries, and they may have to use travel services, such as airlines and hotels for this purpose. Communication is essential for trading partners to initiate and complete a transaction; companies that provide telephone or telegraph services, carry mail or packages, or provide courier services make the communication possible. Goods shipped from one country to another must be insured against damage and theft in transition; hence, the services of insurance companies are needed. Transfer of goods or services in one direction requires transfer of money in the other direction, and banks make this possible. Services of lawyers are needed to prepare the necessary documents for trade between two parties and deal with many issues relating to laws and regulations of the countries involved. In addition to these, many other service providers, such as advertising professionals, accountants, customs experts, translators, and the like, will be needed for international trade to take place.

4.3 WHY SERVICE COMPANIES GO GLOBAL

This section reviews the reasons for service companies to go global through international trade or foreign direct investment. First, for clarification, brief definitions of some important terms are presented in Exhibit 4-2. As can be seen from these definitions, the most important differences among various types of companies are in their competitive strategies and the way they are organized. With these differences in mind, we will use the terms *globalization* and *internationalization* interchangeably to refer to the process of entering the international stage in one form or another, assuming that such a company may eventually evolve into a "global" corporation or even a "transnational" one.

Companies invest in other countries to reduce costs, expand markets, or as a strategic move. As domestic markets become saturated, many service companies look abroad for new business opportunities. Many service companies believe that the success they achieved in their home market can be replicated in foreign markets after some modification to the service concept and/or delivery system. This is not necessarily a correct as-

EXHIBIT 4-2   A Classification of Firms from an International Perspective

Domestic Enterprise: Operates within the boundaries of its own country; buys mostly from domestic suppliers and sells to domestic customers.	**Exporter/Importer:** Exporter sells its goods and services in other countries, usually through independent distributors. Importer sells products of foreign companies in its own country.
International Enterprise: Has sales, distribution, and/or production organizations and facilities in other countries. Units in other countries operate independently of each other and compete against local companies. However, strategy, technology, and resource allocation are centralized. Technology transfer constitutes the key relationship between headquarters and country units.	**Multinational (Multidomestic) Enterprise:** A replica of the company is created in different countries, and each is run by local managers. A multinational company hopes to be seen as a national company and thus gain a competitive advantage. Domestic operations are supplemented by globally sourced resources, skills, and technology.
Global Enterprise: Sees the whole world as a single market and its operations in this market as a single operation. It has standardized global products. Its products can be produced anywhere and can be sold anywhere in the world. It has one coordinated and centralized strategy for its worldwide operations and competition.	**Transnational Corporation:** A transnational corporation combines the advantages of international, multinational, and global corporations: it has the technology transfer capability of international, local responsiveness of multinational, and the efficiency of global enterprises. In other words, a transnational corporation tries to excel in all three forms at once.

Source: Adapted from Stephen H. Rhinesmith, *A Manager's Guide to Globalization*, 2nd ed. (Chicago, Irwin Professional Publishing, 1996), pp. 5–11; and Christopher A. Bartlett and Sumantra Ghoshal, *Managing Across Borders: The Transnational Solution* (Cambridge, MA, Harvard Business School, 1989).

sumption as many international companies discover that considerable challenges exist in going global. Lovelock and Yip identify eight reasons service firms go global[5]:

Common Customer Needs

Theodore Levitt was probably the first to identify the trend for the homogenization of consumer tastes around the world when he wrote: "Everywhere everything gets more and more like everything else as the world's preference structure is relentlessly homogenized."[6]

Consumer services that are good candidates for standardization across countries are limited to those services that do not involve customers, or when customers' involvement can be closely controlled, and when customization can be limited by the service company. Fast-food and airline services are two examples for global services; in both cases, customers' involvement is closely controlled and choices are limited for customization. Some service companies have the opportunity to offer a standard core service around the world and nationally customize it with the addition of a carefully selected set of supplementary services. For example, Club Med can use local entertainers to supplement its global core service, Club Med Vacation.

Global Customers

When a global company sets up shop in a foreign country, some service companies follow them to the same market. That was what the accounting firm Coopers & Lybrand did when Ford Motor Company established a venture in Hungary.[7] It quickly moved to open a branch office in this new market because of the concern that one of its competitors, already established in Hungary, may begin to build a relationship with its client. The uniformity of service is sought also by clients in other fields, for example, by airlines in aircraft maintenance and global manufacturers in factory and machinery maintenance and repair.

In addition, many American travelers feel more comfortable going into a McDonald's restaurant in a foreign country rather than a local restaurant. Similarly, they may prefer renting a car from an American company with which they are familiar.

Global Channels

The Internet created a global channel for the sale and distribution of many goods and services. Services, such as banking, entertainment, software, and travel services can be purchased through this electronic channel. Hence, even very small service companies may be able to offer their services through the Internet without establishing a presence in other countries.

Global Economies of Scale

Services provide few opportunities for economies of scale. The main reason for this is the fact that for most services the demand is geographically dispersed; hence, building large service facilities to exploit economies of scale in operations is usually not possible. In many cases, service capacity and workforce employed exceed average demand. Consequently, idle capacity is not uncommon in service facilities. When economies of scale is possible, it creates an incentive for a service organization to go global.

---

[5] Christopher H. Lovelock and George S. Yip, "Developing Global Strategies for Service Businesses," *California Management Review*, vol. 38, no. 2 (winter 1996), pp. 64–86.

[6] Theodore Levitt, "The Globalization of Markets," *Harvard Business Review* (May–June 1983), pp. 92–102.

[7] Gary W. Loveman, "The Internationalization of Services," Harvard Business School Module Note, 9-693-103 (June 7, 1994).

Favorable Logistics

Costs of travel and transportation have been declining for many years. This has made some previously inaccessible services economically feasible for people in other countries. Lower air travel costs have increased tourism all around the world. Also, some specialized services, such as health care and higher education in developed countries, have become affordable for the newly emerging middle class in many developing countries. For example, London hospitals attract many patients from the Middle East. Similarly, American hospitals and doctors attract patients, and American universities attract students, from all around the world.

Advances in Technology

For many services that generate, process, or use information, the developments in computer and telecommunications technologies have not only eliminated some barriers for internationalization of services, they have also created opportunities for new services and new forms of service production and delivery. They also contribute to foreign direct investment in service industries. For example:

> India has built a flourishing computer-software industry around Bangalore. Its exports more than doubled between 1990 and 1993, to $270m. India is now attracting back-office work from airlines such as Swissair and British Airways. Some of Hong Kong's paging services are manned from China. In Perth, in Western Australia, EMS Control Systems monitors the air-conditioning, lighting, lifts and security in office blocks in Singapore, Malaysia, Sri Lanka, Indonesia, and Taiwan.[8]

Government Policies and Regulations

Governments can and do restrict trade and foreign direct investments in their countries. Many instruments exist for this purpose, such as tariffs and import quotas, export subsidies for domestic companies, local content requirements, currency and capital flow restrictions, and ownership restrictions. In most cases, the main objectives of these restrictions are to protect the domestic firms against foreign companies and improve trade balance and foreign exchange reserves. Imposition of such restrictions and barriers may reduce both the trade and foreign direct investment. Conversely, the elimination or reduction of these restrictions would stimulate globalization of services. The current worldwide trend seems to be in that direction.

Transferable Competitive Advantage

A very important reason for many service companies to go global is the ability to replicate their domestically successful service concept and delivery system in foreign countries. When service companies develop a new service or a delivery system, they do not have the patent protection some manufacturers enjoy. Their advantage lies in the network they own and in the management know-how; otherwise, practically any service or delivery system can be imitated. For example, any bank or financial company can offer a credit card, but if the card does not belong to one of the existing networks (i.e., Visa, MasterCard, or American Express) it does not have much chance for success. Establishing such a network would be a very costly and challenging undertaking. However, an established company, such as American Express, can introduce new

---

[8] "Telecommunications Survey—Communicating Freely," *The Economist* (September 30, 1995), pp. 27–28.

services and establish itself in a foreign country with relative ease because of its existing network, managerial experience, and know-how accumulated through many years of operations in international markets.

4.4   GLOBAL ENVIRONMENT FOR SERVICE BUSINESSES

Any company entering the international business arena, whether in the form of exporting, importing, or foreign direct investment, must be aware of the different conditions under which it will operate, such as political conditions; the role of governments; economic, social, and cultural environments; and technological conditions. In most cases, international companies cannot change these conditions; therefore, they have to accept them as given and learn to reduce their risks when operating in these environments. Frequently, their success in global markets depends on these conditions and how well they adjust to them. A service company that has global aspirations has to think, act, and behave globally. A global company has to remember that it is not dealing with a single culture, single religion, or single set of rules and regulations anymore and therefore must abandon its nationalistic approach to service. Robert Ayling, chief executive officer of British Airways, who is trying to transform his company to a global airline, recently emphasized the importance of this when he said: "We don't want to ram our Britishness down people's throats."[9] We will discuss these environmental factors in the following paragraphs.

Political Conditions   Political stability is one of the most important conditions all international companies seek before setting up operations and investing in a country. Political instability, such as civil war or a government with an uncertain future, increases risks for an international company.

The Role of Governments   Governments may bring many restrictions to trade and foreign direct investment. A major objective of many governments in dealing with international companies is to maximize the benefits from the international company while minimizing the risks (e.g., national security risks). Governments frequently require foreign companies to acquire local partners when they set up operations in their countries. Another common requirement is that the international company hire a specified proportion of its employees from among locals and set up training programs for these employees. Governments may also impose licensing requirements in many professional services such as engineering, accounting, and financial services.

The Economic Environment   The demand for services in general increases as the level of income increases. International service companies look at such statistics as GDP when they assess the attractiveness of a new market. Also important are the current level of economic development and predictions for the future performance of the economy in the candidate country. Finally, the intensity of competition in an industry is another important factor to consider before investing in a foreign country.

The Social and Cultural Environments   Understanding the cultural and the social environment in a country is very important for service managers because of the customer contact involved. If the encounter is not designed carefully with the host country's social and cultural norms in mind, it may turn into a clash of cultures and the service company loses.

The Technological Environment   Delivery of high-quality reliable service depends on the existence of a reliable and modern communications infrastructure, as well as

---

[9] R. B. Lieber, "Flying High, Going Global," *Fortune* (July 7, 1997).

the availability of the necessary equipment for the service delivery and services to maintain the equipment. A well-developed financial services system, such as a banking system, is also crucial for international service companies to operate successfully in a foreign country.

4.5   FORMS OF GLOBALIZATION

Like manufacturers, service companies may enter the international business world in several forms. In general, these can be grouped as trade and foreign direct investment. This section will review these forms and which services are likely to use each different form.

International Trade

Exports/Imports   When a domestic service company sells to the resident of a foreign country, it is a service export. Similarly, when a resident individual of your country buys a service from a foreign company, it is a service import. The nature of services (specifically, intangibility, inseparability, perishability, and customer contact and involvement) puts limits on the number of opportunities for import/export of services. Information- and knowledge-based services or services that can be delivered from a distance are most likely to be traded. Some of these services are embodied in physical products, such as music on compact discs (CDs), movies on videotape, and software on disks or CD-ROM. For example, software engineers in Bangalore, India, are exporting their services to clients located in different parts of the world. There are other forms of service trade. Tourists traveling to other countries are importing a service from the country they are visiting. A service provider's traveling to the country of the customer is another form of exports/imports, for example, a consultant's going to another country to deliver a seminar or perform consulting services.

Licensing/Franchising   Licensing is an agreement between two companies that gives one (licensee) the right to produce and sell a good or service using the patents, technology, or trademarks that belong to the other company (licensor). The licensor receives money, called royalty, for granting these rights. Franchising is an additional form of international service trade.

Management Contracting   Management contracting is another form of exporting by a company that has special expertise in managing a particular service system. The service company supplies the managerial know-how as well as the management team to run the service facility for a fee. Management contracting has been observed in hotel management, aviation, and retailing.

Foreign Direct Investment

When the nature of a service makes its export difficult or impossible, a service company has no choice but to set up facilities in foreign countries for marketing its services. As services grow in importance for most economies, foreign direct investments in services have also been growing. According to the United Nations, in the mid 1990s, they accounted for half of the world's foreign direct investment stocks and about 60 to 65 percent of foreign direct investment flows.[10]

---

[10] *World Investment Report 1996: Investment, Trade and International Policy Arrangements* (New York, United Nations, 1996), p. 87.

The main difference between international trade in services and foreign direct investment is that sales revenues, commissions, fees, or interest charges are collected when services are sold to foreigners, while in foreign direct investment, profits are sought from foreign-based equity.[11] There are a few, but interesting, exceptions to this purpose. For example, New York Life, an insurance company, ships health insurance claims overnight to Ireland. Claims are processed and returned via dedicated telecommunications lines to the data processing center of the company in New York, where a check or a reply is mailed to the customer. In an altogether different industry, American Airlines operates an information and data services facility in Barbados to process accounting data and ticket coupons. In both cases, the facilities in foreign countries have been established to reduce labor costs rather than obtaining profits from overseas investments.[12] Whatever the purpose may be, foreign direct investment implies establishment and staffing of a service facility in another country and consequently taking more risks than exporting.

Foreign direct investment may take one of several forms. A company's having minority ownership of a foreign company is one form of direct investment; the investor may have some say in the management of the company but does not control the enterprise. A second form may be equal ownership, and a third is majority ownership in which the international firm has more control. In all of these forms, the ownership, management, and risks are shared by two or more companies. Finally, whole ownership of a company in a foreign country is the fourth form of direct investment; this is the form in which the investor has the full control of the company and assumes all the risks of the business venture.

Alliances

An important development of the 1990s in the services sector is the growth of alliances between various companies, including competitors. Most of these alliances do not involve any equity exchanges but focus on sharing networks and resources. In many cases, partners supplement each other's competencies. For example, in July 1996, Microsoft and AT&T announced a distribution alliance; they agreed to market each other's products. Under the agreement, AT&T will promote Microsoft's Internet browser software to users of AT&T's WorldNet Internet-access service. Microsoft will reciprocate by programming AT&T's Internet service into every package of Windows 95 software.[13] Microsoft's alliance with NBC in creating the MSNBC news channel is also well known.

Alliances seem to have much more significance in the airline industry. One of the most recent alliances, the Star Alliance, was announced in 1997 and forms a network of five major international airlines: United, Air Canada, Lufthansa, Scandinavian (SAS), and Thai. Many alliances were formed among airlines during the 1990s, including the one among Delta, Swissair, Sabena, and Austrian Airlines; between Northwest and KLM Royal Dutch Airlines; and between American Airlines and British Airways. These alliances give each partner access to the others' network of routes, make it possible to share passengers and revenues, and enable them to coordinate their sched-

[11] J. J. Boddewyn, M. B. Halbrich, and A. C. Perry, "Service Multinationals: Conceptualization, Measurement, and Theory," *Journal of International Business Studies* (fall 1986), pp. 41–57.

[12] B. M. Hoekman and P. Sauvé, *Liberalizing Trade in Services* (Washington, DC, The World Bank, 1994), p. 6.

[13] J. J. Keller, "AT&T and Microsoft Agree to Market Each Other's Product's for the Internet," *Wall Street Journal* (July 26, 1996).

ules, fares, travel packages, discounts, frequent-flier programs, and even some of the ground operations.[14] For passengers, these alliances may mean easy connections (including baggage transfers between flights) to many destinations around the world.

Trends in Service Globalization

Our discussion of the globalization of services has indicated that some services can be traded more easily than others and some services can be created for the residents of another country only by the presence of service facilities in that country. In this section, current trends in the globalization of particular groups of services will be identified, which group of services tend to globalize through international trade and which group through foreign direct investment.

Vandermerwe and Chadwick identified six groups of services in terms of their globalization potential and the form of globalization they tend to use.[15] They used two dimensions to organize services for the purpose: "relative involvement of goods" and "degree of consumer/producer interaction." (See Exhibit 4-3.) The first dimension represents the degree to which a good is essential for service delivery, and the second dimension represents the degree to which interaction between the service provider and consumer is essential for service delivery.

> **Sector 1: Low Goods/Lower Interaction.** The first group consists of "pure" services for which consumer–producer interaction is minimal and the role goods play in their delivery is not significant. These services have very limited globalization potential, because they may exist in any country, and there is very little profit potential for an international company in this market.
> **Sector 2: Medium Goods/Lower Interaction.** In this group are services that require some interaction, and goods play a more significant role. This group has a higher potential for globalization because of the ease with which the facilitating goods can be taken to foreign countries.
> **Sector 3: High Goods/Lower Interaction.** Services in this sector are either embodied goods or can be transmitted through a telecommunications network, and they require very little, if any, interaction between the consumer and the producer. They are the easiest services to export.
> **Sector 4: Low Goods/Higher Interaction.** Most of the services in this group are professional services and characterized by high interaction between the provider and the client, but goods do not play a prominent role in their delivery. Globalization of these services require the movement of people; usually the service provider travels to the client's country, or it requires an institutional presence in the client's country, usually in the form of a branch or subsidiary of the service company.
> **Sector 5: Medium Goods/Higher Interaction.** Customer/producer interaction is important in this group of services, and goods play a relatively significant role. Also important in the delivery of these services are telecommunications facilities and technology. Globalization may be in various forms, such as foreign direct investment, franchising, licensing, or management contracting.

[14] S. McCartney, "Airline Alliances to Alter Overseas Travel," *Wall Street Journal* (June 11, 1996); S. McCartney, "AMR and British Air to Share Profits, as Well as Passengers, From Alliance," *Wall Street Journal* (June 12, 1996); and A. Q. Nomani, "Airline Pacts' Antitrust Question Sparks Controversy," *Wall Street Journal* (January 3, 1997).

[15] This section is largely based on the following paper: Sandra Vandermerwe and Michael Chadwick, "The Internationalization of Services," *The Service Industries Journal* (January 1989), pp. 79–93.

Sector 6: High Goods/High Interaction. Both dimensions are at their highest levels in this group of services, and telecommunications networks and technology in general play a very significant role in delivery. Globalization potential for this group is increasing with advances in technology.

At first glance, services tend to converge to one of three forms of globalization. (See Exhibit 4-3.) The first cluster is "exportable" services, consisting of services embodied in goods. This form requires very little investment or presence in the country of destination; it also involves very little control of the distribution and use of the service. The second cluster consists of services that can go global with relative ease through franchising, licensing, or management contracts. This form requires some

EXHIBIT 4-3   Clustering of Services and Internationalization Modes

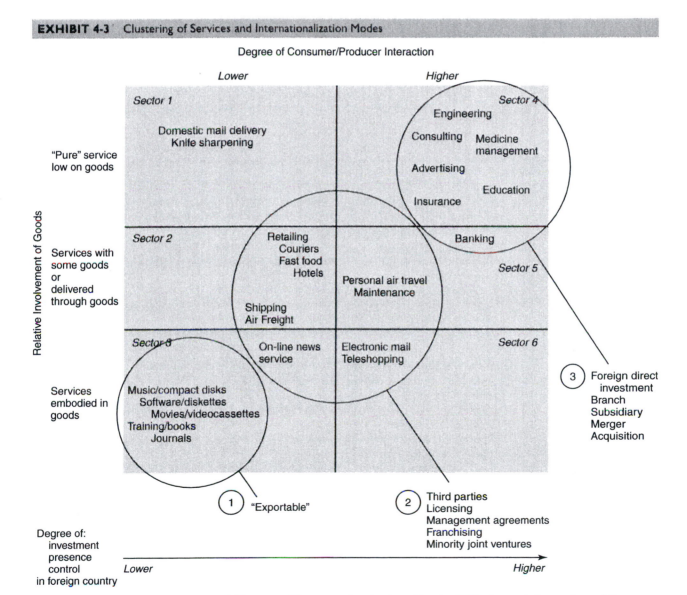

Source: Sandra Vandermerwe and Michael Chadwick, "The Internationalization of Services," *The Service Industries Journal* (January 1989), pp. 79–93.

presence; usually managers from the service company are stationed in the foreign country to deliver the service, and it may require some investment. Foreign direct investment seems to be the most appropriate form for the third cluster of services.

4.6   SUMMARY

This chapter focused on the globalization of services and related issues. The globalization of services may occur as international trade or as foreign direct investments. This chapter reviewed reasons for globalization, the environment in which global service companies have to operate, the different forms of going global, and recent trends in service globalization. The general increase in demand for services and increase in international trade of goods are major reasons for the increase in international service trade. Service companies go global to take advantage of common customer needs, global customers, global channels, economies of scale, favorable logistics, favorable policies and regulations of the government of the host country, advances in technology, and competitive advantages that can be transferable to markets in other countries.

The conditions and factors in the international arena that a service organization must be aware of before deciding whether to go global or set up operations in other countries was also discussed, as well as the three different forms of globalization for service companies: international service trade, foreign direct investment, and foreign alliances. The chapter concluded with a look at trends in service globalization.

Discussion Questions

1. Discuss how services may be "exported" from the United States and "imported" from other countries into the United States. Give some examples of individuals as well as companies engaged in service "export" and "import."
2. What is the difference between "foreign trade" and "foreign direct investment" in services? How would they differ in terms of resource commitment and risks?
3. Describe the forms of foreign trade in services.
4. Describe the forms of foreign direct investment.
5. What is meant by "common customer needs"? What is the significance of these needs for service internationalization?
6. How would "global customers" contribute to the globalization of service companies?
7. How would globalization of a service create economies of scale?
8. What role do computer and telecommunications technologies play in the globalization of services?
9. Discuss the role of host governments in encouraging and discouraging in the globalization of services.
10. What is meant by the "global environment" of service companies? What are the components of this environment?
11. What is a business alliance? What are the benefits of such alliances? Give at least one example of a recent alliance between service companies.
12. Discuss the three clusters of services with respect to their different forms of globalization.

CASES

CASE 4–1 Peters & Champlain

Piet de Lesseps studied the fax he had just received from Robert Poirot, audit director of Montini Van Buren (MVB), a major engineering and construction company. De Lesseps, based in Belgium, was a highly regarded client service partner of Peters & Champlain (P&C), one of the Big Six international accounting firms. He was eager to cement the relationship that had united his old firm, Peters & Heinz, with one of its former rivals, ABNZ Stone Champlain. Poirot's company was also the product of a recent merger and was now seeking to consolidate its auditing relationships around the world. De Lesseps scented a great opportunity to raise Peters & Champlain's profile worldwide.

In his fax, Poirot stated that his board wished to cut the number of accounting firms serving MVB worldwide from the current 34 to just one. Proposals were being sought from all Big Six firms, and MVB intended to select a shortlist of three from which, after further discussions, a single winner would then be chosen.

Later in the day, de Lesseps met with Jacques van Krabbe, managing partner of the Brussels office, to discuss MVB's request. The two recognized that such an engagement would be of great interest to their firm on an international basis. As de Lesseps declared, "We've had their Belgian business for years. This new request makes them more than just another large national client and potentially a worldwide gain for P&C." The partners concluded that it would be appropriate to turn to P&C/Europe in Paris for support in developing a suitable proposal.

Van Krabbe took one more look at the fax. "You'd better get cracking, Piet!" he said. "It's already early December and Poirot says here that he wants proposals by January 31."

MONTINI VAN BUREN

MVB was an international engineering and construction company. It had been formed in 1990 by the merger of an Italian company, Ing. Umberto Montini SpA of Milan, and a Franco-Belgian firm, Van Buren, Walschaert, Lesage SA, whose headquarters were in Brussels. Van Buren's traditional expertise had been in tunnelling, hydroelectric and irrigation projects, and port construction. Montini was best known for its innovative work in bridge design and construction; the firm had also been active in building airports, and both firms had had a number of large highway construction contracts. Although Van Buren had been profitable in recent years, Montini had lost money in two of the three preceding fiscal years. The merged company consolidated its headquarters activity in Luxembourg, while also retaining major administrative functions in Brussels, Milan, and Paris.

Montini Van Buren planned and executed major construction projects around the world, sometimes as the consulting engineers, sometimes as the primary contractor, and sometimes as a subcontractor. For really large projects, MVB might enter into consortium agreements with other firms. Significant current activities included work on the Channel Tunnel, preliminary engineering studies for a new transalpine rail tunnel, a deep-water port in Indonesia, building hydroelectric dams in Canada, India, and Argentina, a new subway line in Mexico City, several large bridges on three continents, airport expansion projects in Nigeria, Australia and several European countries, and highway construction around the world, notably in Asian and African countries. Most projects on which MVB worked ran for three to five years or more, although it would sometimes bid on smaller projects that would provide high visibility, entrée to new markets, or exposure to significant engineering challenges. Many projects were commissioned by government agencies and some, such as bridges and dams, extended across national frontiers.

MVB operated in 53 countries, some of which were sales offices working to obtain future contracts. Its accounts were audited on a country-by-country basis by no less than 34 different accounting firms. Local firms held more than 50% of these engagements, with the balance being held by the Big Six—notably P&C, Jones Pittman, and Coulson & Stuart, which also audited the consolidated accounts in Luxembourg. Peters & Champlain were MVB's auditors in seven countries, including Belgium. Many of these relationships extended back a decade or more. In Belgium, for example, Piet de Lesseps had landed the Van Buren, Walschaerts, Lesage engagement as a junior partner 12 years earlier.

Client Concerns

Two days later, de Lesseps travelled to Luxembourg to meet Robert Poirot. He had learned before the meeting that Poirot, who was French, had been recruited by MVB just four months earlier. It was he who had persuaded the board to consolidate the company's auditing relationships. However, de Lesseps had also learned from phone conversations with several P&C partners in different countries that a number of MVB offices were unhappy with the plan, having only recently gone through a similar change due to the merger of formerly separate Montini and Van Buren offices in many countries where both predecessor firms were operating. In fact, P&C had lost the audit engagement for MVB's merged Caracas office to another Big Six firm, Jones Pittman. In three other locations, however, P&C had been the winner, merging with a local firm in two cases and beating out Martin Amundsen, another Big Six firm, in the third instance.

Poirot impressed de Lesseps with his intellect, professionalism, and ambition for both himself and his new company. He came straight to the point, acknowledging his recent arrival at MVB and prefacing his remarks with the comment, "You know more about this organization than I do!" He told de Lesseps that the decision on selection of worldwide auditors for MVB would involve inputs from a number of other senior executives, including the managing director, Mr. Garelli (former chief executive of Montini), the deputy MD, Mr. Brecht (former CEO of Van Buren, Walschaerts, Lesage), the finance director, Mr. D'Amato, and his deputy, Mr. Brugge, and would have to be ratified by the board of directors. Poirot told de Lesseps that he had had some contact with P&C in his previous position with a large chemicals company and had not been overly impressed. "However, I'm approaching this proposals process with an open mind," he declared. "All existing relationships are up for change in the

interests of selecting a single firm to conduct our audit engagements worldwide." Poirot also emphasized that MVB had no interest in follow-on services and was seeking proposals that were strictly limited to audit services.

De Lesseps left Luxembourg impressed by Poirot, but wondering whether other individuals involved in the selection process at MVB would share the audit director's specific expectations for the outcome. From his own experience in serving MVB's Belgian operations, he knew that the firm perceived relatively little difference between competing Big Six auditors and tended to drive a hard bargain on fees. However, he was not sure how firmly this view was held by former Montini executives, such as the managing director, Mario Garelli, or the finance director, Carlo D'Amato (who reported to Garelli).

A few days later, de Lesseps managed to arrange a meeting in Paris between Garelli, who was in town to visit MVB's French office, and Christopher Diebold, P&C's executive partner from the New York office. The meeting at Garelli's hotel was brief but cordial. Garelli told the other two that he had personally commissioned Poirot to organize the process of selecting new auditors worldwide and had been pleased with his presentation to the board. He also emphasized the matrix structure of the firm which was organized both geographically and by major activity groups, such as tunnelling, bridge construction, marine facilities, and so forth.

De Lesseps had known Michel Brugge, the deputy finance director, for several years, since he had formerly been with Van Buren. D'Amato was approaching retirement age, and it seemed likely that his deputy might succeed him within the next two years—or possibly sooner. Brugge had told de Lesseps in the past that he could not envisage replacing Coulson & Stuart as the auditors on the consolidation accounts. Since Brugge appeared to be the strongest person with respect to appointment of new auditors, it was felt unlikely that Garelli would attempt to overrule him.

THE PROPOSAL TEAM GETS TOGETHER

Following his meetings with Poirot and Garelli, de Lesseps moved quickly to create a proposal team in Brussels. The European office in Paris provided him with a writer/researcher, Marie-Laure Cot. A partner from the Milan office, Ugo Bianchi, who knew the construction business well, agreed to participate in the team's initial strategy session.

The team's first meeting was held two days before the Christmas holidays. Ms. Cot had prepared a dossier summarizing key information about MVB's operations around the world. This included a table listing MVB's 53 country offices and its current auditors in each one (refer to Exhibit 4-4).

Opening the meeting, de Lesseps declared:

Winning this proposal would be very significant for Peters & Champlain. It's not just the revenues from the worldwide engagement that we're interested in, but also the opportunity for P&C to put into place the "One Firm, Worldwide" concept that we've talked about so often since the merger. To get this type of business, it's not sufficient to demonstrate that we have a worldwide network of strong local firms—we have to be perceived as truly international in outlook.

EXHIBIT 4-4   Countries with MVB Operations and Names of Auditors as of December 1991

Region/Country	Current Auditors[a]	Region/Country	Current Auditors[a]
Europe/Near East		*Central & South America*	
Austria	Local firm	Chile	Local firm
Belgium	P&C (Peters & Champlain)	Costa Rica	Local firm
		Ecuador	Local firm
Cyprus	FBG-WB (FBG-Wills Boswell)	Guyana	Local firm
		Panama	JP
Denmark	JP (Jones Pittman)	Venezuela	JP
Finland	Local firm		
France	Local firm	*North Africa/Arabia*	
Germany	C&S (Coulson & Stuart)	Egypt	Local firm
Greece	Local firm	Iraq	Local firm (office closed)
Hungary	unaudited	Kuwait	Local firm
Italy	C&S	Morocco	Local firm
Netherlands	P&C	Saudi Arabia	DMC
Norway	Local firm		
Portugal	Local firm	*Central & Southern Africa*	
Spain	Local firm	Ivory Coast	Local firm
Sweden	JP	Kenya	C&S
Switzerland	DMC (Davis, Miller, & Campbell)	Nigeria	FBG-WB
		South Africa	Local firm
Turkey	Local firm	Zimbabwe	Local firm
United Kingdom	Local firm		
		Asia-Pacific	
North America & Caribbean		Australia	P&C
Bahamas	Local firm	Hong Kong	P&C
Canada	P&C	India	Local firm
Dominican Republic	JP	Indonesia	Local firm
Jamaica	Local firm	Japan	Local firm
Mexico	Local firm	Malaysia	C&S
Trinidad	P&C	New Zealand	Local firm
United States	C&S	Singapore	P&C
		Taiwan	DMC
Central & South America		Thailand	Local firm
Argentina	JP		
Brazil	MA (Martin Amundsen)	*CONSOLIDATION* (Luxembourg)	C&S

[a] Only Big Six firms are named.

We're dealing here with some very distinct differences in culture. On the one hand, there's Van Buren, which is Belgian and where most of top management is Flemish; however, they have given considerable autonomy to their French minority interests, especially in view of all the work they brought in on the Channel Tunnel. The French would never allow themselves to be run by the guys in Brussels! Then there's the old Montini operation based in Italy, but also very strong in Switzerland and Germany, where Van Buren was never able to make much headway. The merger has greatly strengthened the company around the world. Separately, each firm was active in about 35 countries, jointly MVB now operates in 53. And they have a broader array of expertise now; Montini had an outstanding reputation on bridges, highways, and airport construction, while Van Buren was big in dams, tunnelling, and seaports.

From my conversations with MVB it's clear that they see audit work as a commodity—a low price commodity. This was particularly true of Van Buren. Their head office in Brussels would make a short list for their office in each country to choose from. They always claimed that industry knowledge was less important than price.

Poirot told me that he saw all Big Six firms as fairly equal in quality, but that MVB would be concentrating on global reach, and how each firm would approach the audit and deliver the feedback—the product that they would like to get out of the audit. He said they would concentrate much more on that than on the industry focus itself. What he is interested in knowing is how we propose to approach the audit, how we will manage the audit—how we would organize ourselves, set up our reporting procedures, and so on. He kept emphasizing the end product. He downplayed the opinion on the consolidated financial statements and focused more on the feedback we might be able to offer.

Examining the Audit Process

De Lesseps rose from his chair, walked to the board, picked up a blue marker, and sketched out a rectangle which he divided into four columns. At the top of the first column, he wrote "Planning." The second was headed "Execution," the third "Reporting," and the fourth "Follow Up." Turning to the group, he remarked:

You could describe the audit process like this. You do your planning based on significant areas that you identify. You can apply this to various things, such as the budget, which is the precalculation of the profitability of an engagement. In the follow up, you can determine whether it was actually profitable or not. My point is that for each stage there are products. The products for the planning stage are the audit plan and the approach plan. For the execution stage, there are audit programs and working papers. Under reporting we have the audit report and management letter. Finally, under follow up, there's the invoice.

With his marker, de Lesseps circled the entire group of products at the bottom of the four columns (refer to Exhibit 4-5). "Some clients consider the whole thing to be a commodity," he declared. "But my point is that a commodity consists of a number of detailed products. And you can differentiate your service by adding value to some of these products." He then underlined "management letter," "audit plan," and "approach plan," adding:

Here's where the big opportunity to add value takes place—the management letter. And the contents and value of that letter are dependent on what you do in the audit plan and approach plan, such as identifying weak spots. You don't start working until you understand what you need to do, you know what the significant areas are and document them to management. You can increase your likelihood of coming up with comments that are likely to be of value to management in terms of how they are running their company.

An audit is much more than adding or taking away numbers. We're talking about understanding the business, risk analysis, and so forth. When you're dealing with multinational clients, it becomes much more important to understand the business in a global sense. With a local client, you can deal with a local environment and focus on local issues, local tax laws, and so forth. In companies like MVB, your primary contacts on the top level are often a small group of managers who have a huge multinational company and feel a little bit uncomfortable in terms of their ability to control the whole system. They look to the auditors to give them additional comfort with respect to the quality of

EXHIBIT 4-5   Framework Sketched by Piet De Lesseps

Stages	PLANNING	EXECUTION	REPORTING	FOLLOW UP
	Significant Issues	Significant Issues	Significant Issues	Significant Issues
	– – – – – – – – –	– – – – – – – – –	– – – – – – – – –	– – – – – – – – –
	– – – – – – – – –	– – – – – – – – –	– – – – – – – – –	– – – – – – – – –
	– – – – – – – – –	– – – – – – – – –	– – – – – – – – –	– – – – – – – – –
	– – – – – – – – –	– – – – – – – – –	– – – – – – – – –	– – – – – – – – –
	– – – – – – – – –	– – – – – – – – –	– – – – – – – – –	– – – – – – – – –
	– – – – – – – – –	– – – – – – – – –	– – – – – – – – –	– – – – – – – – –
	– – – – – – – – –	– – – – – – – – –	– – – – – – – – –	– – – – – – – – –
	– – – – – – – – –	– – – – – – – – –	– – – – – – – – –	
Products	Audit Plan Audit Approach	Audit Program Working Papers	Audit Report Management Letter	Invoice

the international operation—are the numbers reliable, do they have control over their operations, do they know what kinds of assets they have, and do they collect cash on their assets? This is what should be reflected in the management letter.

De Lesseps opened the floor to discussion. One of the senior managers present, Caroline O'Brien, raised an issue:

Mr. Poirot says he doesn't want us to do anything that isn't material to the consolidation.

But legal reporting requirements in many countries still have to be observed. He wants us to bring down fees, but I'm not sure he understands that MVB's legal structure requires substantially more audit work than might be necessary for purely business reasons.

"That's a good point," de Lesseps admitted. "I think Poirot still has quite a lot to learn about MVB. But it doesn't alter the fact that the market for audit service is changing from a cost plus basis to a price-led situation." ■

SOURCE: Christopher H. Lovelock, *Services Marketing*, 3rd ed. (Upper Saddle River, NJ, Prentice Hall, 1996), pp. 628–632. Copyright © 1992 by IMD (International Institute for Management and Development), Lausanne, Switzerland. IMD retains all rights. Not to be reproduced or used without written permission directly from IMD, Lausanne, Switzerland.

CASE QUESTIONS

1. What is the potential value of the MVB business to P&C?
2. What does MVB really want? Why have they decided to go from 34 audit firms to 1?
3. How well placed is P&C relative to other "Big Six" firms?
4. What is the decision-making unit at MVB, who are its members, and how much influence do they wield?
5. How can auditors add value to an engagement for the client?
6. Recommend a strategy to be included in MVB's short list and then win the second round.

CASE 4–2 Pizza Hut in Moscow: The Pre-Coup Vision

INTRODUCTION

Pizza Hut opened two restaurants in Moscow in what was then the USSR in September of 1990. This was the outcome of a joint venture agreement with the Moscow City Council. Today, the venture is profitable despite operating in a volatile environment where political, monetary, social and economic infrastructures are continuously changing en route to free markets. Since the introduction of *perestroika* (the policies designed to adopt more market oriented approaches toward production and distribution of products and services) change has been progressing exponentially. The attempted political *coup* which failed in 1991 ultimately resulted in the resignation of Mikhail Gorbachev and the rise of Boris Yeltsin as leader.

PEPSICO BACKGROUND

Pizza Hut, which had gained the number one leadership position in the pizza food service market, was acquired by PepsiCo in 1977. PepsiCo had developed early formal business ties to the Soviet Union which dated back to 1972. At that time, an agreement was reached to trade Pepsi for Stolichnaya vodka which would be sold by PepsiCo in the West as a means of generating hard currency. Pepsi-Cola has become the major consumer product in the former USSR and is ranked as Pepsi-Cola's fourth largest national market worldwide.

PepsiCo's substantial interests in the USSR, and the company's contacts made at high levels within the Soviet political system, reflected the drive and commitment to the development of the Soviet market from the very top of the company. According to company reports, PepsiCo's Chairman, Donald Kendall, "was himself pushing hard for the opportunity to open restaurants in the USSR in the mid-1980s."

Kendall made some of his first visits to the USSR in the early 50's, introducing the concept of Pepsi-Cola to Khruschev and initiating negotiations. The 20 or so years of negotiation and preparation that followed ultimately culminated in Pepsi-Cola becoming the widest spread foreign product trademark in the USSR. This history was invaluable in helping the firm establish a full operating business and laid the groundwork for the Pizza Hut venture in Moscow (Exhibit 4-6).

EXHIBIT 4-6 Chronology of Events for Start-Up Joint Venture

	1972	Agreement reached to trade Pepsi for vodka
September	1987	Letter of intent signed with Moscow city council
	1988	Feasibility studies conducted
February	1989	Contracts signed
	1989	Moscow general manager (Alex Antoniadi) employed
January	1990	Building work began
April	1990	$3 billion trade deal signed
June	1990	Staff fully employed; training began
September	1990	First two restaurants opened
April	1991	Andy Rafalat returned to London

Adapted from Pizza Hut, "Pizza Moscow," 1991.

Some of the data for the writing of this case was adapted and edited by the case writers from "Pizza Moscow," a study commissioned by Pizza Hut International from the London Business School in June of 1991 and co-authored by Assheton Don, Claire Don, Amy Stoner, and Andy Rafalat. Additionally, data was collected through personal interviews, surveys, and observations of company documents and archival records. Prepared by Sandra Honig-Haftel and Ronald L. Christy, Wichita State University. Reprinted with permission.

THE EARLY VISION

The restaurant business as it is known in the West and in Europe was culturally alien to the USSR. Kendall had no rules and no recognizable ways of proceeding. There was only a vision and an intention that this thing had to be done. According to Steve Bishopp, Vice President of Finance for Pizza Hut International, Kendall really was the one who sparked the idea. "Don has always been involved with the Soviet Union in business, and saw opportunity to develop business with them, because Pizza Hut was one of the businesses in his corporation when he was Chairman."

An early letter from the Politburo in the Kremlin suggested that the Soviet Union of the mid-1980s did not cater to families. Alcoholism was focused upon as a serious problem and officials were looking for ways to provide a family environment where families could be fed and entertained. Pizza Hut was determined to provide a wholesome non-alcoholic setting, one that could contribute to solving this social problem. The missionary work by Kendall was followed by invitations to Pizza Hut managers to see for themselves what was possible.

In 1985, a team was sent by PepsiCo to evaluate pizzerias in Moscow. A team member observed, "From that very first moment when we got on the plane, we recognized that the conventional rules of business had to be put to one side. We had to look at what we saw with objectivity and common sense to be able to react to it in an unbiased way."

According to Andy Rafalat, then Director of Technical Services for PepsiCo's Eurafme (Europe, Africa, and the Middle East) catering operation, "We all knew that potential customers were there, but we also recognized that the system really didn't allow free enterprise to take place. On that November day (in 1985) it really was the start of an adventure into the unknown, an unknown where there were no points of reference."

With the Pizza Hut team reporting on familiarity with and ready acceptance for pizza, particularly among young people in Moscow, PepsiCo chose Pizza Hut as the vanguard of the push into the USSR. According to a company document, "Its major attraction was the relatively simple, cheap and widely available nature of most of the ingredients." Flour, tomato paste, oil, and many items for the salad bar could all be purchased from Soviet sources.

By early 1987, when joint ventures were permitted in the USSR, Kendall visited the Mayor of Moscow. In September of that year, a letter of intent was signed with *Mosobschepit*, the catering arm of the city council. This was the first joint venture agreement signed between the Soviets and a U.S. company.

Much of the foundation for the eventual success of the negotiations, which were concluded in 1989, is attributed to the single-minded way that Kendall developed his contacts in the U.S., and with Soviet and Eastern European politicians. A company executive observed, "He was a unique man, and the Chairman of a big international company. Yet he always found the time to regularly visit these market places, to make it his business not only to know the leaders, but also to gain an understanding of how those systems were actually working. He had a strong opinion, his own opinion, because he actually saw what was taking place. That was a unique perspective, a chief executive who actually spent time in those markets and understood the problems and really was able to lead his team from the front."

Skilled at networking and making business contacts, Kendall met the former Soviet Ambassador in Washington. "Don was able to meet the man, not only the Ambassador but the man who had a family with him, the man who enjoyed sidling down to the Pizza Hut on a Sunday morning and who was able to share his thoughts and deep perspective of the Russian psyche and mentality."

Contacts were essential and Kendall ensured that invitations were forthcoming from a number of organizations. In the early and mid-1980s few Western business people knew how to establish business contacts in the Soviet Union, then the world's largest government bureaucracy. Kendall secured those contacts and reminded PepsiCo and Pizza Hut executives that they should visit these countries. Kendall's persistence, demonstrated through meetings, extensive contacts and letters to organizations, resulted in the creation of a plan of action for how to do business with the Soviets.

PLAN OF ACTION

By 1987, the laws had changed and joint ventures were now permitted. According to Rafalat, "It was now feasible for an organization to work with a Soviet organization and develop something resembling a private enterprise. We started to recognize the importance of having locally driven businesses. . . . We also recognized the importance of 'living off the land,' which meant using local facilities and resources to maximum effect."

In 1987, a letter of intent was signed delineating each partners objectives and expectations for the new joint venture. Early in the planning process, two Moscow restaurants were conceptualized, one taking rubles and the other hard currency. It was planned that the joint venture would maximize local sourcing and would possibly be expanded at a later date.

The operation would generate both a positive ruble and hard currency cashflow. Although rubles could not be converted into the firm's home currency for the benefit of shareholders in the short term but hard currency could, it was thought that the first restaurants would give the company a toehold in a potentially huge market and that "rubles could well become convertible in the longer term." Furthermore, opening the two restaurants was seen as a valuable learning experience of how things actually work in the USSR. The company would be building contacts with Soviet authorities and training a core force of local employees. According to company reports, the media coverage was also an added benefit to Pizza Hut's worldwide operations. PepsiCo's primary motivations were to initiate actions towards "the long-term goal of a significant restaurant presence in this potentially huge market."

NEGOTIATING THE CONTRACT

Negotiations begun in 1987 took almost two years to complete. The partners were eager to explore the new opportunities offered by the joint venture, which they regarded at the time as "almost a fashionable thing to do." They were content to be led by Pizza Hut and had little desire to control the business. Yet culture and language became a barrier toward completing negotiations in a timely manner.

"We were talking two different languages whose words conveyed different meanings because we were from different systems where everything was incomparable . . . even dictionaries became to an odd extent useless, . . . Negotiation took close to two years, eighteen months. I think we recognized that they were going to take a long time. . . . How we progressed, how we learned, how once we were negotiating [with] Moscow was changing around the thinking, the laws, the gradual acceptance of pizza *Perestroika* and the market forces."

After the letter of intent was signed in 1987, things did not go smoothly. The partners failed to keep the many timetables set, delayed their planned visit to the UK, neglected to arrange supplier visits for Pizza Hut representatives, failed to arrange translations of many necessary documents, and even told the firm that previously confirmed restaurant sites were now unavailable. There seemed to be a complete lack of willingness or knowledge of how to overcome obstacles. This was viewed as symptomatic of a lack of understanding of how a market-based business worked.

"We had a small, flexible negotiating team. There was Scott, a lawyer who was able to detail the structure of an agreement, presenting options and scenarios for both us and the Soviets. There was David Williams, our Vice President who was able to bring in his tremendous experience in negotiating joint ventures in different countries. I was very much the local element, spending time in Moscow looking at various sites, learning how Russian operations work, trying to understand the supply structures and what we needed to do. We also brought in our Finance Director when required to produce numbers and calculations. Between us, we had a good balance.

"We found, however, that the Russians approached negotiations very differently. There seemed to be no real seriousness attached to the operation. The negotiating team was frequently being changed. This was so new to them that they really didn't know how to handle a structured negotiation. One of our biggest problems was always negotiating through an interpreter. It really was only through the many days and weeks that we were spending on these negotiations that we really started to appreciate the huge differences and gaps which we would have to recognize and overcome.

"We spent weeks and months negotiating details which in hindsight proved to be totally useless. For example, we negotiated for the number of telephone lines we ought to have for days. When we actually moved to Moscow, these efforts proved useless because there was no power to get a telephone line. None of us really knew how to get these things done. That's just part of doing business in that part of the world. We were all learning."

RESTATING PROBLEMS AS OPPORTUNITIES

Problems were not considered insurmountable by the Pizza Hut team. According to Andy Rafalat, "Failure is not a word used with us. Problems may occur if management in a given venture is weak or inexperienced." Generally, new business opportunities were viewed as arising from technological or market changes. The company viewed itself as more oriented towards developing existing resources than towards the pursuit of new opportunities.

After the Pizza Hut team learned more about the Moscow market, team members felt that success was assured. What may have been perceived as problems by others was constantly restated as an opportunity by Pizza Hut. This consistent philosophy propelled the venture forward. Eventually, the Soviets fulfilled all of the required commitments and the two parties moved towards signing a legal contract. Contracts were concluded in February of 1989. The first two restaurants were planned to open at the end of 1989. The joint venture was to have a Board of six members, three nominated by each partner, and a Soviet Citizen as Director General. The Director General and a Deputy Director General would jointly decide all major issues.

The contracts detailed the partners' roles. Pizza Hut would provide personnel and training and the partners would deal with negotiating local matters such as visas, customs, utilities and supplies. By-laws were also drawn up stating how the partnership would resolve disputes and how the chain of command would operate. A standard franchise agreement was also signed between Pizza Hut and the new joint venture detailing the initial franchise fee at $25,000 and the monthly service fee (royalty) at 4% of gross sales.

Two feasibility studies ran in parallel with the joint venture negotiations. Although many of the early assumptions turned out to be false, these studies succeeded in formulating the basic operating conditions for the venture.

"Pizza Hut was to provide experienced personnel and training, their partners would deal with the local matters such as utilities, visas, customs, and suppliers. The contract also stipulated in what order claims could be made on any hard currency earned in the business. Royalties to Pizza Hut came first, followed by other payments . . . to PepsiCo before the Soviet party could make claims."

FINANCING THE VENTURE

The foundation for financing the initial joint venture between Pizza Hut and the Moscow City Council relied upon earlier agreements made by PepsiCo. In 1990, a $3 billion countertrade arrangement (see Chronology of Events) between PepsiCo and Soviet authorities was finalized. This extended the trade of vodka and Pepsi to the year 2000, called for 25 additional Pepsi plants for a total of 50, and introduced a new component: the building of ten Soviet commercial ships for sale and lease internationally. This barter arrangement set the scene for financing the first two Pizza Hut restaurants.

At market exchange rates, the upfront cost of the project was very low. Pizza Hut was able to pay for the hard currency costs in rubles, acquiring them through a Soviet bank loan and converting them into hard currency at the official exchange rate. The new business was capitalized at $2.96 million, contributed by the partners as follows:

Soviet Party	*$000*	*Pizza Hut*	*$000*
Land/building	1200	Equipment	856
		Plans & drawings	184
Start-up expenses	120	Start-up expenses($)	200
Reconstruction	200	Reconstruction	200
TOTAL	1520		1440
	(51%)		(49%)

STRATEGY AND ORGANIZATION

Andy Rafalat was assigned to Moscow in 1988 as a full-time chief executive. As stated by Rafalat, "By now, I had been with this project three and a half years. Once the realization came that it was going to happen, I think the truth dawned on me that a project has to have a person behind it. Somebody has to lead it, and it was also an automatic that for it to be transformed to reality, I would have to lead it and really own it. Then the realization came that . . . relocation to the Soviet Union would be required.

"We then gave thought to the hiring of key people, how they would be trained both in London and the Soviet Union, and how systems would have to be developed. We would have to tackle supplies and logistics in an area where there was a total lack of any infrastructure that made sense in any commercial way of thinking. There was no business structure in Moscow.

"I told my family that we would be moving to Moscow in the wintertime. The kids had to change schools, we had to find living quarters and learn how to adapt to an environment where shopping and services were unavailable. Finally in February, 1990 the actual move to Moscow took place."

The management strategy was to staff the venture with Soviet personnel. As their abilities strengthened, Rafalat would withdraw and return to London where he was based, focusing more on the potential expansion of the business rather than overseeing day-to-day operations.

A management team was recruited, with Alex Antoniadi as General Manager to instill Pizza Hut's management theory into the system with hands-on responsibility of daily business management. (See Exhibit 4-7.) Alex Antoniadi formerly ran five restaurants in Moscow and brought this experience into the new venture along with his industry contacts and high food and staff quality standards. His mission was to convey the Pizza Hut culture of high standards for cleanliness, quality, staff performance, and service.

Antoniadi accepted a proposal to come to London for training only after he was assured the General Manger's position and allowed to select his own restaurant managers—Boris Paiken and Sacha Youdin. Antoniadi's high personal work standards helped to permeate Pizza Hut's management standards throughout the venture. A hard worker, Antoniadi quickly became a local celebrity. His long-

term associations and Rafalat's persistence in pursuing the venture in combination with ongoing open communications with the partners provided the strategic foundation for effectively managing the partnership relationship. Antoniadi's contacts were also invaluable in helping to obtain approval documents from various state agencies and authorities.

Pizza Hut pursued a *laissez faire* strategy with Rafalat, empowering him with full entrepreneurial operating responsibility. This seemed to be the general style of the firm. As stated by one executive, "While the company tends to carry out as much homework as realistic on new ideas and markets, once they are established, these projects are handed over to small teams or to individuals to guarantee ownership and provide freedom of action for the relevant individual in charge. This ensures that projects have definite sponsors on whom success or failure rests."

Consistent with *laissez faire* philosophy, Rafalat was empowered with the management of the venture and with the objective of moving out as quickly as possible by empowering local people with a sense of ownership and management.

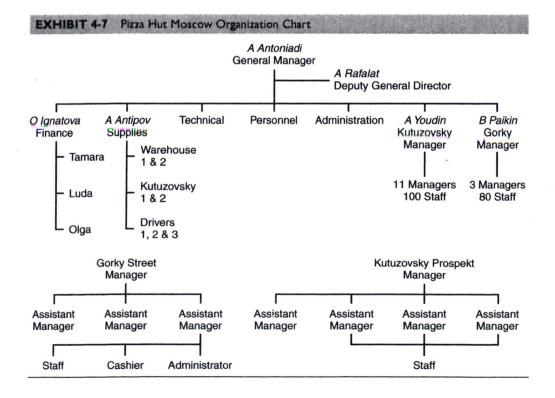

EXHIBIT 4-7 Pizza Hut Moscow Organization Chart

SITE LOCATION AND CONSTRUCTION OF THE FIRST TWO RESTAURANTS

In 1988, recognizing that site selection was critical, proposed locations for the first two restaurants were evaluated according to the following ideal features:

1. Size—250–300 square meters
2. One level
3. Frontage—10 meter minimum
4. Corner with return frontage
5. Heavy pedestrian flow
6. Parking capacity for automobiles
7. Proximity to offices, shops and apartments
8. Proximity to tourist hotels for hard currency

Early identified sites were rejected and the Soviets pursued tours of low-grade sites. This suggested a lack of will to move the project forward or a genuine ignorance as to the nature of the project. Finally, detailed Pizza Hut location maps were provided and suitable sites for the two proposed Pizza Huts in Moscow would be finalized—one on Gorky Street and the second on Kutuzovsky Prospekt. Preliminary drawings of the restaurants were rendered for both sites and were included in the 1988 Feasibility Study.

Construction began in January, 1990. Both restaurants, although conversions of existing buildings, required considerable work. Soviet builders were initially employed but with little performance success. Forced to turn to a West European contractor with multi-national experience, the partners gave the 6 million dollar construction contract to Taylor Woodrow, a UK company.

"The quality of work demanded by Pizza Hut necessitated a large proportion of imported materials and labor; only 10% of the building materials and none of the finishing materials were sourced locally. The Soviet partners found it hard to understand why the operation should need to import cement, for instance, but delivery times were as much of an issue as the quality of materials. None of the local suppliers were able to respond quickly to demands or to guarantee delivery dates. Local supplies of equipment were also very unreliable. Taylor Woodrow was unable to ensure that a crane, for instance, would be available on a certain date, and the workforce was obliged to flag down drivers of passing machinery and pay them to lift the heavy loads."

Construction crews consisted of people from six countries: the United Kingdom, Sweden, Italy, Portugal, Poland, and the USSR. The Western crew members assisted the Soviet builders, training them on various building techniques.

After about eight months of building, the two restaurants opened on September 11, 1990. Considerable fanfare and celebration brought extensive free media coverage of the event.

SOURCING

Although Pizza Hut committed early on to "living off the land," this was sometimes quite difficult. For example, the kitchen equipment had to fit in with Pizza Hut's unique production system and was therefore imported, as were the crockery and restaurant furniture. There simply was no Soviet supplier able to make the product to Pizza Hut's specifications.

"We were told how important it was to get local people involved at each step of the way. The phrase 'living off the land' was very much overused in our negotiation strategy, but every time we said it, it conveyed to us an image of where we were going to find local managers and local people to work in our new venture. We were going to try to localize the supplies as much as we could. And we were going to finalize the concept to every extent possible to get it to run in the country. That really shaped our thinking.

"We started focusing on the sole issue of local supplies. I think that if there was one area that frightened us, it was how to get local sourcing to work. Having seen the disastrous state of most Soviet food factories, the poor controls, storage and distribution, we knew that we were going to have to get right into the food production network. Yet we did not want to do the food producer's job.

"We sent out a clear message to suppliers that we would be willing to pay market prices for their goods in rubles, whatever that market price was. We wanted to negotiate with them. We sent signals of encouragement to the supply community at large with Pizza Hut was open for business, paying market prices for goods."

Pizza Hut gained agreement to initially import all food items with no customs duty, although the intent was to source most of the required products locally over time. This would reduce importation costs over 5 years and increase generation of hard currency. These products would also be marketable as export goods and would generate more hard currency for the USSR. Using local food supplies as much as possible would put the inconvertible ruble currency earned in the ruble restaurants to good use. Aligning costs and sales in the same currency would also minimize the operation's future margin exposure to exchange rate swings. Antoniadi's network of local supplier contacts became crucial to the venture and also made it difficult to recreate the operation outside of Moscow. Outside of Moscow, local recruits would be needed to establish local supply networks to replicate the Moscow structure.

Some suppliers negotiated long term contracts to supply Pizza Hut. Vegetables came from cooperatives. Other products, such as flour, were allocated to Pizza Hut on a centralized basis through the state plans. Although a cheese factory had been identified to produce Mozzarella to Pizza Hut specifications, by winter the quality of the cheese became unacceptable. All cheese supplies had to be sourced from the West, along with some of the meat products, proprietary in-house dough and spice blends. Other products, such as the wooden tables and chairs and Turkish cooking oil, were imported.

THE FUTURE

Envisioning the future as one with a possible 5000 units, Rafalat dedicated the success of the venture

". . . to all the visionaries who knew it was possible." Describing the world behind Soviet borders during the mid-1980s, Rafalat said, "It was a world of secrecy, of relatively unknown languages and of cultures that we knew very little about." It was ". . . the unpredictable Wild East, to be avoided by all but the most daring. There were, however, individuals, visionaires, who realized that despite the current situation, the region presented huge opportunities for future generations. These opportunities would yield enormous payback, not only in commercial terms, but also in providing bridges between two cultures, bridges which would bring these contrasting cultures and unknown systems closer."

Now, after the pre-start negotiations and construction, the task ahead was to develop and implement the major operating systems. Employees had to be recruited and trained. Management and control systems had to be developed, and a new financial system—a hybrid accounting system—had to be developed to reflect doing business in two currencies—hard currency and rubles. Rafalat and Antoniadi went to work to put in place systems for employee compensation and rewards, pricing, purchasing, warehousing and distribution, marketing and tracking of sales performance. They were propelled in their mission by ". . . a powerful vision of a chain of restaurants stretching across the Soviet Union, from Odessa to Vladivostok." ■

SOURCE: Kamal Fatehi, *International Management: A Cross-Cultural Approach* (Upper Saddle River, NJ, Prentice Hall, 1996), pp. 419–427.

CASE QUESTIONS

1. What are joint ventures? How do they differ from other forms of partnership agreements?
2. Describe potential difficulties associated with joint venturing with a government agency (Moscow City Council) versus with a privately owned business organization.
3. Identify key environmental factors confronting the Pizza Hut management team. Which would be considered barriers to entry? Barriers to development? Which would be considered opportunistic?
4. Which problems did Pizza Hut's management team restate as opportunities?
5. What elements could be identified that are similar to more traditional start-up situations in the United States? What elements are unique

to the opening of a new business in the former Soviet Union?
6. Given the volatility of the business environment in the former Soviet Union, what do you think the reasons were for Pizza Hut to embark on such a risky venture?
7. Could a smaller business enterprise without the support of a major international company like PepsiCo have been successful in new business operations in Moscow? Why or why not? Elaborate on the risks that a smaller business entity might have faced which Pizza Hut did not because of PepsiCo's corporate sponsorship.
8. What were identified by Pizza Hut that led them to believe that their restaurants could be successful in Moscow?

References

Bartlett, Christopher A., and Sumantra Ghoshal, *Managing Across Borders: The Transnational Solution* (Cambridge, MA, Harvard Business School Press, 1989).

Boddewyn, J. J., M. B. Halbrich, and A. C. Perry, "Service Multinationals: Conceptualization, Measurement, and Theory," *Journal of International Business Studies* (fall 1986), pp. 41–57.

Economic Report of the President, 1997 (Washington, DC, United States Government Printing Office, 1997).

"Telecommunications Survey—Communicating Freely," *The Economist* (September 30, 1995), pp. 27–28.

Hoekman, B. M., and P. Sauvé, *Liberalizing Trade in Services* (Washington, DC, The World Bank, 1994).

Keller, J. J., "AT&T and Microsoft Agree to Market Each Other's Product's for the Internet," *Wall Street Journal* (July 26, 1996).

Levitt, Theodore, "The Globalization of Markets," *Harvard Business Review* (May–June 1983), pp. 92–102.

Lieber, Ronald B., "Flying High, Going Global," *Fortune* (July 7, 1997).

Lovelock, Christopher H., and George S. Yip, "Developing Global Strategies for Service Businesses," *California Management Review*, vol. 38, no. 2 (winter 1996), pp. 64–86.

Loveman, Gary W., "The Internationalization of Services," Harvard Business School Module Note, 9-693-103 (June 7, 1994).

McCartney, Scott, "Airline Alliances to Alter Overseas Travel," *Wall Street Journal* (June 11, 1996).

McCartney, Scott, "AMR and British Air to Share Profits, as Well as Passengers From Alliance," *Wall Street Journal* (June 12, 1996).

Nomani, Asra Q., "Airline Pacts' Antitrust Question Sparks Controversy," *Wall Street Journal* (January 3, 1997).

Porter, Michael E., *Competitive Advantage of Nations*, (New York, The Free Press, 1990).

Rhinesmith, Stephen H., *A Manager's Guide to Globalization*, 2nd ed. (Chicago, Irwin Professional Publishing, 1996).

Sauvant, Karl P., "The Tradability of Services," in P. A. Messerlin and K. P. Sauvant (eds.), *The Uruguay Round, Services in the World Economy* (Washington, DC, The World Bank, 1990), pp. 114–122.

Vandermerwe, S., and M. Chadwick, "The Internationalization of Services," *The Service Industries Journal* (January 1989), pp. 79–93.

Vernon, Raymond, Louis T. Wells, and Subramanian Rangan, *The Manager in the International Economy*, 7th ed. (Upper Saddle River, NJ, Prentice Hall, 1996).

World Economic and Social Survey 1996 (New York, United Nations, 1996).

World Investment Report 1996: Investment, Trade and International Policy Arrangements (New York, United Nations, 1996).

CHAPTER 5

Service Strategy
and Competitiveness

5.1   INTRODUCTION

A firm survives and prospers if it can create value for its stakeholders on a continual basis. A firm's stakeholders include customers, employees, shareholders, suppliers, and the community at large. A firm that provides value equally well as its rivals, or better than its rivals, will be a competitive firm. Why is creating value so important? A customer who believes that he has received good, or better yet, exceptional service will be a satisfied customer. A satisfied customer will be a loyal customer, and a loyal customer means repeat business for the firm in the months and years to come. A satisfied customer also helps recruit new customers for the firm. Satisfied customers are more likely to buy other services from the firm. Consequently, satisfied customers are not only a long-term source of revenues for the firm, they also provide free advertising and free marketing services for the firm by word-of-mouth. In general, the higher the value a customer sees in the service, the higher the price she is willing to pay. As long as the firm keeps its customers satisfied, its revenues will continue to grow.

To be competitive, a service firm must also provide value to its other stakeholders. For example, a service firm can create value for its shareholders in the form of profits and/or higher share value. Satisfied customers generate the revenues for the service firm, but managers must be able to control costs without jeopardizing the value-generating ability of the firm.

The realities of public service organizations are different. A public service organization has no shareholders, but it has many stakeholders, such as taxpayers, public officials, unions, or anyone who uses its services. Most of the stakeholders are also customers. Stakeholders, of course, do not receive any income as a result of the public service organization's operations. However, they do receive value through a higher-quality service, lower tax burden (as a result of efficient operations), or increased variety and scope of services. Many public service organizations generate either very little or no revenue and hence depend on public funds for their existence. Police, firefighters, and K–12 school systems are some examples. Public service organizations, such as the U.S. Postal Service, generate significant amounts of revenue but may still rely on public funds for their operations.[1] In either case, satisfied stakeholders are the best assurance for a public organization's continued existence.

Finally, value will be created for employees when they are satisfied as internal customers of the organization. Employees will be satisfied if they like their work and the environment they work in, have job security, and perceive the income and benefits they receive as fair and adequate. Satisfied external customers provide the revenues for a company to offer attractive salaries and greater job security to satisfy the employees. Satisfied employees are much more likely to make both internal and external customers happy and keep them satisfied. Hence, the cycle is complete.

5.2   VALUE

Brief Historical Background on Value

The concept of economic value has been a subject of study and debate among philosophers and economists for more than 2,000 years.[2] Adam Smith (1723–1790) identified two different types of value: *value in use* and *value in exchange*. In his well-known work, *The Wealth of Nations*, he wrote:

> The things which have the greatest value in use have frequently little or no value in exchange; and on the contrary, those which have the greatest value in exchange have frequently no value in use. Nothing is more useful than water, but it will purchase scarce anything: scarce anything can be had in exchange for it. A diamond, on the contrary, has scarcely any value in use: but very great quantity of other goods may frequently be had in exchange for it.[3]

Another well-known economist, Alfred Marshall (1842–1924), defined value in microeconomic terms of *marginal utility* and *marginal cost*. Marshall defined value as the equilibrium price formed when the marginal cost equaled the marginal utility.[4] Hence, the marginal analysis indicates that the exchange value is determined not by the total usefulness of a good but the last unit of it that is consumed. Price of a good formed in the marketplace reflects not only the marginal use of it for a consumer, but also the marginal cost of producing the last unit of that good.

More recently, scholars in various fields of management and engineering have paid increased attention to the concept and measurement of value and inevitably have come up with different definitions. These range from value being simply equal to "price" to more elaborate definitions. For example, Harvard Professor Michael Porter defines value as

---

[1] The U.S. Postal Service has been profitable for many years; it has not received any taxpayer support since 1982. The USPS had a surplus of more than a billion dollars three years in a row between 1995 and 1997. Mary Beth Regan, "The Post Office Delivers a Banner Year," *Business Week* (January 19, 1998), p. 38; and Douglas Stanglin, "Don't Return to Sender," *U.S. News and World Report* (October 7, 1996).

[2] See, for example, Hannah R. Sewall, *The Theory of Value Before Adam Smith* (New York, Augustus M. Kelley Publishers, 1968); and Jeffrey T. Young, *Classical Theories of Value: From Smith to Sraffa* (Boulder, CO, Westview Press, 1978).

[3] Adam Smith, *An Inquiry into the Nature and Causes of the Wealth of Nations* (New York, The Modern Library, 1937), p. 28.

[4] Phyllis Deane, *The Evolution of Economic Ideas* (London, Cambridge University Press, 1978), p. 118.

. . .what buyers are willing to pay,. . .superior value stems from offering lower prices than competitors for equivalent benefits or providing unique benefits that more than offset a higher price.[5]

De Marle, however, uses quite a different approach to defining value. His approach is rooted in science and engineering and focuses on the design of goods:

Value is the primary force that motivates human actions. It is dichotomous, centered in people and the objects they desire. Value is a potential energy field between us and objects we need. It draws us to items in our environment that we find appealing. When this attraction is large, we expend our energy to acquire, possess, use, and exchange objects that are rewarding.[6]

Definition of Value

For the purposes of this book, the following definition is proposed:

Value is the ability of a good or service to satisfy a need or provide a benefit to a customer.

According to this definition, a good or service has value only if it satisfies a need or provides a benefit to a customer (a person or organization). Value is subjective; its existence depends on the perception and particular needs of the customer. A car may be valuable for a person who needs transportation. However, the same car has very little or no value for someone who lives on a small island with no paved roads.

More importantly, value in a good or service either exists for a customer or it does not; if something has no value for a customer, improving its components (e.g., increasing its quality or lowering its price) does not make it valuable. A choice steak may be just what a hungry person needs, and therefore is very valuable to her. However, the same steak has no value for a vegetarian, no matter how high a quality it may have in the eyes of nonvegetarians, how tastefully it is prepared and served, or how inexpensive (or free) it may be. A day care center in the neighborhood may be a very valuable service for a single parent or a couple with young children. However, the same day care center has no value for a single person or a couple with no children, or with adult children.

A Model of Service Value

The service value model used in this book is a modified version of the Zeithaml model focusing on customer value.[7] The model includes perceived quality, intrinsic attributes, extrinsic attributes, monetary price, and nonmonetary price as the components of perceived value. We expand this model by adding time as the sixth component of service value. (See Exhibit 5-1.)

Perceived Quality   Quality is frequently defined as "fitness for use." This definition applies to both manufactured goods and services. However, a more appropriate definition of quality for services may be "customer satisfaction" or "external and internal

[5] Michael E. Porter, *Competitive Advantage: Creating and Sustaining Superior Performance* (New York, The Free Press, 1985), p. 3.

[6] David J. De Marle, "The Value Force," in M. Larry Shillito and David J. De Marle, *Value: Its Measurement, Design, and Management* (New York, John Wiley & Sons, 1992), pp. 3–4.

[7] Valarie A. Zeithaml, "Consumer Perceptions of Price, Quality, and Value: A Means-End Model and Synthesis of Evidence," *Journal of Marketing*, Vol. 52 (July 1988), pp. 2-22.

EXHIBIT 5-1   The Service Value Model

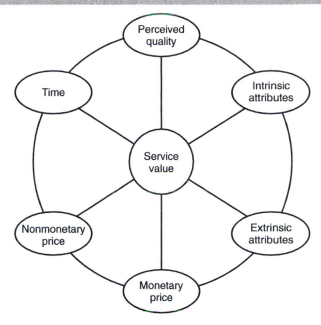

customer satisfaction."[8] This definition captures the essence of quality for services by emphasizing the important fact that quality exists in the eyes of the customer. The customer is the final arbiter of quality; quality exists as the customer perceives it. Customers' expectations are formed through word-of-mouth communication, personal needs, past experience, and external communications from the service organization.

It is clear that if customers' perceptions of what they received matches or exceeds their expectations of the service, they will be satisfied and hence value will have been created for the customer. The higher the perceived quality, the higher the perceived value of the service.

Intrinsic Attributes   Intrinsic attributes of a service are the benefits provided to customers. Intrinsic attributes may be considered in two groups: core service and supplementary services. Core service is the basic, or minimum, benefit a customer expects from the service. For example, in passenger air transport, the core service may be defined as "transporting customers on an airplane from one airport to another safely and comfortably." Supplementary services include preassigned seats, food and beverages, newspapers, movies, pillows and blankets, and connecting flight information by airline representatives at the gate.

Some supplementary services are needed for delivery of the core service. Without them, the service will be impossible. Yet others enhance the value for a customer. The relative importance of supplementary services depends on the nature of the service. Clearly, a service organization that fails to deliver the core service often will not survive long; hence, providing the core service without failure and as expected by cus-

---

[8] J. M. Juran and Frank M. Gryna, *Quality Planning and Analysis* (New York, McGraw-Hill, 1993), p. 5.

tomers is the first and fundamental step in creating value for customers. However, that is usually not enough to be competitive. Consequently, a service organization can create more value for its customers by both increasing the variety of supplementary services that are appreciated by its customers and performing them at least as well as customers expect.

Extrinsic Attributes   Extrinsic service attributes are related to the service, but they exist outside the service package. The reputation of a university as being the "best" in a certain discipline provides extrinsic value to a degree obtained from that school in that particular discipline. Locating a service facility in a fashionable neighborhood may provide added value to customers in addition to the core and supplementary services. In short, all the psychological benefits associated with the service constitute extrinsic attributes. A service organization normally has no direct and immediate influence or control over these attributes. It may, however, create these attributes, and hence create value for its customers in the long run.

Monetary Price   The sum of the expenses incurred by a customer to obtain a service is the monetary price. This includes the price charged by the service organization, as well as other expenses a customer has to incur to access the service. A heart patient who needs a bypass operation may have to travel to a distant city to have access to an expert surgeon. In addition to hospital charges and surgeon's fees, this patient has to consider other expenses, such as airfare and lodging for himself and perhaps for a companion. Monetary price is sometimes the most important factor for customers in making purchase decisions. It is not uncommon to hear consumers define *value* as "low price." A service organization, therefore, can create significant value for its customers if it can lower its prices without causing a deterioration in the other attributes of the service.

Nonmonetary Price   Any perceived sacrifice, other than financial, that a customer has to make to access and receive a service is defined as nonmonetary price. Nonmonetary sacrifice includes time spent searching for the right service or provider, inconvenience for the customer to access the service provider, time spent traveling to and from the service location, and time spent waiting for and during the service performance. Nonmonetary price also includes psychological costs such as perception of risk, and anxiety felt before, during, and after the service. For example, it is very natural for a patient to feel considerable anxiety before surgery. Stress experienced before or during the service, such as waiting in line that feels like forever, and pain experienced in a dentist's chair, can also be part of the nonmonetary price customers perceive they are paying.

Time   Time plays an important role in value creation in services in three ways:

1. *Time needed to use the service.* Some services require minimal involvement by a customer; therefore, the time spent by the customer is usually not significant. Establishing phone service at a new address, for example, usually takes a phone call to the local phone company and consumes only a few minutes. Yet some services require considerable expenditure of time. College education, for instance, normally takes at least four years to complete. Time spent in accessing, waiting for, and receiving a service may mean a significant sacrifice in terms of other activities or earnings lost. In general, the less the required time to use a service, the higher the value of the service for the customer.

There is also an important connection between time and service quality. For example, service quality dimension "responsiveness" is defined as "willingness to help customers and provide prompt service."[9] Time becomes a critical factor in many service failures. When a service failure occurs, even if the service company takes necessary measures to correct the problem, the customer usually ends up losing time, and no corrective measure can restore the lost time. For example, a canceled flight due to a mechanical problem means loss of time for passengers until the airline solves the problem or finds alternative flights. This loss may be very significant for some customers, especially if it means missing an important business appointment or missing an important event such as a wedding.

As discussed earlier, time is also an important element in perceived nonmonetary price. Customers consider the amount of time they have to spend for a service in making purchase decisions. For example, amusement parks are usually very crowded on weekends; therefore, the wait is longer for rides. This means that either a customer has to spend much more time in the park than is normally necessary during the week, or forgo the enjoyment of some rides. Consequently, some customers may prefer to schedule their trip to the amusement park during the week. Reducing the service time usually adds value to service for many customers; sometimes benefit to customers is so significant that they may even be willing to pay a premium price for the time savings. For example, a flight from New York to Paris on a regular jetliner takes about seven hours; the same flight on a supersonic Concorde jet takes about three and a half hours and costs three times as much. Obviously, for some customers, the reduction in flight time is so valuable that they pay extra for it.

2. *Service as a time-saving alternative to another service.* Many services are offered as alternatives to existing services; they create value in a very important way, they provide the same service faster, and save time for the customer. Many of these services have been enthusiastically embraced by customers. Federal Express provides an alternative to regular mail; letters or small packs are delivered overnight rather than in several days with the U.S. Postal Service's regular service. Fax machines provide an even faster alternative over the phone lines. When first introduced, air travel provided a new alternative and a huge advantage over land transportation. Millions of people still use airlines every day for domestic travel as the preferred alternative to travel by train, bus, or car, because of the time savings achieved. For transoceanic travel, of course, airlines provide the only sensible alternative for time-conscious passengers.

3. *The time horizon within which the service provides benefits.* Benefits provided by services create value to customers for very different lengths of time. Four possibilities may be identified:

   a. *Value now and for a short period of time.* Some services provide immediate benefits to customers that last for a limited length of time. A haircut, for example, has immediate benefits for the customer that last for a few weeks; the benefits, however, decrease with time. A stay in a hotel provides shelter and an opportunity to rest immediately, and the benefits continue as long as the customer does not check out.

   b. *Value now and for an indefinite period of time.* Services such as telephone, TV broadcast, police protection, mail delivery, nutrition counseling, and inocula-

---

[9] V. A. Zeithaml, A. Parasuraman, and L. L. Berry, *Delivering Quality Service: Balancing Customer Perceptions and Expectations* (New York, Free Press, 1990), p. 26.

tions for various diseases are examples of services that provide benefits immediately and continuously for an indefinite period of time.

c. *Value in the future for a limited period of time.* Some services provide value for customers or potential customers in a future time period and for a limited time. A new elementary school to be built in the neighborhood may mean an increase in the property taxes for all the residents of a town; however, the new school will provide value for some families only in the future. A couple with no school-aged children will benefit from this service in the future if the couple has preschool-aged children or are planning to have children later. When the benefits accrue, they last for a limited time—until the kids finish school.

d. *Value in the future for an indefinite period of time.* Services such as college education or a dentist's service to straighten the teeth of a youngster take a long time to complete but provide benefits for the rest of the recipient's life. Major benefits usually do not accrue to the recipient until the service is completed. For example, a college student normally will not be able to find a full-time job in the field she has chosen until graduation. There may, of course, be occasional visits back to the service provider for updates (e.g., courses to bring graduates up to date on new techniques), but most services continue to provide benefits even without these updates.

In summary, a service organization can create value for customers by improving the quality of service. It can create value by designing a core service that meets customers' needs and supplementary services that are valued by customers. A service organization can also create value for customers indirectly by creating perceived intrinsic attributes. This is usually accomplished through many years of delivering consistently high-quality reliable service. It can also be accomplished through advertising and creating a high-value service image. When the monetary price of a service is reduced, customers usually perceive an increase in value. Finally, if access, waiting, and delivery times for service can be reduced, and benefits can be made available sooner and last longer, additional value is created for the customer. For example, the Motor Vehicles Department in New Jersey increases access time for vehicle inspection through extended hours—one day a week till 7:30 P.M. and on Saturdays till noon—so that motorists can have their cars inspected without losing time from work. Shouldice Hospital in Toronto, Canada, performs hernia operations so well that its patients return to work in half the time it takes patients of other hospitals. Also, the recurrence rate of all operations at Shouldice is 0.8 percent whereas the recurrence rate for hernias performed in U.S. hospitals is 10 percent. This means that benefits Shouldice patients receive from their operations on average last for a much longer period of time.

The service value model we have presented provides a framework for crafting strategies to create value for customers through the design, development, and delivery of services. The design and development of services and the design of service delivery systems will be discussed in chapter 8. The remainder of this chapter will focus on strategy and related issues.

5.3 STRATEGY

Customers buy goods and services when they perceive value in them. They will continue to purchase goods and services as long as they are satisfied—or better yet, delighted—with what they have received. The survival and prosperity of a service organization is closely linked with this outcome. So how should a service organization approach this most important task? Clearly, not in a haphazard or random way; successful service companies do not happen by accident, they are created as a result of determined efforts by their employees and managers that are aimed at customer satisfaction. Just having a strategy, of course, is no guarantee for success. This section reviews basic concepts of competitive strategy and discusses how a successful service strategy can be developed for creating value for the customer. First, some basic concepts and definitions.

Definition of Strategy

Bruce D. Henderson offers the following definition and perspective on strategy:

> Strategy is a deliberate search for a plan of action that will develop a business's competitive advantage and compound it. For any company, the search is an iterative process that begins with a recognition of where you are and what you have now. . . . The differences between you and your competitors are the basis of your advantage.[10]

It is clear from this definition that an organization needs a good understanding of its environment to develop an effective strategy. Then it can embark upon designing plans to respond and shape this environment to its advantage. The issue of developing effective strategies will be discussed later in this chapter; however, it is important to note that not all firms follow a well-organized, step-by-step procedure in developing a competitive strategy. Strategy may appear in many different forms[11]:

- *Strategy as plan.* Strategy may be developed as a plan that is designed before an action takes place to achieve certain goals. It is a way for executives to steer the organization in the desired direction.
- *Strategy as ploy.* Strategy may sometimes be a ploy, "just a specific 'maneuver' to outwit an opponent or competitor."
- *Strategy as pattern.* Consistent behavior, or a theme, in a series of activities may be identified as evidence of strategy whether or not the pattern was planned.
- *Strategy as position.* This definition implies positioning of an organization in its environment, or carving itself a niche in this environment. It indicates how an organization is trying to cope with its competitors and survive.
- *Strategy as perspective.* Strategy may also be defined as an organization's "personality," that is, "an ingrained way of perceiving the world."

Strategy may appear in one or more of these forms at any one time. Together, they provide a more comprehensive description of strategy than a single definition might convey. Following are a few more definitions of terms that will be used in discussing strategy.

- *Strategic goals (or objectives).* Goals emanate from strategy and specify targets for the organization's efforts. In other words, strategic goals define what is to be achieved for survival and competitiveness.
- *Tactics.* Tactics are action-oriented plans with shorter time horizons than strategy. Their main function is to focus an organization's efforts on specific tasks that when accomplished will help achieve the objectives of a strategy. The distinction between a strategy and tactic may depend on the level of organization where it resides, the scale of action, or the perspective of the leader. For exam-

[10] Bruce D. Henderson, "The Origin of Strategy," *Harvard Business Review* (November–December 1989).
[11] Henry Mintzberg, "Five Ps for Strategy," *California Management Review* (fall 1987).

ple, what a chief executive officer considers a tactic may be a strategy to a lower-level manager.[12]

- *Policies.* Policies define the limits within which the organization will operate, conduct business, and resolve conflicts when there is disagreement among various objectives.

Why an Organization Needs Strategy

Mintzberg identified four main reasons for an organization's need for a strategy[13]:

First, an organization needs strategy to draw a route to desired outcomes, that is, to defend itself against competitors, to remain competitive and prosper. In this sense, strategy provides a sense of direction, a destination to aim for. Second, strategy helps an organization focus its activities and energies on certain ends and promote the coordination of these activities. It provides a sense of purpose and direction. In other words, a strategy may help the whole organization pull together in one direction. Third, strategy helps define an organization as character or personality defines an individual. In this sense, strategy provides meaning for the members of an organization as well as outsiders.

Finally, Mintzberg argues that "providing consistency" may be the clearest reason for strategies. A properly designed strategy helps reduce uncertainty for an organization and its members. It helps them organize, interpret, and deal with experiences and incoming information in a consistent way. Reducing uncertainty helps members function more efficiently and feel less stress. In this sense, strategy also simplifies various tasks for the members of the organization. For example, it reduces the need to learn to deal with every new situation, it provides them with a standard way of responding to most situations.

The preceding arguments explain why organizations need strategies, but they also provide implicit guidelines for service organizations for designing their competitive strategies as well as designing services and service delivery systems.

Understanding the Competitive Environment

A profound understanding of the environment an organization operates in is a prerequisite to developing an effective strategy. An organization that does not know its rivals or understand its industry and the rules of competition will not be able to develop an effective competitive strategy. Porter[14] identifies five forces in any industry that define the competitive environment: the entry of new competitors, the threat of substitutes, the bargaining power of buyers, the bargaining power of suppliers, and the intensity of rivalry among the existing competitors. (See Exhibit 5-2.) An organization develops a strategy to determine how to respond to competitors and, better yet, how to change the environment and the rules of competition to its advantage.

New Entrants   New entrants into an industry usually means new competitive challenges for the existing firms. A new entrant may bring additional capacity to an industry if it brings facilities and workforce that were not previously in that industry. A new entrant means new challenges or possibly increased competition, because a new entrant may be bringing new ideas, new technology, and new services to an industry in addition to increased capacity. For the existing firms, this may mean loss of customers, loss of market share, and a reduction in profits.

---

[12] James B. Quinn, *Strategies for Change: Logical Incrementalism* (Homewood, IL, Richard D. Irwin, 1980).

[13] Henry Mintzberg, "The Strategy Concept II: Another Look at Why Organizations Need Strategies," *California Management Review* (fall 1987), pp. 25–32.

[14] Michael E. Porter, *Competitive Advantage*, pp. 4–5.

EXHIBIT 5-2   Elements of Industry Structure

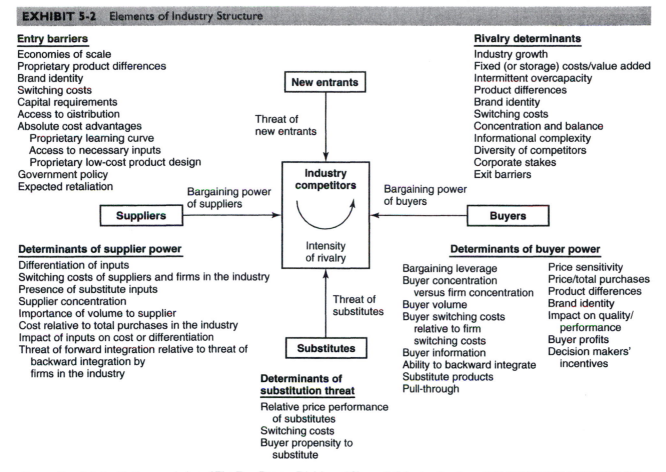

Entry barriers
Economies of scale
Proprietary product differences
Brand identity
Switching costs
Capital requirements
Access to distribution
Absolute cost advantages
    Proprietary learning curve
    Access to necessary inputs
    Proprietary low-cost product design
Government policy
Expected retaliation

Rivalry determinants
Industry growth
Fixed (or storage) costs/value added
Intermittent overcapacity
Product differences
Brand identity
Switching costs
Concentration and balance
Informational complexity
Diversity of competitors
Corporate stakes
Exit barriers

Threat of new entrants

New entrants

Industry competitors

Bargaining power of suppliers

Suppliers

Bargaining power of buyers

Buyers

Intensity of rivalry

Determinants of supplier power
Differentiation of inputs
Switching costs of suppliers and firms in the industry
Presence of substitute inputs
Supplier concentration
Importance of volume to supplier
Cost relative to total purchases in the industry
Impact of inputs on cost or differentiation
Threat of forward integration relative to threat of
    backward integration by
    firms in the industry

Threat of substitutes

Substitutes

Determinants of buyer power

Bargaining leverage
Buyer concentration
    versus firm concentration
Buyer volume
Buyer switching costs
    relative to firm
    switching costs
Buyer information
Ability to backward integrate
Substitute products
Pull-through

Price sensitivity
Price/total purchases
Product differences
Brand identity
Impact on quality/
    performance
Buyer profits
Decision makers'
    incentives

Determinants of substitution threat
Relative price performance
    of substitutes
Switching costs
Buyer propensity to
    substitute

Source: Reprinted with the permission of The Free Press, a Division of Simon & Schuster, Inc. from COMPETITIVE ADVANTAGE: Creating and Sustaining Superior Performance by Michael E. Porter. Copyright © 1985 by Michael E. Porter.

The seriousness of this type of threat for an organization depends on the barriers to entry as well as the competitive strength and determination of the organization to meet the challenge. Porter identified the following barriers to entry[15]:

- *Economies of scale.* Unit costs decline as the volume of production increases when accompanied by increased capacity (i.e., a larger factory). This phenomenon may be observed not only in the manufacture of goods but also production of services. The major reason for this is that fixed costs will be divided among a larger number of customers served.
- *Product differentiation.* If the existing companies in an industry have brand identification and loyal customers, and product differentiation, a potential entrant may face a difficult barrier to overcome. Many banks entering the credit card market offer Visa or MasterCard with no annual fee and reduced interest rates for a limited time to attract customers from other card issuers.

---

[15] Michael E. Porter, *Competitive Strategy: Techniques for Analyzing Industries and Competitors* (New York, The Free Press, 1980), pp. 7–14.

- *Capital requirements.* Some industries require substantial up-front investment to be a player. Investment may be required not only for equipment and facilities, but also for advertising, research and development, and setting up an order taking and processing system. Clearly, large investment requirements make many service industries, such as airline and health care industries, inaccessible for all but companies with substantial financial resources.
- *Switching costs.* Another barrier new entrants may face is the reluctance or unwillingness of customers in an industry to switch to another company due to the costs involved. Customers may be unwilling to switch for other reasons, such as to not give up the comfort of familiar routine or change well-entrenched habits.
- *Access to distribution channels.* Finding a distribution channel or establishing a new one may be a significant barrier for new entrants. Existing competitors in an industry may have exclusive arrangements with distributors that prevent them from accepting business from new or existing competitors. For example, rules of Visa prevent its member banks in the United States from issuing American Express cards.[16]
- *Cost disadvantages independent of scale.* Another barrier for new entrants may be cost advantages existing firms have achieved independent of their size or scale of operations. Some of these advantages originate from the learning curve effect a company enjoys for being in business longer than its competitors.
- *Government policy.* Federal, state, or local governments may create barriers to entry in many industries. For example, licensing requirements exist in industries such as health care, law, and education.
- *Expected retaliation.* Another important deterrent to entry may be the expected behavior of the existing competitors. If companies in an industry have a history of meeting a newcomer by fierce competition, a potential entrant may have to think twice before drawing such a hostile reaction from well-established competitors.

Intensity of Rivalry among Existing Competitors   Rivalry among competitors may occur in various forms, including price wars, advertising, new-product introduction, and increased customer service or guarantees. Several reasons can be listed for the intensity of rivalry among the existing competitors[17]:

- *Equally balanced competitors.* When firms in an industry are about equal in size and resources, their fight may be fierce and last a long time.
- *Slow industry growth.* Competition in a slow-growing industry means someone's market share gain is someone else's share loss.
- *High fixed costs.* High fixed costs create pressures to use the capacity of a firm at full capacity, which may lead to intense price competition.
- *Lack of differentiation or switching costs.* If the service is considered a commodity, price competition may result.
- *Capacity augmented in large increments.* If increment is big enough to disrupt the balance of industry supply and demand, it may lead to overcapacity, which in turn may lead to price wars.
- *Diverse competitors.* When the strategies, goals, or personalities of competitors differ significantly from each other, they will usually be unable to read each other's intentions and end up in direct clashes.

---

[16] Suzanne Oliver, "The Battle of the Credit Cards," *Forbes* (July 1, 1996), pp. 62–66.
[17] Michael E. Porter, *Competitive Strategy*, pp. 17–21.

- *High strategic stakes.* Some diversified firms may place a high priority on success in a particular industry as part of their overall corporate strategy.
- *High exit barriers.* Specialized assets, labor contracts, and government and social restrictions may create barriers to exit.

Substitutes   A substitute for a service is another service that performs the same basic function or functions. Which function is expected from a service or which function is valuable depends on the customer's needs. A frozen dinner from a supermarket or a sandwich from a deli may be a substitute for a meal in a restaurant if the function is to provide nourishment. However, frozen dinners and sandwiches are not substitutes for someone who wants a dining experience in a pleasant atmosphere with a companion. Substitute products reduce the profit potential of an industry.

Buyers (Customers)   Customers create competitive pressures on the organizations in an industry by their search and demand for lower prices, higher quality, or more services, and by playing them against each other. The impact of such behavior on a competitor will be significant if the customer's purchases from the company constitute a major portion of the company's sales.

Suppliers   Similarly, suppliers may create pressures over the members of an industry by their demands for higher prices, or by lowering the quality of products they supply. An important supplier group in service industries is labor (blue- and white-collar workers or professional athletes). Organized labor may play a very important role in an industry, as baseball players' strikes in recent years have shown.

Generic Competitive Strategies

Formulation of a strategy should include an appraisal of all five forces and their interrelationships. Specifically, an organization developing a strategy should assess its own strengths and weaknesses, including its competencies and resources, as well as opportunities and threats that exist in its industry.[18] Also relevant are the values an organization shares, especially of those who implement strategy, and societal impact of such factors as government policy, social concerns, and evolving mores.[19] Exhibit 5-3 summarizes the relationship between competitive strategy and internal and external environment. Consequently, each organization's strategy is unique. However, it is possible to identify patterns in strategy selection. Porter identified three such generic strategies, which are distinctly different in their approach to achieving competitive advantage.[20] This section is based on his classification and description of these generic strategies.

Cost Leadership   An organization is following a cost leadership strategy if it is striving to be the low-cost producer in its industry. Typically, a low-cost producer offers a set of standard, no-frills products (goods and/or services). This approach covers *many segments* of an industry; it is not limited to one particular segment of the market. Cost advantage of a low-cost producer may originate from various sources, including economies of scale, learning curve effects, innovative or proprietary technology, and preferential access to raw materials. The focus on costs, however, does not mean a cost leader can ignore the differentiation aspects of competition; to remain

[18] See, for example, chapter 3, in Kenneth R. Andrews, *The Concept of Corporate Strategy* (Homewood, IL, Irwin, 1987).

[19] Michael E. Porter, *Competitive Strategy*, p. xvii.

[20] Michael E. Porter, *Competitive Advantage*, pp. 12–20, and *Competitive Strategy*, pp. 34–46.

EXHIBIT 5-3 Context in Which Competitive Strategy Is Formulated

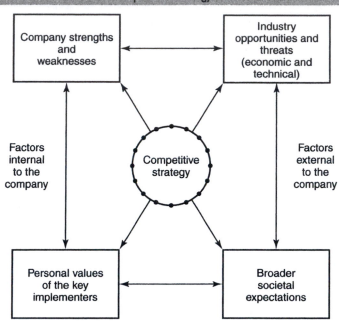

Source: Reprinted with the permission of The Free Press, a Division of Simon & Schuster, Inc. from COM-PETITIVE STRATEGY: TECHNIQUES FOR ANALYZING INDUSTRIES AND COMPETITORS by Michael E. Porter. Copyright © 1980 by The Free Press.

competitive, it must be equal, or close, to its competitors in the bases of differentia-tion. If the cost leader does not have parity in differentiation, it should be close enough so that the price reduction it has to offer to gain and maintain market share does not eliminate its cost advantage. An organization following the cost leadership strategy must pay close attention to cost control and overhead minimization, and work hard to exploit the learning curve effect when it exists.

Cost leadership provides protection for the organization against the five forces of its industry in various ways. Customers cannot put too much pressure on the organiza-tion to reduce its prices—they are already at the lowest levels. Suppliers will not have much power against a low-cost producer if it has economies of scale, and hence is a significant customer for the supplier. Cost leadership also provides protection against new entries and substitutes.

An example provided at the end of this chapter discusses Southwest Airlines and its operations. As will be clear from the example, cost leadership is a part of South-west's strategy; it provides very low-cost air transportation on all routes it flies.

Differentiation   Differentiation strategy requires that an organization be unique in a way that is valued by its customers. Uniqueness is *industry-wide* and may in-clude product attributes, delivery system, or marketing that meet specific needs of a group of customers. Differentiation strategy is based on the assumption that cus-tomers are willing to pay a premium price for the uniqueness the firm offers. Usu-ally, differentiation is obtained through activities that increase costs for the organi-zation. However, the organization cannot completely ignore costs; if its prices are too high, competitors' low cost may overcome the attraction of uniqueness for cus-tomers.

This strategy also helps protect an organization against the five forces of its industry. If the organization is successful in creating differentiation of its goods or services in customers' minds, it may achieve loyalty among them and thus reduce customers' bargaining power, at the same time create a barrier for potential entrants, and provide a defensible position against competitors and substitutes. In general, this strategy leads to higher profit margins but low market share.

Focus   This strategy is built on the concept of serving a limited segment of the potential market very well. By focusing on a limited segment of the market, an organization may be able to tailor its products, operations, and all the relevant activities to serve the selected segment effectively and efficiently. It has two forms: *cost focus* and *differentiation focus*. The difference between these and the previous two generic strategies is that the latter encompass the entire industry or wide industry segments; cost focus and differentiation focus, however, are very limited in scope. They are designed to achieve competitive advantage in costs or differentiation in the selected segment.

For any of the focus strategies to be successful, the selected segment must be somehow neglected by competitors who are trying to serve an entire industry or broad segments of it. Cost focus may be successful if, for example, an organization can identify customers that are inexpensive to serve. Shouldice Hospital in Toronto, for example, performs only inguinal hernia operations and accepts only healthy patients; consequently, it selects customers that are less expensive to serve. Because of this, it can charge a price that is about one third of what its competitors charge.

Differentiation focus in services may be achieved if a segment of the market with special needs can be identified and served to meet those special needs. Jiffy Lube, Midas Muffler, and AAMCO each focus on meeting a particular need of car owners. It is, of course, possible to follow both cost and differentiation focus for a limited segment and be successful at it, as demonstrated by Shouldice Hospital.

Fragmented Industries   A phenomenon that is particularly relevant to services is a fragmented industry. An industry in which no firm has a dominant position or a significant market share is said to be fragmented. These industries usually have a large number of small and medium-size firms, none of which is able to influence industry practices. This is a common phenomenon in many services such as dry cleaning and auto repair. Reasons for industry fragmentation are shown in Exhibit 5-4.

EXHIBIT 5-4   Reasons for Industry Fragmentation

Low overall entry barriers
Absence of economies of scale or experience curve
High transportation costs
High inventory costs or erratic sales fluctuations
No advantages of size in dealing with buyers or suppliers
Diseconomies of scale in some important aspect
Diverse market needs
High product differentiation, particularly if based on image
Exit barriers
Local regulation
Government prohibition of concentration
Newness of the industry

Source: Michael E. Porter, *Competitive Strategy: Techniques for Analyzing Industries and Competitors* (New York, The Free Press, 1980), pp. 196–200.

5.4 FORMULATING A COMPETITIVE SERVICE STRATEGY

Value is created for a customer when a service satisfies a customer's need(s) or provides some benefit to the customer. The higher the value a customer sees in a service, the higher the price he is willing to pay. A customer who perceives value in the service will be a satisfied customer, and a satisfied customer is like an insurance policy for the future of the service organization. Consequently, the purpose of a service strategy must be to create value for its customers. This section focuses on formulating and developing a service strategy to create value for the customer. Strategic service vision is discussed and Southwest Airlines presented as an example of its application.

James L. Heskett developed the concept of "strategic service vision" in his book, *Managing in the Service Economy*.[21] Strategic service vision consists of four basic and three integrative elements. These elements are represented in Exhibit 5-5 with accompanying questions that help construct them.

Basic Elements of the Strategic Service Vision

Target Market Segment   Like most goods, most services are valuable only to some people; a service organization cannot satisfy everybody. Consequently, it should carefully select and identify customers it is able and willing to serve. This is called segmentation. Segmentation tries to identify a group of customers with common characteristics, needs, purchasing behavior, or consumption patterns. Effective segmentation results in a grouping of customers that are very similar on these or other relevant dimensions, but at the same time very different from other segments. Segmentation may be based on geographic, demographic, psychographic, or any other relevant basis.

Service Concept   A service concept describes the service for customers, employees, and other stakeholders. A service must be defined in terms of outcomes or benefits it provides to customers. The service concept flows from the definition of an organization's business. In other words, the answer to the question "What business are we in?" defines the service concept. The definition of the business an organization is in should be broad enough not to eliminate future extensions that may arise because of advances in technology, change in consumption patterns, or other opportunities. Also, a narrow definition may expose the organization to surprise attacks from organizations in related industries. However, it should not be too broad to lead to businesses outside the organization's abilities and competencies.

Operating Strategy   Operating strategy is a set of strategies, plans, and policies concerning an organization's operations, financing, marketing, human resources, and control so that it can bring its service concept to life. It includes hiring, organization policies, control of quality and costs, and ways of leveraging value over cost.

Service Delivery System   A service delivery system is how an organization prepares for and conducts itself in service encounters. It includes facilities and their layout, technology and equipment used, processes for delivering the service, and job descriptions for employees and the roles they and customers play during a service encounter. A service delivery system must be designed to achieve maximum customer satisfaction. Most service concepts can be copied by competitors, but a well-designed service delivery system may not be easily duplicated, and hence may serve as a barrier to potential competitors.

---

[21] James L. Heskett, *Managing in the Service Economy* (Boston, Harvard Business School Press, 1986).

EXHIBIT 5-5 Basic and Integrative Elements of a Strategic Service Vision

Target market segments	Positioning	Service concept	Value/cost leveraging	Operating strategy	Strategy/system integration	Service delivery system
What are common characteristics of important market segments?	How does the service concept propose to meet customer needs?	What are important elements of the service to be provided, stated in terms of results produced for customers?	To what extent are differences between perceived value and cost of service maximized by	What are important elements of the strategy? Operations? Financing? Marketing? Organization? Human resources? Control?	To what extent are the strategy and delivery system internally consistent?	What are important features of the service delivery system, including The role of people? Technology? Equipment? Layout? Procedures?
What dimensions can be used to segment the market? Demographic? Psychographic?	How do competitors meet these needs?	How are these elements supposed to be perceived by the target market segment? By the market in general? By employees as a whole?	Standardization of certain elements? Customization of certain elements? Emphasizing easily leveraged services? Management of supply and demand?	On which will the most effort be concentrated?	Can needs of the strategy be met by the delivery system?	What capacity does it provide? Normally? At peak levels?
How important are various segments?	How is the proposed service differentiated from competition?	How is the service concept perceived?	Control of quality through	Where will investments be made?	If not, what changes must be made in The operating strategy? The service delivery system?	To what extent does it Help insure quality standards? Differentiate the service from competition? Provide barriers to entry by competitors?
What needs does each have?	How important are these differences?	What efforts does this suggest in terms of the manner in which the service is Designed? Delivered? Marketed?	Rewards? Appeal to pride? Visibility/ supervision? Peer group control? Involving the customer? Effective use of data?	How will quality and cost be controlled? Measures? Incentives? Rewards?	To what extent does the coordination of operating strategy and service delivery system insure High quality? High productivity? Low cost? High morale and loyalty of servers?	
How well are these needs being served?	What is good service?		To what extent does this effort create barriers to entry by potential competition?	What results will be expected versus competition in terms of Quality of service? Cost profile? Productivity? Morale/loyalty of servers?	To what extent does this integration provide barriers to entry to competition?	
In what manner? By whom?	Does the proposed service concept provide it?					
	What efforts are required to bring customer expectations and service capabilities into alignment?					

Basic element

Integrative element

Source: Reprinted by permission of Harvard Business School Press. From *Managing in the Service Economy* by James L. Heskett. Boston, MA, 1986, p. 30. Copyright © 1986 by the President and Fellows of Harvard College; all rights reserved.

Integrative Elements of the Strategic Service Vision

Integrative elements help the basic elements fit together for a consistent service strategy. They provide guidelines for planning actions to implement the service vision and include positioning, leveraging value over cost, and strategy system integration.

Positioning   How an organization differentiates itself from its competitors is called positioning. It requires profound knowledge and understanding of customers' needs, the organization's capabilities, and competitors' service offerings and capabilities, as well as the ability of the service concept to meet customers' needs. Once these elements are understood, the organization seeks a unique set of attributes to match the service concept with the selected segment's characteristics. Uniqueness may be achieved in terms of costs, service features, advertising and promotion, distribution channels, and delivery system.

Value/Cost Leveraging   A well-designed and -positioned service concept provides unique benefits to customers, and hence creates value or more value than competitors provide. In general, such uniqueness justifies premium prices for the service, but it also costs more to create. If an organization manages to deliver such high perceived value without driving its costs too high, it is said to leverage value over cost and enjoys higher margins than its competitors. In other words, value is leveraged over cost when the perceived additional value in dollar terms far exceeds the costs of creating it. Clearly, this requires great skill. Various tactics may be used in leveraging value over cost, including customizing certain features that are highly valued by customers, and standardizing others, carefully managing quality at critical points in the service process, managing demand and supply, and involving the customer in service creation.

Strategy/System Integration   In addition to consistency between target segment and service concept, and between service concept and operating strategy, operating strategy must be consistent with the delivery system for this collection to become a whole. An excellent service organization achieves consistency between its operating strategy and service delivery system by carefully designing its hiring policies, service processes, and facilities. It also pays close attention to its employee compensation, promotion, and reward policies. Excellent service companies know that without satisfied employees they cannot have satisfied customers.

An Example: Southwest Airlines

This chapter closes with an example of how an excellent service organization achieves success through its strategy. Although there is no evidence to suggest that Southwest Airlines consciously applied the strategic service vision, its practices fit the model.[22] Southwest's practices were summarized in Exhibit 5-6, which has the same format as Exhibit 5-5 in which the elements of strategic service vision and their relationships are represented.

Air Southwest Co. (later Southwest Airline Co.) was founded by Rollin W. King and was granted a permission to fly between the three largest cities of Texas: Dallas, Houston, and San Antonio. Southwest chose Dallas's Love Field as its headquarters. Southwest purchased three brand new Boeing 737s and started flying on June 18, 1971, between the three major Texas cities at low prices, $20 each way on all its routes versus competitors' $27 and $28, and with a very different image than its competitors.

[22] Information for this example, unless otherwise indicated, has been gathered from the following sources: Southwest Airlines homepage: *www.southwest.com/press/factsheet.html*; Kristin Dunlap Godsey, "Slow Climb to New Heights," *Success* (October 20, 1996); Kenneth Labich, "Is Kelleher America's Best CEO?" *Fortune* (May 2, 1994); "Southwest Airlines (A)," Harvard Business School Case 575-060 Rev. 2/85.

EXHIBIT 5-6   Strategic Service Vision as Applied to Southwest Airlines

Target Market Segment	Positioning	Service Concept	Value Cost Leveraging	Operating Strategy	Strategy System Integration	Service Delivery System
Cost-conscious traveler (business, individuals, and families)	Short, point-to-point (rather than hub-and-spoke system) flights	Safe, no frills, low-cost air travel: mass transportation	Despite the "no frills" image, passengers are provided with a standard meal which has their choice of soft drink and a small bag of peanuts labeled "frills"	Load and unload planes quickly for on-time arrivals and save time for passengers and increase aircraft utilization	Free advertising and promotion through off-the-wall events	An efficient system for maintaining, loading, and unloading planes
	A large number of flights between targeted cities	Convenient schedules	Point-to-point flights save time for passengers in addition to their savings in ticket price	Keep (training, record keeping, parts inventory, maintenance, and crew scheduling) costs down by using one type of plane	No tickets, passengers with a reservation show a picture ID at the gate	Single type of aircraft: Boeing 737, ultimate in delivery system standardization
	"Fun-loving rebel airline" image	Save time for passengers with point-to-point flights and on-time arrivals	Flight attendants with a sense of humor entertain and amuse passengers. Attractive uniforms (earlier hot pants, now shorts)	Make employees the first priority: • Profit-sharing plan for employees • Job security • Airline as a "family"	No assigned seats for quick loading of planes and low cost. Plastic cards with numbers determine boarding order	Employees deliver service with a sense of humor
	Keep the corporate culture at the heart of every campaign	Make flying fun		Hire people who have a sense of humor and "who know how to have fun"	Board 30 passengers at a time for quick loading	
				Train employees for necessary skills, create a sense of responsibility and ownership. Encourage trying new ideas as long as safety is not compromised	Planes are unloaded and loaded in 20 minutes	
				Disciplined, fiscally prudent growth keeps financial costs down	Language of the airline: "love potions" (drinks), "love bites" (peanuts), "love machines" (ticketing machines), employee newsletter "Luv Lines"	
				Encourage employees to think like entrepreneurs	Create a strong company culture: Deliver on "We Care About You" promise. Employees own about 13% of the company and receive a share of profits	

103

By 1975, the airline expanded its flight schedule to eight more cities. By 1978, it was one of the country's most profitable airlines. As of the end of 1998, Southwest had been profitable for 26 consecutive years, never had layoffs, and never had an accident. The airline started with 195 employees in 1971; the number of employees reached almost 26,000 in 1998. From a regional carrier with three planes and three routes, it became a major airline in 1989 when its revenues exceeded the billion dollar mark.

Southwest's business philosophy is: Provide affordable and safe air travel and job security for employees, and make maximum profit possible. Howard Putnam, a consultant and early CEO of the airline, described the company as follows: "We weren't an airline. We were mass transportation."[23] Southwest achieves high levels of profit by keeping its costs down and controlling growth. Costs are kept low by an efficient system of operations including ticketing, maintenance, baggage handling, training, and servicing planes. For example, after a plane pulls into a gate, Southwest could turn it around and fly again in 20 minutes. The industry average is 45 minutes.

Southwest uses only Boeing 737 planes, making it possible to switch crews from one flight to another when need arises. Using only one type of plane keeps its training, record keeping, maintenance, and inventory costs very low. Most of Southwest's flights are about an hour; this implies that it does not have to serve meals. Its ticketing system is also kept very simple. Passengers are given reservations and they just show a picture ID at the gate. There are no assigned seats on Southwest flights; when they arrive at the gate, passengers are issued plastic boarding passes with a number indicating the order in which they board the plane. This strategy keeps costs down and operations simple; the airline does not have to print boarding passes, passes may be used many times, and fewer employees are needed at the gate.

Major airlines use a hub-and-spoke system, where passengers are flown to a central airport from outlying areas and then make connections to their destinations. Most of Southwest's flights are short, point-to-point flights; that is, passengers are flown to their destinations directly. Together with a 20-minute plane turnaround, this saves time and money for both the airline and its customers by keeping planes in the air longer, resulting in higher efficiency. Passengers save time because they do not have to wait at hub airports for their connecting flights. Southwest has achieved a very competitive cost position in its industry. For example, its cost per available passenger mile is 7 cents, while all other major airlines have higher costs, as can be seen in Exhibit 5-7. It also has extremely high labor efficiency in terms of passengers per employee and employees per aircraft. In addition, Southwest's distribution system helps keep its costs down. Most major airlines use computerized reservations systems through which travel agents make reservations for passengers. Southwest does not use that system; agents have to call the airline to book flights, and many customers make the call them-

EXHIBIT 5-7   How Productivity Pays Off for Southwest

	AMR	Delta	Northwest	Southwest	UAL	USAIR
Cost per available seat mile	8.9	9.4	9.1	7.0	9.6	10.8
Passengers per employee	840	1,114	919	2,443	795	1,118
Employees per aircraft	152	134	127	81	157	111

Source: Kenneth Labich, "Is Herb Kelleher America's Best CEO?" Reprinted from the May 2, 1994 issue of *Fortune* by special permission; copyright 1994, Time Inc.

[23] Scott McCartney, "Turbulence Ahead: Competitors Quake as Southwest Air Is Set to Invade Northeast," *Wall Street Journal* (October 23, 1996).

selves, resulting in annual savings of about $30 million in commissions for the company.

Another very important result of the efficient operations system is Southwest's on-time performance. According to the Department of Transportation's Air Travel Consumer Report for July 1996, Southwest ranks No. 1 in percentage of on-time arrivals and gets the least number of mishandled baggage complaints per 1,000 passengers.[24]

Southwest has a distinct company culture and hiring policy. Herb Kelleher, the president and CEO, makes this very clear by putting employees first. He reasons, if they are happy, satisfied, and dedicated, they will make customers happy and satisfied; satisfied customers come back, and that makes shareholders happy.[25] In 1998, *Fortune* magazine ranked Southwest Airlines as number one among the best companies to work for in America.[26]

The company's hiring policy requires that employees have a sense of humor; recruiting brochures and employment ads stress that it seeks employees who are comfortable with themselves and know how to have fun. Southwest has a profit-sharing plan; about 15 percent of net profits are given to employees, and employees own about 13 percent of the company. Once hired, employees go through training for skills and teamwork. The airline tries to create a sense of responsibility and ownership. Employees are encouraged to try new ideas without compromising safety. The informality of corporate culture and fun-loving attitude does not mean Southwest is run haphazardly. Growth is carefully managed; fast growth is avoided.

Other airlines tried to imitate Southwest's successful strategies without much success. For example, United Airlines launched "Shuttle by United" in California in 1994, hoping to duplicate the low costs and quick turnaround times of Southwest. After 16 months of operations, United could only achieve an 8 cents a mile per available seat mile, well above Southwest's 7.1 cents.[27] As a result, United withdrew from many routes in California, and Southwest increased its California business. Kelleher has this to say about competition:

> They can imitate the airplanes. They can imitate our ticket counters and all the other hardware. But they can't duplicate the people of Southwest and their attitudes.[28]

5.5 SUMMARY

A service organization's survival and prosperity depends on its ability to create value for its customers, employees, suppliers, and shareholders. Satisfied employees lead to satisfied customers; satisfied customers mean repeat business for the organization and prosperity. Prosperity of the service organization keeps suppliers in business and makes shareholders happy. Consequently, value creation should be the main strategy of a service organization.

[24] Susan Carey, "St. Louis Blues: TWA Struggles to Improve Performance," *Wall Street Journal* (September 27, 1996).
[25] Kristin Dunlap Godsey, "Slow Climb to New Heights."
[26] Anne Fisher, "The 100 Best Companies to Work for in America," *Fortune* (January 12, 1998), pp. 69–95.
[27] Scott McCartney and Michael J. McCarthy, "Southwest Flies Circles Around United's Shuttle," *Wall Street Journal* (February 20, 1996).
[28] Kristin Dunlap Godsey, "Slow Climb to New Heights."

We defined value as the ability of a good or service to satisfy a need or provide a benefit to a customer. Then we presented a model of service value to provide an insight into how a service organization may create value for its customers. The model has six components: perceived quality, intrinsic attributes, extrinsic attributes, monetary price, nonmonetary price, and time. Customers will be satisfied and hence value will be created for them if their perception of what they received matches or exceeds their expectations of the service. The higher the *perceived quality*, the higher the perceived value of the service. *Intrinsic attributes* of a service are the benefits provided to customers. To create value for customers, a service organization must deliver the core service flawlessly and reliably. *Extrinsic attributes* are related to the service but they exist outside the service package, that is, all the psychological benefits associated with the service.

The sum of the expenses incurred by a customer to obtain a service is the *monetary price*. Extra value is created for the customer, if the organization can deliver the same service at lower monetary cost with no deterioration of quality. Any perceived sacrifice, other than financial, that a customer has to make to access and receive a service is defined as *nonmonetary price*.

Time plays an important role in value creation in services. A service organization can create value for its customers by reducing the time needed to use the service, offer a service as a time-saving alternative to another service, or by extending the time horizon within which the service provides benefits.

The survival and prosperity of a service organization is closely linked with the outcome of the value creation process. To achieve this end, an organization must have a strategy. Strategy is a deliberate search for a plan of action that will develop a business's competitive advantage and compound it. Strategy can also be seen as a plan, a ploy, a pattern, a position, or as a perspective.

The competitive environment in any industry is defined by five forces: the entry of new competitors, the threat of substitutes, the bargaining power of buyers, the bargaining power of suppliers, and the intensity of rivalry among the existing competitors.

In this chapter, three generic strategies were discussed as a possible starting point for developing strategy: cost leadership, differentiation, and focus. Then, the strategic service vision was discussed as a specific approach to developing strategy for a service organization. This model has four basic elements (target market segment, service concept, operating strategy, and service delivery system) and the integrative elements (positioning, value/cost leveraging, and strategy/system integration) that tie the basic elements together. Finally, Southwest Airlines was used as an example of how this model can be applied in a service organization.

Discussion Questions

1. Explain the difference between the use value and exchange value. Does the exchange value concept apply to services? Explain.
2. What is value in a service? Why is it subjective?
3. Briefly describe the service value model presented in this chapter.
4. Explain perceived quality and why it is important in services.
5. Explain intrinsic and extrinsic attributes of services.
6. Explain nonmonetary price of services. How would it influence purchase decisions of customers?
7. Explain how time plays a role in service value creation.
8. Explain what strategy means for a service organization.

9. Does every service organization need a strategy? Explain.
10. Why is it important for a service organization to understand its competitive environment?
11. Briefly explain the forces in the competitive environment.
12. What are barriers to entry? Explain with examples from service industries.
13. Explain the cost leadership strategy.
14. Explain the differentiation strategy.
15. Explain the focus strategy.
16. What is the difference between cost focus and cost leadership strategies?
17. Describe the basic elements of the strategic service vision.
18. Describe the integrative elements of the strategic service vision. What role do they play in the model?

CASES

CASE 5–1   Strategy Seems to Make Wal-Mart Unstoppable

Retailing during the 1980s changed dramatically. Nowhere has this been more true than in the discount store business, a sector that has grown rapidly with increasing value consciousness by consumers. The expansion in this sector has already left some non–discount department store chains badly hurt. For example, Sears lost many of its customers to discounters and was forced to copy some of their tactics. Even among the discounters themselves, a war of attrition has been raging. Of the top ten discounters in 1962, none even existed thirty years later. In the struggle to succeed, the weaker chains inevitably died, often forced out of business by huge takeover debts, recession, and demographic and social change. And as the mid-1990s approached, it looked as though there would be a fight to the death among three of the biggest contenders.

The largest of the three contenders—measured in number of stores—is Kmart, with a 1992 total of 2,200 stores. Ahead of Kmart in sales turnover is Wal-Mart, with 1,590 stores. The third contender is Target, a division of Dayton Hudson, with a chain of 420 stores. In 1990, the three chains between them had 70 percent of the nationwide discount store business. At that time, Wal-Mart directly competed in only about 35% of Kmart's markets. With new store openings, the two chains will be directly competing in more than 75 percent of their markets by 1995. All three will overlap in 40 percent of each other's markets. Wal-Mart opened 165 new stores in 1991, with a strong emphasis on California, which was already a stronghold of Kmart and Target. Further growth will see its network spread from its southern base to the northeast and far west. Target, on the other hand, is setting its sights on Florida as it expands from its strongholds in California and the Midwest.

What is so remarkable is that the three retailers have adopted broadly similar business formats and are trying to pursue similar strategies. All have focused on quite similar product areas. Kmart has focused its efforts on a dozen departments that it considers essential to family life, including clothing, home fashion, home office, fix-it, outdoor, toys, entertainment, and pharmacy. Target aims a range of fashion clothing to the more discerning department store customers who may be looking for better quality, higher-priced apparel while matching other discounters on everyday household items. Wal-Mart has developed a product range broadly similar to that of Kmart. Analysts have speculated that the discount market is large enough for only two of the big three discounters. With similar strategies, success will come to the chain that is best able to execute its strategy.

One of Kmart's big advantages is that it grew before Wal-Mart, allowing it to get hold of the best retail sites in many towns. Research commissioned by the company had indicated that location topped the list of factors influencing customers' choice of discount store, ahead of other factors such as price, product range, and quality. In a decade when convenience will be at a premium, Kmart's store locations could be an extremely valuable asset. However, Kmart is handicapped by the relatively small size of many of its older stores. Too many are 40,000 square feet or less, when 70,000 square feet is considered the minimum to be able to carry the range the customers expect.

All three chains use the offer of low prices to attract customers. The chain that is best able to achieve sustainable low prices will be the one that is most effective in cutting its operating cost levels. All three have invested heavily in checkout scanning systems that give real-time sales data, which are relayed instantaneously to computerized inventory systems. However, the acknowledged industry leader in information distribution is Wal-Mart, whose satellite communication network and computer power allow it instantaneous access to sales information. Wal-Mart has also led in its attempts to cut suppliers' costs. It was the first to insist that suppliers accept orders from computer to computer, and it has dealt with suppliers as partners rather than as adversaries. In this way, both get to share information and new product development, to the advantage of Wal-Mart.

All three have a strategy of achieving customer satisfaction through the performance of its employees, and all have invested heavily in staff training and incentive programs. Again, Wal-Mart seems to be implementing this aspect of strategy more effectively than its rivals. Its training of salespeople (or "associates") and profit-sharing bonuses have inspired legendary loyalty from an otherwise poorly paid workforce.

Overall, Wal-Mart seems to be meeting customers' needs better than its rivals. In a study undertaken by analysts Burnstein & Co., discount shoppers in cities where all three stores operated claimed to be most satisfied with Wal-Mart. They were least satisfied with Kmart.

Wal-Mart's successful pursuit of its strategy on many fronts has resulted in a productivity loop. With higher sales volumes, it can afford to pay for extra bag packers and greeters, which in turn generates more business, making the whole operation achieve even greater economies of scale in buying and distribution, leading to lower prices and still higher sales volume.

The final proof that Wal-Mart had pursued its strategy more effectively than its competitors came on its bottom line. For the year ended January 1991, it earned $2 billion in pre-tax profits, compared to just $1 billion earned by Kmart on just about the same level of sales. As for the future, both Wal-Mart and Kmart have attempted to widen their battlefield beyond the traditional discount stores. Both have been involved in deep discount membership clubs—Wal-Mart with Sam's Club and Kmart with Pace. Both have experimented with having their very large stores sell groceries in addition to the existing lines. Critics have wondered whether Wal-Mart's seemingly unstoppable progress will be slowed down if it enters the very different and competitive grocery sector already inhabited by efficient operators such as Kroger and Safeway. ■

SOURCE: Adrian Palmer and Catherine Cole, *Services Marketing: Principles and Practice* (Upper Saddle River, NJ, Prentice Hall, 1995), pp. 322–324.

CASE QUESTIONS

1. Identify strategies by which Kmart and Target could achieve profitable growth. What risks are associated with these strategies? How can these risks be minimized?
2. In what ways could the contenders use positioning strategy to increase their profits?

3. Assume that you have been hired to advise the owners of downtown businesses in a small farming community in Kansas. Wal-Mart is planning to locate on the highway running through town. How could the small downtown business owners compete against Wal-Mart?

CASE 5–2   NovaCare Inc.*

NovaCare was one of the largest and most rapidly growing national providers of contract rehabilitation services to health care institutions. Between 1988 and 1991, NovaCare had grown at 37.5% per year to $151 million in revenues. It provided speech-language, occupational, and physical therapy to patients with physical disabilities principally resulting from stroke, degenerative neurological disorders, or orthopedic problems. In 1991, NovaCare had over 3,000 contracts to provide rehabilitation services in approximately 1,800 facilities in over 32 states (see Exhibit 5-8). Despite its outstanding successes, NovaCare faced several important strategic issues.

Chief among these was how to position itself in the rapidly changing, problem-ridden health care industry of the early 1990s. Second was how to develop and organize its professional staff to provide the most efficient, highest-quality care in the rehabilitation field. Third was how best to develop the information, control, and incentive systems necessary to achieve these goals. An important portion of these efforts would be the development of Nova-Net, an information system designed to accelerate the collection of field operations, administrative, and billing data. NovaCare had just completed pilot testing of NovaNet, but the system had not achieved

* Research assistants on this case were William Little and Patricia Higgins. The kind generosity and assistance of NovaCare, Inc., are gratefully acknowledged.

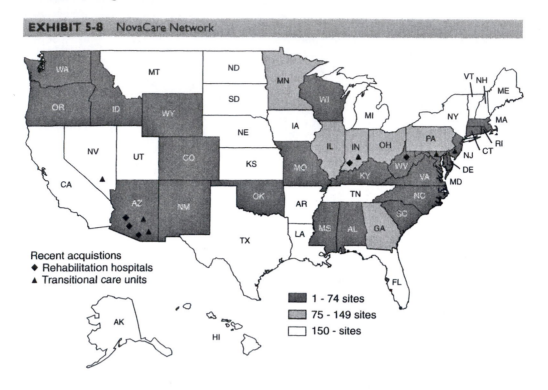

EXHIBIT 5-8 NovaCare Network

Recent acquistions
◆ Rehabilitation hospitals
▲ Transitional care units

■ 1 - 74 sites
▨ 75 - 149 sites
□ 150 - sites

anticipated productivity results. Chief Executive Officer John Foster wondered whether NovaNet should be released to the field, developed further, or designed for other purposes. NovaNet could be a key element in the company's future strategy.

NOVACARE'S EARLY HISTORY

NovaCare began as a company named Inspeech, which coordinated a group of clinicians acting as entrepreneurs; each contracted independently and managed his or her own professional activities. Inspeech provided some common support services, financing, and professional management activities for which the clinicians were not specially trained. By 1985 Inspeech had become the largest speech rehabilitation practice in the country, with about 120 clinicians and $5 million in revenues. But Inspeech was operating in a crisis mode: the company had problems meeting its payroll, and its credit line was running out. Seeking further capital and management support, Inspeech sold out to Foster Management Company, a venture capital firm with about $130 million of capital under management. John Foster was the senior general partner of Foster Management Company (FMC).

After some initial excitement about the new ownership and the security its capital infusion gave,

the clinicians' productivity suddenly plummeted. They began to question the motivation of the new management. They saw the FMC group as "businesspeople" concerned about profitability rather than as caregivers concerned about patient wellness. At this point, John Foster decided to take a more direct role as CEO, and his management team began emphasizing both patient care and the need for productivity. For 18 months, the new management team worked at rationalizing the business and made several complementary acquisitions with FMC funds. In November 1986, Inspeech made a public offering and raised about $40 million of equity.

Foster Management had recognized that there was a cluster of rehabilitation therapies in nursing homes which might be offered on a complementary basis. The most closely related of these were speech, physical, and occupational therapy. In 1987, it diversified into the last two. Inspeech then grew quickly through market development and acquisition of other therapists' practices. Unfortunately, the company's rapid growth was accompanied by problems. John Foster said,

We had very high levels of clinician turnover and a broad level of dissatisfaction throughout the company, partly reflecting indigestion from the 19 acquisitions we had made. Most health care professionals had never worked inside a large successful organization. They were, by tradition, sole practitioners. They were caregivers, and therefore highly sensitive, sensitized people. It was a very subtle thing to bring the concepts of business and productivity to a group of people who have been trained into a special mind-set, who have another language, and who were so sensitive to quality of care. Their view generally was that productivity and quality were mutually exclusive.

The company reached a low point in early 1988; customers were confused about how to interface with the company's multiple services. Its stock price was dropping. The clinician staff was quitting, and the company was missing its performance goals. Hal Price, Divisional Vice President, commented about this period,

> It was very confusing. . . . We had different sets of standards, different benefits. . . . It was all a result of trying to bring different businesses into the company and not doing a smooth job of integrating them. Despite the fact that the financial results were not good, we knew that at a local facility level we were delivering good service.

In July 1988, the company reorganized into four geographic divisions each with a staff organization to support its business. Bud Locilento, Vice President of Human Resources, noted,

> We had been working from a highly centralized model of management. As we continued to grow very rapidly, we were losing our efficiency as an organization and made the decision to move to a more decentralized model. We would grow by penetrating new market areas and then densifying existing markets. We would modify our structure to reflect that approach.

A NEW VISION

In addition to decentralizing significantly, the company undertook a process that was widely referred to as a "healing event," following its many acquisitions and rapid growth. In 1989, the company's name was changed to NovaCare to reflect its broader spectrum of rehabilitation services. It also undertook to develop and document a complete new set of vision and culture statements. These consisted of a Vision Statement, a Statement of Pur-

pose, and a Statement of Beliefs. John Foster said, "These are integral to the culture of the company and the employee/manager relationship. These beliefs are an agreement between the corporation and the employee and create a report card that everyone can use to evaluate the performance of the company." NovaCare's Statement of Purpose begins with the words,

> We are fundamentally a clinical organization. All investment and organizational resources are intended to support the successful interaction of a clinician and the patient.
>
> The Direct Care Provider is the key person in our organization. All the corporate staff and resources exist to support the clinician in providing care to the patient. Line management supports the clinician in direct patient care. Technical experts, in turn, support line managers in providing the highest quality programs. This structure enables each Direct Care Provider to make the best clinical judgments.

The company's Vision Statement makes the following key points:

- "We apply our clinical expertise to benefit our patients through creative and progressive techniques.
- Our people are our most valuable asset. We are committed to the personal, professional, and career development of each individual employee. We are proud of what we do and dedicated to our company. We foster team work and create an environment conducive to productive communications among all disciplines.
- Our customers include national and local health care providers who share our goal of enhancing the patient's quality of life. In each community, our customers consider us a partner in providing the best possible care. Our reputation is based on our responsiveness, high standards, and effective systems of quality assurance. Our relationship is open and proactive.
- NovaCare is people committed to achieving excellence.
- Our ethical and performance standards require us to expend every effort to achieve the best possible results."

The company's Statement of Beliefs documented and detailed four major principles: (1) respect for the individual, (2) service to the customer,

(3) pursuit of excellence, and (4) commitment to personal integrity. These were elaborated in a 16-page pamphlet that was widely distributed and constantly reinforced. John Foster said, "I have spent a great deal of time on the road and in the field articulating our purpose and our beliefs. In time, the soul of the company will come to be less a matter of 'it feels good to be here' and more a matter of an articulated set of values and highly precise purposes." Larry Lane, Vice President of Regulatory Affairs, echoed the statements and added, "The Purpose and Beliefs Statements provide very strong language about making a difference, empowering clinical behavior, service, advocacy, training, and commitment to professional skills. These concepts are central to our success and the way we operate on a day-to-day basis."

PROFESSIONAL STAFFING ISSUES

Demand for clinical professionals was significantly greater than supply. In late 1991, the company employed approximately 2,300 full-time equivalent (FTE) therapists in the provision of patient care. At that same date, the company had open positions for 800 additional full-time therapists who, if hired, could generate revenues immediately. The company employed 23-recruiters in eight regions, representing the largest recruiting function in the rehabilitation services industry. It differentiated its professional opportunities by offering a career ladder which was typically unavailable in other institutional settings. This allowed a trained professional to progress through clinician, team leader, district clinical coordinator, district manager, area manager, clinical consultant, and possibly divisional vice president. In addition, clinicians might choose to do administrative activities like recruiting, sales, or quality assurance.

The company performed sophisticated national salary surveys to ensure that its compensation programs were competitive. It provided excellent benefits and incentive bonuses for clinical productivity that exceeded industry averages. It awarded incentive stock options—commencing at the district manager level—on the basis of performance. It also invested significantly in clinical and management training programs for its professionals. It offered clinical training at company and independent university seminars, it had developed an interactive self-study video library for clinicians to use at

home, and an expanding management training curriculum was mandatory for all district and area managers. As a result of these and other employee relations programs, NovaCare had increased its number of new hires by 130% from fiscal 1988 to fiscal 1990 and had reduced its therapist turnover from 55% in 1988 to 27% in 1991. Its number of FTEs (excluding therapists from acquired companies) had increased at a 33% compound annual growth rate. Nevertheless, the shortage continued. John Foster estimated that each turnover cost the company $5,000 in recruiting costs and about $20,000 in lost revenue.

A THERAPISTS' COMPANY

A unique attribute of the company was that "NovaCare was a therapy company managed by therapists. It was a relatively young organization, hard charging, tending to be athletic, and 90% female," according to John Foster. He noted, "Clinicians tend to be high-caring, highly affiliated people. NovaCare employs many working mothers. This has important implications in terms of training, traveling, continuing education, and promotional opportunities." In 1991, the company was seeking clinicians in all of its fields, including:

- *Speech-language pathology*—the diagnosis and treatment of speech, language, swallowing, and hearing disorders usually arising from stroke, head injury, degenerative neurological disorders, or cancer. The speech-language pathologist is a licensed clinician with a baccalaureate degree and a clinically specific master's degree.
- *Occupational therapy*—improving muscular and neural responses to overcome patients' deficiencies for the basic activities of daily living. Occupational therapists were licensed professionals with a clinically specific baccalaureate degree; certified occupational therapy assistants (COTAS) could provide therapy under the supervision of an occupational therapist. Occupational therapy involved (1) restoring sensory functions; (2) teaching compensatory techniques to improve independence for daily living activities such as feeding, toileting, or bathing; and (3) designing, fabricating, and fitting assistive devices.
- *Physical therapy*—improves muscular and neural responses to enhance patients' physical strength and range of motion. The physical

EXHIBIT 5-9 NovaCare Revenue Breakdown, 1987–1991

	1987	1989	1991 Year	2Q	3Q
Speech-language pathology	79%	51%	39%	39%	38%
Occupational therapy	16%	30%	39%	39%	40%
Physical therapy	5%	19%	22%	22%	22%

Source: Estimates by Alex Brown, Inc.

therapist was a licensed clinician with a clinically specific baccalaureate degree. Physical therapy comprised the application of stimuli like heat, cold, water, electricity, massage, or exercise.

NovaCare's revenue breakdown between the therapies is estimated in Exhibit 5-9.

AN INVERTED ORGANIZATION

NovaCare refers to its organization as "inverted." The entire company exists to support the clinician in the delivery of service to the patient. John Foster considers himself "the lowest man in the inverted organization with everyone between me and the clinician in place solely to support the clinician. . . . This is a very important piece of understanding, not only for our clinical people to have in the field, but also for all of us as staff members to understand what role and relative importance we play in the organization." Vice President of Human Resources Bud Locilento says, "Our goal today is to get each clinician to have a high sense of empowerment, to make decisions for the patient, for the customer, and for their own well-being—instead of having them feel like they are swimming upstream against a pyramidical organization."

Running and maintaining an inverted organization required constant training, empowerment, and reinforcement. It was often confusing to hear executives referring to "my bosses," meaning those people closer to the field contact point, rather than the corporate center. Mr. Foster continued to try to find ways to get feedback or "instructions" from the field. He had established a Chairman's Council consisting of 15 to 20 people from around the entire country who met twice a year. These were representatives, clinical and managerial, from different divisions who represented a cross section of opinion

and thought. Before each meeting, the representatives were to canvass their local groups to collect information and feedback for discussions. The company also had a bimonthly newsletter to keep clinicians informed, reinforce positive happenings in the company, pose issues for feedback, and reinforce the vision of the company. NovaCare clinicians, as sole practitioners operating in a remote nursing home or health facility, had to be independent decision makers. Yet in their formal training, they were not educated for this, nor were they prepared to make the compromises often required within a health care facility or nursing home environment.

A Clinician Focus

Patient screening, or who goes on the caseload and when, is a critical issue for both NovaCare's and the health care facility's profits. Given the limited number of trained clinicians and the desire of all parties to show maximum patient benefit, it was often difficult to make choices among those who needed care, who would not benefit from care, and who could pay for care. Treatments eligible for repayment varied among different insuring groups. Unfortunately, when clinicians were trained, they were taught how to treat a particular condition, not how to identify from a pool of patients those whose conditions could be adequately and economically treated. Larry Lane, Vice President of Regulatory Affairs, said, "Our orientation has been to empower the clinicians to use professional judgment first and then fall back on to the other issues—are there constraints that will inhibit my professional judgment from being fully carried out?"

Within these limits, a clinician would assess and diagnose a patient and determine a strategy of treatment. The clinician had to establish long-term objectives for the treatment and define success on a case-by-case basis. From the fiscal intermediary's perspective, as long as the clinician had selected a legitimate therapy strategy for a disorder that fell under that payor's guidelines—and as long as the patient showed measurable progress—treatment might proceed. However, the clinician's time availability, specific skill capabilities, and psychic energy levels were also important. Certain forms of rehabilitation could be extremely taxing for the clinician. For example, the continuous physical and psychic drain of treating geriatric or seriously impaired individuals could rapidly "burn out" a clinician.

Hence, it was essential to allow some significant variation in the types of patients, disorders, and locations that a clinician experienced. It was also important that the clinician not have to travel extensively between facilities. A number of subjective judgments were required to obtain the right balance.

The Support Organization

The organization supporting the field clinicians (also called direct care providers, or DCPs) was structured regionally. Each clinician belonged to a group called a district. Each district earned annual revenues of approximately $1 million and was home for an average of 15 FTE clinicians. Clinicians were coordinated by a district manager, district managers by an area manager, and area managers by a division vice president. An area had approximately $7–10 million in business. There were three to four area managers per division and four national divisions organized by geography. The four division vice presidents were coordinated by a vice president of field operations. In 1991, the business was managed on a weekly basis; clinicians scheduled their weekly activities in conjunction with their district manager. On Friday, clinicians telephoned their district managers to report their results—both clinical and administrative—for the week. The district manager consolidated these data and reported a summary to corporate headquarters on the following Monday.

An area manager described the weekly work activity as follows:

Our whole company travels Tuesday through Thursday. On Friday, DCPs call the District Manager and report how many patients they've seen, how many evaluations they've done, how much time they've spent in preparation and documentation, and how many units of therapy service they've delivered. On Monday, I spent 9 hours on the telephone with each one of my District Managers going over each of the clinician reports. By 3:00 p.m. that afternoon I report to my Division Manager, who consolidates the information to be sent to the Corporate Operations Officer by 8:00 a.m. Tuesday morning. We are spending 20–25% of our time relaying information.

The district manager's job was to handle customer relations and develop good relations with each clinician. One of the division vice presidents, Hal Price, commented, "We've worked hard to reduce the number of facilities so the District Manager can spend as much time as possible with customers listening to their issues, addressing their problems, trying to constantly reassure them. You need to be constantly in front of the facility's management and staff. . . . Because employee retention is such a major concern for the company, the District Manager's role is critical to ensuring a happy work force." A key management challenge at the district level was the ratio of facilities covered to the number of clinicians. The converse of this question frequently got posed: "How many patients are going unserved in a given facility?"

Timothy Foster (no relation to John Foster), NovaCare's CFO, described the problem this way:

Our central operations problem is that our service, as we charge it to the customer, is priced for the amount of time we spend with each patient, specific to that patient. So for every 15 minutes we spend treating a patient, we are reimbursed a given rate. Any individual therapist works in two or three facilities. That's the premise of our business—there isn't enough reimbursable activity to employ a full-time therapist in any one facility. We are a consolidator of the practice in each facility and among several facilities.

Since the therapist is a fixed cost, we are motivated to optimize billable activity, or production, much as lawyers would be motivated to optimize their productivity/billable time. On the other hand, a Director of Nursing in a facility is looking for many other behaviors that have nothing to do with billable time—team work, consulting or advising, in-servicing, and so on—that contribute to the long-term good of the facility and its caregiving capacity. But our therapist is not incented to do that by virtue of the way our incentive bonus program is oriented toward personal productivity, which may suggest that they get out of the facility quickly when there aren't any more patients to treat on a direct basis that day and go to the next facility.

Complexity of the Customer

NovaCare contracted with nursing home chains and independent operators for the provision of rehabilitation services to their patients. Contracts were written for one year, but could be canceled on

90 days' or less notice by either party. NovaCare was compensated on a fee-for-service basis from the nursing home, which in turn usually collected from a third-party payor, for example, an insurance company. NovaCare usually indemnified its customers against payment denials by third-party payors. For success, NovaCare had to serve many different constituencies. Each constituency had a different set of needs and expectations. Any group of people who had the ability to influence performance or contract termination directly at a customer facility was considered a constituency.

- *The patient* expects to get well by the treatment and expects a good personal relationship with the clinician. As the ultimate recipient of the service, although frequently not the direct payor, the patient could also influence third-party payors like insurance companies or local Medicare administrators. Their insurers—usually the ultimate payors for the service—would tell the nursing home they were unhappy, and the service would be canceled.
- *The director of nursing* has a strong caregiving orientation and is immediately attendant to the patient's needs. However, the director also has to coordinate the therapist's activities with all of the other patient support activities in the nursing area.
- *The nursing home administrator* is concerned with the quality of care and efficiency of operations as well as having a financial responsibility. The administrator's compensation is usually measured in financial terms. Consequently, administrators look for optimal financial performance, with minimum risk, for the rehabilitation unit which NovaCare was contracting to serve or manage.
- *Owner-managers* were frequently removed from clinical issues, other than as they impacted regulatory compliance. Their primary responsibility was financial performance.
- *Third-party payors* were interested in maximizing therapeutic effects for lowest cost.

Each constituency had its own special array of needs and expectations from tender patient care and improved wellness, through smooth hassle-free service, to efficiency and optimal reimbursement, to defending the institution from any possible negative impacts like lawsuits or loss of reputation. NovaCare served not just individual nursing fa-

cilities, but also many of the major nursing home chains on a national level. For these customers, NovaCare provided an additional level of services. Dr. Arnold Renschler, Chief Operating Officer, said,

> We provide our major customers, for example, a quarterly report that tells them what we're doing in terms of the generation of revenues for them on a therapy-by-therapy basis, and a location-by-location basis. That's a capability a smaller operator simply would not have. We have a full-time officer of the company who stays abreast of regulatory changes, changes in reimbursement, and the implications of potential future changes. He is seen as a resource to our major customers on all-regulatory issues.

The corporate staff of NovaCare numbered slightly over 100. The staff's size and functions were carefully tracked as a percentage of revenue, and this percentage had continued to shrink with time. Bud Locilento attributed this to "getting better people, increasing our reliance on technology and systems, and moving many of the staff functions into the field."

Incentive Systems

An elaborate compensation system supported the highly decentralized, "inverted" organization of NovaCare. Starting in the days of Inspeech, the company had defined productivity in terms of 15-minute "units of billable time." The primary billable activity was direct patient care. But "units" included any time spent documenting what was done with the patient, consulting with other professionals, direct preparation time, patient care meetings, or anything done directly on behalf of the patient. In December 1984, the productivity standard was set at 100 units (or 25 hours) of billable time per week for each clinician. Above this, a bonus system came into effect. The remainder of the clinician's time was to allow them to do practice building, engage in marketing activities, and create a steadier flow of patients. The most productive therapists actively sought out opportunities to develop their practice and worked with doctors and other nursing home staff personnel to get patients needing care into their caseload.

NovaCare had developed state-of-the-art marketing programs to help make the facilities in which its clinicians worked real magnets for referrals from the community. NovaCare wanted potential referral sources (doctors, nurses, patients, nursing home directors, etc.) to recognize both the availability and quality of its service delivery. The therapist was the key link in converting the company's service concept into a reality. Each clinician was paid a bonus based on the number of units of patient care delivered each week over the agreed-upon standard. However, since speech and occupational therapy were the higher-margin services offered within a nursing home, the physical therapy bonus system was quite different.

NovaCare earned 100% of its revenues from service activities. These were dependent on the ability of its clinicians to form and cultivate one-to-one relationships with patients, facilities, and key personnel in those facilities. The company's revenues were constrained by the available time per clinician, available billable time per clinician, and the number of clinicians. NovaCare's management went to great lengths to educate its clinician work force that productivity and quality of care were in fact synonymous. It went even further, pointing out to the therapist that "In the process of being productive we are, in fact, enhancing our professions, enhancing the quality of care, and demonstrating the professional qualifications of our clinical staff."

Quality and Revenue Control

Quality was an assumed ingredient in the delivery of health care services, although it was not precisely defined or measured by institutions, insurance companies, or other payors. NovaCare, through its systems and management practices, had attempted to "set the standard of care for its field" and to take the lead position within its industry. Hal Price said, "I don't think there is anyone in the country that comes close to doing what we do—delivering on a consistent basis, on a similar scale, the quality of care that we now deliver to our customers." NovaCare constantly sought areas for minor improvements leading to perfection in the delivery of its therapies. Quality control was a basic responsibility of therapists.

District managers were measured on the revenue side of the business only. They were not accountable for managing costs. They were rewarded for (1) productivity, (2) gross unit production measured against budget, (3) retention of people, and (4) supplemental goals contained in personally agreed-upon management objectives. Productivity, production, and retention each accounted for 30%

of the district manager's measured performance. Ten percent was allocated to the supplemental goals.

Area and division managers had incentives on three components: (1) gross operating profit, (2) retention, and (3) supplemental goals. Gross operating profit was 50%, retention 30%, and supplemental goals 20% of their performance measurement package. Operating profit incorporated both net revenue and margin performance targets.

NOVACARE'S STRATEGY AND FUTURE MARKETS

NovaCare's basic strategy had been to grow by consolidating practices of rehabilitation services through a program of disciplined internal growth and acquisitions. The strategy was designed to capitalize upon several external structural factors: (1) an unserved and growing demand for rehabilitation services, (2) an increasing concern with health care costs and the needs of the elderly, and (3) a highly fragmented competition made up of smaller regional firms and care centers. By 1991, the U.S. health care industry was in a state of crisis. The United States spent over $2,500 per person on health care and in the aggregate over $700 million. Medicare alone cost roughly twice what Britain's entire national health service cost. It was estimated that at least 20% of all health care spending in the United States was on administration. Deep concerns had been expressed about the quality of health care in the United States. Yet the Congressional Budget Office projected that federal spending on health care programs would increase to almost 20% of its budget in 1996. There was an extensive national debate about (1) how to finance health care in the future, (2) access to the health care system for much of the population, and (3) the problems of delivering quality care to an increasing percentage of an aging or disabled population.

An industry report on the rehabilitation marketplace read:

We expect the medical rehabilitation market, which had annual revenues of about $11 billion in 1990, to grow at an annual rate of 15–20% through the 1990s.

Operating margins for well-managed, mature operations exceed 20%. We expect to see growth in this market for the following reasons:

- The number of people who experience activity limitations is increasing, as is the age and size of the population.
- The availability of rehabilitation is growing, as are consumers' and third-party payors' awareness of its benefits.
- Technological advances are expanding the pool of patients who can benefit from rehabilitation.
- The current focus on physical fitness, independence, and quality of life is expected to continue.
- The rehabilitation setting is cost effective relative to services in the acute care setting. Increasingly, insurers using a managed care approach are recognizing the economic benefits of rehabilitation. Studies have shown that for every dollar spent on rehab, anywhere from $11 to $38 is saved.

Under the Medicare program, reimbursement for therapy services was cost based in all but the inpatient, acute care hospital setting. Coverage of rehabilitation therapies by Medicare had been expanded to include outpatient care for occupational therapy in 1987 and swallowing disorders in 1989. Regulators and third-party payors viewed rehabilitation services favorably because of the cost effectiveness of these services relative to acute care facilities. The principal settings for rehabilitation therapies were acute care hospitals, dedicated rehab hospitals, comprehensive outpatient rehab facilities, nursing homes, schools, outpatient clinics, psychiatric hospitals, and the patient's home. Among these providers, small (fewer than 350 bed) institutions frequently contracted with third-party suppliers to manage their rehabilitation requirements. The estimated contract therapy market is shown in Exhibit 5-10.

According to industry data, in 1988 more than 71% of nursing homes outsourced their occupational therapy as did over 90% of those providing speech-language pathologies therapy. The same data indicated that rehab services compromised less than 1% of nursing home expenses. A greater number of homes provided physical therapy services, but 67% contracted for these as well. The Omnibus Budget Reconciliation Act of 1987 mandated that as of October 1, 1990, all nursing homes must be able to provide all three rehabilitation therapies. However, cost and other factors made this difficult to do internally. According to a professional association survey, only 14,000 of the 129,000 therapists certified in 1989 worked in a long-term care setting. There was a ratio of less than one speech-language pathologist for every ten facilities and one occupational therapist for every eight facilities. NovaCare's ratios were one speech-language pathologist for every three facilities it served and one occupational therapist for every two facilities. The changing mix of its services is shown in Exhibit 5-11.

NovaCare's competition was made up of some regional companies, sole proprietors, and small-group practices within communities. The largest regional firms were approximately one-third to one-half NovaCare's size. Many of NovaCare's nursing home customers were national companies. In addition to an aggressive acquisition strategy, NovaCare focused its sales strategy on increasing the density of customers in existing markets to reduce the impact of travel on employee morale and productivity. By integrating its therapy programs, the company had realized significant growth through bringing to the attention of the caregiving institution the other therapies that NovaCare offered. As Exhibit 5-12 indicates, NovaCare's growth had been extremely

EXHIBIT 5-10   Estimated Contract Therapy Market, 1988–1993 (in millions of dollars)

	Speech			Occupational		
	1988	1993E	CGR	1988	1993E	CGR
Nursing homes	$250	$ 365	8%	$250	$ 550	17%
Hospitals, other[a]	300	420	7	300	460	9
Home health	250	365	8	300	505	11
Therapy total	**$800**	**$1,150**	**8**	**$850**	**$1,515**	**12**

CGR—Compound growth rate.

[a] "Wholesale" pricing, that is, revenues generated by providers.

Source: Robertson, Stephens & Co. estimates.

EXHIBIT 5-11 Product Mix Breakdown by Facility and Type of Contract, 1990–1991

Contract Types	12-31-90	6-30-91	9-30-91	9-Month % Change
Total Facilities	1,813	1,724	1,797	-0.5
Speech-language pathology contracts only	815	589	574	−29.6
Occupational therapy contracts only	45	49	59	31.1
Physical therapy contracts only	49	51	49	0.0
Speech-language pathology and occupational therapy contracts only	321	348	365	13.7
Speech-language pathology and physical therapy contracts only	44	23	22	−50.0
Occupational therapy and physical therapy contracts only	29	33	34	17.2
Speech-language pathology, occupational therapy, and physical therapy contracts	510	631	694	36.1
Total Contracts	3,227	3,390	3,606	11.7
Total speech-language pathology contracts	1,690	1,591	1,655	−2.1
Total occupational therapy contracts	905	1,061	1,152	27.3
Total physical therapy contracts	632	738	799	26.4

Source: Alex. Brown, Inc., reports.

EXHIBIT 5-12 NovaCare Financial Performance History, 1988–1991 (in thousands, except earnings per share)

	1991	1990	1989	1988
Net revenues	$151,532	$102,110	$69,975	$56,612
Gross profit	56,403	39,478	25,586	11,505
Gross profit margin	37%	39%	37%	20.3%
Operating profit	29,875	19,534	8,999	3,162
Operating profit margin	20%	19%	13%	5.6%
Loss on marketable securities	—	—	—	(2,468)
Net income (loss)	20,315	12,382	5,107	(1,045)
Net income per share	0.64	0.43	0.19	(0.04)
Working capital	66,721	41,680	33,294	31,515
Total assets	127,489	87,912	73,609	72,386
Total indebtedness	1,037	14,075	15,908	18,915
Total liabilities	13,975	25,107	23,831	27,781
Stockholders' equity	113,514	62,805	49,778	44,605
Return on average equity	23.0%	22.2%	10.9%	(2.4%)
Annual average FTEs	1,929	1,375	na	na
Revenues per FTE	79	74	na	na
Annual average therapist turnover rate	27.0%	32.0%	39.0%	na

Source: *Rehabilitation Today*, November–December 1991, and company reports.

rapid and its stock market performance spectacular (see Exhibit 5-13).

NovaNet: An Information Strategy

In its 1990 10K Report, the company described its new NovaNet initiative:

The company has implemented, on a pilot basis, a laptop computer network enabling each clinician to record and transmit billing, payroll, productivity, and clinical documentation informa-

tion daily. This innovation is designed to (1) eliminate much of the clinician's administrative burden, increasing time available for patient care; (2) reduce selling, general and administration expenses associated with information gathering and data processing; (3) accelerate the billing cycle thereby reducing days sales outstanding in receivables; and (4) improve the company's ability to capture and correlate clinical data in support of quality assurance standards. Management believes that this proprietary system will further distinguish the

EXHIBIT 5-13   NovaCare Stock Market Performance, 1989–1992E

Physical			*Totals*		
1988	*1993E*	*CGR*	*1988*	*1993E*	*CGR*
$ 300	$ 420	7%	$ 800	$1,335	11%
1,000	1,470	8	1,600	2,350	8
550	900	10	1,100	1,770	10
$1,850	**$2,790**	**9**	**$3,500**	**$5,455**	**9**

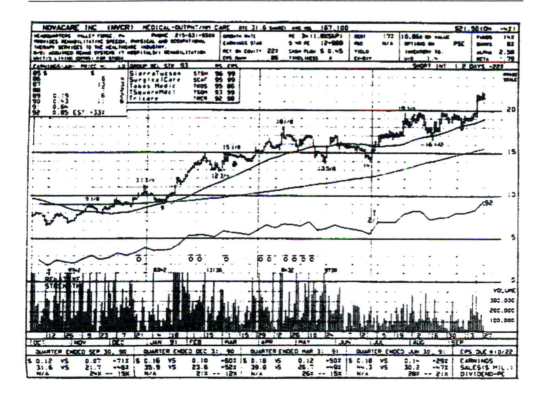

Share Price Data

	1988	1989	1990	1991
High	$7^5/_8$	$8^1/_4$	$11^9/_{16}$	$29^7/_8$
Low	$1^{15}/_{16}$	$2^7/_{16}$	$6^1/_2$	$12^3/_4$

(*continued*)

EXHIBIT 5-13   NovaCare Stock Market Performance, 1989–1992E *(continued)*

EARNINGS PER SHARE

	1989		1990		1991		1992E	
	Amount	*Y/Y % Change*	*Amount*	*Y/Y % Change*	*Amount*	*Y/Y % Change*	*Amount*	*Y/Y % Change*
1Q	$0.04	NM	$0.08	100.0%	$0.14	75.0%	$0.19	35.7%
2Q	0.04	NM	0.09	125.0	0.15	66.7	0.21	40.0
3Q	0.05	NM	0.12	140.0	0.17	41.7	0.23	35.3
4Q	0.07	NM	0.14	100.0	0.18	28.6	0.24	33.3
FY	$0.20	NM	$0.43	115.0	$0.64	48.8	$0.87	35.9

SOURCES OF PROFIT

	1991	1992
Therapy services	91%	87%
Rehabilitation centers	—	11
Interest income	9	2
Total	100%	100%

ANNUAL FINANCIAL DATA (IN MILLIONS OF DOLLARS)

	1989	1990	1991	1992E
Total revenues	$70.0	$102.0	$151.5	$281.8
Cash flow	6.0	13.3	21.2	34.5
Pretax margin	11.2%	18.6%	20.2%	17.0%
Return on average equity	12.8%	22.0%	23.0%	NE
Return on average assets	7.0%	15.3%	19.0%	NE

NE—No estimate. NM—Not meaningful. Y/Y—Year to year.

Source: Alex. Brown & Sons, October 2, 1991.

company as the employer of choice for therapists.

NovaNet was projected to be a $7–10 million information systems investment, the largest investment in systems NovaCare had ever made. The system would allow each clinician to report results daily. John Foster stated, "We believe NovaNet will have significant short-term, positive implications for clinician productivity. Over the long term, as we learn from the data that we collect, it will have a substantial impact on total productivity."

The NovaNet system had two components—an administrative and a clinical component. The administrative component was intended to eliminate duplicate forms, redundant or erroneous data entry, and administrative paperwork. Quality of documentation was important to NovaCare's customers to satisfy state and federal health care standards and to

both NovaCare and the customer for reimbursement. Another objective was to free up time for clinicians so they could have more time to spend with patients. The system was intended to replace existing manual systems and telephone call reporting. Part of the design philosophy was to automate the front end of the manual process—the collection of data from the clinicians—without altering back-end processing systems. The latter included the billing system—which was provided by Shared Medical Systems—and a number of in-house management systems.

NovaNet was seen as providing several initial advantages. It provided accurate documentation for reports and billings, and it eased the administrative burdens of clinicians. Further, NovaNet would give clinicians a communication vehicle they currently did not have, allowing them to communicate electronically with their supervisors or other clinicians.

One feature under consideration that excited many clinicians was potential use of the technology in the treatment of their patients. NovaCare management had initially targeted a 3% gain in productivity, that is, clinicians billing 103 units per week rather than 100 standard units. But much greater potentials were available. On average, clinicians spent 35% of their time in activities unrelated to direct patient care, that is, documentation, meetings, and traveling. Management also expected to be able to extend district managers' "spans of communication" beyond the current average of 15 clinicians, yet provide more time to improve the quality of relations with therapists and customer institutions.

NovaNet had been designed by a multifunctional team, including a project committee made up of the company's controller, vice president of MIS, vice president of professional services, and vice president of operations. Under this committee's supervision, a small design team had defined the parameters of the system and laid out its major design objectives. The team was made up of clinicians and staff people. The project's review and cost-benefit analysis had calculated a 1.7-year direct payback for the initial investment and a 33% return over a 5-year period. But various executives saw other less measurable quality, morale, flexibility, information exchange, and strategic applications as providing even greater long-term benefits. The question was how to implement the system best to achieve these longer-term potentials at the same time as NovaNet achieved desired short-term payback goals.

NovaCare only had a small systems group and made extensive use of outside service bureaus. It also had a strategy to outsource as much of the programming work as would be compatible with its goals. Given the breadth and scope of NovaNet, the company contracted with CompuServe to develop and deliver the system. CompuServe proposed to write the PC software, provide the telecommunications network, and staff an "800 number support desk" for questions. NovaCare's Board gave approval for the project, and system design began in January 1990.

Implementation and Questions

Prior to the implementation of the NovaNet pilot, a time study had looked at how clinicians spent their time. This data was compared with similar data from groups participating in the NovaNet pilot after a period of use. It was found that productivity had not increased. Pat Larkins, Vice President of Professional Services, commented, "Our clinicians had to get used to the technology. I don't think you could get the desired increase in productivity by just teaching them how to input information, as opposed to also showing them how to use the information as a means of changing their established behaviors." Nevertheless, with the initial results at the clinician level less than promising, management began to look to other areas of productivity improvement to pay for the system in the short run, while it developed longer-term strategic uses.

Meanwhile, various government agencies were increasing their demands for information from all health care providers. The Health Care Finance Administration (HCFA), which managed the Medicare program, was attempting to define standards for basic data formats and electronic data submissions. The government and insurers had a vital interest in how effective their expenditures were in delivering better health care to patients. The Medicare program in particular was moving to a more outcomes-oriented approach in how it reimbursed for patient care. John Foster noted:

As the largest service provider in our field, we should have some economies of scale in the collection and use of data that are not available to anyone else. In fact, if we develop the system right, it might provide the ultimate barrier to entry for other competitors. Along with our other strategic initiatives to penetrate existing markets further and to acquire entry into new markets, NovaNet could be among our most important strategic investments.

Dr. Arnold Renschier said,

One of the issues being debated internally right now is: "Do we go ahead and roll out a successful administrative function (which is already available) before we have a successful clinical component for NovaNet?" Once we resolve that question, the administrative piece could be rolled out almost immediately. The big opportunity, though, in terms of improved productivity, consistency of treatment, and the potential to measure outcomes derives from the clinical piece. . . . If only the administrative piece is rolled out, the clinician will not feel the same degree of affirmation that they would experience if the clinical piece were working.

Yet if NovaCare did not go ahead, there could be significant public and employee relations problems for NovaCare. Internally, many clinicians had knowledge of the pilot and were eager to obtain the help it offered. Externally, NovaCare had announced its plans for NovaNet, and therefore many investment houses, customers, and shareholders might have anticipated benefits from the system.

NovaCare had to proceed cautiously. It operated within a highly regulated environment: 80–90% of its billings were dependent on Medicare reimbursement. Said Tim Foster, "The biggest strategic threat in any health care business is the regulatory environment and the questions of reimbursement from the public or private sector." Regulations or interpretations of existing laws could quickly change to stimulate, redirect, or curtail specific therapies or their reimbursement. Intermediaries also constantly used their ability to interpret or change reimbursement. These and the constant flow of new rehabilita-

---

EXHIBIT 5-14 Competitor Situation: Brief Profiles

In October–November 1991, *Rehab Management* ran an article profiling the rehab industry's largest providers. The following is summarized from that source.

Baxter Health Care Corp's Physical Therapy Division was purchased by $8 billion Baxter in 1984. Its history was in sports medicine. Baxter established the division as an entrepreneurial company within the parent. In 1991, the division had started a growth campaign to add as many as 150 centers in five years. Its stated intention was to focus on the outpatient market. The division handled roughly 100,000 patient visits a year and was establishing data bases on treatment, outcomes, and quality control.

MedRehab, Inc. had three primary business lines: contractual services in long-term care settings (350 nursing home sites); its own operation in 39 outpatient clinics; and 51 hospitals where it provided physical, occupational, speech, and respiratory therapy services. Founded in May 1987 as a start-up company, MedRehab had acquired a number of existing regional rehab companies. MedRehab saw the switch from inpatient to outpatient professionals at work and claimed to be maintaining a retention rate of better than 80% on an annualized basis. It had affiliations throughout the country with 75 universities which trained physical, occupational, and speech therapists.

HealthSouth Rehabilitation Corp. was an entrepreneurial company formed in 1984 and taken public in 1986. It had attempted to build outpatient rehab centers and hospitals that would be more cost effective than keeping patients in higher cost settings. It had built 40 facilities in its first five years and had continuing growth plans in similar directions. With 3,000 counties in the United States and only 175 comprehensive rehab facilities. HealthSouth saw no barriers to its development. Using careful financial controls, it had maintained a strong balance sheet and was able to move rapidly and price competitively.

Rehab Hospital Services Corp. was founded in 1979 and purchased by National Medical Enterprises in 1985. Since then, it had grown from six facilities to 33 facilities, 18 managed units, and two transitional living centers. It had one rehab outpatient facility of its own and was currently building three more. Its plans stated that it would seek to build five to ten freestanding hospital facilities per year. In 1991, it claimed to be the largest rehabilitation company in the country. It was aggressively managed and would consider all forms of expansion, both internal and through acquisitions. In public statements, it emphasized its "one to two referral marketing" program to generate new business. In each of its areas, it tried to develop "focused administrators," willing to take risks and aggressively pursue opportunities. It claimed its distinctive advantage was its human resources capability.

Continental Medical Systems was founded in 1986. It had a presence in 36 states, with 22 operating rehab hospitals in 11 states, 57 outpatient centers in 18 states, and four contract therapy companies which had a presence in 30 states. With over 7,500 employees, it had opened eight new hospitals in 1991 and was planning another eight in 1992. Its target was to be a billion-dollar company in the mid-1990s. It had purchased three of its 22 operating hospitals and all four of its contract service companies.

Healthfocus, Inc. was started in 1963 as a partnership. It was purchased by Hyatt in 1971 and then acquired by American Medical International (AMI) in 1980. It had started a rehab division in 1985 which officers and employees later purchased in a leveraged buyout. Healthfocus had 55 freestanding clinics in 13 states and contracts with 85 hospitals in 31 states. In 1991 it was looking at work-health programs to augment its rehab and hospital activities.

There were also a number of other smaller regional players with specialized services, facilities, or capabilities. However, acquisition prices were increasing rapidly because of the success of these "Big 7" players and NovaCare.

tion needs and therapeutic techniques were a continuing challenge.

Other threats included competition for rehabilitation patients from nursing homes themselves. Many nursing homes were trying to move out of the "hotel and beds" portion of the business and into higher-margin activities. Growing nursing homes might obtain a sufficient number of patients to justify employment of internal therapists. If consolidation occurred around these centers, NovaCare could be left primarily with the smaller facilities, with fewer patients, and highly dispersed from a travel standpoint. In addition, if the government undertook a massive program for training therapists, the labor situation could change from a shortage to a surplus condition, seriously affecting NovaCare's margins. It was in this context that NovaCare's top

management had to consider how best to position the total company, its organization, its controls and incentives, and its NovaNet information system for maximum future effectiveness. (See Exhibit 5-14 for brief profiles of NovaCare's competitors.)

Referring to the company's purposes and beliefs, John Foster noted,

As we make these decisions and we look around at successful leadership companies, we observe that those companies with the highest integrity also have the highest returns on capital and the highest profit margins on sales. Therefore, we are satisfied that if we are prepared to do whatever we do right, the yield should be outstanding financial performance. Quality, productivity, and integrity are the things that serve our shareholders best in the long run. ■

SOURCE: Henry Mintzberg and James Brian Quinn, *The Strategy Process: Concepts, Contexts, and Cases*, 3rd ed. (Upper Saddle River, NJ, 1996), pp. 517–529. Case Copyright © by James Brian Quinn.

CASE QUESTIONS

1. What is the basis for NovaCare's current competitive edge? How can it develop a permanent competitive edge against its many potential future rivals?
2. What should be the future directions of NovaCare's growth? What new fields should it enter? Why? In what sequence? What are the important timing parameters? What are the limiting factors on growth? How should these be handled?
3. What will be the effects of growth on NovaCare's organization structure? Management style? What are the critical factors for organizational success from NovaCare's viewpoint? The

clinician's viewpoint? Client's viewpoint? Patient's viewpoint? How should NovaCare deal with conflicts among these?
4. How should NovaCare position NovaNet for maximum future impact? Should it go ahead with the proposed rollout? What priorities in functions should NovaNet seek to achieve? How can NovaNet most contribute to the development of NovaCare's distinctive maintainable competitive edge? What will be the important questions to deal with in implementation of NovaNet? How can NovaNet be leveraged into other opportunities for NovaCare?

References

Andrews, Kenneth R., *The Concept of Corporate Strategy* (Homewood, IL, Irwin, 1987).

Carey, Susan, "St. Louis Blues: TWA Struggles to Improve Performance," *Wall Street Journal* (September 27, 1996).

Deane, Phyllis, *The Evolution of Economic Ideas* (London, Cambridge University Press, 1978).

De Marle, David J., "The Value Force," in M. Larry

Shillito and David J. De Marle (eds.), *Value: Its Measurement, Design, and Management*, (New York, John Wiley & Sons, 1992).

Fisher, Anne, "The 100 Best Companies to Work for in America," *Fortune* (January 12, 1998), pp. 69–95.

Godsey, Kristin Dunlap, "Slow Climb to New Heights," *Success* (October 20, 1996).

Henderson, Bruce D., "The Origin of Strategy," *Harvard Business Review* (November–December 1989).

Heskett, James L., *Managing in the Service Economy* (Boston, Harvard Business School Press, 1986).

Juran, Jospeh M., and Frank M. Gryna, *Quality Planning and Analysis* (New York, McGraw-Hill, 1993).

Labich, Kenneth, "Is Herb Kelleher America's Best CEO?," *Fortune* (May 2, 1994).

McCartney, Scott, and Michael J. McCarthy, "Southwest Flies Circles Around United's Shuttle," *Wall Street Journal* (February 20, 1996).

McCartney, Scott, "Turbulence Ahead: Competitors Quake as Southwest Air Is Set to Invade Northeast," *Wall Street Journal* (October 23, 1996).

Mintzberg, Henry, "Five Ps for Strategy," *California Management Review* (fall 1987).

Mintzberg, Henry, "The Strategy Concept II: Another Look at Why Organizations Need Strategies," *California Management Review* (fall 1987), pp. 25–32.

Oliver, Suzanne, "The Battle of the Credit Cards," *Forbes* (July 1, 1996), pp. 62–66.

Porter, Michael E., *Competitive Strategy: Techniques for Analyzing Industries and Competitors* (New York, The Free Press, 1980).

Porter, Michael E., *Competitive Advantage: Creating and Sustaining Superior Performance* (New York, The Free Press, 1985).

Quinn, James B., *Strategies for Change: Logical Incrementalism* (Homewood, IL, Irwin, 1980).

Regan, Mary Beth, "The Post Office Delivers a Banner Year," *Business Week* (January 19, 1998), p. 38.

Sewall, Hannah R., *The Theory of Value Before Adam Smith* (New York, Augustus M. Kelley Publishers, 1968).

"Shouldice Hospital Limited," Harvard Business School Case 683-068 Rev. 6/89.

Smith, Adam, *An Inquiry into the Nature and Causes of the Wealth of* Nations (New York, The Modern Library, 1937).

"Southwest Airlines (A)," Harvard Business School Case 575-060 Rev. 2/85.

Stanglin, Douglas, "Don't Return to Sender," *U.S. News and World Report* (October 7, 1996), pp. 49–50.

Young, Jeffrey T., *Classical Theories of Value: From Smith to Sraffa* (Boulder, Colorado, Westview Press, 1978).

Zeithaml, Valarie A., "Consumer Perceptions of Price, Quality, and Value: A Means-End Model and Synthesis of Evidence," *Journal of Marketing*, vol. 52 (July 1988), pp. 2–22.

Zeithaml, Valarie A., A. Parasuraman, and Leonard L. Berry, *Delivering Quality Service: Balancing Customer Perceptions and Expectations* (New York, The Free Press, 1990).

CHAPTER 6

Positioning and Marketing of Services

6.1   INTRODUCTION

The marketing of *services*, as distinct from the marketing of goods, is receiving increased attention from marketing scholars and practitioners. This change in emphasis is due to many factors other than the obvious growth of the service economy. With the deregulation of such industries as airlines, trucking, financial services, and telecommunications, marketing strategies are needed to address issues previously decided by the government regulations, such as service offerings, pricing, and promotion. With new competitors entering the marketplace, markets for some firms are narrowing and becoming increasingly segmented. For others, market opportunities are rapidly expanding. In the face of these developments, it became clear that the original "4 Ps" of product, place, price, and promotion were not sufficient to embrace all the activities marketers perform in services marketing. Consequently, some marketing scholars proposed three additional Ps, *participants*, *physical evidence*, and *process* to expand the traditional set of 4 Ps.[1]

Issues such as product design, process design, quality, and site selection are traditional operations management topics that also concern service marketers. On the other hand, service operations managers and researchers are developing an interest in issues that are considered to be in marketing's domain, such as customer satisfaction, service encounters, customer retention, and consumer behavior. These issues are also covered in this book to help managers deal with the multitude of problems faced in managing service organizations. This overlap (or integration) of topics is due to the closeness that the marketing and operations functions enjoy in services. The purpose of this chapter is to explore the integration of marketing and operations, to examine the differences between goods and services marketing, to expand the tradi-

---

[1] B. H. Booms and Mary Jo Bitner, "Marketing Strategies and Organization Structures for Service Firms," in J. H. Donnelly and W. R. George (eds.), *Marketing of Services* (Chicago, American Marketing Association, 1981), pp. 47–52. Also see A. J. Magrath, "When Marketing Services, 4 Ps Are Not Enough," *Business Horizons* (May–June 1986), pp. 44–50.

tional marketing mix to incorporate service-oriented concerns, and to discuss some strategic issues such as market segmentation, targeting, and positioning of services as well as customer retention, also known as *relationship marketing.*

6.2 INTEGRATION OF MARKETING AND OPERATIONS

In chapter 2, the important characteristics of services were reviewed, including intangibility, perishability, inseparability, and variability, which imply customer contact, involvement of customers in service production, and high personal judgment required of service providers. These characteristics make service encounters special events in which operations, marketing, and human resources functions of a business are all interested. At the same time, these characteristics necessitate cooperation and coordination among the three functions to create value and customer satisfaction. The situation is very different in a manufacturing firm. Goods are manufactured in a plant under the supervision of operations people, and then shipped to regional warehouses, then to stores or retail outlets where customers buy them. Once the goods leave the factory, marketing people assume responsibility and they are the ones in contact with customers. In other words, they form a link between operations and customers. Also, operations and marketing responsibilities are fairly well defined and separated in manufacturing firms; they do not have to interact frequently, and almost never in the presence of customers. In most services, this distinction and separation of the operations and marketing functions does not exist. Neither does the separation of producers and customers; front-line employees have to perform both functions.

Operations constitutes the core function in most service organizations, because it is operations that puts together the service system and processes and delivers the actual service to customers. However, they can and should invite the input and support of marketing people in many decisions such as service design, site selection, scheduling, and customer retention. In addition, the marketing department can perform very useful activities, independently or in cooperation with operations, such as collecting information on customer needs and satisfaction, evaluating and selecting market segments, pricing, preparing demand forecasts, collecting information on competitors and their standing in the marketplace.[2]

Some other activities that are traditionally within the marketing domain, such as advertising and promotion, will be performed exclusively by the marketing department. Some service companies may still maintain a marketing department to carry out these traditional marketing activities. Whether or not they do this, it is crucial that these two functions cooperate and coordinate their activities; otherwise, value creation and customer satisfaction will be seriously compromised. Some firms, such as Federal Express, have been successful in doing so. Case 6–1 tells the Federal Express story of balance and support between marketing and operations.

Despite its importance, the integration of operations and marketing activities is neither easy nor without problems. The source of a major problem is the different and frequently conflicting orientations and objectives of managers in each group. Historically, operations managers have been evaluated and rewarded according to measures of output, operational efficiency, and costs. Attaining high output levels and operational efficiency implies long runs of the same product (i.e., good or service), which in turn implies less variety and customization. In some services, labor cost is very significant; lowering labor costs may result in longer waiting time for customers, poor ser-

---

[2] Christopher H. Lovelock, *Services Marketing*, 3rd ed. (Upper Saddle River, NJ, Prentice Hall, 1996), p. 511.

vice quality, and overall low levels of customer satisfaction. Marketing managers, however, face different criteria: sales revenues and customer satisfaction, which frequently depend on the availability of a variety of products and fast response to customer demand. Also, a no-less-important contributing factor in services is the presence of customers during service delivery. Customers provide input and sometimes labor to the service process. They also exhibit great variability in their behavior and cannot be controlled easily by the service provider; hence, they increase the variability of service output. There are also various specific issues for which operations and marketing managers may have conflicting objectives. (See Exhibit 6-1.)[3]

Human resources also occupies an important place in service management because of the critical role service providers play in value creation and customer satisfaction. A service company has to select, hire, and train the right people for the job and keep them happily employed with the company. These are usually the tasks and responsibilities of the human resources department. The role of the human resources function in service organizations will be discussed in more detail in chapter 9.

6.3   DIFFERENCES IN GOODS AND SERVICES MARKETING

Goods typically are first produced, then sold, and then consumed. Most services, however, are first sold, then produced and consumed simultaneously.[4] This unique order of processes and the inseparability of the production of a service (an operations issue) from its consumption (a marketing issue) significantly change the role of marketing in a service firm. This difference is verified by marketing managers who have transferred from goods-producing firms to service-performing firms. The differences between goods and services marketing may be viewed in terms of:

- Output tangibility
- Organizational features
- Ownership, use, and consumption
- The scope of marketing activities
- The consumer's role

Tangibility

In earlier chapters of this text, the difficulties in dealing with the intangible nature of services were discussed from an operations management point of view. The problem is no less serious for the marketing of intangibles. In fact, the greater the presence of intangible elements in a service, the greater will be the divergence from goods marketing principles and approaches.[5]

For example, consumer goods marketing attempts to enhance a physical object through abstract association. Coca-Cola is associated with authenticity and youth; Dr.

---

[3] For a more detailed discussion of different objectives of operations and marketing and how they may be resolved, see Benjamin Schneider and David E. Bowen, *Winning the Service Game* (Boston, Harvard Business School Press, 1995), pp. 200–218. Also see two articles by Christopher H. Lovelock, "A Basic Toolkit for Service Managers," and "The Search for Synergy: What Marketers Need to Know about Service Operations," both in Christopher H. Lovelock, *Managing Services Marketing, Operations and Human Resources*, 2nd ed. (Upper Saddle River, NJ, Prentice Hall, 1992), pp. 17–30 and pp. 392–405, respectively.

[4] This idea was first put forth by W. J. Regan, "The Service Revolution," *Journal of Marketing*, vol. 27 (July 1963), pp. 57–62.

[5] This view is strongly expressed in G. Lynn Shostack, "Breaking Free From Product Marketing," *Journal of Marketing* (April 1977), pp. 73–80. Many of the examples in this section are from the Shostack article.

EXHIBIT 6-1 Operations and Marketing Perspectives on Operational Issues

Operational Issues	Typical Operations Goals	Common Marketing Concerns
Productivity improvement	Reduce unit cost of production	Strategies may cause decline in service quality
Make-versus-buy decisions	Trade off control against comparative advantage and cost savings	"Make" decisions may result in lower quality and lack of market coverage; "buy" decisions may transfer control to unresponsive suppliers and hurt the firm's image
Facilities location	Reduce costs; provide convenient access for suppliers and employees	Customers may find location unattractive and inaccessible
Standardization	Keep costs low and quality consistent; simplify operations tasks; recruit low-cost employees	Consumers may seek variety, prefer customization to match segmented needs
Batch versus unit processing	Seek economies of scale, consistency, efficient use of capacity	Customers may be forced to wait, feel "one of a crowd," be turned off by other customers
Facilities layout and design	Control costs; improve efficiency by ensuring proximity of operationally related tasks; enhance safety and security	Customers may be confused, shunted around unnecessarily, find facility unattractive and inconvenient
Job design	Minimize error, waste, and fraud; make efficient use of technology; simplify tasks for standardization	Operationally oriented employees with narrow roles may be unresponsive to customer needs
Learning curves	Apply experience to reduce time and costs per unit of output	Faster service is not necessarily better service; cost saving may not be passed on as lower prices
Management of capacity	Keep costs down by avoiding wasteful underutilization of resources	Service may be unavailable when needed; quality may be compromised during high-demand periods
Quality control	Ensure that service execution conforms to predefined standards	Operational definitions of quality may not reflect customer needs, preferences
Management of queues	Optimize use of available capacity by planning for average throughput; maintain customer order, discipline	Customers may be bored and frustrated during wait, see firm as unresponsive

Source: Christopher H. Lovelock, "The Search for Synergy: What Marketers Need to Know about Service Operations," in Christopher H. Lovelock, *Managing Services Marketing, Operations and Human Resources*, 2nd ed. (Upper Saddle River, NJ, Prentice Hall, 1992), p. 403.

Pepper suggests originality and risk taking; and 7-Up is light, clean, and buoyant. Tangible products are given intangible images.

For service marketing, however, the opposite strategy should be used. Services are already intangible. Abstractions are not needed. What the marketer can do is provide tangible evidence as to the reality of the service. Thus, an investment management service described in terms of "sound analysis," "careful portfolio monitoring," and "strong research capability" does not achieve the credibility or the customer draw of Merrill Lynch's bull charging through an advertisement. Other examples of making the intangible tangible can be found in the insurance industry.

- "You're in good *hands* with Allstate."
- "I've got a piece of the *rock*." (Prudential)
- "Under the Traveler's *umbrella*."
- "Nationwide's *blanket* of protection."

Firms with a mixture of goods and services offerings can follow a mixed marketing strategy. McDonald's, for instance, markets its food product as *nutritious* (two all-beef patties, etc.), *fun* (Ronald McDonald), and *helpful* ("We Do It All For You," "You Deserve a Break Today," etc.). Its service, in contrast, is marketed through a tangible uniformity of environment, including color, style of graphics, apparel, and golden arches. It is clear from these examples that there are similarities as well as differences between marketing of goods and services. Professor Theodore Levitt of Harvard Business School expressed this succinctly: ". . . a key area of similarity in the marketing of intangibles and tangibles revolves around the degree of intangibility inherent in both. Marketing is concerned with getting and keeping customers. The degree of product intangibility has its greatest effect in the process of trying to get customers. When it comes to holding on to customers—to keeping them—highly intangible products run into very special problems."[6]

Organizational Features

As mentioned earlier in this chapter, operations personnel in manufacturing firms are not normally engaged in marketing activities, except in rare cases of custom-made items. The marketing department is a separate department within the company. In contrast, any service that has personal contact with the customer conducts marketing activities as it provides the service. In addition, many services companies, particularly the larger ones, have a separate marketing department that carries out traditional marketing functions. These two marketing components may be identified respectively as *service interface marketing* (SIM) and *functional marketing* (FM).

In Exhibit 6-2, the contrast between the marketing of high-contact services (i.e., personal services) and low-contact services (i.e., impersonal or mass services) is depicted. In personal services, the marketing organization may be small or nonexistent. Service interface marketing is more predominant. For impersonal services, such as utilities and credit card systems, as well as for manufacturing companies, the formal marketing department carries out practically all marketing activities. Marketing is well established in the organizational structure.

EXHIBIT 6-2 Organizational versus Informal Marketing

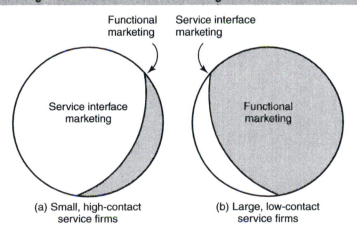

(a) Small, high-contact
service firms

(b) Large, low-contact
service firms

[6] Theodore Levitt, "Marketing Intangible Products and Product Intangibles," *Harvard Business Review* (May–June 1981), pp. 94–102.

The need for the integration of marketing and operations in services has already been suggested. To formalize this integration, several researchers have promoted the idea of reorganizing service firms so that marketing, human resources, and operations can work more closely together.[7]

Ownership, Use, and Consumption

A company that manufactures and markets a good is essentially selling a physical item, even though the promotional technique may imply a service. For example, IBM does not picture itself as selling hardware but rather a system that is a service to the customer. Perfume firms do not emphasize the perfume as a physical item but rather as a producer of fantasies.

The focus of the marketing activities of a service organization is always the service itself. Even in embedded services, it is the service, not the package, that is more important. If the service is immaterial to the package, then the subject of the transaction is a good. There are significant differences between goods and services in terms of ownership, use, and consumption. We may purchase a service but we do not own anything as a result of this transaction. We obtain only the right to enjoy the benefits of the service, usually for a limited period of time. For example, in the case of an airline ticket, a passenger purchases transportation service to carry him and his luggage from point A to point B. The purchase gives him the right to occupy a seat on a particular flight operated by the airline. The passenger does not become an owner of anything other than the piece of paper the ticket is printed on, but the ticket is only a symbol, or evidence of the purchase of the service; it has no value by itself. Today, some airlines do not even issue a ticket—the passenger only has to show a picture ID to board the plane. Furthermore, a passenger's right to use the airline's plane is limited to a particular date and flight, not for an indefinite period, and unlike goods, his right is limited to one-time use only.

Almost all services are like this—customers only obtain the *use* of a service for limited time periods. There are only a few exceptions to this rule. Exceptions occur when the service is embodied in a physical product such as a book or recorded music. However, even in these cases, ownership is limited to that one copy and to the physical product, because the consumer has only purchased the right to enjoy the service, not the ownership of its contents. In other words, one cannot duplicate the book or the music and sell to others. These different ownership, use, and consumption options present additional opportunities and challenges for services marketing.

Scope of Marketing Activities

The scope of marketing activities is defined by a basic marketing concept called **marketing mix.** An organization's marketing mix consists of all the variables that are controllable by the organization in communicating with and satisfying its target market.

The traditional, goods-oriented marketing mix can be categorized into four elements: product, price, place, and promotion. With some adjustment, these elements are important to service marketing as well. However, there are other variables in the service environment that can be controlled and coordinated to communicate with and

---

[7] See Christian Grönroos, "Innovative Marketing Strategies and Organization Structures for Service Firms," in *Emerging Perspectives on Services Marketing*, Proceedings of the 1983 Conference on Services Marketing (Chicago, American Marketing Association, 1983); and Christopher H. Lovelock, *Managing Services: Marketing, Operations and Human Resources*, 2nd ed. (Upper Saddle River, NJ, Prentice Hall, 1992).

satisfy service customers.[8] These include the service employees and customers, the physical environment in which the service is provided, and the service process itself. Thus, the 4 Ps of goods marketing currently incorporated in the marketing mix need to be expanded to the 7 Ps for services to include

- *Participants* (employees and customers)
- *Physical evidence* (building, uniforms, and other tangible evidence)
- *Process* (the actual procedures and flow of activities involved in providing the service)

This expanded marketing mix for services is discussed in more detail in the next section. (Also refer to chapter 2, in which the role these 3 Ps play in service encounters is discussed.)

The Consumer's Role

Consumer behavior is a more difficult process to study for services than for goods because the customer may be involved in the creation and delivery of the service. In addition, because purchase and consumption of the service occur simultaneously in most services, consumer behavior *during* the service encounter must also be considered.

Consumers evaluate services differently from goods. Most goods are relatively easy to evaluate because evaluations can be based mainly on visible, touchable, quantifiable qualities that can be searched *prior* to purchase, and then evaluations can be backed up with the qualities experienced *after* the purchase. Most services, however, are more difficult to evaluate because people base their evaluations on qualities they experience and even on some qualities that they believe are present in the service but of which they cannot be sure. Following is a summary of the three criteria:

- *Search qualities*—attributes that a consumer can determine prior to purchasing a good or service, such as color, style, fit, feel, smell, core and supplementary services and their prices, service duration, and schedule of the service facility
- *Experience qualities*—attributes that can only be determined after purchase or during consumption, such as taste, wearability, pain, pleasure, and comfort
- *Credence qualities*—attributes that the consumer may be unaware of or lack the technical knowledge to evaluate even after consumption, such as appendix operations and brake relinings

Marketing of experience qualities and credence qualities is a more difficult task than marketing search qualities. These different evaluative qualities also imply that when customers buy services, their prepurchase and postpurchase behaviors may be different when they buy goods. The need for marketing activities may actually be greater after the purchase of a service than *before* the purchase!

6.4 MARKETING MIX

As mentioned earlier, the marketing mix recommended for services consists of seven elements: product (service), price, place, physical evidence, participants, promotion, and process. These are variables that can be controlled and manipulated by the organization for competitive advantage. A service organization should select its marketing

---

[8] This discussion of expanded product mix is adapted from Mary Jo Bitner and Valarie A. Zeithaml, "Fundamentals in Services Marketing," in *Proceedings of the 1988 Conference on Services Marketing* (Chicago, American Marketing Association, 1989), pp. 7–11. The original idea for an expanded marketing mix appeared in B. H. Booms and Mary Jo Bitner, "Marketing Strategies and Organization Structures for Service Firms," in *Marketing of Services*, Proceedings of the 1981 Conference in Services Marketing (Chicago, American Marketing Association, 1983), pp. 47–52.

mix to support its strategy and competitive position in its market. Elements of the extended marketing mix and examples of related activities are shown in Exhibit 6-3. Each element is now discussed.

Product (Service)

The "product" element of the marketing mix for services refers to the variety and depth *of services* offered within a particular service package. It is concerned with the matching of services to target markets. The core and supplemental services and their quality must be determined by market demand and competitive positioning. Also part of this element are after-sales service and warranties. Much of the material discussed in chapter 8 concerning service design is relevant to this aspect of marketing mix.

Price

Pricing policy concerns such issues as the list price, discounts, allowances, payment period, and credit terms and is much more complex for services than for goods.[9] For ex-

---

EXHIBIT 6-3 The Marketing Mix for Services

Product (Service)
Target markets
Services
Service level
Rent, lease, or sell
After-sales service
Warranties

Price
Rent, lease, or sell
Structure and time
Discounts
Payment terms
Flexibility
Customer's perceived value

Place
Location
Accessibility
Channels of distribution
Distribution coverage

Promotion
Advertising
Publicity
Public relations
Selling by salespeople
Selling by service providers
Employee training in customer relations

Physical Evidence
External appearance of the site
Internal appearance and ambiance
Appearance of employees
Credentials of employees
Equipment
Materials

Participation
Interpersonal behavior
Skills
Attitudes
Commitment
Discretion used
Frequency of customer contacts
Duration of customer contacts
Selling activities
Training

Process
Customer needs and wants
Customer involvement
Demand control
Quality control
Customer follow-up
Policies and procedures
Flow of activities

---

[9] Philip Kotler, *Marketing for Nonprofit Organizations*, 2nd ed. (Upper Saddle River, NJ, Prentice Hall, 1982), p. 108.

ample, it can play an important role in managing demand; the price for the same service may be different for different times of the day (at theaters) or seasons of the year (for resorts). Price may be scaled to match the steps of a service versus the entire service (upper body massage versus total body massage).

For services, pricing not only affects the level of customer demand, but also sends a message to customers concerning their expectations of a service.[10] This is especially important for intangible and professional services. Because price is an indicator of value, service firms typically use factors other than the cost of a service to set prices. Federal Express provides a good example of a service pricing strategy.[11] The pricing decisions at FedEx are worked out jointly between the marketing staff and the corporate financial staff. The trick is to set prices at a high enough level to protect company profit margins while at the same time making absolutely certain that the company is not pricing itself out of the market. Marketing strategy must then convince customers that Federal Express charges the prices it does because it is rendering a superior type of service.

Place

Place basically refers to the location and distribution of services. Some services are delivered right to the home or business. Such delivery may be optional, as in the case of a music teacher or a business consultant. In other services, such as cleaning a house or servicing a pool, delivery is essential. The decision to bring a customer to a fixed service location or to take the service to the customer depends on the market for each type of service, the price, the cost, and the competition.

Services may be transportable, location bound, or a combination, depending on the degree to which the service or parts of it may be separated from its production.[12] Thus, a computer database service may serve anyone anywhere there are telephone lines. On the other hand, a restaurant is location bound, although a franchised chain reduces this limitation somewhat. A financial service may require local representatives, but the major part of the service production may be performed anywhere. Channels of distribution for services include agents (insurance) and franchises (U-Haul, restaurants).

As will be discussed in chapter 10, the location decision is extremely important for a service firm because accessibility can ultimately determine whether a service succeeds or fails. It may be true, at least for some services, that the three most important elements for success in a service business are location, location, and location.

Physical Evidence

Physical evidence is an important element of the marketing mix because the customer is usually in contact with at least some part of the service production facilities, equipment, and personnel. In addition, because services are intangible and thus difficult to evaluate, physical evidence provides clues as to service quality. A simple example is the "gold" credit card that promotes a superior package of credit services. The grade of paper and print, form, and language of letters and statements also af-

---

[10] See Valarie A. Zeithaml, "How Consumer Evaluation Processes Differ between Goods and Services," in *Marketing of Services*, Proceedings of the 1981 Conference on Services Marketing (Chicago, American Marketing Association, 1981), pp. 186–190.

[11] This example is taken from R. A. Sigafoos and R. R. Easson, *Absolutely, Positively Overnight!* (Memphis, TN, St. Luke's Press, 1988), p. 154.

[12] See J. J. Boddewyn, Marsha Baldwin Halbrich, and A. C. Perry, "Service Multinationals: Conceptualization, Measurement, and Theory," *Journal of International Business Studies* (fall 1986).

fect the perception of service quality. Similarly, credentials indicated by diplomas hung on the wall or certification initials in advertisements are physical evidence of service quality.

Airlines are well known for their ability to create service identity through consistency in the decor of their planes, their graphics, their advertising, and their uniforms. As another example, Fred Smith of Federal Express does not want anyone to have a neutral reaction to the brazen purple, orange, and white emblem on his planes, delivery trucks, and advertising material. He also stresses personal grooming of his employees—clean-cut, no beards, and no trendy hairstyles. Even the selection of courier uniforms is a major corporate event.[13]

Physical evidence adds substance to the service concept. Service marketers should therefore be involved in the design, planning, and control of such physical evidence.

Participants

Participants refers to any and all people who play a role in the service encounter. This includes a particular customer, employees, and other customers. The attitudes and actions of employees can certainly affect the success of a service encounter. It is also likely that the behavior of other customers, in a movie theater, restaurant, or classroom, can affect an individual's service.

Employee behavior must be strongly customer oriented in services. Employees in contact with the customers should truly be considered salespeople. Throughout its development, AT&T has been noted for the friendliness of its telephone operators. Florida Power & Light is another example of a company in which the employees do their utmost to answer queries and assist customers. In contrast, most of us have had contact with uncaring salespeople, rude service people, and discourteous managers. In services, marketing is everyone's job. Thus, it is important to have employees with the skills, attitudes, commitment, and ability to use discretion in dealing with customers.

Promotion

Services utilize the traditional methods of promotion, including advertising, publicity, sales promotion, and personal selling. However, because of the interactive and intangible nature of services, there are some differences in how promotions are carried out.

Determining a message content for a promotion is more difficult in services. Tangible clues of service quality are needed. Customer expectations have to be determined and put into words. Personal selling is by far the most commonly used promotion for services. Everyone who has contact with the customer "sells" the service and the organization. Employees must be trained in customer relations to promote the service while the service process is ongoing.

Nordstrom, a retailer known for its high-quality service, does little advertising. The money it saves goes into employee training, which, in turn, improves service quality and increases its word-of-mouth reputation.

An important part of service promotion takes place *after* the sale and delivery of the service. Since many services are dependent on repeat business, maintaining relationships with existing customers is very important. "Reselling" service benefits, customizing services, rewarding existing customers with special attention or promotions, and quickly and effectively resolving problems are all part of the after-sale marketing

---

[13] Sigafoos and Easson, *Absolutely, Positively Overnight!*, p. 154.

activities known as **relationship marketing.**[14] Relationship marketing has broader, strategic implications for service organizations.

Process

A major objective of marketing is to identify the needs and wants in the marketplace, so that the organization may design the service to fulfill these needs. This concern extends to the design of the service process and the service delivery system, which are within the domain of operations. Ultimately, the service and the process that creates it reflect how all the marketing mix elements are coordinated to create value for the customer.

Insufficient attention to the service process leads to poor service quality and dissatisfied customers. Services are created and delivered as a result of one or more processes. In a sense, process is the service. In a manufacturing company, the outcome of the production process is important, but the process itself is irrelevant to most customers. In most services, however, the process that creates the service as well as its outcome are very important to the customer, especially when the customer is present during the process. For example, a competently performed root canal treatment by a dentist would not lead to customer satisfaction if the patient had to wait for a long time, was treated rudely by the dentist and the office personnel, given no explanation about the treatment procedure, and never inquired about her pain or discomfort. Can you separate the process and the outcome in this situation? Probably not, because to a large extent the outcome is the process.

Marketing and operations should share the responsibility to ensure that the service encounter is a positive one and that service quality is maintained. Thus, marketing must be involved in designing the service process and is often involved in, or responsible for, quality control in services.

6.5   STRATEGIC ISSUES

Consumers exhibit great variety in terms of their lifestyles, needs, expectations, perceptions, and buying habits. An organization that wants to satisfy its customers by tailoring its goods or services to match each individual in terms of these variables faces a tremendous challenge because of the large number of possible combinations and the costs involved. Furthermore, an organization may not be equipped to serve every potential customer. Consequently, organizations have to select customers they can serve competently and profitably. In chapter 5, strategic service vision was discussed as a possible approach to developing a strategy for a service organization.[15] One of the basic elements of this approach is market segmentation, and its integrative element is positioning. Segmentation and positioning are among the traditional marketing activities. Marketing professionals in an organization should work together with operations people in identifying market segments, targeting them, and positioning services for a service strategy that creates customer value and satisfaction.

Segmentation, Positioning, and Targeting

A **market segment** is a group of customers who have the same or similar characteristics, needs, and buying behavior. The purpose of segmentation is to identify customer groups that have as much similarity as possible within the group, but dissimilarity with

14 See Theodore Levitt, "After the Sale Is Over," *Harvard Business Review*, vol. 62, no. 5 (September–October 1983), pp. 87–93; Leonard Berry, "Relationship Marketing," in *Proceedings of the 1983 Conference on Services Marketing* (Chicago, American Marketing Association, 1983), pp. 25–28; and Mary Jo Bitner and Valarie A. Zeithaml, "Fundamentals in Services Marketing," pp. 7–11.
15 James L. Heskett, *Managing in the Service Economy* (Boston, Harvard Business School Press, 1986).

other groups with respect to the relevant characteristics.[16] The next step is **targeting,** that is, deciding which group or groups of customers the organization is equipped to serve and can do so profitably. Finally, the organization should decide how to **position** its service(s) in the minds of its current and potential customers. It should be recalled that an organization develops a service strategy to differentiate itself and its service(s) from the competition.

In the extreme case, an organization may define each customer as a separate segment—in other words, a segment of one. This is a very expensive strategy and cannot be economically justified for most companies. A segment of one makes sense when the customer's purchases constitute a significant portion of the company's business volume. For example, an advertising agency may identify each automobile manufacturer in the United States as a segment of one and develop a separate strategy for each. This may be justified because there are so few of these companies and revenues from serving one of them as an exclusive ad agency would be very significant.

In most cases, however, an organization should segment its market so that each segment is meaningful and offers a sales potential worth pursuing. Markets may be segmented according to various criteria. Some of the most common criteria are geographic, demographic, psychographic, and behavioral. Exhibit 6-4 provides examples of how customers may be grouped according to these criteria. Kotler and Armstrong identify four characteristics of effective segmentation[17]:

- *Measurability.* Marketers must be able to measure the size and purchasing power of the segments. The ease with which this can be done is called the measurability. This is instrumental in determining whether the sales potential and profitability justify the investment in time, effort, and costs.
- *Accessibility.* For a segment to be meaningful, consumers in the segment must be accessible to the organization through various advertising and marketing vehicles.
- *Substantiality.* This is the degree to which segments offer a large enough sales potential and are profitable.
- *Actionability.* Market segments must also be defined so that effective services and marketing programs can be developed to attract and serve customers. For example, a service organization may be able to identify several segments but may lack the resources to develop a different service and a separate marketing program for each one.

Once the segmentation criteria are selected, marketers must identify segments and try to achieve the four characteristics listed above; clearly, not all segments may have all four characteristics. In addition, marketers must make sure that the segments are really different from each other.

Assuming that some segments have all four characteristics, the next step is to select one or more of them to serve. This is known as targeting, and the segments selected are called **target markets.** In making this decision, the organization has to consider the sales volume and profit potential each segment offers, the number and strength of competitors in each segment, and whether the segment has growth potential. Also, if more than one segment is going to be targeted, the organization must make sure that these segments are compatible. For example, if different segments are to be served using the same facilities at the same time, they must be compatible, even

---

[16] Christopher H. Lovelock, *Services Marketing*, 3rd ed., p. 165.

[17] Philip Kotler and Gary Armstrong, *Principles of Marketing*, 4th ed. (Upper Saddle River, NJ, Prentice Hall, 1989), p. 228.

EXHIBIT 6-4   Common Segmentation Criteria for Consumer Markets

Variable	*Typical Breakdowns*
Geographic	
Region	Pacific, Mountain, West North Central, West South Central, East North Central, East South Central, South Atlantic, Middle Atlantic, New England
County size	A, B, C, D
City or MSA size	Under 5,000; 5,000–20,000; 20,000–50,000; 50,000–100,000; 100,000–250,000; 250,000–500,000; 500,000–1,000,000; 1,000,000–4,000,000; 4,000,000 or over
Density	Urban, suburban, rural
Climate	Northern, southern
Demographic	
Age	Under 6, 6–11, 12–19, 20–34, 35–49, 50–64, 65+
Sex	Male, female
Family size	1–2, 3–4, 5+
Family life cycle	Young, single; young, married, no children; young, married, youngest child under 6; young, married, youngest child 6 or over; older, married, with children; older, married, no children under 18; older, single; other
Income	Under $10,000; $10,000–$15,000; $15,000–$20,000; $20,000–$30,000; $30,000–$50,000; $50,000 and over
Occupation	Professional and technical; managers, officials, and proprietors; clerical, sales; craftsmen, foremen; operatives; farmers; retired; students; homemakers; unemployed
Education	Grade school or less; some high school; high school graduate; some college; college graduate
Religion	Catholic, Protestant, Jewish, other
Race	White, black, Asian, Hispanic
Nationality	American, British, French, German, Scandinavian, Italian, Latin American, Middle Eastern, Japanese
Psychographic	
Social class	Lower lowers, upper lowers, lower middles, upper middles, lower uppers, upper uppers
Lifestyle	Belongers, achievers, integrateds
Personality	Compulsive, gregarious, authoritarian, ambitious
Behavioristic	
Purchase occasion	Regular occasion, special occasion
Benefits sought	Quality, service, economy
User status	Nonuser, ex-user, potential user, first-time user, regular user
Usage rate	Light user, medium user, heavy user
Loyalty status	None, medium, strong, absolute
Readiness stage	Unaware, aware, informed, interested, desirous, intending to buy
Attitude toward product	Enthusiastic, positive, indifferent, negative, hostile

Source: Philip Kotler and Gary Armstrong, *Principles of Marketing*, 4th ed. (Upper Saddle River, NJ, Prentice Hall, 1989), p. 217.

if the service package offered to each segment is different. When this is not possible, the service must be offered at different times and/or in different facilities so that the incompatible groups do not have to interact.

There are some other very important criteria in selecting target segments. First, the organization has to choose segments that are consistent with its objectives and overall strategy. Second, it must make sure that it has the resources and competencies to serve a particular segment, and that these competencies provide a competitive advantage in that segment.

We must note that it is also possible that an organization may decide to ignore the segment differences and offer one service to all consumers. This approach focuses on what is common in customers' needs rather than on what is different among segments.[18] This is known as *undifferentiated* marketing.

Identifying customer groups that can be served profitably, targeting them, and developing services to serve these segments is not enough for success. An organization has to find a unique **position** in the minds of consumers for itself and/or its services so that it differentiates itself and/or its services from those of its competitors. The discussion in chapter 5 emphasized the importance of differentiation in gaining competitive advantage in the marketplace. Positioning is a very important step in this process and is also a relevant issue in service design and development.

Consumers are bombarded with advertisements, messages, and product (good or service) information daily. When they have to make a purchase decision, however, consumers cannot organize or evaluate such a large volume of information; actually, they may not even remember most of it. What they may do instead is to organize products into categories; in other words, they "position" these products or companies in their minds. "A product's position is a complex set of consumer perceptions, impressions, and feelings consumers hold for the product compared with competing products."[19]

Naturally, marketers do not want to leave this important element of strategy to chance but try to find a unique place for their product in consumers' minds. We must emphasize that positioning is not what marketers do to a good or service, but it is what they do to the mind of the consumer.[20] However, positioning is not tricking customers into believing you are something that you are not. It is finding an effective way to communicate to consumers what an organization stands for and what they can expect from the organization's product.[21] For example, Avis car rental company used the famous slogan "We're number two, so we try harder" to position itself as an underdog against the number one Hertz. Also consider how airlines try to differentiate themselves from competitors. At one time, American Airlines described itself as the "on-time machine" to differentiate itself in terms of on-time arrivals. Delta used the slogan "Delta is ready when you are" for on-time departures, and United used its "Fly the friendly skies of United" slogan to position itself as a friendly airline in the minds of customers.

Positioning can be used for reemphasizing the position of an old product, or to move it to a new position, as well as for new products. Services can be positioned on a large number of possible dimensions. For example, services may be positioned on the five dimensions of service quality (i.e., reliability, responsiveness, assurance, empathy, and tangibles) as well as service evidence (i.e., people, physical evidence, and processes).[22] In making positioning decisions, managers frequently use a graphical tool called a *positioning map* or *perceptual map*, which portrays the relative positions of competing organizations as they are perceived by consumers with respect to two or more attributes. Perceptual maps will be discussed in chapter 8 when service design and development are discussed.

---

[18] Kotler and Armstrong, *Principles of Marketing*, 4th ed., p. 228.

[19] Kotler and Armstrong, *Principles of Marketing*, 4th ed., p. 233.

[20] Al Ries and Jack Trout, *Positioning: The Battle for Your Mind* (New York, McGraw-Hill, 1981), p. 3.

[21] Margaret L. Friedman, "Positioning Strategies for Differential Advantage," in Carole A. Congram and Margaret L. Friedman (eds.), *Handbook of Marketing for the Service Industries* (New York, American Management Association, 1991), pp. 39–53.

[22] Valarie A. Zeithaml and Mary Jo Bitner, *Services Marketing* (New York, McGraw-Hill, 1996), pp. 288–294.

Relationship Marketing: Focus on Customer Retention

At various points throughout this book, the importance of customer satisfaction for the survival and prosperity of an organization has been emphasized. Also, in this chapter, the importance of segmenting the market and then selecting a target market was discussed. The reason this is so important is that an organization cannot be all things to all customers; it has to determine those customers it is capable of serving profitably. Naturally, not all companies are successful in doing this all the time; they sometimes end up trying to serve customers that are not right for them and end up disappointing these customers. The best solution in these cases seems to be to avoid those customers and concentrate on the ones the company can satisfy profitably. This is the best way to survive and prosper in the service business—serve only customers whose needs can be met by the organization's competencies and capabilities, and serve them very well. This section focuses on the importance of keeping these customers for long-term survival and profitability.

There is plenty of research evidence to indicate that a strong relationship exists between customer satisfaction and profitability.[23] However, recent research suggests that although customer satisfaction is necessary, it may not be sufficient for profitability in some service industries. Researchers have found the link between customer loyalty (or retention) and profitability to be very strong. Leading in this area of research are three Harvard professors, Heskett, Sasser, and Schlesinger, who proposed a model that describes a relationship between profitability and a host of relevant factors in a chainlike relationship.[24] Their model is called "the service profit chain," which they describe as "an evolving set of ideas." The model (see Exhibit 6-5) is based on seven propositions:

1. Profit and growth are linked to customer loyalty.
2. Customer loyalty is linked to customer satisfaction.
3. Customer satisfaction is linked to service value.
4. Service value is linked to employee productivity.
5. Employee productivity is linked to loyalty.
6. Employee loyalty is linked to employee satisfaction.
7. Employee satisfaction is linked to internal quality of work life.

The major reason for the new focus on the relationship between customer loyalty and profitability seems to be the fact that customers switch companies even if they are "satisfied."[25] For example, Xerox discovered that the "totally satisfied" customers are six times more likely to buy again from Xerox over the next 18 months than are "satisfied" customers.[26] Similarly, in the auto industry, while 85 to 95 percent of customers

---

[23] For a brief review of research on the issue, see, for example, Roland T. Rust, Anthony J. Zahorik, and Timothy L. Keiningham, "Return on Quality (ROQ): Making Service Quality Financially Accountable," *Journal of Marketing* (April 1995), pp. 58–70; and Claes Fornell, Michael D. Johnson, Eugene W. Anderson, Jaesung Cha, and Barbara E. Bryant, "The American Customer Satisfaction Index: Nature, Purpose, and Findings," *Journal of Marketing*, vol. 60 (October 1996), pp. 7–18.

[24] James L. Heskett, W. Earl Sasser, Jr., and Leonard A. Schlesinger, *The Service Profit Chain* (New York, The Free Press, 1997). Also see James L. Heskett, T. O. Jones, G. W. Loveman, W. Earl Sasser, Jr., and Leonard A. Schlesinger, "Putting the Service-Profit Chain to Work," *Harvard Business Review* (March–April 1994), pp. 164–174.

[25] In most customer satisfaction surveys, respondents are usually given five choices to express their satisfaction with a good or service: extremely dissatisfied, somewhat dissatisfied, neither satisfied nor dissatisfied, satisfied, and totally satisfied.

[26] Thomas O. Jones and W. Earl Sasser, "Why Satisfied Customers Defect," *Harvard Business Review* (November–December 1995), pp. 88–99.

EXHIBIT 6-5   The Service Profit Chain

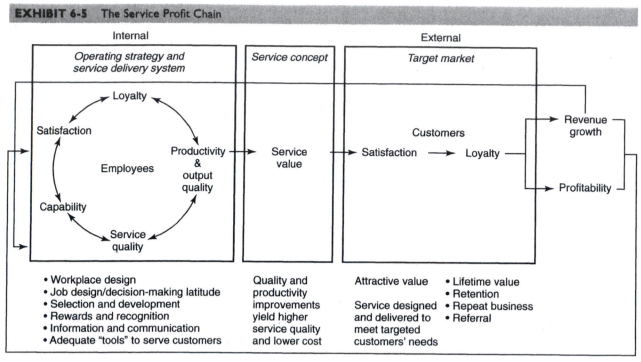

say they are satisfied, repurchase rates average only 40 percent.[27] Consequently, this implies that the relationship between satisfaction and loyalty is not linear. (See Exhibit 6-6.) It should also be emphasized that this relationship depends on the industry. It is strongest in very competitive industries, in which consumers have many choices, and very weak in monopolistic situations, such as local telephone service, in which customers have to stay with the service provider because there is usually no other alternative.

Why is customer retention or "loyalty" so important? First of all, acquiring new customers is usually an expensive process. For example, institutions that issue credit cards are estimated to spend an average of $51 for each new customer.[28] If a service organization can hold on to its customers, it will not have to get too many new customers, and therefore it does not have to spend much for advertising, promotion, and other marketing activities aimed at attracting new customers. Second, most managers would agree that loyal customers are more profitable to serve because they tend to increase their purchase as they stay longer with the firm. They also tend to purchase at full price and provide free advertising for the firm if they are satisfied. Repeat customers are more profitable than new customers because they are less expensive to serve; they do not need training or guidance in the use of services, and they know what they want; hence, loyal customers consume less company time and resources.

---

[27] Frederick F. Reichheld, "Loyalty Based Management," *Harvard Business Review* (March–April 1993), pp. 64–73.

[28] Frederick F. Reichheld and W. Earl Sasser, Jr., "Zero Defections: Quality Comes to Services," *Harvard Business Review* (September–October 1990), pp. 105–111.

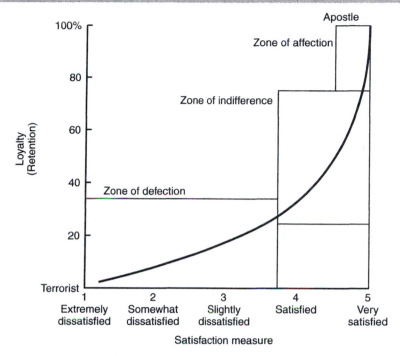

EXHIBIT 6-6   Relationship Between Customer Satisfaction and Loyalty

Source: James L. Heskett, Thomas O. Jones, G. W. Loveman, W. Earl Sasser, Jr., and Leonard A. Schlesinger, "Putting the Service-Profit Chain to Work," *Harvard Business Review* (March–April 1994), pp. 164–174.

When a loyal customer switches to a competitor, the organization loses the future stream of revenues from a very profitable type of customer. Reichheld estimated the increase in customer net present value corresponding to as little as a 5 percent increase in retention rate for various industries.[29] (See Exhibit 6-7.) For example, if an auto service company can hold on to an additional 5 percent of its customers (e.g., increasing its retention rate from 60 to 65 percent), it will enjoy an average of 81 percent increase in the total lifetime profits from a typical customer.

Why Service Customers Switch

Customer switching behavior among manufactured goods is a well-researched phenomenon in business literature. However, switching in services has not yet received the same attention. Consequently, there is little established knowledge on why consumers switch from one service provider to another beyond the obvious reasons of "dissatisfaction" or "price." There are many interesting and important questions that await research for answers to such questions as, "What role do particular events, such as core service failure, supplementary service failures, and the like, play in the decision of a customer to defect?", "How important are each of various possible factors in decisions to switch?", and "What roles do service encounters play in the defection of customers?". Susan M. Keaveney reported results of a critical incident study among more than 500 service consumers to help understand service switching behavior from

---

[29] Frederick F. Reichheld, *The Loyalty Effect* (Boston, Harvard Business School Press, 1996).

EXHIBIT 6-7   Impact of a 5-Percentage-Point Increase in Retention Rate on Customer Net Present Value

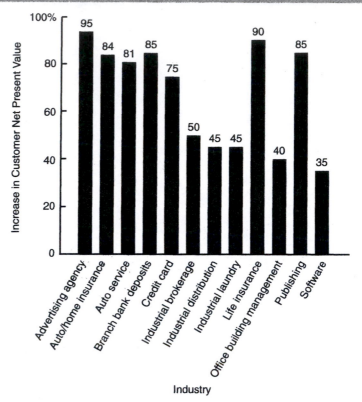

Source: Frederick F. Reichheld, *The Loyalty Effect* (Boston, Harvard Business School Press, 1996), p. 36.

the customer's point of view.[30] Critical incidents are those events between a customer and a service organization that, singly or in combination, caused the customer to switch to another service provider. The survey uncovered more than 800 critical behaviors of service organizations that caused customers to defect. Reasons customers gave for switching service providers have been categorized into eight general categories: pricing, inconvenience, core service failures, service encounter failures, employee responses to service failures, attraction by competitors, ethical problems, and involuntary switching.

6.6   SUMMARY

Marketing aims to establish, maintain, and enhance long-term relationships with customers so that customers receive value and the company makes a profit and prospers in the long term. Segmenting the market to determine groups of customers with similar needs is an important step in this direction. Then the service organization must target the segments it is capable of serving at a profit. This is necessary, because most service organizations cannot service all potential customers and make a profit. Once the

---

[30] Susan M. Keaveney, "Customer Switching Behavior in Service Industries: An Exploratory Study," *Journal of Marketing*, vol. 59 (April 1995), pp. 71–82.

target market is selected, the organization has to position itself and its services in the minds of its current and potential customers.

These steps are essential for creating value and satisfaction for the customers and prosperity for the organization. In achieving these goals, a service organization has to select the right mix of marketing variables for its target market. These variables, also known as the 7 Ps, include product, price, place, physical evidence, participants, promotion, and process. This is an extended version of the traditional marketing mix. Expansion was needed because of the additional challenges created by services. These challenges originate from the differences between goods and services marketing, such as output tangibility; organizational features; ownership, use, and consumption; the scope of marketing activities; and the consumer's role. The presence of customers during service delivery makes most service encounters special events in which marketing, human resources, and operations functions are interested. This necessitates the cooperation and coordination of the activities of these three functions.

Discussion Questions

1. How does the marketing of services differ from the marketing of goods?
2. Why is it especially important that the marketing and operations functions be integrated for services?
3. To what does the "marketing mix" refer? Why is the marketing mix for services larger than the marketing mix for products?
4. Describe the seven elements of marketing mix for services.
5. How do goods and services differ in terms of ownership, use, and consumption?
6. What role does tangibility play in marketing goods and services?
7. Why is "process" included in the marketing mix? What is the justification?
8. What is "physical evidence," and how is it different from "place" in the extended marketing mix?
9. What strategic role does the extended marketing mix play in services?
10. Why is segmentation important for a service organization?
11. Explain the four desirable characteristics of effective segmentation.
12. What is positioning of services, and why is it important?
13. Given that many services have a very large pool of current and potential customers, is it important for a service organization to have loyal customers? Why?
14. What happens when a customer defects to a competitor?
15. What are some of the reasons for customer defections?
16. What is the relationship between customer loyalty and satisfaction? When do the customers defect?
17. What are the implications of the service profit chain for service managers?

CASES

CASE 6–1   The Marketing/Operations Strategy at Federal Express

Fred Smith, owner, operator, and creator of Federal Express, knew that if he were to attract interest from investors and customers for his proposed service, he would need to successfully differentiate his service from the general hauling of air freight. Smith told the business world:

Federal Express is in the transportation, communication, and logistics business.

We're a freight service with 550-mile per hour delivery trucks.

We're an intermodal transportation system using jet cargo planes.

But the business world was skeptical that anyone could successfully combine an airline and a trucking company. And they didn't understand why Federal would transport just small packages.

Smith responded

This company is nothing short of being the logistics arms of a whole new society that is building up in our economy—a society that isn't built around automobile and steel production, but that is built up instead around service industries and high-technology endeavors in electronics and optics and medical science. It is the movement of these support items that Federal Express is all about.

Transporting small packages represents a clear, unambiguous image to the public. We have found our niche in the market. We're not carrying mice and elephants on the same plane like a lot of cargo outfits such as Airborne Freight, Emery Air Freight and Flying Tigers. We carry what a person can lift.

To make his new service a reality, Fred Smith had to support his *marketing vision* with an equally strong *operations vision*. Federal's management knew from their extensive market research that throughout the United States each day there was a quantifiable demand for so many computer parts,

for so many pieces of diagnostic medical equipment, and for so many sets of architectural plans. Of course, the mystery—that is, the source of the demand—was the unknown. The demand was quantifiable, but the distribution random. They borrowed from the telephone company's switching system to come up with its "hub and spokes" concept. All packages and documents would be flown nightly, Monday through Friday, to a central sorting hub before being transshipped to their ultimate destination. As far as the customer was concerned, it really made no difference that his package was not flown in a linear fashion, or directly, from City A to City B. Since the package was an inanimate object which could not complain during its journey between pickup and delivery, the only concern originated with the customer who wanted Federal Express to deliver it to the consignee the next day on time.

The nonlinear system permitted service to a far greater number of points with fewer aircraft. And in addition, the central hub system helped reduce mishandling and delay in transit, because Federal Express kept total control over the packages from the pickup point through delivery. The system also permitted Federal Express the opportunity each night to match aircraft flights with package loads and reroute flights when the load volume required it. This flexibility permitted considerable savings in operating costs.

Smith located the sorting hub at the Memphis International Airport. His radial distribution system was unique, effective, and visionary. He could now describe Federal Express operationally as "a special expedited service where the packages never stop moving with the primary conveyer being the airplane."

A MARKETING PLAN

Vince Fagan was Federal's top marketing executive, and he was a masterful man. In developing a marketing plan, he stressed that the company needed to address the question of a two-tiered market. One market was the traditional distribution sector. These were the shipping departments and the mail rooms and loading docks of business and industry— what the company called the "back door market." The other market was called the "front door market," since it consisted of executive offices or what are sometimes called the "papermills of America." In this front door market were the ad agencies, architectural firms, banks, consultants, law firms, and similar business and financial services.

In the first tier market, or back door business, Federal Express had to compete head-to-head with Emery, Airborne, United Parcel Service, and the whole gamut of air freight forwarders and commercial airlines. The other tier was a nontraditional market, and a market that few people had precisely identified or understood very well. Within this first tier of potential customers were those in the business and professional service industries. At best, those in the second tier may have shipped by air on rare occasions. But Vince Fagan felt these front office groups might constitute a strong customer base if given a sufficient reason to use air express overnight service. His strategy was to get the attention of the people in the mailroom or the shipping departments as well as the secretaries who daily make decisions about what mode of transportation will be used to ship packages and documents and which air express company will be called.

Fagan recognized soon after his arrival in Memphis that the company needed to identify precisely what marketing approach should be taken to build volume quickly. His choice was to use advertising to reach a mass market versus the traditional direct "cold call" approach to reach individual accounts.

He saw little use for a separate sales force and recommended that Federal spend another $1 million on advertising and do away with its salesmen.

This was quite a controversial and risky recommendation, especially when the details of Fagan's plan were revealed. He proposed that heavy emphasis be given to television advertising with secondary support from print media advertising. No one in the air freight industry had ever used TV before—it was a radical plan.

Over the years 1974–1983, Federal's marketing department, in collaboration with the New York advertising agency Ally and Gargano, launched five basic campaigns. Each was well-planned and memorable. (See Exhibit 6-8.)

Federal's media campaign was enormously successful in building business volume. But as one marketing executive said, "You could probably overdo it, if you relied solely on this strategy. The ability to deliver service is really the main determinant of how well you do."

NEW COMPETITION

In 1982, Federal Express faced its toughest competitive challenge—UPS decided to enter the overnight air service market. Smith had always admired UPS because of its financial success and its efficient management. During Federal's startup in 1973, it relied heavily on the technical help of ex-UPS employees. It adopted many of UPS's administrative procedures and selling techniques until Federal had time to devise its own. Privately, it wished that it did not have to meet head-to-head competition from UPS.

EXHIBIT 6-8 Federal's Five Basic Campaigns

Campaign Purpose	Campaign Slogan
Build public awareness	America, You've Got a New Airline. But Don't Get Excited Unless You're a Package. No First Class, No Meals, No Movies. In Fact, No Passengers. Just Packages
Dominate competition (Emery, specifically)	Twice As Good As the Best in the Business
Stress service efficiency	Take Away Our Planes and We'd Be Just Like Everybody Else
Stress dependability of service	Absolutely, Positively Overnight
Reinforce customer recognition of Federal	Various humorous ads, including Dingbat Air Freight, Untouched by Civil Servants, Fast Paced World, and The Paper Blob

Federal's counterattack was based again on differentiating itself from its competitor, but this time differentiation was based on the *quality* of service. Smith sent out this message:

> UPS is the best in the business at what they do—moving low priority, consumer-oriented parcels where emergency is not a factor. But Federal, in turn, is best at what it does—movement of the most vital and time-sensitive parcels and documents. We want to dispel in the minds of the customers the idea that competitors are the equal of us when in fact they are not. We are not going to let competitors equal Federal Express. We will offer 10:30 A.M. delivery, more service options, Saturday pickups, package tracing, and call-backs to shippers informing them that the packages have been delivered.

To support this strategy, operations had to become even more streamlined and efficient. New technology was added. Modern computer technology enabled the company to develop a professional customer-service function located at four interlinked call centers across the country. Electronic "order blanks" on cathode-ray tube (CRT) screens replaced paper records, and a sophisticated information and retrieval system allowed customer service agents (CSAs) to call up data on a regular customer simply by keying in that customer's account number. Since all packages were now computer coded and passed through optical scanners at each stage in the transportation and sorting process, information on package movements could be entered in the central computer and was easily accessible to CSAs for tracing purposes. Problems beyond the capabilities of a CSA to solve were transferred promptly to specialist personnel. ■

SOURCE: Adapted from Robert A. Sigafoos and Roger R. Easson, *Absolutely, Positively Overnight! The Unofficial Corporate History of Federal Express* (Memphis, TN, St. Luke's Press, a division of Plaintree Publishing, Ltd., 1988), chaps. 5, 10, 11, and 12 (reprinted by permission of the publisher); and Christopher H. Lovelock, "Developing and Managing the Customer-Service Function in the Service Sector," in John Czepiel, Michael Solomon, and Carol Surprenant (eds.), *The Service Encounter* (Lexington, MA, Lexington Books, D. C. Heath & Co., 1985), p. 270 (reprinted by permission of the publisher, copyright 1985 D. C. Heath & Co.).

CASE QUESTIONS

1. Summarize in your own words how FedEx integrates its marketing and operations strategies.
2. Which parts of the marketing mix does FedEx use successfully?
3. What aspects of FedEx's marketing plan are unique?
4. What factors differentiate FedEx's operations from its competitors?
5. In your opinion, does the marketing function or operations function play a bigger role in FedEx's success?

CASE 6–2 Fare Combat

An air war has broken out on the Eastern front.

After years of relative insulation from the pitched airline rivalries elsewhere in the U.S., the East Coast is feeling the blitzkrieg of dramatic fare cuts.

While travelers are cheering, this structural shift in the country's largest air-travel market threatens to wreak havoc on high-cost carriers, notably USAir, and could trigger a shakeout among some of the low-cost aspirants making strafing runs in the region.

The battle amounts to much more than a passing fare war. It is a strategic fight between two different kinds of airlines: lean, nimble carriers offering value pricing, and large, full-service "majors" charging higher fares.

And the East Coast, which represents 37% of U.S. air travel and encompasses many of the nation's important business cities, is well worth fighting for. USAir and Delta Air Lines, in particular, are facing a showdown over their historically profitable bread-and-butter business: sales people packing shuttle flights between Boston and Washington, executives flying to Pittsburgh from New York, Northeastern families seeking the sun in Orlando. Low-cost aggressors see the incumbent carriers as vulnerable, but also believe the vast East Coast market will yield more fruit if fares are substantially lowered—and that is exactly what they are doing.

TURF BATTLES

In late January, Continental Airlines announced plans to expand its low-fare "CALite" flights—now operating mostly in the Southeast—up and down the coast, starting next week. To defend its turf, normally somnolent USAir jolted the industry by preemptively slashing ticket prices as much as 70% to many coastal cities—and by making the new fares permanent.

Soon after, Southwest Airlines, a paragon of low-price, no-frills flying, said it planned to beef up its East Coast beach-head in Baltimore, adding six new gates by next fall to its two already there. And America West, another lower-cost carrier, announced it would make its Philadelphia debut in April.

To guard its ground, Delta, one of the slow-moving, high-cost majors, extended indefinitely a program offering low fares in 12 Southeastern cities. Beginning to nip at the edges are as many as 28 start-up carriers that have formed in the past two years, targeting Eastern cities stretching from Boston to Miami.

"The time was ripe for the East Coast high-fare structure to crumble," says Harold Shenton, a vice president of Avmark Inc., an Arlington, Va., consulting firm.

Between 1982 and 1992, fares in the Eastern U.S. more than doubled in short-haul markets, helping drive passenger traffic down 12%, according to a study by ATX Inc., an airline-in-planning headed by former Continental and Eastern airlines chief Frank Lorenzo. By contrast, the Western U.S., populated by expanding low-cost lines such as Southwest, saw a 75% jump in traffic over the decade, with fares rising by only 5%. ATX, which still lacks government permission to fly, has targeted the East because, as Mr. Lorenzo declared last year: "It's so obvious. The public is begging for an alternative product."

Tom Parsons, publisher of *Best Fares* magazine, says, "Nobody has really challenged the East Coast

since PeopleExpress." In the early 1980s, that Newark N.J., carrier bought its way into Eastern markets by charging 30% to 90% less than competitors. (It later failed, a victim of too-rapid expansion and an ill-fated move overseas.)

PASSENGERS BENEFIT

The airlines' battle for the East will be a windfall for long-suffering passengers. And it probably will stir more discretionary flying and lure some travelers from cars and trains. Some aviation consultants think air traffic could jump 50% in some cities.

And why not? Until last month, a round-trip flight from Providence, R.I., to Orlando, Fla., cost $986, while one from Boston to Charlotte, N.C., cost $808. Today, the first costs $458 and the other $598. A round trip between Newark and Greenville/Spartanburg, N.C., priced at $682 before, now is $298 (see Exhibit 6-9). Unlike heavily restricted promotional fares of the past, these are refundable tickets requiring no advance purchase.

But some airline specialists worry that these unrestricted low fares could provoke a financial debacle similar to the disastrous summer of 1992. That was when AMR Corp.'s American Airlines launched a so-called value-pricing program that sparked a 50%-off fare war nationwide. The U.S. airline industry had a $2.5 billion operating loss that year.

USAir's cuts "could be the son of value pricing," warns Robert Harrell, vice-president of American Express Co.'s airfare management division. USAir cut business fares up to 50% and leisure fares up to 70% on roughly a quarter of its routes.

EXHIBIT 6-9 Continental Divide

Fliers on the East Coast face much higher airfares than their counterparts on the West—even after major discounts hit Eastern cities earlier this month.

For flights of	East Coast Fares Run
100–199 miles	103% more
200–299	199%
300–399	42%
400–499	30%
500–599	31%
600–699	8%

Source: American Express Co.'s airfare management division.

Some newcomers, such as Kiwi International Air Lines of Newark and Valujet Airlines of Atlanta, could get hurt despite their lower costs. "Some of the smaller airlines won't survive," predicts Avmark's Mr. Shenton. "As fares decrease, people won't need to go out of their way to get low fares" from the smaller carriers.

FIRST PAINS

But with costs more than 50% higher than Continental's and 60% higher than Southwest's, USAir could be the first major airline to suffer the effects of sharply lower revenue, airline specialists predict. Some of the higher costs are unavoidable for the airline, a unit of USAir Group Inc. of Arlington, Va. Its dense networks in the Northeast and Florida consist mostly of short routes, traditionally more expensive to operate. The Northeast also has higher labor costs, sometimes brutal winters and normally congested airports.

For now, USAir's major cost-cutting drive is its "Project High Ground," a plan begun last month to speed the way it services and turns around planes at airports. Borrowing a page from Southwest, USAir is trying to halve the time its planes spend on the ground. Instead of waiting for all the passengers to leave before cleaning a cabin, for instance, USAir's cleaning crews have begun entering the rear of the plane, picking up behind people as they exit out the front.

USAir expects to turn planes around fast enough to generate at least one more daily departure per plane. In the 18 markets where the project is under way, USAir figures it could sell 3,500 more seats at no extra operating cost.

Industry specialists, however, believe USAir can achieve only limited success with the program. What the airline really needs, they contend, is an overhaul of its entire cost structure, starting with labor. "The kind of flexibility USAir needs isn't in existing labor contracts," says Rose Ann Tortora, an analyst with Donaldson, Lufkin & Jenrette. "If you've got to remodel the house, you need the cooperation of all the residents."

LABOR'S ROLE

USAir had a shot at a major remodeling and blew it. In 1992, it persuaded its unions to make wage concessions. But the airline struck a one-year-only deal and saved $170 million. Wages have since snapped back, and the unions now are sitting atop multiyear, no-furlough guarantees, an obstacle to a company already burdened with headquarters staff in three cities and a fat work force of about 46,000.

USAir acknowledges costs must fall, but says it had to slash its fares quickly. "I can't afford to let the other guy get established here" in the East, says Robert Fornaro, a USAir senior vice president.

For their part, Continental and Southwest merely wish to parlay their lower costs into competitive advantage in USAir's backyard. Despite the severity of the new discounts, Easterners still face comparatively steep ticket prices. On flights of 300 miles or less, East Coast passengers currently are being charged fares that on average are more than double those charged Westerners, says a study by the American Express air-fare group. A 190-mile flight, which averages about $156 round trip out West, currently runs $319 in the East.

The price gap prompted Southwest and Continental to invade USAir's hub at Baltimore/Washington International Airport last fall. The groundwork the two began laying last summer for their separate assaults ultimately forced USAir into its defensive posture.

Baltimore, which offers a preview of what is likely to come, seems an unlikely spot for a first skirmish among the majors. Commanding 55% of the Baltimore airport's daily flights, USAir appeared to have a lock on the mid-Atlantic region, especially with its other hubs in Philadelphia, Pittsburgh and Charlotte.

Baltimore held attractions for the newcomers. Landing fees are lower than at nearby airports, and gate rentals are reasonably priced. Proximity to Washington and southern Pennsylvania makes the city a huge travel market. With low fares to entice them, the masses could easily be funneled into the airport by an efficient interstate-highway system and 30 trains that roll into the airport's rail station daily.

In Baltimore, Southwest's first East Coast destination, the airline employed its time-tested start-up formula. It dispatched the "diamond team"—a half-dozen planners from marketing and sales, promotion, advertising and public relations that handle all new cities.

The team subscribed to the *Baltimore Sun* newspaper and pored over specially prepared demographic data, and quietly fanned out in search of events, sports teams or cultural institutions to sponsor. Southwest quickly signed up the Orioles baseball team for advertising and joint-marketing promotions, including ticket contests. And to ensure that the locals didn't mistake Southwest for some fly-by-night operator, the airline flooded the market with newspaper and TV ads, stressing its young jet fleet and industry-beating profitability.

Then Southwest did what it does best. It offered rock-bottom prices, including introductory one-way fares of $19 to Cleveland. Baltimore responded. In the fourth quarter, passenger boardings at the airport jumped more than 30%, and USAir's market share slipped four percentage points, to 51%. Southwest now says Baltimore is one of its most successful new cities, and it wants to add more flights as soon as it gets the needed planes and its six new gates.

Continental already had eight flights a day from Baltimore, but it targeted the city and others served by USAir for its low-fare CALite operation. Not quite a carbon copy of Southwest, CALite provides assigned seats, offers a first-class cabin and awards frequent-flier miles.

Continental had to retrain its CALite personnel, many of whom were accustomed to the more leisurely pace of non-hub cities. Workers who once had hours to stock galleys and load baggage now have only minutes. In Greensboro, N.C., for example, workers who once handled three flights a day had to gear up for 30.

LIGHTER LOAD

Since emerging from Chapter 11 bankruptcy proceedings with a far lighter debt load last April, Continental has shed money-losing Pacific routes, shrunk its unprofitable Denver hub and beefed up short-haul service. But its boldest move has been CALite, an attempt to exploit its less-restrictive union contracts.

Starting next month, Continental will begin boosting CALite flights to more than 800 a day from 300. By year's end, CALite service will account for nearly two-thirds of Continental's flights. Though some analysts wonder if Continental is expanding CALite too quickly, others are enthusiastic. "There's no reason why Continental Airlines shouldn't be one of the profitable U.S. carriers," says Sam Buttrick, a Kidder, Peabody & Co. analyst. So far, Continental's approach hasn't translated into profits, but the carrier expects it will by year end.

Southwest, the only consistently profitable airline flying short routes, remains the model. And it doesn't like this wave of emulation, however flattering. Speaking before financial analysts this month, Southwest Chairman Herbert Kelleher warned Continental and USAir that he would retaliate in their long-haul markets if they "plan on coming into our niche in a way that irritates us."

And just what would constitute provocation? "Basically," he said, "it's when we get very, very angry." ∎

SOURCE: Case prepared by Michael J. McCarthy and Bridget O'Brian. "Fare Combat. Lean, Nimble Airlines Head East, Targeting Region's Plump Prices," *Wall Street Journal*, February 28, 1994. Reprinted by permission of the *Wall Street Journal*, © 1994 by Dow Jones & Company, Inc. All rights reserved worldwide. As seen in C. H. Lovelock, *Services Marketing*, 3rd ed. (Upper Saddle River, NJ, Prentice Hall, 1996), pp. 442–445.

CASE QUESTIONS

1. Who are the key players and how are they positioned?
2. How serious is the threat to USAir?
3. How likely are Southwest and CALite to be successful?
4. What marketing strategy should USAir adopt for the future?
5. As a USAir marketing strategist, what other information would you like to have?

References

Berry, Leonard, "Relationship Marketing," in *Proceedings of the 1983 Conference on Services Marketing* (Chicago, American Marketing Association, 1983), pp. 25–28.

Bitner, Mary Jo, and Valarie A. Zeithaml, "Fundamentals in Services Marketing," in *Proceedings of the 1988 Conference on Services Marketing* (Chicago, American Marketing Association, 1989), pp. 7–11.

Boddewyn, J. J., Marsha Baldwin Halbrich, and A. C. Perry, "Service Multinationals: Conceptualization, Measurement, and Theory," *Journal of International Business Studies* (fall 1986).

Booms, B. H., and Mary Jo Bitner, "Marketing Strategies and Organization Structures for Service Firms," in J. H. Donnelly and W. R. George (eds.), *Marketing of Services* (Chicago, American Marketing Association, 1981).

Booms, B. H., and Mary Jo Bitner, "Marketing Strategies and Organization Structures for Service Firms," in *Marketing of Services*, Proceedings of the 1981 Conference in Services Marketing (Chicago, American Marketing Association, 1983), pp. 47–52.

Fornell, Claes, Michael D. Johnson, Eugene W. Anderson, Jaesung Cha, and Barbara E. Bryant, "The American Customer Satisfaction Index: Nature, Purpose, and Findings," *Journal of Marketing*, vol. 60 (October 1996), pp. 7–18.

Friedman, Margaret L., "Positioning Strategies for Differential Advantage," in Carole A. Congram and Margaret L. Friedman (eds.), *Handbook of Marketing for the Service Industries* (New York, American Management Association, 1991), pp. 39–53.

Grönroos, Christian, "Innovative Marketing Strategies and Organization Structures for Service Firms," in *Emerging Perspectives on Services Marketing*, Proceedings of the 1983 Conference on Services Marketing (Chicago, American Marketing Association, 1983).

Grönroos, Christian, *Service Management and Marketing* (Lexington, MA, Lexington Books, 1990).

Heskett, James L., *Managing in the Service Economy* (Boston, Harvard Business School Press, 1986).

Heskett, James L., W. Earl Sasser, Jr., and Leonard A. Schlesinger, *The Service Profit Chain* (New York, The Free Press, 1997).

Heskett, James L., Thomas O. Jones, G. W. Loveman, W. Earl Sasser, Jr., and Leonard. A. Schlesinger, "Putting the Service-Profit Chain to Work," *Harvard Business Review* (March–April 1994), pp. 164–174.

Jones, Thomas O., and W. Earl Sasser, Jr., "Why Satisfied Customers Defect," *Harvard Business Review* (November–December 1995), pp. 88–99.

Keaveney, Susan M., "Customer Switching Behavior in Service Industries: An Exploratory Study," *Journal of Marketing*, vol. 59 (April 1995), pp. 71–82.

Kotler, Philip, and Gary Armstrong, *Principles of Marketing*, 4th ed. (Upper Saddle River, NJ, Prentice Hall, 1989).

Levitt, Theodore, "After the Sale Is Over," *Harvard Business Review*, vol. 62, no. 5 (September–October 1983), pp. 87–93.

Lovelock, Christopher H., *Managing Services: Marketing, Operations and Human Resources*, 2nd ed. (Upper Saddle River, NJ, Prentice Hall, 1992).

Lovelock, Christopher H., *Services Marketing*, 3rd ed. (Upper Saddle River, NJ, Prentice Hall, 1996).

Regan, W. J., "The Service Revolution," *Journal of Marketing*, vol. 27 (July 1963), pp. 57–62.

Reichheld, Frederick F., and W. Earl Sasser, Jr., "Zero Defections: Quality Comes to Services," *Harvard Business Review* (September–October 1990), pp. 105–111.

Reichheld, Frederick F., "Loyalty Based Management," *Harvard Business Review* (March–April 1993), pp. 64–73.

Reichheld, Frederick F., *Loyalty Effect* (Boston, Harvard Business School Press, 1996).

Ries, Al, and Jack Trout, *Positioning: The Battle for Your Mind* (New York, McGraw-Hill, 1981).

Rust, Roland T., Anthony J. Zahorik, and Timothy L. Keiningham, "Return on Quality (ROQ): Making Service Quality Financially Accountable," *Journal of Marketing* (April 1995), pp. 58–70.

Shostack, G. Lynn, "Breaking Free From Product Marketing," *Journal of Marketing* (April 1977), pp. 73–80.

Sigafoos, R. A., and R. R. Easson, *Absolutely, Positively Overnight!* (Memphis, TN, St. Luke's Press, 1988).

Zeithaml, V. A., "How Consumer Evaluation Processes Differ Between Goods and Services," in *Marketing of Services*, Proceedings of the 1981 Conference on Services Marketing (Chicago, American Marketing Association, 1981), pp. 186–190.

Zeithaml, Valarie A., and Mary Jo Bitner, *Services Marketing* (New York, McGraw-Hill, 1996).

CHAPTER 7

Technology and Its Impact on Services and Their Management

7.1   INTRODUCTION

Every day we watch on TV and read in our newspapers news about advances in technology such as the following:

- Artificial organs
- Cloning
- Optical fibers
- Distance learning
- Smart cards
- Compact discs
- Automated language translation
- Digital, wireless communications
- Space travel
- Telecommuting
- Genetic engineering

Technology is the practical application of science to any human endeavor. Technology includes the resources and knowledge needed to achieve an objective.[1] Hence, when early humans used flint to make fire, or bows and arrows to kill animals for food, they were using technology. We use the word *technology* in this broadest sense. Clearly,

---

[1] Gerard H. Gaynor, "Management of Technology: Description, Scope, and Implications," in G. H. Gaynor (ed.), *Handbook of Technology Management* (New York, McGraw-Hill, 1996), pp. 1.3–1.17.

we try to achieve many objectives through our activities and try to solve numerous problems, such as space exploration, producing goods and services for our needs, protecting the environment, finding cures for diseases, generating energy economically, and communicating with others, to name just a few. When science is used for such purposes, a technology is created for that area of human activity, such as space technology, manufacturing technology, environmental technology, medical technology, and communications technology. Naturally, all these technologies influence our lives and organizations that produce goods and services. However, information technology is probably the technology that has the greatest impact on how services are created and delivered. Therefore, this chapter is devoted to a discussion of information technology and its impact on services and their management. This chapter also focuses on how technology can be turned into a competitive weapon for service organizations.

7.2 PROCESS TECHNOLOGY AND INFORMATION TECHNOLOGY

A **process** is any purposeful activity or group of activities that result in an outcome. A process requires input such as human intelligence, information, machines, and materials, and may produce a physical output or service. In manufacturing, many different technologies are used, such as computer-aided design (CAD) to design goods and chemical, electrical, metallurgical, or mechanical technologies to produce them. Batch, continuous, or mass production technologies are used, depending on the goods being produced or the quantity needed. Processes are also essential for the creation and delivery of services. As a matter of fact, any service is the result of a process. Service processes, however, cannot be easily classified or labeled as is done in manufacturing. Service processes are numerous and varied. The types of activities and inputs required for service processes depend on the service. For example, surgeons operating on a patient in a hospital use information about the patient and medical technology, and follow well-established medical procedures. An investment banker uses financial information and information technology, and follows the established principles of her profession, as well as the applicable laws. Clearly, these two groups of professionals use very different process technologies; however, they both rely on information technology.

Information technology (IT) consists of computer and telecommunications technologies. **Computer technology** is based on hardware and software and is essential for storing and processing data and information. **Telecommunications technology** consists of both equipment and software and is needed for transmitting data and information.

7.3 TECHNOLOGY IN SERVICES

The stereotype of a service firm is a small-scale, labor-intensive establishment with unsophisticated processes that require little or no investment in technology. This dated view of services is not supported by evidence; there have been significant investments in IT since the early 1980s. For example, it is estimated that the health care industry alone spent $15 billion on information technology in 1997. This sum is expected to nearly double by the year 2001.[2] It is also estimated that about 85 percent of all investments in IT hardware are in services. It is interesting to note that, although investments in capital and technology usually lead to higher productivity in manufacturing,[3] no linkage has been found between investments in IT in services and higher

---

[2] Erick Schonfeld, "Can Computers Cure Health Care?" *Fortune* (March 30, 1998), pp. 111–116.

[3] Productivity is simply defined as the output divided by inputs that are used to create the output. In chapter 13, service productivity will be discussed in more detail.

productivity or profitability. The slow growth in service productivity despite the significant investments in IT is known as the "information technology paradox."[4] A recent report by a committee of National Academy of Sciences offers several possible explanations for this so-called paradox[5]:

1. *Wasteful and inefficient use of IT.* Although IT provides very powerful tools for service workers at all levels, there is no assurance that these tools are used competently or correctly. In many cases, IT had been used to automate inefficient systems or processes without streamlining the system first.
2. *Impact of other problems.* It may be that IT has increased productivity in services, but other problems caused a slowdown in productivity growth, since IT is only one of the factors that affect productivity.
3. *Outdated methods of productivity measurement.* A third possibility is that IT did have a positive impact on service productivity but these improvements have been missed by current methods of measurement. For example, existing data on productivity do not capture important elements of service quality.
4. *Lagged effect.* It is possible that IT does have a positive effect on service productivity but it takes time for the results to emerge.
5. *Level of aggregation.* Finally, a fifth possible explanation is that we should look at the impact of IT expenditures on service productivity at lower levels (i.e., firm level) of aggregation rather than macro levels.

Paul A. Strassmann, former chief information officer of Xerox, summarized the result of his many years of research on the issue as follows: "The lack of correlation of information technology spending with financial results has led me to conclude that it is not computers that make the difference, but what people do with them. . . . The problem seems to rest not with the inherent capabilities of the technologies, which are awesome, but with the managerial inability to use them effectively."[6] Peter F. Drucker, probably the most influential management thinker of our time, reaches the same conclusion by looking at the issue from a different perspective: ". . . capital cannot be substituted for labor (i.e., for people) in knowledge and service work. Nor does new technology by itself generate higher productivity in such work. In making and moving things, capital and technology are *factors of production*, to use the economist's term. In knowledge and service work, they are *tools of production*. Whether they help productivity or harm it depends on what people do with them, on the purpose to which they are being put, for instance, or on the skill of the user."[7]

7.4   WHY SERVICE COMPANIES INVEST IN TECHNOLOGY

It is safe to say that all service industries use some technology. However, the level of sophistication of the technology and the degree of utilization varies across industries. This is largely due to the nature of the business. Some organizations, such as tele-

---

[4] There have been several publications confirming this phenomenon. See, for example, Gregory P. Hackett, "Investment in Technology—The Service Sector Sinkhole?," *Sloan Management Review* (winter 1990), pp. 97–103; Stephen S. Roach, "Services Under Siege—The Restructuring Imperative," *Harvard Business Review* (September–October 1991), pp. 82–91; and Paul A. Strassmann, "Will Big Spending on Computers Guarantee Profitability?" *Datamation* (February 1997), pp. 75–85.

[5] Committee to Study the Impact of Information Technology on the Performance of Service Activities, *Information Technology in the Service Society* (Washington, DC, National Academy Press, 1994), pp. 27–29.

[6] Paul A. Strassmann, "Will Big Spending on Computers Guarantee Profitability?"

[7] Peter F. Drucker, *Managing for the Future: The 1990s and Beyond* (New York, Truman Talley Books/Dutton, 1992), pp. 95–96.

phone companies, software developers, and Internet service providers, are in the business of developing IT. Some others, however, invest in technology for other reasons, mainly to stay competitive. Banks, for example, are among the biggest spenders, not only of the service sector, but also of corporate America. According to Denis O'Leary, the chief information officer and an executive vice-president of Chase Manhattan Bank, "In the Seventies credit was a central competency in banking, the dominant source of new revenues. In the Eighties and early Nineties it was capital markets and then consumer banking. From the mid-1990s going forward it is clear that technology and information management are becoming not only a central competency of successful banks but of any kind of business."[8]

In Section 7.6, applications of technology in services are reviewed, but first the major reasons why many service organizations invest in technology and rely on it are reviewed. These are identified by a Committee of the National Academy of Sciences from the many interviews they conducted with service industry executives.[9]

1. *Preserving or expanding market share.* Although it may sometimes be an inappropriate and misleading indicator, market share is used as a key measure of performance by some companies. Market share may also be used as a basis for obtaining marketing power and favorable terms from suppliers as well as improved economies of scale or scope. Some service companies may feel compelled to invest heavily into technology to maintain their share, even though it does not necessarily increase their output or profitability.

2. *Avoiding risks or alternative costs.* Some organizations invest in technology to reduce or avoid risks. For example, hospitals may invest in the state-of-the-art technology to avoid malpractice suits in addition to the benefits from improved diagnostic and treatment capabilities provided by the new technology. Airports are installing explosives detection devices against terrorist attacks. Similarly, many airports are installing advanced radar systems to detect wind shear, which has been blamed for many airline accidents at or in the vicinity of airports.

3. *Creating flexibility for changing business environment.* A constant in today's business world seems to be change. Changes in government regulations (increases as well as deregulations), increased competition, complexity of operations, and changing consumer tastes, all contribute to the uncertainty and complexity of the environment in which service organizations operate. Flexible IT systems often help service organizations cope with the rapidly changing environment.

4. *Improving the internal environment.* Many organizations invest in technology to make their employees' jobs easier and create a happier work environment by eliminating tedious tasks and making jobs more interesting. Also, the use of IT improves data collection and processing, as well as forecasting abilities of the organization, thereby providing greater stability to the organization's operations.

5. *Improving the quality of services and interactions with customers.* Quality and customer satisfaction are clearly the focus of many service organizations today. Some of the elements of customer satisfaction and quality service are reliability, consistency, accuracy, and speed of service. When used competently and efficiently, IT can help a service organization deliver all these elements for long-term customer loyalty. Investments in technology also enhance the positive perception of both customers and employees about the organization and its services.

---

[8] Matthew Schifrin, "The New Enablers—Chief Information Officers," *Forbes* (June 2, 1997), p. 142.

[9] *Information Technology in the Service Society*, pp. 12–13.

7.5   TECHNOLOGY AS A COMPETITIVE EDGE

Despite the discouraging lack of a universal positive relationship between IT investments and profitability or productivity, there is no denying that technology has made and continues to make a huge impact on our daily lives through many goods and services. Think about the many conveniences of modern life, such as television, video cassette recorders (VCRs), fax machines, cellular phones, voice mail, e-mail, automated teller machines (ATMs), the World Wide Web on the Internet, air travel, and modern medicine, to name a few; they are all outcomes of technological progress. Consequently, even if IT is no guarantee for profits, it is clear that it has provided many benefits to millions of consumers. On the other hand, there are many organizations that made big investments in IT and achieved huge success. This section discusses how service companies can use technology as a competitive edge and become very profitable.

By being the first to use new technology, as well as using it competently, a service organization may gain an important edge over its competitors. *Competitive edge* is what distinguishes an organization from its competitors. It is an asymmetry that appeals to prospective buyers of a service. A competitive edge may be the speed of service, increased scope of the service package, lower price for the same quality, or better "fit" to the customer, and technology may help an organization achieve these objectives.

Information technology can help a service organization differentiate its service offerings from competing services. For example, customers of FedEx can prepare their own shipping documents by filling out electronic forms and request pickup at its Web site. Later, they can check the status of their shipment through FedEx's Web page.[10] United Parcel Service (UPS) has a similar system. These service organizations differentiate their services from competitors' with the aid of IT.

Advances in IT may also lead to new business practices that were not possible earlier. A case in point is the strategic **alliances** among many large service organizations. These alliances may be between organizations within the same industry or between organizations in different industries. An example of the first kind is the alliances between airlines that have become commonplace in the airline industry. Northwest Airlines and Continental, Continental and America West, Northwest and KLM Royal Dutch Airlines, American and US Airways,[11] and the Star Alliance of United, Air Canada, Lufthansa, SAS, and Thai airlines are some examples. Alliances between airlines usually involve establishing systems for code sharing. Code sharing involves linking flight schedules and helps airlines channel passengers to each other by selling tickets on each others' flights. Code sharing helps airlines expand their networks to other parts of the country, or the world, without making any new investments in new planes or routes. This type of alliance also provides benefits to airline passengers in the form of easy connections, baggage transfers, and frequent flier miles that they can use on any airline in the alliance. There is also evidence, however, that some alliances may reduce the number of choices for passengers and lead to higher prices.[12]

Alliances may also be formed between organizations in different service industries. For example, Citibank and American Airlines, and Northwest Airlines and First Bank of Minneapolis have established an **information partnership.** American Airlines

---

[10] Thomas Hoffmann and Kim S. Nash, "Couriers Deliver New Net Services," *Computerworld* (January 6, 1997), p. 2.

[11] Susan Carey, "Airline Marketing Linkups Draw Opposition," *Wall Street Journal* (April 27, 1998).

[12] Scott McCartney, "Airline Alliances Take Toll on Travelers," *Wall Street Journal* (February 18, 1998).

awards one mile in its frequent flier program for every dollar spent using the Citibank credit cards. American and Northwest also have alliances with MCI; for every dollar of long-distance billing, airlines award one frequent flier mile to an MCI customer.[13]

In the case of alliances between airlines, a sophisticated computer reservation system is essential for the partnership, and in the airline–bank alliance, linking of computer information systems makes the partnership possible.

Companies today aggressively seek competitive advantage by monitoring new technical advances or conducting applied research themselves. Professor Leonard L. Berry provides the following guidelines to increase the chances of achieving competitiveness through technology[14]:

1. *Take a holistic approach.* Technology is not an end in itself—it should serve as a tool to help the service organization achieve its goals and objectives. In other words, the use of technology should support the overall strategy of the organization. This requires a clear vision of the destination the organization is trying to reach, as well as its strengths and weaknesses and its competencies. Top managers of the organization must be involved in the formulation of a technology strategy to make sure that it supports the organizational strategy and monitor its implementation. "Management must tell the technologists what the technology must do; management, not the technologists, must be in charge of the technology strategy."

2. *Automate efficient systems.* Technology does not make an inefficient service process or system efficient. As many organizations have learned from unsuccessful implementations of technology, automating an outdated, inefficient system does not increase output or profits significantly. Before making any investment in technology, an organization should study the existing service system and its processes for tasks and practices that do not add value for customers, create needless delays, or make employees' jobs unnecessarily difficult and boring. Special attention must be paid to processes that cross traditional organizational or departmental boundaries, or processes that involve many handoffs. Systems and/or processes with such undesirable characteristics must be redesigned with customer and employee satisfaction in mind, and if possible, with their input, before an advanced technology is introduced.

3. *Solve a genuine problem.* To be effective, technology should be used to solve a real problem of customers, internal or external. This requires identification of customers, finding out their needs, and obtaining their input to decisions concerning the choice of technology and system design. "Investing in technology strictly to lower operating costs rarely produces optimum results. Users need to benefit, not just the investors. The technology should help service providers perform more effectively, with more authority, confidence, creativity, quickness, and/or knowledge. Or the technology should offer external customers more convenience, increased reliability, greater control, lower prices, or some other value adding property."

4. *Offer more—not less—control.* The basic reason why technology is developed in the first place is to improve the benefits of the existing technology or create new benefits for users. One of the greatest benefits technology can provide to service employees and their customers is to give them more choices and more control.

[13] Kenneth C. Laudon and Jane P. Laudon, *Management Information Systems*, 5th ed. (Upper Saddle River, NJ, Prentice Hall, 1998), p. 62.

[14] Leonard L. Berry, *On Great Service: A Framework for Action* (New York, The Free Press, 1996), pp. 147–155.

Customers should have more choices so that they can choose freely what they need. Service employees should have more authority and control over their actions so that they can serve their customers better, or act quickly to solve problems. In short, technology should empower service providers and their customers.

5. *Optimize basic technologies.* Every service system or process, regardless of the level of sophistication of its technology, may have some low-tech components. Failure or inefficiencies in these low-tech components may significantly reduce the ability of the organization to service its customers. Consequently, great attention must be paid to components of the system that are basic to the creation and delivery of the service; they must be the first to get the benefit of advanced technology. Even after the installation of advanced technology, there may remain low-tech components. Implementers of technology must make sure that high- and low-tech components are compatible and are well integrated into producing results for the customers. The following quote illustrates a failure in this integration:

> Consider my experience while checking out of a hotel. The receptionist quickly computed my bill on the monitor in front of her, transformed it into a paper copy on the adjacent printer, and asked me to sign the credit card slip; but then she walked off, papers in hand, to the far end of the long reception desk. There she remained several minutes, standing beside a couple of her colleagues. I began to fear that something horrible had happened to my credit line. Other customers behind me muttered restlessly. Finally the receptionist returned. "You're all set!" she said. "What was the problem?" I asked. She gave me a tired smile. "Oh, we've only got one stapler on the desk, so I had to wait my turn to staple your bill and credit card slip together." For want of a low-tech, $3 stapler, was lost a sizable chunk of the potential gains in employee productivity and customer satisfaction to be derived from a computer system that probably cost ten thousand times as much! (Of course, assuming that a paper receipt is needed in the first place, a better solution would be to integrate bill and card receipt into a single document.)[15]

6. *Combine high tech with high touch.* When used competently and efficiently, technology will increase the speed of service when it is desirable, and improve accuracy and consistency of outcomes. However, some customers are technology averse; they prefer to deal with humans rather than machines and computers, even if machines provide some advantages. Also, some customers may feel that the service is rather impersonal when they have to subject themselves to tests or go through processes involving machines. Technology may be seen as the culprit in these situations, but it can also be a very powerful tool when the organization, or service providers, manage to add human touch to the high-tech environment. Technology may create extra time for service providers to pay personal attention to customers by reducing the service time and/or performing tedious tasks for them.

7.6   APPLICATION AREAS OF TECHNOLOGY IN SERVICES

Technology applications in service industries are plentiful, as shown in Exhibit 7-1. For example, in banking, which is just one part of financial services, such technologies as electronic funds transfer (EFT), electronic imaging, ATMs, and magnetic ink character

---

[15] Christopher H. Lovelock, *Product Plus—How Product + Service = Competitive Advantage* (New York, McGraw-Hill, 1994), p. 181.

EXHIBIT 7-1 Examples of Technology Use in Services

Service Industry	Example
Financial services	Debit cards, electronic funds transfer, automated teller machines, electronic imaging, magnetic ink character recognition
Education	Multimedia presentations, electronic bulletin boards, library cataloging systems, Internet
Utilities and government	Automated one-man garbage trucks, optical mail scanners, airborne warning and control systems
Restaurant and foods	Optical checkout scanners, wireless orders from waiters to the kitchen, robot butchering
Communications	Electronic publishing, interactive TV, voice mail, "notepad" computers, cellular phones
Hotels	Electronic check-in and checkout systems, electronic key/lock systems
Wholesale/retail trade	Point-of-sale electronic terminals, electronic communication between store and supplier, bar-coded data, automated security systems
Transportation	Automatic toll booths, satellite-directed navigation systems
Health care	Magnetic resonance imaging scanners, sonograms, patient-monitoring systems, online medical information systems
Airlines	Ticketless travel, computer scheduling, computer reservation systems

recognition (MICR) readers for encoding checks are widely used to increase productivity. Similar advances in technology are evident in other services. In health care services, technologies such as computed tomography scanners and fetal monitors are diagnostic in nature, while technologies such as pacemakers and dialysis machines aid in managing existing illnesses. Unlike most other services, advancements in health care have concentrated on improving the quality of care rather than on reducing its cost.

Technology may create a competitive edge by *improving* an existing service process. Such improvements may be in the form of speed, offering more choices to customers, or increased quality. **Office automation,** for example, helps office workers become more efficient and effective by integrating IT into their processes. Word processing software increases efficiency in document preparation by reducing the time needed to type, revise, check spelling, and print. Similarly, spreadsheets help reduce the time needed to gather, analyze, and manipulate large amounts of numerical data for decision making.

Technology may also change the entire process through *substitution*. In the first case, examples are wide-screen movie theaters, fiber optics to transmit information, or desktop publishing services. Examples of substitution include electronic mail as a substitute for hard-copy mail, television as a substitute for radio, air travel as a replacement for train travel, teleconferencing to air travel or in-person meetings, automated car washing as a substitute for hand washing, and computer-programmed stock trading as a substitute for judgmental trading.

Technology may be applied for four different purposes in the service business:

- Processing the customer
- Processing the customer's possessions
- Processing information
- Creating new services

Processing the Customer

Processing the customer is typical of personal services such as health care, cosmetics, transportation, education, and entertainment. It is one of the growing challenges in services. Several factors contribute to this problem. One factor is that customers are becoming less tolerant to waiting in service systems. Another is the high cost of staffing service outlets to meet peak demand. Consequently, service organizations sometimes reduce staffing levels to lower their costs. A third factor is the nonuniform demand for service during the day. The problem seems to be particularly acute at airports. A recent *Wall Street Journal* article described the situation as follows: "These days, getting from the curbside to gate can take nearly as long as the flight itself, with long waits to check bags and obtain boarding passes."[16]

Alaska Airlines is trying a range of high-tech innovations to process passengers through airports to their planes. The essence of the approach is to process passengers through different channels if they do not have any problems that need to be solved at the check-in counter. For example, passengers who purchased their tickets electronically on the Internet can go to a computer kiosk at the airport for self check-in, which takes about one minute. Some kiosks also issue bar-coded baggage tags. Another innovation the airline has implemented is roving customer-service agents with a hand-held computer and a tiny printer attached to their belts; they check in passengers on the spot and issue boarding passes.[17] These innovations help Alaska Airlines reduce lines and waiting at its check-in counters and save time for customers, and are all made possible by advanced information technology.

Computers seem to follow us from cradle to grave. Consider, for example, how John McDonough, a funeral director in Lowell, Massachusetts, uses technology in arranging funerals. "Doing a funeral is like putting together a puzzle with tons of pieces," says McDonough.

> The pieces start coming together during a bereaved family's first visit. Having wired the entire house so that he can hook up a computer almost anywhere, McDonough sits with his Macintosh PowerBook, guiding customers through 50 to 100 questions, ranging from the deceased's date of birth to what clubs he or she belonged to. As he types in the information, his assistant, Paula Clark, sits in an office, watching the answers appear in real time on *her* Macintosh screen.
>
> Clark begins creating a standard obituary, pulling in the specifics as her boss enters them. When it is finished, she sends it via modem to the local newspaper, the *Lowell Sun*. At the same time, the system is automatically importing the information into various required forms residing in a FileMaker Pro 3.0 database. As a result, "every necessary form—from social security to veterans benefits—has been filled out and is waiting to print seconds after the meeting," says McDonough.
>
> When he's done collecting personal information, McDonough moves on to the funeral arrangements. He types in the family's preferred time and location, and notes that they want "Amazing Grace" played as mourners file into the service and "Danny Boy" played as they file out. While he is still talking with the family, Clark is on the phone with the church, setting everything up.[18]

---

[16] Susan Carey, "New Gizmos May Zip Travelers through Airport Lines," *Wall Street Journal* (January 4, 1999).

[17] Susan Carey, op. cit.

[18] Sarah Schafer, "Mourning Becomes Electric," *Inc.* (September 16, 1997), pp. 65–71.

Processing the Customer's Possessions

The second area on our list of technology applications involves processing a customer's equipment or materials. A prominent example of new technology applied to the processing of a customer's possession is the COSMOS (Customer, Operations, Service, Master On-line System) of Federal Express.[19] This is a worldwide information system network transmitting information about the customer's letters or packages to a central database in Memphis, Tennessee. Every package shipped by FedEx has a 10-digit bar code. When a courier picks up a package, he scans this number with his hand-held computer (Supertracker) and enters the destination zip code and the type of service. In his van, the courier fits the computer into a port in the dispatch computer, which then transmits the data to Memphis. When packages arrive in Memphis, or one of the regional hubs, they are sorted and loaded on planes for their final destination and are scanned again by a Supertracker. When another courier delivers the package at the destination city, she scans the bar code one last time and enters the location of the delivery and recipient information, which is then transmitted to the COSMOS system in Memphis. This system enables customers to track, via the Internet or FedEx software, where their packages are at any point in the cycle.

A second component of FedEx's information system is the digital dispatch system, which communicates with 30,000 couriers through interactive screens in their vans. This helps them respond to pickup and delivery requests quickly. FedEx also installs PowerShip computer systems in its customers' offices; by the end of 1994, more than 50,000 PowerShip systems were in place.[20] This system consists of an electronic scale, a computer terminal, bar-code scanner, and a printer. The PowerShip system enables FedEx customers to print labels for their packages, download transactions to FedEx, manage accounts receivable, and track packages through COSMOS.

Processing Information

The third area in which technology may be applied to improving services is data and information processing. This topic is so important that it will be discussed in more detail later in the chapter. Basically, information comes into a firm, is edited, and is converted to a standard form. Multiple copies are prepared and distributed to different work sequences where operations are performed. The copies finally end up in files, are sent to some outside agency such as a customer or vendor, or are destroyed. Some opportunities for increasing the level of technology are electronic data interchange (EDI), computer-to-copier reproduction, and the automatic generation of orders as electronically monitored needs are detected. Consider the following example.

One of the most successful organizations in the use of technology is United Services Automobile Association (USAA), a mutual insurance company providing auto and home insurance to its members who are active or retired military officers.[21] CEO Robert F. McDermott, now retired, took over the company in 1968 and made it one of the most successful in the insurance business. USAA went from a $200 million com-

[19] Information on FedEx COSMOS and Powership, unless otherwise indicated, is based on Halsey M. Cook, "Federal Express—The Cost of Poor Quality," Darden Graduate Business School Case, 1992. Revised March 1994.

[20] Robert Frank, "Federal Express Grapples with Changes in U.S. Market," *Wall Street Journal* (July 5, 1994).

[21] Information on USAA, unless otherwise indicated, is based on Thomas Teal, "Service Comes First: An Interview with USAA's Robert F. McDermott," *Harvard Business Review* (September–October 1991), pp. 117–127.

pany with 650,000 members to $20.7 billion in assets and 2 million customers and policyholders. McDermott had made four important decisions and implemented them: (1) automate the insurance policy-writing system; (2) reduce the work force by attrition; (3) implement an education and training program; and (4) decentralize decision making. In short, USAA "empowered" its employees through IT (by providing them all the data and information they need to serve customers), education and training (by giving them the necessary knowledge), and decentralized decision making (by giving them the authority to make decisions and solve customers' problem). To accomplish these, USAA invested heavily in technology, and education and training; in the mid-1990s, it was investing 7 percent of its revenues in technology and 3 percent in education and training.[22] McDermott explains the results as follows:

> Now when you want to buy a new car, get it insured, add a driver, and change your coverage and address, you can make one phone call—average time, five minutes—and nothing else is necessary. One-stop, on-line, the policy goes out the door the next morning about 4 A.M. In one five-minute phone call, you and our service representative have done all the work that used to take 55 steps, umpteen people, two weeks, and a lot of money.[23]

USAA also uses electronic imaging for storing and processing all of its documents. **Document imaging systems** convert documents and images into digital form and store them in a computer data environment. USAA receives more than 150,000 pieces of mail every day, 60 to 65 percent of which are checks. Most of the rest of the documents do not even leave the mailroom; they are scanned and stored on optical disks, and they instantly become available for any service representative of the company. Chase Manhattan Bank uses electronic imaging for its check-clearing operations; checks are scanned and stored as electronic images. This reduces the handling of checks from 12 to 6 "touches" by employees and saves both time and money; manual processing of paper checks costs 10.5 cents per check, whereas electronic processing of check images costs 5.7 cents.[24]

Creating New Services

Finally, technology may create completely new services through development of new products or processes. The development of television created the services of television programming and broadcasting and, later, cable TV. The invention of VCRs brought with it the era of video rental stores. Knowledge and information are the essence of many new services. For example, software, computer games, information services such as Dow Jones News Service (business/financial), Lexis (legal), America Online, Compuserve, and Prodigy (general interest/business) are all products of advancements in information technology. And think of all the services and benefits created by the introduction of the World Wide Web on the Internet! People can obtain practically anything on the Web: a new or used car, a car loan, mortgage loan, a home, groceries, or even look for a college. They can read newspapers and magazines and retrieve information from government agencies, or numerous other sources. These are just a few of the new services created by IT.

---

[22] Frederick F. Reichheld, *The Loyalty Effect* (Boston, Harvard Business School Press, 1996), pp. 118–119.

[23] Thomas Teal, op. cit.

[24] Matt Murray and Raju Narisetti, "Bank Mergers' Hidden Engine: Technology," *Wall Street Journal* (April 23, 1998).

7.7   INFORMATION SYSTEMS

A recent *Fortune* article declared that "Corporate America is now built on intellectual capital rather than bricks and mortar—and that is changing everything."[25] Many researchers and observers of the business world agree and even go as far as characterizing the economy of the United States and other developed nations as a "knowledge- and information-based service economy." Most economic activities require information as an input. However, information plays a very critical role in services. Almost all services require information as an input, and almost all services generate information as part of the service, and for some services, information is the output. A service cannot happen without information. Information is generated from data by an information system.

An information system can be defined as a system of "interrelated components working together to collect, process, store, and disseminate information to support decision making, coordination, control, analysis, and visualization in an organization."[26] An information system performs three basic activities: input, processing, and output. Facts, numbers, words, strings of characters or symbols, or uninterpreted observations are called **data.** Data are the **input,** or the raw material, for an information system. **Information** is the **output** of an information system; it is data that have been transformed into a useful and meaningful form for human beings. Transformation of data into information is the **processing** function of an information system.

Information systems existed in all organizations before computers and telecommunications technology were developed. However, an information system without these components would be very rare, even unthinkable, in developed countries today. Consequently, it must be clear that information systems in service organizations are **computer-based information systems.**

Most service organizations have multiple information systems. These systems are usually developed at different times for different purposes as they are needed. Consequently, a service organization may have separate information systems for its operations, marketing, finance, accounting, and human resources functions. It may also have different information systems serving different organizational levels: operational-level, knowledge-level, management-level, and strategic-level systems. Exhibit 7-2 summarizes these possibilities.[27]

Operational-Level Systems

Operational-level systems are designed to support operational-level managers by supplying them with information about day-to-day operations and transactions, such as sales, receipts, cash deposits, and payroll. These systems are called **transaction processing systems.** They collect the necessary data and generate information needed by operational managers to conduct their daily activities. Business processes at this level are highly structured and well defined. For example, a decision regarding whether to grant an increase in credit limit to a credit card customer can be made by a lower-level manager by simply determining whether the customer meets predetermined criteria.

---

[25] Thomas A. Stewart, "Brain Power: Who Owns It . . . How They Profit From It," *Fortune* (March 17, 1997), pp. 105–110.

[26] Kenneth C. Laudon and Jane P. Laudon, *Management Information Systems*, 5th ed. (Upper Saddle River, NJ, Prentice Hall, 1998), p. 7.

[27] The material on information systems has been adapted from Laudon and Laudon, *Management Information Systems*, 5th ed., pp. 37–48.

EXHIBIT 7-2   Types of Information Systems and Groups They Serve

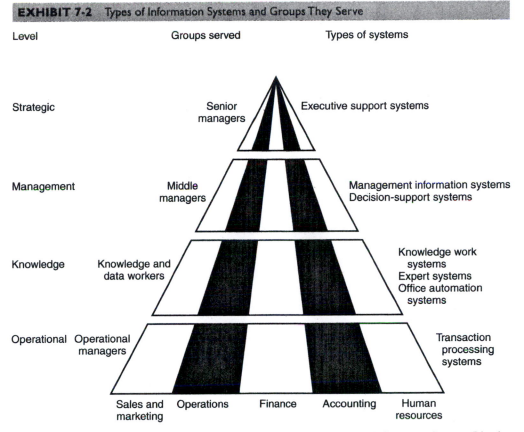

Source: Adapted from: Kenneth C. Laudon and Jane P. Laudon, *Management Information Systems,* 5th ed. (Upper Saddle River, NJ, Prentice Hall, 1998), pp. 37–39.

Knowledge-Level Systems

These systems are designed to support knowledge and data workers. Knowledge workers are those who contribute to a service organization by applying their knowledge to organization's problems or by creating new knowledge. They usually hold college degrees or more advanced degrees and are usually members of a recognized profession, such as scientists in a research lab, faculty members at a university, doctors, engineers, and economists. Information systems that serve knowledge workers are known as **knowledge work systems.**

There are a number of information systems designed to serve knowledge workers. Some of these systems are listed and organized as to their specific function in supporting knowledge workers in Exhibit 7-3. For example, a workstation and software for CAD used an engineer at an engineering consulting firm is one of the most frequently used systems. Another knowledge-level system that is being used in service organizations is expert systems. Simply put, an **expert system** (ES) is a computer program that captures the knowledge and experience of an expert in a narrow, well-defined area of knowledge. Experts can solve difficult problems, explain the result, learn from experience, restructure their own knowledge, and determine the relevance of certain data in making decisions. When used to solve a problem or to make a decision, a well-designed ES imitates the reasoning processes experts use in solving that specific problem. ES can be used as a training device, or as a knowledgeable assistant

EXHIBIT 7-3 Contemporary Information Systems to Support Knowledge Workers

Share knowledge		Distribute knowledge
Group collaboration systems • Groupware • Intranets	**Office automation systems** • Word processing • Desktop publishing • Imaging • Electronic calendars • Desktop databases	
Artificial intelligence systems • Expert systems • Neural nets • Fuzzy logic • Genetic algorithms	**Knowledge work systems** • CAD • Virtual reality • Investment workstations	
Capture and codify knowledge		Create knowledge

Source: Kenneth C. Laudon and Jane P. Laudon, *Management Information Systems,* 5th ed. (Upper Saddle River, NJ, Prentice Hall, 1998), p. 553.

by an expert.[28] Expert systems are in use in almost every industry and functional area.[29] The significant role they play in decision making and training in services is likely to increase as these systems are improved.

Data workers tend to have less formal educational degrees. They contribute to a service organization by collecting, recording, and processing relevant data. Secretaries, accountants, filing clerks, and data entry clerks are among the data workers. **Office automation systems** (OAS) such as word processing, spreadsheets, desktop publishing, and document imaging systems are examples of OAS. These systems also support and are used by knowledge workers.

Management-Level Systems

These systems serve middle managers in their duties such as planning, controlling, and decision making. Generally, two types of information systems exist to support middle managers: management information systems and decision support systems. **Management information systems** (MIS) provide middle managers with weekly, monthly, or yearly summary reports on important performance indicators. MIS usually provide answers to structured questions that are known in advance. **Decision support systems** (DSS) also serve middle managers. However, they go one step further than MIS by aid-

---

[28] Efraim Turban and Jay E. Aronson, *Decision Support Systems and Intelligent Systems*, 5th ed. (Upper Saddle River, NJ, Prentice Hall, 1998), p. 440.

[29] For applications in finance and accounting, see R. M. O'Keefe and D. Rebne, "Understanding the Applicability of Expert Systems," *International Journal of Expert Systems*, vol. 1, no. 1 (September 1993); and L. C. Foltin and L. M. Smith, "Accounting Expert Systems," *The CPA Journal*, vol. 64, no. 11 (November 1994), pp. 46–53.

ing the manager in making decisions, rather than simply providing the information. It is an interactive, user-friendly, computer-based system that utilizes both data and mathematical models to help solve unstructured or semistructured problems. The ability of the user to query the DSS concerning the effect of different potential scenarios of a decision (called "what if" analysis) is an important attribute of decision support systems.[30]

Strategic-Level Systems

Strategic-level systems are designed to serve senior managers. Senior managers deal with problems and issues that concern the well-being of an organization in the long run. They have to deal with issues and problems that are internal to the organization as well as external. Information systems that provide information to senior managers for these purposes are called **executive support systems** (ESS). ESS address unstructured decisions, and they provide information both from within the organization and from outside. These systems use advanced graphics and communications software and are very user friendly.

7.8 ENTERPRISE RESOURCE PLANNING SYSTEMS

As we discussed in the previous section, many organizations have developed information for different functions at different times. A major problem with these systems is that usually they do not "talk" to each other. In other words, they are not compatible. This approach to information system design leads to inefficiencies and inaccuracies in data and information because the same type of data are collected and stored by different systems and usually information from these systems do not agree. **Enterprise resource planning** (ERP) systems have been developed to solve this problem—namely, to create an information system for the entire organization and its various functions and departments that provides seamless integration of information from different sources and functions.

An ERP system consists of "a set of integrated business applications, or modules, to carry out most common business functions, including inventory control, general ledger accounting, accounts payable, accounts receivable, material requirements planning, order management, and human resources, among others."[31] An ERP system uses a common database and common set of definitions; hence, its various modules can communicate with each other. Another very important characteristic of ERP systems is that they require the organization to follow a specific model of doing business. Usually, processes assumed in ERP software reflect the state of the art for the particular area and represent best industry practices. Therefore, before an ERP system can be implemented, an organization must change its business practices to conform to the model assumed by the system. Resistance to change usually creates the greatest obstacle in implementation.

Several software companies have developed ERP systems. The leading vendors are SAP, Baan, J. D. Edwards, Oracle, and People Soft. Among these, SAP has been the most successful ERP system developer to date.

SAP and Its ERP Systems

SAP (Systems, Applications, and Products in Data Processing) was founded in 1972 in Waldorf, Germany. By the end of the 1990s, SAP was the fifth largest independent software company in the world, and more than 6,000 companies in over 50 countries were

---

[30] For more information on DSS, see Turban and Aronson, *Decision Support Systems and Intelligent Systems*; and George M. Marakas, *Decision Support Systems in the 21st Century* (Upper Saddle River, NJ, Prentice Hall, 1999).

[31] W. W. Martin, C. V. Brown, D. W. DeHayes, J. A. Hoffer, and W. C. Perkins, *Managing Information Technology: What Managers Need to Know*, 3rd ed. (Upper Saddle River, NJ, Prentice Hall, 1999), p. 191.

using SAP software. The company offers two ERP software packages: R/2 and R/3. R/2 is designed to run on mainframe computers; R/3 is built for a client/server system, and it is the newer version of R/2. A client/server system is a model of a networked computer system. The system consists of clients, such as desktop computers, workstations, or laptops, and servers, such as more specialized computers that provide data storage or computational services. The system assigns functions and tasks, such as data storage and computations, to machines that are most capable to perform the function.

SAP software was developed to solve the problem of fragmented data and computer systems of large organizations. It adopts the perspective of the organization as a whole rather than a collection of separate functions and departments. However, R/3 is built from modules for a variety of functions and purposes to accommodate different levels of implementation. An organization does not have to install all modules to benefit from R/3, but all modules use a single database and are integrated. The modules of R/3 can be grouped into three categories: financial, human resources, and manufacturing and logistics.

The financials group includes five major modules: financial accounting, controlling, investment management, treasury management, and enterprise controlling. The human resources group provides the full set of capabilities to hire, manage, schedule, and pay employees. The modules in the manufacturing and logistics category perform traditional operations management tasks, such as production planning and control, project management, materials management, quality management, and plant maintenance. This group also includes modules for sales and service management.[32]

Many organizations have implemented SAP's R/2 and R/3 and ERP systems by other vendors. In general, results are very positive. However, there are also failures. The greatest benefits of ERP systems are perhaps increases in efficiency and improvement in bottom lines. These usually result from replacing incompatible and fragmented information systems with a single well-integrated system. The disadvantages of ERP systems include costs (they are very expensive), complexity of the software, and the difficulty of implementation. Perhaps the greatest challenge in implementing an ERP system is that the organization has to change its way of doing business; there is widespread agreement among the experts that failures are not caused by SAP or R/3, but by resistance to change from the organization.[33]

7.9 TECHNOLOGY AND THE FUTURE OF SERVICES

"The overwhelming majority of revenues we get by the end of the decade will be from services and products that have not yet been invented"[34] were the words of John C. Malone, CEO of Tele-Communications, Inc., at the news conference in 1993 announcing the merger of his company with Bell Atlantic. Given the dizzying speed of technological developments during the last two decades, this prediction may become true for many other service organizations. Technological developments are the triumph and product of human intelligence, that is, brainpower. And that is what will be

---

[32] W. W. Martin, C. V. Brown, D. W. DeHayes, J. A. Hoffer, and W. C. Perkins, *Managing Information Technology: What Managers Need to Know*, p. 191; also see Nancy H. Bancroft, Henning Seip, and Andrea Sprengel, *Implementing SAP R/3*, 2nd ed. (Upper Saddle River, NJ, Prentice Hall, 1998); and Thomas Curran and Gerhard Keller, *SAP R/3 Business Blueprint: Understanding the Business Process Reference Model* (Upper Saddle River, NJ, Prentice Hall, 1998).

[33] See, for example, Thomas H. Davenport, "Putting the Enterprise into the Enterprise System," *Harvard Business Review* (July–August 1998), pp. 121–131; and Bancroft, Seip, and Sprengel, *Implementing SAP R/3*, 2nd ed.

[34] Edmund L. Andrews, "When We Build It, Will They Come?" *New York Times* (October 17, 1993).

driving the economy in the twenty-first century. Traditional manufacturing, as well as mining and agriculture, will continue to exist and play a role, but man-made brain-power industries will be the driving force of the U.S. economy and economies of other developed countries.

In the nineteenth and part of the twentieth century, natural resources, such as coal, oil, minerals, and timber, gave some countries a comparative economic advantage and made them rich. Also, availability of capital was a very important factor in a country's prosperity. However, this is no longer true, says Massachusetts Institute of Technology economics professor Lester C. Thurow: "Today knowledge and skills now stand alone as the only source of comparative advantage. They have become the key ingredient in the late twentieth century's location of economic activity. Silicon Valley and Route 128 are where they are simply because that is where the brainpower is. They have nothing else going for them."[35] He also adds that knowledge has become the only source of long-run sustainable competitive advantage.

Professor Thurow is not alone in this view. Management philosopher Peter F. Drucker made the same assessment several years earlier from a micro-perspective: "The basic economic resource—'the means of production,' to use the economist's term—is no longer capital, nor natural resources (the economist's 'land'), nor 'labor.' *It is and will be knowledge.* . . . Value is now created by 'productivity' and 'innovation,' both applications of knowledge to work. . . . In fact, knowledge is the only meaningful resource today. The traditional 'factors of production' . . . have not disappeared, but they have become secondary. They can be obtained, and obtained easily, provided there is knowledge. . . . These developments, whether desirable or not, are responses to an irreversible change: *knowledge is now being applied to knowledge.*"[36]

The emerging picture seems to be clear. In the future, our lives as well as our prosperity will depend more and more on the creation and use of knowledge. Manufacturing, mining, and agriculture will certainly be impacted by technological developments, but most services will exclusively depend on brainpower and knowledge. For example, service industries such as software development, telecommunications, biotechnology, and pharmaceuticals, as well as computer and telecommunications hardware producers and medical equipment manufacturers, are all in the knowledge creation and application (i.e., technology) business. In addition to brainpower, two of the essential ingredients in knowledge creation and application are data and information. Information technology expert Don Tapscott summarizes the situation with the following prediction:

> The new economy is all about competing for the future, the capacity to create new products or services, and the ability to transform businesses into new entities that yesterday couldn't be imagined and the day after tomorrow may be obsolete.[37]

7.10 SUMMARY

Services have traditionally been known for low productivity and the difficulty of substituting machines for humans. This is probably the main reason for the "productivity paradox" in services. During the past two decades service companies as well as manu-

[35] Lester C. Thurow, *The Future of Capitalism: How Today's Economic Forces Shape Tomorrow's World* (New York, William Morrow and Company, 1996), p. 68.

[36] Peter F. Drucker, *Post-Capitalist Society* (New York, Harper Business, 1993), pp. 8, 42.

[37] Don Tapscott, *The Digital Economy: Promise and Peril in the Age of Networked Intelligence* (New York, McGraw-Hill, 1995), p. 43.

facturers have made huge investments in IT with no apparent increase in productivity in services. The most likely explanation for this paradox seems to be that the impact technology makes on productivity and profits depends on what managers and service workers do with it. In other words, technology is not a magic wand that can be waved over poorly designed and inefficient systems or processes.

Although there is no universal correlation between technology investments and productivity or profits, there are many organizations (e.g., USAA and FedEx) that have been very successful in the use of technology. These companies created a competitive advantage through technology and became very profitable in the process. Information technology can be used to create competitive advantage by taking a holistic approach; automating only efficient systems and processes; solving real problems of customers, whether they are internal or external; giving more control to customers and service workers; optimizing basic technologies; and combining high touch with high tech.

Technology has many uses and applications in services. Main categories of applications are processing the customer, processing the customer's equipment or material, processing information, and creating new services. Processing information is clearly a very important application because many services create and sell information, but all services use information and they need information systems. An information system can be defined as a system of "interrelated components working together to collect, process, store, and disseminate information to support decision making, coordination, control, analysis, and visualization in an organization." Several forms of information systems that are frequently used in services have been discussed in the chapter. Information systems may be developed for operational, knowledge, managerial, or strategic levels of an organization. They include transaction processing systems, knowledge work systems, office automation systems, expert systems, management information systems, decision support systems, and executive support systems. Information systems may also be designed to support a particular function, such as operations, marketing, finance, accounting, or human resources.

Another important type of information system that has been implemented by many large organizations is enterprise resource planning systems. An ERP system is an information system for the entire organization and its various functions and provides seamless integration of information from different sources and functions. An ERP system consists of a set of integrated business applications, or modules, to carry out most common business functions, such as inventory control, general ledger accounting, accounts payable, accounts receivable, material requirements planning, order management, and human resources.

Knowledge will be the driving force of economic activity in the twenty-first century. Traditional manufacturing, mining, and agriculture will continue to exist, but our lives as well as our prosperity will depend more and more on the creation and use of knowledge. In addition to brainpower, data and information are essential raw materials for the creation of knowledge, but they are also the outcomes of knowledge creation processes. Organizations that are able to create new knowledge and turn it into new goods and services that consumers need will survive and prosper in the new century.

Discussion Questions

1. What is the information technology paradox?
2. What are some possible explanations of the information technology paradox?
3. In what ways is technology important to services?

4. Why do service organizations invest in technology?
5. What should a service organization do to create competitive advantage through technology?
6. What are the application areas of technology in services?
7. How can technology be used in processing customers?
8. How can technology be used in processing customers' possessions?
9. How can technology be used in processing information?
10. Define *information system*. Differentiate between information and data.
11. How is a decision support system different from a management information system?
12. In what ways are decision support systems and expert systems different?
13. Can a service organization have information systems at all four levels (operational, knowledge, managerial, and strategic) simultaneously?
14. Why are expert systems particularly well suited to services?
15. What is an enterprise resource planning system (ERP)? Why did ERP systems emerge?
16. How are recent advances in telecommunications changing the way we work?
17. Some writers characterize the economy of the United States in the twenty-first century as a "knowledge economy." Explain what knowledge economy means. What role will technology play in this new economy?

CASES

CASE 7–1   David Battles Goliath for the Power of Information on the Internet

In an information-based economy, control of information is the key to power. Many believe that is the source of the 1995 conflict between the London Stock Exchange and a tiny startup, Electronic Share Information Ltd. The London Stock Exchange (LSE), the Goliath in the battle, was formally organized 250 years ago to replace a 150-year-old informal system of trading shares in London coffee houses. LSE has undergone some computerization, but some of its activities remain manual and paper based. Today, although LSE is one of the five premier stock exchanges in the world, it is coming under increasing competitive pressure. The European Association of Securities Dealers plans an automated screen-based trading system soon, while Tradepoint Financial Networks has already established a stock exchange that delivers its services electronically.

Electronic Share Information (ESI), the David in the battle, was established in June 1993 for the purpose of becoming the "world's first cyberspace stock market." Being a British company, it planned to start with British stocks, going head-to-head with the LSE. The new company's leadership was convinced that the Internet would change the way people do business, and it saw an opportunity to develop new tools to support the globalization of the financial markets.

The conflict originated with the plans of ESI to create the first on-line stock exchange. Its founders wanted to phase in the exchange, beginning with a conventional Internet-based information service that provided up-to-the-minute stock prices, company news, and analyst reports. During phase two they would develop an on-line stock exchange for small companies. Their planned service required them to deliver instant real-time market data to the computers of paying customers. The only source for the data was the London Stock Exchange. In the spring of 1995 the LSE signed a contract to supply ESI with market data for a year. Originally ESI planned to develop the whole system itself; however, the World Wide Web of the Internet grew far faster than any of them (or anyone else) expected, and ultimately they decided to base their service on the Web.

Although ESI would not become a stock exchange during its first phase, it did need to offer a brokerage service to transact orders, something that it was not licensed to do. So it turned to David Jones, the founder and chief executive officer of ShareLink Ltd., an established retail brokerage firm that uses modern telecommunications to reduce the cost of brokerage services, thus enabling discount prices. Jones agreed to provide ESI with a Web-based full-brokerage service, including client portfolio tracking.

With everything in place the pilot began on May 20, 1995. The ESI pilot site offered free stock market information, including delayed stock prices, price histories, and company data. By the end of August, 3000 potential clients had registered, a positive enough response for ESI to decide to launch the service. The launch was scheduled for September 8.

On September 4, the LSE backed out, announcing its decision to discontinue the data feed to ESI and to end the contract to supply ESI with real-time market data. Without real-time data, ESI could not continue in business—real-time prices are a linchpin to any market trading service in the electronic information age. The feed was not cut immediately, and ESI decided to go ahead with the launch as planned but to challenge the LSE by publicizing its action to explain its (ESI's) own lack of service. ESI also decided to fight the stock exchange because ESI's contract with LSE still had eight months to run.

On September 8, Jones gave a public TV interview in which he alleged that the LSE had improperly changed the terms of its contract with ESI. On September 11, the LSE cut its price feed in the middle of the afternoon, and on September 13 it held a press conference at which it rejected allegations that it had cut the feed to prevent a new competitor from being established. It announced a defamation suit against Jones, claiming that Jones's remarks on September 8 constituted "conduct detrimental to the interests of the Exchange."

The Office of Fair Trading, a British regulatory body, quickly undertook an investigation into whether the LSE's cancellation of the ESI contract was "intended to distort, restrict, or prevent competition." With this great pressure on the LSE, secret negotiations commenced, and on September 27, both sides dropped their legal proceedings and the contract between them was renewed. The details of the settlement remain secret, but on September 28, the data feed to the ESI Web site resumed and soon thereafter Jones publicly apologized.

Jones later indicated his belief that the episode was a battle for control of information. He stated that the Internet undermines control of informa-tion, and therefore power, by giving individuals more direct access to information. The London Stock Exchange continues to claim that the whole affair was merely a contract dispute. Observers point out that the LSE is certainly unable to control the new Internet technology and has reason to be concerned about being undermined.

By early November 1995, ESI had 8,500 users registered for the free service and 250 customers paying for access to full on-line service, including real-time data and brokerage services. The company indicated that it expected to break even by the end of 1995, and early in 1996, ESI began another round of raising investment capital to begin the second phase, the development of a cyberspace stock market for small capitalized companies. By early 1996 the company already had 17 inquiries from groups in various countries interested in franchising its virtual stock exchange model. ∎

SOURCES: E. E. Baatz, "Hostile Exchanges," *WebMaster*, January/February 1996; Faegre & Benson Limited Liability Partnership, "London Stock Exchange—New Market to be Launched," http://www.faegre.com/areas/area_ib5.html.

CASE QUESTIONS

1. How are the Internet and information technology changing the way stock exchanges are conducting business?

2. How important is the role of information systems in ESI's new venture? Discuss.

3. Describe the management, organization, and technical challenges to building this cyberspace stock exchange.

CASE 7–2 National Technological University

INTRODUCTION

The National Technological University (NTU) is a very unusual university:

- Its mission focuses exclusively on advanced technical education.
- It has no central campus but instead uses a satellite and other telecommunications technologies to deliver instruction.
- Its "campus" consists of forty-five member universities that provide an excellent faculty, hundreds of courses, and outstanding teaching facilities.
- Its students are working adults with challenging jobs in high-techology organizations.

- Its subscribing organizations include many of the best companies in the world—they are selective, enlightened, creative, and successful.

With a critical mission, sweeping curriculum, exceptionally strong faculty, and a nationwide delivery system, NTU truly symbolizes a higher order of education.

For the U.S. economy to remain vital, particularly with respect to manufacturing, a large percentage of working engineers and technical managers will have to continue their education beyond the undergraduate level. This will likely be especially true for older engineers and technical managers who were not exposed to technological changes during their formal education.

172 PART II Building the Service System

However, many companies cannot afford the time or cost to send their engineers and technical managers to full-time graduate programs at universities. But they recognize that what these employees need to enhance their productivity is career-long education that does not disrupt full-time work.

The National Technological University was established as a separate nonprofit, private educational corporation in January 1984. As an institution of higher education, it has the unique mission of serving the advanced educational needs of graduate engineers, technical professionals, and managers. It awards master's degrees to qualified individuals and provides research seminars in selected disciplines. It operates a modern telecommunications delivery system for convenient, flexible, and on-site service and offers noncredit short courses, tutorials, seminars, and research symposia to introduce advanced technology concepts to a broad range of technical professionals.

Three major building blocks comprise NTU: the service suppliers (the member universities), the service customers (the reception sites at the various facilities of the associated organizations), and the administration of the service delivery system (the coordination and other services provided by NTU headquarters).

NTU'S SERVICE SUPPLIERS

NTU offers graduate programs of study leading to master of science degrees in eleven disciplines:

- Computer engineering
- Computer science
- Electrical engineering
- Engineering management
- Hazardous waste management
- Health physics
- Management of technology
- Manufacturing systems engineering
- Materials science and engineering
- Software engineering
- Special majors

NTU's participating universities are chosen on the basis of their academic standing and reputation, experience with long-distance learning, and the interest of their faculty in the program. Exhibit 7-4 lists

---

EXHIBIT 7-4   NTU Participating Universities

Arizona State University	University of Alaska at Fairbanks
Boston University*	Unversity of Arizona
Colorado State University	University of California—Berkeley
Columbia University	University of California—Davis
Cornell University	University of Colorado—Boulder
George Washington University	University of Delaware
Georgia Institute of Technology	University of Florida
GMI Engineering & Management Institute*	University of Idaho
Illinois Institute of Technology	University of Illinois at
Iowa State University	Urbana–Champaign
Kansas State University	University of Kentucky
Lehigh University	University of Maryland
Michigan State University	University of Massachusetts
Michigan Technological University	University of Michigan
New Jersey Institute of Technology	University of Missouri—Rolla
New Mexico State University	University of New Mexico
North Carolina State University	University of Notre Dame*
Northeastern University	University of South Carolina
Oklahoma State University	University of Southern California*
Old Dominion University	University of Tennessee—Knoxville
Purdue University	University of Washington
Rensselaer Polytechnic Institute*	University of Wisconsin—Madison
Southern Methodist University	

*Contributes only to noncredit Advanced Technology and Management Program

the leading U.S. universities that participated during the 1992–1993 school year. Some universities participate in all eleven disciplines, whereas others provide courses only in selected subject areas. The *NTU Bulletin* lists more than 890 courses from these participating universities. Many of the universities produce the majority of the noncredit courses, tutorials, and research teleconferences offered by NTU; private companies, independent consultants, and private individuals produce the rest. Additional universities continue to join the NTU network.

NTU'S SERVICE CUSTOMERS

NTU's service customers are its subscribing corporations or government agencies. NTU today delivers instruction to 649 sites, each located at a facility operated by one of 131 sponsoring organizations. Six Canadian and Mexican sites are in NTU's satellite network, and NTU member corporations have 46 sites outside of North America. Additionally, 59 government sites are on the NTU network, and the NTU has community sites and is interconnected with other networks. NTU aired 528 graduate credit courses and 321 noncredit courses during the 1992–1993 academic year.

All NTU students are employees of a subscribing organization. Eighty-four percent of the students are men and 16 percent are women; their average ages are thirty-four and thirty-two, respectively. The predominant entry degree is the bachelor of science (60 percent); 30 percent hold master of science degrees, 5 percent hold doctorates, and the remainder bachelor of arts, master of business administration, or other degrees.

NTU'S ADMINISTRATION

The administrative headquarters for NTU, located in Fort Collins, Colorado, consists of two divisions, the credit and noncredit programs. The credit program consists of the eleven master's degree programs, each of which is offered on the basis of individual courses supplied by NTU member universities. Academic committees formed by professors from participating universities establish minimum requirements and standards for individual students, courses, credits, and all other academic matters. Students can earn and accumulate credits from any NTU member university, and transferring a limited amount of credits from

nonmember universities is possible. NTU has established its own set of graduate requirements, which is independent of those at its member institutions.

The main function of the administrative headquarters is coordinating the supply and demand for courses, registering students, organizing broadcasts, and training and providing support for the local site coordinators. For the noncredit program NTU headquarters has main responsibility for marketing and producing the individual short courses or seminars. NTU headquarters also has the strategic objective of expanding the bases of supply and demand for all types of courses.

THE NTU SERVICE DELIVERY SYSTEM

NTU is a truly unique institution of higher education, not only in the United States but throughout the world. It built and operates a sophisticated satellite telecommunications network. More important, it put together and operates a unique academic network that meets the advanced educational needs of thousands of technical professionals and managers at hundreds of geographically dispersed work sites.

Exhibit 7-5 shows the major components of the NTU satellite network. The NTU network uses Telstar 401, a new Ku-band domestic communications satellite, to provide fourteen compressed digital video channels throughout the day and night. The satellite operates in the 12/14/GHz band. NTU has installed a series of satellite uplink stations, and a network of television receive-only terminals is at each organizational site of participating graduate students. The technical operations of the network are controlled at the NTU Network Control Center, which prepares schedules and monitors satellite channels for technical quality.

To make optimum financial use of satellite transponder time and to deal with the realities of the working students' class time, courses are transmitted around the clock, seven days a week. Videotape machines record most courses at the students' sites for use at the convenience of the students. Electronic mail, fax, telephone, U.S. mail, and overnight mail service are the primary means that students and instructors use to communicate, although computer conferencing is also available. All students can participate and interact with students at other sites as well as with the instructors. Normal

EXHIBIT 7-5 Major Components of the NTU Satellite Network

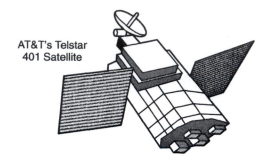

AT&T's Telstar
401 Satellite

Range: Nationwide

40 digital uplinks

300 downlinks

workday hours on the network are used for seminars, conferences, and classes that require real-time interaction.

NTU students use instructional services provided by the sponsoring organizations, including the instructional areas, computer access, selected equipment, laboratories, telecommunications equipment, and educational offices. Finally, the institutional and organizational libraries, combined with the public and academic libraries where the students are located, provide the learning materials the students need for their studies. Because of the satellite delivery facilities students have access to a range of materials beyond the normal capacity of any single institution.

A PERSPECTIVE ON NTU

NTU has awarded degrees to 373 individuals since 1986; 118 were conferred in 1993. In the 1992–1993 academic year saw 5,213 course enrollments, up more than 11 percent from the previous year. By 1995 NTU is expected to become a top-ten provider of master's degrees in engineering. Virtually all

graduates report that they would not have been able to get graduate degrees by any other means.

How do the employers evaluate NTU? Eastman-Kodak recently made an in-depth study of NTU, summarizing its findings as follows:

- Undergraduate level education is not enough to prepare our technical employees for many of the challenges they face in performing the required tasks.
- Master's level education significantly improves job performance.
- Courses are applicable to work assignment; students are able to apply many of the new tools immediately.
- National Technological University's faculty provide state-of-the-art information.
- The variety of courses offered by National Technological University is extremely important; it gives students/employees the pertinent information, when needed.[1]

---

[1] Lionel Baldwin, "The National Technological University in Early 1989," unpublished paper, p. 8.

In the Eastman-Kodak study technical professionals estimated that their effectiveness on the job had increased by 25 to 35 percent as a result of completing the NTU graduate program of study. They also cited specific examples of significant project savings in dollars and time that resulted from advanced study.

NTU has been guided by a clear set of goals from its inception—enhancing personal and corporate productivity by providing America's engineers and technical managers with a set of excellent classes, taught by excellent professors, at their work sites. It has been remarkably successful at providing a long-distance education service, and it has shown great flexibility in producing, transmitting, and distributing its educational services in a cost-effective manner. Its future seems secure and promising, and its mandate is likely to expand and diversify, both in the United States and abroad. ■

ACKNOWLEDGMENTS

The preparation of this case was greatly assisted by Dr. Lionel V. Baldwin, president, National Technological University. Material for the case was drawn from the following sources:

Baldwin, Lionel V. "The National Technological University in Early 1989," unpublished paper.

Fwu, Bih-jen et al. "National Technological University (NTU): A Case Study on Growth and Expansion in Distance Education" (paper presented at the XVth World Conference of the International Council of Distance Education, Caracas, November 1990).

Graham, Ellen. "Distance Education Uses Electronic Links to Recast the Campus," *Wall Street Journal,* September 13, 1991, pp. A1, A5.

National Technological University. *Long Range Plan, 1990–1995.* Fort Collins, Colo., October 1990.

_____. *National Technological University Bulletin.* Fort Collins, Colo., May 1991.

_____. *National Technological University Annual Report, 1992–1993,* Fort Collins, Colo., August 1993.

SOURCE: Robert E. Markland, Shawnee K. Vickery, and Robert A. Davis, *Operations Management: Concepts in Manufacturing and Services* (St. Paul, MN, West Publishing Company, 1995), pp. 642–645.

CASE QUESTIONS

1. What are some of the factors that make the National Technological University such an unusual university?
2. What are the major buiding blocks of NTU's service delivery system?
3. What types of technology does NTU use in its service delivery system?
4. Evaluate the unique mission of NTU.
5. What sorts of competitive pressures is NTU likely to confront in the future?

References

Andrews, Edmund L. "When We Build It, Will They Come?," *New York Times* (October 17, 1993).

Bancroft, Nancy H., Henning Seip, and Andrea Sprengel, *Implementing SAP R/3,* 2nd ed. (Upper Saddle River, NJ, Prentice Hall, 1998).

Berry, Leonard L., *On Great Service: A Framework for Action* (New York, The Free Press, 1996).

Carey, Susan, "Airline Marketing Linkups Draw Opposition," *Wall Street Journal* (April 27, 1998).

Carey, Susan, "New Gizmos May Zip Travelers through Airport Lines," *Wall Street Journal* (January 4, 1999).

Committee to Study the Impact of Information Technology on the Performance of Service Activities, *Information Technology in the Service Society* (Washington, DC, National Academy Press, 1994).

Cook, Halsey M., "Federal Express—The Cost of Poor Quality," Darden Graduate Business School Case, 1992. Revised March 1994.

Curran, Thomas, and Gerhard Keller, *SAP R/3 Business Blueprint: Understanding the Business Process Reference Model* (Upper Saddle River, NJ, Prentice Hall, 1998).

Drucker, Peter F., *Managing for the Future: The 1990s and Beyond* (New York, Truman Talley Books/Dutton, 1992).

Drucker, Peter F., *Post-Capitalist Society* (New York, Harper Business, 1993).

Foltin, L. C., and L. M. Smith, "Accounting Expert Systems," *The CPA Journal,* vol. 64, no. 11 (November 1994), pp. 46–53.

Frank, Robert, "Federal Express Grapples with Changes in U.S. Market," *Wall Street Journal* (July 5, 1994).

Gaynor, Gerard H., "Management of Technology: Description, Scope, and Implications," in G. H. Gaynor (ed.), *Handbook of Technology Management* (New York, McGraw-Hill, 1996), pp. 1.3–1.17.

Hackett, Gregory P., "Investment in Technology—The Service Sector Sinkhole?," *Sloan Management Review* (winter 1990), pp. 97–103.

Hoffmann, Thomas, and Kim S. Nash, "Couriers Deliver New Net Services," *Computerworld* (January 6, 1997), p. 2.

Laudon, Kenneth C., and Jane P. Laudon, *Management Information Systems,* 5th ed. (Upper Saddle River, NJ, Prentice Hall, 1998).

Lovelock, Christopher H., *Product Plus—How Product + Service = Competitive Advantage* (New York, McGraw-Hill, 1994).

Marakas, George M., *Decision Support Systems in the 21st Century* (Upper Saddle River, NJ, Prentice Hall, 1999).

Martin, W. W., C. V. Brown, D. W. DeHayes, J. A. Hoffer, and W. C. Perkins, *Managing Information Technology: What Managers Need to Know,* 3rd ed. (Upper Saddle River, NJ, Prentice Hall, 1999).

McCartney, Scott, "Airline Alliances Take Toll on Travelers," *Wall Street Journal* (February 18, 1998).

Murray, Matt, and Raju Narisetti, "Bank Mergers' Hidden Engine: Technology," *Wall Street Journal* (April 23, 1998).

O'Keefe, R. M., and D. Rebne, "Understanding the Applicability of Expert Systems," *International Journal of Expert Systems,* vol. 1. no. 1 (September 1993).

Reichheld, Frederick F., *Loyalty Effect* (Boston, Harvard Business School Press, 1996).

Roach, Stephen S., "Services Under Siege—The Restructuring Imperative," *Harvard Business Review* (September–October 1991), pp. 82–91.

Schafer, Sarah, "Mourning Becomes Electric," *Inc.* (September 16, 1997), pp. 65–71.

Schifrin, Matthew, "The New Enablers—Chief Information Officers," *Forbes* (June 2, 1997), pp. 138–143.

Schonfeld, Erick, "Can Computers Cure Health Care?" *Fortune* (March 30, 1998), pp. 111–116.

Stewart, Thomas A., "Brain Power: Who Owns It . . . How They Profit From It," *Fortune* (March 17, 1997), pp. 105–110.

Strassmann, Paul A., "Will Big Spending on Computers Guarantee Profitability?" *Datamation* (February 1997), pp. 75–85.

Tapscott, Don, *The Digital Economy: Promise and Peril in the Age of Networked Intelligence* (New York, McGraw-Hill, 1995).

Teal, Thomas, "Service Comes First: An Interview with USAA's Robert F. McDermott," *Harvard Business Review* (September–October 1991), pp. 117–127.

Thurow, Lester C., *The Future of Capitalism: How Today's Economic Forces Shape Tomorrow's World* (New York, William Morrow and Company, 1996).

Turban, Efraim, and Jay E. Aronson, *Decision Support Systems and Intelligent Systems,* 5th ed. (Upper Saddle River, NJ, Prentice Hall, 1998).

CHAPTER 8

Design and Development of Services and Service Delivery Systems

8.1 INTRODUCTION

Service design and development is a very important step in creating value and satisfaction for the customer. In chapter 2, service encounters were defined as "any episode in which the customer comes into contact with any aspect of the organization and gets an impression of the quality of its service." It was also emphasized that a service organization is made, or "created" in the minds of customers during a service encounter. Most important service encounters are those during which a service is delivered. These involve the customer, the service provider (employee), the delivery system, the physical evidence, and, of course, the service itself, which is an act or performance by service providers and/or equipment of the delivery system. It is clear that when so much rides on an event like a service encounter, it cannot be left to chance; service encounters and everything associated with them must be carefully designed, planned, and executed. In other words, the service, its delivery system, and the physical evidence must be carefully designed, and service providers must be prepared for the encounter. This chapter focuses on the first three of these, and chapter 9 will discuss human resource issues.

8.2 WHY THE DESIGN IS SO IMPORTANT

In chapter 5, the concept of value and creation of service value for customers was discussed, because this is what an organization must do to survive and prosper. Customers do not buy goods or services—they buy solutions to their problems or satisfactions for their needs or benefits they enjoy. Consequently, a service organization creates value by creating solutions, satisfactions, or benefits for customers. The process that does all this is called *service*. To achieve its objectives, a service must be a well-thought-out and planned process. In other words, it must be designed and cannot be left to chance. Design also affects costs, quality, and the image of the service as well as the company.

It is clear, then, that for success a service organization must start with a well-designed service. However, it will not end there, because service design is not a one-time undertaking. An organization must create new services or improve existing ones, because customers' needs are changing rapidly and new needs are emerging. Also, changes in consumers' tastes and lifestyles make some of the existing services obsolete or inadequate in meeting customers' needs. Consequently, an organization's vitality and competitiveness often depends on how well it discovers the shifts in consumers' needs and the emergence of new ones and meets them with new services or with improvements in existing services.

In addition to the reasons given above, other factors exist that motivate organizations to design and develop new services. These reasons will be discussed later in this chapter, but first an important note about what is meant by the "design and development" of services. Service design includes the development of a service concept and the design of a system through which it is delivered. Both of these are the products of an evolutionary process; that is, they evolve and change as the design progresses. It is also important to note that when service design and development are referred to in this book, both the service concept and the delivery system are included, because they are inseparable. We now turn our attention to another important issue, what is meant by "new" in services, or how "new" they may be.

Categories of Product Innovation

We all are accustomed to hearing advertisers claim that their products are "new," "all new," or "new and improved." Naturally, having some familiarity with the product, many consumers are unimpressed by these claims, or worse, confused by them, because it is not at all clear what is "new" in the advertised product. Because the topic of this chapter is the design of "new" or "improved" services, it may be appropriate to shed some light on what the advertisers may mean when they make such claims or what alternatives exist for an organization contemplating designing new services.[1]

1. *Major innovations.* These are "new to the world" services for which markets are as yet undefined and undimensioned. They involve a high degree of uncertainty and risk. Federal Express's overnight delivery of small packages was an example of this type of innovation.
2. *Start-up businesses.* Some new services may provide new and innovative solutions to generic needs of customers that have been served by existing services. These new services may be in the form of bundling existing services in a new package, such as health maintenance organizations that bring together general practitioners and specialists, as well as labs, x-ray facilities, and sometimes pharmacies under one roof for one-stop visits for patients.
3. *New products for the currently served market.* This category includes new services offered to the existing customers that were not previously available from the service organization. Examples include banks that introduce their Visa or MasterCard, or offer mutual funds, money market funds, or insurance services, or museums that open gift and souvenir shops and restaurants for their patrons.

[1] These categories were suggested by Donald F. Heany, "Degrees of Product Innovation," *Journal of Business Strategy* (spring 1983), pp. 3–14, adapted to services by Christopher H. Lovelock, "Developing and Implementing New Services," in W. R. George and C. E. Marshall (eds.), *Developing New Services* (Chicago, American Marketing Association, 1984), pp. 44–64.

4. *Product line extensions.* Additions to the existing lineup of services that enhance the current offerings are called product line extensions. Examples include call waiting, caller ID, and redial services offered in addition to regular phone service from the phone company; new routes for an airline; or new courses offered by a university.

5. *Product improvements.* Product improvements consist of changing certain features of a service to give customers better quality or increased value. These may be in the form of performing an existing service faster or enrichments or embellishments, that is, addition of "bells and whistles." For example, many automated teller machines (ATMs) print account balances after each deposit or withdrawal. Another example is the free car wash some automobile dealers provide with any service they perform, including oil change.

6. *Style changes.* These are the most modest but often highly visible forms of service improvements, and they include renovating and refurbishing the building where service is provided, new uniforms for employees, a new logo, and so forth.

The discussion of service design and development in this chapter assumes that the new service falls in one of the first three categories. However, what is offered in this chapter can easily be adapted for other categories.

Factors That Motivate the Design and Development of New Services

Chapter 4 pointed out some global trends that lead not only to a general increase in demand for existing services, but also to an increase in demand for new services in many countries of the world. Earlier in this section, it was stated that the main reason for the design and development of new services is to meet new and changing needs of consumers. There are other reasons that motivate organizations to design and develop new services. Some of the most important factors will be reviewed in the following paragraphs.[2]

Financial Goals   Management in many service organizations is under constant pressure to achieve financial goals of profit, market share, or revenue. These goals may be achieved by improving service quality and customer satisfaction with the existing services. Another way, however, is to introduce new services. As we just noted, several degrees of "newness" exist for services. However, only the first three are most likely to lead to increases in market share and revenue, and help the organization achieve its financial goals.

Competitive Actions   One of the strongest motivations for developing new services emerges when a competitor introduces a new service. Standing still and doing nothing usually leads to an erosion of market share and profits. Consequently, introduction of a new service promotes similar actions from competing organizations. For example, when Merrill Lynch introduced the cash management account, which combined brokerage, debit card, and bank checking services in a single package, its competitors had to develop and offer similar services.

Globalization   The increase in global trade and foreign direct investment, establishment of the European Union, and the collapse of the Soviet Union created new markets and opened up many opportunities for service firms. These developments

---

[2] These factors have been adapted from the following two sources: Glen L. Urban and John R. Hauser, *Design and Marketing of New Products*, 2nd ed. (Upper Saddle River, NJ, Prentice Hall, 1993), pp. 6–12; and Christopher H. Lovelock, "Developing and Implementing New Services," pp. 44–64.

created a need for the design and development of new services or modification of existing ones to meet the needs of different countries and cultures.

Technology With its new products and capabilities, technology creates new needs which require new services. In chapter 7, how new services were motivated by technological advances was discussed. Here, an organized look is taken at some possible ways technology may be responsible for the creation of new services or advances in existing services.

1. *New consumer goods.* New consumer goods, such as video cassette recorders (VCRs) and personal computers, create a need for related services, such as video rentals, VCR and computer repair services, and training services for newly developed software.
2. *New equipment.* Advances in engineering technology helped manufacturers and service organizations introduce new equipment or implement many improvements in existing equipment. These developments in turn led to faster delivery of existing services as well as the introduction of new services. For example, faster computers increased data storage and computation speed for all sorts of data processing and made the development of new and complex software possible; invention of ATMs made some banking services available 24 hours a day.
3. *Electronic networks.* Electronic networks, such as the Internet and World Wide Web, electronic data banks, and online information systems are among the most important technological developments of the late twentieth century, which made the creation and delivery of many new services possible.

Regulation/Deregulation Several important industries in the United States have been deregulated during the last three decades of the twentieth century, including airlines, trucking, telecommunications, and banking and financial services. These deregulations allowed many companies to enter into markets that had not been open to them previously and offer new services or offer consumers innovative bundling of existing services. An example is Merrill Lynch's cash management account mentioned earlier. While some industries are being deregulated, new regulations are created, such as environmental protection and consumer safety regulations. Such regulations usually create a need for improvements in consumer goods and manufacturing equipment, or new ones. They also create a need for new services, such as legal, engineering, and consulting services specializing in environmental protection and safety issues.

Elimination of Professional Association Restrictions Paralleling deregulation of some important industries by the government, professional associations also relaxed some of their restrictions on their members' practices. For example, codes of ethics for legal, medical, accounting, and architectural professionals have been changed to allow them to advertise. Lifting of such restrictions usually leads to the development of new services and innovative delivery systems such as health maintenance organizations, franchise chains of small business accounting services, and legal clinics in shopping malls.

Growth of Franchising A franchise is a type of business in which a person (franchisee) receives a license to produce and/or sell a well-known good or service in return for an initial fee and a percentage of gross receipts to be paid to the grantor of franchise (franchisor). Some well-known franchises include McDonald's, H&R Block Tax Services, Mail Boxes Inc., Howard Johnson's, and automobile dealerships. This system makes it possible for the franchisor to focus on and spend money for formal research in service innovations, product line extensions, product enhancement, and development of new delivery systems.

Balancing Supply and Demand   Many service organizations have limited capacities but face fluctuating demand for their services. When the demand exceeds the capacity of an organization, either customers are lost or their satisfaction level will be lower because of excessive waiting. However, when the demand falls short of supply, expensive equipment and personnel stand idle. Manufacturers can manage this problem by building inventories when the demand falls short of supply, and use inventories when it exceeds supply. However, perishability of most services eliminates this practice as an alternative for service organizations. A plausible alternative is offering services that are countercyclical to the existing portfolio of services. In other words, a service organization facing fluctuating demand can try developing new services that will have high demand when the demand for the existing services is low, and vice versa.

8.3   DESIGNING QUALITY AND VALUE

Humans have been designing and making tools and consumer goods for thousands of years. Technical aspects of design and manufacture of goods have been taught in engineering schools, and the process of product design and development has been studied by business scholars for many years. Service design and development, on the other hand, has never received this much scrutiny or study. Only recently, more attention is being paid to the design of services, mainly because the ever-increasing significant role of services in our economy has become very obvious.

Consequently, the current level of service design and development experience and knowledge is nowhere near the level of experience and scientific knowledge accumulated for goods. This naturally leads many service researchers to the body of knowledge on goods for answers or clues to questions that concern service design and development. Hence, we start from the same place and see what can be learned from manufacturing, and which tools and practices that have been successful in the design of goods can be used in designing services. First, the differences and similarities between goods and services are considered from a design perspective, and then some of the successful practices and tools employed in designing quality and value into goods that may also be used in the design and development of services are discussed.

Designing Goods and Services: Similarities and Differences

As pointed out earlier, customers do not buy goods or services; they buy solutions to their problems, satisfactions to their needs, or benefits they can enjoy. Therefore, the most important similarity between goods and services is that they are designed to provide a solution, satisfaction, or benefit. For example, George Eastman, founder of Kodak, once said, "Kodak sells memories," and Charles Revson of Revlon said: "In the factory we make cosmetics; in the store we sell hope."

The second similarity is that designs of both goods and services are products of human creativity. The human mind first creates something new in concept and then figures out how this is going to be made.

The third similarity is that consumers rarely ask for the creation of a specific good or service. Consumers may express some vague needs but cannot usually articulate them in terms of goods or services; they only respond to what is offered to them. Hence, these unarticulated needs must be discovered and met with the benefits offered by a new product.

We now note some of the important differences. Manufacture of goods requires many resources, such as raw materials, semi-finished products, labor, and energy. These resources are essential for the production of a good. The outcome of the design activity is a set of standards and specifications, such as the type, grade, and quantity of materials to use, dimensions of various parts, and tolerances. Most of these specifications are expressed in a drawing called a *blueprint*. Conformance to standards and specifications in manufacturing is essential; deviations from them, beyond tolerances, will render the manufactured good unusable or defective and sometimes dangerous. The concept of a good can be visualized on paper, and a prototype can be made and studied, measured, tested, and put into actual use. Once the design is finalized and manufacturing begins, all the goods will be identical with only minor variations in dimensions.

In services, raw materials are rarely used; tools and equipment are utilized, but they are not always essential. Airplanes are essential for air transportation service, but a couch is not essential for a psychiatrist's services. The outcome of service design is a concept, or an idea, and a description of a process for performance of the concept. Service design may have standards, but usually there are very few, and deviations from these standards do not necessarily make the service "defective" or create undesirable consequences. No drawing of a service is possible, because a service is performance. A service can be tested in a mock trial, but each performance will be different whether in test or in actual implementation because of the involvement of different customers and service providers. Once the design is finalized and service is offered to customers, no two service performances will be the same, and each customer's experience will be unique.

Another important difference between goods and services is that changes become more and more expensive in manufacturing as the design progresses. This is usually expressed as the 85/15 percent rule, which implies that approximately 85 percent of the cost of a good is determined by decisions made during the first 15 percent of the design period. Once it is finalized and frozen, the design for a good cannot be changed easily, and manufacturing will follow the same design for all units produced. Service design, on the other hand, is not a static or rigid document; modifications and adaptations on the fly are possible and sometimes required for meeting widely varying customer needs and requirements. Furthermore, design changes in services are not likely to be as costly as in manufacturing. These characteristics create a risk; instead of improving a service, accumulation of unplanned changes may cause a slow deterioration of the service in the long run.

Tools for Designing Quality and Value

The now famous adage, "You cannot inspect quality into products, it must be built in," was in response to the decades-long practice in manufacturing of relying largely on inspection to make sure that poor quality goods did not leave the factory. In the early 1980s, manufacturers and quality professionals began to learn from Japanese manufacturers that many quality problems can be solved by improving the manufacturing process, but even more dramatic improvements can be obtained in the design stage.

It is clear that most services do not lend themselves to inspection. There are very few things you can inspect before or after a service performance. For example, you can inspect the appearance of service employees, measure the waiting time and time for the service, and count the number of mistakes made by service providers. These measurements, of course, do not prevent service failures or guarantee customer satisfaction. Furthermore, the service quality is not judged by quality inspectors or service employees—it is judged by customers. Consequently, inspection is not an alternative for quality assurance in services. Just like in making superior-quality goods, quality must be built into the design of a service and its delivery system.

The realization of the importance of design of goods and their manufacturing processes led many manufacturers to try new tools and practices as well as rediscovery of old ones. In the following paragraphs, some of these concepts and tools that can be used in the design and development of services will be reviewed.

Concurrent Engineering

Design and development of goods include many steps, such as idea generation, opportunity identification, design, prototype, process design, procurement, packaging design, and design of the distribution system. The traditional approach was to conduct these activities one at a time, sequentially. One problem with the traditional approach was that it took too long. For example, American automobile manufacturers used to spend about five years designing and developing a new car, whereas Japanese manufacturers did it in three years. Another, equally important problem was costly design changes and quality problems. In the traditional system, design engineers would "throw the design over the wall" to manufacturing engineers, who would then try to figure out how to manufacture the product. This meant designers and manufacturing engineers did not talk to each other. Usually, manufacturing engineers would find many problems with the design, such as parts that cannot be produced as designers envisioned, and throw it back over the wall. It was not unusual for this to be repeated several times during the design process. Once the problems between the design and manufacturing are resolved, procurement would get the design for parts to be purchased from suppliers. Inevitably, they would find problems with the design, such as parts that are too expensive or no longer made by suppliers. The design would go back to the designers.

Japanese manufacturers used a parallel approach to design that also included cross-functional team work. American manufacturers began using this approach after seeing its benefits and called it *concurrent,* or *simultaneous* engineering. One of the major advantages of this approach is that all functions (design, manufacturing, procurement, distribution, marketing, etc.) are represented on the design team and communicate with each other. If possible, customer participation, or at least, customer input should be solicited.

For service design and development, participation of the front-line employees is equally important for various reasons.[3] First, front-line employees are psychologically and physically close to customers and therefore can identify customer needs as the new service is developed. Second, employee involvement will increase the chances of acceptance and understanding of the new service by all front-line employees. Third, they will warn designers against the possibility of organizational efficiency concerns to overwhelm the needs and interests of the customer. Finally, front-line employees are a good source of useful ideas for improvements in service quality.

Concurrent engineering also helps eliminate many quality problems. Most problems are avoided or solved early in the process before they become major headaches and lead to costly design changes. This approach avoids many design modifications by allowing product and process designs to be developed simultaneously.[4]

Concurrent engineering is a logical approach to designing goods, and there is no reason for not using it in the service design and development. For one thing, as indicated earlier, design and development of the service concept and its delivery system are inseparable, so this alone is a strong incentive for using concurrent engineering in services.

---

[3] Benjamin Schneider and David E. Bowen, "New Services Design, Development and Implementation and the Employee," in W. R. George and C. E. Marshall (eds.), *Developing New Services* (Chicago, American Marketing Association, 1984), pp. 82–101.

[4] For more information on concurrent engineering, see Alfred Rosenblatt and George F. Watson (eds.), "Special Report: Concurrent Engineering," *IIIE Spectrum* (July 1991), pp. 22–37; Biren Prasad, *Concurrent Engineering Fundamentals*, vols. I & II (Upper Saddle River, NJ, Prentice Hall, 1996, 1997); J. W. Dean and G. I. Susman, "Organizing for Manufacturable Design," *Harvard Business Review* (January–February 1989), pp. 28–36.

Also, service delivery involves interactions and handoffs between many departments and implies potential service failures. To avoid these problems, all functions or departments of an organization must participate in the design so that they understand each other and what is expected of them for seamless transitions and superior service delivery.

Quality Function Deployment

Professor Yoji Akao of Japan's Tamagawa University developed quality function deployment (QFD) as a structured approach for integrating customer requirements (i.e., "customer's voice") into product design.[5] "In other words, this is a method for developing design quality aimed at satisfying the consumer and then translating the consumer's demands into design targets and major quality assurance points to be used throughout the production stage."[6] Also known as "The House of Quality,"[7] QFD involves several tables that translate customer requirements into product design characteristics, product design characteristics into part characteristics, part characteristics into process parameters, and process parameters into operating instructions for machine operators. QFD can and should be used in the design and development of services; it is actually one of the most sensible tools that can be borrowed from manufacturing. Any organization that aims at creating customer value and satisfaction has to design its services to meet customers' needs, and QFD is a very effective tool for this purpose.

Exhibit 8-1 shows the structure of the House of Quality and Exhibit 8-2 is an example of how QFD can be used to translate customer's voice into the redesign of a dry cleaning service. Customer requirements are listed on the left. The dry cleaner would like to meet all the requirements as much as possible, but notices that not all requirements are equally important to customers. The most important customer requirement in this example is that the clothing item is completely cleaned—it has a ranking of 1 (highest in importance). What the dry cleaner has to do to meet customer requirements is listed in the technical requirements section. In the middle section of the house is a matrix where the relationship between customer requirements and technical requirements are shown. For example, to meet customers' "completely clean" requirement, "clean solvent," "clean filters," "no rust in steam-press lines," and "good equipment maintenance" are essential. Each cell in the roof of the house represents the relationship between two technical requirements, whether they affect each other positively or negatively. If there is no relation, it is left blank. As the boxes on the right and on the bottom indicate, the house of quality also requires competitor evaluations with respect to both customer and technical requirements. As this simple example illustrates, QFD can be a very powerful tool in designing a service that meets customers' needs and creates value for them.

Robust Design

Robust design is a very powerful idea and design practice developed for the manufacture of goods by Genichi Taguchi.[8] The basic idea behind robust design is making the product so that its performance is unaffected by adversities in the environment beyond normal operating conditions. For example, a handheld calculator is not sup-

[5] Yoji Akao (ed.), *Quality Function Deployment: Integrating Customer Requirements into Product Design* (Cambridge, MA, Productivity Press, 1990).

[6] Yoji Akao, "An Introduction to Quality Function Deployment," in Yoji Akao (ed.), *Quality Function Deployment: Integrating Customer Requirements into Product Design*, pp. 3–24.

[7] John R. Hauser and Don Clausing, "The House of Quality," *Harvard Business Review* (May–June 1988), pp. 63–73.

[8] Genichi Taguchi and Don Clausing, "Robust Quality," *Harvard Business Review* (January–February 1990), pp. 65–75.

EXHIBIT 8-1   The House of Quality

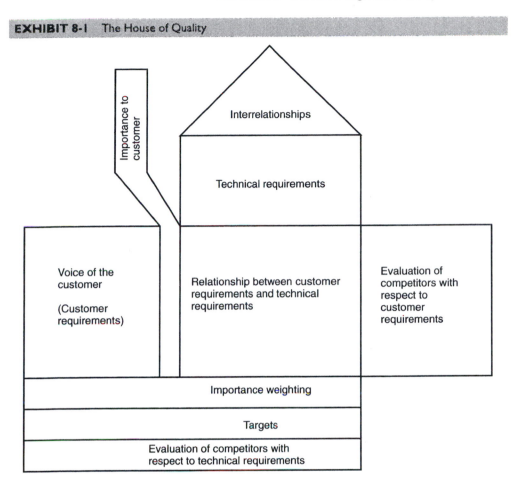

posed to be dropped or used in a very hot and steamy environment such as a steam bath. However, if the calculator endures such harsh conditions and operates as expected, it is said to be a robust product.

Service providers and customers are human. The differences in personalities and demographic characteristics they exhibit may create situations that are not normal operating conditions. Also, failures in delivery or support systems, such as a computer crash, power outage, or failure of a vendor to deliver supplies, may create these adverse conditions in which service has to be delivered. No design can make a service or a good to withstand all adverse conditions under all circumstances. However, services can be designed with possible extreme conditions in mind, and measures can be taken to prevent them. Or alternative services and emergency procedures can be built into the system. The next two tools may be very helpful in making services robust.

Design Failure Mode Analysis[9]   This is a systematic procedure of examining a design to determine possible ways its parts can fail. For each potential failure, the cause, its effect on the system, and its criticality are estimated. This helps designers develop

[9] Joseph M. Juran and Frank M. Gryna, *Quality Planning and Analysis*, 3rd ed. (New York, McGraw-Hill, 1993), p. 266; and Joseph M. Michalek and Richard K. Holmes, "Quality Engineering Techniques in Product Design/Process," *Quality Control in Manufacturing*, Society of Automotive Engineers, SP-483, pp. 17–22.

EXHIBIT 8-2 House of Quality for a Dry Cleaning Service

Correlation:
◎ Strong positive
○ Positive
✕ Negative
✳ Strong negative

Customer requirements / Importance to customer		Good training	Clean D.C. solvent	Clean D.C. filters	No rust in S.P. lines	Firm press pads	Good equipment maintenance	Competitive evaluation
Completely clean	1	○	◎	◎	◎		◎	AB ✕ (4–5)
Perfect press	2	○				◎	◎	BA ✕ (1–2)
No delay at counter	5	○						✕ AB (3–4)
Quick turnaround	3	○					△	✕ AB (2–3)
Friendly service	4	○						AB ✕ (1)
Importance weighting		15	9	9	9	9	19	
Target values		4-hr formal 2-wk OJT	Visual daily	Visual daily; clean monthly	Visual daily	Change monthly	Monthly, plus as needed	

Competitive evaluation:
X = Us
A = Comp. A
B = Comp. B
(5 is best) 1 2 3 4 5

Relationships:
◎ Strong = 9
○ Medium = 3
△ Small = 1

Technical evaluation:

Scale	Good training	Clean D.C. solvent	Clean D.C. filters	No rust in S.P. lines	Firm press pads	Good equipment maintenance
5	B		A		B	✕
4				✕	✕	A
3		✕		B	A	B
2	✕	A	✕	A		
1	A	B	B			

Source: Richard J. Schonberger and Edward M. Knod, Jr., *Operations Management Continuous Improvement*, 5th ed. (Burr Ridge, IL, Irwin, 1994), p. 66. Reproduced with permission of The McGraw-Hill Companies.

preventive measures. Failure mode analysis can be used in evaluating and improving service designs. If a blueprint of service is developed, potential failure points can be identified and measures such as poka-yokes can be developed and implemented.

Poka-Yoke or Fail Safe Methods[10]   This is a simple but very useful concept that also came from Japan; the late Shigeo Shingo developed this approach to designing and manufacturing goods.[11] Poka-yokes are devices or procedures that signal that a

---

[10] For more information on the application of poka-yoke methods in services, see Richard B. Chase and Douglas M. Stewart, "Make Your Service Fail-Safe," *Sloan Management Review* (spring 1994), pp. 35–44.

[11] Shigeo Shingo, *Zero Quality Control: Source Inspection and the Poka-yoke Systems* (Cambridge, MA, Productivity Press, 1986).

mistake is about to be made. *Warning* poka-yokes signal the existence of a problem, and control poka-yokes stop production when a mistake is made and force the operator to correct the problem before proceeding with the operation. The concept of fail-safing a process is similar to a combination lock that opens only when the correct sequence of numbers is supplied. Manufacturers sometimes implement this concept by designing parts of a product so that there is only one way that they can fit, eliminating the possibility of assembly mistakes. Poka-yoke methods can and should be used in service design. However, services must be designed to prevent mistakes not only by service employees but also customers when they are involved in the process. There are many ways poka-yokes can be used in services. A bank, for example, believes that eye contact with customers is very important, and to ensure eye contact, it requires tellers to mark the eye color of each customer on a checklist before they start a transaction.

Blueprints   Design specifications and standards for goods are traditionally represented in the form of drawings on a special blue-colored paper. The blueprint is a visualization of the designer's concept of the product together with its dimensions and tolerances. Lynn G. Shostack applied this concept to the design and development of services: A service blueprint is simply a picture of a service system and its processes.[12] Service blueprints will be discussed in more detail later in the chapter.

Value Analysis/Value Engineering   Value analysis, also known as *value engineering,* was developed by Lawrence D. Wells of General Electric in the late 1940s.[13] It is a systematic approach to identifying the function of a good or service, it establishes the value of its parts, and tries to provide the function, or benefit, at the lowest possible cost without sacrificing quality or value.[14] Its basic concern is "providing good value for the customer's dollar, at a fair profit to the supplier."[15] Typical questions asked during the analysis include "Is the function necessary?", "Can the function of two or more parts or steps of a service process be combined into one and performed for a lower cost?", and "Can the process be simplified?". These are clearly useful questions to streamline a service process for better quality and higher value for customers. Value analysis can be used effectively after a blueprint of the service has been prepared.

Benchmarking[16]   Benchmarking was developed at Xerox Corporation in the late 1970s as a result of one of various quality improvement programs. It is an approach to setting goals and standards for improvements in goods, parts, or processes. It searches for the best-in-class practice in any industry to use as a source of learning and target for the process to be improved. For example, a manufacturer may benchmark L. L. Bean for order filling operations. Benchmarking is not simply copying ideas from other organizations. Its main objective is finding out what performance levels are pos-

---

[12] G. Lynn Shostack, "How to Design a Service," *European Journal of Marketing,* vol. 16, no. 1 (1982), pp. 49–63.

[13] Lawrence D. Wells, *Techniques of Value Analysis and Engineering* (New York, McGraw-Hill, 1961).

[14] Edward D. Heller, *Value Management: Value Engineering and Cost Reduction* (Reading, MA, Addison-Wesley, 1971), pp. 13–14. Also see pp. 187–208 for some applications of value analysis/value engineering in services.

[15] Carlos Fallon, "The All Important Definition," in William D. Falcon (ed.), *Value Analysis Value Engineering: The Implications for Managers* (New York, American Management Association, 1964), pp. 9–24.

[16] For more information on benchmarking, see Robert C. Camp, *Benchmarking: The Search for Industry Best Practices That Lead to Superior Performance* (Milwaukee, WI, ASQC Quality Press, 1989); and Robert C. Camp, *Business Process Benchmarking: Finding and Implementing Best Practices* (Milwaukee, WI, ASQC Quality Press, 1995).

sible for various processes and learning from best performers. This approach would be very useful in service design and development, especially reducing the learning pains of implementing a new service or process, and setting standards for processes or parts of processes. Service companies already use benchmarking for their existing services. For example, Marriott benchmarked fast-food companies for its hiring, training, and pay practices, and Houston's Second Baptist Church, serving 12,000 members, benchmarked Disney World's parking and people practices in its quality improvement program.[17]

8.4 PRINCIPLES OF SERVICE DESIGN

"Service industries" in the business literature refers to groups of organizations that offer similar services. The degree of similarity may justify the term *industry,* but even within each industry the number and variety of services is truly staggering. For example, think about the "transportation industry": It has several subindustries, such as airlines, trucking, passenger and freight rail transportation, passenger bus transportation, and marine shipping. Organizations in each of these subsectors offer hundreds or thousands of different services. The same is true for most service industries. As discussed earlier in this chapter, there are many reasons that motivate organizations to develop new services or enhance and augment existing ones. Even manufacturing firms offer many services to their internal and external customers. This immense variety raises an important question: Are there principles that apply to designing services regardless of the industry for which they are designed, or is each service so unique that there are very few principles that apply to all sectors and services? Despite the uniqueness of each service, there are some basic principles that can and must be applied to designing services if the objective is to create customer value and satisfaction. The following are general principles for designing and developing services.

1. *Know your customers.* If the objective is creating customer value and satisfaction, the most important principle is to know your customers and their needs. A typical service organization cannot serve all potential customers; hence, it has to determine who it wants as its customers. Knowing your customer implies learning everything possible and relevant about the target market at a reasonable cost, including demographic information, such as age, sex, income, geographic distribution, and lifestyle. Information such as this will help an organization determine the needs of potential customers. When possible and economical, information about customers' needs must also be solicited from them directly. The following quote from the chief executive officer of an excellent service company emphasizes the role "knowing your customer" plays in designing winning services:

> One of our newest innovations—The Room That Works—grew out of a listening-to-the-customer exercise. A couple of years ago, we set out to design a better guest room for business travelers. We pulled together some focus groups and quickly discovered that high on their wish list was a change in the placement of electrical outlets in our rooms. Guests wanted them to be visible.[18]

2. *Determine which of the customers' needs will be satisfied.* It is clear that customers have many needs. It must also be clear that an organization cannot possibly meet all

[17] Richard J. Schonberger and Edward M. Knod, Jr., *Operations Management: Continuous Improvement,* 5th ed. (Burr Ridge, IL, Irwin, 1994), p. 39.

[18] J. W. Marriott, Jr., and Kathi Ann Brown, *The Spirit to Serve: Marriott's Way* (New York, Harper Business, 1997), p. 57.

the needs of all its customers; therefore, it has to focus on one or a few of them it can competently meet and make a reasonable profit. The service that will meet the most basic and important customer need will be the core service. There are usually other services that provide additional benefits to customers. These are called *supplementary services.*

Supplementary services are designed and offered to meet needs that may not be common to all customers. They are often optional and may carry additional costs. Lovelock identified eight clusters of supplementary services: information, consultation, order taking, safekeeping, exceptions, hospitality, billing, and payment.[19] Customers usually need *information* about the service, especially when they use it the first time. There are a large number of items about which customers may need information. Some of these include price, what is included in the service (i.e., core and supplementary services), directions to the service facility, instructions about using the service, hours of operation, and payment options. *Consultation* goes beyond providing such basic facts and involves provision of information in a more customized manner. A service employee has to find out customers' needs and try to provide the best advice to meet those needs. *Order taking* may include obtaining and recording relevant information from a customer, making reservations and providing confirmation numbers, scheduling the performance of the service, providing physical evidence (e.g., a ticket) for the order. *Safekeeping* services include safekeeping of valuables in a hotel, safely transporting baggage on an airliner, and safety of a customer's car in a garage or parking lot. *Exceptions* are provided when a service organization accommodates a customer with special needs, such as serving a low-salt meal on a flight to those who request it. *Hospitality* basically means "taking care of the customer"—providing a welcoming environment and treating customers with courtesy. *Billing* should provide an accurate, timely, and easy-to-understand document about the service charges. A service company should set up the payment system to make bill paying easy and convenient for customers.

Not all the supplementary services exist or are relevant for all services. Some of the supplementary services are needed for the delivery of the core service. Without them, the service will be impossible. Yet others enhance the value for a customer. Relative importance of supplementary services depend on the nature of the service.

Clearly, a service organization that fails to deliver the core service often will not survive long; hence, providing the core service without failure and as expected by customers is the first and the fundamental step in creating value for customers. The core service must be the focus of the design effort. The system must be designed for flawless delivery of the core service. A failure in the core service means the failure of the service and the organization in the eyes of the customer, no matter how well supplementary services are designed and delivered. However, providing the core service well is almost never enough to be competitive, because competitors probably exist that can deliver the same basic service without failure. Consequently, a service organization can create more value for its customers by both increasing the variety of supplementary services that are appreciated by its customers and performing them at least as well as customers expect.

Determination of core and supplementary services leads to the "service concept." In other words, a service concept is an expression of the benefits to be provided, problems to be solved, or results to be achieved for a customer. An organization must also make sure that it has the basic competencies necessary to turn the service concept

[19] Christopher H. Lovelock, "Competing on Service: Technology and Teamwork in Supplementary Services," *Planning Review* (July–August, 1995), pp. 32–47.

into reality. If these competencies do not exist in the organization, it must have a plan to acquire them before going forward with the design effort.

3. *Develop a service strategy, and position the service for competitive advantage.* The basic question to be answered here is: "How do we differentiate our service from those of competitors and on what basis we give the most value to the customer for the cost of the service?" Part of this issue relates to the "operating strategy" in the "strategic service vision" model discussed in chapter 5, and the other part is related to "positioning," discussed in chapter 6. Differentiation is the major vehicle of competitiveness. An organization can differentiate its service on the basis of various benefits, including cost, reliability, uniqueness of benefits, speed, personalized service, convenience, accessibility, prestige, or long-lasting effects. The service should ideally be positioned to give it a unique place in the consumers' minds relative to competitors' services. The service strategy must support and complement the organization's overall strategy. One way this may be violated is the new service's being incompatible with the existing services. If such conflicts exist, they should be resolved to support the overall strategy.

4. *Design the service, delivery system, human resource requirements, and tangibles simultaneously.* This principle can be summarized as: "Use the concurrent engineering approach to design." When applied to service design, concurrent engineering includes the simultaneous, or parallel, design and development of the service and its delivery system, as well as the design of physical evidence, development of personnel selection criteria, and site selection criteria if a new site is required. As discussed in the previous section, concurrent engineering requires a cross-functional approach and teamwork. In other words, the design should be a team effort by the representatives of all the parties that will be involved in the creation and delivery of the service. Input of all departments, or functional areas, is a very important ingredient in the design of services that deliver superior quality and value. If possible and economical, customers should also be represented on the design team.

5. *Design service processes from the customer's/employee's perspective.* Once the right service concept is developed, the most important aspect of design is the design and development of processes. Because almost all services are basically processes, process design must receive special attention. If the customer's body (e.g., a physical exam at a hospital) or mind (e.g., a concert) is the recipient of the service, the process must be designed from the customer's perspective. This needs special emphasis, because very often the concerns of various departments, such as accounting, operations, marketing, human resources, and shipping, dictate the parameters and nature of the process, and their objectives will be optimized in the design. Very often, the result is extended waiting for the customer, unnecessary tasks he has to perform, waste of his time, and overall frustration with the whole process.

On the other hand, if the recipient of the service is the customer's possession or information and the customer's presence is not required during the performance, processes must be designed from the service provider's perspective. The objective here is to help the service provider deliver the service with the least amount of effort possible and make the task as pleasant as possible for her, so that she can deliver the highest quality service she is capable of.

It must be emphasized that using the customer's or the employee's perspective as the guiding light for the process design does not imply a complete disregard of the other. In other words, if the customer's perspective is taken in the design, this does not mean that the needs of the service provider are ignored; nor does it mean that one should be unconcerned if the process is such that it would make a service employee's life miserable. Interests of both parties must be promoted and protected. The issue is finding the proper balance.

6. *Minimize handoffs.* Many services involve processing of the customer or his possessions by more than one service employee or department. This usually increases the probability for something to go wrong. The problem is usually caused by miscommunication or lack of communication. To reduce these problems, service must be delivered by a single service provider from the beginning to the end. Recall the example of USAA in chapter 7; USAA service employees have access to all the relevant information about a customer on a computer screen and can answer any questions from a customer and solve practically any problem without handoffs. If this is not possible, a team approach can be followed; a team that works together and is responsible for a particular customer from the beginning to the end.

7. *Design back room operations to support front room operations.* The front room, or office, is where most of the service encounters take place, and that is where the customer's opinion of the service and organization is formed. However, practically everything done in the back room has an impact on the front room operations and hence on customer satisfaction. Consequently, it is important that this dependence is taken into consideration when the service system is designed. For most services, back room processes are very much like manufacturing operations, and the back room can be run like a factory. The first priority, however, is that back room operations must be designed so that the front room operates flawlessly. Once this is established, traditional operations management techniques can be used to optimize the back room operations.

8. *Incorporate data collection in process design.* A service organization needs data for monitoring and measuring customer satisfaction, for performance measurement, and for quality improvement efforts, in addition to data needed for accounting and management decision making. Data collection mechanisms installed after a service is launched may create problems and make the service provider's job harder. Data needs for various purposes must be determined during the service design and incorporated into the system to create the least amount of interference with service delivery and minimize any additional work required from the employee or the customer.

9. *Determine the extent of customer contact and participation.* As emphasized several times throughout this book, the customer's involvement in the service process creates many challenges for management as well as opportunities for a great service experience. For most services, the extent of customer contact and participation are determined by the nature of the service. However, it is usually possible to modify these parameters. For example, if an organization desires less customer involvement in the service delivery, it may automate certain aspects of the service or hire more service employees to relieve customers from some of the tasks required. On the other hand, increased involvement usually implies higher risks for mistakes and may require a higher level of customization and therefore higher costs. The degree of customer involvement determines the type and nature of skills and information the customer must have to participate. The organization must determine these needs and provide the necessary information for effective and efficient customer participation in the service delivery.

10. *Build flexibility and robustness into the system.* There will always be customers whose needs create situations that were not anticipated by designers. Also, there may be failures caused by outside factors, such as natural disasters, power outages, and failure of vendors. Service systems must be able to respond to these unplanned situations

and be able to continue the service. A very important step in this direction is to build flexible rules and processes. Rigid rules and processes make the service employee's job harder and frustrate customers. Most importantly, empowered employees act quickly and decisively to respond to a situation and ensure customer satisfaction. Flexibility is important in processes in which customers are present. Back room processes that may be characterized as "manufacturing" type can have much less flexibility for efficiency in operations and consistency in results. Marriott is one of the most successful companies in the hospitality industry and is also well known for its attention to detail and obsession with processes. Chairman and CEO J. W. "Bill" Marriott, Jr., explains this passion as follows:

> We are sometimes teased about our passion for the Marriott Way of doing things. If you happen to work in the hospitality industry, you might already be familiar with our encyclopedic procedural manuals, which include what is probably the most infamous of the bunch: a guide setting out sixty-six separate steps for cleaning a hotel room in less than half an hour. Maybe we *are* a little fanatical about the way things should be done. But for us, the idea of having systems and procedures for everything is very natural and logical: If you want to produce a consistent result, you need to figure out how to do it, write it down, practice it, and keep improving it until there's nothing left to improve. (Of course, we at Marriott believe that there's *always* something to improve.)[20]

11. *Design employee and customer loyalty into the system.* In chapter 6, the importance of loyalty of both customers and employees was discussed; recall "The Service Profit Chain" model: "Profit and growth are linked to customer loyalty, customer loyalty is linked to customer satisfaction, customer satisfaction is linked to service value, service value is linked to employee productivity, employee productivity is linked to loyalty, employee loyalty is linked to employee satisfaction, employee satisfaction is linked to internal quality of work life."[21] Therefore, it is crucial that customer and employee loyalty must be one of the principles of service design. If the principles listed earlier are followed, a significant step toward customer satisfaction will be taken. Ensuring employee satisfaction would be another major step in the same direction. In addition, other mechanisms can be used to encourage customer loyalty, such as frequent flier programs offered by airlines or frequent guest programs offered by hotel chains.

Fair compensation, benefits, treatment with respect, and a pleasant place to work, are the main ingredients for employee satisfaction. Employee satisfaction also depends on advancement opportunities, rewards for performance beyond the standard job requirements, and empowerment. These are human resource management issues and will be discussed in more detail in chapter 9. However, requirements for various tasks and the corresponding job descriptions can be developed in parallel with the service design. Another component that may play a crucial role in employee satisfaction is empowerment, which can also be designed into the delivery system and its processes during the design. Briefly, service employees must be able to serve customers in the best way they can and solve customers' problems quickly and efficiently

---

[20] J. W. Marriott, Jr., and Kathi Ann Brown, *The Spirit to Serve: Marriott's Way*, p. 16.

[21] James L. Heskett, W. Earl Sasser, Jr., and Leonard A. Schlesinger, *The Service Profit Chain* (New York, The Free Press, 1997). Also see James L. Heskett, Thomas O. Jones, G. W. Loveman, W. Earl Sasser, Jr., and Leonard A. Schlesinger, "Putting the Service-Profit Chain to Work," *Harvard Business Review* (March–April 1994), pp. 164–174.

without waiting for authorization from management. There are many good examples of this type of empowerment. For example, the Ritz-Carlton Hotel Company, a winner of the 1992 Malcolm Baldrige National Quality Award, has a list of 20 basic service standards, called Gold Standards, printed on a wallet-size card carried by every employee. The following three describe how employees are empowered to solve problems:

- Any employee who receives a customer complaint "owns" the complaint.
- Instant guest pacification will be ensured by all. React quickly to correct the problem immediately. Follow-up with a telephone call within twenty minutes to verify the problem has been resolved to the customer's satisfaction. Do everything you possibly can to never lose a guest.
- Guest incident action forms are used to record and communicate every incident of guest dissatisfaction. Every employee is empowered to resolve the problem and to prevent a repeat occurrence.[22]

12. *Improve continuously*. As indicated earlier, designs in manufacturing are usually difficult and costly to change. Modifications to service designs, however, are relatively easier to implement and they are generally less costly. This gives most services a significant advantage, because they can be modified and improved in light of customer input and changing needs, as well as changing competitive conditions. In other words, services lend themselves to continuous improvement much more than goods. Continuous improvement[23] has become a widely accepted and well-established approach to achieving superior goods and services, and it should also be a principle of service design. The process of continuous improvement must be in place for the life of the service.

8.5 DESIGN PROCESS

Ideas for new goods or services are products of human creativity. Although creativity cannot be programmed, or achieved as a result of a step-by-step procedure, service design and development should be a well-thought-out and organized undertaking. Research by the consulting firm Booz, Allen, & Hamilton suggests that manufacturing firms that are active in designing and developing new goods follow a seven-step process: (1) new product development strategy, (2) idea generation, (3) screening and evaluation, (4) business analysis, (5) development, (6) testing, and (7) commercialization.[24] There also exist many other similar processes developed by business researchers.[25] Since service design and development does not have a long history, most models suggested for services are modifications of processes originally developed for goods. In this section, a service design and development model will be described, which goes well beyond a simple modification of a manufacturing model and takes into account the complexity of service design. The model (see Ex-

---

[22] "Ritz-Carlton's Gold Standards," reprinted in Leonard L. Berry, *On Great Service: A Framework for Action* (New York, The Free Press, 1996), p. 74.

[23] Most books on quality cover continuous improvement process; however, probably the most detailed and comprehensive treatment of the subject can be found in Masaaki Imai, *Kaizen: The Key to Japan's Competitive Success* (New York, McGraw-Hill, 1986).

[24] Booz, Allen, & Hamilton, *New Products Management for the 1980s* (New York, Booz, Allen, & Hamilton Inc., 1982).

[25] Other product development processes may be found in Edgar A. Pessemier, *Product Management* (New York, John Wiley, 1977); Yoram J. Wind, *Product Policy: Concepts, Methods and Strategy* (Reading, MA, Addison-Wesley, 1982); and Glen L. Urban and John R. Hauser, *Design and Marketing of New Products* (Upper Saddle River, NJ, Prentice Hall, 1993).

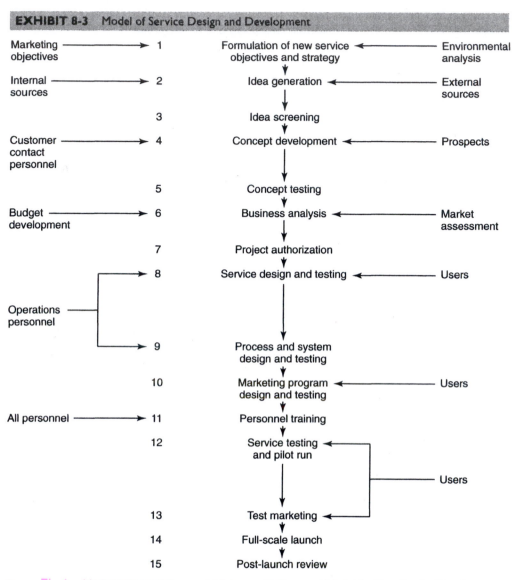

EXHIBIT 8-3 Model of Service Design and Development

Marketing objectives →	1	Formulation of new service objectives and strategy ←	Environmental analysis
Internal sources →	2	Idea generation ←	External sources
	3	Idea screening	
Customer contact personnel →	4	Concept development ←	Prospects
	5	Concept testing	
Budget development →	6	Business analysis ←	Market assessment
	7	Project authorization	
	8	Service design and testing ←	Users
Operations personnel	9	Process and system design and testing	
	10	Marketing program design and testing ←	Users
All personnel →	11	Personnel training	
	12	Service testing and pilot run ←	Users
	13	Test marketing ←	
	14	Full-scale launch	
	15	Post-launch review	

Source: Eberhard E. Scheuing and Eugene M. Johnson, "A Proposed Model for New Service Development," *The Journal of Services Marketing*, vol. 3, no. 2 (spring 1989), pp. 25–34.

hibit 8-3) has been suggested by Scheuing and Johnson.[26] It consists of 15 steps and can be described in four stages: direction, design, testing, and introduction. It also indicates key influences at each step both from within and outside the service organization.

Direction

The first stage includes activities that determine the direction of the development effort.

---

[26] Eberhard E. Scheuing and Eugene M. Johnson, "A Proposed Model for New Service Development," *The Journal of Services Marketing*, vol. 3, no. 2 (spring 1989), pp. 25–34.

1. *Formulation of new service objectives and strategy.* This is the first step of the whole process. As discussed in the previous section, the service strategy must support the organization's overall strategy, and it must be directed at satisfying selected needs of customers in the target market or solving a particular problem for them. Once this determination is made, strategy is the decision as to how value will be leveraged over costs, in other words what kind of service value will be created for the customer for the price he paid. (Refer to the discussion of "A Model of Service Value" in chapter 5).

Customers make their purchase decisions on the basis of their perception of benefits. Consequently, positioning a new service with respect to benefits and relative to competing services is critical for its success. A useful tool for positioning is a perceptual map. Perceptual maps are graphic representations of positions of products (goods or services) with respect to customer needs or desired benefits. Perceptual maps help managers and designers discover opportunities for new products, or improvements in existing products, by providing a visual representation of how customers perceive and evaluate competing products in a category with respect to important benefits. Consider the following example of positioning of new transportation services[27]:

> **EXAMPLE.** Suppose you are a public transit manager considering the introduction of new services to increase the utilization of public transportation. First, you need to find out what your customers' needs are. This can be done through one-on-one interviews, focus groups, or other formal and informal methods. Suppose that the following three primary needs have been discovered from customer research: (1) speed and convenience; (2) ease of travel; and (3) psychological comfort, together with how consumers rate each of the four existing modes of transportation.[28] The results of how consumers perceive various modes of transportation may be as shown in Exhibit 8-4. Careful examination of this map reveals that there may be a need for a transportation service that provides ease of travel and psychological comfort. This is indicated by the fact that there is no transportation service in that sector of the perceptual map.

2. *Idea generation.* Ideas for new services may come from many different sources, including customers, customer complaints, service employees, competitors, and suppliers.

3. *Idea screening.* Naturally, not every idea for a new service is viable. There may be many ideas, but only a few will be successful as new services in the marketplace. This step involves a crude sorting procedure separating promising ideas from others. Feasibility and potential profitability are the main concerns behind this activity. Care must be exercised not to throw out ideas just because they seem to be unusual.

Design

The design stage consists of steps 4 through 11, and they focus on designing a new service and its delivery system.

4. *Concept development.* Ideas that survived the screening process are developed a step further into service concepts. A service concept is a description of the bundle of

---

[27] This example has been adapted from Glen L. Urban and John R. Hauser, *Design and Marketing of New Products*, pp. 205–218.

[28] For a detailed discussion of data collection and construction of perceptual maps, see Urban and Hauser, *Design and Marketing of New Products*, chapters 8–11.

EXHIBIT 8-4 Perceptual Map of Transportation Services

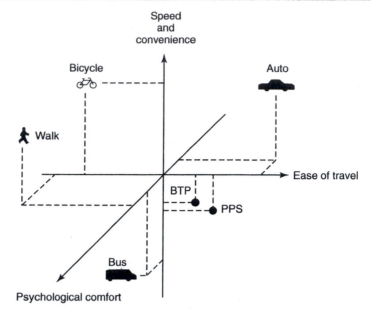

Source: Glen L. Urban and John R. Hauser, *Design and Marketing of New Products* 2nd ed. (Upper Saddle River, NJ, Prentice Hall, Inc., 1993), p. 218.

benefits, solutions, and value the service is supposed to provide to a customer. The following are examples of two service concepts:

> *A professional financial counseling service offered by your bank.* This counseling service is designed to assist you in determining and developing priorities for your financial goals (such as children's college education, retirement, purchase of a home) and to aid in the selection of a program tailored to achieve these goals. Your overall financial situation would be confidentially reviewed (including insurance policies, pension benefits, savings) so that various investment alternatives could be explored. The service would provide for periodic review. Price for average yearly usage would be $100 for the initial year and $25 for each year thereafter.
>
> *Vision care insurance.* A plan that pays $20 for each of the following annual vision care expenses: eye examination, single lens prescription, bifocal lens prescription, trifocal lens prescription, and a set of frames.[29]

5. *Concept testing.* The purpose of concept testing is to determine potential consumers' responses to the service concept so that service ideas that are not attractive to consumers may be eliminated from further consideration. It also helps designers sharpen and focus the benefits of attractive concepts on what consumers really want. "A concept test of a new service is a research technique designed to evaluate whether a prospective user (1) understands the idea of the proposed service, (2) reacts favorably to it, and (3) feels it offers benefits that answer unmet needs."[30]

---

[29] Yoram J. Wind, *Product Policy: Concepts, Methods and Strategy* (Reading, MA, Addison-Wesley, 1982), pp. 281–282.

[30] Scheuing and Johnson, "A Proposed Model for New Service Development," p. 32.

EXAMPLE (continued). After discovering the gap in the coverage of consumers' needs, particularly the unmet needs of ease of travel and psychological comfort, you decide to consider two new service concepts. The first concept is Budget Taxi Plan (BTP), which provides a service similar to that provided by taxi services but at a lower price. Also, the driver may pick up or drop off other passengers on the way to your destination. BTP is to be provided by a private company. A second new service concept is called Personalized Premium Service (PPS). This is the same as BTP, except minibuses are used instead of taxis, and it is to be publicly owned and operated. These concepts can be tested by asking potential customers to evaluate them with respect to the three dimensions, speed and convenience, ease of travel, and psychological comfort. The results of testing of these two concepts are shown in Exhibit 8-4 as BTP and PPS. These two service concepts are perceived to be significantly higher than bicycling, walking, and riding the bus on the speed, convenience, and ease of travel dimensions. On the psychological comfort dimension, however, they are perceived to be better than auto, equal to bicycle, but lower than walking and bus.

6. *Business analysis.* If a new service survives the concept testing, it is next subjected to a much closer scrutiny. The most important question designers try to answer is: "Is this service concept economically sound?" In other words, is there a large enough market for it and can it be produced and sold for a reasonable profit? Consequently, this step includes market assessment, demand analysis, revenue projections, and cost analysis. If the result of this analysis is promising, the new service is recommended to top management for implementation.

7. *Project authorization.* If the results of the business analysis and profit projections meet the top management's criteria, the project will be approved and resources will be committed to the design and implementation of the new service and its delivery system.

8. *Service design and testing.* This is the stage at which a detailed service description is developed together with the specific features and characteristics of the service that differentiates it from its competitors. Although steps 8 and 9 are listed separately, they must be performed simultaneously, or in parallel, if two different teams are responsible for them. This is where the application of concurrent engineering principles must begin, if it has not been in place already. A cross-functional team approach should be used for the entire design process, steps 1 through 15. However, if that has not been the case, this is where the team approach to design must begin, as well as parallel design efforts on other components, such as marketing program, development of employee selection criteria, site selection criteria, and the design of physical evidence.

9. *Process and system design and testing.* As emphasized earlier, most services are performances, and therefore they are the outcomes of processes. In other words, service processes create the service. This is the stage in which the most detailed design work is done. This is also where quality and value can be built into the service, and hence concepts and tools for building quality and value into services can and should be used at this stage.

Before those concepts and tools are discussed, however, there are some general issues to consider. First of all, designers must take into consideration the influence of the following service characteristics on process design: (1) the nature of customer contact, (2) the degree of customer participation in the service production, (3) the degree of customization, (4) the role of goods and equipment in service delivery, (5) the recipient of the service (i.e., customer's body, mind, or possessions), and (6) anticipated demand. Second, designers must also be conscious of the influence of these characteristics on what is above and below the line of visibility, the imaginary line that separates the front room and back room. The front room consists of what the customer would be seeing, or in contact with, during the service encounter. The back room includes all the personnel, facilities, and processes that support the front room operations but need not be visible to the customer.

For example, if the customer's body is the recipient of the service, say a visit to the hospital for a physical exam, the customer (patient) has to be present in the facility. The front room consists of doctors, nurses, receptionists, waiting rooms, examination rooms, nurses' station, x-ray room, and so forth. Some of the front room processes include gathering information from the patient (e.g., filling out forms), preparing the patient for the doctor's exam (e.g., taking blood pressure, temperature, providing an examination gown, etc.), physical exam, and drawing a blood sample for tests. Back room processes include tests performed in the lab; ordering, receiving, and stocking of medical supplies; maintenance of the facility; and billing. Most of the important services in this example are created and delivered by the processes of the front room. In this case, they have to be designed for one patient at a time, and the performance is customized for each patient. The operational rule of the front room is appointment or first come first served.

Consider another service, say dry cleaning, in which a customer's possession is the recipient of the service. Here the front room consists of a counter and an employee behind it to receive the items to be cleaned, give the customer a receipt, and a date when they can be picked up. There is no need for a waiting room or elegant facilities, as the customer will be in the store for only a few minutes. The back room consists of the equipment used for cleaning operations and the personnel who operate them, supplies, and customers' items waiting to be cleaned and those that have been cleaned and are ready to be picked up. Although sometimes visible, customers are not allowed in the back room, which is organized for optimal operational efficiency. Unlike the hospital, items in a dry cleaner can be cleaned in any order, they can be processed in batches, and there is very little customization.

As mentioned earlier, this is the design stage in which the tools and concepts discussed in Section 8.3 should be used to build quality and value into a service. Probably the most important tool for the purpose is quality function deployment, or the house of quality. This tool not only requires that designers find out customers' needs, but it also forces them to study and evaluate competitors' services. Consequently, it helps designers develop a service that meets customers' needs and determine performance levels they need to achieve to beat competitors. If the service designers also perform a benchmarking study to determine the best performances relevant to the new service, they can use those as their design targets instead of competitors' performances.

A tool that was briefly mentioned in Section 8.3 is a service blueprint. A blueprint is a picture of a service system and its processes; it provides a bird's-eye view of the service system. It shows the steps of processes and interactions among processes as well as the interaction of a customer with the system. One of the most important benefits of blueprints is that they are more precise than verbal descriptions of service processes and therefore reduce ambiguity and the likelihood of misunderstandings that may originate from them. Blueprints are also educational. Preparing a service blueprint forces one to learn more about that system and probably helps him realize how little he actually knows about the functioning of the entire system.[31]

Another important advantage is that service blueprints allow the creation, study,

---

[31] G. Lynn Shostack, "Understanding Services through Blueprinting," in T. A. Swartz, D. E. Bowen, and S. W. Brown (eds.), *Advances in Services Marketing and Management: Research and Practice*, vol. 1, (Greenwich, CT, JAI Press, 1992), pp. 75–90.

and testing of services conceptually on paper before a costly implementation. Service blueprints are task oriented. They display activities involved in a process. This characteristic makes them useful for training, communication, and quality improvement purposes. These last characteristics allow the application of value analysis to the evaluation of new or existing services for cost reductions and efficiency improvements. Service blueprints also allow the application of failure mode analysis (discussed in Section 8.3) to determine potential areas where service failures may occur. These are called *fail points,* and they are where poka-yoke methods can be applied. Exhibit 8-5 presents an example of fail-safing a service design. The exhibit shows a blueprint of an automotive service operation and how poka-yoke can be used to prevent service failures and create a robust service.

Although there are some differences, service blueprints use the flowcharting conventions. Exhibit 8-6 presents a sample blueprint of a florist service. Exhibit 8-7 presents a more complicated example—a discount brokerage service. Notice that this chart also includes the expected time to complete various operations and identifies fail points.[32]

The importance of building quality and value into the service at the design stage has been emphasized and several concepts and tools suggested. Application of these tools and concepts will also help make the new service more robust.

Although the model represented in Exhibit 8-3 suggests an orderly and smooth progression of steps, the reality is never orderly or smooth; at the least it involves many iterations, revisions, redefinitions of concepts, and redesigns. Even when all these have been done several times, the process is not over; what has been designed must be tested. Tests at this stage correspond to prototype testing in manufacturing. However, they do not involve offering the service to the public—they are done internally. If possible, service and process designs must be tested under as realistic conditions as possible with real customers. When this is not possible, service may be offered to employees and their families.

10. *Market program design and testing.* A marketing program for the introduction, distribution (if relevant), and sale of the new service must be developed and tested with potential customers.

11. *Personnel training.* As previously indicated, criteria for employee selection (new hires or current employees) must be developed in parallel with the service and process design. Once the selection is completed, employees must be trained not only in their specific tasks, but they must be knowledgeable about the whole service system. They should also be given as wide authority as possible to serve customers and solve their problems.

Testing

12. *Service testing and pilot run.* This is live testing in which the service is offered on a limited basis at one or a few locations, but the service, employees, and customers are real. The purpose of this step is to determine consumer acceptance from firsthand knowledge. Another goal is to make necessary refinements and adjustments based on the information collected from customers.

---

[32] For more information on service blueprinting, in addition to Shostack's previously cited works, see G. Lynn Shostack and Jane Kingman-Brundage, "How to Design a Service," in Carole A. Congram and Margaret L. Friedman (eds.), *Handbook of Marketing for the Service Industries* (New York, American Management Association, 1991), pp. 243–261; G. Lynn Shostack, "Service Design in the Operating Environment," in W. R. George and C. E. Marshall (eds.), *Developing New Services* (Chicago, American Marketing Association, 1984), pp. 27–43; Jane Kingman-Brundage, "The ABCs of Service System Blueprinting," in Mary Jo Bitner and L. A. Crosby (eds.), *Designing a Winning Service Strategy* (Chicago, American Marketing Association, 1989).

EXHIBIT 8-5 Fail-Safing a Typical Automotive Service Operation

Failure: Customer forgets the need for service.
Poka-Yoke: Send automatic reminders with a 5 percent discount.

Failure: Customer cannot find service area, or does not follow proper flow.
Poka-Yoke: Contact method— clear and informative signage directing customers.
Failure: Customer has difficulty communicating problem.
Poka-Yoke: Joint inspection— service advisor repeats his or her understanding of the problem for confirmation or elaboration by the customer.

Failure: Customer does not understand the necessary service.
Poka-Yoke: Preprinted material for most services, detailing work, reasons, and possibly a graphic representation.

Failure: Bill is illegible.
Poka-Yoke: Top copy to customer, or plain paper bill.

Failure: Customer not located.
Poka-Yoke: Contact method— Issue beepers to customers who wish to leave facility.

Failure: Feedback not obtained.
Poka-Yoke: Motion step—customer satisfaction postcard given to customer with keys to vehicle.

Customer calls for service appointment	→	Service department schedules appointment
Customer arrives with vehicle	→	Greet customer
Customer specifies problem	←	Obtain vehicle information
		Problem is diagnosed
Customer approves service	←	Cost and time estimate is prepared
		Waiting room or service shuttle provided
		Schedule work
		Retrieve parts from stockroom
		Perform required work
		Work verified
Customer pays bill	←	Vehicle cleaned
		Customer invoice prepared
Customer departs	←	Vehicle is retrieved

Line of visibility

Failure: Customer arrival unnoticed
Poka-Yoke: Contact method—use bell chain to signal arrivals.

Failure: Customers not served in order of arrival.
Poka-Yoke: Place numbered markers on cars as they arrive.

Failure: Vehicle information incorrect and process time consuming.
Poka-Yoke: Maintain customer database and print forms with historical information.

Failure: Incorrect diagnosis of the problem.
Poka-Yoke: High tech check list such as expert systems and diagnostic equipment.

Failure: Incorrect estimate.
Poka-Yoke: Check lists itemizing costs by common repair types.

Failure: Service shuttle is inconvenient.
Poka-Yoke: Fixed value method—seating in available shuttles is allocated when scheduling appointments. Lack of free spaces indicates that customers needing shuttle service should be scheduled for another time.

Failure: Parts are not in stock.
Poka-Yoke: Contact method—limit switches activate signal lamps when part level falls below order point.

Failure: Vehicle not cleaned correctly.
Poka-Yoke: Successive check—person retrieving vehicle inspects, orders a touch-up if necessary, and removes floor mat in presence of customer.

Failure: Vehicle takes too long to arrive.
Poka-Yoke: Motion step method—when cashier enters customer's name in order to print the bill, information is electronically sent to runners, who retrieve vehicle while the customer is paying.

Source: Richard B. Chase and Douglas M. Stewart, "Fail-Safing Services," in Eberhard E. Scheuing and William F. Christopher (eds.), *The Service Quality Handbook* (New York, American Management Association, 1993), pp. 347–357. Reprinted from *The Service Quality Handbook* by Eberhard E. Scheuing, et al. Copyright © 1993 AMACOM, a division of American Management Association International. Reprinted by permission of AMACOM, a division of American Management Association International, New York, NY. All rights reserved. http:/www.amanet.org.

EXHIBIT 8-6   Blueprint for Florist Service

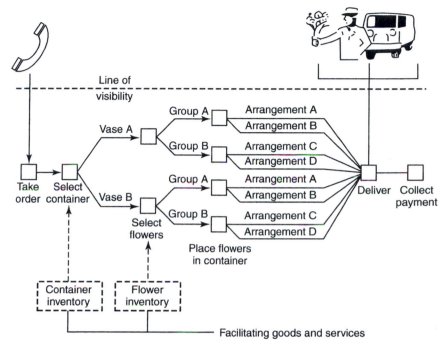

Source: Reprinted from G. Lynn Shostack, "Service Positioning through Structural Change," *Journal of Marketing*, vol. 51, no. 1, published by the American Marketing Association, January 1987.

13. *Test marketing.* Test marketing investigates the salability of the new service. In this case, service is offered on a limited basis but at a larger scale than in step 12 (e.g., at a few branches or in one region). The marketing program is also tested for its effectiveness. Information collected in this step includes customers' reactions to the new service and results of different marketing mixes, such as demand corresponding to different prices charged for the service. These results are reviewed, and if necessary, modifications to the marketing plan are made.

Introduction

14. *Full-scale launch.* With all tests completed and adjustments and modifications implemented, the service is ready for a full-scale launch, and is offered to the entire market.

15. *Post-launch review.* The purpose of this step is to determine the degree of achievement of the objectives and decide whether further adjustments and modifications are needed. This step should not be the termination of the design and development process. Reviews should be conducted at regular intervals, with input from customers and front-line employees, to evaluate the success of the new service and adjust the service to changing conditions and make improvements.

8.6   SUMMARY

This chapter focused on the design and development of services and their delivery systems. Service design is an important step in creating value and satisfaction for the customer. A service is supposed to satisfy the needs of customers, or solve their prob-

EXHIBIT 8-7 Blueprint for Discount Brokerage

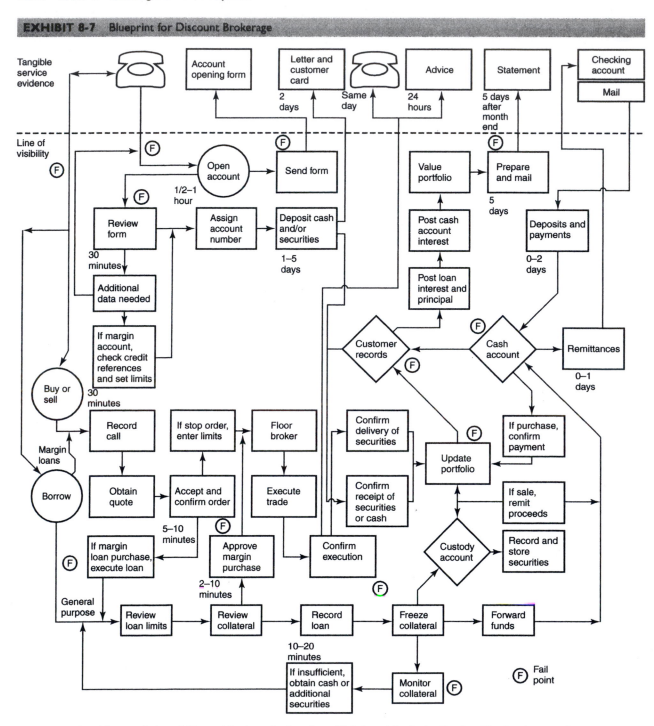

lems; the purpose of the design is to determine the best and most profitable way for doing this. Service design is also important because it influences quality, costs, customer value, and the image of the organization. Various categories of "newness," or innovation, in services were reviewed: major innovations, start-up businesses, new products for the currently served market, product line extensions, product improvements, and style changes.

In addition to meeting customers' needs, sometimes organizations are motivated by other factors to design and develop new services. Among the factors reviewed were financial goals, competitive actions, globalization, technology, changes in government regulations, elimination of professional association restrictions, growth of franchising, and balancing demand and supply.

Experience in manufacturing makes it clear that the best way to achieve quality and value in services is to build them in at the design stage. To provide an appropriate background for understanding how this can be done, the similarities and differences between goods and services were first reviewed with respect to design. Then, a brief review of tools and concepts that were successfully used in designing, developing, and manufacturing goods that provide superior value and quality was provided. Included among them are concurrent engineering, quality function deployment (or the house of quality), robust design, design failure mode analysis, poka-yoke (or fail-safe methods), blueprints, value analysis (or value engineering), and benchmarking. Suggestions were provided regarding how these concepts and tools may be used in designing and delivering services that provide superior value and quality.

Section 8.4 provided 12 basic principles for design and development of services that provide superior value and quality:

1. Know your customers.
2. Determine which of the customers' needs will be satisfied.
3. Develop a service strategy, and position the service for competitive advantage.
4. Design the service, delivery system, human resource requirements, and tangibles simultaneously.
5. Design service processes from the customer's/employee's perspective.
6. Minimize handoffs.
7. Design back room operations to support front room operations.
8. Incorporate data collection in process design.
9. Determine the extent of customer contact and participation.
10. Build flexibility and robustness into the system.
11. Design employee and customer loyalty into the system.
12. Improve continuously.

In the last section, all these principles were put together to develop services that provide superior value and quality. Scheuing and Johnson's model for service design and development process was used. The model consists of 15 steps that can be accomplished in four stages: direction, design, testing, and introduction. Through this model, how the twelve design principles can be implemented and concepts and tools for building value and quality can be used in the process was explained.

Discussion Questions

1. Explain the major reasons for the importance of service design.
2. Discuss what "new" may mean in new services. Give an example for each category.
3. Discuss the reasons for which new services are designed and developed.

4. In Section 8.2, eight factors that motivate the design and development of new services were discussed. Discuss with examples if and how these same factors may make existing services obsolete and motivate their elimination.

5. Compare and contrast goods and services with respect to design.

6. Explain how an organization can build quality and value into a service.

7. Explain the basic idea behind concurrent engineering. How can it be useful to designers of new services? How can it be useful to customers?

8. Explain the basic idea behind quality function deployment. How can it be useful to designers of new services? How can it be useful to customers?

9. What does "robust service" mean? How can one make a service robust?

10. What is a service blueprint? What benefits does a service blueprint provide?

11. Develop a service blueprint for a service of your choice. Be sure to indicate fail points. Provide time estimates where relevant.

12. Refer to discussion question 11. Explain how you would apply design failure mode analysis to the blueprint you have developed. Recommend poka-yokes where necessary. Explain how each poka-yoke will prevent failures or make them less likely. Explain how you would apply value analysis/value engineering to this service.

13. Refer to Exhibit 8-6 (blueprint for florist service). Suppose the owner of this service wants to augment her service offering. In other words, she wants to continue the florist service, but offer something new. What "new" service can you recommend to her? Justify your recommendation. Which category of product innovation would your recommendation fall into? Develop a "service concept" for this "new" service. Modify the blueprint to incorporate the new service.

14. Explain the basic idea behind benchmarking. How can it be useful to designers of new services? How can it be useful to customers?

15. Choose a service with which you are familiar. Identify a major process of this service and briefly describe the process. Identify one or more performance measures for this process that are important to a customer. Where would you go to benchmark this process (i.e., which industry and which organization)?

16. "Know your customer" was listed as the first among the principles of service design. Explain what "knowing the customer" means for a service organization and suggest ways of accomplishing this.

17. How can an organization build employee loyalty and customer loyalty into its services?

18. Is flexibility a desirable characteristic of a service? Explain.

18. Explain what a "perceptual map" is and how it can be used in service design and development.

19. Describe the four major stages of Scheuing and Johnson's model of service design and development. What are the objectives of each stage?

20. How would the front room and back room operations differ? What are the major objectives in the design of each?

CASES

CASE 8–1   Streamlining the Refinancing Process

First National Bank has been swamped with refinancing requests this year. In order to handle the increased volume, they divided the process into five distinct phases and assigned several persons to each stage. (Each stage, in fact, became a department.)

The process begins with a customer completing a loan application for a *loan agent*. The loan agent discusses the refinancing options with the customer and performs quick calculations based on customer-reported data to see if the customer qualifies for loan approval. If the numbers work, the customer signs a few papers to allow a credit check and goes home to wait for notification of the loan's approval.

The customer's file is then passed on to a *loan processor,* who requests a credit check, verification of loans or mortgages from other financial institutions, an appraisal of the property, and employment verification. If any problems are encountered, the loan processor goes to the loan agent for advice. If items appear on the credit report that are not on the application or if other agencies have requested the credit report, the customer is required to explain the discrepancies in writing. If the explanation is acceptable, the letter is placed in the customer's file and the file is sent to the loan agent (and sometimes the bank's board) for final approval.

The customer receives a letter of loan approval and is asked to call the *closing agent* to schedule a closing date and to lock in a loan rate if the customer has not already done so.

The closing agent requests the name of the customer's attorney in order to forward the loan packet. The attorney is responsible for arranging a termite inspection, a survey, a title search, and insurance and for preparing the closing papers. The attorney and the closing agent correspond back and forth to verify exact fees, payment schedules, and payoff amounts.

The *loan-servicing specialist* makes sure the previous loan is paid off and the new loan is set up properly. After the closing takes place, the bank's *loan-payment specialist* takes care of issuing payment books or setting up the automatic drafting of mortgage fees and calculating the exact monthly payments, including escrow amounts. The loan-payment specialist also monitors late payment of mortgages.

It is difficult to evaluate the success or failure of the reengineered process, since the volume of refinancing requests is so much greater than it has ever been before. However, customer comments solicited by the loan-servicing specialist have been disturbing to management.

CUSTOMER COMMENTS:

- I decided to refinance with the same bank that held my original loan, thinking erroneously that I could save some time and money. You took two months longer proccessing my loan than the other bank would have, and the money I saved on closing costs was more than eaten up by the extra month's higher mortgage payments.
- I just got a call from someone at your bank claiming my mortgage payment was overdue. How can it be overdue when you draft it automatically from my checking account?
- How come you do everything in writing and through the mail? If you would just call and ask me these questons instead of sending forms for me to fill out, things would go much quicker.
- If I haven't made any additions to my house or property in the past year, you appraised it last year, and you have access to my tax assessment, why bother with another appraisal? You guys just like to pass around the business.
- I never know who to call for what. You have so many people working on my file. I know I've repeated the same thing to a dozen different people.
- It took so long to get my loan approved that my credit report, appraisal report, and termite inspection ran out. I think you should pay for the new reports, not me.
- I drove down to your office in person today to deliver the attorney's papers, and I hoped to return them with your signature and whatever else you add to the closing packet. The loan specialist said that the closing agent wouldn't get to my file until the morning of the scheduled closing and that if she hit a snag, the closing could

be postponed! I'm taking off half a day from work to attend the closing and "rescheduling" is not convenient. I know you have lots of business, but I don't like being treated this way.

- I received a letter from one of your loan-payment specialists today, along with a stack of forms to complete specifying how I want to set up my mortgage payments. I signed all these at closing—don't you read your own work? I'm worried that if I fill them out again you'll withdraw the payment twice from my account! ∎

SOURCE: Roberta S. Russell and Bernard W. Taylor III, *Production and Operations Management: Focusing on Quality and Competitiveness* (Upper Saddle River, NJ, Prentice Hall, 1995), pp. 320–321.

CASE QUESTIONS

1. Identify the steps of the refinancing process. What is the purpose of each step?
2. Develop a blueprint for the process. Indicate fail points and, where possible, indicate time for each step.
3. Do you see any steps that can be eliminated? Which steps do you think create value for the customer?
4. How can the overall process be improved?
5. Which of the service design and development principles discussed in Section 8.4 did the bank use in developing this service? Which principles do you think the bank needs to implement?
6. Which of the concepts and tools recommended for building quality and value into services did the bank use in developing this service? Which concepts and tools do you think the bank should use?

CASE 8-2   The Shuttle by United

United Airlines designed the Shuttle by United to compete in the short-haul air service market. Up to mid-1994, United had been steadily losing market share in the short-haul markets to new carriers with lower costs. It seized an opportunity created by an employee buyout through an employee stock ownership plan (ESOP) to reestablish itself as a competitor in those markets. Using a combination of market research, employee teams, and process analysis, United reduced its costs by 30 percent, increased plane utilization, and cut turnaround time in half from its existing air service. Its efforts have resulted in higher customer satisfaction, improved market share, reduced costs, and increased profitability.

It is 9:30 A.M. on October 1, 1994. "Three, two, one, ignition!" Rono Dutta, vice-president of shuttle development, is chanting this countdown with a group of Shuttle by United employees at Los Angeles International airport. As he presses a large button labeled "Launch," the San Francisco-bound passengers on flight 2018 holding zone 1 boarding passes start to board. Zone boarding is a concept initiated by the Shuttle by United to help the air-

line regain market share in the short-haul markets. In those markets, niche carriers, such as Southwest, America West, and other low-cost carriers, have steadily pushed out the more established, higher-cost airlines, such as American, Delta, and United. The niche carriers offer low fares, no-frills service, and frequent flights, a formula that has been fully endorsed by the marketplace.

When designing the shuttle, United targeted the west coast of the United States. United has a strong, well-established consumer franchise in the busy and demanding west coast market. For example, it operates 40 round trips per day between Los Angeles and San Francisco, the largest air travel market in the United States. In this crucial west coast market, United's share eroded from 50 percent in 1989 to 34 percent in 1994, mainly due to Southwest entering the fray in the late 1980s and increasing its market share from zero to 50 percent. As United announced its plans for the shuttle for the fall of 1994, both USAir and American Airlines announced major reductions in intrastate flights.

To compete successfully in the short-haul market, United needed to reduce its costs by 30 percent. When its employees bought out United Airlines Corporation through an ESOP (employee stock ownership plan), it had an opportunity to make this happen. The lower pay scales and more flexible work rules resulting from the ESOP package, combined with increased aircraft utilization, helped United close its cost gap with its short-haul competitors.

THE EMPLOYEE BUYOUT

As part of the employee buyout of United Airlines, employees traded nearly five billion dollars in wage, benefit, and work-rule concessions for a 55 percent stake in United. The buyout was sought and driven by the pilots and machinists unions. Flight attendants withdrew from the labor coalition in 1993. In exchange for the right to select three of the 12 directors on the United board, the employees put up $4.9 billion in wage and benefit concessions over five years, ranging from 8.25 percent in givebacks for nonunion office workers and ticket agents to 14.7 percent for ground crews and 15.7 percent for pilots. The entire package will reduce United's labor costs by 14 percent.

United strategists sought to leverage this reduction in labor costs to develop a new product competitive with Southwest Airlines. The cost target for the new product was set at 7.4 cents per available seat mile (down from the pre-ESOP 10.5 cents). To achieve its 7.4 cents goal, United needed to decrease costs in two other areas: assets and distribution. It reduced asset costs through higher utilization of aircraft and facilities and reduced distribution expenses through greater reliance on direct ticketing

(Exhibit 8-8). At 7.4 cents, United would be at a 0.4 cent disadvantage to Southwest. It compensated for this disadvantage by obtaining additional revenue with its superior yield management tools and from its higher average revenue per passenger. The shuttle routinely matched Southwest fares to the penny on the same routes. Even at fare parity, the shuttle would enjoy a higher average simply because of its first-class service and a greater proportion of connecting passengers.

THE COMPETITION: SOUTHWEST AIRLINES

Southwest Airlines was the major competitor for United in the west coast market. Southwest has succeeded because of its well-focused strategy centered on high frequency point-to-point service of routes under 750 miles and a fleet built around a single aircraft type, the Boeing 737. Southwest leads the industry in on-time performance, baggage handling, and rate of consumer complaints and bills itself as the only holder of the "Triple Crown" in the industry. Its success is largely credited to a highly enthusiastic, motivated, and productive work force and high aircraft utilization, resulting in a low-cost structure. Southwest is a very different airline: it offers no meals, no first-class section, and no assigned seats. To avoid booking fees, it has repeatedly refused to join the computerized reservatons systems sponsored by the big three carriers (American, Delta, and United). Thanks to a simpler product and simpler processes, it consistently achieves a 20-minute turnaround time (the period from when a plane arrives at the gate until it leaves the gate) and

EXHIBIT 8-8

Expense Category	Southwest	Current United	United Shuttle
Wages and Benefits	$0.024	$0.035	$0.026
Fuel and Oil	$0.011	$0.011	$0.011
Aircraft Ownership	$0.007	$0.008	$0.007
Aircraft Maintenance	$0.006	$0.003	$0.002
Commissions (excluding international)	$0.005	$0.010	$0.006
Advertising	$0.002	$0.002	$0.003
Food and Beverage	$0.000	$0.005	$0.000
Other	$0.017	$0.031	$0.019
Total	$0.072	$0.105	$0.074

Shuttle by United costs slightly exceed those of Southwest. Southwest outsources a higher percentage of maintenance work than United does. Thus, its aircraft maintenance cost is higher than United's, but its unit labor expense related to maintenance is lower (from UAL Corporaton, Proxy Statement, June 10, 1994).

high aircraft utilization. Its open-seating policy encourages passengers to arrive at the gate early to get the best seats. Its boarding process is a prime example of a simpler process. Passengers are issued plastic boarding cards numbered from 1 to 126 (the number of seats on the airplane) on a first-come, first-served basis. These cards are issued only at the gate, which eliminates the need for expensive and extensive computer networks throughout the airport. Passengers are boarded in groups of 30, and carry-on baggage rules are strictly enforced to speed up the boarding process. Carry-on bags not meeting the size requirements are tagged at the gate and brought down to the baggage compartment in the plane cargo bay by any available employee.

Once on board, passengers can sit in any available seat. Flight attendants assist passengers with seating and carry-on storage. In-flight service is limited to peanuts and drinks, which simplifies aircraft servicing and reduces costs.

The practice of cross-utilizing employees makes the Southwest workplace productive and has created a strong team atmosphere. Southwest's low-cost structure, combined with its high load factor and high customer satisfaction, has led to its enormous success and its status as the only profitable US airline in the early 1990s with a net margin of five percent or better.

DEVELOPMENT OF THE SHUTTLE

"It is our firm belief that if we do what is right for our customers and what is right for our employees, then shareholders' value will be maximized." This vision of the shuttle was translated into an implementation plan by 22 cross-functional employee teams. According to Rono Dutta, vice-president of shuttle development, their mandate was to set up the shuttle as a "customer-friendly and hassle-free" product, build "a fiercely loyal customer base," instill ownership and enthusiasm in its employees, and ultimately achieve profitability. Over a two-month period, these teams developed operating procedures (*playbooks* in shuttle parlance) from the ground up. These playbooks covered such areas as airport, flight, and in-flight operations. In addition, the airline set up city teams to develop a public awareness campaign targeted at specific communities. These "city" teams typically consisted of a flight attendant, a pilot, a baggage handler, a reser-

vations agent, and a sales account executive who lived in a particular metropolitan area. Involving a broad cross-section of front-line employees in designing a new product represented a radical departure from past United management practices.

MAIN GOALS

To compete with Southwest, United needed to make a profit at Southwest's price. United asked its employee teams to increase aircraft utilization, which implied reducing time on the ground. Turn-around time is affected by several factors: the deplaning rate (in passengers per minute), the enplaning rate (in passengers per minute), baggage handling time, and other servicing time. If the airline reduced ground time, it would require fewer gates and less ground equipment. If it could increase aircraft utilization, it would increase the revenue generated by each plane. Southwest flew its planes 11 hours per day. The Shuttle by United made matching that number its goal.

THE ORIGINAL PROCESS

Before designing the Shuttle by United, the teams analyzed the existing procedures of United and Southwest. They performed detailed time studies for deplanement, enplanement, baggage handling, and fueling services. These studies served as the basis for the design of the Shuttle by United.

On United's regular flights, passengers received assigned seats and, upon request, boarding passes, when they bought their tickets. Families with children, children traveling alone, and people needing extra assistance were preboarded, followed by first-class passengers and premier passengers (the top level of United's frequent flyer program). After this, the airline boarded by row numbers from the rear of the plane forward. Passengers in the back third of the plane boarded first, then passengers in the middle of the plane, and finally passengers in the front part of the coach section. United restricted carry-on baggage to two bags per person but did not strictly enforce size and number restrictions.

A flight attendant greeted passengers as they boarded the plane while other flight attendants set up the in-flight service in the galleys. The gate attendant or a flight attendant could restrict what a passenger carried on but had to call a baggage handler for assistance.

The United teams performed time studies on the components of ground time for both Southwest and United. It did both time studies on 737 aircraft using a single door jet bridge. Southwest and United Airlines had the same deplaning rate (17 passengers per minute), but the team observed that Southwest had an enplanement rate of 11 passengers per minute while United had an enplanement rate of only 8.5 passengers per minute.

When flights arrived at the gate, the plane door was opened so passengers could deplane. Southwest took a half minute to open the door and United one minute. Southwest had a gate agent who waited at the jetway door to meet the plane and open the door from the outside, whereas the United gate agent often had to be called in from other duties. Once the door was open, passengers were deplaned (six minutes for both airlines), and the inflight crew did minor cabin cleaning. Departing passengers were then boarded: at an 80 percent load factor, observations showed that Southwest took 12.5 minutes to board passengers while United took 14.2 minutes. Finally, the crew asked passengers to settle into their seats and closed the door. This process took 2.5 minutes on both airlines. The entire boarding process on United took approximately 23.7 minutes compared to 21.5 minutes for Southwest Airlines.

Ramp service consists of baggage handling and fueling service. The team assumed a 128-seat plane with an 80-percent load factor, 0.9 bags per passenger, and 500 pounds of cargo (on and off). The baggage handling process was sequential and consisted of six steps: (1) open the doors and set up the belt loaders (3.0 minutes), (2) unload the bags (7.7 minutes, (3) unload the cargo (1.7 minutes), (4) load the base (7.7 minutes), (5) load the cargo (1.7 minutes), and (6) remove the belt loaders and close the doors (3.0 minutes). The baggage-handling process took approximately 24.8 minutes. The fueling process occurred concurrently and was usually shorter than the baggage-handling procedure.

THE REENGINEERED PROCESS

The current United enplaning process was too slow. Time studies showed that the open seating method Southwest used was faster than United's assigned seating approach. However, many passengers did not like scrambling for a seat. Even with Southwest's open seating, bottlenecks still occurred. Most

passengers preferred aisle or window seats, which left only middle seats for late-boarding passengers. They either climbed over the aisle passengers or displaced them and created a bottleneck in the aisle. In addition, bottlenecks occurred when passengers stowed their baggage in the overhead compartments. Southwest anticipated this problem, and its flight attendants actively assisted passengers with stowing their carry-on bags.

The United team experimented with open seating on 40 flights. The results showed that open seating reduced boarding time from an average of 14.2 minutes to 13.3 minutes, which was still higher than the Southwest time of 12.5 minutes, but customer comments were largely unfavorable. The employee team decided that it needed "a better mousetrap."

In team meetings about the boarding process, an industrial engineer who had worked for a trucking company noted that trucks were loaded from the outside in to minimize loading time. Couldn't the same concept be applied to an airplane? The initial reactions to her idea varied, but United decided to test the plan. Passengers holding window seats were to be boarded first, followed by those holding middle seats and finally followed by those holding aisle seats.

The boarding process, code-named WILMA (window-middle-aisle), uses zones to identify seating order. When passengers select their seats, zone numbers are automatically assigned and printed in large letters on their boarding passes. Zone 1 seats are window seats on the right side of the plane; Zone 2, window seats on the left side of the plane; Zone 3, middle seats on the right; Zone 4, middle seats on the left; Zone 5, aisle seats on the right; and Zone 6, aisle seats on the left. Zone 1 and 2 passengers are boarded first, followed by Zone 3 and 4 passengers, followed by Zone 5 and 6 passengers. Premier customers are not offered early boarding but instead boarded when their zone is called. Early boarding is still provided for passengers needing special assistance.

Tests of the new boarding procedure resulted in an average enplanement rate of 11.5 passengers per minute on planes with a load factor of 80 percent. The boarding time was reduced by 2.5 minutes to 11.7 minutes (slightly lower than the Southwest boarding time of 12.5 minutes). United performed time studies on selected Southwest flights, on United Airlines advanced-seat-assignment flights, and on United Airlines WILMA flights. The results

EXHIBIT 8-9

Flight	Open Seating Time	United Advanced Seating Time	WILMA Time
1	10.0	13.9	11.3
2	16.7	12.6	13.3
3	14.8	18.0	13.3
4	11.8	14.7	12.4
5	11.6	13.9	13.3
6	15.0	13.8	9.6
7	13.8	14.0	13.3
8	10.2	12.7	8.8
9	12.3		10.9
10	11.7		10.5
11	12.3		
12	12.9		
13	10.1		
14	12.3		
15	12.6		
Average	12.5	14.2	11.7

This summary of boarding times on 15 flights shows the advantage of the WILMA system (window, middle, aisle). We assumed that all planes had 128 seats and had an 80 percent load factor. All times are in minutes.

(Exhibit 8-9) showed that the use of WILMA resulted in a 17.6 percent reduction in boarding time.

A problem that surfaced early on was the issue of passengers traveling together. What would happen if a family with small children all received different zone numbers? United modified the zone assignment algorithm to issue the same zone number to passengers traveling together.

Boarding passes with the zone number printed in large block letters are issued to all passengers. United modified its printers so they could print the shuttle boarding passes. In addition, during the launch period, it clearly displayed cards describing the Shuttle by United at ticket counters and gate areas.

Before the boarding process begins, the gate agent makes an announcement explaining how the plane will be boarded by zones and emphasizing the enforcement of the carry-on baggage policy. Passengers requiring extra time or assistance are preboarded. Passengers seated in Zones 1 and 2 are boarded first. If the gate attendant notices passengers boarding out of order, he or she politely asks them to wait for their zones. Zones 3 and 4 are then boarded, followed by Zones 5 and 6.

The teams identified several factors that could disrupt the WILMA process. Reducing the standard deviation around the WILMA mean is critical to maintaining consistency. Potentially disruptive factors included advanced seat assignments, carry-on baggage, overhead bins, preflight beverage service, and provision of in-flight materials.

1. In the original process, passengers could request boarding passes with their seat assignments when they bought their tickets. On the day of travel, passengers with advance seat assignments tended to arrive at the last minute and board out of sequence, which defeated the WILMA scheme. The team decided on a best of both worlds approach: keep seat assignments, a feature demanded by frequent flyers, but issue them only at the airport when they checked in. This gives passengers an incentive to arrive early at the airport.

2. Carry-on baggage was a problem. Most airlines restrict passengers to two carry-on bags of a certain size, but restrictions are unevenly enforced. Passengers with too much carry-on luggage or with over-sized carry-on luggage often have problems finding places to store it. While these passengers search for places to store their bags, the passengers behind them have to wait, and the boarding process is disrupted. These passengers can impede the deplaning process as they go against the flow to gather their belongings. The shuttle teams came up with several ways to handle this problem. Clearly marked boxes at the ticket counter, the gate, and the gate door illustrate the largest acceptable size of carry-on baggage. Ticket and gate agents offer to check any oversize and excess bags. To expedite this process, United relied on the newly created position of flight coordinator. The flight coordinator patrols the gate area before boarding looking for over-size and excessive bags and coordinates loading these bags onto the plane with the baggage handlers.

3. Overhead bins are to be opened before boarding and flight attendants are to keep the overhead bins open as long as possible. Passengers can then easily see whether a bin is full or not without having to open and close it.

4. Traditionally, first-class passengers are boarded first and offered predeparture beverages. The beverages are difficult to deliver because flight attendants have to dodge in and out of other

boarding passengers disrupting boarding process. United eliminated the predeparture beverage service on the shuttle.

5. Traditionally, magazines are placed at the front of the first class cabin, and pillows and blankets are located throughout the plane. The teams observed that as passengers enplaned, they sometimes stopped to peruse the magazine rack or to pick up a pillow or blanket. To eliminate these distractions, United stores in-flight reading material on the shuttle out of sight in the overhead bins. Pillows and blankets are kept at a central location and distributed on request by the flight attendants.

In addition to WILMA, the team identified other time savers that helped ensure a consistent 20-minute turnaround:

The flight coordinator waits on the jetway for the airplane to arrive. Previously, the airplane sometimes had to wait for the agent.

Pilot and flight attendant crew changes are minimized and occur simultaneously. This reduces cases in which the pilots are onboard but the flight attendants are on their way from another flight (or vice versa). Because of contractual differences between pilots and flight attendants, building common schedules for these two groups increased costs significantly. Yet, after a period of hesitation, the shuttle team decided to implement this concept because of its favorable impact on on-time performance.

To reduce the time needed to provision the aircraft and the frequency of provisioning, United greatly simplified meal service. It now provides only beverages and light snacks (peanuts or cookies). In most cases, it can pack enough supplies on the aircraft at the beginning of the day to last six flight segments. This decision was supported by market research studies: on flights of less than 750 miles, passengers have repeatedly stated that on-time performance and low fares are more important to them than a meal.

Flight attendants no longer use beverage carts so aisles remain clear during flights; instead they take beverage orders and bring them to passengers on trays. Toward the end of the flight, attendants collect newspapers, used cups, and napkins from the passengers to reduce cabin-servicing time on the ground.

Airline ground personnel are divided into upstairs employees (gate and ticket agents) and downstairs employees (baggage handlers, cabin service employees, and mechanics). On the shuttle, the up-

stairs and downstairs employees work together as teams with common goals. For example, they are jointly responsible for on-time departure performance. To reinforce team spirit, all ground employees connected with the shuttle wear the common shuttle uniform. This uniform was designed by a cross-functional employee team and consists of a red, white, and blue shirt worn with dark pants or a dark skirt. A common uniform is a powerful symbol, especially at large airports where the downstairs employees are unionized but the upstairs ones are not. In the shuttle operations, for example, it has become routine for mechanics or gate agents to help with loading last-minute bags.

United redesigned the baggage handling process so crews could handle both cargo bays concurrently: both cargo doors are opened at once and a team of employees works on each door. The concurrent process requires two additional employees. Both doors are opened and equipment set up in 2.0 minutes, bags are unloaded in 4.6 minutes, cargo is unloaded in 1.0 minute, bags are loaded in 4.6 minutes, cargo is loaded in 1.0 minute, and the doors are closed and equipment removed in 2.0 minutes, for a total of 15.2 minutes.

SHUTTLE PERFORMANCE

The Shuttle by United began operations on October 1, 1994 with 92 round-trip flights to eight west coast cities. By November 1, 1994, the shuttle expanded to 130 round-trip flights to 12 markets; by December 1, 1994, to 143 daily round-trip flights to 14 markets. By April 2, 1995, it had grown to 362 flights to 16 markets (Exhibit 8-10).

Performance can be measured in a number of ways: turnaround time, passenger load factor, and on-time arrivals and departures. On-time arrival and departure performance is based on the difference between actual and scheduled arrival or departure times. The U.S. Department of Transportation defines on-time arrival as within 14 minutes of scheduled arrival. United uses the 14-minute guideline, but also computes five-minute and zero-minute percentages.

Consumer research indicates that the key indicator of performance for the customer is arrival performance. Departure delays are irrelevant as long as the flight arrives at the destination close to on-time. After the inclement winter of 1994 (which eroded the percentage of on-time arrivals and de-

EXHIBIT 8-10

City Pair	October	November	December	One-Way Miles
San Francisco/Burbank	20	22	22	326
San Francisco/Las Vegas	18	18	18	414
San Francisco/Ontario	14	20	22	363
San Francisco/San Diego	18	20	20	447
San Francisco/Seattle	28	26	26	678
San Francisco/Los Angeles	58	62	62	337
Los Angeles/Sacramento	10	10	10	373
Los Angeles/Oakland	18	18	20	337
Los Angeles/Las Vegas		18	20	236
Oakland/Burbank		14	14	325
Oakland/Ontario		12	14	361
Oakland/Seattle		10	10	671
San Diego/Sacramento		10	10	480
Los Angeles/Phoenix			18	370
Total Flights	184	260	286	

The total daily flights have increased over three months from 184 to 286 (from United Airlines: "Friendly Skies").

partures), in early 1995, the shuttle recovered to a level of 75 percent of arrivals within five minutes of schedule (Exhibit 8-11). During the fall of 1994, average ground time was reduced from 37.5 minutes in October 1994 to 24.7 minutes in December 1994.

United conducts regular surveys of its customers to assess their satisfaction with its service. In general, customers were pleased with the shuttle service and both premier and regular passengers were more satisfied with the shuttle than with the main airline (Exhibit 8-12).

In San Francisco immediately after the shuttle was launched, some passengers complained about the gates used for the shuttle. Before the shuttle, San Francisco/Los Angeles flights left from gates 68–75, but after the shuttle started, its flights used gates 76–79. Passengers had to walk further to get to these gates and some resented the extra time and effort. United argued that by using gates that were farther out, the taxi time of the shuttle planes was reduced by several minutes, and the minute or two increase in walking time was justified. After two to three months, this complaint subsided.

Management was particularly concerned with the reaction of the premier passengers. On nonshuttle flights, premier passengers are allowed to preboard the plane along with first-class passengers. On the shuttle, premier passengers must board by zone with everyone else but receive preferential seating. A survey of premier passengers resulted in 28 percent positive comments, 28 percent neutral, and 44 percent negative. The major complaint (about 30 percent) was that the shuttle did not offer preassigned seats. Another 20 percent resented the loss of early boarding privileges. About 10 percent complained about the fare; 10 percent were an-

EXHIBIT 8-11

Month	Passenger Load Factor	Average Daily Departures Completed	Arrivals On-Time :05	Arrivals On-Time :15	Departures On-Time :00	Average Ground Time
Oct-94	69.80%	180	92%	96%	85%	37.5 min
Nov-94	65.10%	246	79%	86%	63%	27.9 min
Dec-94	59.10%	283	73%	83%	54%	24.7 min
Goal			78%	88%	75%	

Shuttle by United performance statistics show decreases in all factors except daily departures.

EXHIBIT 8-12

Service	Shuttle Premier	Shuttle Other	Mainline Premier	Mainline Other
Overall	4.3	4.5	3.7	3.8
On-Time	4.7	4.6	3.6	3.8
Courtesy	4.6	4.6	3.8	3.9
Check-in Efficiency	4.4	4.5	—	—
Boarding Efficiency	4.4	4.6	—	—
Overall Flight Attendant Service	4.5	4.6	3.8	3.9
Flight Attendant Friendliness	4.6	4.6	3.9	3.9
Beverage Service	4.2	4.4	—	—
Aircraft Cleanliness	4.2	4.4	3.6	3.8

10/94 Customer satisfaction surveys show that customers were more satisfied with the shuttle than with the main airline (scale: 1–5).

noyed by a change in frequent-flier-mile computations (with the shuttle, passengers earned actual flight miles, instead of the former 500-mile minimum), 10 percent felt that first-class service fell short of first class, and another 20 percent complained about various other factors.

Among positive comments, passengers liked the on-time performance, the schedule, the potential for upgrade, the friendly employees, and earning miles in the Mileage Plus program. In an earlier survey of shuttle passengers, 94 percent of the respondents said they would fly United instead of Southwest if the schedule and fares were identical. On the other hand, the Southwest loyalists liked Southwest gate location, its friendly staff, and its two-for-one companion fares.

United did not expect the shuttle to meet the goal of a 20-minute ground time for the first few months of operation. The flight schedule allowed an average of 40 minutes between flights during October. The employee-owners decided to first develop experience with the new procedures in a low-stress situation before attempting to achieve a 20-minute ground time. In November 1994, United tightened the flight schedule to allow an average of 35 minutes between flights. It reduced this to an average of 25 minutes between flights by early 1995.

CONTINUOUS IMPROVEMENT

In its first nine months, the shuttle has operated very successfully. The challenge is to avoid complacency and to improve the process continuously while staying focused on the customer. Since its

launch, all shuttle airports have had daily "huddles" to identify cross-functional problems and resolve them. In addition, airport and corporate support staff meet for corporate huddles bimonthly. United encourages its corporate staff members to spend a day at the shuttle to stay in touch with operating and market realities. Some of the issues addressed during the huddles are carry-on bags, seat assignments for connecting passengers, fare surcharges, duplicate seat assignments, accurate passenger counts, and the potential for ticketless travel.

The design of the original "yardstick" box for carry-ons was inadequate. Gate personnel routinely had arguments with customers about what size carry-ons were acceptable. United designed a new box illustrating the acceptable carry-on size and its introduction greatly improved the interpretation and enforcement of the carry-on policy for both gate personnel and passengers.

Moving oversized carry-ons from the gate to the plane was cumbersome and labor intensive. Employees carried the bags down the jetway stairs two to four at a time, which often caused delays. To solve this problem, the San Francisco team installed bag slides along the jetway stairs.

Connecting passengers are given seat assignments on the shuttle when they check in for their first flight. If connecting passengers are late and hold window or middle seats, the boarding process is disrupted. However, if most aisle seats are reserved for connecting passengers, other passengers might be unhappy with their seat assignments. On flights with a large number of connecting passengers, the shuttle team decided to set aside entire rows of seats for them and thus minimize disruption to the WILMA boarding.

Over half of the shuttle passengers travel on some sort of discount fare. Most of these fares do not allow passengers to change flights or travel dates unless they pay a surcharge. Passengers arriving early at the airport usually want to move up to an earlier flight. Because flights are very frequent in many shuttle markets, this situation has become a common situation resulting in some heated arguments at the gates. Adding and collecting the surcharge had become the most frequent cause of passenger complaints. To conform with the hassle-free vision of the shuttle, the team decided to remove the surcharge.

Partly because flights are so frequent and ground times so short, a few passengers would get confused between flights and end up boarding the wrong flight. The common manifestation of this problem was for another passenger to find a person in his seat. This severely disrupted the boarding process as the mistaken passenger went against the flow to exit the airplane. The solution to this problem is for the gate agent to check boarding cards at the gate door prior to allowing passengers to get on the airplane.

A second problem, which called for a similar solution, was to determine the number of empty seats on the aircraft at departure time so the shuttle could accommodate stand-by passengers. The primary causes of discrepancy between the computer check-in inventory of seats and the actual inventory were no-shows and passengers who missed their connections. To reconcile such potential discrepancies, someone usually boarded the aircraft to count empty seats, which often resulted in a delay. United decided to test a boarding-pass reader at the gate door. This device reads the magnetically encoded boarding pass and verifies that the passenger is boarding the correct flight. It also checks off the passenger's seat as boarded so that the gate personnel have an accurate count of available seats. In the spirit of WILMA, the team named this device FRED (Fast Reconciliation Enplanement Device). United is currently testing FRED at the San Francisco Airport.

To encourage passengers to book directly with United or through self-service media, such as United Connections on Compuserve, the shuttle launched electronic ticketing with a $10 promotional fare between Los Angeles and San Francisco on Thanksgiving Day. With electronic ticketing, passengers make their reservations ahead of time and pay by credit card. At the airport, they are issued boarding passes when they present their credit cards or some other form of identification, and the need for a printed ticket is eliminated.

FUTURE PLANS

The buyout agreement placed certain constraints on the shuttle operation. The Shuttle by United is limited to 130 737-size planes for its first five years of operation. With the exceptions of Los Angeles and San Francisco, the shuttle is not allowed to fly between United hub cities. The maximum length of any shuttle flight is 750 miles. In addition, total flight hours on the shuttle are restricted to 20 to 25 percent of total United hours.

Since its launch on October 1, 1994, the shuttle has added several new cities including Las Vegas, Phoenix, Reno, and Portland. The shuttle has triggered vigorous reaction from its competitors, mainly in the form of protracted fare wars, which have shifted the battleground from operational excellence to financial strength.

The Shuttle by United is an excellent example of reengineering in action. By listening to its customers, benchmarking its competition, and involving its employees, United has demonstrated that it is a company that can translate its vision into action—a key to success in a highly competitive marketplace. ■

SOURCE: Sheryl Kimes and Franklin S. Young, "The Shuttle by United," *Interfaces,* vol. 27, no. 3 (May–June 1997), pp. 1–13. Copyright © 1997, Institute for Operations Research and the Management Sciences.

CASE QUESTIONS

1. What was the vision for the shuttle service? How did United plan to operationalize this vision?
2. What was the "service concept" for the shuttle?
3. Who were the competitors of United's Shuttle? How did United position its service relative to competitors' services?
4. Which of the service design and development

principles discussed in Section 8.4 did the design teams use? Next, consider the ones they did not use. Why do you think they did not use them? Do you recommend that they use them in future iterations? How?

5. Which of the concepts and tools recommended for building quality and value into services did the design teams use? Next, consider the ones they did not use. Why do you think they did not use them? Do you recommend that they use them in future iterations? How?

6. Identify the steps of the service design process United used in developing the shuttle service. What similarities and differences do you see between United's process and Scheuing and Johnson's model?

7. Identify front room and back room processes for the shuttle service. From whose point of view were they designed?

8. Identify the elements of physical evidence. Did they match the service concept and design?

9. What performance measures did United use? Do you agree that these are the appropriate measures for this service? Can you recommend any additional performance measures?

10. How did the design team find out what the customer wanted? How did they translate the "customer's voice" into service characteristics?

References

Akao, Yoji, "An Introduction to Quality Function Deployment," in Y. Akao (ed.), *Quality Function Deployment: Integrating Customer Requirements into Product Design* (Cambridge, MA, Productivity Press, 1990), pp. 1–24.

Berry, Leonard L., *On Great Service: A Framework for Action* (New York, Free Press, 1996).

Booz, Allen, & Hamilton, *New Products Management for the 1980s* (New York, Booz, Allen, & Hamilton Inc., 1982).

Camp, Robert C., *Benchmarking: The Search for Industry Best Practices That Lead to Superior Performance* (Milwaukee, WI, ASQC Quality Press, 1989).

Camp, Robert C., *Business Process Benchmarking: Finding and Implementing Best Practices* (Milwaukee, WI, ASQC Quality Press, 1995).

Chase, Richard B., and Douglas M. Stewart, "Fail-Safing Services," in Eberhard Scheuing and William F. Christopher (eds.), *The Service Quality Handbook* (New York, American Management Association, 1993), pp. 347–357.

Chase, Richard B., and Douglas M. Stewart, "Make Your Service Fail-Safe," *Sloan Management Review* (spring 1994), pp. 35–44.

Dean, James W., and Gerald I. Susman, "Organizing for Manufacturable Design," *Harvard Business Review* (January–February 1989), pp. 28–36.

Fallon, Carlos, "The All Important Definition," in William D. Falcon (ed.), *Value Analysis Value Engineering: The Implications for Managers* (New York, American Management Association, 1964), pp. 9–24.

Hauser, John R., and Don Clausing, "The House of Quality," *Harvard Business Review* (May–June 1988), pp. 63–73.

Heany, Donald F., "Degrees of Product Innovation," *Journal of Business Strategy* (spring 1983), pp. 3–14.

Heskett, James L., W. Earl Sasser, Jr., and Leonard A. Schlesinger, *The Service Profit Chain* (New York, The Free Press, 1997).

Heskett, James L., Thomas O. Jones, G. W. Loveman, W. Earl Sasser, Jr., and Leonard A. Schlesinger, "Putting the Service-Profit Chain to Work," *Harvard Business Review* (March–April 1994), pp. 164–174.

Imai, Masaaki, *Kaizen: The Key to Japan's Competitive Success* (New York, McGraw-Hill, 1986).

Juran, Joseph M., and Frank M. Gryna, *Quality Planning and Analysis,* 3rd ed. (New York, McGraw-Hill, 1993).

Kingman-Brundage, Jane, "The ABCs of Service System Blueprinting," in Mary Jo Bitner and L. A. Crosby (eds.), *Designing a Winning Service Strategy* (Chicago, American Marketing Association, 1989).

Lovelock, Christopher H., "Developing and Implementing New Services," in W. R. George and C. E. Marshall (eds.), *Developing New Services* (Chicago, American Marketing Association, 1984), pp. 44–64.

Marriott, J. W., Jr., and Kathi Ann Brown, *The Spirit to Serve: Marriott's Way* (New York, Harper Business, 1997).

Michalek, Joseph M., and Richard K. Holmes, "Quality Engineering Techniques in Product Design/Process," *Quality Control in Manufacturing*, Society of Automotive Engineers, SP-483, pp. 17–22.

Pessemier, Edgar A., *Product Management* (New York, John Wiley, 1977).

Rosenblatt, Alfred, and George F. Watson (eds.), "Special Report: Concurrent Engineering," *IIIE Spectrum* (July 1991), pp. 22–37.

Scheuing, Eberhard E., and Eugene M. Johnson, "A Proposed Model for New Service Development," *The Journal of Services Marketing*, vol. 3, no. 2 (spring 1989), pp. 25–34.

Schneider, Benjamin, and David E. Bowen, "New Services Design, Development and Implementation and the Employee," in W. R. George and C. E. Marshall (eds.), *Developing New Services* (Chicago, American Marketing Association, 1984), pp. 82–101.

Schonberger, Richard J., and Edward M. Knod, Jr., *Operations Management: Continuous Improvement*, 5th ed. (Burr Ridge, IL, Irwin, 1994).

Shingo, Shigeo, *Zero Quality Control: Source Inspection and the Poka-yoke Systems* (Cambridge, MA, Productivity Press, 1986).

Shostack, G. Lynn, "How to Design a Service," *European Journal of Marketing*, vol. 16, no. 1 (1982), pp. 49–63.

Shostack, G. Lynn, and Jane Kingman-Brundage, "How to Design a Service," in Carole A. Congram and Margaret L. Friedman (eds.), *Handbook of Marketing for the Service Industries* (New York, American Management Association, 1991), pp. 243–261.

Shostack, G. Lynn, "Service Design in the Operating Environment," in W. R. George and C. E. Marshall (eds.), *Developing New Services* (Chicago, American Marketing Association, 1984), pp. 27–43.

Shostack, G. Lynn, "Understanding Services through Blueprinting," in T. A. Swartz, D. E. Bowen, and S. W. Brown (eds.), *Advances in Services Marketing and Management: Research and Practice*, vol. 1 (Greenwich, CT, JAI Press, 1992), pp. 75–90.

Taguchi, Genichi, and Don Clausing, "Robust Quality," *Harvard Business Review* (January–February 1990), pp. 65–75.

Turino, Jon, *Concurrent Engineering* (Campbell, CA, Logical Solutions Technology, 1991).

Urban, Glen L., and John R. Hauser, *Design and Marketing of New Products*, 2nd ed. (Upper Saddle River, NJ, Prentice Hall, 1993).

Wells, Lawrence D., *Techniques of Value Analysis and Engineering* (New York, McGraw-Hill, 1961).

Wind, Yoram J., *Product Policy: Concepts, Methods and Strategy* (Reading, MA, Addison-Wesley, 1982).

CHAPTER 9

Human Resource Management in Services

9.1 INTRODUCTION

Human resource management (HRM) consists of all the activities in an organization involving the acquisition and utilization of human resources. Good human resource management must meet the needs and rights of employees and at the same time recognize the demands of the community, minorities, governmental concerns, and other parts of society. Line managers are ultimately responsible for managing human resources. The HRM department has staff responsibilities for providing technical advice on compliance with equal employment opportunity and other employment-related laws; hiring, firing, training, and the like; and maintaining services such as record keeping and benefit plan development. The most important activities of HRM are human resources planning, recruiting and selecting, training and developing, utilizing, and rewarding employees.

9.2 THE NATURE OF HUMAN RESOURCE MANAGEMENT

The human resource function in each organization is unique to that organization and may exhibit great variety from one organization to another. What follows is a group of activities most likely to be found within the domain of human resources departments in many organizations.

Human Resources Planning

Human resources planning makes sure that a firm has the right number and mix of people at the right times and places. Such planning must be part of the firm's strategic plan, intermediate plan, and operating plan. In large service firms, human resources planning is similar to that of manufacturing firms. In small service firms or small units such as a Burger King outlet, human resources planning is very short range. It may consist largely of tracking employees who are seeking advancement to management positions, those who will return to school or part-time work, or those who regard their job as only a temporary one.

217

It is apparent, then, that in services, human resources planning varies from long-range planning for large, stable companies to short-range crisis planning for thousands of small companies employing low-skilled and low-paid workers. Exhibit 9-1 suggests a general classification of the time horizon for human resources planning by type of service. The length of the planning horizon establishes the forecasting lead time. The choice of forecasting method to be used may be a difficult one, as will be discussed in chapter 15. Large companies must forecast both human resources requirements and the supply of people with required skills. Human resource needs must take into account corporate objectives and policies, new hires, training and development, turnover, promotion, new jobs, and attrition. These factors and others are shown in Exhibit 9-2.

Referring to Exhibit 9-2, corporate objectives help define the organizational structure; establish policies on the use of temporary, part-time, or subcontracted personnel; and develop a framework for forecasting the service demand. These are all inputs into the forecast of human resource needs. Constraints on human resource requirements include limitations on overtime, natural attrition, equipment capacity, and cash-flow constraints. Finally, the need for human resources is affected by the leadership and motivation of current personnel, the effectiveness of training programs, and the efficiency with which employees do their jobs. The efficiency of work and how to measure it is discussed in the supplement to this chapter.

One feature of human resources planning for services that differentiates it from manufacturing is the great number of firms with very few employees. Retail shops, repair shops, personal services firms, and local real estate firms are examples. When a firm's employees consist of highly skilled people such as lawyers, financial analysts, systems analysts, insurance underwriters, physicians, or public accountants, the loss of an individual is serious and the time required to replace such a person may be lengthy. Therefore, the manager of such a firm must know where to go to find good people quickly. She must maintain contacts within the profession, with universities, and even with "headhunters."

At the other extreme, many service firms employ unskilled workers. Although replacing unskilled workers is usually not a problem, their rapid turnover is a cause for concern. Such employees may tender their resignation by just not showing up one morning, and the loss of an employee will likely affect operations immediately, as in

EXHIBIT 9-1 Manpower Planning in Service Businesses

Type of Business	Length of Planning Horizon		
	Short (days to months)	Medium (months to 1 year)	Long (years)
Fast-food restaurants	X		
Traditional restaurants		X	
Real estate sales		X	
Colleges			X
Architectural firms			X
Hospitals		X	X
Resorts	X	X	X
Airlines			X
Lawn maintenance		X	
Banks			X
Temporary-help service	X		

EXHIBIT 9-2 Inputs to Forecasting Manpower Requirements

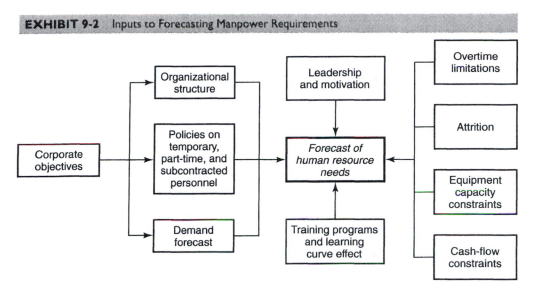

the case of a restaurant. Human resources planning consists largely of having a pool of potential employees who appear to be reliable and being able to access them rapidly. Some industries, such as fast-food restaurants and tourism, which have traditionally relied on teenage employees, have experienced spot shortages of employees because of the dwindling numbers of 15- to 18-year-olds. One solution: Many have chosen to raise pay above minimum wage and to seek out a new source of employees—senior citizens.

Recruiting and Selecting

Recruiting means identifying and attracting people who could fill positions within the firm and then securing them as applicants. The starting point for recruiting is to prepare a good job description for the position and a specification of skills and abilities the candidate should have. A pool of potential applicants may be developed from replies to newspaper ads, membership lists in professional organizations, government or private employment agencies, walk-ins, "head hunters" who seek and screen for a specific position, friends and relatives of employees, high school and college career offices, and business/professional conventions.

Recruiting managers, professional people, and many white-collar workers for services is similar to that for manufacturing management. In services, however, many white-collar workers are engaged in serving the customer, often while the customer is waiting or is in contact with the employee. There is no buffer between the customer and the surly or shoddy worker. For these reasons, employee recruiting and selection are extremely important for the service firm, and many service firms are highly selective in their employment practices. This is why for some of the most successful service companies, such as Southwest Airlines and Marriott, employees come first.[1] J. W. "Bill" Marriott, Jr., chairman and chief executive officer (CEO) of Marriott says:

> The cornerstone of our corporate culture has always been: "Take care of your employees, and they'll take care of your customers." . . . The philosophy of

---

[1] See the quote from Herb Kelleher, CEO of Southwest Airlines, in chapter 2, section 2.5.

putting employees first is particularly important in our industry, because Marriott is in the *people* business, not just the service business.[2]

Employee selection should be based on clearly established criteria for performance of the job. The application form should be designed to uncover the applicant's skills and abilities for job performance. Other selection techniques include testing, interviews, references, and probationary periods of employment.

In personal service firms in particular, it is important that the candidate have a strong customer service and sales orientation. This requires the proper motivation (sometimes called *internalized need*) to provide good service and extend oneself beyond the perfunctory performance of minimum job requirements. Everybody has motivation toward some goals. In the selection process, the manager must determine whether the individual's motivation can be compatible with company goals. The hiring of an employee is a psychological contract in which the employee should truly feel committed to the work and its rewards. Disney World has done a masterful job of motivating its employees to provide high-quality, consistent service.

In those service firms in which the pay is low and the work is routine, education is not likely to be a major criterion. In services in which manual skills and knowledge are important, the same may be true. ServiceMaster is an example of a successful service company that employs unskilled, poorly educated workers but has used their desire to obtain more education as a route to reducing employee turnover and increasing the quality of the service provided.

Service work often requires certification or licenses to be held by the applicant. A *certification* means that a person has passed required course work (as in a teaching certificate) and, in some cases, is also permitted by city or state law to practice in public. A certified public accountant is an occupation in which certification is required to practice, but a license to operate a business also may be required. A licensed barber may be required if a firm is hiring barbers. In contrast, an engineering firm may hire unlicensed engineers to perform work as long as there is a licensed engineer to approve the work. Engineers who are registered professional engineers have taken required formal course work, passed state examinations, and paid the state a registration fee. Exhibit 9-3 gives a number of examples of certification, licensing, and registration requirements for services.

Training and Development

Training is a systematic method for changing an employee's behavior to prepare the employee for a job or upgrade the employee's performance on the job. For example, a new waiter or waitress in a restaurant may be trained to handle difficult customers, or a real estate agent may be trained to organize his or her time better. **Development** is *person-oriented.* It is the preparation of a person for broader responsibilities and higher-level positions within the company. A senior systems analyst in a company may be prepared by on-the-job training, job rotation, and night courses for advancement toward the position of vice-president of information systems. In service firms, training and development (T&D) programs are usually differentiated among the following groups:

- Managers
- Professional personnel

---

[2] J. W. Marriott, Jr., and Kathi Ann Brown, *The Spirit to Serve: Marriott's Way* (New York, Harper Business, 1997), pp. 34–35.

EXHIBIT 9-3   Certification, Licensing, and Registration Requirements for Some Occupations and Professions

Occupation or Profession	*Certified*	*Licensed*	*Registered*
Beautician	X	X	
Bar owner		X	
Airplane mechanic	X	X	
High school teacher	X		X
Real estate broker		X	X
Certified pubic accountant	X		X
Doctor	X	X	X
Lawyer	X	X	X
Physical therapist	X	X	X
Airline pilot	X	X	
Stockbroker		X	X

- Office and clerical (including information processors)
- Technicians (such as lab assistants or auto repair mechanics)
- Operative employees (such as mail clerks, janitors, bus drivers, and generally people who do physical work)

Training and development programs can vary significantly from firm to firm, as well as by type or size of service organization. Some firms pay only modest attention to T&D. Personal service firms generally hire specialists who are already trained, certified, or licensed and provide little further training other than in the procedures and services of the company. If unskilled entry-level people are hired, as in both small and large retailing stores and chains, the new employee is usually trained on the job by another employee. The owner or manager may assist with weekly reviews of the employee at first. Development in larger stores, in resort and other hospitality businesses, and in real estate firms is generally limited to encouraging the employee to take outside courses at nearby schools. Other firms have extensive, long-term T&D programs. Electronic Data Systems (EDS) has such an extensive and valuable training program that new employees must pledge a three-year commitment to the company or reimburse the company for training expenses if they leave EDS before the three years are up.

Many corporations are taking T&D to a new level; they are starting and running their own universities. In the early 1980s, there were about 400 corporate universities; by the end of 1990s, the number was estimated to be more than 1,600. Most of the corporate universities, such as Tennessee Valley Authority University, or Holiday Inn University, have been established for training and development of their employees and managers. However, some others, such as Bellcore Learning Services of Bellcore and Symbol University of Symbol Technologies, also serve their customers, vendors, or other companies.

Technological developments and cost considerations are likely to change the form and nature of training in the future. Computer-based learning systems such as interactive videodisc/CD training programs are becoming more popular as the computer technology advances and prices of hardware decline. Similarly, advances in telecommunications combined with computer technology are making other forms of training possible and economical. For example, some institutions of higher learning now offer **distance learning** as an alternative to traditional classroom delivery of education. Also, many corporations are relying more and more on courses and seminars transmitted through satellite linkages and videoconferencing.

Another trend in organizational training and development is self-directed learning (SDL). Self-directed learning can be defined as a process in which "individuals take the initiative, with or without the help of others, in diagnosing their learning needs, formulating learning goals, identifying human and material resources for learning, choosing and implementing appropriate learning strategies, and evaluating learning outcomes."[3] Among the advantages of SDL are: (1) greater relevance to the particular needs of the individual learner, (2) sharper focus on the subject, (3) flexibility in the schedule of learning, (4) frequent updates of skills and knowledge, and (5) lower cost compared to more traditional approaches.[4]

The procedures for developing and carrying out T&D programs are covered in numerous HRM texts. Exhibit 9-4 shows a typical flowchart for the development and execution of a training program. Note that a training program starts with certain objectives and ends with an evaluation of the extent to which the objectives were achieved. If the objectives are not stated clearly in measurable terms, then it will be difficult to determine when the training is complete (i.e., has been effective).

In addition to following an organized procedure for training, successful training and development systems should take certain points into consideration.[5]

1. *Focus on the particular skills that make the service distinctive.* Entry-level employees have more customer contact than managers. Thus, a retail clerk's training should focus on knowledge of the merchandise and communication skills rather than on how to operate a cash register.
2. *Treat all employees as potential career employees.* Federal Express's typical employee is a part-time college student, and yet each receives more extensive training than most skilled workers in America's factories!
3. *Spend time and money generously on training.* One highly successful grocer spends over $1,000 for training per employee per year, offering to send anyone—including part-time bag boys—to a full 14-week, $600 Dale Carnegie course. Why the expense for menial employees? Because each unhappy customer is a potential loss to the store of $50,000,[6] and cashiers, stock boys, and bag boys are essential to the service delivery process.
4. *Retrain on a regular basis.* Employees at every level should have their skills broadened and sharpened through training programs that are considered an important part of their job.
5. *Provide training at various levels of skill, regardless of the employee's current position.* ServiceMaster and Embassy Suite Hotels have extensive training programs to accompany their promotion-from-within policies. Through company-sponsored training, a housekeeper at Embassy, for example, can be certified to run the front desk. This additional training raises the housekeeper's base pay and allows him to fill in at the new position whenever needed.[7]
6. *Be line-driven.* This means that training programs should be developed with input from or at the request of the workers actually doing the jobs. Another way of

---

[3] M. S. Knowles, *The Adult Learner: A Neglected Species* (Houston, TX, Gulf Publishing Co., 1990).

[4] Paul J. Guglielmino and Robert G. Murdick, "Self-Directed Learning: The Quiet Revolution in Corporate Training and Development," *SAM Advanced Management Journal* (summer 1997), pp. 10–18.

[5] These suggestions are adapted from Tom Peters, *Thriving on Chaos: Handbook for a Management Revolution* (New York, Knopf, 1987), pp. 326–329. Copyright © 1987 by Excel, a California Limited Partnership. Reprinted by permission of Alfred A. Knopf, Inc.

[6] $50,000 is the "value" of a customer, assuming good customers spend $100 per week on groceries 50 weeks a year over their estimated 10-year lifetime as a customer.

[7] Bro Uttal, "Companies That Serve You Best," *Fortune* (December 7, 1987), p. 102.

EXHIBIT 9-4   The Training and Development System

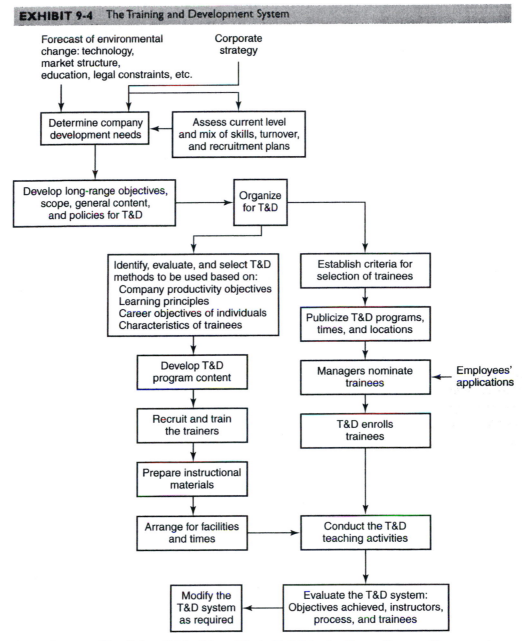

Source: Lawrence Klatt, Robert G. Murdick, and Frederick E. Schuster, *Human Resource Management* (Columbus, Ohio, Merrill, 1985), Exhibit 11.2. Reprinted by permission of the authors.

stating this recommendation is that training should be relevant and useful. For example, while it is important that service employees have a good attitude toward the customer they are serving, training must go beyond typical motivational seminars and so-called smile-and-dial courtesy skills. Training should teach how the job is to be done. Employees should be empowered, through proper design, tools, methods, authority, and training to offer the best possible service they can.

7. *Teach the organization's vision and values.* Top management should use every training program as an opportunity to discuss and transmit its vision of the ser-

vice concept. The best training is by example, and the best examples come from the top. Witness the impact of Bill Marriott, Walt Disney, Fred Smith (Federal Express), Sam Walton (Wal-Mart) and Jan Carlzon (SAS Airlines) on their respective organizations.

Employees learn what is expected of them in a job from sources other than training programs; they learn from observing the behavior of other employees and management. **Social learning theory** says that learning and behavior depend on continuous cognitive and behavioral interaction of a person with the environment. Social learning may be illustrated by "socialization" of a new employee. He or she observes the culture and behavior of coworkers. Rewards occur as the new employee bonds with the informal group. Failure to meet group norms may lead to hostility of coworkers.

Cognitive learning theory hypothesizes that people can recognize relationships between signs in the environment and their own goals. As an illustration, a worker wishes to buy a new automobile. She notes that coworkers who do well in a certain training program have a high probability of being promoted. Promotions lead to a series of wage increases with associated probabilities for each. Therefore, the employee's behavior is directed toward learning the most she possibly can from the training program.

Fortunately, no matter what theory we subscribe to, in practice we try to identify the goals of each individual and relate training and development to that individual's goals, as well as to company objectives.

Utilizing Human Resources

Utilizing workers means arranging their work to make them both productive and motivated. The factors that determine the effectiveness of human resource utilization are the following:

- Job structure and work that provide an opportunity for "stretch" performance
- Participation in decisions that have a direct effect on the person's job
- Open communications and equitable scheduling of assignments
- Competent supervision and organizational flexibility
- Economic and noneconomic rewards that recognize achievement and equity
- Opportunity for growth
- A culture that encourages caring for both customer and worker needs

Let us first consider the small employee service firms that are successful. Employees may be encouraged to take initiative and be given a variety of tasks and responsibilities. The "shop" operates like a family, with workers participating in decisions and communicating freely with a manager who provides experienced support. Noneconomic rewards, such as flexibility in working hours, time off when needed, and an atmosphere of general caring about other people, are important.

In large, successful service firms, the work may be organized so that small teams share responsibility for key tasks. Here, economic rewards and opportunity for growth are likely to be greater than in the small service firm. The culture of caring about others, both inside and outside the work group, must exist here also.

Perhaps the major difference between utilization of human resources in service and manufacturing firms is the technocratic perspective of the manufacturing firm. Rational organizational structure, subdivision of labor, rigid scheduling based on machines, and a focus on units of output per period are common to American manufacturing firms. Although service firms can be strongly results-oriented, they tend to be strongly people-oriented as well. Attention must be paid to the employees if the employees are expected to pay attention to the customers. Heskett goes so far as to suggest that the service concept be "turned inward to our employees, as well as outward to our customers."[8] Similarly, Albrecht and Zemke consider management itself to be a service to employees.[9] This attention and concern for employees translates into higher employee motivation and higher service quality.

Rewarding Employees

In many service organizations, the discretionary content of an employee's job may be large compared with the prescribed content. This is one of the reasons that developing a compensation plan and achieving perceived equity are so difficult in many service organizations. For example, a teacher may be *required* to present only certain instructional material to the students and to assess their progress in the completion of the material. However, the best teachers also design special materials, programs, or experiences for students at different levels of progress. In addition, they relate to the students on a personal level and engage the help of parents or other professionals in understanding and motivating student performance. Merit pay for teachers has not been widely used, in part because the variability or discretion inherent in teaching makes it difficult to determine what constitutes "merit."

Another problem for many service organizations is the low wages they offer relative to those in manufacturing. This makes it difficult to recruit, reward, and hold employees. Thus, the standard principles of wage and salary administration in services must be expanded to include an array of low-cost benefits that provide employee satisfactions. Further, candidates who are selected must be those to whom these benefits appeal. Methods for compensating employees in order to attract and retain them may include the following:

1. *Develop a public image of the company such that employees have pride in working for the firm.* Private colleges and college preparatory schools do this quite well. Professions such as teaching, nursing, and law enforcement have to rely on their mission of helping others to attract good people.
2. *Provide flextime working conditions* so that people may fit their work to their personal needs and lifestyle, including working at other jobs.
3. *Reward employees for participating in suggestions that can make their work more productive* (or that might even eliminate their present jobs without fear of loss of employment). This especially includes ideas for improved methods and automation. Through natural attrition, then, output per worker will increase and employees may share in the monetary gains.
4. *Structure jobs so that employees have control over their work and responsibilities that challenge them.*
5. *Provide first-class facilities,* such as private offices, lounges, cafeterias, and the like. For example, a modern building with carpeting instead of linoleum, advanced communications systems, modern conference rooms, an attractive cafeteria, and the name of the employee on the door or entry wall of partitioned areas may be much cheaper than the cost of turnovers due to hiring and training costs.
6. *Reduce the cost of employment for the worker.* For example, uniforms and a cleaning allowance are usually provided for law enforcement and other emer-

[8] James L. Heskett, "Lessons in the Service Sector," *Harvard Business Review* (March–April 1987), pp. 120–124.

[9] K. Albrecht and R. Zemke, *Service America! Doing Business in the New Economy* (Homewood, IL, Dow Jones-Irwin, 1985), p. vi.

gency personnel. This idea could be applied in modified form to dress clothes for store sales personnel (who also may serve as models), receptionists, school teachers, or bank clerks. The cost of such a program is small compared with cumulative wage increases. In addition, the use of well-designed uniforms in companies that do not usually use them (bus drivers, for example) may provide an identity and sense of pride for the employees. Other "perks" of employment include "company" cars; cafeteria compensation plans; transportation tokens; YMCA, health club, or country club memberships; child care facilities or vouchers; vacation packages; and stock options.

7. *Compensate by salary or commission.* This may induce increases in productivity and result in higher income for employees.

8. *Design the service so that the customer does more of the work.* Self-service stores, cafeterias, government agencies, shuttle airlines, and banks (automated tellers) are examples of services that have increased productivity per employee by this method. Any increase in productivity, of course, offers a firm the opportunity to share these benefits with employees and to possibly reduce employee turnover.

9.3   NEW CHALLENGES

The decade of 1990s witnessed many changes in the workplace; probably the most talked about is the massive downsizing many large companies were engaged in to cut costs and become more competitive. Downsizing was, of course, not the only change we witnessed in the 1990s. A *Business Week* Special Report on the new world of work had this to say about the changes:

> Mobility. Empowerment. Teams. Cross-training. Virtual offices. Telecommuting. Reengineering. Restructuring. Delayering. Outsourcing. Contingency. If the buzzwords don't sound familiar, they should: They are changing your life. The last decade, perhaps more than any other time since the advent of mass production, has witnessed a profound redefinition of the way we work.[10]

In this section, two of the issues listed in the above paragraph are discussed: *empowerment* and *teamwork*. These issues and how they are handled are decided at the top levels of management. However, they require involvement or at least input from the human resources function of an organization.

Empowerment

"Empowerment is the process of giving employees the power to make decisions about their work."[11] In other words, empowerment is the process through which management shares its decision-making power with employees who do not have such authority in traditional organizations. However, empowerment does not mean abdication of authority and responsibility by the management, nor does it mean unlimited power with no accountability for employees.

The basic belief behind empowerment is that employees are more likely to be productive, innovative, and concerned with the overall well-being of the organization if they share the decision-making authority and responsibility. Hence, the objective of empowerment is to tap into employees' intellectual potential, knowledge, and experi-

---

[10] Keith Hammonds, Kevin Kelly, and Karen Thurston, "Special Report: Rethinking Work—The New World of Work," *Business Week* (October 17, 1994), pp. 76–87.

[11] Don Harvey and Donald R. Brown, *An Experiential Approach to Organization Development*, 5th ed. (Upper Saddle River, NJ, Prentice Hall, 1996), p. 227.

ence, and unleash their creativity for problem solving, improvements, and overall customer satisfaction.

Empowerment and teamwork are relatively new management practices initiated by the quality movement that started in the 1980s. Another important factor for the emergence of empowerment as a favored approach is the advancement in information technology and reduction in communication costs that made information widely available and affordable in many organizations.[12] It is estimated that the percentage of U.S. firms using self-managed teams, a form of empowerment, was about 20 percent in 1990, and it is expected to rise to 50 percent by the year 2000.

Empowerment may be at individual and/or team level. An individual service provider may have the authority to do whatever is reasonably necessary to solve a customer's problem and in general satisfy customers. For example, in chapter 8 Ritz-Carlton's Gold Standards were quoted, which included the following statements: "Do everything you possibly can to never lose a guest. . . . Every employee is empowered to resolve the problem and to prevent a repeat occurrence." Another example of empowerment of individual service providers is the Nordstrom rule: "Rule #1—Use your good judgment in all situations. There will be no additional rules." A more recent example is United Airlines, which empowered its telephone reservation agents to lower fares within existing market prices.[13] For most service organizations, empowerment of front-line, or front room, employees is most important because they are the ones customers encounter.

Empowerment may also be at team level when a group of employees is authorized to change its operational environment. For example, some federal court administrations around the country have been implementing a "Maximizing Productivity in the Courts" program, which they developed with the Federal Judicial Center. In their team-based management approach, employee teams are empowered to take responsibility for such things as:

- Setting their work schedules (within certain limits determined by management)
- Making work assignments within the team
- Providing backup in the event of absences
- Identifying resources they need to do their jobs as a team and requesting additional training, equipment, or management assistance[14]

Empowerment cannot be achieved simply by sharing authority with employees. It is not very meaningful—actually, it could be disastrous—to empower employees without providing them with the necessary knowledge, information, and tools. For knowledge and tools, service providers must be trained. For information, they must have easy access to all the relevant information. Recall the example of United Services Automobile Association (USAA) from chapter 7; employees have instant access to all the documents in a customer's file, because such information has been computerized and available to all employees. Without such availability and ease of access, empowerment at USAA would not have been meaningful.

What are the main advantages and disadvantages of empowerment? David E. Bowen and Edward E. Lawler III identify the following advantages and disadvantages:

---

[12] For a more detailed discussion of the impact of information technology and declining costs of communication on the centralization and decentralization of decision making, see Thomas W. Malone, "Is Empowerment Just a Fad? Control, Decision Making, and IT," *Sloan Management Review* (winter 1997), pp. 23–35.

[13] Carleen Hawn, "The (Truly) Friendly Skies," *Forbes* (January 13, 1997), p. 39.

[14] David K. Hendrickson, "Improving Productivity in Federal Courts through Participation," *Journal for Quality and Participation* (January–February 1997), pp. 20–29.

ADVANTAGES OF EMPOWERMENT

1. *Quicker online responses to customer needs.* Empowered service providers do not waste the customer's or the company's time by checking with their supervisors every time they encounter a nonstandard customer need; they respond and meet the customer's needs quickly.

2. *Quicker online responses to dissatisfied customers during service recovery.* Not every service delivery goes perfectly all the time; service failures do occur, sometimes due to employee error and sometimes due to customer behavior. Regardless of who caused the failure, it is very important that the service organization recover quickly. Quick recovery almost always leads to a satisfied, or even a loyal, customer. Empowered employees need not go through layers of management to take corrective measures.

3. *Employees feel better about their jobs and themselves.* Feeling in charge of one's work makes people feel good about themselves and gives them a sense of ownership. This leads to higher productivity and customer satisfaction and reduces absenteeism and turnover.

4. *Employees will interact with customers with more warmth and enthusiasm.* Most service encounters are person-to-person encounters with customers. A service provider's happy and enthusiastic attitude could be contagious and make customers feel happy and satisfied about the service experience.

5. *Empowered employees can be a great source of service ideas.* Employees who have a sense of ownership of their job would naturally want to improve the service process if they see no threat to their job security. Consequently, they would not hesitate to offer new service ideas and suggestions for improving existing ones.

6. *Great word-of-mouth advertising and customer retention.* Happy and satisfied employees who take pride in their jobs are most likely to treat customers right and make them satisfied customers. Satisfied customers are the best advertising a service organization can get. That is why Nordstrom's advertising budget is 1.5 percent of its sales, whereas the industry average is 5 percent.[15]

DISADVANTAGES OF EMPOWERMENT

1. *A greater dollar investment in selection and training.* Great service organizations look for the right attitude in the employees they hire and then train them to give the necessary skills and tools. Finding the right employee is not always easy or inexpensive. It takes a good deal of time, effort, and money to screen candidates and select those who are right for the kind of service being offered. Training also has a significant cost.

2. *Higher labor costs.* Well-qualified employees are in demand in almost every industry; hence, a company must pay them well and provide attractive benefits, such as health insurance, to keep them in the organization.

3. *Slower or inconsistent service delivery.* Empowered employees responding to nonstandard or unusual requests or solving a customer's problem tend to spend a lot more time with those customers. In such cases, other customers will inevitably wait longer for service. Also, when a service employee has too much discretion about service delivery, service output may become nonuniform. This may lead to customer complaints.

---

[15] David E. Bowen and Edward E. Lawler, III, "The Empowerment of Service Workers: What, Why, How, and When," *Sloan Management Review* (spring 1992), pp. 31–39.

4. *Violations of "fair play."* Research evidence exists to suggest that customers associate adherence to set procedures with fair treatment.[16] When they realize that some customers get special deals, they may perceive this as "unfair."
5. *Giveaways and bad decisions.* Some managers may fear that empowerment may result in employees' giving too much away to the customer. In some cases, giveaways may lead to increased customer loyalty, but this may not be the case in every situation. Also, in some cases breaking the rules may have a negative impact on other parts of the organization that the service provider does not anticipate.

It is clear from the above discussion that empowerment is not all benefit and no cost, these costs and benefits must be weighted carefully by the management. We must also point out that benefits of empowerment are not guaranteed in every type of service work. Some services may reap great benefits from empowerment, but others may be better off with an approach to service delivery that relies on well-defined and limited duties and responsibilities for service employees. Empowerment would be appropriate if the service is designed to deliver customized and personalized service to customers for whom cost and speed are not the major issues. An elegant French restaurant and a five-star hotel are examples of organizations in which empowerment will be the right approach.

Empowerment may be the best approach when the tie to the customer is supposed to be long term. In other words, if the service organization values a long-term relationship with its customers, as in the case of management consulting, or financial planning for wealthy people, empowerment is the right approach.

Technology plays a very important role in deciding whether empowerment is the right approach for a service organization as well as the degree of empowerment. Services that are delivered automatically and routinely by a system, such as automated teller machine services, may have very little employee involvement; hence, there is no need for empowerment. However, as the system and the technology gets more complex and requires employee involvement in its operation, empowerment becomes more appropriate. An example of this type is technical troubleshooting services provided by computer manufacturers to their customers over the phone.

The business environment in which the service organization operates also has a strong influence on whether empowerment is appropriate. Some service organizations operate in uncertain environments, which may disrupt operations and may make planning difficult for nonstandard conditions. Airlines, for example, are affected by weather, mechanical problems, and competitors' actions. Empowered employees who have been trained to handle nonstandard situations are most likely to provide the best responses in uncertain environments.

Whether empowerment is appropriate for an organization also depends on the types of people employed by the organization as managers and service providers. Douglas McGregor identified two general types of beliefs by managers.[17] Theory X managers believe that people dislike work, they have to be coerced and threatened to do good work, they need to be closely supervised, they avoid responsibility, and they want security. Theory Y managers, however, believe that people do not inherently dislike work, they just do not like rigid controls or threats. They do not necessarily avoid responsibility; they want security but they have other needs such as esteem and self-

[16] C. Goodwin and I. Ross, "Consumer Evaluations of Responses to Complaints: What's Fair and Why," *Journal of Services Marketing*, vol. 4 (1990), pp. 53–61.

[17] Douglas McGregor, *The Human Side of Enterprise* (New York, McGraw-Hill, 1960).

actualization. Clearly, theory Y types would thrive and become valuable contributors in an empowered service organization. Theory X types, on the other hand, would not feel comfortable in an empowered environment, neither as managers nor as employees. A recent *Wall Street Journal* article[18] indicated that while many companies and their employees in the United States are embracing the idea and practice of empowerment enthusiastically, not all employees in these companies are happy with either the idea or its practice.

Teamwork

Teamwork is another management practice that gained prominence during the 1980s, and it is predicted that it will be the dominant form of work in the future. Five factors can be identified that motivated the emergence of teams and popularity of teamwork: (1) global competition has increased the need to reduce the time required to design and develop new products; (2) today's employees are better educated and informed and hence are able to contribute more meaningful input into the development of new products as well as routine work; (3) success of teamwork at other companies convinced skeptical managers about the effectiveness of teams; (4) when combined with empowerment, teamwork leads to more job satisfaction and a feeling of ownership, which in turn leads to higher productivity and creativity from employees[19]; and (5) downsizing strategies in many organizations eliminated supervisors and middle managers and delegated many of their duties to self-managed teams.[20]

A team is a group of employees who work together to achieve a common set of goals. Team members usually have complementary skills that are instrumental in reaching the team goals. Work teams may be of two types.[21] The first type is a **natural work team,** which is a group of employees whose jobs constitute parts of a process. In other words, it is natural for team members to work together. The difference is that members prefer to assume responsibility for the whole process rather than the limited responsibility of their individual jobs. In most cases, the team is empowered; therefore, the team has more authority and does a lot more than the sum of their individual tasks. The team sets its own objectives, allocates tasks to members, evaluates performance of the team and its members, makes day-to-day decisions, and sometimes is involved in hiring and firing of team members. These teams are also called autonomous, or self-managed work teams.

The second type is the **temporary task team.** This type of team is formed for a specific purpose and therefore has a limited life. Temporary teams may be formed for design and development of new products, quality improvement projects, or any particular problem facing the organization. These teams frequently are formed by experts and representatives from various parts of the organization to capitalize on the expertise of members in different fields and the advantages of a multidisciplinary approach to problem solving.

Teamwork is most effective when the process is complex and requires expertise in different areas. For example, as discussed in chapter 8, the design and development of

[18] Timothy Aeppel, "Missing the Boss: Not All Employees Find Idea of Empowerment as Neat as It Sounds," *Wall Street Journal* (September 8, 1997).

[19] The first four of these factors have been suggested by Michael R. Carrell, Norbert F. Elbert, and Robert D. Hatfield, *Human Resource Management,* 5th ed. (Upper Saddle River, NJ, Prentice Hall, 1995), p. 658.

[20] Davis A. Kolb, Joyce S. Osland, and Irwin M. Rubin, *Organizational Behavior: An Experiential Approach,* 6th ed. (Upper Saddle River, NJ, Prentice Hall, 1995), p. 217.

[21] Don Harvey and Donald R. Brown, *An Experiential Approach to Organization Development,* 5th ed. (Upper Saddle River, NJ, Prentice Hall, 1996), p. 267.

goods or services is a very complex process and for high quality and value results, it requires the expertise in many different disciplines. Consequently, a cross-functional design team may be the most effective approach to design and development of products. Teamwork may also be appropriate when the problem faced by the organization is atypical, consequential, unprecedented, and has an impact on more than one part of an organization.[22]

Positive results from teamwork are not automatic; an organization must prepare for teamwork. First of all, a team must have a meaningful purpose and goals shared by its members. Second, teams need top management support. Third, employees who are going to participate in teamwork must be trained. The necessary skills for team members are technical, administrative, and interpersonal.[23] They need to know a lot more about the process or problem beyond their particular tasks; sometimes, team members may have to switch tasks, so they have to be skilled in more than one area. They also need to know more about the whole process than before so that they can make intelligent decisions. Administrative skills are needed to manage the team meetings and team's relationships with the rest of the organization. Interpersonal skills such as communication, conflict resolution, and problem solving are essential for effective and efficient teamwork.

9.4 TYPES OF SERVICE EMPLOYEES

There are many different types of service employees. In this section, four categories are examined to help determine how best to utilize, motivate, and compensate different employees. The classifications are: (1) private-profit, not-for-profit, and government workers; (2) full-time versus contingent workers; (3) blue-collar versus white-collar workers; and (4) professional service employees versus consumer service employees.

Private-Profit, Not-for-Profit, and Government Employees

Private, profit-driven service firms cover the gamut of compensation and organizational complexity. Accounting firms, large financial firms such as Bank of America or Sears, small "mom and pop" service businesses, and small outlets of large chains such as Burger King illustrate the variety. There are by far more low-paid positions than high-paid positions in these firms.

Not-for-profit organizations vary from the Salvation Army to the Ford Foundation. In many of these services, we see people who are dedicated to a cause and work for bare subsistence wages. Large philanthropic organizations, however, are likely to pay high salaries. The same is true for not-for-profit research organizations, such as the Institute for Advanced Study in Princeton, New Jersey; the Institute for Defense Analysis in Arlington, Virginia; or the Rand Corporation in Santa Monica, California, and Washington, D.C. The survival of these organizations depends on employing top-notch people and hence paying high salaries. In such organizations, a collegial management style and flexibility in assignments are likely to be found.

Government agencies are mainly information processors, although there are some exceptions (such as the National Park Service). Compensation plans in federal, state, and local governments are rigid and can be changed only by law. More flexibility may appear in quasi-government agencies such as the Postal Service, at the top of

---

[22] Harvey and Brown, *An Experiential Approach to Organization Development*, p. 268.

[23] Kolb, Osland, and Rubin, *Organizational Behavior*, p. 217.

some agencies, or in special agencies such as the Central Intelligence Agency (CIA). Productivity increases that parallel technology gains are difficult to achieve in most government agencies. Couple these difficulties with nonmonetary objectives and you will find that some individuals are unlikely to find satisfaction working for government agencies. Compensation and benefits provided by the federal government for lower-level employees often exceed those for private service firms. At the top levels, however, the reverse tends to be true. City and state governments tend to pay less than federal agencies and may offer less job security.

Full-Time versus Contingent Workers

Large, centralized service organizations tend to follow traditional patterns by employing full-time career employees. Large, decentralized service companies such as food chains, retail consumer goods firms, and financial firms tend to fulfill human resource requirements by a combination of full-time employees and contingent employees. **Contingent employees** are part-time people and temporary help who usually do not receive the fringe benefits of full-time employees. In addition, with the proliferation of computers and corporate downsizing, there has been an increase in people who work full-time at home, acting as subcontractors. As such, they do not receive fringe benefits either. There are also a number of firms such as Manpower Temporary Services, Inc., that *lease* people for a variety of jobs. Other firms specialize in subcontracting services such as security, industrial office cleaning, computer services, or accounting.

White-Collar versus Blue-Collar Workers

The terms **white collar** and **blue collar** have generally differentiated between office workers and factory workers. In services, however, there are many people engaged in the productive or conversion process who cannot be clearly put into one of these classes. Is a waiter wearing a tuxedo a blue-collar worker? Is a nurse, a retail salesperson, or a computer service technician a white-collar or blue-collar worker? Additional descriptors such as skilled/unskilled or hourly/salaried/commissioned help to define a new set of categories for managing human resources in services. They suggest a basis for recruiting, selecting, training, and compensating employees.

Professional Service Employees versus Consumer Service Employees

Another way to look at different types of service employees is by their background and the level of service provided.[24] A **professional service employee,** for example, refers to doctors, lawyers, accountants, consultants, and other highly skilled customized service providers. This type of employee typically has a higher level of education, a higher level of perceived status, more responsibility and authority, and considerably higher earnings than the normal service employee. The individual is usually self-motivated, with strong ego-gratification needs. Further, it is often difficult to separate the service from the employee providing the service. In other words, the professional service employee *is* the company, and thus retention of good employees is essential.

Consumer service employees, however, provide relatively standardized services to the public, as typically seen in retail stores, restaurants, and delivery services.

[24] The distinction between professional and consumer service employee is described in W. Earl Sasser, Jr., R. P. Olson, and D. Daryl Wyckoff, *Management of Service Operations* (Boston, Allyn and Bacon, 1978), pp. 401–405.

EXHIBIT 9-5   Human Resource Management in Service Organizations

	Characteristics of the Organization		
Type of service	Small, custom service	Large, mass service	Professional service
Examples	Beauty parlors, interior decorators, restaurants, travel agencies	Telephone, financial (credit card, banks), TV, fast food	Law firms, accounting firms, brokerage firms, real estate firms
Geographic dispersion	Single or multiple local sites	Central headquarters, local sites	Local, regional, national, international
Transaction or service rate	Low	High	Low
Value of transactions	Moderate to low	Low	High
Type of operating personnel	Semiskilled	Low-skilled	Professional
Type of middle management	None	Professionally trained	Professional
Entry-level skills	None to certified	Semiskilled	Professional
Training and development	On-the-job	On-the-job and company T&D	Advanced T&D and on-the-job
Customer contact	High	Low to none	High
Quality control	High	Medium to high	High
Customer loyalty	To the high-quality provider	To the concept and the best price	To the firm
Working facilities	Small	Large office buildings, small local offices	Luxurious office buildings
Compensation	Low or commission	Low to medium	High

These employees perform jobs that are more routine and that require only minimum levels of education. However, consumer service employees must interact with the public and therefore require significant interpersonal skills. Typically, pay is low and advancement is slow. Managers must pay attention to motivating factors to maintain a sufficient level of job satisfaction or face poor service performance and high turnover.

Exhibit 9-5 summarizes the dynamics of human resource management in service organizations with examples by type of service.

Establishing a Service Culture

The following are some important components of a company culture.[25]

Shared Cultures	Example
Important shared understandings	The company will support you if you are acting in the customer's interest with reasonable costs to the company.
Shared things	Most employees eat in the company cafeteria.
Shared sayings	We live up to our commitments to employees and the community.
Shared doings	We all pitch in together to solve a customer's major problem.
Shared feelings	If you are not willing to cooperate by going the extra mile, you do not fit in here.

[25] For a more thorough discussion on corporate culture, see Desmond Graves, *Diagnosis and Change* (New York, St. Martins Press, 1986); and Frederick E. Schuster, *The Schuster Report* (New York, Wiley, 1986).

If there is one value that permeates the culture of successful service organizations, certainly it is the emphasis on serving the customer. The bored, gum-chewing clerk, the argumentative maintenance person, the service representative who conducts personal phone conversations while the customer waits, and the government bureaucrat who knows little and cares less represent a service culture that is rapidly becoming intolerable.

In its place, a service culture is emerging in which superlative service is the norm. Consider the phenomenal success of the Seattle-based retailer Nordstrom, Inc. Nordstrom's advertising budget is a small fraction of the industry's average, yet its sales are three times higher than the industry norm. Its secret? Customer service and customer loyalty—almost fanatic loyalty. The service culture at Nordstrom is created by a CEO with a focused customer orientation (Jim Nordstrom on returns: "I don't care if they roll a Goodyear tire into the store, if they say they paid $200 for it, give them the $200"[26]), an overstaffed sales force providing personalized service (they remember names, send birthday flowers and personal notes, and routinely go out of their way for the customers[27]), salespersons who are multifunctional (they can cash checks, take returns, and gift wrap), and a sparkling store environment (with fresh flowers in the dressing rooms).

Employer Expectations

High-customer-contact services put tremendous pressure on the service provider. Employers, as well as customers, expect service employees to be courteous, competent, and caring *at all times,* even to unruly customers and in unpleasant situations. Whether the job is as a waitress, a bank teller, a teacher, or a sales clerk, the constant requirement to be "on stage" serving the customer creates a stressful situation. Doctors, nurses, firefighters, police officers, and others in similar professions have the added burden of dealing with life-and-death situations on a day-to-day basis and sometimes with unsavory "customers."

The resulting stress is a common cause of *burnout* for service providers, which leads to either high employee turnover or a progression from high absenteeism to deteriorating performance to unresponsive employees for the service firm. Employee health problems due to stress are also common.

Employers should expect that this stress will occur, be able to recognize stress-related problems, and take steps to compensate for stress incurred by high-contact service-related jobs. More specifically, in order to preserve the value of their human resources, managers of service firms should provide:

1. *Opportunity for positive reinforcement for a job well done,* especially in difficult circumstances. For example, most police officers see only criminals and other undesirables (or even worse, their victims) day and night. It is easy to become skeptical and hardened about the customers they serve.

2. *Periods of reduced stress,* such as ample breaks during the day, rotating schedules, rotating tasks, or rotating positions. For example, at a university, the student personnel administrator in charge of the judicial system spends each and every day hearing cases of student misconduct and handing down punishment. To give the administrator a different perspective on the student population, she might

---

[26] Tom Peters, *Thriving on Chaos* (New York, Knopf, 1987), p. 90.

[27] Says one customer, "When a blouse I wanted wasn't in stock, the clerk volunteered to get one from another store, and drop it by my house." From Amy Dunkin, "How Department Stores Plan to Get the Registers Ringing Again," *Business Week* (November 18, 1985), p. 67.

also be assigned as the advisor of a national leadership honor society or other highly motivated, successful student group.

3. *Avenues to alleviate stress,* such as open communication, clear and reasonable expectations of performance, group help sessions, opportunities for physical exercise, and stress avoidance training.

9.5   ORGANIZATIONAL STRUCTURE FOR THE SERVICE FIRM

An organization's structure can be defined along the following dimensions:

- *Standardization*—the degree to which procedures have been established for regular activities
- *Formalization*—written rules and regulations
- *Specialization*—division of labor
- *Centralization*—the degree to which authority is concentrated at the top
- *Configuration*—span of management, number of levels of management, number of supervisors to nonsupervisors
- *Flexibility*—the ability of the organization to restructure itself to adapt to external (environmental) changes[28]

In large service firms, departmentalization may be based on function and service lines just as manufacturing or conglomerates are organized. If we closely examine the structure of most service firms, however, we would find that they are very different from typical manufacturing firms, and the higher the customer contact of a service, the more different the organizational structure becomes. Consider the following principles on structure from organizational theory, based on studies of manufacturing firms.[29]

1. *As task complexity increases, the span of control decreases.* This makes sense because as tasks become more varied and complex, supervisors have less time to assist their subordinates. However, this is not borne out in service industries. There is no particular relationship between task complexity and the number of people under a manager's supervision. Further, the span of control for services is considerably less than in manufacturing. This is probably due to the fact that even the simplest of jobs in services (e.g., retail clerk) involve relatively complex tasks, a variety of tasks, uncertainty with each different customer, and decision-making responsibilities with each transaction.

2. *As the complexity of technology increases, the number of people responding to the CEO increases.* For manufacturing firms, the increase in technology makes certain groups within the company more self-governing. This means that the CEO has less direct impact on these groups and can therefore supervise more of them, providing general policy guidelines. But the reverse is true for services! The number of people reporting to the CEO actually decreases as the complexity of the customer encounter increases. In services, the more complex interactions are handled by lower levels of employees. CEOs manage at the administrative level, sheltered from direct customer contact, in a more certain, ordered environment. The difference in environment allows the CEO to supervise more people on a regular basis.

---

[28] These dimensions are taken from P. K. Mills, *Managing Service Industries* (Cambridge, MA, Ballinger, 1986), p. 56.

[29] This section is a summary of the material presented in P. K. Mills, *Managing Service Industries*, chapter 4.

3. *As the complexity of technology increases, the number of levels of management increases.* This is primarily due to the number of support systems necessary to protect the technology in manufacturing-oriented firms. Again, in service organizations, the opposite is true. The number of levels of management is inversely related to the complexity of the service encounter. Service organizations tend to be much flatter than manufacturing organizations because customer-contact personnel must be given authority and autonomy to complete the service process. In addition, the more levels of management, the longer it takes to make and implement a decision and, owing to the lapse of time in receiving feedback, the riskier the decision becomes. Services, by their nature, require that decisions be made on the spot and that any feedback on those decisions be immediate.

4. *As organizations increase in size, their organizational structure becomes more complex.* Thus, as the number of people employed increases, there is a tendency in manufacturing-oriented firms to specialize, standardize, and increase the levels of management control. But some service organizations, regardless of their size, tend toward unbureaucratic forms of organization and a less formal organizational structure.

These contradictions of traditional organizational theory support the contention that to succeed in a service industry, one must "turn the organization chart upside down."[30]

Peter Drucker, a well-known management expert, further suggested that large businesses of every type will follow the lead of services in drastically reducing their levels of management and their numbers of managers and giving more autonomy to the front-line worker. He predicted that the typical business of the twenty-first century is more likely to resemble a hospital, a university, or a symphony orchestra than the manufacturing companies of today.[31] Considering the widespread use of teams and empowerment of employees, his predictions seem to have turned out to be true.

9.6 SUMMARY

Most services are labor-intensive. Further, service personnel tend to have more contacts and interactions with customers. The management of personnel who employ such discretionary responsibilities on a continuous basis requires different emphases than managing factory or back-office personnel. Therefore, although some HRM activities (payroll, fringe benefits, and so on) may be the same for all types of employees, the selection, training and development, utilization, and reward of high-contact service personnel requires special treatment.

Recently, international and domestic competition has forced companies to reduce labor costs by downsizing. Technology also has provided some relief. Finding and utilizing lower-cost labor sources have provided more. This has led to a great expansion in the number of *contingency* workers, such as part-time, temporary, and subcontracted workers. Corporate downsizing has been identified as one of the reasons for the expanding use of teams and empowerment of employees in U.S. companies. Another reason is the quality movement and the desire to provide superior quality goods and services to customers.

---

[30] D. S. Davidson, "How to Succeed in a Service Industry: Turn the Organization Chart Upside Down," *Management Review* (April 1978), pp. 13–16.

[31] Peter F. Drucker, "The Coming of the New Organization," *Harvard Business Review* (January–February 1988), pp. 45–53.

The organizational structure of a service firm must be designed to support a service culture that provides a high level of service quality. Many times, this means decentralization of authority, fewer levels of management, and more flexibility than traditional bureaucratic organizations.

Discussion Questions

1. Name five activities associated with human resource management. Who in a firm is responsible for HRM?
2. How does human resources planning for services differ from that for manufacturing?
3. What are some typical criteria that should be used to select service employees?
4. List and explain several factors involved in successful training and development programs.
5. In general, service firms pay relatively low wages. What other benefits can they provide to attract and retain employees?
6. Discuss the advantages and disadvantages of empowerment.
7. Describe the type of organization for which empowerment is an appropriate approach.
8. Discuss the factors that motivated the use of teamwork in U.S. companies.
9. Discuss the types of teams that can be formed in service organizations.
10. Differentiate between
    a. White-collar and blue-collar service workers.
    b. Professional service employees and consumer service employees.
11. Discuss the implications of managing a large contingent work force.
12. What is a service culture? Give examples of firms with strong service cultures.
13. What do customers typically expect from service employees? Why are service jobs particularly stressful?
14. Most of the theories on organizational structure are based on studies of manufacturing firms. How does organizational structure differ for service firms?

CASES

CASE 9–1   Pool Delight, Inc.

Pool Delight, Inc., is a small pool service and remodeling company located on the southwest coast of Florida near Sarasota. It consists of the president of the firm and three permanent "subcontractors," who are individuals roughly equivalent to employees.

The president of Pool Delight, Bill Gordon completed two years of study at Broward Community College. He then worked from 1981 to 1984 for a large pool service company in Sarasota. While employed there, he worked weekends on his own time to develop a list of residential clients south of Sarasota. In 1985, Bill left his employer and founded Pool Delight. Initially, he concentrated on increasing his list of residential clients and taking on some commercial accounts. Florida has a high density of pools in middle- and upper-class areas.

It was apparent to Bill that he could not both service pools and market for Pool Delight if he were to survive and expand. He proposed to a friend, Jim McGuire, that Jim work as an independent contractor by cleaning and servicing pools and working on remodeling of pools with him. He offered to supply Jim with clients to be serviced. Jim would bill Bill. Bill would bill and collect from the customers and give 60 percent to Jim.

Jim was required to supply his own pickup truck, pay about $60 to $80 per week for chemicals used, and pay about $150 per month for health insurance.

Servicing a pool consists of brushing the pool and the walk and taking a chemical count of the water. Once a week the pool must be vacuumed. The service time is about fifteen to twenty minutes including vacuuming. A service contract normally consists of one service per week, for which the monthly charge is $55. One competitor charges only $50 per month and pays his employees a 35 percent commission. If the pool area is surrounded by heavy foliage and trees, $60 is the monthly charge.

In May of 1986, Bill purchased the customer list of a quality competitor who was retiring from business. The customers were being charged only $55 per month for two services per week, and Bill agreed to maintain this rate for three years for them. As a result of this purchase, Bill had to find another person as a "subcontractor." He knew a number of young men who did lawn maintenance work and selected one named Derek Rohr.

A few months later, Bill received complaints and lost several accounts of wealthy out-of-state people. They had dropped in at their Florida homes and found their pools in bad shape. Bill then severed his contract with Jim McGuire who was responsible for these pools. Bill again had to find a new subcontractor immediately while he worked weekends to maintain Jim's client list. Within two weeks, he had hired Jill Pole.

By the end of 1986, Bill had been operating smoothly for six months. He had taken on a number of pool remodeling jobs, most hinging on remarsiting the pool surface. He used a high-quality subcontractor with three employees to apply the finish after he and Derek did the rough work and acid etch. The three workers took about ten hours to remarsite a standard fifteen- by thirty-foot pool surface. Pool Delight remodels about thirty pools per year.

At the end of 1986, Derek was servicing sixty residential pools and four commercial pools. Jill serviced fifty residential pools and five commercial pools. She also took care of the bookkeeping and sending out bills. Bill handled five commercial pools and did the marketing. Derek and Jill usually worked from 8:00 A.M. to 2:00 P.M. on Monday through Friday on pools. In addition, Jill spent about ten hours per week on bookkeeping for $7.00 per hour.

Bill was considering expanding by opening a pool supply store. ■

CASE QUESTIONS

1. Assume that all of Pool Delight's subcontractors are employees. Draw an organizational chart.

2.
   a. Assume fringe benefits run about 10 percent of direct labor costs. Make four different assumptions about labor rates ranging from minimum wage to $10 per hour. If Pool Delight hires its subcontractors as employees, paid an hourly rate with benefits, estimate the total labor costs per year for each labor rate assumption.
   b. Estimate current annual costs if subcontractors are paid a 35% commission.
   c. What conclusions can you draw from comparing your answers to parts a and b?

3. How could Bill go about recruiting employees who are reliable and good workers?

4. What should Bill do to prevent a recurrence of the problem whereby the subcontractor skips servicing of pools? Remember, Bill has very little time to check on pools, and these pools are scattered over a wide area.

5. Evaluate Bill's idea of operating a pool store. Hazardous chemicals for pool work are currently stored at some distance outside the city, while the safer chemicals are stored in a small warehouse.

6. What kind of training for what period of time should be required for this work? Who should conduct the training? Are pool service workers unskilled, skilled, or professional workers?

7. How large do you think this business can grow? What could hinder its growth? What changes in management practices would you anticipate as the business gets larger?

CASE 9–2   Lewis Foods Fleet Management*

On June 1, Lee Foods, an Omaha based distributor of cheese and other foodstuffs, acquired Wisconsin Food Distributors, a similar company also based in Omaha to form Lewis Foods. Lee Foods distributed cheese and other foodstuffs to fast food restaurants, pizzerias, and Mexican restaurants throughout the states west of the Mississippi River. Lee Foods owned a fleet of 160 tractors and 230 refrigerated trailers. Wisconsin Foods was a distributor of perishables to retail grocery stores in a nine state area centered in Omaha. Wisconsin Food Distributors had 90 tractors and 160 refrigerated trailers. A total of 26.5 million miles was driven by the two fleets in 1988, and that figure is remaining constant through this year. Management anticipated that a total of 31.5 million miles, an additional 5 million miles, will be driven next year to support new customers.

At Lee Foods, John Richards, the chief mechanic, had also been serving as the dispatcher/fleet supervisor for the past year. At Wisconsin Foods, Al Lopez was the chief dispatcher with responsibilities similar to John's. After talking to both Al and John, Harlan Highsmith, the President of Lewis Foods, had the uneasy feeling that in the excitement generated by the potential savings in overhead costs, the increased productivity and efficiency due to economies of scale, and the larger market area, upper management may have overlooked some major issues in the merger of the two fleets. As a result, he created the position of fleet manager to oversee the entire fleet. John Richards was to be named chief mechanic for Lewis Foods, the newly formed company, and Al Lopez was to take the position of chief dispatcher when the merger of the two fleets was completed. Harlan Highsmith knew who he wanted as fleet manager. He contacted Bill Carnes and offered him the job. He voiced his uneasy feelings and emphasized that he wanted a smooth changeover.

On July 15, Bill Carnes became the Fleet Manager for Lewis Foods. His first concern was to merge the operation and management of the two groups of trucks into a single fleet rather than continue to operate two separate fleets. The warehouse division of the company had completed their plans and expected to close the Wisconsin Foods facility in about 90 days. At that time all route planning and dispatching of loads would be out of the main warehouse.

Bill began his job of integrating the two groups into a single unit by evaluating the past performance of the two fleets. The major expenditures in

---

*By Carl R. Ruthstrom, University of Houston–Downtown, and David Cross and Arthur Nelson, Stephen F. Austin State University. Used by permission of the authors and NACRA.

EXHIBIT 9-6   Operating Performance—Industry Averages

Fuel economy	5.7 mpg
Engine overhauls	Every 450,000 miles to 475,000 miles
Tire life	Recapped at every 150,000 miles, replaced at 500,000 miles

fleet operations are for fuel, engine maintenance, and tires. The staff anticipated Bill's information needs and prepared a report on fuel economy, maintenance, and tire life for the trucking industry as shown in Exhibit 9-6 and a comparison of the two fleets as shown in Exhibit 9-7.

This report failed to identify the strengths and weaknesses of the operations of the two fleets. Bill Carnes visited both terminals and obtained the following additional information.

At Lee Foods, John Richards, the chief mechanic provided much of the information Bill wanted. The Lee fleet consists of tandem Kentworth and Peterbilt tractors. Eighty percent of the tractors are powered by the Cummins 350 Big Cam III governed at 1800 RPM. The phrase "governed at 1800 RPM" means that a governor or speed control device is installed on the engine to limit the maximum engine speed to 1800 revolutions per minute. This extends the operating life of the engines. The other twenty percent of the fleet's engines are Caterpillar 3406Bs governed at 1600 RPM. The Lee fleet uses eight Goodyear 167 radial tires, four on each of the two drive axles, and two Goodyear Unisteel IIs on the single steering axle of each tractor. The trailers have another eight tires, four on each of the two axles. Tires removed from the steering axles are recapped and used on trailers. At the third recap, drive axle tires are moved back to the trailers. Only recapped tires are used on the trailers.

Two years ago, Lee had improved the fuel economy to 5 miles per gallon (mpg) by using fuel saving devices such as Paccar's Varashield air deflectors, Rudkin Wiley cab extenders, Rockford viscous fans, and lower horsepower engines. "But,

somehow we seem to have hit a plateau and cannot get above 5 mpg," said John Richards.

Driver comfort and safety have always been important considerations at Lee Foods as shown by the cabs with their deluxe carpeted interiors, AM/FM radio-tape players, air conditioning and seats with air-ride suspensions. The estimated cost of upgrading the interiors is $2000 per tractor. In addition, Lee has awarded drivers completing one million miles of safe driving with a $1000 bonus check. Every month, each driver attends a half-day driver safety and improvement class conducted by company instructors. As a result, Lee has one of the lowest driver turnover rates in the trucking industry at three percent. John Richards said, "There are not any labor problems at Lee. The only new drivers we have hired replaced those lost to retirement or physical disability."

At Wisconsin Foods terminal, Al Lopez, the chief dispatcher, provided similar information. The Wisconsin fleet is entirely Kentworth tractors powered by the Cummins 350 Big Cam III engines governed at 1800 RPM. Fuel saving devices similar to those used by Lee are installed on all the tractors. Drivers are allowed to customize their tractors at their own expense resulting in interiors similar to the Lee tractors.

Two and one-half years ago, Wisconsin implemented a transportation improvement (TRIM) program. The program includes Stemco's on-board computer monitoring system (trip recorder) and Stemco's vehicle management system (VMS) software package. The recorders are installed in all Wisconsin's tractors. The hardware for this system averages $2200 per tractor. The memory cartridges are

EXHIBIT 9-7   Lee/Wisconsin Performance Comparisons

	Lee Averages	*Wisconsin Averages*
Fuel economy	5.0 mpg	5.8 mpg
Engine overhauls	330,000 miles	450,000 miles
Tire life	Recapped at every 100,000 miles, replaced at 345,000 miles	Recapped at every 150,000 miles, replaced at 500,000 miles

in the tractors when the drivers are dispatched. At the end of a trip, the last thing a driver does is to remove the cartridge and turn it into dispatch. There he is given a blank cartridge, which he installs before leaving for the day. The driver enters his identification, the vehicle number, and the route number at the start of the trip. In addition, he enters the number of gallons of fuel purchased for the trip. The computerized recorder stores times, engine RPM, speed in MPH, foot brake applications, and stops. The data for each trip is downloaded from the memory cartridge to an IBM PC and subsequently stored on a floppy disc. The VMS program analyzes the data and prints out a Basic Trip Summary. Included in this summary are the statistics of various performance criteria management selected to evaluate driver performance, such as engine on time, idle time, road time, speed, RPM, and fuel consumption plus a grade (from 0 to 100) of the driver's performance. The drivers were introduced to the TRIM program in meetings of 10 to 15 drivers. In these meetings, the emphasis was on improving fleet performance by identifying the problem areas in each driver's performance. Initially, the computer trip summaries showed 50% to 60% of the drivers were speeding (running above 58 MPH).

Al Lopez said, "We knew that the greatest savings for large tractors can be achieved through improved gas mileage and reduced wear on the vehicle. Better efficiency in either area would make a very visible difference in costs. We started informally counseling the drivers with emphasis on driver awareness of economical driving habits. The nonthreatening approach produced dramatic results in reducing our fleet costs. Our fuel economy rose rapidly to 5.8 mpg where it remains today. Tire wear and engine maintenance costs have declined noticeably."

The single most noteworthy incident occurred when one of the drivers blew a Cummins engine in Texas. Cummins claimed it was attributable to over-revving and speed. The driver brought the memory cartridge with him when he flew back to Omaha. The VMS program analyzed the data and showed no speeding or over-revving saving the company a $17,000 engine repair bill.

"The most disappointing thing about the TRIM program is that we have never reached the anticipated 6–7 mpg that the Stemco salesmen assured us could be attained. In addition, we seem to be continually training new drivers on the system. Over

40% of our drivers have less than one year with the company," volunteered Al Lopez.

Further discussion with Al Lopez revealed that while 20–25% turnover of drivers was not unusual in the trucking industry, other underlying problems did exist. Both the chief dispatcher and the drivers feel that all the benefits of the computerized vehicle management system are reserved for the company. The drivers are of the opinion of having "a cop" in the cab limits their potential earnings and does not allow the driver much freedom in terms of length of driving day, breaks, and sleep time. Therefore most of the turnover of drivers is generated by the lure of higher incomes and more individual freedom in other trucking companies.

Upon his return to his office, Bill Carnes decided to review the data in Exhibits 9-6 and 9-7 to compare the performance differences in fuel consumption, maintenance, and tire wear. After reviewing the data in Exhibit 9-7, he decided to visit accounting and acquire cost data comparisons for the two fleets. Since the two fleets had continued operating separately, accounting had maintained separate books. The data Bill needed was readily available and Bill constructed the following table (see Exhibit 9-8).

Before leaving, he questioned the accounting supervisor, Shirley Williams, about the differences in operating costs per mile between the two fleets. Shirley confirmed his finding that the Lee trucks were reporting higher fuel, tire, and engine repair costs per truck than the Wisconsin fleet. Shirley Williams had begun investigating the differences in operating costs and found that both fleets were reporting approximately the same unit costs for fuel, tires, and engine overhauls as listed in Exhibit 9-9. Shirley also found that the company policies for both fleets included the replacement of 15 percent of the fleet with new tractor-trailer rigs each year.

At first she was puzzled by the difference in the drivers' cost per mile. "Both groups of drivers are

EXHIBIT 9-8 Lee/Wisconsin Cost Comparisons

	Lee Averages	Wisconsin Averages
Cost per mile		
Equipment	$0.82	$0.65
Drivers	$0.61	$0.58
Miles per year		
Per tractor	112,708	94,075
Per driver	77,420	73,127

EXHIBIT 9-9 Unit Costs

Item	Unit Price
Engine overhauls	$7000 per engine
Diesel fuel	$1.15 per gallon
New tires	
Steering axles	$175 per tire
Drive axles	$195 per tire
Recapping	$65 per tire

paid union scale. I'll have to look into this for you," Shirley said. As Shirley reviewed the records used to calculate the drivers' cost per mile for the two fleets, the only differences she could find were the safe driving bonuses paid to Lee drivers and lower pay to Wisconsin drivers during their initial probationary period. Shirley did find that the total pay and benefits package was larger for the Lee drivers because of the greater number of miles driven annually.

As Bill Carnes walked back to his office, he remembered Al Lopez's final remark, "Over 40% of our drivers have less than one year with the company." He made a mental note to confirm this with Shirley Williams in the morning.

When Bill Carnes returned to his office at 4:00 P.M., his secretary handed him a message to call Harlan Highsmith immediately. Bill is surprised when Harlan Highsmith answers the phone without the assistance of a secretary.

After the preliminary salutations, Harlan Highsmith says, "Bill, you have been with the company long enough to evaluate our current fleet operations. I've scheduled you to present your plans for integrating the Lee and Wisconsin fleet operations

into a single fleet for 3:00 P.M., tomorrow. Have a good evening."

Bill Carnes realizes that his recommended program must address both fleet operating costs and employee relations. He realizes that capital investments may be needed in both fleets to achieve improvements in these areas.

At 6:00 P.M., before leaving the office, he calls both John Richards and Al Lopez at home. He explains why he is calling and solicits their help in preparing for the 3:00 P.M. meeting. Both men agree to be in Bill Carnes' office at 9:00 A.M. the next morning to assist in developing the plans for integrating the two fleets.

At 9:00 A.M. the next morning John Richards and Al Lopez report to Bill Carnes' office. By this time, Bill Carnes has begun to feel the same uneasiness that Harlan Highsmith, the President, had expressed when he hired Bill.

Bill Carnes begins, "After tossing and turning all night, I finally got dressed and prepared a list of questions that need to be answered."

"I have been listening to all of the drivers' comments at Lee and can give you a long list of answers for those first two questions," exclaimed John Richards.

"I'll bet my list of gripes is longer," said Al Lopez.

"Great! John, if you and Al will work on the first two questions, I'll get to work on the last three. Remember that we need more than just a list of gripes. We need a plan detailing how we are going to integrate the two groups of drivers without creating more problems. Let's meet back here at 11:00 A.M. and see what progress we have made." ∎

SOURCE: Joseph C. Latona and Jay Nathan, *Cases and Readings in Production and Operations Management* (Boston, Allyn and Bacon, 1994), pp. 105–110.

CASE QUESTIONS

1. What problems do you anticipate from the employees reactions to the merging of the two fleets if we do not make any changes in the treatment of the two groups of drivers?
2. What issues do you anticipate will cause the most concern among the drivers and what approach should we use to integrate the two fleets without alienating the drivers?
3. Some of the drivers already qualify for the safe driving bonus. Could we continue this and add

a bonus of $.03/mile for every mile driven under 58 MPH?
4. Since any changes or improvements will cost money, where will we get the money to implement our plans?
5. Assuming that we decide to upgrade the tractors, would your first action be to install the Stemco trip recorders in all the Lee tractors or upgrade the driver comfort items in the Wisconsin tractors? Why?

References

Aeppel, Timothy, "Missing the Boss: Not All Employees Find Idea of Empowerment as Neat as It Sounds," *Wall Street Journal* (September 8, 1997).

Albrecht, K., and R. Zemke, *Service America! Doing Business in the New Economy* (Homewood, IL, Dow Jones-Irwin, 1985).

Bowen, David E., and Edward E. Lawler III, "The Empowerment of Service Workers: What, Why, How, and When," *Sloan Management Review* (spring 1992), pp. 31–39.

Carrell, Michael R., Norbert F. Elbert, and Robert D. Hatfield, *Human Resource Management,* 5th ed. (Upper Saddle River, NJ, Prentice Hall, 1995).

Davidson, D. S., "How to Succeed in a Service Industry: Turn the Organization Chart Upside Down," *Management Review* (April 1978), pp. 13–16.

Drucker, Peter F., "The Coming of the New Organization," *Harvard Business Review* (January–February 1988), pp. 45–53.

Dunkin, Amy, "How Department Stores Plan to Get the Registers Ringing Again," *Business Week* (November 18, 1985), p. 67.

Goodwin, C., and I. Ross, "Consumer Evaluations of Responses to Complaints: What's Fair and Why," *Journal of Services Marketing,* vol. 4 (1990), pp. 53–61.

Graves, Desmond, *Diagnosis and Change* (New York, St. Martins Press, 1986).

Guglielmino, Paul J., and Robert G. Murdick, "Self-Directed Learning: The Quiet Revolution in Corporate Training and Development," *SAM Advanced Management Journal* (summer 1997), pp. 10–18.

Hammonds, Keith, Kevin Kelly, and Karen Thurston, "Special Report: Rethinking Work—The New World of Work," *Business Week* (October 17, 1994), pp. 76–87.

Harvey, Don, and Donald R. Brown, *An Experiential Approach to Organization Development*, 5th ed. (Upper Saddle River, NJ, Prentice Hall, 1996).

Hawn, Carleen, "The (Truly) Friendly Skies," *Forbes* (January 13, 1997), p. 39.

Hendrickson, David K., "Improving Productivity in Federal Courts Through Participation," *Journal for Quality and Participation* (January–February 1997), pp. 20–29.

Heskett, James L., "Lessons in the Service Sector," *Harvard Business Review* (March–April 1987), pp. 120–124.

Knowles, M. S., *The Adult Learner: A Neglected Species* (Houston, TX, Gulf Publishing Co., 1990).

Kolb, Davis A., Joyce S. Osland, and Irwin M. Rubin, *Organizational Behavior: An Experiential Approach*, 6th ed. (Upper Saddle River, NJ, Prentice Hall, 1995).

Levitt, Theodore, "Production-Line Approach to Service," *Harvard Business Review* (September–October, 1972), pp. 41–52.

Levitt, Theodore, "The Industrialization of Service," *Harvard Business Review* (September–October, 1976), pp. 63–74.

Malone, Thomas W., "Is Empowerment Just a Fad? Control, Decision Making, and IT," *Sloan Management Review* (winter 1997), pp. 23–35.

Marriott, J. W., Jr., and Kathi Ann Brown, *The Spirit to Serve: Marriott's Way* (New York, Harper Business, 1997).

McGregor, Douglas, *The Human Side of Enterprise* (New York, McGraw-Hill, 1960).

Mills, P. K., *Managing Service Industries* (Cambridge, MA, Ballinger, 1986).

Peters, Tom, *Thriving on Chaos* (New York, Knopf, 1987).

Sasser, W. Earl, Jr., R. P. Olson, and D. Daryl Wyckoff, *Management of Service Operations* (Boston, Allyn and Bacon, 1978).

Schuster, Frederick E., *The Schuster Report* (New York, Wiley, 1986).

Uttal, Bro, "Companies That Serve You Best," *Fortune* (December 7, 1987), pp. 98–116.

Zeithaml, Valarie A., A. Parasuraman, and Leonard L. Berry, *Delivering Quality Service: Balancing Customer Perceptions and Expectations* (New York, The Free Press, 1990).

CHAPTER 9 SUPPLEMENT

Work Measurement in Services

S9.1   INTRODUCTION

One of the problems faced by human resource managers in chapter 9 is the effective use of service personnel. Good management means knowing what can be expected from employees, and that requires some sort of labor standards. Such standards are needed to determine

- Labor content of the service performed (labor cost)
- Staffing needs of the organization (how many people are needed on duty to meet customer demands)
- Cost and time estimates prior to performing services (to assist in a variety of decisions)
- Productivity expectations (both supervisor and employee should know what constitutes a fair day's work)
- Basis of wage-incentive plans (what provides a reasonable incentive)
- Efficiency of employees (a standard is needed against which efficiency is determined)

Properly set labor standards represent the amount of time it should take an average employee to perform specific job activities under normal working conditions.

How are labor standards set? There are three major ways:

1. Time studies
2. Predetermined time standards
3. Work sampling

This supplement covers each of these techniques.

S9.2   TIME STUDIES

The classical stopwatch study, originally proposed by Frederick W. Taylor in 1881, is still a widely used time-study method. A **time-study procedure** involves timing a sample of a worker's performance and using it to set a standard. A trained and experienced person can establish a standard by following these eight steps:

1. Define the job to be studied.
2. Decide how many times to measure the job (the number of cycles or samples needed).
3. Break down the job into precise elements (parts of a job that often take no more than a few seconds).
4. Choose a worker to observe. Time and record how long it takes the worker to complete each element. Rate the worker's performance.
5. Compute the **average cycle time** for *each* job element:

$$\text{Average cycle time} = \frac{\begin{array}{c}\text{sum of the times recorded}\\\text{to perform each element}\end{array}}{\text{number of cycles observed}} \qquad \text{(S9.1)}$$

6. Compute the **normal time** for each job element:

$$\text{Normal time} = (\text{average cycle time}) \times (\text{rating factor}) \qquad \text{(S9.2)}$$

The rating factor, based on the performance of the observed worker, adjusts the average cycle time to what a normal worker could expect to accomplish. For example, a normal worker should be able to walk three miles per hour. He or she also should be able to deal a deck of 52 cards into four equal piles in 30 seconds. There are numerous films specifying work pace on which professionals agree, and activity benchmarks have been established by the Society for the Advancement of Management. However, performance rating is still something of an art.

7. Sum the normal times for each element to develop a total normal time for the job.
8. Compute the **standard time** for the job. This adjustment to the total normal time provides for allowances such as personal needs, unavoidable work delays, and worker fatigue.

$$\text{Standard time} = \frac{\text{total normal time}}{1 - \text{allowance factor}} \qquad \text{(S9.3)}$$

Personal time allowances are often established in the 4 to 7 percent of total time range, depending on nearness to restrooms, water fountains, and other facilities. Delay standards are often set as a result of the actual studies of the delay that occurs. Fatigue standards are based on our growing knowledge of human energy expenditure[1] under various physical and environmental conditions. A sample set of personal and fatigue allowances is shown in Exhibit S9-1.

Time-Study Example

As an example, let us consider Management Sciences Associates, a firm that promotes its management development seminars by mailing thousands of individually typed letters to various firms. A time study has been done on the task of preparing the letters for mailing. Based on the observations in Exhibit S9-2, Management Science Associates wants to develop a time standard for the task. The firm's personal, delay, and fatigue allowance factor is 15 percent. The procedure after the data have been collected is as follows:

---

[1] Ernest J. McCormick, *Human Factors in Engineering and Design* (New York, McGraw-Hill, 1976), pp. 171–178; also see Haim Gershoni, "Allowances for Heat Stress," *Industrial Engineering* (September 1979), pp. 20–24.

EXHIBIT S9-1   Rest Allowances for Various Classes of Work (in percentage)

A. Constant allowances:	
1. Personal allowance	5
2. Basic fatigue allowance	4
B. Variable allowances:	
1. Standing allowance	2
2. Close attention:	
a. Fairly fine work	0
b. Fine or exacting	2
c. Very fine or very exacting	5
3. Noise level:	
a. Continuous	0
b. Intermittent—loud	2
c. Intermittent—very loud	5
d. High pitched—loud	5
4. Mental strain:	
a. Fairly complex process	1
b. Complex or wide span of attention	4
c. Very complex	8
5. Monotony:	
a. Low	0
b. Medium	1
c. High	4
6. Tediousness:	
a. Rather tedious	0
b. Tedious	2
c. Very tedious	5

Source: Excerpted from B. W. Niebel, *Motion and Time Study*, 8th ed. (Homewood, IL, Irwin, 1988), p. 393. Copyright © 1988 by Richard D. Irwin, Inc.

1. Delete all unusual or nonrecurring observations, such as those marked with an asterisk. (They might be due to an unscheduled business interrruption, a conference with the boss, or a mistake of an unusual nature: these are not part of the job.)
2. Compute the average cycle time for each job element.

$$\text{Average time for } A = \frac{8 + 10 + 9 + 11}{4}$$
$$= 9.5 \text{ minutes}$$

EXHIBIT S9-2

Job Element	Observations (in minutes)					Performance Rating
	1	2	3	4	5	
(A) Type letter	8	10	9	21*	11	120%
(B) Type envelope address	2	3	2	1	3	105%
(C) Stuff, stamp, seal, and sort envelopes	2	1	5*	2	1	110%

$$\text{Average time for } B = \frac{2+3+2+1+3}{5}$$
$$= 2.2 \text{ minutes}$$
$$\text{Average time for } C = \frac{2+1+2+1}{4}$$
$$= 1.5 \text{ minutes}$$

3. Compute the normal time for each job element.

$$\text{Normal time for } A = (\text{average time}) \times (\text{rating})$$
$$= (9.5)(1.20)$$
$$= 11.4 \text{ minutes}$$
$$\text{Normal time for } B = (2.2)(1.05)$$
$$= 2.31 \text{ minutes}$$
$$\text{Normal time for } C = (1.5)(1.10)$$
$$= 1.65 \text{ minutes}$$

Normal times are computed for each element because the rating factor may vary for each element, which it did in this case.

4. Add the normal times for each element to find the total normal time (the normal time for the whole job).

$$\text{Total normal time} = 11.40 + 2.31 + 1.65$$
$$= 15.36 \text{ minutes}$$

5. Compute the standard time for the job.

$$\text{Standard time} = \frac{\text{total normal time}}{1 - \text{allowance factor}}$$
$$= \frac{15.36}{1 - 0.15}$$
$$= 18.07 \text{ minutes}$$

Thus, 18.07 minutes is the time standard for this job.

Sampling Error

Time study is a sampling process, and the question of sampling error in the average cycle time naturally arises. Error, according to statistics, varies inversely with sample size. In order to determine just how many cycles should be timed, it is necessary to consider the variability of each element in the study.

The easiest means of finding the necessary sample size is to use standard charts such as the one in Exhibit S9-3. Such charts help estimate sample sizes that offer the user 95 or 99 percent confidence that the average cycle time from the sample will be within 5 percent of the true average.[2] To use the chart, we follow four steps.

---

[2] The sample size formula on which this chart is based is

$$N = \left(\frac{Zs}{h\overline{X}}\right)^2$$

where Z = standard normal deviate for the desired confidence coefficient
    h = desired accuracy level
    $s/\overline{X}$ = coefficient of variation

EXHIBIT S9-3 Chart for Estimating Sample Size with ±5 Percent Accuracy for Given Coefficient of Variation Values

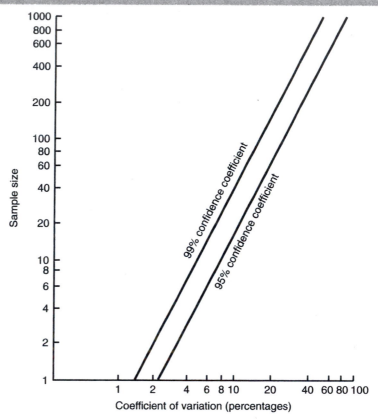

Source: A. Abruzzi, *Work Measurement* (New York, Columbia University Press, 1952), p. 161. Copyright © 1952 by Columbia University Press. Used by permission.

1. Compute the average cycle time $\bar{X}$.
2. Find the standard deviation s based on the sample data.

$$s = \sqrt{\frac{\Sigma(each\ sample\ observation - \bar{X})^2}{\text{number in sample} - 1}} \qquad \textbf{(S9.4)}$$

3. Compute the coefficient of variation, which is just the standard deviation divided by the mean, that is,

$$\text{Coefficient of variation} = \frac{s}{\bar{X}} \qquad \textbf{(S9.5)}$$

4. Find the appropriate coefficient of variation on the horizontal axis in Exhibit S9-3, proceed up to the curve that gives the confidence coefficient desired, and then read the sample size on the left-hand scale.

As an example, we take a sample of 12 cycles in a study of insurance data entry clerks. The result is an average cycle time of 2.80 minutes with a standard deviation of 0.56 minute. In order to be 95 percent confident that the resultant standard time is within 5 percent of the true average, we need to know whether this sample size of twelve observations is large enough.

To find the answer, we compute the coefficient of variation.

$$\frac{s}{\overline{X}} = \frac{0.56}{2.80}$$
$$= 0.20$$

Turning to Exhibit S9-3 for a coefficient of variation of 20 percent, we see that the required sample size is about 60 cycles. Thus, the sample of 12 cycles is not large enough and the observation process should continue.

S9.3   PREDETERMINED TIME STANDARDS

A third way to set service labor standards is to use predetermined time standards. **Predetermined time standards** divide manual work into small basic elements that have established times (based on very large samples of workers). To estimate the time for a particular task, the time factors for each basic element of that task are added together. For any given service firm to develop a comprehensive system of predetermined time standards would be prohibitively expensive. Consequently, a number of systems are commercially available. The most common predetermined time standard is *methods time measurement* (MTM), which is a product of the MTM Association.[3] *Computerized standard data* (CSD) is a product of Rath and Strong, a management consulting firm. Predetermined time standards are an outgrowth of basic motions called **therbligs.** Therbligs include activities such as select, grasp, position, handle, fasten/loosen, move, reach, hold, rest, and inspect. These activities are stated in terms of time measurement units (TMUs), which are each equal to only 0.00001 hours or 0.0006 minutes. MTM values for various therbligs are specified in very detailed tables. Exhibit S9-4 provides, as an example, the set of time standards for the motion GET and PLACE. To use GET and PLACE (which is the most complex in the MTM system), one needs to know what is "gotten," its approximate weight, and where and how far it is placed. Two illustrations will help clarify this concept.

Pouring a Tube Specimen in a Hospital Lab

A simple example of how standard time data are developed is provided in Exhibit S9-5. The sample tube is in a rack, and the centrifuge tubes are in a nearby box. A technician removes the sample tube from the rack, uncaps it, gets the centrifuge tube, pours, and places both tubes in the rack.

The first work element involves getting the tube from the rack. Suppose the conditions for GETTING the tube and PLACING it in front of the technician are

- Weight—less than two pounds
- Conditions of GET—easy
- Place accuracy—approximate
- Distance range—8 to 20 inches

Then the MTM element for this activity is AA2 (as seen from Exhibit S9-4). The rest of Exhibit S9-5 is developed from similar MTM tables. Most MTM calculations, by the

---

[3] MTM is really a family of products available from the Methods Time Measurement Association, a non-profit corporation based in Des Plaines, IL. All MTM systems are based on original research, and many of these serve specific groups of activities. For example, MTM-HC deals with the health care industry. MTM-C handles clerical activities. MTM-M involves microscope activities. MTM-V deals with machine shop tacks, and so on. In addition to the United States, there are MTM Associations in 12 countries. MTM-UAS, used in setting laboratory standards, was developed by the German MTM Association.

EXHIBIT S9-4 Sample MTM Table, for GET and PLACE Motions

MTM® ASSOCIATION	UNIVERSAL ANALYZING SYSTEM			UAS		
January 1984	IF TRAINING IN MTM AND UAS IS LACKING, USAGE OF THIS TABLE LEADS TO WRONG RESULTS	\multicolumn{4}{l}{TIME UNITS}			
		TMU	SEC	MIN	HRS	
		1	0.036	0.0006	0.00001	

TIME VALUES IN TMU

GET AND PLACE			DISTANCE RANGE IN in.	<8	>8 <20	>20 <32
WEIGHT	CONDITIONS OF GET	PLACE ACCURACY	CODE	1	2	3
<2 LBS	EASY	APPROXIMATE	AA	20	35	50
		LOOSE	AB	30	45	60
		TIGHT	AC	40	55	70
	DIFFICULT	APPROXIMATE	AD	20	45	60
		LOOSE	AE	30	55	70
		TIGHT	AF	40	65	80
	HANDFUL	APPROXIMATE	AG	40	65	80
>2 LBS <18 LBS		APPROXIMATE	AH	25	45	55
		LOOSE	AJ	40	65	75
		TIGHT	AK	50	75	85
>18 LBS <48 LBS		APPROXIMATE	AL	80	105	115
		LOOSE	AM	95	120	130
		TIGHT	AN	120	145	160

PLACE	CODE	1	2	3
APPROXIMATE	PA	10	20	25
LOOSE	PB	20	30	35
TIGHT	PC	30	40	45

Source: Copyright © 1984 by the MTM Association for Standards and Research. No reprint permission without written consent from the MTM Association, 1111 East Touhy Ave. Des Plaines, IL 60018.

way, are computerized, so the user need only key in the appropriate MTM codes, such as AA2.

Computer Data Entry Analysis

As a second illustration, we may refer to Exhibit S9-6. This exhibit shows MTM coding to develop standard times for entering a computer system, providing user identification, and requesting a specific program or procedure.

EXHIBIT S9-5 MTM-HC Analysis: Pouring Tube Specimen

Element Description	Element	Time	Frequency	Total
Get tube from rack	AA2	35	1	35
Get stopper, place on counter	AA2	35	1	35
Get centrifuge tube, place at sample tube	AD2	45	1	45
Pour (3 seconds)	PT	1	83	83
Place tubes in rack (simo)	PC2	40	1	40
			Total TMU	238
			Total MIN	.14

Source: A. S. Helms, B. W. Shaw, and C. A. Lindner, "The Development of Laboratory Workload Standards Through Computer-Based Work Measurement Technique, Part 1," *Journal of Methods—Time Measurement*, vol. 12, p. 43. Used with permission of MTM Association for Standards and Research.

EXHIBIT S9-6   MTM Standard Data Development for Computer Entry Task

Code: L4   Name: computer entry

Description	Element	Time	Frequency	Total
Enter system	UBA1	10	5	50
Password	UBA1	10	4	40
Initials	UBA1	10	4	40
User code	UBA1	10	6	60
Visual	UVA	15	1	15
Lab procedure	UBA1	10	4	40
Department procedure	UBA1	10	4	40
User code	UBA2	25	5	125
Visual	UVA	15	1	15
Work station	UBA1	10	4	40
Work sheet	UBA1	10	4	40
Visual	UVA	15	1	15
			Total TMU	520
			Stnd. minutes	0.3120

Source: A. S. Helms, B. W. Shaw, and C. A. Lindner, "The Development of Laboratory Workload Standards Through Computer-Based Work Measurement Techniques, Part II," *Journal of Methods—Time Measurement*, vol. 12, p. 48. Used with permission of MTM Association for Standards and Research.

Advantages

Predetermined time standards have several advantages relative to direct time studies. First, they may be established in a laboratory environment, which will not upset service activities (which time studies tend to do). Second, the standard can be set before a task is done and can be used for planning. In addition, no performance ratings are necessary—and the method is widely accepted by unions as a fair means of setting standards. Predetermined time standards are particularly effective in firms that do substantial numbers of studies where the tasks are similar. In these cases, standard data tables, tailored to the particular firm's procedures may be developed for a group of similar tasks. Some service firms use both time studies and predetermined time standard to ensure accurate labor standards.

S9.4   WORK SAMPLING

The third method of developing service labor standards, work sampling, was developed by an Englishman, L. Tippet, in the 1930s. **Work sampling** estimates the percentage of time that an employee spends working on various tasks. The method involves random observations to record the activity that the worker is performing.

The work-sampling procedure can be summarized in seven steps.

1. Take a preliminary sample to obtain an estimate of the parameter value (such as percentage of time a worker is busy).
2. Compute the sample size required.
3. Prepare a schedule for observing the employee at appropriate times. The concept of random numbers (discussed in chapter 11) is used to provide for random observation so that a representative sample of activities can be obtained.
4. Observe and record employee activities; rate the employee's performance.
5. Record the number of units produced (such as paychecks written) or services rendered during the applicable portion of the study.

6. Compute the normal time per service.
7. Compute the standard time per service

To determine the number of observations required, management must make a statement about the desired confidence level and accuracy. But first the work analyst must select a preliminary value of the parameter under study (step 1 above). The choice is usually based on a small sample of perhaps fifty observations. The following formula then gives the sample size for a desired confidence and accuracy.

$$n = \frac{Z^2 p(1-p)}{h^2}$$

(S9.6)

where

n = required sample size
Z = standard normal deviate for the desired confidence level ($Z = 1$ for 68 percent confidence, $Z = 2$ for 95.45 percent confidence, and $Z = 3$ for 99.7 percent confidence—these values are derived from the normal table in Appendix)
p = estimated value of sample proportion (of time employee is observed busy or idle)
h = accuracy level desired, in percent.

Word-Processing Pool Example

To illustrate work sampling, we examine a word-processing typing pool. The head of the unit estimates the operators are idle 25 percent of the time. The supervisor would like to take a work sample that would be accurate within 3 percent and wants to have 95.45 percent confidence in the results.

In order to determine how many observations should be taken, the supervisor applies the equation

$$n = \frac{Z^2 p(1-p)}{h^2}$$

where

n = sample size required
$Z = 2$ for 95.45 percent confidence level
p = estimate of idle proportion = 25 percent = 0.25
h = accuracy desired of 3 percent = 0.03

It is found that

$$n = \frac{(2)^2(0.25)(0.75)}{(0.03)^2} = 833 \text{ observations}$$

Thus, 833 observations should be taken. If the percentage of idle time noted is not close to 25 percent as the study progresses, then the number of observations may have to be recalculated and increased or decreased as appropriate.

Random Observation

To obtain the random sample needed for work sampling, a manager divides a typical work day into 480 minutes. Using a random-number table to decide what time to go to an area to sample work occurrences, the manager records observations on a tally sheet such as the one that follows.

Status	Tally	Frequency
Productively working	JHT JHT JHT I	16
Idle	IIII	4

In this case, the supervisor made twenty observations and found that employees were working 80 percent of the time. So, out of 480 minutes in an office workday, 20 percent, or 96 minutes, was idle time, and 356 minutes was productive. Note that this procedure describes what a worker *is* doing, not necessarily what he or she *should* be doing.

S9.5   SUMMARY

Labor standards are required for efficient service operations. They are needed for manpower planning, costing, and evaluating performance. They can also be used as a basis for incentive systems. Standards may be established by time studies, predetermined time standards, and work sampling. In particular, MTM-HC is gaining acceptance as a tool for setting standards that improve productivity in the health care field. Work sampling is a tool with unlimited potential in most service and white-collar jobs where service output is not easily quantified.

Discussion Questions

1. What is the difference between normal time and standard time?
2. Consult a production management or reference text and locate a sample of MTM measurement tables. How do tables used in factories differ from those in clerical or hospital jobs?
3. Why do managers need labor standards?
4. Contact a service organization that uses work-measurement techniques and describe the tasks analyzed and results reached.

Problems

S9.1. An office worker is clocked performing three work elements, with the results shown in Exhibit S9-7. The allowance for tasks such as this is 15 percent.
 a. Find the normal time per cycle.
 b. Find the standard time per cycle.
S9.2. Installing mufflers at the Ross Garage in Queens, New York, involves five work elements. Richard Ross times workers performing these tasks seven times. The times are shown in Exhibit S9-8. By agreement with his workers, Ross allows a

EXHIBIT S9-7

Job Element	Observations (in minutes)						Performance Rating
	1	2	3	4	5	6	
1	13.0	11.0	14.0	16.0	51.0	15.0	100%
2	68.0	21.0	25.0	73.0	26.0	23.0	110%
3	3.0	3.3	3.1	2.9	3.4	2.8	100%

EXHIBIT S9-8

Job Element	Observations (in minutes)							Performance Rating
	1	2	3	4	5	6	7	
1. Select correct mufflers	4	5	4	6	4	15	4	110%
2. Remove old muffler	6	8	7	6	7	6	7	90%
3. Weld/install new muffler	15	14	14	12	15	16	13	105%
4. Check/inspect work	3		24	5	4	3	18	100%
5. Complete paperwork	5	6	8	—	7	6	7	130%

10 percent personal time factor. To compute standard time for the work operation, Ross excludes all observations that appear to be unusual or nonrecurring.

    a. What is the standard time for the task?

    b. How many cycles are needed to ensure a 95 percent confidence level?

    c. How many are needed to ensure a 75 percent confidence level?

S9.3. Sample observations of a hospital lab worker made over a 40-hour work week revealed that the worker completed a total of 320 tests. The performance rating was 125 percent. The sample also showed that the worker was busy testing specimens 80 percent of the time. Allowances for work in the hospital total 10 percent. Find the normal time and standard time for this task.

S9.4. A bank wants to determine the percentage of time its tellers are working and idle. It decides to use work sampling, and its initial estimate is that the tellers are idle 30 percent of the time. How many observations should be taken to be 95.45 percent confident that the results will not be more than 5 percent away from the true result?

S9.5. A work operation consisting of three elements has been subjected to a stopwatch time study. The observations recorded are shown in Exhibit S9-9. By union contract, the allowance time for the operation is personal time 5 percent, delay 5 percent, and fatigue 10 percent. Determine the standard time for the work operation.

S9.6. A preliminary work sample of an operation indicates the following:

Number of times operator working	60
Number of times operator idle	40
Total number of preliminary observations	100

What is the required sample size for a 99.7 percent confidence level with ± 4 percent precision?

S9.7. Sharpening your pencil is an operation that may be broken down into eight small elemental motions. In MTM terms, each element may be assigned a certain number of TMUs, as shown:

Reach four inches for the pencil	6 TMU
Grasp the pencil	2 TMU

EXHIBIT S9-9

Job Element	Observations (in minutes)						Performance Rating
	1	2	3	4	5	6	
A	0.1	0.3	0.2	0.9	0.2	0.1	90%
B	0.8	0.6	0.8	0.5	3.2	0.7	110%
C	0.5	0.5	0.4	0.5	0.6	0.5	80%

Move the pencil six inches	10 TMU
Position the pencil	20 TMU
Insert the pencil into the sharpener	4 TMU
Sharpen the pencil	120 TMU
Disengage the pencil	10 TMU
Move the pencil six inches	10 TMU

What is the normal time for sharpening one pencil? Convert this time to minutes and seconds.

References

Aft, Lawrence S., *Productivity Measurement and Improvement.* (Reston, VA, Reston Publishing, 1983).

Barnes, Ralph M., *Motion and Time Study.* (New York, Wiley, 1980).

Denton, D. Keith, "Work Sampling: Increasing Service and White Collar Productivity," *Management Solutions* (March 1987), pp. 36–41.

Helms, Ashley S., et al., "The Development of Laboratory Workload Standards Through Computer-Based Work Measurement Techniques: Part III," *Journal of Methods—Time Measurement*, vol. 12, pp. 51–54.

Karger, Delmar W., *Advanced Work Measurement.* (New York, Industrial Press, 1982).

Konz, Stephen, *Work Design* (Columbus, OH, Grid, Inc., 1975).

Lindner, Carl A., "The Application of Computer-Based Work Measurement in a Community Hospital," Working Paper, University Community Hospital, Tampa, Florida, March 10, 1986.

Nadler, Gerald, *Work Design: A Systems Concept.* (Homewood, IL, Irwin, 1976).

Neibel, Benjamin W., *Motion and Time Study.* (Homewood, IL, Irwin, 1976).

CHAPTER 10

Locating Facilities and Designing Their Layout

10.1 INTRODUCTION

One of the most important long-term revenue decisions a service organization makes is where to locate its operation. This decision follows the design of the service and service delivery systems (the topic of chapter 8) and consists of two parts: finding a *location* and then finding a *site* within it for the service delivery system. Once the location and site have been selected, the facility layout must be designed. The layout problem involves finding the best arrangement of the physical components of the service system possible within the time, cost, and technology constraints of the situation. Attention in this chapter first focuses on the location options available, and then turns to facility layout.

Service organizations may have to make location decisions for various reasons. Offering service at new locations may be part of a growth strategy the organization is pursuing. Another reason may be increased demand; the current service facility may be unable to meet the additional demand; hence, a new facility or expansion may be needed. Of course, the opposite may also be true. That is, demand at one location may fall below the level at which the service organization can survive; hence, a new location with sufficient demand may be needed. When a service organization faces a location decision, there are basically three options:

1. Enlarge an existing facility at the present site.
2. Close the present facility and construct one or more new ones on new sites.
3. Open a new site or sites.

Location selection is a macro decision involving which countries, regions within a country, and communities (within a region, county, or city) are appropriate for locating the service units. **Site selection** is a micro decision as to the specific piece of property (or properties) on which to establish the service. This chapter first examines the location selection decision by describing the effect of:

- The business profile
- Dominant location factors
- General selection criteria
- Common mistakes made in selection
- Multiple locations

A variety of quantitative methods for evaluating locations, ranging from simple factor weighting to complex mathematical models, are examined. Designing the layout of service facilities will be discussed in the second half of this chapter.

10.2   LOCATION SELECTION

Location and site selection is a strategic decision because it is usually a decision that will have long-term effects on costs, demand, and profitability. Because location is such a significant cost driver, the consulting firm McKinsey believes "location ultimately has the power to make (or break) a company's business strategy."[1] This is a particularly important decision for service organizations, because most services are produced and consumed simultaneously. Also, most services require the customer's presence. These characteristics of services make service location an extremely important factor in consumers' buying decisions. Service organizations have no choice but to make their facilities accessible to as large a customer group as possible.

Business Profile

Before considering alternative locations (and sites), a business profile should be prepared. The profile describes the nature of the business and the needs of the business in terms of location and site. It also includes an analysis of the dominant location factors presented in the next section. A comparison is then made of the profile versus the firm's strategic plan, as shown by the model in Exhibit 10-1. The overall strategy of the organization should serve as the guiding principle and framework for locating any business.

Dominant Location Factors

The selection of location and site for a service obviously depends on a number of factors and trade-offs among benefits and costs. However, there may be a particular factor that *dominates* the selection process and limits the number of feasible locations to be evaluated. Below are nine dominant factors relating to location and site selection.

1. *Customer based.* If convenience of location determines where a customer shops, banks, or dines, the service is said to be customer based. Hence, the service should be located in close proximity to its customers. Retail stores, health care and other personal services, theaters, branches of banks and brokerage houses, and restaurants are examples of organizations with customer-based locations.

---

[1] See Andrew D. Bartness, "The Plant Location Puzzle," *Harvard Business Review* (March–April 1994), pp. 20–37.

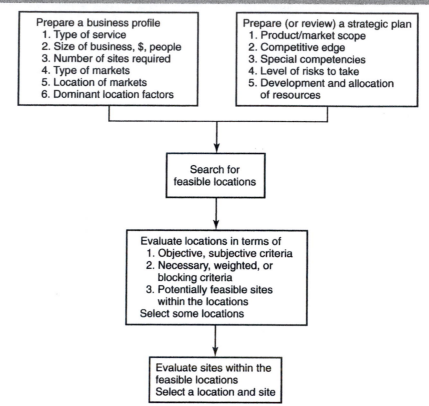

EXHIBIT 10-1   Location and Site Selection Evaluation

Prepare a business profile
1. Type of service
2. Size of business, $, people
3. Number of sites required
4. Type of markets
5. Location of markets
6. Dominant location factors

Prepare (or review) a strategic plan
1. Product/market scope
2. Competitive edge
3. Special competencies
4. Level of risks to take
5. Development and allocation of resources

Search for feasible locations

Evaluate locations in terms of
1. Objective, subjective criteria
2. Necessary, weighted, or blocking criteria
3. Potentially feasible sites within the locations
Select some locations

Evaluate sites within the feasible locations
Select a location and site

2. *Cost based.* Most specialty shops, wholesalers, and clerical services find that operating cost is their dominant location factor.

3. *Competitor based.* Some businesses prefer to locate near their competition to observe, share resources, and draw customers from a distance. For example, in manufacturing, there are garment districts, furniture towns, and textile areas. Similarly, in services, there are clusters of car dealerships, antique shops, and fast-food restaurants.

4. *Support systems.* Many companies locate in areas where support systems are available. For example, a hotel may locate near a university medical research center. A bullion firm may locate in a city with good police protection. For Disney World, location at a site with good airline and road support systems, as well as good electric utility service, was essential.

5. *Geographic or environmental factors.* Ocean resorts, ski resorts, and outdoor health ranches or spas illustrate geographic or environmental constraints on location.

6. *Business climate.* When a service business has only minor constraints on its location, the business climate of a state or city may provide the major factor in site location. Insurance companies, private educational institutions, and gaming resorts are likely to fall in this category.

7. *Communication based.* Financial services usually require rapid communication with other companies and perhaps even with governments throughout the world. This is one of the reasons that large banks locate in large, highly devel-

oped cities with excellent communications. Further, as telecommunication systems continue to replace transportation of documents by mail, this factor will become more important.

8. *Transportation based.* Mail-order businesses and private express delivery services tend to make location decisions based on entry to a good transportation network.

9. *Personal desires of the CEO.* Despite the preceding factors, many companies have moved their headquarters based on the desire of the president or chief executive officer. When Justin Dart took over Rexall Drug, for example, he moved the headquarters from Boston to Los Angeles because of a personal preference.

General Criteria for Location Selection

In addition to dominant location factors, there are many other general criteria that should be considered in selecting a location, such as labor availability/cost, climate/ weather, and state taxes. Many of the items listed in Exhibit 10-2 apply regardless of the type of service business. In making comparisons among locations, it is well to group the criteria according to:

1. Subjective criteria
   a. Quantifiable (e.g., management's estimate of risk)
   b. Nonquantifiable (e.g., acceptance by the community, zoning, and legal factors)
2. Objective criteria
   a. Quantifiable (e.g., cost of construction)
   b. Nonquantifiable (e.g., lower cost of living)

EXHIBIT 10-2   General Criteria for Location Selection

1. Labor availability and costs
2. Labor history and culture
3. Educational centers
4. Recreational and cultural centers
5. Electric power
6. Transportation and road networks
7. Health and welfare system
8. Climate and weather
9. Geography and environmental protection management
10. State business climate and incentives
11. State taxes
12. Health care system
13. Suppliers and supporting service companies
14. Population and population trends
15. Communication systems
16. Preference of management
17. Cost of living
18. Community attitudes
19. Cost of land and construction
20. Potential for expansion

Common Mistakes

Oversights and common mistakes in the location decision have been identified by various writers.[2] Some of these errors are:

- Failure to forecast trends. Too often, the long-range location decision is based on factors at the present time without regard to potentially adverse changes or future opportunities. The growth of the Sun Belt in the 1970s and the decay in the North Central states are examples.
- Failure to develop a company profile. In this case, the company simply looks for a place to put a building rather than a place to enhance its business.
- Paying too much attention to land costs. High land costs may accompany a highly desirable area. Also, they *may* indicate the possibility of large growth in value in case the company decides to move its business at some future time.
- Failure to understand the costs of moving people.
- Allowing prejudices of executives to override what should be a business decision; loss of key people who do not favor the new location.
- Failure to take into account the culture of the workers at the location.
- Paying too much attention to wage rates rather than productivity.
- Failure to coordinate construction and moving with the ongoing operations of the business.

Multilocations

Multilocation selection decisions differ in some important aspects from single-location selection decisions. For example, a new competitor to Club Med could lay out a plan for locations all over the world, taking into account many factors. But when Club Med adds a new location, consideration must be given to its present locations and the specific recreations offered at each. As another example, suppose yet another competitor to Federal Express were to start up. It may wish to limit the first 50 locations of its offices to a specified region of the United States. Federal Express, on the other hand, must take into account present locations served throughout the United States to avoid overlapping and to provide synergy. Banking firms, brokerage firms, resorts, TV networks, motel chains, franchise services, and airlines all face the multilocation as well as the single-location problem.

10.3   QUANTITATIVE METHODS FOR LOCATION SELECTION

Quantitative techniques for location selection vary from the simple to the complex. We will give an overview of a few common methods,[3] starting with factor weighting.

Factor Weighting

Factor weighting is a simple numerical method that has six steps:

1. Develop a list of relevant factors.
2. Assign a weight to each factor to reflect its relative importance in the firm's objectives.
3. Develop a scale for each factor (for example, 1 to 5, 1 to 10, or 1 to 100 points).

[2] See, for example, Richard Muther, *Systematic Layout Planning*, 2nd ed. (Boston, Cahners Books, 1973).

[3] For a state-of-the-art survey of quantitative models and their applications to facility location decisions, see Zvi Drezner (ed.), *Facility Location: A Survey of Applications and Methods* (New York, Springer-Verlag, 1995).

4. Have management score each location for each factor, using the scale in step 3.
5. Multiply the score times the weights for each factor, and total the score for each location.
6. Make a recommendation based on the maximum point score, considering the results of qualitative approaches as well.

A simplified illustration is provided in Exhibit 10-3 for location of a new ski resort. The rating sheet in the exhibit provides a list of not easily quantifiable factors that management has decided are important, their weights, and their ratings for three possible sites: California, Colorado, and New England. The factor-weighting analysis indicates that New England, with a total weight of 147, is preferable to both the California and Colorado locations. By changing the weights slightly for those factors about which there is some doubt, the sensitivity of the decision can be analyzed.

Center of Gravity Method

The center of gravity method is a mathematical technique used for finding a location for a single distribution center that services a number of retail stores. The method takes into account the location of markets, the volume of goods shipped to those markets, and shipping costs in finding a best location for a distribution center.

By way of an example, consider the case of Quain's Discount Department Stores, a chain of four large Kmart-type outlets.[4] The firm's store locations are in Chicago, Pittsburgh, New York, and Atlanta. They are currently being supplied out of an old and inadequate warehouse in Pittsburgh, the site of the chain's first store. Data on demand rates at each outlet are shown in Exhibit 10-4.

The firm has decided to find some "central" location in which to build a new warehouse. Since the number of containers shipped each month affects cost, distance alone should not be the principal criterion. The center of gravity method assumes that cost is directly proportional to both distance and volume shipped. The ideal location is that which minimizes the weighted distance between the warehouse and its retail outlets, where the distance is weighted by the number of containers shipped.

EXHIBIT 10-3   Factor Weighting in Selection of Ski Resort Location

		Location Scores			Weighted Scores		
Factor	Importance Weight	California	Colorado	New England	California	Colorado	New England
Average snowfall/year	8	5	4	3	(8)(5) = 40	(8)(4) = 32	(8)(3) = 24
Topography	9	4	5	4	(9)(4) = 36	(9)(5) = 45	(9)(4) = 36
Size of nearest market	7	3	2	5	(7)(3) = 21	(7)(2) = 14	(7)(5) = 35
Transportation to ski resort	5	4	4	5	(5)(4) = 20	(5)(4) = 20	(5)(5) = 25
Government incentives	3	3	4	4	(3)(3) = 9	(3)(4) = 12	(3)(4) = 12
Number and size of competitors	3	2	5	5	(3)(2) = 6	(3)(5) = 15	(3)(5) = 15
				Totals	132	138	147

Factor scoring scale: 5 = excellent, 4 = good, 3 = fair, 2 = poor, 1 = unacceptable.

[4] This example is from Jay Heizer and Barry Render, *Production and Operations Management*, 5th ed. (Upper Saddle River, NJ, Prentice Hall, 1999), pp. 302–303.

EXHIBIT 10-4   Demand for Quain's Discount Stores

Store Location	Number of Containers Shipped per Month
Chicago	2,000
Pittsburgh	1,000
New York	1,000
Atlanta	2,000

The first step in the center of gravity method is to place the existing store locations on a coordinate system. This is shown in Exhibit 10-5. The origin of the coordinate system and the scale used are arbitrary, just as long as the relative distances are correctly represented. This can be done easily by placing a grid over an ordinary map. The center of gravity is determined by equations 10.1 and 10.2.

$$C_x = \frac{\sum_i d_{ix} W_i}{\sum_i W_i} \tag{10.1}$$

$$C_y = \frac{\sum_i d_{iy} W_i}{\sum_i W_i} \tag{10.2}$$

where

C_x = x-coordinate of the center of gravity
C_y = y-coordinate of the center of gravity
d_{ix} = x-coordinate of location i
d_{iy} = y-coordinate of location i
W_i = volume of goods moved to or from location i

EXHIBIT 10-5   Coordinate Locations of Four Quain's Department Stores

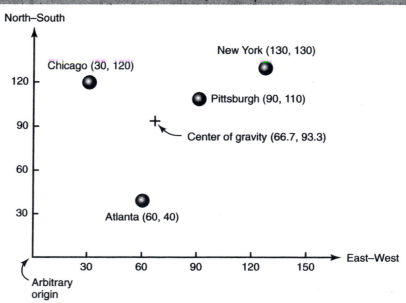

For example, location 1 is Chicago, and from Exhibits 10-4 and 10-5, we have

$d_{1x} = 30$
$d_{1y} = 120$
$W_1 = 2,000$

Using the data in Exhibits 10-4 and 10-5 for each of the other cities, in equations (10.1) and (10.2), we find

$$C_x = \frac{(30)(2,000) + (90)(1,000) + (130)(1,000) + (60)(2,000)}{2,000 + 1,000 + 1,000 + 2,000} = \frac{400,000}{6,000}$$

$$= 66.7$$

$$C_y = \frac{(120)(2,000) + (110)(1,000) + (130)(1,000) + (40)(2,000)}{2,000 + 1,000 + 1,000 + 2,000} = \frac{560,000}{6,000}$$

$$= 93.3$$

This location (66.7, 93.3) is shown by the crosshair in Exhibit 10-5. By overlaying a U.S. map on this exhibit, we find that this location is near central Ohio. The firm may well wish to consider Columbus, Ohio, or a nearby city as an appropriate location.

Warehouse Multisite Locations and Sizes

Bowman and Stewart developed a warehouse location model that can be readily adapted to a wholesaling service company that desires to set up warehouses to cover a regional area such as New England.[5] Their technique answers the question of how many square miles of area each warehouse should serve. The more warehouses in the system, the smaller is the area served by each, and hence the smaller are the warehouses.

Here are the economics of the problem as analyzed by Bowman and Stewart. Warehousing costs per dollar of goods handled tend to decrease with increasing volume (since costs of supervision and other overhead are spread over more units and since labor can usually be used with a lower proportion of idle time). They further reasoned that distance traveled would be the main factor determining costs associated with area and that this cost would tend to vary approximately with the square root of the area (radius and diameter vary with the square root of the area of a circle). The following terms for the model are defined:

C = total cost per dollar of goods distributed in warehouse region
K = sales density, in dollar volume of goods per square mile handled by a warehouse
A = area in square miles served by warehouse
a = cost, per dollar's worth of goods, which is not affected either by warehouse volume or area served (variable cost per dollar unit)
b = fixed costs associated with warehouse operation
c = costs that vary with the distance from the warehouse

The total costs per dollar of merchandise handled are

$$C = a + \frac{b}{KA} + c\sqrt{A} \tag{10.3}$$

---

[5] E. H. Bowman and J. B. Stewart, "A Model for Scale of Operations," *Journal of Marketing* (January 1956), pp. 242–247.

To minimize cost, we take the first derivative of C with respect to A, set it equal to 0 and solve for A. The following formula results:

$$A= \left[\frac{2b}{cK} \right]^{2/3} \tag{10.4}$$

Also dealing with warehouse location and sizing decisions, Effroymson and Ray developed a branch-and-bound algorithm,[6] while Atkins and Shriver tackled the problem through linear programming.[7]

10.4   SITE SELECTION

Site selection may sometimes be divided into two stages: community (within the location area) and specific site selection. The site chosen should be appropriate to the nature of the service operation, so clearly the factors involved will differ depending on the type of business. Exhibit 10-6 provides a sample listing of some criteria for site selection.

Locating a Retail Store with the Gravity Model

When deciding where to locate a retail outlet such as a furniture or appliance store, a firm's objective is usually to maximize profits. The size and site of the store are two decision variables. The retailing literature is rich with variations of the so-called gravity or spatial interaction model, first proposed by Reilly in 1929, which can be used to estimate consumer demand.[8] Based on the work of Reilly and many others, a number of empirical observations have been found to affect retail trade:

EXHIBIT 10-6   A Guide to Criteria for Site Selection

1. Area available relative to area required
2. Appropriateness of buildings, if any on site
3. Zoning
4. Traffic, access, and parking
5. City road network
6. Neighborhood character
7. Labor availability, history, and costs
8. Taxes
9. Community attitudes
10. Educational, recreational, and cultural centers
11. Air and water pollution
12. Communications network
13. Banking system
14. Fire and police protection
15. Sewage and waste removal
16. Proximity to airports
17. Local market for the company's services

---

[6] M. A. Effroymson and T. L. Ray, "A Branch and Bound Algorithm for Plant Location," *Operations Research* (May–June 1966), pp. 361–368.

[7] Robert J. Atkins and Richard H. Shriver, "A New Approach to Facilities Location," *Harvard Business Review*, vol. 46, no. 3 (May–June 1968), pp. 70–79.

[8] W. J. Reilly, *The Law of Retail Gravitation* (New York, Putnam and Son, 1931).

1. The proportion of consumers patronizing a given shopping area varies with their distance from the shopping area.
2. The proportion of consumers patronizing various shopping areas varies with the breadth and depth of merchandise offered by each shopping area.
3. The distances that consumers travel to various shopping areas vary for different types of product purchases.
4. The "pull" of any given shopping area is influenced by the proximity of competing shopping areas.

The probability that a consumer at a given place of origin i will shop at a particular shopping center j is expressed by David L. Huff in the following model[9]:

$$P_{ij} = \frac{S_j / T_{ij}^{\lambda}}{\sum\limits_{j=1}^{n} (S_j / T_{ij}^{\lambda})} \tag{10.5}$$

where

P_{ij} = probability of a consumer at a given point of origin i traveling to a particular shopping center j

S_j = size of a shopping center j (measured in terms of square footage of selling area devoted to sale of a particular class of goods)

T_{ij} = travel time involved in getting from a consumer's travel base i to a given shopping center j

λ = a parameter that is to be estimated empirically to reflect the effect of travel time on various kinds of shopping trips

In Huff's initial pilot study, λ was found to be 2.7 for furniture shopping trips and 3.2 for trips involving clothes purchases. The greater the value of λ, the less time expenditure for a given trip purpose.

The expected number of consumers at a given place of origin i that shop at a particular shopping center j is equal to the number of consumers at i multiplied by the probability that a consumer at i will select j for shopping. That is

$$E_{ij} = P_{ij} C_i \tag{10.6}$$

where

E_{ij} = expected number of consumers at i likely to travel to shopping center j
C_i = number of consumers at i

The Gravity Model in Nonretail Services

Variations of Huff's and Reilly's gravity models also have been applied to the services supplied by hospitals, recreational facilities, and colleges. For example, the model was used to determine the service areas of existing hospitals in St. Louis by Ault, Bass, and Johnson.[10] Attractiveness of each hospital complex was estimated to be proportional to the total number of services offered there, and cost was measured in minutes to reach the hospital from each sector of the city. Morrill and Kelley used a similar grav-

---

[9] David L. Huff, "Defining and Estimating a Trading Area," *Journal of Marketing*, vol. 28 (1964), pp. 34–38.

[10] David Ault, Stephen Bass, and Thomas Johnson, "The Impact of New Hospital Construction on the Service Areas of Existing Hospital Complexes," *Proceedings of the American Institute for Decision Sciences* (St. Louis, 1971).

ity model to study flows of patients to hospitals.[11] Cesario developed a model to measure competition among northeastern Pennsylvania state park facilities in drawing vacationing residents of that state.[12] As a measure of trip cost, he employed road mileages from each county to each park. Finally, Render and Shawhan's model examined the competition among seventy public colleges in Ohio in attracting students from each county to attend their school.[13] All these applications indicate the potential for the use of gravity models in locating a wide variety of service-sector facilities and determining their success in drawing clients away from existing competition.

Factor-Weighting Method

Just as cities and communities can be compared for location selection by the factor-weighting model, as we saw earlier in this chapter, so can actual site decisions be helped. Exhibit 10-7 illustrates four factors of importance to Washington, D.C., health officials charged with opening that city's first public AIDS clinic. Of primary concern (and given a weight of 5) was location of the clinic so it would be as accessible as possible to the largest number of patients. The annual lease cost also was of some concern due to a tight budget. A suite in the new City Hall, at 14th and U Streets, was highly rated because its rent would be free. An old office building near the downtown bus station received a much lower rating because of its cost. Equally important as lease cost was the need for confidentiality of patients and, therefore, for a relatively inconspicuous clinic. Finally, because so many of the staff at the AIDS clinic would be donating their time, the safety, parking, and accessibility of each site were of concern as well.

From the three right-most columns in Exhibit 10-8, the weighted scores are summed. It appears that the bus terminal area can be excluded from further consideration, but that the other two sites are virtually identical in total score. The city may now consider other factors, including political ones, in selecting between the two remaining sites.

EXHIBIT 10-7 Potential AIDS Clinic Sites in Washington, D.C.

		Potential Locations*			Weighted Scores		
Factor	Importance Weight	Homeless Shelter (2nd and D, SE)	City Hall (14th and U, NW)	Bus Terminal Area (7th and H, NW)	Homeless Shelter	City Hall	Bus Terminal Area
Accessibility for infectives	5	9	7	7	45	35	35
Annual lease cost	3	6	10	3	18	30	9
Inconspicuous	3	5	2	7	15	6	21
Accessibility for health staff	2	3	6	2	6	12	4
				Total scores	84	83	69

* All sites are rated on a 1 to 10 basis, with 10 as the highest score and 1 as the lowest.

[11] R. L. Morrill and M. B. Kelley, "The Simulation of Hospital Use and the Estimation of Location Efficiency," *Geographical Analysis*, vol. 2 (1970), pp. 283–300.

[12] Frank J. Cesario, "A Generalized Trip Distribution Model," *Journal of Regional Science*, vol. 13 (1973), pp. 233–248.

[13] Barry Render and Gerald Shawhan, "A Spatial Interaction Model for the Allocation of Higher Education Enrollments," *Socio-Economic Planning Sciences*, vol. 11 (1977), pp. 43–48.

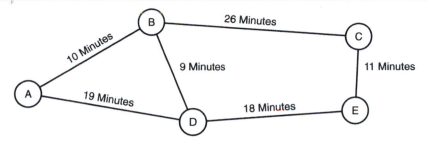

EXHIBIT 10-8   Zone Connections for Arlington County

Multisites

Within a city or metropolitan area, various services require multiple sites for offices, warehouses, outlets, branches, or service areas for vehicles. Examples range from fire stations to branch banks to auto quick-lube shops. The measures of benefits that arise from an arrangement of sites within a metropolitan area are (1) *distance,* (2) *time,* and (3) *cost.* These three criteria are not necessarily related. For example, a customer may travel a longer distance by bus to reach the service site than traveling by cab. Again, a longer route over an expressway may be much quicker than driving through crowded inner-city streets.

The preceding criteria of distance, time, and cost may apply to a service business (1) that delivers goods or services where time is not a factor, (2) that must service people quickly (as in the case of a private ambulance business), or (3) when transportation costs are high and visits to clients frequent. On the other side of the coin, the sites selected may depend on the distance, time, and cost criteria taken from the point of view of the customer who must travel to the service site.

A trade-off occurs when a service business adds more sites at a greater total cost to the firm. This may reduce the value of one or more of the preceding criteria. Also, the greater the proximity of sites, the more likely it is that some will draw trade from others.

Quantitative methods for finding the minimum number of sites to cover a specified market area are very rough in terms of meeting multiple realistic criteria. For example, geometric distance on a grid is sometimes used as a substitute for actual distance or time of travel. In one method, a table is set up in which markets served and potential sites are matched. When we want to find the minimum number and location of facilities to serve all customers within a specified service time or distance, we face what is called the **location set-covering problem.**

To illustrate, Arlington County, Virginia, which currently has five fire stations, wishes to place highly sophisticated emergency medical vehicles in one or more of those stations. The county's objective is to find a site or sites that will minimize response times to medical emergencies. Although regular firefighters and firetrucks are equipped to deal with minor medical problems, the county now wishes to provide its residents with a higher level and quality of care for severe cases. Exhibit 10-8 identifies the location of each of the current fire stations, its zone of the county, and the distance in time along major roads between zones. The question faced is where the medical vehicle or vehicles should be located. If the objective is to select a site so that maximum response time to any other zone is as small as possible, our analysis in Exhibit 10-9 provides several insights.

For example, if the county is satisfied responding to all medical calls within 30 minutes, then *one* station located in *either* zone B *or* zone D will suffice. If a 15-minute

EXHIBIT 10-9 Possible Sites for Arlington County Emergency Medical Units with Differing Response Rates

	Set of Zones Served from Stations in This Zone		
Zone in County	*Within 10 Minutes*	*Within 15 Minutes*	*Within 30 Minutes*
A	A, B	A, B	A, B, D
B	A, B, D	A, B	A, B, C, D, E
C	C	C, E	B, C, D, E
D	B, D	B, D	A, B, C, D, E
E	E	C, E	B, C, D, E
Possible locations to meet time constraints	B, C, E	B, C *or* B, E	B *or* D

response time is the county's objective, then locating medical units in zones B and C *or* B and E will suffice. Finally, if a 10-minute response time is desired, the county must place units at three stations, with one each in zones B, C, and E.

Another version of the location set-covering problem is called **maximal covering.** The goal of maximal covering is to maximize the population covered within a desired service distance. First described by Church and Revelle, the approach begins by mapping the population density for a metropolitan area.[14] The first site selected is the one that maximizes the population served within a specified travel distance. Then, a second site is selected that serves the maximum of the remaining population. This process is continued until the population served by the last site meets the criterion for level of population to be served.

10.5 OBJECTIVES OF FACILITY LAYOUT[15]

Once the location and site have been selected, the facility layout must be designed. The layout problem involves finding the best arrangement of the physical components of the service system possible within the time, cost, and technology constraints of the situation. The objectives of designing a good layout are:

1. Movement of people, materials, and paperwork must be over the minimum distance possible. One of the largest components of cost in many wholesalers' warehouses is the handling and movement of materials.
2. High utilization of space, balanced with means for expansion. There should be some space available for growth that will have low utilization, or else the building should be constructed so that a wing or floor may be easily added on.
3. Flexibility for rearrangement, services, and growth. Changes in product or service, changes in output required, and improvements in layout make modification of layout desirable from time to time.
4. Satisfactory physical environment for workers. This includes good lighting, temperature control, low noise, cafeterias, rest rooms, and exits. Fixed equipment, such as boilers, should be external to the work area.

---

[14] Richard Church and Charles Revelle, "The Maximal Covering Location Problem," *Papers of the Regional Science Association* (fall 1974), pp. 101–118.
[15] Portions of the rest of this chapter were adapted from Jay Heizer and Barry Render, *Production and Operations Management* (copyright © 1988 by Allyn and Bacon).

EXHIBIT 10-10   Some Types of Layout Strategies in the Service Sector

	Product	*Process*	*Office*	*Retail*	*Warehouse*
Example	Cafeteria serving line	Insurance company	Hospital	Retail store	Distributor
Problem	Balance work from one serving station to the next	Locate workers requiring frequent contact close to one another	Flow to various services differs with each patient	Expose customer to high margin items and impulse items at exit	Lower cost of storage and material handling

5. Convenience for customers during the service.
6. Attractive appearance of room office arrangements for management and customers. An example is the use of planter boxes and foliage to separate areas in banks and offices.

A variety of layout strategies are available to management depending on whether the firm is dealing with arranging processes, stores, warehouses, assembly lines, or offices. Exhibit 10-10 provides examples of five types of service layouts.

10.6   INPUTS TO THE LAYOUT PROBLEM

This section presents a brief discussion of six issues that need to be addressed before tackling service layout problems. Richard Muther developed a five-item key to unlocking *factory* layout problems.[16] Exhibit 10-11 shows a six-item service variation called the **OPQRST key.** The inputs are as follows:

O. *Objectives of the company.* Those objectives related to layout are diversification plans, cost objectives, expansion plans, and so on.
P. *People/services—nature and number.* Whether the company is providing a single service or a mix of heterogeneous services, the degree of customer contact and personalization will have an impact on the layout.
Q. *Quantity demanded.* Layout will be affected by whether high volume or low volume throughput is required.
R. *Routing—*processes, equipment, materials, information, and customer participation in the process.
S. *Space and services.* The square feet, the cubic feet, and the shape (rectangular, square, L-shaped) of the space available or desired are important to layout decisions. The type and location of services are also inputs.
T. *Timing—*flexibility for change over time and timing for additional space needed.

10.7   LAYOUT STRATEGIES

Now that these six inputs to the layout decision have been addressed, each of the strategies available to managers will be introduced.

Product Layout

A **product layout** is one in which a limited number of services is provided, one after the other, to a large number of customers. These services, such as food stations in a student cafeteria, are arranged in the sequence in which they are to be performed.

---

[16] Richard Muther, *Systematic Layout Planning*, 2nd ed. (Boston, Cahners Books, 1976).

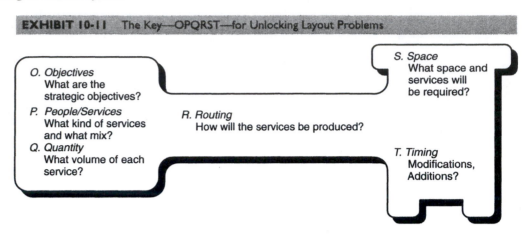

EXHIBIT 10-11 The Key—OPQRST—for Unlocking Layout Problems

O. Objectives
   What are the strategic objectives?

P. People/Services
   What kind of services and what mix?

Q. Quantity
   What volume of each service?

R. Routing
   How will the services be produced?

S. Space
   What space and services will be required?

T. Timing
   Modifications, Additions?

The idea is to maintain a smooth flow of customers through the stations so that bottlenecks can be avoided and the time needed by each individual server or station is equalized. This is the familiar assembly-line layout problem found in the manufacture of cars, toasters, and even jet fighter airplanes.

Assembly lines can be "balanced" by moving tasks from one individual to another. The central problem in product layout planning is to find the ideal balance so a continuous flow of customers is maintained along the service line with a minimum of idle time at each workstation.

To illustrate, assume that you enter your cafeteria, pushing your tray ahead of you, and request various items for your meal. The line is inflexible and some servers may even have specializations that cannot be assigned to others (such as being trained to act as cashier). The ideal (i.e., balanced) line is one where each server is assigned tasks that take an equal amount of time. Exhibit 10-12 indicates that there are six service stations in the cafeteria. Exhibit 10-13(a) illustrates how five workers have currently been assigned to staff the service stations. Workstation (WS) 4 consists of one employee who serves both desserts (15 seconds) and drinks (10 seconds). The problem, however, is that this line is poorly balanced. Workstation 5, the cashier, requires 60 seconds per customer on average, meaning that only 60 customers per hour can be served. The other workers are idle anywhere from 30 to 40 seconds of every minute or customer "cycle."

In Exhibit 10-13(b), management has reduced costs by eliminating two workstations (and hence two workers) by merging vegetables and entrees into one station (50 seconds) and soup, dessert, and drinks into a second station (45 seconds), and

EXHIBIT 10-12 Cafeteria Service Times

Sequence	Service Station	Average Service Time
1	Serve vegetables	20 seconds
2	Serve entree	30 seconds
3	Serve soup	20 seconds
4	Serve dessert	15 seconds
5	Serve drink	10 seconds
6	Collect money	60 seconds

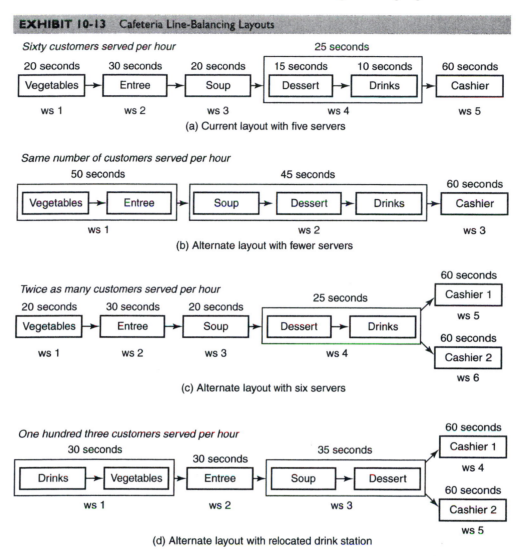

EXHIBIT 10-13 Cafeteria Line-Balancing Layouts

Sixty customers served per hour

(a) Current layout with five servers

Same number of customers served per hour

(b) Alternate layout with fewer servers

Twice as many customers served per hour

(c) Alternate layout with six servers

One hundred three customers served per hour

(d) Alternate layout with relocated drink station

placing a cashier at the third (still 60 seconds). Although this first alternative lowers costs, service is still slowed to a pace of 60 customers per hour, or one per minute, on average.

If the real problem is the need for increased throughput, alternatives 2 and 3 [see Exhibit 10-13(c) and (d)] may be explored. In Exhibit 10-13(c), the current layout is retained but for the opening of a second cashier station. With the reduction of that bottleneck, 120 customers may now be served, albeit at a higher labor cost, since there are now six workers.

The final alternative shown is one in which the drink equipment is relocated to the beginning of the cafeteria line and assigned to the worker currently serving vegetables. The soup and dessert tasks are assigned to workstation 3, and the freed worker is trained to work as a second cashier. There will be some costs of reconfiguring the service line, but labor costs will not increase. Now 103 customers can be handled per hour. The new bottleneck is workstation 3, which requires 35 seconds per customer.

Many services can be viewed in the context of product layout, even though they are not as rigid as this assembly-line example. Oil change/lube shops, for example, provide well-defined services, require special equipment for different tasks, and work well with a division of labor. Again, the service output is limited to the slowest activity.

Process-Oriented Layout

Whereas product layouts are arranged to deliver a specific product, **process-oriented layouts** are arranged by similar process function. Most service organizations use this approach, for it can simultaneously handle a wide variety of services. It is very efficient when dealing with customers of law offices, insurance companies, or travel agencies, typical situations in which each customer has a different need. Another good example of the process-oriented layout is a hospital or clinic. A continuous inflow of patients, each with his or her own request, requires routing through records areas, admissions, laboratories, operating rooms, intensive care areas, pharmacies, nursing stations, and so on.

A big advantage of process layout is its flexibility in equipment use and in employee assignments. In the hospital example, there may be several obstetricians on duty available to deliver an unexpected baby in a number of similar delivery rooms. However, if a specialist is unavailable, there are other doctors with broad enough skills to step in during an emergency. The service provided is enhanced by the personalization found in the process approach. The downside of this approach is that while operational efficiency is being optimized, customers' convenience, time, and travel distances are probably sacrificed. In chapter 8, the principles of service and delivery system design were discussed. One of those principles is *"Design service processes from the customer's/employee's perspective."* Process layout will probably violate this principle. However, if the cost savings from increased operational efficiency are reflected in the prices charged, customers may prefer such a compromise.

In process layout planning, the most common tactic is to arrange departments or service centers in the most convenient locations. This often entails placing departments with large interdepartmental flows of people or paperwork next to one another. Costs in this approach depend on (1) the number of people or documents moving during some period of time between two departments and (2) the distances between departments. The best way to understand the steps of process layout is to look at an example.

Example: North Slope Hospital

The North Slope Hospital is a small, emergency-oriented facility located in a popular ski resort area in northern Vermont. Its new administrator decides to reorganize the hospital using the process layout method she studied in business school. The current layout of North Slope's eight rooms is shown in Exhibit 10-14. The only physical restriction perceived by the administrator is the need to keep the entrance and initial processing room in its current location. All other departments or rooms (each 10 ft × 15 ft) can be moved if the layout analysis indicates it would be beneficial.

The first step is to analyze records in order to determine the number of trips made by patients between departments in an average month. The data are shown in Exhibit 10-15. The objective is to lay out the rooms so as to minimize the total distance walked by patients who enter for treatment. The administrator writes her objective as

EXHIBIT 10-14 North Slope Hospital Layout

| Entrance/Initial processing | Exam room 1 | Exam room 2 | X-ray | 15' |
| Laboratory tests/EKG | Operating room | Recovery room | Cast-setting room | 15' |

← 40' →

$$\text{Minimize patient movement} = \sum_{i=1}^{8} \sum_{j=1}^{8} N_{ij} D_{ij}$$

where

N_{ij} = number of patients (or trips) per month moving from department i to department j and from department j to department i

D_{ij} = distance in feet between departments i and j (which, in this case, is the equivalent of cost per load to move between departments)

i, j = individual departments

Departments next to one another, such as the entrance and examination room 1, are assumed to carry a walking distance of 10 feet. Diagonal departments are also considered adjacent and assigned a distance of 10 feet. Nonadjacent departments such as the entrance and examination room 2 or the entrance and recovery room are 20 feet apart, while nonadjacent rooms such as the entrance and x-ray are 30 feet apart. (Hence, 10 feet is considered 10 units of cost, 20 feet is 20 units of cost, and 30 feet is 30 units of cost.)

Given this information, we can redo the layout of North Slope Hospital and improve its efficiency in terms of patient flow. Using North Slope's current layout flow, shown in Exhibit 10-16, the patient movement may be computed.

EXHIBIT 10-15 Number of Patients Moving between Departments in One Month

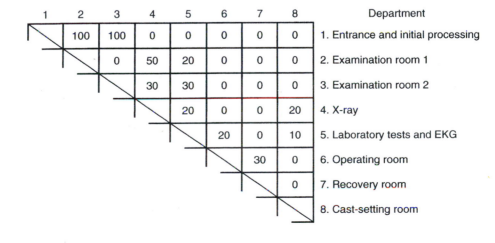

	1	2	3	4	5	6	7	8	Department
		100	100	0	0	0	0	0	1. Entrance and initial processing
			0	50	20	0	0	0	2. Examination room 1
				30	30	0	0	0	3. Examination room 2
					20	0	0	20	4. X-ray
						20	0	10	5. Laboratory tests and EKG
							30	0	6. Operating room
								0	7. Recovery room
									8. Cast-setting room

EXHIBIT 10-16 Current North Slope Patient Flow

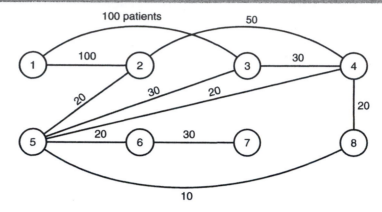

Total movement = $(100 \times 10 \text{ ft}) + (100 \times 20 \text{ ft}) + (50 \times 20 \text{ ft})$
 1 to 2 1 to 3 2 to 4

$+ (20 + 10 \text{ ft}) + (30 \times 10 \text{ ft}) + (30 \times 20 \text{ ft})$
 2 to 5 3 to 4 3 to 5

$+ (20 \times 30 \text{ ft}) + (20 \times 10 \text{ ft}) + (20 \times 10 \text{ ft})$
 4 to 5 4 to 8 5 to 6

$+ (10 \times 30 \text{ ft}) + (30 \times 10 \text{ ft})$
 5 to 8 6 to 7

$= 1{,}000 + 2{,}000 + 1{,}000 + 200 + 300 + 600 + 600$
$+ 200 + 200 + 300 + 300$

$= 6{,}700 \text{ feet}$

It is not generally feasible to arrive at an "optimal" solution, but we should be able to propose a new layout that will reduce the current figure of 6700 feet. Two useful changes, for example, are to switch rooms 3 and 5 (reducing patient movement by 1000 feet) and to interchange rooms 4 and 6 (reducing patient movement by an additional 900 feet). The revised layout is shown in Exhibit 10-17.

The revised patient movement is calculated as

Total movement = $(100 \times 10 \text{ ft}) + (100 \times 10 \text{ ft}) + (50 \times 10 \text{ ft})$
 1 to 2 1 to 3 2 to 4

$+ (20 \times 10 \text{ ft}) + (30 \times 10 \text{ ft}) + (30 \times 20 \text{ ft})$
 2 to 5 3 to 4 3 to 5

$+ (20 \times 10 \text{ ft}) + (20 \times 20 \text{ ft}) + (20 \times 10 \text{ ft})$
 4 to 5 4 to 8 5 to 6

$+ (10 \times 10 \text{ ft}) + (30 \times 10 \text{ ft})$
 5 to 8 6 to 7

$= 1{,}000 + 1{,}000 + 500 + 200 + 300 + 600 + 200$
$+ 400 + 200 + 100 + 300$

$= 4{,}800 \text{ ft}$

Further improvement may be possible. Do you see where it could take place?

EXHIBIT 10-17   Improved Layout

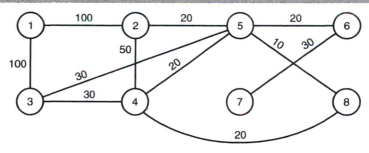

Computerized Layout

The graphic approach we have been discussing is adequate for finding a reasonable layout for small service centers.[17] When 20 departments are involved in a layout problem, over 600 trillion (or 20!) different department configurations are possible. Fortunately, computer programs have been written to handle layouts of up to 40 departments. The best-known of these is CRAFT (Computerized Relative Allocation of Facilities Technique),[18] a program that produces "good," but not always "optimal" solutions. CRAFT is a search technique that systematically examines alternative departmental rearrangements to reduce the total movement cost. CRAFT has the added advantage of not only allowing the number of people and distance to be examined, but also introducing a third factor: a difficulty rating.

Computerized techniques have been developed for both two-dimensional and three-dimensional cases. The two-dimensional case is a one-story facility successfully addressed by CRAFT; the three-dimensional case is a multistory facility addressed by SPACECRAFT.[19] And, as we have discussed, manual as well as computer techniques exist.

Another computerized approach to facility layout design is simulation. (We discuss simulation in the supplement to chapter 11.) Various simulation packages exist to help decision makers review alternative layouts. ServiceModel and MedModel are two of these packages that have been developed by ProModel Corporation. ServiceModel is a full-scale simulation program for service system modeling. In addition to simulating various operations of service organizations, one of its capabilities is to assist decision makers in facility layout and design. With this software, a decision maker can create an office layout, locate service employees and machines in the layout, observe the operation of the system, such as movement of customers and bottlenecks in various processes, and collect data on important performance measures for intelligent decision making. ServiceModel has been used in designing the layout of service facilities such as banks and airport terminals. MedModel has been developed for similar purposes of health care organizations.

---

[17] Also see Richard Muther, *Systematic Layout Planning*, for a similar approach to what the author calls simplified layout planning.

[18] E. S. Buffa, G. S. Armor, and T. E. Vollman, "Allocating Facilities with CRAFT," *Harvard Business Review*, vol. 42, no. 2 (March–April 1964), pp. 136–159.

[19] R. V. Johnson, "SPACECRAFT for Multi-Floor Layout Planning," *Management Science,* vol. 28, no. 4 (1982), pp. 407–417. A discussion of CRAFT, COFAD, PLANET, CORELAP, and ALDEP is available in James A. Tompkins and James M. Moore, *Computer Aided Layout: A User's Guide,* Publication Number 1 in the Monograph Series (Norcross, GA: American Institute of Industrial Engineers, 1977), p. 77-1.

10.8   OFFICE LAYOUT

Office workers are concerned with the movement of information. Movement of information is carried out by

- Individuals in face-to-face conversations
- Individuals conversing by phone and computers simultaneously
- Mail, hard-copy documents
- Electronic mail
- Group discussions or meetings
- Intercom speakers

A Checklist for Office Layout Design

If all work were carried out by phone and telecommunications, the layout problem would be greatly simplified. It is the movement of people and hard documents that largely dictates the nature of office facility layouts. A design checklist to consider in laying out office facilities is as follows:

1. Workers within groups usually have frequent contacts with each other.
2. Some groups interact frequently with certain other groups.
3. Some firms require conference rooms, especially those who supply professional services to clients.
4. Some service work is best done in private offices, whereas other work, such as high-volume routine processing of paper forms, is best suited to large open areas (frequently called "bullpens").
5. Areas visited by customers should be more aesthetic than standard work areas.
6. Aisles should be designed so that all offices may be quickly reached, and yet high traffic past private offices should be avoided to the extent possible.
7. Individual offices usually reflect the status of the workers by size, location, and window space.
8. Shared facilities such as computers and files should be convenient for users.
9. Reception areas may be required, and they should be attractive and convenient for customers.
10. Rooms for storage of supplies may be needed.
11. Generally, restrooms and coat rooms for employees are required. If the service is in a suite of an office building, restrooms may be provided already.
12. A central computer room or an information center may be required.

Workstations

The office layout depends on the total office area, its shape, the process to be performed, and the relationships among the employees. Each employee has a workstation designed for (hopefully) optimal efficiency in terms of the work system as a whole and the tasks of the worker at the station. Different types of jobs require different kinds of working surfaces, equipment, space, and privacy.

Workstation variations are:

- Desks packed together in rows in an open area
- Desks or work areas separated by bookcases, foliage, or file cabinets
- Partitions about the work area—metal and glass—varying in height from about four to eight feet, which can be installed in about one day
- Floor-to-ceiling partitions around a group of workstations
- Offices that are built as part of the building construction

By making effective use of the vertical dimension in a workstation, some office designers expand upward instead of outward. This keeps each workstation unit (what designers call the "footprint") as small as possible.

10.9 RETAIL STORE LAYOUT

In retail organizations, the objective is to maximize the net profit per square foot of display space. Because the retail grocery store is pervasive and widely studied, it will be used it as an example in this section. Most grocery stores target a wide range of customer groups, and this discussion of retail store layout is based on that assumption. However, this is not the only possible strategy; the retail store layout may be tailored for a particular segment of consumers. Consider, for example, the strategy followed by Ames, a very successful discount department store chain. Ames targets consumers with limited means; people with annual incomes of $25,000 to $35,000—waitresses, clerks, laborers, and retirees. In addition to its strategy of selling low-cost items, it designs the layouts of its stores to make it convenient for its target segment: "Ames makes a point of staying down around 60,000 [square-] feet. Seniors get tired in giant stores, . . . and working mothers want to be able to get in and out quickly. . . . Ames has given some stores a 'race-track' aisle circling the central apparel area, making it easy for seniors or hurried shoppers to get the merchandise they want."[20]

A hypothesis that has been widely accepted for the retail case is that sales vary directly with customer exposure to products. Consequently, a requirement for good profitability is to expose customers to as many products as possible.

Studies do show that the greater the rate of exposure, the greater the sales and therefore the higher return on investment. The service manager has two distinct variables to manipulate: the overall arrangement or flow pattern for the store and the allocation of space within that arrangement to various products.

Although some authors suggest that there is no longer any set pattern for store layouts, we can still note six ideas that are helpful for determining the overall arrangement of many stores.

1. Locate the high-draw items around the periphery of the store. Thus, we tend to find dairy products in one corner of a supermarket and bread and bakery products in another.
2. Use prominent locations such as the first or last aisle for high-impulse and high-margin items such as housewares, beauty aids, and shampoos.
3. Remove the crossover aisles that allow customers the opportunity to move between aisles. Place continuous shelves the length or width of the store. In the extreme case, customers are allowed only one path through the store.
4. Distribute what are known in the trade as "power items"—items that may dominate a purchasing trip—to both sides of an aisle, and disperse them to increase the viewing of other items. This results in a "bounce" pattern of shopping that increases exposure and hence sales of those items located adjacent to the power items.
5. Use end-aisle locations because they have a very high exposure rate.
6. Convey the image of the store by careful selection in the positioning of the lead-off department. Produce remains a popular choice in stores, but managers who want to convey a low-price message may want to start off with a wall of values.

[20] William M. Bulkeley, "Ames to Please: Discounter Rebounds by Targeting a Clientele below the Wal-Mart Set," *Wall Street Journal* (Monday, January 11, 1999).

Others will position the bakery and deli up front to appeal to convenience-oriented customers who want prepared foods.

With these six ideas in mind, we move to the second phase of retail store layout, which is to allocate space to various products.

The objective is to maximize profitability per product per square foot of shelf space. The criteria may be modified to the needs of the product line by using linear foot of shelf space in lieu of square foot of shelf space. "Big-ticket," or expensive, items may yield greater dollar sales, but the profit per square foot may be lower. Additionally, determining actual cost per item means determining spoilage, pilferage, breakage, and returns, as well as the necessary labor to stock and sell. There are, of course, other issues, such as having a full line of merchandise regardless of margin. A drugstore selling only high-margin shampoo would have met the criteria, but it would have a different set of problems.

Rapid manipulation of data by means of computers, accurate reports, and the capture of sales data through point-of-sale terminals allows retail store managers an opportunity to find optimal allocation of space. A number of computer programs exist that can assist managers in evaluating the profitability of various merchandise.

One such program is SLIM (Store Labor and Inventory Management), which can assist store managers in determining when shelf space is adequate to accommodate another full case. Sales and restocking information can be collected directly from a point-of-sale terminal, combined with a program such as SLIM, and the profitability can be established per product. This is a strong management tool for retail store layout.

Another software package is COSMOS (Computerized Optimization and Simulation Modeling for Operating Supermarkets). COSMOS matches shelf space with delivery schedules, allocating sufficient space to minimize out-of-stock between loads. A disadvantage of COSMOS is that analysis traditionally has been based on warehouse withdrawal figures rather than on actual store sales. This means that a good bit of the product could still be in the store. Once again, point-of-sale terminals, providing prompt information, can supply comprehensive and current data to aid retail store layout.

10.10 WAREHOUSING AND STORAGE LAYOUTS

The objective of warehouse layout is to find the optimal tradeoff between handling cost and warehouse space (Exhibit 10-18). Consequently, management is to maximize the utilization of the total "cube" of the warehouse—that is, utilize its full volume while maintaining low materials handling costs. **Materials handling costs** are defined here as all the costs related to the incoming, storage, and outgoing transport of the materials. These costs are related to equipment, people, type of materials, supervision, insurance, obsolescence, shrinkage, spoilage, and depreciation. Management minimizes the sum of the resources spent on finding and moving materials plus the deterioration and damage to the materials themselves. The variety of items stored and the number of items "picked" have direct bearing on the optimal layout. A warehouse storing a few items lends itself to higher density more than a warehouse storing a variety of items. Modern warehouse management is, in many instances, an automated procedure utilizing automatic stacking and picking cranes, conveyors, and sophisticated controls that manage the flow of materials. Of course, with the recently demonstrated success of just-in-time concepts in cutting inventory costs, the whole issue of ware-

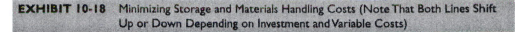

EXHIBIT 10-18   Minimizing Storage and Materials Handling Costs (Note That Both Lines Shift Up or Down Depending on Investment and Variable Costs)

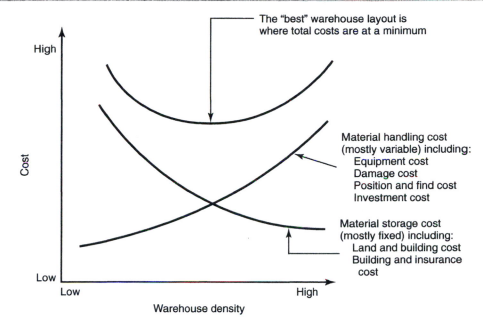

housing costs needs to be reexamined. There probably will always be some situations in which inventory storage is unavoidable.

Using POM for Windows to Solve Location Decision Problems

The Location module in POM for Windows includes two different models. The first, the qualitative weighting model (also known as the factor-weighting method) is used to solve the Ski Resort Location Selection example as shown in Exhibit 10-19. The second, the center of gravity method, is applied to the Quain's Discount Department Store example as shown in Exhibit 10-20.

10.11   SUMMARY

Part of the design of the service conversion or delivery process consists of location and site selection. Location selection is the macro decision about the general regions or metropolitan areas in which the business is to be established. Site selection is the micro decision as to the specific pieces of property for the business location. Several methods for evaluating locations, including factor weighting, center of gravity and Bowman and Stewart's warehouse model were discussed. For the site-selection problem, a variety of gravity or spatial interaction models, along with another factor-weighting example, and the location set-covering approach were presented.

Service location analysis differs in many ways from industrial location analysis. The focus in the industrial sector is usually on minimizing cost, while revenue maximization is the focus of most private-sector service firms. This is so because manufacturing costs tend to vary substantially between locations, but in service firms, costs

EXHIBIT 10-19 POM for Windows Factor Weighting Model Applied to Ski Resort Location Selection Example

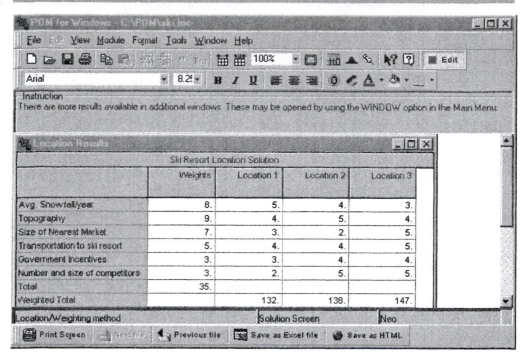

EXHIBIT 10-20 POM for Windows Center of Gravity Method Applied to Quain's Discount Department Store Example

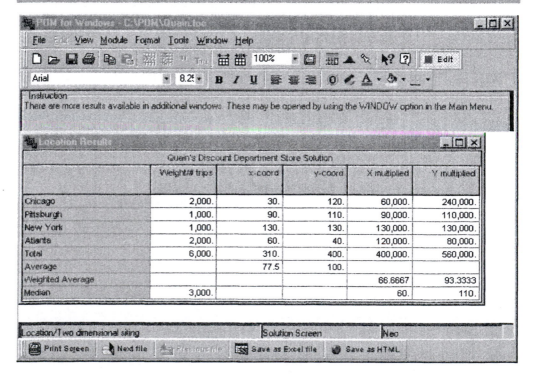

vary little within a region. The location decision focus for service firms should thus be on determining the volume of business and revenue.

The layout problem is the determination of the most nearly optimal arrangement of the physical components of the service system within time, cost, and technology constraints. A six-point list of inputs to the layout problem (called OPQRST) was given in this chapter, and a number of layout strategies were described. Different approaches to designing layout in service facilities have been discussed including product layout, process layout, and computerized layout. In addition, approaches to designing layouts for efficient operations in offices, retail establishments, and warehouses were discussed. Despite all the quantitative techniques available and substantial research effort, layout decisions remain something of an art.

Discussion Questions

1. Explain the assumptions behind the center of gravity method. How can the model be used in a service facility location?
2. How do service facility location decisions differ from industrial location decisions?
3. What considerations would be important to a police department opening a new station? What information would be useful in making the site-selection decision?
4. Explain the concept of Reilly's gravity model. What is the meaning of λ?
5. Propose an application of the gravity or spatial interaction model other than in retail-store location analysis.
6. Describe the set-covering approach. Why is it popular with public-sector organizations?
7. List the factors you think are most important in deciding where to locate
   a. A distribution warehouse
   b. A retail gift shop
   c. A health clinic
   d. A government employment office
8. This chapter concludes with the statement, "Despite all the quantitative techniques available and substantial research effort, layout decisions remain something of an art." Explain why this might be the case in
   a. Office layout
   b. Supermarket layout
   c. Department store layout
9. What is the layout strategy of your local "quick copy" or print shop? Draw it on grid paper.
10. How would you go about collecting data to help a small business, such as a print shop, improve its layout?
11. In what service organizations are customer waiting-room aesthetics of major concern? Compare a variety of waiting rooms you have visited by listing the characteristics of each.
12. Describe the objective of each of the major categories of layout discussed in this chapter.
13. What layout variables might you want to consider as particularly important in an office layout where computer programs are written?
14. Most supermarkets have placed long continuous shelves the length (or width) of the store so that customers will have to pass more items as they shop. Why are some stores rethinking this concept? Talk to a few store managers in your town and ask their opinions about this and other changes in layout.

Problems

10.1. A Detroit seafood restaurant is considering opening a second facility in the suburb of West Bloomfield. Exhibit 10-21 shows its ratings of five factors at each of four potential sites. Which site should be selected?

10.2. In placing a new medical clinic, county health offices wish to consider three sites. The pertinent data are given in Exhibit 10-22. Which is the best site?

10.3. The main post office in Tampa, Florida, is due to be replaced with a much larger, more modern facility that can handle the tremendous flow of mail that has followed that city's growth since 1970. Since all mail, incoming or outgoing, travels from the seven regional post offices in Tampa through the main post office, its site selection can mean a big difference in overall delivery and movement efficiency. Using the data in the following table, calculate the center of gravity for the proposed new facility.

Regional Post Office	X, Y Map Coordinates	Truck Round-Trips per Day
Ybor City	(10, 5)	3
Davis Island	(3, 8)	3
Dale-Marbry	(4, 7)	2
Palma Cera	(15, 10)	6
Bayshore	(13, 3)	5
Temple Terrace	(1, 12)	3
Hyde Park	(5, 5)	10

10.4. Todd's Video, a major video rental and TV sales chain headquartered in New Orleans, is about to open its first outlet in Mobile, Alabama, and wants to select a site in that city that will place it in the center of the city's population base. Todd examines the seven census tracks in Mobile, plots the coordinates of the center of each from a map, and looks up the population base in each to use as a weighting. The information gathered appears in the following table. At what center of gravity coordinates should the new store be located?

Census Tract	Population in Census Tract	X, Y Map Coordinates
101	2,000	(25, 45)
102	5,000	(25, 25)
103	10,000	(55, 45)
104	7,000	(50, 20)
105	10,000	(80, 50)
106	20,000	(70, 20)
107	14,000	(90, 25)

EXHIBIT 10-21

Factor	Weight	Site			
		1	2	3	4
Affluence of local population	10	70	60	85	90
Construction and land cost	10	85	90	80	60
Traffic flow	25	70	60	85	90
Parking availability	20	80	90	90	80
Growth potential	15	90	80	90	75

EXHIBIT 10-22

Location Factor	Weight	Scores		
		Downtown	Suburb A	Suburb B
Facility utilization	9	9	7	6
Average time per emergency trip	8	6	6	8
Employee preferences	5	2	5	6
Accessibility to major roadways	5	8	4	5
Land costs	4	2	9	6

10.5. The police chief wants to locate enough police stations so that each sector of the city has an average response time of 6 minutes. Using the data in Exhibit 10-23 determine the minimum number of facilities needed and their locations.

10.6. Exhibits 10-8 and 10-9 dealt with the location of emergency medical units at fire stations in Arlington County, Virginia. If the county finds a 25-minute response time is acceptable, how many ambulance sites are needed? What combinations of possible sites will suffice?

10.7. Jeri Ross is proprietress of two exclusive women's clothing stores in Miami. In her plan to expand to a third location, she has narrowed her decision down to three sites—one in a downtown office building, one in a shopping mall, and one in an old Victorian house in the suburban area of Coral Gables. She feels that rent is absolutely the most important factor to be considered, while walk-in traffic is 90 percent as important as rent. Further, the more distant the new store is from her two existing stores the better, she thinks. She weights this factor to be 80 percent as important as walk-in traffic. Jeri developed Exhibit 10-24 where she graded each site on the same system used in her MBA program in college. Which site is preferable?

10.8. Walters Printing Company's management wants to rearrange the six departments of its print shop in a way that will minimize interdepartmental materials handling costs. Each department is 20 feet by 20 feet, and the building is 60 feet long and 40 feet wide. Exhibit 10-25 shows the current flow of materials (in

EXHIBIT 10-23

City Sector	Response Time in Minutes from this Sector				
	1	2	3	4	5
1	1	2	8	20	15
2		1	3	12	10
3			1	16	5
4				1	4
5					1

EXHIBIT 10-24

	Downtown	Shopping Mall	Coral Gables House
Rent	D	C	A
Walk-in traffic	B	A	D
Distance from existing stores	B	A	C

EXHIBIT 10-25 Walters Printing Company Data

Number of loads per week

Department	1	2	3	4	5	6
1		50	100	0	0	20
2			30	50	10	0
3				20	0	100
4					50	0
5						0
6						

loads per week) from department to department, while Exhibit 10-26 illustrates the current layout. The cost of moving one load between adjacent departments is estimated to be $1. Moving a load between nonadjacent departments costs $2. Try to improve this layout to establish a reasonably good arrangement of departments.

10.9. You have just been hired as the director of operations for Bellas Chocolates, in Blacksburg, Virginia, a purveyor of exceptionally fine chocolates. Bellas Chocolates has four kitchen layouts under consideration for its recipe making and testing department. The strategy is to provide the best kitchen layout possible so that the food scientists can devote their time and energy to product improvement, not wasted effort in the kitchen. You have been asked to evaluate these four kitchen layouts and prepare a recommendation for your boss, Mr. Bellas, so that he can proceed with placing the contract for building the testing kitchens. (See Exhibit 10-27.)

10.10. Using the kitchen layouts in Problem 10.9, collect load data (the number of trips between workstations) from an operating kitchen of your choosing, perhaps at home, and determine which is the best layout.

EXHIBIT 10-26 Building Dimensions and Current Department Layout for Walters Printing

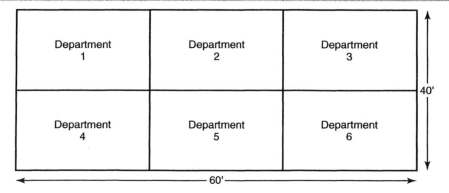

EXHIBIT 10-27   Layout Options

Number of trips between work centers

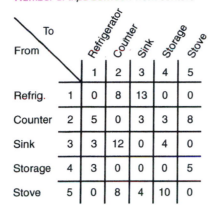

From \ To		Refrigerator 1	Counter 2	Sink 3	Storage 4	Stove 5
Refrig.	1	0	8	13	0	0
Counter	2	5	0	3	3	8
Sink	3	3	12	0	4	0
Storage	4	3	0	0	0	5
Stove	5	0	8	4	10	0

Kitchen layout #1

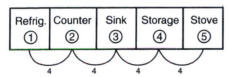

Kitchen layout #2

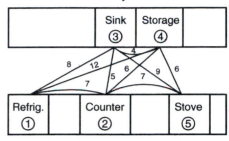

Kitchen layout #3

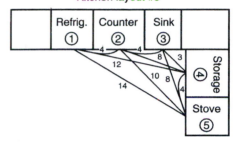

Kitchen layout #4

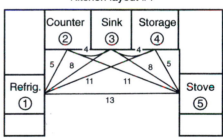

10.11. Using load data (number of trips) collected from an operating kitchen, determine which of the five layouts (the four in Problem 10.9 and the one from which you collected data) is best.

10.12. Georgetown Phone Directory prints and distributes a yellow page phone book for the northwest area of Washington, D.C. Its white-collar staff of clerical and managerial employees currently occupies the first floor of a U-shaped office building in Washington that is configured as shown in Exhibit 10-28. (The firm's warehouse and production facilities are next door.) This organization loses time and money because of unnecessary personnel, information, and materials movements. Without moving the production or shipping departments, see if you can reorganize the facility and create shorter communications distances.

10.13. The preinduction physical examination given by the U.S. Army involves the following seven activities:

Activity	Average Time (minutes)
Medical history	10
Blood tests	8
Eye examination	5
Measurements (i.e., weight, height, blood pressure)	7
Medical examination	16
Psychological interview	12
Exit medical evaluation	10

These activities can be performed in any order, with two exceptions: the medical history must be taken first and the exit medical evaluation is the final step. At present there are three paramedics and two physicians on duty during each shift. Only a physician can perform the exit evaluation or conduct the psychological interview. Other activities can be carried out by either physicians or paramedics.

a. Develop a layout and balance the line. How many people can be processed per hour?

b. What activity is the current bottleneck?

c. If one more physician and one more paramedic can be placed on duty, how would you redraw the layout? What is the new throughput?

10.14. The cafeteria discussed in this chapter (see Exhibits 10-12 and 10-13) has just decided to eliminate soup from the current servings because of spoilage and demand factors. To compensate, more elaborate desserts can now be ordered, including banana splits and hot fudge sundaes. The average time to serve a dessert is estimated to increase by 33 percent, however. Lay out this line:

a. With 3 workers

b. With 4 workers

c. With 5 workers

d. With 6 workers

For each of these four cases, identify the throughput per hour and the bottleneck station.

EXHIBIT 10-28 Layout for Georgetown Phone

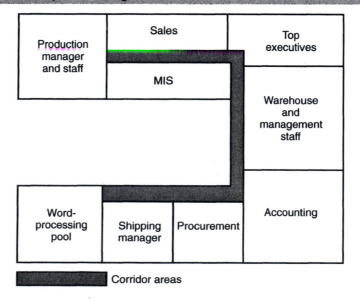

Corridor areas

CASES

CASE 10–1   Red River Blood Center

Red River is a community of 65,000 people in which there are three hospitals with a total of 287 beds. The Red River Blood Center was formed four years ago to provide the needed whole blood and plasma for emergency and surgical use within the three hospitals. The blood center is also part of a statewide network that shares blood resources. The Center is located downtown next to the largest of the three hospitals. It is on the fourth floor of a doctors' office building.

Given the size of the Red River community, the blood center does relatively poorly in attracting a sufficient number of blood donors. The administrator of the Red River Blood Center is constantly calling on other members of the network to provide blood needed in emergency cases. On the other hand, Red River is very seldom able to help other members of the network in their emergencies. During the initial two years of operations, the adminis-tration believed that newness of the center was the cause for "substandard" donor performance. But, now that the center has been operating for four years, that "excuse" will no longer hold up. Donors have often complained of the horrible traffic condi-tions downtown and the fact that parking is so scarce.

One of the lab technicians who recently moved from a larger community commented about the use of a mobile blood unit and setting up temporary clinics in meeting halls and other public facilities. She indicated that numerous civic and religious or-ganizations had helped in organizing blood drives through their memberships. The new assistant ad-ministrator even commented about the possibility of moving from the downtown location to an outly-ing shopping center. The administrator argued that the blood center was located where it was to be close to the hospitals. ■

SOURCE: Jack R. Meredith, *The Management of Operations*, 3rd ed. (New York: Wiley, 1987), pp. 217–218. Copyright © 1987 by John Wiley & Sons, Inc. Reprinted by permission of John Wiley & Sons, Inc.

CASE QUESTIONS

1. What location/transportation trade-offs have been made here?
2. Comment on the "demand(s)" made by the blood center's constituents.
3. What factors should be considered in compar-ing the benefits and costs of mobile or tempo-rary units with a shopping center–based unit?

CASE 10–2   Des Moines National Bank

Des Moines National Bank (DNB) recently fin-ished construction on a new building in the down-town business district. Moving into a new building provides an opportunity to arrange the various de-partments to optimize the efficiency and effective-ness of the operations.

One primary operation of DNB is its check-processing division. This division acts as a clearing-house for commercial and personal checks. These checks are received from the tellers downstairs as well as from other, smaller financial institutions that DNB has contracted for check processing. Checks are sorted to be sent to the bank from which they are drawn, using the magnetic-ink char-acters located at the bottom of the check. The rec-oncilement area ensures that the incoming and out-going totals balance, and the crediting area makes the entries to complete the transaction. Finally, the sorted checks are bundled and shipped from the distribution area.

The personnel in this division are also responsible for processing government checks and for handling any returned checks coming back through the system. Because these checks require very different processing operations, they are placed in separate departments from the commercial check operations but are located on the same floor.

The service elevator only travels from the basement to the second floor, so it has been decided that the check-processing division will be located on the second floor of the new DNB building. The second floor is divided into eight equal-sized rooms, as shown in Exhibit 10-30. (We call them rooms even though they are not separated by walls.) Each room is 75 feet square. Fortunately, this will not be a concern to bank management as each of the eight departments to be located on this floor require roughly 5,000 square feet; these rooms will allow for some additional-storage space and for future expansion.

The physical flow of materials—such as the checks being processed and computer printouts for the reconcilement and crediting areas—will be on aisles that run between the centers of the rooms, as shown in Exhibit 10-29. The checks will arrive and be distributed from the service elevator, so it is necessary to put the distribution departments in the room with the elevator. There are no other physical restrictions that require any department to be placed in a given room.

For the first step in this analysis, it was necessary to determine the amount of workflow that travels between the departments. Data collected for several weeks determined the average daily traffic—measured in the number of trips between de-

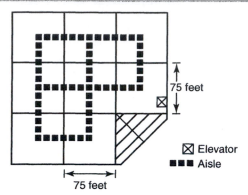

EXHIBIT 10-29 Floor Plan of the Second Floor of the DNB Building

75 feet

75 feet

⊠ Elevator
■■■ Aisle

partments. Although there is some fluctuation in the number of checks processed during the different days of the week, these average figures provide a good estimate of the relative workflow between each pair of departments.

A review of the workflow data revealed that several important relationships were not being considered. For example, although no material flows directly between the commercial check-sorting area and the government check area, they use the same type of equipment. This equipment is very noisy and requires a "soundproof" wall to control the noise, so it is necessary to keep all of this equipment together to minimize the construction cost. Also, due to this noise, it is desirable to keep this department removed from areas that require concentration, such as the reconcilement area and the offices. To account for these types of concerns, closeness ratings were identified for each pair of departments using the following rating scheme:

EXHIBIT 10-30 Workflow and Closeness Relationships between Departments

Department	1	2	3	4	5	6	7	8
1. Check sorting	—	50	0	250	0	0	0	0
2. Check reconcilement	X	—	50	0	0	0	0	0
3. Check crediting	X	A	—	0	0	0	0	10
4. Check distribution	U	U	U	—	40	60	0	0
5. Government checks	A	U	U	E	—	0	0	0
6. Returned checks	U	U	U	E	U	—	12	0
7. Credit adjustment	X	A	A	U	U	E	—	10
8. Offices	X	I	I	U	O	O	I	—

A—*A*bsolutely necessary

E—*E*specially important

I—*I*mportant

O—*O*rdinary closeness OK

U—*U*nimportant

X—*Not* desirable

Exhibit 10-30 provides the average daily workflow between departments in the upper-right portion and the closeness ratings in the lower-left portion. For example, the workflow between the check sorting and reconcilement departments is 50 units per day, and there is a closeness rating of "X." ■

SOURCE: Professor Timothy L. Urban, The University of Tulsa. Reprinted from Jay Heizer and Barry Render, *Production and Operations Management*, 5th ed. (Upper Saddle River, NJ, Prentice Hall, 1999), pp. 358–360.

CASE QUESTIONS

1. Develop a layout that minimizes the total workflow.
2. Develop a layout using the relationships defined by the closeness ratings.
3. Develop a layout that considers both the workflow and closeness relationships between departments.
4. Comment on the various layouts developed.
5. Discuss any other factors that should be considered when developing a layout of the check-processing division.

References

Atkins, Robert J., and Richard H. Shriver, "A New Approach to Facilities Location," *Harvard Business Review*, vol. 46, no. 3 (May–June 1968), pp. 70–79.

Ault, David, Stephen Bass, and Thomas Johnson, "The Impact of New Hospital Construction on the Service Areas of Existing Hospital Complexes," *Proceedings of the American Institute for Decision Sciences* (St. Louis, 1971).

Bartness, Andrew D., "The Plant Location Puzzle," *Harvard Business Review* (March–April 1994), pp. 20–37.

Bowman, E. H., and J. B. Stewart, "A Model for Scale of Operations," *Journal of Marketing* (January 1956), pp. 242–247.

Buffa, E. S., G. S. Armor, and T. E. Vollman, "Allocating Facilities with CRAFT," *Harvard Business Review*, vol. 42, no. 2 (March–April 1964), pp. 136–159.

Bulkeley, William M. "Ames to Please: Discounter Rebounds by Targeting a Clientele below the Wal-Mart Set," *The Wall Street Journal* (Monday, January 11, 1999).

Cesario, Frank J., "A Generalized Trip Distribution Model," *Journal of Regional Science*, vol. 13 (1973), pp. 233–248.

Drezner, Zvi (ed.), *Facility Location: A Survey of Applications and Methods* (New York, Springer-Verlag, 1995).

Effroymson, M. A., and T. L. Ray, "A Branch and Bound Algorithm for Plant Location," *Operations Research* (May–June 1966), pp. 361–368.

Heizer, Jay, and Barry Render, *Production and Operations Management*, 5th ed. (Upper Saddle River, NJ, Prentice Hall, 1999).

Huff, David L., "Defining and Estimating a Trading Area," *Journal of Marketing*, vol. 28 (1964), pp. 34–38.

Johnson, R. V., "SPACECRAFT for Multi-Floor Layout Planning," *Management Science*, vol. 28, no. 4 (1982), pp. 407–417.

Morrill, R. L., and M. B. Kelley, "The Simulation of Hospital Use and the Estimation of Location Efficiency," *Geographical Analysis*, vol. 2 (1970), pp. 283–300.

Manners, Steven, "Optimizing the Cube," *Administrative Management* (October 1986), pp. 19–21.

Muther, Richard, *Systematic Layout Planning*, 2nd ed. (Boston, Cahners Books, 1976).

Reilly, W. J., *The Law of Retail Gravitation* (New York, Putnam and Son, 1931).

Render, Barry, and Gerald Shawhan, "A Spatial Interaction Model for the Allocation of Higher Education Enrollments," *Socio-Economic Planning Sciences*, vol. 11 (1977), pp. 43–48.

Sunderesh, Heragu, *Facilities Design* (Boston, PWS Publishing Company, 1997).

Tompkins, James A., and James M. Moore, *Computer Aided Layout: A User's Guide*, Publication Number 1 in the Monograph Series (Norcross, GA: American Institute of Industrial Engineers, 1977), p. 77-1.

CHAPTER 11

Managing Demand and Supply in Services

11.1   INTRODUCTION

One of the biggest challenges service operations managers face is matching demand for service and the capacity (or supply) of the service. This is also a challenge for manufacturing managers, but they have a few more tools and strategies—such as inventories, overtime work, adding another shift, and back ordering—available to them to help meet the challenge. When the demand and supply are matched for a period of 1 to 3 years, the activity is known as **aggregate planning.** Aggregate planning involves determining the resource capacity that a firm will need to meet its demand. The role of aggregate planning is to convert the strategic types of marketing plans or demand forecasts associated with long-range planning into overall capacity requirements. These aggregate capacity requirements will subsequently serve as a framework for the short-range allocation (i.e., disaggregation) of overall capacity to individual services.

Exhibit 11-1 indicates the general characteristics of aggregate planning, planning disaggregated by resources and outputs, and the short-term scheduling of resources. The distinction between manufacturing-like and service-like firms refers to the tangibility of the output. Manufacturing-like firms are those which have tangible outputs or have distinct front-office/back-office operations.

This chapter focuses on strategies and tools available to service organizations to meet the demand for service. Some of these strategies can be implemented over a span of one to three years, and therefore are aggregate planning strategies. Others, however, can be implemented within much shorter periods, such as months, weeks, or days. The discussion of matching demand and supply has been organized in two parts. First, strategies for managing demand are discussed, and then strategies for supply, or capacity, management.

Forecast of demand is of course very important for effective demand management. Forecasting is a broad subject that includes a variety of approaches and techniques that can appropriately be covered in an independent chapter; forecasting is-

EXHIBIT 11-1 Levels of Planning Disaggregation		
Level of Planning	*Manufacturing-Like Firms*	*Service-Like Firms*
Level 1 Aggregate planning	Translation of strategic decisions into productive capacity over 1 to 3 years	Translation of strategic decisions into technology and resource planning over 1 to 3 years
Level 2 Disaggregate planning	Decisions on the individual product lines with regard to capacity and timing for each	Decisions on basic service designs and markets to be matched
	Decisions on capacity disaggregated into facilities, equipment, and human resources with timing for each for 1 year ahead	Decisions on how capacity will be expanded or limited and demand will be managed for 1 year ahead
	Make or buy decisions	
Level 3 Scheduling of resources	Weekly, monthly, and quarterly (or rolling 3-month) plans for production to match capacity to short-term fluctuations in demand	Weekly, monthly, and quarterly (or rolling 3-month) plans for production to match capacity with managed demand
	Raw materials and finished goods inventory decisions	Decisions on raw materials inventory
	Decisions on priorities for products, filling of orders, and assignment of work to individual operations	Decisions on assignment of work to individuals

sues and techniques are presented in chapter 15. Before the important issue of matching demand and supply is discussed, however, the reasons that make this such a challenge for service operations managers should be reviewed.

11.2 WHY MATCHING DEMAND AND SUPPLY IS SUCH A CHALLENGE IN SERVICES

It was mentioned earlier that some of the strategies and tools operations managers use in manufacturing to match demand and supply are not available in services. In this section, the reason is explained, and some other reasons that make this a difficult task are discussed.

1. *Most services are perishable—they are consumed as they are produced.* Thus, it is impossible to produce the service early in anticipation of higher demand at a later time. This eliminates inventory as a tool in managing demand fluctuations or uncertainties for most services. Back ordering of goods is possible when customers are willing to wait. For example, a car buyer is likely to wait a few weeks if his preferred model with all the options he wants is not available on the dealer's lot. A patient with a toothache, however, will not probably wait if her dentist is on vacation. Of course, there are exceptions to these generalizations; for example, the reservation system that services use may be seen as a form of back ordering.

2. *Maximum capacity of some service systems has no flexibility.* Capacity of manufacturing systems can be increased in the short term through such practices as overtime work or additional shifts. Some services can similarly increase their maximum capacity by extending their hours of operation, like amusement parks do in summer months, but not all services can do that. For example, if you are making TV sets, working overtime or adding another shift will increase the number of sets produced, but a hotel manager cannot increase the number of rooms by overtime, or second shift, when all the rooms are booked for the night.

3. *Demand for many services is more difficult to predict.* Compared to predicting demand for most goods, predicting demand for many services is much more difficult, and demand variations are typically more severe and frequent—that is, they occur over shorter time periods. One reason for this is that consumption decisions for some services, such as eating out, going to a movie, or getting a haircut, are usually spur of the moment decisions, induced by the circumstances of the day or week. In other words, people normally do not make long-range plans for some services. Also, demand for some services, such as a visit to a pediatrician for a child's ear infection is never planned. This makes prediction of demand very difficult. Another reason is that the demand for some services occurs in peaks and valleys; in some services, such as fast food, public transportation, and electric power, these peaks and valleys are known and predictable, but in others they are not.

4. *Variability in service time.* Because of (1) the variety of services offered, (2) the individualized nature of services, and (3) the variability of each customer's needs and requirements, the time needed to serve an expected number of customers is difficult to predict. For example, the time required to serve a customer at a bank can vary considerably depending on the number and type of transactions requested by the customer. This may lead to underestimation or overestimation in determining the required capacity. *Units* of capacity also may be hard to define. For instance, should a hospital define capacity in terms of number of beds, number of patients, size of nursing or medical staff, or number of patient hours at each level of care?

5. *Most services are location bound.* Because most services cannot be transported, service capacity must be available at the appropriate *place* as well as at the appropriate time. For a multisite service organization, this may mean while one unit is overwhelmed with customers, another unit at a different location may be underutilized. When such an imbalance occurs for goods, they can be transported from one location to another with relative ease; however, service customers cannot be easily transported or may not be willing to go to another service unit.

11.3 MANAGING DEMAND

Demand management is usually within the realm of marketing management. However, as pointed out earlier in this book, in service organizations, many operations and marketing management tasks overlap, and frequently operations managers have to perform those tasks. Hence, they must be knowledgeable about options available to their colleagues in marketing. Furthermore, even when operations and marketing duties are clearly separated, managers on both sides must coordinate their activities and cooperate for superior service and a profitable organization; therefore, they must be well versed in the tools of each other's field.

Understanding Customers and Their Needs

The simplest and probably the most important requirement for managing demand effectively is knowing who the customers are and understanding their needs. This may be a simple requirement, but it is an often overlooked ingredient of demand management. A service organization must collect data on its customers' demographic characteristics, such as age, sex, income, and occupation, as well as lifestyle characteristics and their needs and requirements, or any other relevant data that can be found. It must also know what motivates them to buy the service. Collecting data on these dimensions is neither easy nor inexpensive; therefore, it is not always economically feasible to build a complete data set. However, whatever information can be economically gathered about the customers is better than no information.

Understanding customers and their needs will help a service organization decide which of the strategies and tools discussed in this section will be most effective in managing demand for its services. For example, lower prices may be used to shift service demand from peak to off-peak periods. However, if the customers are affluent people insensitive to small price changes, this strategy may be ineffective and, worse yet, may lead to a perception of lower quality by those customers.

Understanding customers and their needs will also help identify and separate, if they exist, different components of demand. For example, hospital or health clinic managers discovered long ago that demand for their services can be grouped as emergency and regular care. To meet these two types of demand more effectively, they allocate part of their facilities and some of their doctors and nurses to emergency cases while the rest attend regular visits. Clearly, each component has a different demand pattern. For example, most people do not schedule a hospital visit for a check-up on weekends, but emergency room visits may actually increase on weekends.

Studying the Nature and Pattern of Demand

Knowing the customers and understanding their needs is necessary but not sufficient for effective demand management. Service managers must also study the nature and pattern of the demand, because many factors, such as weather and social, political, or sporting events in the community, influence the demand for services. Some of these influences may be regular, some may not be. Discovering patterns and understanding the behavior of demand requires data. Again, data may not always be easy or inexpensive to collect, but without an understanding of the nature and patterns of demand, effective management is not possible. Clearly, knowing the demand pattern not only helps the operations manager determine which strategies to use to influence demand, but it also helps her manage service supply effectively.

Strategies for Influencing Demand

Demand for services is not under the direct control of the service organization. It is influenced and shaped by many factors such as price, competitors' offerings and prices, income level of potential customers, accessibility, and so forth. A service organization, however, may exert some influence on demand by using one or more of the strategies discussed in this section. We must point out, however, that not all these strategies are appropriate or feasible for every service organization.

Pricing   This is probably the most obvious of strategies; for most services, reducing the price will increase demand, and increasing it will create the opposite effect. Another common use of pricing is in short-term price changes. Some service organizations offer their services at lower-than-normal prices to shift peak period demand to off-peak periods. Price incentive may be strong enough for some customers to use the service during periods of low demand, thereby reducing the severity of fluctuations in demand. Examples of this practice include reduced-rate long distance or cellular telephone service at night and on weekends, movies before 6 P.M., and red-eye specials on airlines. Shifting peak period demand, of course, is important for efficient use of resources, such as work force and facilities. If demand cannot be smoothed by shifting, the service organization either has to build enough capacity to meet the maximum demand or lose customers who demand service during the peak period. The result of the first alternative will be inefficient use of resources; facilities and employees will be underutilized during the off-peak period. The consequence of the second may be a significant reduction in profits or even failure of the company.

Reservations/Appointments   Another very common strategy in demand management used by many service organizations is to offer their services through reservations or appointments. This can be seen as "inventorying" or "backlogging" demand for service. This practice is viable for services that are not widely available but highly valuable to customers. Airlines, hotels, health care providers, legal services, and elegant restaurants offer their services through reservations or appointments; service is not guaranteed to walk-in customers. Reservations/appointments usually provide a steady level of demand, and they guarantee that the demand will not exceed a previously set limit. However, there is no guarantee that customers who cannot get an appointment soon enough will come back. This practice also has benefits for the customers. The most important benefit is probably the guarantee of service at the scheduled time. Also, it helps customers save time; they do not have to wait in line. Another benefit a reservation system provides is that it eliminates customer anxiety about if and when the service will be available, or how long they will have to wait for the service.

A disadvantage of reservations systems is no-shows, that is, customers who make a reservation or appointment but fail to show up. This, of course, means loss of revenue for the service organization if it cannot immediately replace the no-show by another customer. This is a problem frequently faced by airlines and hotels. Since finding a new customer on short notice is usually not possible, these service organizations use a practice called *overbooking*. They accept more reservations than they have room for. This reduces the chances of having many empty seats on airplanes or empty hotel rooms, but may also lead to a difficult situation when the number of people who show up exceeds the number of available seats or rooms. The general practice in these cases is to offer some compensation to the passenger whose reservation has not been honored, such as free plane tickets to anywhere in the United States, and put him on the next flight, or in the case of a hotel guest, to find her a room at a comparable hotel nearby at no charge.

Communication Efforts   Sometimes, a simple message to customers may help reduce the peaks in the demand. Signs, advertising, and sales messages may convince customers that using various services, such as public transportation, national parks, museums, and post offices at off-peak periods has many benefits, including lower prices, smaller crowds, and a more comfortable ride or visit. Everyone is familiar with the TV commercials of the U.S. Postal Service reminding us to "mail early for Christmas."[1]

Offering Services That Have Countercyclical Demand Patterns   Some services present extreme challenges in demand management. Demand for these services has a definite and inflexible seasonal pattern and price incentives. Reservations or commu-

---

[1] Christopher H. Lovelock, *Services Marketing*, 3rd ed. (Upper Saddle River, NJ, Prentice Hall, 1996), p. 216.

nications will not usually be effective in changing the pattern or smoothing the peaks of demand. Demand for these services is either extremely low or nonexistent during the "off" season. One possible remedy is to offer additional services that use the same facilities and possibly the same personnel but have a countercyclical seasonal pattern. For example, many landscaping services offer snow removal services during the winter months when there is not much landscaping to be done. Another example is a ski resort offering a dry ski run or an alpine slide (a winding plastic channel for wheeled toboggans), or offering the ski slopes for mountain biking enthusiasts.[2]

Offering Complementary Services.   Loss of patrons because of long waiting lines may be reduced by diverting them to complementary services. During periods of peak demand, complementary services may make the wait for service more bearable for customers and increase the likelihood of their staying in the system or returning at a later date. Thus, a bar or lounge may hold a surge of patrons for a restaurant. A putting green or driving range may keep golfers occupied when starting times are delayed. In essence, a complementary service represents one stage of a two-stage queue.[3] The service time for the first stage may stretch out for a considerable time before a client leaves the service stage to exit from the system.

Advertising and Sales Promotion   Promotional offers and advertising are two additional tools to stimulate demand when the demand is below what is desired. Promotions may offer additional benefits or reduced price for a limited period of time. Holiday tours with extended features, and promotion of late-night movie theater showings with prizes are examples.

Yield Management

Yield management is an approach that originated in the airline industry but is used in hotel and car rental businesses as well. The objective of yield management is to maximize the revenue, or yield, from revenue-generating units that are limited in number for a given time period, such as seats on a flight or rooms in a hotel on a particular day. Yield management is an appropriate approach when: (1) the firm is operating with a relatively fixed capacity, (2) demand can be segmented into clearly identified partitions, (3) inventory is perishable, (4) the product is sold well in advance, (5) demand fluctuates substantially, and (6) marginal sales costs and production costs are low, but capacity change costs are high.[4]

The basic idea behind the yield management is to partition the inventory of revenue-generating units and sell them to different customer segments. For example, airlines have identified different customer segments such as affluent travelers for whom the cost is not the primary concern, a business traveler who has to go somewhere on short notice and be back on a certain date, vacationers for whom cost is an important issue, and people who would visit family and friends or travel for pleasure if the price is right. Airlines offer different levels of service for these groups, such as first class, business class, economy, and super-savers, respectively.

All these different levels of service are offered on the same plane; therefore, the problem is how to allocate the available seats on a particular flight to each one of these groups. Obviously, an airline would like to fill all seats with first-class passengers or full fare–paying business travelers, but because this is not likely to occur many

[2] Lovelock, *Services Marketing*, p. 213.

[3] Queuing theory is discussed in the supplement to this chapter.

[4] Sheryl E. Kimes, "Yield Management: A Tool for Capacity-Constrained Service Firms," *Journal of Operations Management*, vol. 8, no. 4 (October 1989), pp. 348–363.

seats will be empty on most flights. Consequently, they offer the remaining seats to economy and super-saver passengers at reduced prices. This is justified because the marginal cost of flying another passenger when there is an available seat on a flight is almost negligible. Seats are sold long before the departure date; therefore, the issue is how many discount tickets to sell and make sure that there are enough seats left for late-booking travelers who will be willing to pay the full fare.

A yield management system has to address four basic issues to optimize revenues: demand patterns for various rates/fares, overbooking policy, demand elasticities, and information system.[5] Yield management has been successfully used by many companies such as Holiday Inn, Ryder truck rental company, Amtrak, and American Airlines. For example, it is estimated that yield management at American Airlines provided over $1.4 billion quantifiable benefits for a three-year period in the early 1990s.[6]

Management Science Techniques

Management science provides powerful techniques to help service operations managers manage both demand and supply. Two of these, queuing theory and simulation, are especially useful in making decisions in managing both demand and supply. Queuing models help determine some important performance characteristics of a service system related to waiting lines that form at peak periods of demand or when demand exceeds service capacity for a limited period of time. Queuing models provide performance measures such as the average time each customer spends in the waiting line and in the system, average number of customers in the system, and average queue length. Knowledge of such important performance measures will help operations managers make intelligent decisions concerning capacity and demand. Simulation is also a powerful and popular tool often used with queuing models. Simulation helps managers collect important information about system performance and provide answers to "what if" questions concerning capacity expansion or reduction. These techniques are discussed in the supplement to this chapter.

Management of Demand in Waiting

Lines that form at cash registers, box offices, toll booths, bank tellers, and post offices are resented by many people, but seen by most as part of daily life. Strategies for managing demand are effective for some service organizations but they do not completely eliminate waiting. In other words, waiting lines, or queues, form even at well-managed service facilities.

Among the many disadvantages of waiting is balking; that is, some customers may give up and leave the system. This may mean loss of some customers in the short term; they may come back at another time, but some may leave the system forever and go to a competitor. Whatever the case might be, it means loss of revenue for the service organization.

Reducing waiting time may be an important component of both demand and supply management. It was mentioned that management science techniques are available to help operations managers make system-related decisions to reduce waiting and its negative impact on customers and service organizations. Now let's look at other, nontechnical approaches to managing demand when waiting lines are formed. The main focus of these approaches is to make waiting a less painful experience for customers

---

[5] Kimes, "Yield Management: A Tool for Capacity-Constrained Service Firms," pp. 348–363.

[6] Barry C. Smith, John F. Leimkuhler, and Ross M. Darrow, "Yield Management at American Airlines," *Interfaces*, vol. 22, no. 1 (January–February, 1992), pp. 8–31.

as well as service providers. To accomplish this, we must understand the psychology of people in waiting lines. David Maister formulated eight propositions about the perceptions and psychology of people in waiting.[7] In the following paragraphs, these propositions are summarized and suggestions are offered as to what management can do to alleviate the problem.

1. *Unoccupied time feels longer than occupied time.* Many service organizations have discovered this perception and provide distractions to keep customers occupied. Some restaurants have a bar where patrons can have a drink and socialize while waiting for their table. Newspapers and magazines found in doctors' and dentists' offices, or TV sets in waiting rooms of auto repair shops all serve the same purpose: take the customer's mind off waiting.

2. *Preprocess waits feel longer than in-process waits.* Waiting seems to be shorter once the service has begun. Anxiety may be higher when waiting to be served. There is the fear of being forgotten by the servers, but once you are in the system and the process is underway, these feelings can easily go away. Some restaurants give menus to patrons waiting for a table, which gives them the impression that service has begun and keeps them occupied. Sometimes, a simple acknowledgment is enough to give the same impression; a letter from the admissions office of a college you have applied may make waiting feel shorter, especially if an approximate date for decision is also provided.

3. *Anxiety makes waits seem longer.* As mentioned in the previous paragraph, "being forgotten" may be one source of anxiety; not knowing how long the wait is going to be, what the service will be like, if you are in the right line, or if you will be able to get in before all tickets are sold out at a sporting event are some other sources. Anything management can do to reduce the customer's anxiety will make the wait feel shorter and less painful. For example, the waiting seems to have become particularly severe at the Statute of Liberty, one of the most-visited monuments in the world. A recent *Wall Street Journal* article reports that "every day thousands of tourists are barred from going to the top of the statute as early as 2 P.M. Worse, hundreds of others each year require medical attention from standing in the heat too long or climbing the stairs."[8]

4. *Uncertain waits are longer than known, finite waits.* Waiting feels longer when you do not know when the service will begin, and as just mentioned, this increases anxiety. Providing an estimate for the wait usually helps customers calm down and accept the situation. Estimates, however, must be carefully made and close to actual, and overestimating usually pleasantly surprises the customer. Disney World and Disneyland, for example, post estimates for each attraction, and they generously overestimate them.

5. *Unexplained waits are longer than explained waits.* When people are told of the reasons for wait they can feel more comfortable and be more understanding, but when they are kept in the dark as to the reason for delay they may get upset. For example, if a nurse explains to patients in the waiting room that the doctor is going to be late because he is attending an emergency case, most people will understand and judge the delay as justifiable. Consequently, service organizations must be honest and forthcoming with customers and explain the reason(s) when there is a delay in the service.

---

[7] David H. Maister, "The Psychology of Waiting Lines," in J. A. Czepiel, M. R. Solomon, and C. F. Surprenant (eds.), *The Service Encounter: Managing Employee/Customer Interaction in Service Businesses* (Lexington, MA: Lexington Books, 1985), pp. 113–123.

[8] Danielle Reed, "Where the Huddled Masses Wait All Day," *Wall Street Journal* (September 19, 1997).

6. *Unfair waits are longer than equitable waits.* Most people would be upset if they see someone cutting in the line, or any other practice that violates the common concept of fairness. Unfortunately, these practices are common at some service organizations. For example, an employee who opens up a new cashier line at a supermarket may take customers from the end of another checkout line rather than the next person in line, or an employee at the service counter who interrupts your service to answer a phone and serves the customer on the line violates people's expectations of fairness. These practices not only anger customers, but also make the wait feel longer than it really is.

7. *The more valuable the service, the longer the customer will wait.* In chapter 5, a model of value was presented, which defined nonmonetary price as any sacrifice customer has to make to receive a service. We also included waiting time as part of this price. Consequently, time spent in waiting is part of the sacrifice consumers are willing to make for the service, and just like monetary price paid for services, the higher the value of the service, the higher the nonmonetary price customers will be willing to pay. Service managers must have a good idea how valuable the service is to customers to make sure that waiting does not exact too high a price from customers.

8. *Solo waits feel longer than group waits.* Waiting for most services is in the company of other customers; hence, customers are not alone in the line in a strict sense. However, because customers normally do not know each other, they may feel as though they are waiting in isolation, especially if there is no conversation among customers or no distractions. Service operations managers should create opportunities, when possible, for customers to socialize and converse among themselves. This will create a sense of community and provide a distraction and make the wait feel shorter.

Research on customer perceptions of waiting conducted at a bank branch in Boston confirmed that as perceptions of waiting time increase, customer satisfaction tends to decrease. Researchers also found that the most important issues for customers include:

- *Fairness.* Can newcomers cut in front of customers who arrived before them, or is the line first come, first served?
- *Interest level.* Are interesting things happening that the customer can watch?
- *Customer attitudes.* What time pressures do customers face?
- *Environment.* Is waiting comfortable? Does the customer have to freeze in the cold or bake in the sun?
- *Value of service.* How important is the result of the transaction to the customer? Could it easily be obtained elsewhere? Can the customer come back another time, or is the transaction urgent?[9]

11.4   MANAGING SUPPLY

Capacity is the extent of the ability of a system to deliver the service it was designed to deliver. Hence, managing supply means managing the capacity. Before strategies for managing supply are discussed, capacity must first be defined and difficulties surrounding the measure of capacity understood. Then, the components that make up or influence capacity will be examined. When there is a solid understanding of capacity

[9] Karen L. Katz, Blaire M. Larson, and Richard C. Larson, "Prescription for the Waiting-in-Line Blues: Entertain, Enlighten, and Engage," *Sloan Management Review* (winter 1991), pp. 44–53.

and its components, the various strategies for managing demand and the process of aggregate planning may be discussed.

Capacity

Capacity is usually defined as the maximum rate of output. This simple definition, however, hides an inherent difficulty with the concept, and that is the measure of output in services. As discussed in chapter 2, two of the characteristics of services are that they produce an intangible output, and the output is not standard and may exhibit considerable variability. A third reason for the difficulty is that service organizations rarely offer a single, uniform service. For example, how is the output of a hospital measured? Should the number of beds occupied, number of patients treated, number of physician hours, or number of nurse hours be used? None of these measures provides a satisfactory measure to truly reflect the service provided at a hospital. For example, if the number of beds occupied is used, this measure does not tell anything about the difference in resources needed to treat a patient with cancer and a patient who is in the hospital with a broken leg. Even if two cancer patients are compared, the severity of their cases, required treatments, and the resources needed for their treatment and their costs can be very different.

Another interesting fact, and a challenge for service operations managers, is that even with the same number of employees and same facilities, capacity of a service organization may not be the same from day to day. This is so because of the variability customers exhibit in terms of their needs and requirements as well as variability due to service employees. For example, two customers who arrive at a bank teller may require considerably different amounts of service from the teller; one may be just depositing his paycheck and take 30 seconds of the teller's time. The second customer, on the other hand, may be depositing 15 checks for a small business and transferring money between accounts of the company and may take several minutes. When the bank has too many of the second type of customers on a particular day, say Friday, the capacity of the bank will be reduced. Thus, it is clear that a service organization must choose its output measure carefully, if possible, to avoid all these problems.

Components of Capacity

The seven basic components of capacity are human resources, facilities, equipment, tools, time, customer participation, and alternative sources of capacity.

Human Resources   Human resources are directly related to aggregate output. The number of people, the level of skills, and the mix of skills are major factors. Highly skilled people organized into motivated groups and supplied with the best equipment can have an enormous impact on productivity. Further, if the leadership is excellent and the environment is rewarding, the twin factors of leadership and motivation may increase capacity. Human resources are also a highly flexible capacity component. Workers can be hired and fired easier than equipment can be bought and sold. Labor can work full time, part time, or overtime. Workers can be cross-trained to perform a variety of jobs.

Facilities   Facilities are needed to house employees and equipment. Some services are provided over the phone, through computer networks, through mail, or on the air such as TV broadcasts; hence, they do not need to consider customers in facility design. However, many other organizations receive customers in their facilities to deliver a service.

Equipment and Tools   Although much of equipment planning has already been determined in the design of the service delivery system and capital budgeting stage of the strategic plan, sometimes simple, inexpensive equipment substitutions or modifications may yield increases in productivity and thereby expand capacity. As an example, Sears introduced a computer terminal for order takers in its catalog department to replace hand completion and filing of forms. At the same time, it introduced a terminal stand in which customers enter their home phone numbers, and then the storage location of their packages appears on the screen. Each customer goes to the storage shelf, picks up the package, and takes it to the cashier. Formerly, a Sears clerk had to retrieve the location number from a desk file. In this example, the work was simplified and shifted to the customer, but customer waiting time was greatly reduced.

Time   Time is a component in two ways. First, capacity may be altered by changing the mix between two time periods or shifting output to another time period. This is especially appropriate for services subject to peak demand periods. Second, in a larger sense, extending the hours of operation increases the total capacity relative to demand for a specified time period.

Customer Participation   Another important component of capacity in some services is customer participation. Many services rely on customers' labor for service delivery. For example, a customer does all the work at an automated teller machine to withdraw money from his account. In other services, the customer may supply only part of the required labor.

Alternative Sources   Alternative sources of capacity may be internal or external. Internal sources may consist of mothballed machines or facilities, extended work hours, or multiple shifts. External sources may consist of subcontracting, acquiring another company, or increasing automation. The leasing of resources also allows for a wide range of capacity expansion alternatives.

Strategies for Management of Supply

Service operations managers have a much greater control of and influence on the supply of services than they have on the demand. However, even a higher degree of control of the supply of services does not guarantee a perfect match between the demand and supply. Following are some strategies operations managers can use to increase or decrease the supply of services. These strategies inevitably rely on skillful use of one or more capacity components in changing the service capacity, and hence the supply. As with demand management strategies, it must be pointed out that not all of these strategies are appropriate or feasible for all service organizations.

Changing the Level of Work Force   This is a strategy that can be used effectively only in the medium-term, that is, over a planning period of 3 to 12 months. Anticipating an increasing or decreasing trend in demand, managers can gradually increase or decrease the number of employees. Also, anticipating seasonal peaks and valleys in demand, a service organization may hire workers for the length of the season. The major disadvantage of this strategy is the high cost of hiring, training, and termination of employees, and the difficulty of developing loyalty among employees.

Cross-Training Employees   Most services involve several tasks. The level of demand for each task may not be equal at all times. Training employees in tasks other than their regular assignments and empowering them to serve will help increase service capacity during peak demand periods. This has an additional advantage; it helps employees develop themselves by gaining additional skills and reduces boredom that results from doing the same job day-in and day-out.

Part-Time Workers   Many service organizations today rely on part-time employees for a significant portion of their labor needs. It is estimated that a quarter of the work force in the United States is employed on a temporary, part-time, or contract basis.[10] Part-time employees may be most appropriate when the daily labor needs of the service exhibit a clear and pronounced pattern, as is the case in fast-food restaurants and package delivery services. When feasible, the use of part-time workers adds significant flexibility to service capacity and give operations managers better control of service supply.

Increasing Customer Participation   As mentioned earlier, customers may be a valuable source of labor in the delivery of some services, and some service organizations make clever use of this source. For example, in some restaurants, patrons prepare their own salad at the salad bar, but the waiter brings their food to the table. At Shouldice Hospital, patients are encouraged to walk out of the operating room to a rest area after a hernia operation, rather than hospital personnel transporting the patient in a wheelchair as done in most hospitals after surgery. Increasing customer participation, in general, reduces the labor input from the service organization and increases the service speed, thereby increasing the capacity. However, there is also a risk in increasing customer participation; if customers are not skillful in performing their tasks, they may slow things down and cause a reduction in the capacity.

Renting Equipment   Equipment is an important component of service capacity in many services. Hence, just increasing the number of employees may not be enough to increase the capacity. An increase in the equipment availability must usually accompany the increase in employment. When the increase in employment is only temporary, purchase of equipment may not be economically justified. When this is the case, the service organization may rent or lease the necessary equipment. This is a common practice in the airline industry; airlines that face increased demand during summer rent or lease airplanes from other airlines or freight carriers.

Expanding/Renovating Facilities   Often, output may be increased by moving to a new building with a better space pattern or by developing a better layout of equipment in the old building. Better lighting, air-conditioning, and heating improvements also may contribute to productivity and thereby expand capacity.

Automation   Automation of tasks performed by humans has been used in manufacturing for many years. Major advantages of automation are lower cost, higher output, consistency of output, and hence higher quality. Automation has not always been seen as desirable in services, because it usually implies impersonal service. However, speed and lower cost, in addition to other benefits it provides, are making automation an attractive alternative to human delivery of some services. For example, hotel chains such as Hyatt, Hampton Inns, Embassy Suites, and Homewood Suites have been installing kiosks for quick check-ins and checkouts. A hotel industry executive predicts that these kiosks will become the norm in the hotel industry in the future.[11]

Extending Service Hours   Some service organizations may increase their capacity by extending their hours of operation under special circumstances or during periods of increased demand. For example, some retailers stay open all night during Christmas shopping, some post offices receive mail until midnight on April 15 to help taxpayers make the deadline, and amusement parks have extended hours in summer months and on weekends.

---

[10] Keith Hammonds, Kevin Kelly, and Karen Thurston, "Special Report: Rethinking Work—The New World of Work," *Business Week* (October 17, 1994), pp. 76–87.

[11] Jon Bigness, "Impersonal Touch: More Hotels Automate Front Desk," *Wall Street Journal* (June 18, 1996).

Better Scheduling Tools and Practices   Significant increases in capacity may be obtained from better scheduling of service personnel and their activities. Many management science techniques are available to optimize scheduling of service employees, such as nurses at a hospital, airline flight crews, and locating and scheduling emergency medical services. Also, performing nonurgent tasks, such as cleaning and maintenance, during periods of low demand is a simple but effective way to increase service capacity.

11.5   SUMMARY

The development of a service system proceeds from the design of the service, to aggregate planning of resources, to building of the system. The basic objective of aggregate planning is to plan a firm's resources so that the firm's capacity and demand for outputs are matched. Thus, aggregate planning may alternatively emphasize adjusting the demand side or the supply side to achieve a desired balance. In this chapter, strategies and tools that operations managers can use in accomplishing the challenging task of balancing demand and supply in services was discussed.

The major reasons that make this a particularly difficult task in services were first reviewed. It was pointed out that for effective performance of this task, an operations manager must be equipped with a sound knowledge of her customers and an understanding of their needs. Then, she must study the nature and pattern of demand to select and implement the appropriate strategies for managing demand. Strategies and tools that help a service organization influence demand include price, advertising and promotions, offering services that have countercyclical demand patterns, using reservations or appointments, communication efforts, and offering complementary services. Yield management as a special form of demand management used by airlines, car rental companies, and hotel chains was also briefly discussed. The discussion of demand management concluded by focusing on the psychological aspects of waiting and what operations managers can do to make waiting less painful, or maybe even an enjoyable experience for customers.

Capacity is the extent of the ability of a system to deliver the service it was designed to deliver and is usually defined as the maximum rate of output. Hence, managing supply means managing the capacity. After pointing out the difficulties surrounding the capacity measurement in services, the major components of capacity for a service organization were discussed. Strategies for managing supply rely on the management of these components of capacity, and include changing the level of work force, cross-training employees, hiring part-time workers, increasing customer participation, renting equipment, expanding/renovating facilities, automation, extending service hours, and using management science techniques for better scheduling and implementing good scheduling practices.

Discussion Questions

1. What is the purpose of aggregate planning?
2. How does aggregate planning differ for services versus manufacturing?
3. Explain why balancing demand and supply is a challenge in services.
4. Discuss how marketing and operations people can cooperate in balancing demand and supply.
5. What type of data would be needed to understand customers and their needs for
   a. A credit card company
   b. An amusement park
   c. A fitness center

6. Which of the strategies for managing demand would be appropriate and which ones would not be appropriate or feasible for the following services. Explain your answers.
   a. A university
   b. A copy center
   c. A prison system
7. Which of the strategies for managing capacity, or supply, would be appropriate, and which ones would not be appropriate or feasible for the following services? Explain your answers.
   a. A hospital
   b. A restaurant
   c. A resort
8. Explain the type of services in which yield management would be most effective.
9. Refer to Maister's propositions about the psychology of waiting in section 11.3. Which of these propositions would be valid for the customers of the following services? Explain.
   a. Mail-order house
   b. Private piano lessons
   c. Airline
10. What is capacity, and why is it so difficult to measure it in services?
11. In what terms would capacity be measured for:
    a. A computer center?
    b. Mass transit?
    c. A police force?
12. Discuss the strategies for managing service capacity that are directly related to labor input.
13. Discuss the strategies for managing service capacity that are directly related to capital input.

CASES

CASE 11–1   Forecasting Nursing Staffing Requirements by Intensity-of-Care Level

The continuing escalation of health care costs has become a matter of considerable national concern. Research is being conducted throughout the nation on cost containment, and much of this effort has recently been devoted to the macro questions on regulation of health care costs. This case reports the results of a project to develop a micro approach to nursing cost containment at a 220-bed, nonprofit community hospital in an urban setting. The hospital administrator is confident that nursing requirements can be influenced by proper planning and that control over costs can be exerted. Considerable savings can result from reduction or more efficient utilization of nursing personnel-hours. Since payroll expenditures typically account for over 50 percent of the operating budget of most hospitals, this area would seem to provide the greatest potential for savings.

PROJECT DESCRIPTION

The overall goal of this project is to enable hospital management to predict nursing personnel-hour requirements by ward, shift, day of the week, and month of the year. Since the nursing personnel-hours required by ward and by shift for any given day are a function of both the number of patients by care level and the standard hours (for that level of care), the research has focused first on the demand, or patient forecast. The first models are expected to predict required nursing hours by ward and shift with greater accuracy and less effort than is currently being accomplished manually. It is important to note that approximately 50 percent of the nursing hours in the hospital are "variable" costs and can be varied with patient requirements.

METHODOLOGY

In order to obtain estimates of the required nursing personnel-hours, statistical models were developed to predict the number of patients by six intensity-of-care levels for each hospital ward by month, day, and shift. The magnitude of the distribution of care levels is shown in Exhibit 11-2. Numerous regression runs were made on the data with the following as independent indicator variables:

WARDS:	ICC/CCU	Intensive care, coronary care
	2N	Psychiatric cases
	3N	Medical cases, surgical and orthopedic overflow
	3T	Medical cases
	4T	Surgical cases
	5T	Orthopedic cases
	PEDS	Pediatrics
	OB	Obstetrics—maternity and gynecology cases
	NSY	Nursery
MONTH:	January through December	
DAY:	Sunday through Saturday	
SHIFT:	Day, evening, night	
TIME:	Day of the year, numbered 1 through 365	

The Ward 2N, the month of May, the day of Wednesday, and the day shift were selected as the reference point and set equal to zero (this is reflected in the constant term). The resulting models predict the number of patients by care level, shift, ward, month, and day of the week. The impact of the shift, day of the week, and other independent variables on the workloads can be determined from the model coefficients shown in Exhibit 11-3.

Using the coefficients in Exhibit 11-3, the regression model for care level 1 predicts the number of patients as follows:

EXHIBIT 11-2 Totals by Level of Care

	Total Census in 1988	Average Patients per Day (Three Shifts)	Average Patients per Shift	Standard Hours of Nursing Care per Patient
CL1	15,226	41.72	13.91	1.5
CL2	94,234	258.18	86.06	2.1
CL3	41,115	112.64	37.55	3.5
CL4	8,131	22.28	7.43	4.7
CL5	1,720	4.71	1.57	6.5
CL6	385	1.05	0.35	8.0

No. of patients =

$$1.03 + 0.49(3N) + 0.67(3T) + 1.75(4T)$$
$$+ 0.84(5T) + 0.27(PEDS) + 5.12(OB)$$
$$+ 5.72(NSY) - 0.45(APRIL) - 0.30(JUNE)$$
$$- 0.35(AUGUST) - 0.36(SUNDAY)$$
$$- 0.33(MONDAY) - 0.31(TUESDAY)$$
$$- 0.18(FRIDAY) - 0.34(SATURDAY)$$
$$- 1.31(NIGHT\ SHIFT) - 0.00097(TIME)$$

For example, if this model were to be used to predict the number of patients requiring level 1 of care in Ward 4T (Surgical Cases) on Monday, July 4, 1988, during the day shift, we would have 4T = 1, Monday = 1, Time = 195, and the following equation:

Estimated no. of CL1 patients
$$= 1.03 + 0.175(1) - 0.33(1) - 0.00097(195)$$
$$= 2.26 \text{ patients}$$

The results of the seven models developed are particularly helpful when compared in the format of Exhibit 11-3. A review of this exhibit by ward clearly shows the distribution of care levels by ward and can be extremely valuable in the distribution of the nursing skill mix (RNs, LPNs, and other) by ward. For example, the care level mix for the surgical ward (4T) reflects the fact that most of the patients require care specified by care level 2 with the following distribution for July 4, 1988, during the day shift.

Care Level	Estimated No. of Patients
CL1	2.26
CL2	24.84
CL3	5.70
CL4	0.05
CL5,6	0.00

An evaluation of the time constant shows that there is relatively little change over time in the number of patients in any care level. However, a review of the monthly data suggests an increase in care level during the later months of the year. The second year of data which has now been collected will be used to clarify these points. Obviously, such information is crucial to the hospital administrator in planning nursing workloads. For weekly scheduling, an evaluation of the daily data is helpful to the administrator. The data clearly show a decreased demand for nursing staff on Fridays, Saturdays, Sundays, and Mondays, which is not unusual. However, the model supports intuition with more precise information. Obviously, with the availability of numerous part-time nurses whose schedules can be a management "variable," management has the ability to bring in this resource as the forecast and actual demand indicate. Predictably, the more acutely ill patients, while showing a seasonal pattern, do not demonstrate any significant daily or by-shift variation. ■

SOURCE: Adapted by permission of F. T. Helmer, E. B. Oppermann, and J. D. Surver, "Forecasting Nursing Staffing Requirements by Intensity-of-Care Level," *Interfaces*, vol. 10, no. 3 (June 1980), pp. 50–56. Copyright 1980 The Institute of Management Sciences, 290 Westminster Street, Providence, Rhode Island 02903 USA.

CASE QUESTIONS

1. Use the regression model given in Exhibit 11-3 to predict the number of patients requiring care level 2 in Ward 5 on Tuesday, July 18, during the evening shift.

2. Examine Exhibit 11-3 and verify the conclusions of the study in regard to
   a. Number of patients in any care level.
   b. Monthly distributions of care level.

EXHIBIT 11-3   Regression (Coefficients) by Care Levels (1988 Data, $n = 8687$)

	CL1	CL2	CL3	CL4	CL4,5	CL5,6	CL4,5,6
Constant	1.03	4.99	1.22	0.98	1.07	0.42	1.50
Time	−0.00097	0.00040	0.00209	−0.00250	−0.00279	−0.00283	−0.00601
Shifts							
Day							
Eve		−1.45	0.66		0.06		
Night	−1.31	−0.24	0.65				
Wards							
ICU/CCU			−2.03	3.19	4.44	1.64	4.84
2N*							
3N	0.49	2.30	1.38	−0.66	−0.70	−0.06	−0.72
3T	0.67	18.90	5.89	−0.68	−0.71	−0.06	−0.73
4T	1.75	21.75	3.82	−0.44	−0.46		−0.45
5T	0.84	22.49	4.93	−0.53	−0.57	−0.06	−0.59
PEDS	0.27	−0.136	1.40		−0.42		−0.39
OB	5.12	2.06	−0.31		−0.13	−0.06	−0.15
NSY	5.72	0.64	−1.56	−0.59	−0.62	−0.06	−0.64
Months							
Jan				−0.23	−0.30	−0.36	−0.67
Feb						−0.22	−0.30
Mar			0.21		−0.19	−0.21	−0.36
Apr	−0.45	0.88					
May*							
Jun	−0.30				0.25	0.12	0.38
Jul		−0.45			0.27	0.15	0.54
Aug	−0.35	−1.42	0.38	0.35	0.33	0.26	0.67
Sep		0.21	0.54	0.32	0.31	0.40	0.80
Oct			0.38	0.23	0.29	0.48	0.81
Nov				0.43	0.50	0.62	1.17
Dec				0.58	0.67	0.69	1.43
Days							
Sun	−0.36	−1.79	−0.55				
Mon	−0.33	−1.98	−0.25				
Tue	−0.31	−0.98	0.30				
Wed*							
Thr					0.07		0.07
Fri	−0.18	−0.77	0.16	0.07	0.01		0.08
Sat	−0.34	−1.89	−0.17				
R^2	0.61	0.89	0.61	0.64	0.74	0.56	0.77
Std error	1.80	3.51	2.21	0.87	0.93	0.47	0.93

* These variables included in constant term.

c. Daily distributions of care level.
d. Distributions of care level by shift.
3. Use Exhibit 11-2 to calculate the nursing requirements per shift by care level.
4. How can your calculations above aid in determining a nursing skill mix (i.e., how many RNs, LPNs, and Nurses' Aides are required)?

5. Considering the value of the information provided in Exhibit 11-2, why is it necessary to predict number of patients by ward, month, shift, and day?
6. What level of nurse staffing would be considered aggregate planning for this hospital? What aggregate planning strategies for meeting nursing requirements do you suggest for the hospital?

CASE 11–2 Developing an Aggregate Capacity Plan for the Campus Police

The campus police chief is attempting to develop a two-year plan for the department that involves a request for additional resources. Recently, the university administration has suggested that the department change its image and operating strategy from that of "policing" to a more comprehensive "public safety" approach.

The department currently has twenty-six sworn officers. The size of the force has not changed over the past fifteen years. Although the size of the student population also has remained stable over that time period, several changes have occurred in the university environment that have prompted the campus police chief to review his operations and request additional resources. These changes include

- The university has expanded geographically. More buildings and other facilities have been added, some in outlying areas miles from the main campus.
- Traffic and parking problems have increased because more students bring their cars to campus.
- More portable, expensive equipment with high theft potential is dispersed across the campus (e.g., there are over 10,000 personal computers on campus).
- Alcohol and drug problems have increased.
- The size of the athletic program and its facilities have increased dramatically.
- The size of the surrounding community has doubled.
- The police need to spend more time on education and prevention programs in an attempt to become more fully integrated into the university community.

The university is located in a small town, thirty-five miles from an urban center. During the summer months, the student population is around 5000. This number swells to 30,000 during fall and spring semesters. Thus demand for police and other services is significantly lower during the summer months. Demand for police services also varies by

- Time of the day (peak time between 10 P.M. and 2 A.M.)
- Day of the week (weekends are the busiest)
- Weekend of the year (on football weekends, 50,000 extra people come to campus)
- Special events (check-in, check-out, Founder's Day, commencement, and so on)

Football weekends are especially difficult to staff. Extra police services are typically needed from 8:00 A.M. to 5:00 P.M. on five football Saturdays. All twenty-six officers are called in to work double shifts. Over forty law enforcement officers from surrounding localities are paid to come in on their own time, and a dozen state police lend a hand free of charge (when they are available). Twenty-five students and local residents are paid to work traffic and parking. During the last academic year (a 9-month period), overtime worked by campus police officers totalled over 2400 hours.

Other relevant data include the following

- The average starting salary for a police officer is $18,000.
- Work-study, part-time students, and local residents who help with traffic and parking are paid $4.50 an hour.
- Overtime is paid to police officers who work over 40 hours a week at the rate of $13.00 an hour. Extra officers who are hired part-time from outside agencies also earn $13.00 an hour.
- There seems to be an unlimited supply of officers who will work for the university when needed for special events.
- With days off, vacations, and average sick leave considered, it takes five persons to cover *one* 24-hour, 7-day a week position.
- The schedule of officers during fall and spring semesters is typically:

	Weekdays	Weekends
1st Shift (7 A.M.—3 P.M.)	5	4
2d Shift (3 P.M.—11 P.M.)	5	6
3d Shift (11 P.M.—7 A.M.)	6	8

Staffing for football weekends and special events is in *addition* to the preceding schedule. Summer staffing is, on average, half that shown above.

The police chief feels that his present staff is stretched to the limit. Fatigued officers are potential problems for the department and the community. In addition, neither time nor personnel have been set aside for crime prevention, safety, or health pro-

grams. Interactions of police officers with students, faculty, and staff are minimal and usually negative in nature. In light of these problems, the chief would like to request funding for four additional officers, two assigned to new programs and two to alleviate the overload on his current staff of officers. He would also like to begin limiting overtime to ten hours per week for each officer. ∎

CASE QUESTIONS

1. Which variations in demand for police services should be considered in an aggregate plan for resources? Which variations can be handled with short-term scheduling adjustments?
2. In what terms would you define capacity for the department? What additional information do you need to determine capacity requirements?
3. Evaluate the current staffing plan. What does it cost? Are 26 officers sufficient to handle the normal workload?
4. What would be the additional cost of the chief's proposal? How would you suggest that the chief justify his request?
5. How much does it currently cost the university to provide police services for football games? What would be the pros and cons of subcontracting this work completely to outside law enforcement agencies?
6. Can you propose any other alternatives? What suggestions do you have for duties of police officers in nonpeak periods?

References

Czepiel, J. A., M. R. Solomon, and C. F. Surprenant (eds.), *The Service Encounter: Managing Employee/Customer Interaction in Service Businesses* (Lexington, MA, Lexington Books, 1985).

Bigness, Jon, "Impersonal Touch: More Hotels Automate Front Desk," *Wall Street Journal* (June 18, 1996).

Hammonds, Keith, Kevin Kelly, and Karen Thurston, "Special Report: Rethinking Work—The New World of Work," *Business Week* (October 17, 1994), pp. 76–87.

Katz, Karen L., Blaire M. Larson, and Richard C. Larson, "Prescription for the Waiting-in-Line Blues: Entertain, Enlighten, and Engage," *Sloan Management Review* (winter 1991), pp. 44–53.

Kimes, Sheryl E., "Yield Management: A Tool for Capacity-Constrained Service Firms," *Journal of Operations Management*, vol. 8, no. 4 (October 1989), pp. 348–363.

Lovelock, Christopher H., *Services Marketing*, 3rd ed. (Upper Saddle River, NJ, Prentice Hall, 1996).

Maister, David H., "The Psychology of Waiting Lines," in J. A. Czepiel, M. R. Solomon, and C. F. Surprenant (eds.), *The Service Encounter: Managing Employee/Customer Interaction in Service Businesses* (Lexington, MA, Lexington Books, 1985), pp. 113–123.

Reed, Danielle, "Where the Huddled Masses Wait All Day," *Wall Street Journal* (September 19, 1997).

Smith, Barry C., John F. Leimkuhler, and Ross M. Darrow, "Yield Management at American Airlines," *Interfaces*, vol. 22, no. 1 (January–February, 1992), pp. 8–31.

CHAPTER 11 SUPPLEMENT

Queuing and Simulation

S11.1   INTRODUCTION

The body of knowledge about waiting lines, often called queuing theory, is a valuable tool for the service operations manager. Waiting lines are a common situation—they may, for example, take the form of cars waiting for repair at an auto service center, printing jobs waiting to be completed at a print shop, or students waiting for a consultation with their professor. Exhibit S11-1 lists just a few uses of waiting-line models. Analysis of waiting-line length, average waiting time, and other factors helps to understand service system capacity.

Service operations managers recognize the trade-off that must take place between the cost of providing good service and the cost of customer waiting time. Managers want queues that are short enough so that customers do not become unhappy and either leave without buying or buy but never return. However, managers are willing to allow some waiting if the waiting is balanced by a significant savings in capacity costs.

EXHIBIT S11-1   Common Queuing Situations

Situation	Arrivals in Queue	Service Process
Supermarket	Grocery shoppers	Checkout clerks at cash register
Highway toll booth	Automobiles	Collection of toll at booth
Doctor's office	Patients	Treatment by doctors and nurses
Computer system	Programs to be run	Computer processes jobs
Telephone company	Callers	Switching equipment to forward calls
Bank	Customers	Transactions handled by teller
Machine maintenance	Broken machines	Repairpeople fix machines
Harbor	Ships and barges	Dockworkers load and unload

EXHIBIT S11-2   The Trade-Off between Waiting Costs and Capacity Costs

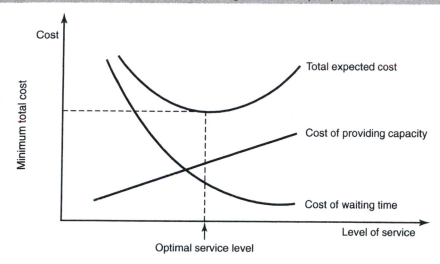

One means of evaluating a service facility is to look at total expected cost, a concept illustrated in Exhibit S11-2. Total cost is the sum of capacity costs plus expected waiting costs.

Capacity costs are seen to increase as a firm attempts to raise its level of service. Managers in *some* service centers can vary their capacity by having standby personnel and machines that can be assigned to specific service stations to prevent or shorten excessively long lines. In grocery stores, managers and stock clerks can operate extra checkout counters when needed. In banks and airport check-in points, part-time workers may be called in to help. As service improves (i.e., speeds up), however, the cost of time spent waiting in lines decreases. Waiting cost may reflect lost productivity of workers while their tools or machines are awaiting repairs or may simply be an estimate of the cost of customers lost because of poor service and long queues. In some service systems (e.g., emergency ambulance service), the cost of long waiting lines may be intolerably high.

S11.2   BASIC QUEUING SYSTEM CONFIGURATIONS

Service systems are usually classified in terms of their number of channels (e.g., number of servers) and number of phases (e.g., number of service stops that must be made). A single-channel queuing system with one server is typified by the drive-in bank that has only one open teller or by a drive-through fast-food restaurant. If, on the other hand, the bank had several tellers on duty and each customer waited in one common line for the first available teller, then we would have a multichannel queuing system at work. Most banks today are multichannel service systems, as are most large barber shops, airline ticket counters, and post offices.

A single-phase system is one in which the customer receives service from only one station and then exits the system. A fast-food restaurant in which the person who takes your order also brings you the food and takes your money is a single-phase system. So is a driver's license agency in which the person taking your application also grades your test and collects the license fee. However, if the restaurant requires you to place your order at one station, pay at a second, and pick up the food at a third service stop, it becomes a multiphase system. Likewise, if the driver's license agency is large or busy, you will probably have to wait in a line to complete the application (the first service stop), then queue again to have the test graded (the second service stop), and finally go to a third service counter to pay the fee. To help you relate the concepts of channels and phases, Exhibit S11-3 presents four possible configurations.

S11.3   MEASURING THE QUEUE'S PERFORMANCE

Queuing models help managers make decisions that balance desirable capacity costs with waiting-line costs. Some of the many measures of a waiting-line system's performance that are commonly obtained in a queuing analysis are

- The average time each customer or object spends in the queue
- The average queue length
- The average time each customer spends in the system (waiting time plus service time)
- The average number of customers in the system
- The probability that the service facility will be idle
- The utilization factor for the system
- The probability of a specific number of customers in the system

S11.4   A SINGLE-CHANNEL QUEUING MODEL

The most common case of queuing problems involves the single-channel, or single-server, waiting line. In this situation, arrivals form a single line to be serviced by a single station (Exhibit S11-3). It is often possible to assume that the following conditions exist in this type of system:

1. Arrivals are served on a first-come, first-served basis, and every arrival waits to be served, regardless of the length of the line or queue.
2. Arrivals are independent of preceding arrivals, but the average number of arrivals (arrival rate) does not change over time.
3. Arrivals are described by a Poisson probability distribution and come from an infinite (or very, very large) population.[1]
4. Service times vary from one customer to the next and are independent of one another, but their average rate is known.
5. Service times occur according to the negative exponential probability distribution.[2]
6. The average service rate is faster than the average arrival rate.

When these conditions are met, the equations shown in Exhibit S11-4 can be developed. These equations allow us to calculate the seven measures of a waiting line

---

[1] The Poisson distribution is established by the formula

$$P(x) = \frac{e^{-\lambda}\lambda^x}{x!} \qquad \text{for } x = 0, 1, 2, \ldots$$

where $P(x)$ = probability of x arrivals per unit of time
   x = number of arrivals per unit of time
   λ = average arrival rate
   e = 2.7183 (which is the base of natural logs)

[2] This distribution takes the form

Probability (service takes longer than x minutes) = $e^{-\mu x}$ \qquad for $x \geq 0$

where μ = average number served per minute

EXHIBIT S11-3   Basic Queuing System Configurations

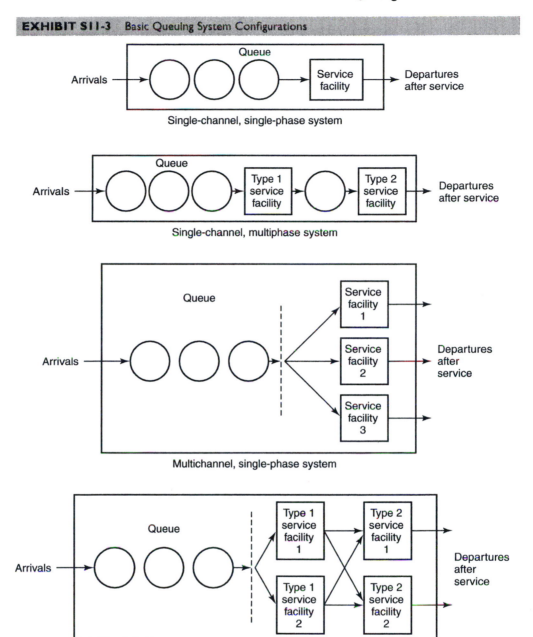

Single-channel, single-phase system

Single-channel, multiphase system

Multichannel, single-phase system

Multichannel, multiphase system

system's performance mentioned earlier. Note that all of the calculations are based in some way on the average number of *arrivals* per time period (λ) and the average number of customers *served* per time period (μ). The following example illustrates how this single-channel model may be used.

Golden Muffler Shop   Jones, the mechanic at Golden Muffler Shop, is able to install new mufflers at an average rate of three per hour (or about one every 20 minutes), according to a negative exponential distribution. Customers seeking this service arrive at the shop on the average of two per hour, following a Poisson distribution.

EXHIBIT S11-4 Equations for the Single-Channel Waiting-Line Model

λ = Mean number of arrivals per time period

μ = Mean number of people or items served per time period

L_s = Average number of units (customers) in the system (waiting line + service)

$$= \frac{\lambda}{\mu - \lambda}$$

W_s = Average time a unit spends in the system (waiting time + service time)

$$= \frac{1}{\mu - \lambda}$$

L_q = Average number of units in the queue

$$= \frac{\lambda^2}{\mu(\mu - \lambda)}$$

W_q = Average time a unit spends waiting in the queue

$$= \frac{\lambda}{\mu(\mu - \lambda)}$$

ρ = Utilization factor for the system

$$= \frac{\lambda}{\mu}$$

P_0 = Probability of 0 units in the system (that is, the service unit is idle)

$$= 1 - \frac{\lambda}{\mu}$$

$P_{n>k}$ = Probability of more than k units in the system, where n is the number of units in the system

$$= \left(\frac{\lambda}{\mu}\right)^{k+1}$$

The customers are served on a first-in, first-out basis and come from a very large population of possible buyers.

From this description, we are able to obtain the operating characteristics of Golden Muffler's queuing system:

$$\lambda = 2 \text{ cars arriving per hour}$$

$$\mu = 3 \text{ cars served per hour}$$

$$L_s = \frac{\lambda}{\mu - \lambda} = \frac{2}{3 - 2} = \frac{2}{1}$$

$$= 2 \text{ cars in the system, on average}$$

$$W_s = \frac{1}{\mu - \lambda} = \frac{1}{3 - 2} = 1 \text{ hour}$$

$$= 1\text{-hour average waiting time in the system}$$

$$L_q = \frac{\lambda^2}{\mu(\mu - \lambda)} = \frac{2^2}{3(3 - 2)} = \frac{4}{3(1)} = \frac{4}{3}$$

$$= 1.33 \text{ cars waiting in line, on average}$$

$$W_q = \frac{\lambda}{\mu(\mu - \lambda)} = \frac{2}{3(3-2)} = \frac{2}{3} \text{ hour}$$

$$= 40\text{-minute average waiting time in the queue per car}$$

$$\rho = \frac{\lambda}{\mu} = \frac{2}{3}$$

$$= 66.6 \text{ percent of time mechanic is busy}$$

$$P_0 = 1 - \frac{\lambda}{\mu} = 1 - \frac{2}{3}$$

$$= 0.33 \text{ probability there are 0 cars in the system}$$

$$P_{n>3} = \left(\frac{\lambda}{\mu}\right)^{k+1} = \left(\frac{2}{3}\right)^{3+1}$$

$$= .198 \text{ or a } 19.8\% \text{ chance that more than 3 cars are in the system}$$

Once we have computed the operating characteristics of a queuing system, it is often important to do an economic analysis of their impact. The waiting-line model described above is valuable in predicting potential waiting times, queue lengths, idle times, and so on, but it does not identify optimal decisions or consider cost factors. As stated earlier, the solution to a queuing problem may require management to make a tradeoff between the increased cost of providing better service and the decreased waiting costs derived from providing that service.

S11.5   A MULTICHANNEL QUEUING MODEL

The next logical step is to look at a multichannel queuing system, in which two or more servers or channels are available to handle arriving customers. Let us still assume that customers awaiting service form one single line and then proceed to the first available server. An example of such a multichannel, single-phase waiting line is found in many banks today. A common line is formed, and the customer at the head of the line proceeds to the first free teller. (See Exhibit S11-3 for a typical multichannel configuration.)

The multichannel system presented here again assumes that arrivals follow a Poisson probability distribution and that service times are exponentially distributed. Service is first-come, first-served, and all servers are assumed to perform at the same rate. Other assumptions listed earlier for the single-channel model apply as well.

The queuing equations for this model are shown in Exhibit S11-5. These equations are obviously more complex than the ones used in the single-channel model, yet they are used in exactly the same fashion and provide the same type of information as the simpler model.[3]

Golden Muffler Revisited   The Golden Muffler Shop has decided to open a second garage bay and to hire a second mechanic to handle muffler installations. Customers, who arrive at the rate of about $\lambda = 2$ per hour, will wait in a single line until one of the two mechanics is free. Each mechanic installs mufflers at the rate of about $\mu = 3$ per hour.

---

[3] See either Barry Render and R. M. Stair, *Quantitative Analysis for Management,* 7th ed. (Upper Saddle River, NJ, Prentice Hall, 2000); or Jay Heizer and Barry Render, *Production and Operations Management,* 5th ed. (Upper Saddle River, NJ, Prentice Hall, 1999), for details.

EXHIBIT S11-5 Equations for the Multichannel Queuing Model

M = Number of channels open

λ = Average arrival rate

μ = Average service rate at each channel

P_0 = Probability that there are zero people or units in the system

$$= \frac{1}{\left[\sum_{n=0}^{M-1} \frac{1}{n!}\left(\frac{\lambda}{\mu}\right)^n\right] + \frac{1}{M!}\left(\frac{\lambda}{\mu}\right)^M \frac{M\mu}{M\mu - \lambda}} \quad for \; M\mu > \lambda$$

L_s = Average number of people or units in the system

$$= \frac{\lambda\mu(\lambda/\mu)^M}{(M-1)!\,(M\mu-\lambda)^2} P_0 + \frac{\lambda}{\mu}$$

W_s = Average time a unit spends in the waiting line or being serviced (namely, in the system)

$$= \frac{\mu(\lambda/\mu)^M}{(M-1)!\,(M\mu-\lambda)^2} P_0 + \frac{1}{\mu} = \frac{L_s}{\lambda}$$

L_q = Average number of people or units in line waiting for service

$$= L_s - \frac{\lambda}{\mu}$$

W_q = Average time a person or unit spends in the queue wating for service

$$= W_s - \frac{1}{\mu} = \frac{L_q}{\lambda}$$

To find out how this system compares to the old single-channel waiting-line system, we will compute several operating characteristics for the $M = 2$ channel system and compare the results with those found in the first example.

$$P_0 = \frac{1}{\left[\sum_{n=0}^{1}\frac{1}{n!}\left(\frac{2}{3}\right)^n\right] + \frac{1}{2!}\left(\frac{2}{3}\right)^2 \frac{2(3)}{2(3)-2}}$$

$$= \frac{1}{1 + \frac{2}{3} + \frac{1}{2}\left(\frac{4}{9}\right)\left(\frac{6}{6-2}\right)} = \frac{1}{1 + \frac{2}{3} + \frac{1}{3}} = \frac{1}{2}$$

$= 0.50$ probability of zero cars in the system

Then

$$L_s = \frac{(2)(3)(2/3)^2}{1![2(3)-2]^2}\left(\frac{1}{2}\right) + \frac{2}{3} + \frac{8/3}{16}\left(\frac{1}{2}\right) + \frac{2}{3} = \frac{3}{4}$$

$= 0.75$ average number of cars in the system

$$W_s = \frac{L_s}{\lambda} = \frac{3/4}{2} = \frac{3}{8} \; \text{hour}$$

$= 22.5$-minute average time a car spends in the system

$$L_q = L_s - \frac{\lambda}{\mu} = \frac{3}{4} - \frac{2}{3} = \frac{1}{12}$$

= 0.083 average number of cars in the queue

$$W_q = \frac{L_q}{\lambda} = \frac{0.083}{2} = 0.0415 \text{ hour}$$

= 2.5-minute average time a car spends in the queue

We can summarize these characteristics and compare them to those of the single-channel model as follows:

	Single Channel	*Two Channels*
P_0	0.33	0.5
L_s	2 cars	0.75 car
W_s	60 minutes	22.5 minutes
L_q	1.33 cars	0.083 car
W_q	40 minutes	2.5 minutes

The increased service has a dramatic effect on almost all characteristics. In particular, time spent waiting in line drops from 40 minutes to only 2.5 minutes. This is consistent with the trade-off curve illustrated earlier in Exhibit S11-2.

S11.6   MORE COMPLEX QUEUING MODELS AND THE USE OF SIMULATION

Many practical waiting-line problems that occur in service systems have characteristics like the models just described. Often, however, *variations* of this specific case are present in an analysis. Service times in an automobile repair shop, for example, tend to follow the normal probability distribution instead of the exponential distribution. A college registration system in which seniors have first choice of courses and hours over all other students is an example of a first-come, first-served model with a preemptive priority queue discipline. A physical examination for military recruits is an example of a multiphase system, one that differs from the single-phase models discussed earlier. A recruit first lines up to have blood drawn at one station, then waits to take an eye examination at the next station, talks to a psychiatrist at the third, and is examined by a doctor for medical problems at the fourth. At each phase, the recruit must enter another queue and wait his or her turn.

Models to handle these cases have been developed by operations researchers. The computations for the resulting mathematical formulations are more complex than the earlier ones, though. And many real-world queuing applications are too complex to be modeled analytically at all. When this happens, analysts usually turn to computer simulation.

Simulation, our next topic, is a technique in which random numbers are used to draw inferences about probability distributions (such as arrivals and services). Using this approach, many hours, days, or months of data can be developed by a computer in a few seconds. This allows analysis of controllable factors, such as adding another service channel, without actually doing so physically. Basically, whenever a standard analytical queuing model provides only a poor approximation of the actual service system, it is wise to develop a simulation model instead.

S11.7   SIMULATION AS A SCHEDULING TOOL

When a system contains elements that exhibit chance in their behavior, the **Monte Carlo method** of simulation may be applied. The basis of Monte Carlo simulation is experimentation on the chance (or *probabilistic*) variables through random sampling.

The simulation technique breaks down into five simple steps:

1. Set up a probability distribution for important variables.
2. Build a cumulative probability distribution for each variable.
3. Establish an interval of random numbers for each variable.
4. Generate random numbers.
5. Actually simulate a series of trials using the random numbers to obtain values for the variables.

We will demonstrate a Monte Carlo simulation with the aid of Exhibits S11-6 through S11-8. Assume that a single-channel, single-phase queuing system, such as that at a postal substation, is being analyzed. The analyst makes a number of observations of the number of arrivals per five-minute period and the number of services per five-minute period. The data are classified into frequency distributions and then represented as probability distributions, as shown in Exhibit S11-6(a) and (c). Next, the cumulative probability distributions for Exhibit S11-6(a) and (c) are computed as shown in Exhibit S11-6(b) and (d). We now proceed as follows:

EXHIBIT S11-6   Probabilities for a System Simulation

Probability for number of arrivals in a time period

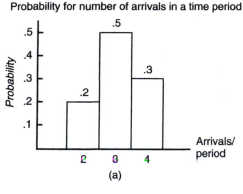

(a)

Probability for number of services/period

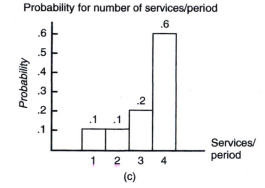

(c)

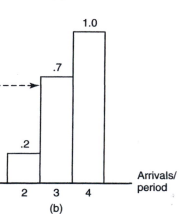

(b)

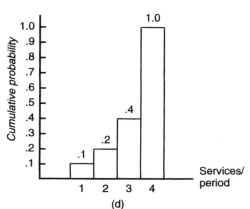

(d)

EXHIBIT S11-7   Simulation of a Postal Substation for Three Time Periods

Period	Random Number	Units Arriving during the Period	Random Number	Units Serviced during the Period*	Units in Line Waiting to Be Serviced at End of Period
1	—	0	—	0	0
2	0.63	3	0.17	2	1
3	0.87	4	0.03	1	4
4	0.11	2	0.42	3	3

* These would proceed to the next station.

1. Set up headings for the time and status of each item in the system, as in Exhibit S11-7. (Items in this case are the number of people arriving or being served.)
2. Obtain a table of random numbers found in management science texts. A portion of such unrelated numbers is shown in Exhibit S11-8.
3. Select a row and column, and then proceed to the random number table. We selected the second column to start and decided to read down. Enter the number 0.63 for the second column and 0.17 for the fourth column in Exhibit S11-7.
4. Go to the first cumulative probability chart [Exhibit S11-6(b)], and find 0.63 on the vertical scale. Draw a horizontal line to the bar it first meets. This is the three-arrivals-per-period bar. Enter 3 in the table in Exhibit S11-7 in the appropriate column.
5. Go to the second cumulative probability chart [Exhibit S11-6(d)] and find 0.17 on the vertical scale. Draw a horizontal line to the bar it first meets. This is the two-units-serviced-per-period bar. Enter 2 in the appropriate column in Exhibit S11-7.
6. Units arriving minus units serviced in the period gives a surplus of one waiting to be served in the next period.
7. Repeat steps 3 through 5, keeping track of units left to be serviced in each following period, if any.

Note that no matter how complex the system may be, simulation consists of examining the inputs, waiting lines, services, and output at one particular time period. Then the "clock" is moved up one time period and the system is examined again. After hundreds (or thousands) of simulations, average waiting periods, or average total service times through many different transactions may be found.

S11.8   THE ROLE OF COMPUTERS IN SIMULATION

Computers are critical in simulating complex tasks. They can generate random numbers, simulate thousands of time periods in a matter of seconds or minutes, and provide management with reports that make decision making easier. A computer approach is almost a necessity in order to draw valid conclusions from a simulation.

EXHIBIT S11-8   Portion of a Table of Random Numbers

5497	6317	5736	9468	5707	8576	2614
0234	8703	2454	6094	1760	3195	0985
9821	1142	6650	2749	3677	4451	4959
9681	5613	9971	0081	7249	3016	1385

Computer programming languages can help the simulation process. General-purpose languages such as FORTRAN, BASIC, COBOL, PL/I, or PASCAL are one approach. Special-purpose simulation languages, such as GPSS, SIMSCRIPT, and DYNAMO have a few advantages: (1) they require less programming time for large scale simulations, (2) they are usually more efficient and easier to check for errors, and (3) they have random-number generators already built in as subroutines.

Commercial, easy-to-use prewritten simulation programs are also available. Some are generalized to handle a wide variety of situations ranging from queuing to inventory. The names of a few such programs are: Witness, Xcell, MAP/I, Slam II, SIMFACTORY, ARENA, Micro Saint, Taylor II, and Extend. There also exist packages specifically designed for simulating various aspects of service systems. Two such programs are ServiceModel and MedModel developed by ProModel Corporation. ServiceModel can be used to simulate facility layout and design, capacity planning, staff and service scheduling, complex paperwork and customer flow, and distribution and logistics of service organizations. MedModel can be used in simulating the emergency room of a hospital.

Spreadsheet software can also be used to develop simulations quickly and easily. Such packages have built-in random-number generators (through the @ RAND command) and develop outputs through "data-fill" table commands.

Using POM for Windows for Queuing Problems

POM for Windows' Waiting Lines (queuing) module can be used to solve problems that fit any one of the models we have discussed in this chapter. Exhibit S11-9 illustrates the solution of the single channel waiting line model of Golden Muffler Shop example (select model M/M/1 from the menu) and a graph of probabilities for the number of customers in the system. In addition, the Waiting Lines module provides a table of probabilities for $P\ (n = k)$. Exhibit S11-10 has the output of the Golden Muffler Shop problem with two servers (multichannel model, M/M/s).

S11.9 SUMMARY

Two management science tools were examined, queuing theory and simulation, which are often useful in scheduling capacity. They can both provide information about the capacity needed so that customers are not forced to wait an unreasonable length of time. When certain mathematical conditions can be met, a series of queuing formulas may describe the parameters of the wait. When the situation at hand does not fit the assumptions of queuing theory, Monte Carlo simulation can be employed as a scheduling tool.

Problems

S11.1. The Tengler Electronics Corporation retains a service crew to repair machine breakdowns that occur on an average of $\lambda = 3$ per day (approximately Poisson in nature). The crew can service an average of $\mu = 8$ machines per day, with a repair time distribution that resembles the exponential distribution.
   a. What is the utilization rate of this service system?
   b. What is the average down time for a machine that is broken?
   c. How many machines are waiting to be serviced at any given time?
   d. What is the probability that more than one machine is in the system? Probability that more than two are broken and waiting to be repaired or being serviced? More than three? More than four?

S11.2. Barry's Car Wash is open six days a week, but its heaviest day of business is always Saturday. From historical data, Barry estimates that dirty cars arrive at the

EXHIBIT S11-9   POM for Windows Solution of the Single-Channel Golden Muffler Shop Example

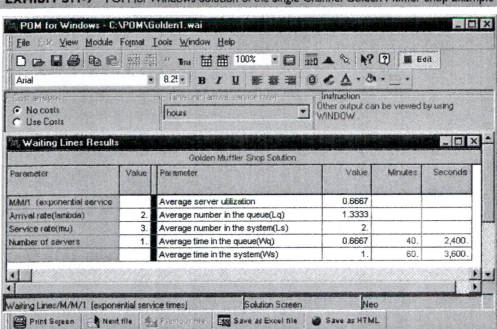

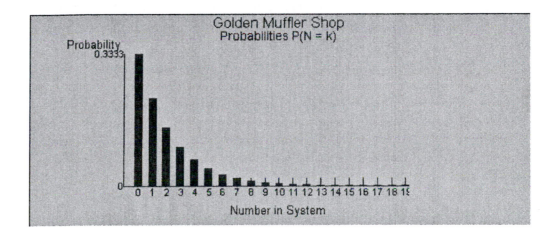

rate of 20 per hour all day Saturday. With a full crew working the hand-wash line, he figures that cars can be cleaned at the rate of one every two minutes. One car at a time is cleaned in this example of a single-channel waiting line.

Assuming Poisson arrivals and exponential service times, find the

a. Average number of cars in line
b. Average time a car waits before it is washed
c. Average time a car spends in the service system
d. Utilization rate of the car wash
e. Probability no cars are in the system

S11.3. Judy Holmes manages a large Montgomery, Alabama, movie theater complex called Cinema I, II, III, and IV. Each of the four auditoriums plays a different film; the schedule is set so that starting times are staggered to avoid the large crowds that would occur if all four movies started at the same time. The the-

EXHIBIT S11-10 POM for Windows Solution of the Two Channel Golden Muffler Shop Example

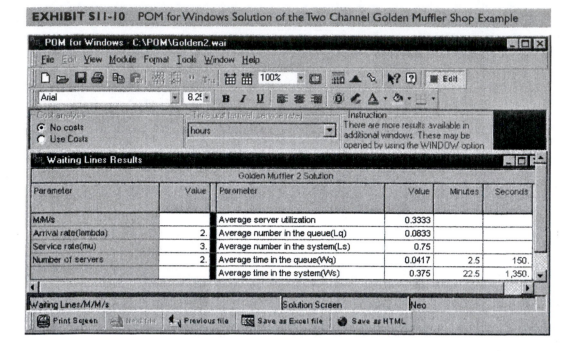

ater has a single ticket booth and a cashier who can maintain an average service rate of 280 movie patrons per hour. Service times are assumed to follow an exponential distribution. Arrivals on a normally active day are Poisson distributed and average 210 per hour.

In order to determine the efficiency of the current ticket operation, Judy wishes to examine several queue operating characteristics.

a. Find the average number of moviegoers waiting in line to purchase a ticket.

b. What percentage of the time is the cashier busy?

c. What is the average time a customer spends in the system?

d. What is the average time spent waiting in line to get to the ticket window?

e. What is the probability that there are more than two people in the system? More than three people? More than four?

S11.4. A university cafeteria line in the student center is a self-serve facility in which students select the food items they want, then form a single line to pay the cashier. Students arrive at a rate of about four per minute according to a Poisson distribution. The single cashier ringing up sales takes about 12 seconds per customer, following an exponential distribution.

a. What is the probability there are more than two students in the system? More than three students? More than four?

b. What is the probability that the system is empty?

c. How long will the average student have to wait before reaching the cashier?

d. What is the expected number of students in the queue?

e. What is the average number in the system?

S11.5. Jerry's Department Store in Dubuque, Iowa, maintains a successful catalog sales department in which a clerk takes orders by telephone. If the clerk is occupied on one line, incoming phone calls to the catalogue department are answered automatically by a recording machine and asked to wait. As soon as the clerk is free, the party that has waited the longest is transferred and answered first. Calls come in at a rate of about 12 per hour. The clerk is capable of taking an order in an average of four minutes. Calls tend to follow a Poisson distribution, and service times tend to be exponential.

The clerk is paid $5 per hour, but because of lost goodwill and sales, Jerry's loses about $25 per hour of customer time spent waiting for the clerk to take an order.

   a. What is the average time that catalogue customers must wait before their calls are transferred to the order clerk?
   b. What is the average number of callers waiting to place an order?
   c. Jerry's is considering adding a second clerk to take calls. The store would pay that person the same $5 per hour. Should it hire another clerk? Explain.

S11.6. The administrator at a large hospital emergency room faces a problem of providing treatment for patients that arrive at different rates during the day. There are four doctors available to treat patients when needed. If not needed, they can be assigned to other responsibilities (for example, lab tests, reports, x-ray diagnoses) or else rescheduled to work at other hours.

It is important to provide quick and responsive treatment, and the administrator feels that, on the average, patients should not have to sit in the waiting area for more than five minutes before being seen by a doctor. Patients are treated on a first-come, first-served basis and see the first available doctor after waiting in the queue. The arrival pattern for a typical day is:

Time	Arrival Rate
9 A.M.—3 P.M.	6 patients/hour
3 P.M.—8 P.M.	4 patients/hour
8 P.M.—Midnight	12 patients/hour

These arrivals follow a Poisson distribution, and treatment times, 12 minutes on the average, follow the exponential pattern.

How many doctors should be on duty during each period in order to maintain the level of patient care expected?

S11.7. The number of cars arriving at Jim Harvey's Car Wash during the last 200 hours of operation is observed to be the following:

Number of Cars Arriving	Frequency
3 or less	0
4	20
5	30
6	50
7	60
8	40
9 or more	0
	200

   a. Set up a probability and cumulative probability distribution for the variable of car arrivals.
   b. Establish random number intervals for the variable.
   c. Simulate 15 hours of car arrivals and compute the average number of arrivals per hour. Select the random numbers needed from Exhibit S11-8.

S11.8. Blacksburg, Virginia's, General Hospital has an emergency room that is divided into six departments: (1) the initial exam station to treat minor problems or make diagnoses; (2) an x-ray department; (3) an operating room; (4) a cast fitting room; (5) an observation room (for recovery and general observation before final diagnoses or release); and (6) an out-processing department (where clerks check patients out and arrange for payment or insurance forms).

The probabilities that a patient will go from one department to another are presented in the accompanying table.

a. Simulate the trail followed by 10 emergency room patients. Proceed, one patient at a time, from each one's entry at the initial exam station until he or she leaves through out-processing. You should be aware that a patient can enter the same department more than once.

b. Using your simulation data, what are the chances that a patient enters the x-ray department twice?

From	To	Probability
Initial exam at emergency room entrance	X-ray department	0.45
	Operating room	0.15
	Observation room	0.10
	Out-processing clerk	0.30
X-ray department	Operating room	0.10
	Cast-fitting room	0.25
	Observation room	0.35
	Out-processing clerk	0.30

From	To	Probability
Operating room	Cast-fitting room	0.25
	Observation room	0.70
	Out-processing clerk	0.05
Casting-fitting room	Observation room	0.55
	X-ray department	0.05
	Out-processing clerk	0.40
Observation room	Operating room	0.15
	X-ray department	0.15
	Out-processing clerk	0.70

S11.9. Fully loaded barges arrive at night in New Orleans following their long trips down the Mississippi River from industrial midwestern cities. The number of barges docking on any given night ranges from 0 to 5. The probability of 0, 1, 2, 3, 4, and 5 arrivals is displayed below.

Number of Arrivals	Probability
0	0.13
1	0.17
2	0.15
3	0.25
4	0.20
5	0.10

A study by the dock superintendent reveals that because of the nature of their cargo, the number of barges unloaded also tends to vary from day to day. The superintendent provides information from which one can create a probability distribution for the variable *daily unloading rate* (see the following table).

Daily Unloading Rate	Probability
1	0.05
2	0.15
3	0.50
4	0.20
5	0.10
	1.00

Barges are unloaded on a first-in, first-out basis. Any barges that are not unloaded the day of arrival must wait until the following day. Tying up a barge in dock is an expensive proposition, and the superintendent cannot ignore the angry phone calls from barge line owners reminding him that "time is money!" He decides that, before going to the Port of New Orleans's controller to request additional unloading crews, a simulation study of arrivals, unloadings, and delays should be conducted. Develop a 15-day simulation.

S11.10. Management of the First Syracuse Bank is concerned over a loss of customers at its main office downtown. One solution that has been proposed is to add one or more "drive-through" teller stations to make it easier for customers in cars to obtain quick service without parking. Chris Carlson, the bank president, thinks the bank should only risk the cost of installing one drive-through. He is informed by his staff that the cost (amortized over a 20-year period) of building a drive through is $12,000 per year. It also costs $16,000 per year in wages and benefits to staff each new teller window.

The director of Management Analysis, Anita Greenberg, believes that the following two factors encourage the immediate construction of two drive-through stations, however. According to a recent article in *Banking Research* magazine, customers who wait in long lines for drive-through teller service will cost banks an average of $1.00 per minute, in loss of goodwill. Also, adding a second drive-through will cost an additional $16,000 in staffing, but amortized construction costs can be cut to a total of $20,000 per year if two drive-throughs are installed together, instead of one at a time. To complete her analysis, Mrs. Greenberg collected one month's worth of arrival and service rates at a competing downtown bank's drive-through stations. These data are shown as Observation Analysis 1 and 2.

a. Simulate a one-hour time period, from 1 to 2 P.M., for a single-teller drive-through.

b. Simulate a one-hour time period, from 1 to 2 P.M., for a two-teller system.

Observation Analysis 1—Interarrival Times for 1,000 Observations	
Time between Arrivals (in minutes)	*Number of Occurrences*
1	200
2	250
3	300
4	150
5	100

c. Conduct a cost analysis of the two options. Assume the bank is open 7 hours per day and 200 days per year.

Observation Analysis 2—Customer Service Time for 1,000 Customers	
Service Time (in minutes)	*Number of Occurrences*
1	100
2	150
3	350
4	150
5	150
6	100

CASE

CASE S11–1   The Winter Park Hotel

Donna Shader, manager of the Winter Park Hotel, is considering how to restructure the front desk to reach an optimum level of staff efficiency and guest service. At present, the hotel has five clerks on duty, each with a separate waiting line, during peak check-in time of 3:00 P.M. to 5:00 P.M. Observation of arrivals during this time show that an average of 90 guests arrive each hour (although there is no upward limit on the number that could arrive at any given time). It takes an average of 3 minutes for the front-desk clerk to register each guest.

Ms. Shader is considering three plans for improving guest service by reducing the length of time guests spend waiting in line. The first proposal would designate one employee as a quick-service clerk for guests registering under corporate accounts, a market segment that fills about 30% of all occupied rooms. Because corporate guests are pre-registered, their registration takes just 2 minutes. With these guests separated from the rest of the clientele, the average time for registering a typical guest would climb to 3.4 minutes. Under plan one, noncorporate guests would choose any of the remaining four lines.

The second plan is to implement a single-line system. All guests could form a single waiting line to be served by whichever of the five clerks became available. This option would require sufficient lobby space for what could be a substantial queue.

The use of an automatic teller machine (ATM) for check-ins is the basis of the third proposal. Given that initial use of this technology might be minimal, Shader estimated that 20% of customers, primarily frequent guests, would be willing to use the machines. (This might be a conservative estimate if the guests perceive direct benefits from using the ATM, as bank customers do. Citibank reports that some 80% of its Manhattan customers use its ATMs.) Ms. Shader would set up a single queue for customers who prefer human check-in clerks. This would be served by the five clerks, although Shader is hopeful that the machine will allow a reduction to four. ∎

SOURCE: Barry Render and R. M. Stair, *Quantitative Analysis for Management,* 7th ed. (Upper Saddle River, NJ, Prentice Hall, 2000).

CASE QUESTIONS

1. Determine the average amount of time that a guest spends checking in. How would this change under each of the stated options?

2. Which option do you recommend?

References

Bechtold, Stephen E., and Michael J. Showalter, "A Methodology for Labor Scheduling in a Service Operation Room," *Decision Sciences,* vol. 18 (1987), pp. 89–107.

Byrd, J., "The Value of Queuing Theory," *Interfaces,* vol. 8, no. 3 (May 1978), pp. 22–26.

Chung, K. H., "Computer Simulation of a Queuing System," *Production and Inventory Management,* vol. 10, no. 1 (1969), pp. 75–82.

Cooper, R. B., *Introduction to Queuing Theory* (New York: Macmillan, 1972).

Cox, D. R., and W. L. Smith, *Queues* (New York, Wiley, 1965).

Deutsch, Howard, and Vince Mabert, "Queuing Theory and Teller Staffing: A Successful Application," *Interfaces,* vol. 10, no. 5 (October 1980), pp. 63–67.

Erikson, W., "Management Science and the Gas Shortage," *Interfaces*, vol. 4, no. 4 (August 1974), pp. 47–51.

Eschcoli, Z., and I. Adiri, "Single-Lane Budget Serving Two-Lane Traffic," *Naval Research Logistics Quarterly*, vol. 24, no. 1 (March 1977), pp. 113–125.

Foote, B. L., "Queuing Case Study of Drive-In Banking," *Interfaces*, vol. 6, no. 4 (August 1976), p. 31.

George, J. A., D. R. Fox, and R. W. Canvin, "A Hospital Throughput Model in the Context of Long Waiting Lines," *Journal of the Operational Research Society*, vol. 34 (January 1983), pp. 27–35.

Gostl, J., and I. Greenberg, "An Application of Queuing Theory to the Design of a Message-Switching Computer System," *Communications of the ACM*, vol. 28, no. 5 (May 1985), pp. 500–505.

Grassmann, Winfried K., "Finding the Right Number of Servers in Real World Queuing Systems," *Interfaces*, vol. 18, no. 2 (March–April 1988), pp. 94–104.

Green, L., and P. Kolesar, "The Feasibility of One-Officer Patrol in New York City," *Management Science*, vol. 30, no. 8 (August 1984), pp. 964–981.

Kaplan, Edward H., "A Public Housing Queue with Reneging and Task-Specific Servers," *Decision Sciences*, vol. 19 (1988), pp. 383–391.

Lambert, Carolyn U., and Thomas P. Cullen, "Balancing Service and Costs Through Queuing Analysis," *Cornell Quarterly* (August 1987), pp. 60–72.

Morse, Philip M., *Queues, Inventories and Maintenance* (New York: Wiley, 1958).

Northcraft, Gregory B., and Richard B. Chase, "Managing Service Demand at the Point of Delivery," *Academy of Management Review*, vol. 10, no. 1 (January 1985), pp. 65–75.

Panico, J. A. *Queuing Theory: A Study of Waiting Lines for Business, Economics and Sciences* (Upper Saddle River, NJ, Prentice-Hall, 1969).

Paul, R. J., and R. E. Stevens, "Staffing Service Activities with Waiting Line Models," *Decision Sciences*, vol. 2 (April 1971), pp. 206–318.

Render, Barry, and R. M. Stair, *Quantitative Analysis for Management*, 7th ed. (Upper Saddle River, NJ, Prentice Hall, 2000).

Sasser, W. Earl, "Match Supply and Demand in the Service Industries," *Harvard Business Review*, vol. 54, no. 6 (November–December 1976), pp. 133–140.

Sasser, W. Earl, Jr., R. Paul Olsen, and D. Daryl Wyckoff, *Management of Service Operations* (Boston, Allyn and Bacon, 1978).

Shannon, R. E., *Systems Simulation: The Art and Science* (Upper Saddle River, NJ, Prentice Hall, 1975).

Solomon, S. L., *Simulation of Waiting Lines* (Upper Saddle River, NJ, Prentice Hall, 1983).

Sze, D. Y., "A Queuing Model for Telephone Operator Staffing," *Operations Research*, vol. 32, no. 2 (March–April 1984), pp. 229–249.

Watson, H. J., *Computer Simulation in Business* (New York: Wiley, 1981).

Welch, N., and J. Gussow, "Expansion of Canadian National Railway's Line Capacity," *Interfaces*, vol. 16, no. 1 (January–February 1986), pp. 51–64.

Worthington, D. J., "Queuing Models for Hospital Waiting Lists," *Journal of the Operational Research Society*, vol. 38 (May 1987), pp. 413–422.

CHAPTER 12

Service Quality and Continuous Improvement

12.1   INTRODUCTION

Quality was one of the most talked about topics in the business world during the 1980s and 1990s. There is, of course, good reason for this. During the late 1970s and 1980s, many large U.S. corporations were affected; some were virtually devastated by competition from foreign companies. Japanese firms, for example, increased their U.S. market share in practically every industry they entered while consumer confidence in goods produced by American companies diminished. Loss of customers led to loss of profits for many American companies and loss of jobs for many of their employees, and hardship for their families. Japanese companies achieved this success in the United States, as well as in many other countries, largely due to the superior quality of their goods.

The shock caused by this situation initiated a quality revolution in U.S. industry. As a result, today most American manufacturers have significantly improved the quality of their goods. The quality revolution that started in the early 1980s was not limited to manufacturing industries. Practically all service organizations, including government organizations at all levels, were also impacted by the movement as consumers came to demand quality in everything they purchased—both goods and services.

This chapter discusses basic issues that determine quality and continuous improvement in services. The supplement to the chapter focuses on the tools and techniques of service quality and continuous improvement.

12.2   WHY QUALITY IS SO IMPORTANT

Quality is no longer a strong competitive advantage possessed by only a relatively few firms in any manufacturing industry. Today, it is simply a prerequisite for being in business. Manufacturers who do not produce quality products will not survive in the years to come. Is this also true for the field of services? We believe the answer is "yes." Although service companies do not have as much foreign competition as manufacturers do, domestic competition is fierce enough to make quality a prerequisite for survival in many services. Thus, the answer to the question as to why service quality is so important is simply "survival." Let's take a look at some of the reasons that make quality so essential for survival.

Higher Customer Loyalty   Quality is a vital ingredient of customer satisfaction. Superior quality leads to higher satisfaction, and higher satisfaction in turn leads to loyal customers. As emphasized in chapter 6, customer loyalty leads to higher profits and growth.

Higher Market Share   Loyal customers provide a solid customer base for the organization. Their word-of-mouth advertising brings new customers, leading to a larger market share for the organization.

Higher Returns to Investors   Research indicates that companies known for their high-quality goods and/or services are profitable companies, and therefore their stocks are good investments. For example, a recent study by the National Institute of Standards and Technology (NIST) found that the winners of Malcolm Baldrige National Quality Award have outperformed the Standard & Poor's 500 stock index by 3 to 1 in terms of return on investment. Even companies that did not win the award but that were finalists in the competition bested the Standard & Poor's 500 by 2 to 1.[1]

Loyal Employees   When an organization produces superior quality goods and/or services, its employees take pride in their work and gain high levels of satisfaction from their jobs. Satisfied employees tend to be loyal and productive. In addition, the organization enjoys low employee turnover.

Lower Costs   Superior quality means doing things right the first time, which means the organization will spend relatively little money to correct mistakes or give refunds to dissatisfied customers. Preventing mistakes increases productivity and lowers cost.

Lesser Vulnerability to Price Competition   Companies like Ritz-Carlton Hotels, known for their superior quality, can usually charge premium prices because they offer something their competitors do not. Consequently, they usually do not have to compete primarily on the basis of price, and when they do have to compete on the basis of price, they are usually in good condition to do so because of their high productivity and low costs.

No organization will enjoy these competitive advantages if its goods and/or services do not have the quality customers want. Another consequence of poor quality is liability for damages or injuries caused by poorly designed or produced goods and/or services. Medical malpractice suits and their financial impact on physicians and health care providers are well known.

12.3   QUALITY DEFINED

Quality is often talked about and much desired, but somewhat difficult to define. The problem lies not in finding definitions as many definitions exist, but in making sure that in any particular situation, customers, service providers, and suppliers understand each others' definitions. Most definitions of quality fall short of reflecting all the relevant perspectives. However, this is not necessarily bad; multiple definitions of quality

---

[1] Otis Port, "The Baldrige's Other Reward," *Business Week* (March 10, 1997), p. 75.

make us aware of the multiple perspectives that should be considered and multiple requirements that must be met to achieve superior quality.

Professor David Garvin identified five categories of quality definitions that reflect five different perspectives[2]:

1. *Transcendent.* According to the transcendent view, quality is innate excellence and can be recognized only through experience. In other words, it can be summarized as "You cannot define quality but you know it when you see it." This, however, provides little practical guidance to managers in the quest for quality.

2. *Product-based.* Product-based definitions rely on measurable quantities to define quality. For goods, the measures may include length of useful life, amount of a desirable ingredient (e.g., "100% cotton") or amount of a desirable output (e.g., "45 miles per gallon"). Examples for services include number of entries in an encyclopedia, number of days within which your order will be shipped, or number of rings before your call will be answered. Since it is based on measurable quantities, this definition allows an objective assessment of quality. The disadvantage of a product-based definition is that it assumes that all customers desire the same attributes and hence fails to account for differences in tastes and preferences of individual consumers.

3. *User-based.* This approach to defining quality begins where the product-based definition ends; it defines quality from an individual consumer's perspective. The "fitness for use" definition of quality is consistent with this approach. In other words, it is based on the premise that "quality is in the eyes of the beholder." For example, a tastefully prepared and presented meal that takes half an hour to deliver to a customer's table may be seen as a sign of poor quality if the meal is for lunch and the customer is in a hurry. The subjectivity of this approach leads to two problems: (1) how to decide which attributes should be included in a good or service to appeal to the largest number of customers; (2) how to differentiate between attributes that provide satisfaction and those that imply quality.

4. *Manufacturing-based.* Manufacturing-based definitions view quality as an outcome of engineering and production processes. According to this approach, quality is "conformance to requirements." In other words, how well does the output match the design specifications. For example, if an airline service specifies arrival within 15 minutes of the schedule, the level of quality in terms of this specification can easily be determined by comparing actual flight arrivals with schedule. The disadvantage of this approach is that, unless specifications are based on customers' needs and preferences, quality becomes an internal issue that helps simplify production control but fails to deliver what customers want.

5. *Value-based.* This approach incorporates value and price into the definition of quality. Quality is defined as a balance between conformance or performance and an acceptable price to the customer.

These different quality definitions represent differences in perspectives of business functions such as marketing, manufacturing, and design. For example, user-based definitions are closest to marketing viewpoint. Designers, on the other hand, prefer a product-based approach, but manufacturing-based definitions reflect manufacturing managers' primary concerns.

Finally, the formal definition developed jointly by the American National Standards Institute (ANSI) and the American Society for Quality (ASQ) should also be

[2] The discussion of the five perspectives has been adapted from David A. Garvin, *Managing Quality* (New York, The Free Press, 1988), pp. 40–46.

given: Quality is *"the totality of features and characteristics of a product or service that bears on its ability to satisfy given needs."*

12.4   DIMENSIONS OF SERVICE QUALITY

Despite the value of the different definitions of quality discussed above, managers of service organizations still have a difficult time understanding the exact meaning of service quality. Garvin identified eight dimensions of quality that help develop a more precise understanding of the concept.[3]

1. *Performance.* The basic operating characteristics of a product that can be measured constitute the performance dimension. For example, the number of seconds it takes a car to reach 60 miles per hour can be considered a performance measure for an automobile.
2. *Features.* These are extras or "bells and whistles" that come with the product but normally not part of the standard package in similar products, such as a CD player and antilock braking system in a car.
3. *Reliability.* Reliability refers to the probability that a product will perform its intended function for a specified period of time under specified environmental conditions, such as the probability that the transmission system will not require a repair for six years when maintained according to the manufacturer's guidelines.
4. *Conformance.* Conformance is the degree to which a product meets design specifications, such as actual number of miles per gallon (mpg) as compared to the mpg design specifications.
5. *Durability.* Durability is the amount of use a consumer gets from the product before it physically deteriorates or continued use becomes uneconomical.
6. *Serviceability.* Serviceability refers to the ease and speed of repairs and the courtesy of repair personnel.
7. *Aesthetics.* This dimension includes subjective traits such as how a product looks, feels, sounds, tastes, or smells.
8. *Perceived quality.* Perceived quality is the perceptions that have been formed in the consumer's mind as a result of advertising, brand promotion, word-of-mouth, or personal experience in use.

Although the meaning of the word *product* includes both goods and services, these dimensions seem more easily interpreted or understood for goods. Zeithaml, Parasuraman, and Berry identified five dimensions with which consumers judge services.[4]

1. *Reliability.* Reliability in services is defined as the ability to perform the promised service dependably and accurately. It means that the service organization performs the service right the first time and also means that the organization honors all of its promises. Some examples include accuracy in billing, keeping records correctly, and completing the service at the promised time.
2. *Responsiveness.* This concerns the willingness or readiness of employees to provide service. It includes timeliness of service such as giving prompt service, mailing a transaction slip immediately, and returning customer calls quickly.

---

[3] David A. Garvin, "Competing on the Eight Dimensions of Quality," *Harvard Business Review* (November–December 1987), pp. 101–109.

[4] The discussion of the five dimensions has been adapted from Valarie A. Zeithaml, A. Parasuraman, and Leonard L. Berry, *Delivering Quality Service: Balancing Customer Perceptions and Expectations* (New York, The Free Press, 1990), pp. 15–33.

3. *Assurance.* This dimension relates to the knowledge, competence, and courtesy of service employees and their ability to convey trust and confidence. Competence means possession of the required skills and knowledge to perform the service. Courtesy involves politeness, respect, consideration, and friendliness of contact personnel. This dimension also includes trustworthiness, believability, and honesty of service employees.

4. *Empathy.* Empathy is defined as the caring and individualized attention provided to customers. It includes the approachability and ease of contact with the service providers and making the effort to understand the customers and their needs.

5. *Tangibles.* Tangibles include the physical evidence of the service such as physical facilities, appearance of service providers, tools or equipment used to provide the service, physical presentation of the service, and other customers in the service facility.

When Zeithaml, Parasuraman, and Berry asked more than 1,900 customers of five nationally known companies to allocate 100 points across the five service quality dimensions, they averaged as follows: reliability 32 percent, responsiveness 22 percent, assurance 19 percent, empathy 16 percent, and tangibles 11 percent. Then, the researchers asked these customers to evaluate the company with which they had a service experience. Customers indicated that their service company's most serious shortcoming was lack of reliability. These results seem to indicate that the most important service quality dimension for customers is reliability. This also seems to be where many service companies fail.

It should be noted that some researchers believe these dimensions do not necessarily apply to all services, while others conclude that only two of the dimensions are significant.[5] These should be seen as dimensions for services in general. An in-depth understanding of quality in any particular service requires a closer study of its characteristics and what customers expect from the service. However, one should not be surprised to find commonalities among the different sets of quality dimensions for different services. For example, a National Consumer Study on Service Quality in Banking identified the following eight dimensions of quality in bank services: accessibility, appearance, clarity, competence, courtesy, features, reliability, and responsiveness.[6] When AT&T designed the Military Card, a special calling card service for military personnel (many of whom do not have local service), it identified the following eight dimensions based on customers' needs: reliability, responsiveness, competence, access, courtesy, communications, credibility, and tangibles.

12.5   THE GAPS MODEL OF SERVICE QUALITY

The research project that helped Zeithaml, Parasuraman, and Berry to identify the five service quality dimensions also led them to develop a model of service quality, which is commonly known as the "gaps" model. This model conceptualizes service quality on the basis of the differences between customers' expectations with respect to the five dimensions and their perceptions of what was actually delivered. If a differ-

---

[5] See, for example, Emin Babakus and Gregory W. Boller, "An Empirical Assessment of the SERVQUAL Scale," *Journal of Business Research,* vol. 24 (May 1992), pp. 253–268; James M. Carman, "Consumer Perceptions of Service Quality: An Assessment of the SERVQUAL Dimensions," *Journal of Retailing,* vol. 66 (spring 1990), pp. 33–35; and Gerhard Mels, Christo Boshoff, and Deon Nel, "The Dimensions of Service Quality: The Original European Perspective Revisited," *The Service Industries Journal,* vol. 17, no. 1 (January 1997), pp. 173–189.

[6] Penny Lunt, "Just What, Exactly, Is Quality Service?" *ABA Banking Journal* (June 1992), pp. 78–81.

ence exists, it is characterized as a "gap." To measure these gaps, they developed a 22-item questionnaire called SERVQUAL.

The gaps model and its SERVQUAL instrument is probably the most frequently used approach to discuss and measure service quality. However, this approach also has some risks. One problem is that it does not allow the possibility that customers can have low quality expectations.[7] For example, if a customer expected poor quality and got slightly better service than expected from a service organization, the service could not logically be characterized as quality service. Also, the satisfaction approach to measuring quality runs into difficulty when services high in credence characteristics are evaluated. For example, complex legal or medical services present particular challenges because customers usually do not know what to expect, and even after the service is delivered, they may never know with certainty how good the service was.[8] Another limitation of the gaps model is that it is appropriate for large service organizations. It may not be an accurate representation of service quality in small firms.[9]

Despite these limitations, the gaps model provides valuable insight into understanding challenges of delivering quality service. A graphic representation of the gaps model is given in Exhibit 12-1.[10]

Gap 1: Not Knowing What Customers Expect   According to the model, the first gap occurs because of the difference between what customers expect and what managers perceive they expect. Major reasons for this gap are lack of marketing research orientation, evidenced by insufficient marketing research, inadequate use of research findings, and lack of interaction between management and customers. Inadequate upward communication from contact personnel to management and too many levels of management separating contact personnel from top managers are the other two reasons for this gap.

Gap 2: The Wrong Service Quality Standards   The difference between what managers think customers expect and the actual specifications they establish for service delivery leads to the second gap. Reasons for the emergence of this gap are *inadequate commitment to service quality, lack of perception of feasibility, inadequate task standardization,* and *absence of goal setting.*

Gap 3: The Service Performance Gap   The discrepancy between service specifications and the actual service delivered creates this gap. In general, this gap is created when employees are unable and/or unwilling to perform the service at the desired level. Various reasons are: *role ambiguity; role conflict, poor employee–job fit, poor technology–job fit, inappropriate supervisory control systems* leading to an inappropriate evaluation/compensation system, *lack of perceived control* on the part of employees, and *lack of teamwork.*

Gap 4: When Promises Do Not Match Delivery   The difference between what a firm promises about a service and what it actually delivers is described as Gap 4. Two factors contribute to this gap: (1) *inadequate communication* among operations, mar-

---

[7] Richard L. Oliver, "A Conceptual Model of Service Quality and Service Satisfaction: Compatible Goals, Different Concepts," in T. A. Swartz, D. E. Bowen, and S. W. Brown (eds.), *Advances in Services Marketing and Management: Research and Practice,* vol. 2 (Greenwich, CT, JAI Press Inc.), 1993, pp. 65–85.

[8] Christopher H. Lovelock, *Services Marketing,* 3rd ed. (Upper Saddle River, NJ, Prentice Hall, 1996), p. 466.

[9] See, for example, Cengiz Haksever, Ronald G. Cook, and Radha Chaganti, "Applicability of the Gaps Model to Service Quality in Small Firms," *Journal of Small Business Strategy,* vol. 8, no. 1 (spring 1997), pp. 49–66.

[10] The discussion of the gaps model is adapted from Valarie A. Zeithaml, A. Parasuraman, and Leonard L. Berry, *Delivering Quality Service: Balancing Customer Perceptions and Expectations,* pp. 51–133.

EXHIBIT 12-1 Service Quality Model

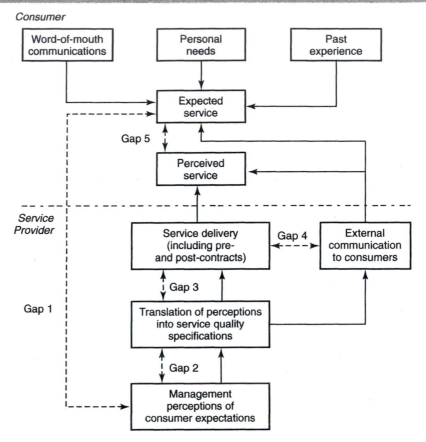

Source: A. Parasuraman, Valarie A. Zeithaml, and Leonard L. Berry, "A Conceptual Model of Service Quality and Its Implications for Future Research," *Journal of Marketing* (fall 1985), p. 44. Reprinted from *Journal of Marketing*, published by the American Marketing Association.

keting, and human resources, as well as across branches; and (2) *propensity to over-promise* in communications.

Gap 5: Expected Service—Perceived Service Gap   Gaps 1 through 4 contribute to the emergence of Gap 5, which is the difference between what the customer expected to receive from the service and what she believes she actually did receive. As the model in Exhibit 12-1 indicates, customers' perceptions are influenced by many sources, which include word-of-mouth communications, personal needs, past experiences, and communications from the service organization. This is the most important gap because, if the perceived service falls short of the customer's expectations, she will be disappointed and dissatisfied. Conversely, if the perceived service exceeds the customer's expectations, she will be not only satisfied but delighted.

12.6 ACHIEVING QUALITY

The American quality revolution that started in the 1980s was to a large extent sparked by Japanese competition. Japanese companies learned the basics of quality from American experience. Quality experts W. Edwards Deming and Joseph M. Juran taught quality to many Japanese managers after World War II. In turn, American quality practitioners learned several things from Japanese companies and their quality practices. Probably the most important lesson was that quality cannot be achieved simply by the mechanical application of a few quality techniques in our factories or service establishments. Creating quality goods and services requires a fundamental change in management philosophy. A second important lesson was that this change cannot be accomplished quickly or easily. It is an endless journey. The third lesson was that we must produce goods and services that are desired by customers, rather than try to sell them what we produce. In other words, we should be customer focused. This also required a fundamental change in how we design and produce goods and services. We must listen to customers and find out what they need and require.

These observations, combined with the accumulated theoretical and practical knowledge of quality of American industry, led to the development of a new philosophy of management initially known as Total Quality Management (TQM). Although most elements of TQM are not new, the way they are put together and practiced today is considered by many as revolutionary because of the fundamental changes it requires in management philosophy. TQM has evolved from the ideas of many quality experts and practices of highly successful companies in the United States and Japan, and it will probably continue to evolve in the future as the needs of customers and the realities of the marketplace change. In this section, the basic principles of this philosophy are briefly reviewed.

Focus on Customer Satisfaction

The first and foremost principle of TQM is customer focus, which means meeting and exceeding customer requirements and expectations the first time and every time. This principle must be embraced by all employees and must become part of an organization's culture. It requires systematic and continual inquiry into customer wants and desires, for their requirements and expectations are ever changing. It must be emphasized that this is quite different from the practice of the past that pretended to acknowledge the significance of customers with slogans like "The Customer Is King," but in actuality focused on what managers thought customers needed.

Leadership

Strong and dedicated leadership is one of the prerequisites for successful TQM implementation. Leadership must come from the highest levels of the organization. The leadership needed goes far beyond writing a memo emphasizing the organization's need for quality or hiring a manager to be "in charge" of quality. These approaches do not work. The type of leadership needed is the kind that starts a revolution in the corporate culture; such a leader is actively and personally involved in the implementation of all the TQM principles and provides examples of the desired behavior.

Senior leadership must create clear quality values, policies and strategies, and high expectations. Among these are innovation, risk taking in trying new ideas and methods to improve product quality and customer satisfaction, pride in work, employee involvement, and continuous improvement of products, processes, and individuals. Finally, there is a need for change in the way managers do their jobs; managers must shift their focus from directing and controlling to identifying and removing barriers that prevent employees from meeting customer requirements and expectations the first time and every time. Managers must become facilitators.

Commitment to Training and Education: Creating a Learning Organization

A major reason for many quality problems is lack of proper employee training. In some industries, service employees are paid the minimum wage because of the minimum skills required. However, some employees do not have even the basic reading and math skills that are needed for any job. Furthermore, employees also need to be trained in the technical requirements of the job they are performing. Of course, these basics are not enough to guarantee quality service delivery. Employees also need to be given training in problem solving and the use of continuous improvement tools. The amount and the type of training should be determined according to the nature of the work.

Participation, Empowerment, Teamwork, and Recognition

Top management involvement and leadership are essential for success; however, they alone are not sufficient. TQM succeeds only when it is embraced by the whole organization. Therefore, employee involvement at every level is another vital principle.

Empowerment is giving employees the authority to make and implement decisions and change the environment in which they work. Teamwork is another way employee involvement can be achieved.[11] Teams may be formed to address operational and quality problems. The advantage of this approach is that people who perform the task usually have the best ideas for solving task-related problems. When their suggestions are implemented and problems are eliminated, team members experience the satisfaction of making a contribution to the success of the firm and are motivated to seek continuing improvements.

Whether they are the result of an individual effort or teamwork, achievements in improving quality and customer satisfaction must be recognized and rewarded. Recognition is probably the best way for the management to reinforce the new values and practices TQM requires. Rewards do not have to be monetary, but they must be meaningful and timely.

Benchmarking

As we discussed in chapter 8, benchmarking is one of the essential methods of determining what to aim for in quality improvements. It helps a service organization determine what is possible in terms of customer satisfaction and quality. Benchmarking does not have to be in one's own industry—it must be global in its scope. The purpose of benchmarking is to determine who is doing the best job in a particular area of interest and learn from the best performer.

Long-Term View and Strategic Approach

It must be clear from the discussion of the TQM principles so far that TQM requires significant changes in an organization's culture. However, the experiences of many large firms indicate that positive results will not be apparent immediately. Hence, an organization on the quality journey needs to take a long-term perspective. This requires strategic thinking and planning on the part of the top management. A strategic plan will identify major tasks to achieve the necessary changes in the organizational culture and the way of doing business. The plan should establish goals and methods for the implementation of TQM. The plan should be updated as the conditions within and outside the organization change.

---

[11] See chapter 9 for a more detailed discussion of empowerment and teamwork.

Management by Fact: Measurement and Analysis

Intuition and experience are two of the most valuable assets of managers. However, intuition and experience alone are not always sufficient for achieving customer satisfaction. To be effective, decisions must be based on facts and results must be measured. Facts can be obtained from data gathered from customers, service delivery processes, and competitors. In other words, a service organization must have a system of collecting and processing relevant data to determine what the customers' requirements are, how well the service design and delivery system conform to these requirements, and the degree with which the services satisfy customers' needs.

Fast Response

The nature of competition, especially in consumer services, has changed in recent decades. It now includes faster introduction of new services, greater variety, and higher quality and value. Consequently, a service organization must be flexible and agile to respond to changing customer needs and requirements as well as competitive threats.

Continuous Improvement

A fundamental view in TQM is that whatever success a company may have achieved in its quality efforts and competitiveness, it has not reached its destination, for there is no destination to reach. TQM is best understood as a journey with no particular end. However, there is a direction to this journey; it is toward customer satisfaction. The reason why there is no end to the journey is that the needs and expectations of customers are constantly changing, and competition is pushing standards to higher levels; hence, customer satisfaction is a moving target. Another reason is that new services are being introduced at a faster pace in recent years. New products tend to use more advanced technology, offer higher quality and value than existing products, and sometimes make some services obsolete. As an organization gains experience with its existing services and improves their quality, it may also introduce technologically advanced new services, which bring new challenges in quality and customer satisfaction. Consequently, continuous improvement is a natural requirement for superior quality and sustained customer satisfaction.

A few points must be emphasized with regard to TQM. The items listed above do not constitute a recipe. They are the principles of quality and continuous improvement as expressed as a management philosophy. Implementing them is a strategic issue, but they *all* should be implemented. There is no one right way to implement TQM; each organization must tailor its quality program to its needs according to these principles. Implementation should not be rushed, but it should proceed with determination.

Another strategic issue is the design and development of service and its delivery system. The principles and tools discussed in chapter 8 must be used for this purpose under the guidance of TQM principles.

12.7   OTHER APPROACHES TO ACHIEVING SERVICE QUALITY

ISO 9000 Standards

ISO is the acronym for the International Organization for Standardization in Geneva, Switzerland. Founded in 1946, this organization has about 110 member countries. Each country is represented by its national organization. The United States is represented by the American National Standards Institute (ANSI).

The standards known as the ISO 9000 series have been developed by ISO in an effort to achieve uniformity among standards of member countries. The impetus was provided by the globalization of business. The economic unification of Europe under the banner of European Union helped the rapid acceptance of common standards throughout the world. When implemented, these standards serve to eliminate nontariff barriers to international trade that arise from differences among national or company standards. Consequently, ISO 9000 standards tend to facilitate international trade.[12]

ISO 9000 standards are designed to define and implement management systems by which organizations design, produce, and deliver and support their products. In other words, they are standards for building a management system that ultimately produces quality goods and/or services, but they are not related to any product or technical specifications.

An organization may adopt one of the ISO 9001, 9002, or 9003 standards to provide evidence to customers that it has a management system capable of producing a satisfactory good or service. The three standards differ only in their comprehensiveness:

- **ISO 9001** provides a model appropriate for an organization engaged in design, development, production, installation, and servicing a product. It is the most comprehensive of the three. Although it usually applies to manufacturing, it can also apply to services such as construction, architecture, and engineering.
- **ISO 9002** includes everything covered by ISO 9001 except the design function.
- **ISO 9003** is the least comprehensive of the three standards and it is appropriate for organizations whose quality of goods and services can be judged primarily by inspection and testing.

ISO also has guidance standards that provide guidelines to help organizations develop an understanding of the standards and select the appropriate standard for implementation.

An organization that adopts one of the ISO standards needs to be certified by an independent agency as an evidence of its compliance with the standards. Registration[13] achieved by an organization indicates that it has a documented quality system, but it does not necessarily imply that the organization produces high-quality products. Essentially, the ISO standards require that an organization document what it does, do what it documents, review the process, and change it when necessary. Therefore, when implemented, ISO 9000 standards do not create a full-fledged quality management system, they just make sure that the registered organization has the building blocks for such a system.[14]

Originally, service organizations did not show much interest in ISO 9000 standards because they were known as standards for manufactured goods. However, competitive pressures led more service organizations to adopt these standards and seek registration. Despite the fact that ISO 9000 standards have a manufacturing flavor, and some aspects of them may not be applicable to services, they can be adopted by service organizations.[15] For example, FedEx achieved ISO 9001 certification for its worldwide operations and renewed it in 1997.

[12] Donald W. Marquardt, "Background and Development of ISO 9000 Standards," in Robert W. Peach (ed.), *The ISO 9000 Handbook,* 3rd ed. (Chicago, Irwin, 1997), pp. 9–30.

[13] Although they have slightly different meanings, *registration* and *certification* are used interchangeably.

[14] Robert W. Peach, "Overview of the ISO 9000 Series Standard," in Robert W. Peach (ed.), *The ISO 9000 Handbook,* 3rd ed. (Chicago, Irwin, 1997), pp. 33–57.

[15] For a more detailed discussion of the applicability of ISO 9000 standards in services and the issues to implementation, see David L. Goetsch and Stanley B. Davis, *Understanding and Implementing ISO 9000 and ISO Standards* (Upper Saddle River, NJ, Prentice Hall, 1998), pp. 103–116; and James L. Lamprecht, *ISO 9000 and the Service Sector* (Milwaukee, WI, ASQC Quality Press, 1994).

The Malcolm Baldrige National Quality Award Program

The Malcolm Baldrige National Quality Award (MBNQA) was established by the U.S. Congress in 1987. The law created a public–private partnership for improving national competitiveness. National Institute of Standards and Technology (NIST) of the Department of Commerce manages the award program with the assistance of the American Society for Quality (ASQ).

The award has been established to help:

- Stimulate American companies to improve quality and productivity
- Recognize the achievements of those companies that improve the quality of their goods and services and provide example to others
- Establish guidelines and criteria that can be used by business, industrial, governmental, and other organizations in evaluating their own quality improvement efforts
- Provide specific guidance for other American organizations that wish to learn how to manage for high quality by making available detailed information on how winning organizations were able to change their cultures and achieve eminence[16]

Originally, the MBNQA was given to for-profit businesses in three categories: manufacturing, services, and small business; a maximum of two awards were given in each category. However, in 1999 the award eligibility was expanded to include education and health care organizations, and the maximum number of awards in each category was increased to three. Nonprofit and for-profit education organizations and health care providers are now eligible to apply for the award.

MBNQA criteria are "designed to help organizations enhance their competitiveness through focus on dual, results-oriented goals:

- delivery of ever-improving value to customers, resulting in marketplace success; and
- improvement of overall organizational performance and capabilities."[17]

MBNQA criteria are based upon a set of core values and concepts:

- Customer-driven quality
- Leadership
- Continuous improvement and learning
- Valuing employees
- Fast response
- Design quality and prevention
- Long-range view of the future
- Management by fact
- Partnership development
- Public responsibility and citizenship
- Results focus

Although the core values and the criteria based on them have been evolving through the years, they basically reflect the principles of TQM as discussed earlier in this chapter. The MBNQA has had a positive effect on many American companies as well as government and private nonprofit organizations. Participants have shown sig-

---

[16] From the "Findings and Purposes Section of Public Law 100-107" signed into law on August 20, 1987.
[17] 1999 Criteria for Performance Excellence, Baldrige National Quality Program.

nificant improvements in productivity, employee relationships, market share, and profitability.

The sound principles and criteria of the MBNQA help organizations develop systems, processes, and a management philosophy for producing superior-quality goods and services. More than 40 states have established their own quality award programs based on MBNQA criteria. In addition to the general service category, the expansion of eligibility to nonprofit and for-profit educational organizations and health care providers creates a greater opportunity for service organizations to improve their services and create more value for their customers by adopting MBNQA criteria and competing for the award.

12.8   REINFORCING QUALITY SERVICE

On several occasions throughout this book, the importance of keeping customers has been emphasized; that is, the question of customer loyalty. In this section, two measures a service organization should take to achieve customer loyalty and reinforce its overall quality efforts are discussed.

Service Recovery

Even the best service organizations experience service failures once in a while. Inexperienced or rude service employees, equipment breakdown, power system failure, flight cancellations, and late delivery by a vendor are just some examples of how a service organization may experience failures. Whether or not the organization is responsible for the failure, it is crucial that it take the necessary steps to solve the problem and restore the service. If that is not possible, it should at least make it less inconvenient for the customers.

Some service failures may occur during the delivery and are obvious to managers and service providers, but some failures may go unnoticed. Some customers may later complain and bring the service failure to the attention of management. Whenever such failure may be discovered, the service organization must act quickly and decisively and resolve the problem as soon as possible to the customer's satisfaction. Failing to do so means a second failure in the service delivery and will probably lead to the loss of that customer. Resolving the problem quickly and to the customer's satisfaction usually means winning that customer's business for the long term.

Customer complaints must be considered as "opportunities" for winning customer loyalty, because there is evidence that a well-handled service failure may ensure the loyalty of many customers. Kent C. Nelson, chairman and chief operating officer of United Parcel Service (UPS), reached the same conclusion as a result of a service recovery effort undertaken by his organization:

> One of our customers is the chairman of several Midwestern banks . . . an avid map collector. He owns many rare and valuable maps, and collects maps that will increase in value over time. Some time ago, he got the idea of sending a die-cut map of the lunar surface to each of the nine astronauts who had walked on the moon, asking them to sign at the spot where they had walked. Over the course of many months, he gathered all of their signatures, ending with Neil Armstrong, who signed it in Las Vegas. It was now one of a kind, and very valuable.
>
> The finished map was shipped from Las Vegas to the bank chairman. It was shipped via UPS. The map never arrived. The banker was devastated. We were embarrassed.

It was one of our customer service managers who decided that the only way to satisfy their customer would be to duplicate the map. He bought a die-cut map of the lunar surface and sent it around to the business development managers in each UPS district where one of the nine astronauts lived. Over the course of several weeks, we obtained each of their signatures and delivered the finished map to the customer. He was delighted. And impressed. And completely satisfied. In fact, I think he was more satisfied by what we did to make up for our mistake than he would have been if the original map had been routinely delivered.[18]

There is also research evidence to support this view. Technical Assistance Research Programs (TARP), a Washington, D.C.–based research and consulting organization, conducted a survey among consumers of various industries with interesting results. Among the customers who complained about a good or service they purchased and were not satisfied with the outcome, only 19 percent expressed repurchase intentions if the purchase was over $100 (see Exhibit 12-2). Of those whose complaints were resolved, 54 percent said they would buy again from the same company. However, if the complaint was resolved quickly, 82 percent would buy again from the same

EXHIBIT 12-2   Consumers' Repurchase Intentions

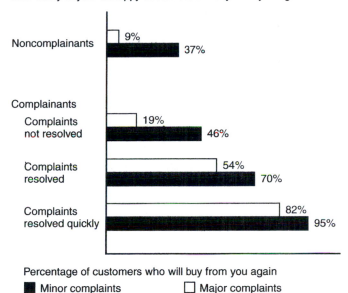

How many of your unhappy customers will buy from you again?

Noncomplainants — 9% / 37%

Complainants
Complaints not resolved — 19% / 46%

Complaints resolved — 54% / 70%

Complaints resolved quickly — 82% / 95%

Percentage of customers who will buy from you again
■ Minor complaints   □ Major complaints

Source: Ron Zemke, "The Art of Service Recovery: Fixing Broken Customers—And Keeping Them on Your Side," in Eberhard E. Scheuing and William F. Christopher (eds.), *The Service Quality Handbook* (New York, American Management Association, 1993), pp. 463–476, based on TARP industry-specific data. Reprinted by permission of AMACOM, a division of American Management Association International, New York, NY. All rights reserved. http://www.amanet.org.

---

[18] Kent C. Nelson, "Quality in a Service Organization: Beyond Grand Gestures," *Executive Speeches* (August–September 1995), pp. 11–14.

company. As can be seen from Exhibit 12-2, percentages are higher for small ($1–$5) purchases.[19]

Recovering from service failures does not happen automatically; an organization must carefully prepare for it. Hart, Heskett, and Sasser recommend the following approach[20]:

1. *Measure the costs.* The old adage "What gets measured gets managed" is the principle here. Service failures have costs to both the customer and the service organization. Some of the costs customers incur include time and money they spend in writing letters or calls to the organization, and the anguish they feel. The organization may have to give a refund or repeat the service, and in extreme cases may have to face a lawsuit and punitive damages that may result from it. Probably the most important cost is the permanent loss of the customer. Most managers underestimate the costs of service failures. Once they understand the magnitude of their losses, they are more likely to focus on prevention measures.

2. *Break the silence and listen closely for complaints.* It is well known that many customers do not complain if they are not happy with a good or service. Among the most frequently given reasons found by TARP research are:

   - It's not worth the time or effort.
   - No one would be concerned with my problem or interested in acting on it.
   - I don't know where to go or what to do.

   Clearly, if a service organization does not know about service failures, it will not do anything about them. Hence, it is important that customers are encouraged to complain when they are not satisfied with the service. There are many ways to hear the customer's voice. Some organizations have toll-free 800 numbers for complaints and questions, whereas others offer rewards for suggestions. Regular surveys, focus groups, and interviews of lost customers are additional ways of uncovering service problems.

3. *Anticipate needs for recovery.* Managers who understand the service and its delivery system can anticipate where failures may occur and can make plans for recovery. In chapter 8, it was recommended that service process and the delivery system be represented by a blueprint on which the failure points are indicated. A plan and a procedure for each potential failure must be developed, and employees must be trained in these procedures.

4. *Act fast.* A service organization that acts quickly to correct the situation will probably impress the customer and make him forget the incident. Long, drawn-out processes and weeks of waiting are not going to make the customer forget the failure easily even if it is eventually resolved satisfactorily.

5. *Train employees.* Effective service recovery is not possible if the employees who handle complaints are not prepared for occasional service failures. Preparation involves training and empowerment. Employees who know what to do in response to various types of service failures and who are authorized to take corrective measures quickly are indispensable for effective recovery. Training should include developing good communication skills, creative thinking, quick

---

[19] Technical Assistance Research Program Institute (TARP), *Consumer Complaint Handling in America: An Update Study*, Parts I and II (Washington, DC, TARP and U.S. Office of Consumer Affairs, April 1986).

[20] Christopher W. L. Hart, James L. Heskett, and W. Earl Sasser, Jr., "The Profitable Art of Service Recovery," *Harvard Business Review* (July–August 1990), pp. 148–156.

decision making, and developing an awareness of customers' concerns. One of the most effective training methods is simulated situations and role playing.

6. *Empower the front line.* Quick and decisive action to remedy a service failure is not possible without empowered employees. If employees have to check the rule book and seek authorization from a supervisor every time they have to handle a complaint, recovery will neither be quick nor satisfactory in customers' eyes. In addition, employee enthusiasm in solving customers' problems will quickly diminish. Many rules and limits on authority are established because of a fear that employees will "give away the store." However, this will not happen with a well-trained and motivated employee, but losing a customer is more likely to happen when her problem is not solved.

7. *Close the loop.* Recovery and complaint handling must be brought to a closure. If the condition that led to the problem cannot be remedied, the customer must be given an explanation. If the complaint leads to a change in the service and/or the delivery system, the customer should be told so. Other ways of effectively closing the loop include asking the customer for suggestions and letting him know what is being done with his suggestions.

Service Guarantees

An effective way to improve the quality image of a service organization in the eyes of its customers and improve service quality is to offer service guarantees, especially unconditional ones. Most service guarantees have financial consequences for the organization. If the organization cannot deliver what it promised, there will be an immediate financial loss, such as refunding the customer's money. This makes the cost of poor quality unbearable.[21] Consequently, when they are done right, service guarantees will help an organization focus on delivering superior-quality service. Only a few service companies offer unconditional service guarantees, but their number will be increasing in the future because of competition and because there are good reasons for offering them. Christopher Hart identifies five reasons for service guarantees[22]:

1. *A guarantee forces you to focus on customers.* Guaranteeing something that customers do not want or value is not meaningful, and worse, it may just backfire. Therefore, a service organization has to find out first what its customers want in a service.

2. *A guarantee sets clear standards.* A meaningful service guarantee must be unambiguous and clear, such as FedEx's delivery promise "absolutely, positively by 10:30." Such clear promises also force the organization to clearly identify the service expectations for its employees, and they in turn know what to shoot for.

3. *A guarantee generates feedback.* When an organization fails to satisfy a customer, it does not necessarily hear from him as indicated in the previous section. In addition to the reasons given earlier, because services are intangible, customers lack evidence for their complaints and many may not know what the standards are. (Is 45 minutes too long for pizza delivery?) When customers do not complain, the service organization gets no feedback. A service guarantee significantly increases the chances of hearing from customers when something goes wrong. The feedback as well as payouts to customers provide invaluable data for quality improvement efforts.

---

[21] Christopher W. L. Hart, *Extraordinary Guarantees* (New York, American Management Association, 1993), p. 17.

[22] Christopher W. L. Hart, "The Power of Unconditional Service Guarantees," *Harvard Business Review* (July–August 1988), pp. 54–62.

4. *A guarantee forces you to understand why you fail.* Data about failures and their costs forces management to look for causes in the way the service and its delivery system is designed and/or employees are selected and trained. Finding the causes of poor quality and eliminating them is the best way to improve quality.

5. *A guarantee builds marketing muscle.* When they are done right, an organization will attract new customers and keep existing ones by offering service guarantees. Especially in services about which customers do not have much knowledge, such as auto repair, existence of a guarantee gives most customers peace of mind and provides a good reason for selecting that organization for the service.

Another benefit is that service guarantees level the field for customers in their relationship with a service provider. Services are intangible and many are hard to evaluate before the actual experience, and some even after they have been delivered. Because of this, customers of some services feel they are at a disadvantage in their relationship with the service organization. Service guarantees play the role of an equalizer and help the organization demonstrate its fairness.[23]

For these benefits to accrue to the service organization, a service guarantee must meet five criteria.[24]

1. *Unconditional.* A guarantee with conditions loses its power and attractiveness to customers. The best service guarantee is without any conditions, such as the one by L. L. Bean, which guarantees 100 percent satisfaction, no strings attached. L. L. Bean, the Freeport, Maine, retailer probably has the ultimate in guarantees. Its customers can return any merchandise any time and get a refund, credit, or replacement.

2. *Easy to understand and communicate.* A guarantee should not look like a legal document. It should be simply worded and easy to understand by any customer. "Delivery by 10:30 or your money back" rather than "Prompt delivery" leaves no doubt as to what is guaranteed.

3. *Meaningful.* A guarantee must promise what is important to the customer. A promise of an error-free bank statement is probably more meaningful than a promise to deliver them before the end of each month. A guarantee must also be meaningful financially. If it promises a payout when the customer is not satisfied, the payout must be in proportion with the cost of the service and the inconvenience to the customer.

4. *Easy to invoke.* If a service guarantee requires the customer to jump through many hoops to invoke it, it loses all of its advantages and probably makes an already unhappy customer even more unhappy or angry.

5. *Easy to collect.* A customer invoking a guarantee should not have to wait too long or go to different units of the organization to collect a payout. The best way for a payout is on the spot, if possible, or automatic credit.

12.9 SUMMARY

Service quality and customer satisfaction are closely related. Satisfaction is a very likely outcome when customers perceive that they have received superior-quality service. Superior quality also leads to higher customer and employee loyalty, higher mar-

---

[23] Leonard L. Berry, A. Parasuraman, and Valarie A. Zeithaml, "Improving Service Quality in America: Lessons Learned," *Academy of Management Executive,* vol. 8, no. 2 (1994), pp. 32–52.

[24] These criteria are adapted from Christopher W. L. Hart, "The Power of Unconditional Service Guarantees."

ket share, higher returns to investors, lower costs, and lower sensitivity to price competition. Even a single one of these reasons is sufficient motivation for a service organization to seek quality and continuous improvement.

In this chapter various definitions of quality were reviewed. We pointed out that each one of these definitions, in addition to representing the viewpoint of different organizational areas, makes a valuable contribution to our understanding of the meaning of quality and related issues.

A definition of quality, however useful it might be, is never sufficient to guide managerial action for customer satisfaction. Managers need to understand what quality means to customers and what characteristics are perceived to contribute to the quality of a service. In other words, managers need to understand the dimensions of quality. We reviewed various approaches to defining the dimensions of service quality. One set of dimensions (reliability, responsiveness, assurance, empathy, and tangibles) may serve well for most services as a generic set, but articulation of additional dimensions for a proper understanding of quality may be needed when closer attention is paid to a particular service. The gaps model is another device to guide managers in delivering high-quality service. This model conceptualizes service quality on the basis of the differences between customers' expectations with respect to the five dimensions and their perceptions of what was actually delivered.

Achieving quality is not a matter of using a particular method or technique; it requires a change in the philosophy of management and organizational culture. Total Quality Management was developed through the 1980s and 1990s to meet that need of American manufacturing and service organizations. Its principles form a whole new approach to managing, and require a long-term commitment from both management and employees.

Even the best service organizations occasionally experience failures in their service delivery. Most customers will forgive these mishaps if the organization manages to solve the problem quickly. Actually, some service organizations manage to win lifelong customers when they masterfully recover from failures. Every service organization must have a recovery system and must train its employees for such emergencies.

An increasing number of service organizations are offering unconditional service guarantees to their customers. The last section of this chapter reviewed the reasons why service guarantees make sense for many service organizations. The characteristics of effective service guarantees were also discussed.

Discussion Questions

1. Discuss the reasons why a service organization should pursue superior quality as an objective.
2. How would the perception of superior-quality service make an organization less vulnerable to competition based on price cutting?
3. Discuss the applicability of Garvin's eight dimensions of quality to services.
4. Describe the five dimensions of service quality of the gaps model.
5. Do you agree that "reliability" is the most important service quality dimension for customers? Explain.
6. Discuss some possible ways of closing Gap 1 in the gaps model.
7. Discuss some possible ways of closing Gap 2 in the gaps model.
8. Discuss some possible ways of closing Gap 3 in the gaps model.
9. Discuss some possible ways of closing Gap 4 in the gaps model.
10. Customer satisfaction is the foundation of TQM philosophy. Do you agree with this view? Why?
11. Why is leadership so important in the TQM philosophy?

12. What is meant by "management by fact" as a principle of TQM?
13. Why is service recovery important, and how can a service organization prepare for service failures?
14. Why should an organization guarantee its service? Is it a good idea for all service organizations?
15. Discuss the characteristics of effective service guarantees.

CASES

CASE 12–1   Falls Church General Hospital

Founded in 1968, the Falls Church General Hospital (FCGH) is a privately owned 615-patient bed facility in the incorporated township of Falls Church, Virginia.[1] Falls Church is four miles from downtown Washington, D.C., and is surrounded by the counties of Arlington, Fairfax, and Alexandria, Virginia, all affluent urban/suburban comunities with a highly educated population composed largely of employees of the U.S. government and high tech engineering firms.

THE HOSPITAL

Falls Church General Hospital, with 895 employees, provides a broad range of health care services, including drug/alcohol abuse wards, emergency rooms, x-ray and laboratory facilities, maternity wards, intensive and cardiac care units, and outpatient facilities. With strong competition from other comprehensive facilities such as George Washington University Hospital, Georgetown University Hospital, Fairfax General, and Arlington Hospital, FCGH has had to concentrate on offering high-quality treatment at reasonable prices. FCGH has not attempted to obtain all of the latest up-to-date diagnostic equipment (such as $350,000 CAT scans) because its board felt it would not be cost effective to try to compete with the more research-oriented university hospitals such as Georgetown or George Washington (the latter being where former President Reagan was taken when he was shot by John Hinkley in 1981). Even though FCGH is considered a "medium-to-large" hospital, it has attempted to stress personal attention to each patient. In January 1990, the hospital began a series of ads in the *Washington Post* highlighting its concerned doctors and nurses, its friendly support staff, and its overall phi-

losophy that its employees care about their work and their patients.

THE ISSUE OF ASSESSING QUALITY HEALTH CARE

Quality health care is a goal all hospitals profess, but few have developed comprehensive and scientific means of asking customers to judge the quality of care they receive. A tremendous amount of effort has been devoted to assessing the clinical quality of hospital care; books, journals, and papers on the topic abound. The problem, however, is that past efforts to measure hospital quality have largely ignored the perceptions of customers—the patients, physicians, and payers. Instead of formally considering customer judgments of quality, the health care industry has focused almost entirely on internal quality assessments made by the health professionals who operate the system. In effect, a system for improving health care has been created that all but ignores the voice of the customer.

The board of FCGH believes that all hospitals need to make the transformation from the current practice of attempting to ensure quality to actually measuring and improving the quality of care from both the external, customer perspective and the internal, provider perspective. Fueled by concerns in recent years about costs and medical practice variation and by the demand for greater social accountability, there is an emerging demand by patients and payers that quality health care be provided at best value.

As board president Dr. Irwin Greenberg recently stated at the annual FCGH meeting,

"As the prices people pay in the future for given levels of service become more similar, hospitals will be distinguished largely on the basis of their quality and value as assessed by customers. We must have accurate information about how our customers, not just the health care professionals, who work here, judge the

---

[1] Some background information for this case was taken from quotes in T. R. Gillem and E. Nelson, "Hospital Quality Trends," in J. W. Spechler (ed.), *When America Does It Right: Case Studies in Service Quality* (Norcross, GA, Industrial Engineering and Management Press, 1989), pp. 117–122.

quality of care in this institution. Many hospitals already have some methods for measuring patient satisfaction. A recent survey of more than two hundred hospitals showed that two-thirds routinely conduct patient satisfaction surveys. Typically, the surveys are distributed at discharge to patients who are free to respond or not. The main value of such surveys is to gain quick knowledge of problems experienced by patients, many of whom often fill out questionnaires because they are disgruntled about some specific aspect of the care they received."

In response to Dr. Greenberg's statement, and in light of the advertising campaign, hospital administrator Carla Kimball called a meeting of her department heads to discuss the issue of quality. "Can we really deliver on our promises? Or are we in danger

of failing to live up to the level of health care our patients expect, and do we risk losing them?" Ms. Kimball asked.

Frances Pruitt, head of nursing, continued the debate.

"I argue that surveys, such as the one Dr. Greenberg mentioned in his speech, are valuable. But how do we measure the quality of our health care? Some patients who leave FCGH happy may have actually received poor treatment here. If we are serious about improving the quality of care, we need more *valid* and *reliable* data on which to act. We need answers to specific, quality-related questions about activities in areas that affect patients—admission, nursing, medical staff, daily care, and ancillary staff."

EXHIBIT 12-3   Steps in TRW's Quality Audit

1. *Quality to the customer.* Is conformance of the product to established quality standards measured? Is quality of the organization's product compared with that of competitors' products?
2. *Quality costs.* Have the costs of quality been measured and have areas for possible cost savings been identified?
3. *Design review.* Do procedures exist to review designs for quality? Are these procedures being carried out?
4. *Product qualification.* Have procedures been established and followed to qualify new products before any deliveries to customers?
5. *Product liability.* Has each product been scrutinized regarding safety and are appropriate records kept? Does a written plan exist for dealing with a major product liability problem?
6. *Process capability.* Has the capability of all processes been measured and is that information used in product design and development?
7. *Incoming inspection.* Are incoming lots inspected in an efficient manner and are appropriate records kept?
8. *Supplier quality.* Are suppliers made aware of their quality responsibilities? Are records kept on nonconformance?
9. *Process control.* Has the company developed policies for controlling processes? Have employees been trained to follow those policies?
10. *Inspection and test planning.* Do inspection and test plans exist for all products and are records maintained on the results? Is all test equipment calibrated regularly?
11. *Quality performance indicators.* Are quality performance indicators regularly published throughout the organization and made available to employees?
12. *Employee involvement program.* Are employees involved in quality improvement through some process such as quality circles?
13. *Multifunctional quality improvement team.* Has a quality improvement team covering all functional areas been established to monitor quality and work to improve it?
14. *Quality business plan.* Has quality been integrated into the organization's business plan—and from there into the overall strategic plan?

Source: John M. Groocock, *The Chain of Quality* (New York, Wiley, 1986) p. 250. Copyright © 1986 John Wiley & Sons, Inc. Reprinted by permission of John Wiley & Sons, Inc.

"I have an idea," said Merrill Warkentin, Kimball's staff director. "I just finished reading a book by John Groocock. He's the Vice-President for Quality at TRW, a big manufacturer. He says there are 14 steps in TRW's internal quality audits. I made a photocopy of those steps (see Exhibit 12–3). Why don't we consider his approach?"

When the meeting ended, Ms. Kimball read Groocock's list again and began to think about the whole issue of quality control in U.S. firms. It had worked in many manufacturing companies, but could the concepts of quality control really be used in a hospital? ■

CASE QUESTIONS

1. Why is it important to get the patient's assessment of health care quality? Does a patient have the expertise to judge the health care he or she receives?
2. How might a hospital measure quality?
3. Using the steps in Exhibit 12-3, discuss how each might apply to FCGH.
4. How can the value of a human life be included in the cost of quality control?

5. There are certain parallels between the evaluation of health care quality and educational quality. How are customer surveys used to evaluate the quality of teaching at your institution? How are the results used? Are any other measures available to assess educational quality? What improvements would you suggest to the current system?

CASE 12–2   The First National Bank of Chicago's Quality Program

The skeptics are now believers, and the experts are downright impressed. The First National Bank of Chicago has earned its praise the hard way: by proving that measuring quality in the service industry not only is possible but truly is a formula for success. Since 1981, First Chicago has tracked and charted its performance on a weekly basis in 500 key customer-sensitive areas. Management at the bank felt that a quality-focused strategy is the most effective way to answer the competition, and was delighted to discover that an emphasis on quality helps monitor costs. At First Chicago, the installation and execution of its quality process has resulted in savings of $9 to $12 million annually. In addition to performance measurement, the bank's four-part quality process includes employee involvement, specialized customer service, and reward and recognition.

"We set out to increase the market share of our subsidiary—The First National Bank of Chicago—by positioning ourselves as the quality provider of corporate operating services," says First Chicago President Richard L. Thomas. "These are noncredit services such as corporate checking, funds transfer, shareholder services, and so on. These kinds of services were traditionally thought of as 'giveaways,' designed to help build a relationship for deposits and lending. We believed they could become profit centers on their own, and that the best way to achieve that goal was to emphasize quality and view it as a strategic marketing weapon."

First Chicago Corporation is the largest bank holding company in the Midwest with assets of $48.5 billion. The First National Bank of Chicago (First Chicago), First Chicago Corporation's principal banking subsidiary, is centered on its major businesses—the Global Corporate Bank and the Superregional Bank. The Global Corporate Bank encompasses all financial and operating services oriented to large domestic and international corporate clients. Within the Global Corporate Bank, the Service Products Group provides operating services focused on cash management, securities processing, and trade finance.

First Chicago is the eleventh largest bank in the United States and was founded in 1863. It is the oldest and largest national bank operating under its original name and charter. There are 18,000 employees working worldwide for First Chicago Corporation and 13,000 shareholders.

Since 1971, the required return on equity of the banking industry has been in a free fall decline. So for banks to remain in business, they must alter their business mix, pricing, and/or cost to recover from the free fall.

First Chicago has opted to set itself apart by concentrating on product offerings that meet client needs while generating a high return on equity. Included in its plan of attack is a focus on the high quality of services. For example, service and quality are key controllable buying determinants in operating services, as determined by a major independent research firm. Therefore, First Chicago is determined to be the highest quality provider in the operating services business.

"Satisfying customer needs and expectations is the number one reason for being in any business," says Aleta Holub, Vice President, Manager, Quality Assurance at First Chicago. "Customer responsiveness and loyalty to products and services will ultimately determine a company's success or failure. Customers' standards are constantly rising. A company's failure to respond to raised expectations is like denying the force of the tide. It can leave you high and dry on the beach, while customers sail off to competitors' ports."

"Our formal measurement program really began to take shape back in 1981," Thomas recalls. "We had a particular product quality problem—a system enhancement that was first delayed and then didn't operate as well as it should. We had to make sure the errors we had made in developing the new system didn't recur.

"So we got all the key players into a room and we realized that we needed some form of measurement to judge how we were doing. There was a lot of disparity around the table about just what we should measure, however, and we finally concluded that there was only one valid opinion: the opinion of our clients."

The bank surveyed many of its corporate clients on a product-by-product basis, emphasizing two key questions about each of its nine operating services: (1) What do you consider quality features of each particular service? And (2) what do you consider good quality in the delivery of those services?

"We wanted to make sure we were doing the right things correctly," says Holub. "We didn't want to be doing the wrong things right. By listening to our clients, we learned that what they most wanted and expected from us was timeliness, accuracy, and responsive service."

The first step the bank took in launching its quality process was to create a roadmap for the journey, better described as the company's mission statement: "Our mission is to be the premier bank in the Midwest with a reputation for excellence in serving clients nationwide and throughout the world . . . Our clients are First Chicago's highest priority . . . We are committed to providing our clients with high quality and innovative services."

Next, the bank altered its organizational framework. Separate strategic business units were created—each based on an individual product family. For instance, the Money Transfer unit's product family includes all domestic and international payment services. Operating under the philosophy that bringing the producer and consumer of a product closer together encourages better quality, the strategic business unit manager suddenly became an entrepreneur. The manager was vested with the power to control not only expenses, but also pricing, product features, promotion, and quality.

This customer-focused framework was enhanced by the bank in January 1989 in order to further support the Global Corporate Bank, one of First Chicago Corporation's major businesses. In 1989, the Global Corporate Bank comprised $34 billion, or 69 percent of the corporation's total assets. The Service Products Group further articulated its role with a mission statement: "To enhance Global Corporate Bank relationships through service excellence, responsiveness, tailored solutions, high quality, and efficient operations."

A logo in the shape of a star was designed to show employees the key elements of the strategy needed to strengthen the Global Corporate Bank's relationships. All of the star's points represent an action included in the new mission statement—responsiveness, service excellence, tailored solutions, efficiency, and quality. Although responsiveness rests at the top of the star, every point is considered equal. Within the center of the star is the word "teamwork," for teamwork is thought of as central to the execution of the strategy. Without it, First Chicago cannot be a "relationship bank."

"Effective teamwork within the Service Products Group and with the Global Corporate Bank is critical to our success in serving our clients," says Holub.

Each Product Area has its own customer service representatives to handle inquiries and problems, and they act as conduits, communicating client concerns to the product area. Through this specialized customer service approach, the client talks to a knowledgeable service representative who is a product specialist. Because the customer service function and production area are in the same location, the representatives are more efficient and responsive. With the client dealing specifically with a product specialist, a closer relationship is possible, which encourages the client to offer feedback on enhancements and new products.

"We realize the client is the ultimate product specialist," says Holub. "They are the ones using the product on a daily basis. We wanted to make sure that our clients were dealing with a very knowledgeable person who 'spoke their language.'"

The operating services area of First Chicago devised a quality process that's today described as one of America's finest. This area's efforts were revolutionary in the financial industry and have been duplicated by other financial institutions.

In 1981, the bank went to work developing an extensive performance measurement system using nearly 500 charts to track weekly every product's performance in relation to the corresponding client concerns. For example, the accurate processing of money transfers and the turn-around time for letters of credit are measured. By focusing on the attributes of each major product and service, First Chicago learns how to fix a quality problem or sustain a quality advantage. Using the client's perspective and industry standards, managers from each area establish Minimum Acceptable Performance (M.A.P.) standards for each indicator, as well as a goal for exceptional performance. At a weekly performance review, data on how each product area is doing relative to these challenging goals are presented to senior management.

"To encourage performance improvement, the M.A.P. and goal lines are continually adjusted upward similar to the high-jump bar always being raised a little higher for the high jumper," says Holub. Managers' commitment to the program is reinforced because their incentive compensation is linked to reaching M.A.P. and goal levels.

"All of this measuring and charting is not simply to encourage in-house competition," Thomas says. "Nor do we do this solely to provide management information. The chief reason we measure, chart, and analyze is to bring about improvement. The objective is to fix a problem, not to place blame."

A very effective twist on the bank's performance measurement program is the invitation extended to both clients and suppliers to attend the weekly performance measurement meetings. First Chicago receives valuable feedback from clients by having them participate in these sessions. And since suppliers began attending, their service levels have improved.

"A two-fold benefit is gleaned by inviting both clients and suppliers to attend these meetings," says Holub. "First, the bank has an additional forum in which to learn about clients' expectations and concerns involving our products and service. We regularly use that knowledge to refine and improve both. More importantly, we are sending a loud and sincere message that the client is our central interest.

"The second benefit is that service levels from our vendors have also improved. Vendors are invited to see how well they are doing in relation to the bank's performance objectives."

Holub elaborates, "At the weekly performance meetings, competing vendors sit next to each other. For example, the IBM representative may sit beside his or her competitor from Tandem. Each has a chance to see the other's graphically shown performance and then prepare ways to top the other. The result is that the bank receives its 'fair share plus' of the vendors' attention and service. And, of course, our vendors' quality is critical to First Chicago's quality."

Employee involvement is another vital element of the bank's quality process, with more than 30 active quality improvement teams in place. These small groups of employees are brought together to identify problems or opportunities and to recommend actions to improve performance.

For example, when Illinois Bell announced a new area code for suburbs surrounding Chicago, an improvement team assumed a proactive role in guaranteeing a smooth transition for those clients affected. The team formed two months before the new area code went into effect, communicating the conversion to clients and employees alike. The area code change was completely painless for First

Chicago clients (and employees) thanks to the work done ahead of time by the team.

The suggestion program within the Service Products Group has generated many excellent ideas for the bank. Handled through the Human Resources Department, suggestion boxes are located throughout the bank and are checked once a week by staff members. Suggestions are numbered and logged, and assigned to a manager and in the Service Products Group or Human Resources to research and respond. The updated log and new suggestions are discussed at the Group head's staff meeting every week. An employee who includes his or her name on the suggestion receives a written response, with a copy sent to the department head of his or her area. The Employee Relations Council also periodically reviews the updated log and those suggestions that are still pending a written response.

One suggestion concerned a work process issue. First shift employees on mail desks in Remittance Banking were working unnecessary overtime, so a proposal was made that changed procedures, improving productivity and lowering costs.

"With the suggestion program, we've learned that follow-up and communication are the most important aspects," Holub stresses. "If you do those two things well, employees will feel they have a voice and can make a change for the better."

The theme of the Service Product Group's Annual Awards Banquet is reward and recognition draped in elegance. The event is as close to the banking world's Oscars as you can get. And that's First Chicago's intention. Impressive is quite an understatement for this evening of celebration.

Positive strokes such as "most improved," "best sustained superior performance," and "most effective in improving quality in a changing environment" are announced emphatically. Yes, First Chicago realizes the importance of recognizing the accomplishments of employee teams within the product areas. These "teams," however, vary in structure. Some employees form a team from their normal work group and address problems affecting their department's productivity.

Then there are teams comprised of employees based on cross functional issues needing attention. These team members might not normally work together. A team can also be a form of recognition for accurate performance by a number of employees. For instance, if an employee consistently does not make errors over a specified time period, he or she is honored by "making" a team. This type of team is an honor group, so to speak, not a problem-solving group.

A dozen employee teams—one for each month—receive this recognition monthly and attend the banquet each year.

"Our objective is to improve the quality of First Chicago's services, recognize groups of employees who have contributed to that improvement, and further develop teamwork," Holub explains.

Each month's winning team receives a plaque and a paid group outing of its choice. The outing is usually dinner, the theater, or a sports event. The group decides on what type of event within the following expense guideline: a maximum of $100 per person with a ceiling of $1,000 per group. Each team member also receives a certificate, and everyone's name is entered in a grand prize drawing held during the annual banquet. The grand prize is round-trip airfare for two to anywhere in the U.S., plus $650 spending money.

"We've created an achievement-oriented culture in which we have asked our employees to work to their potential, rewarding and recognizing them when they do," says Holub.

Last year's November winning team was the Cash Disbursement Team. This group sustained "superior performance in processing currency and coin." The team accepts currency and coin requests from corporate clients and internal bank units. These orders are prepared, verified, packaged, and shipped to their proper destination. In addition, the team maintains an inventory of proper monetary denominations by receiving coin and currency from the Federal Reserve Bank and the bank's Deposit Processing Unit. The team members' accomplishments: since January, 1987, they made only six errors in the 305 million bills, $3.5 billion processed, without a single late delivery.

As mentioned in the opening, First Chicago has fans in respected places, including Tom Peters, who in his syndicated column "On Excellence" cited the bank as having the "quality program of the year." And in 1988, the company became the first financial institution to win the International Customer Service Association's Award of Excellence.

But Holub is quick to put the back-patting into perspective by offering First Chicago's 10 lessons learned during the near decade of quality work. These lessons include:

1. *If you can't measure it, you can't manage it.* Your managers might tell you they can't measure a process. But they've been able to manage it all these years, haven't they?

2. *People respect what you inspect.* And remember to inspect the process. American managers tend to look at problems as though they must be the result of people problems. Japanese managers, on the other hand, look at the process. "It traditionally has been 'whose problem is it?' versus 'what is the problem?' " adds Holub.

3. *Watch out for averages.* Be careful when looking at averages: very hot and very cold can average out to lukewarm. You may be missing important information from "average" performance.

4. *What gets measured gets done.* What you pay for gets done even better, says Holub. The measures included in the bank's annual chartbook give tangible proof of the quality that sets it apart from others.

5. *Make the steak good and don't forget the sizzle.* As an example of this point, Holub refers to a conference of the National Corporate Cash Managers Association. These cash managers—for the most part, treasurers of corporations—are the banks' largest audience. At the close of this conference, the cash managers were asked to rank the best bank exhibit booths. "One bank got the best score for a booth," she recalls. "Only it didn't have a booth at the conference. Obviously, the perception of how that bank does things is well established."

6. *The client is your product specialist.* "We used to have a generalized customer service area. Now we have specialized service representatives—Dedicated Service Reps (DSRs)," says Holub. "This should have been the arrangement from the start." Clients more readily suggest product enhancements to a DSR, who is well informed about their business. And the relationship is just as beneficial for the DSR, because the client directly evaluates his or her job performance by completing an evaluation form. The majority of a DSR's performance appraisal is based on the client's responses to the questionnaire.

7. *Don't underestimate the power of ownership.* "When was the last time you washed a rental car?" Holub asks. Make your employees accountable for their performance.

8. *Wave the right flag.* "I'm not sure we did this at first," Holub confesses. The quality flag shouldn't be cost reduction/expense savings. It's easier to get employees involved when you wave the flag of Quality of Work Life or say the quality process will "take them out of an error-prone environment," says Holub. Be certain that management understands that quality improvement calls for the empowerment of people at all levels. If First Chicago were given the opportunity to start over again, Holub feels that the bank would make the connection between teamwork and improvement more explicit from the very beginning. Several years ago, changing the culture became more of a priority. One key to this culture change is the chance for an employee's peers from across the bank to evaluate his or her performance.

9. *Know the client's heartbeat so you know when your quality process needs a bypass.* Already well into its quality process, First Chicago began to actively involve clients in resolving problems. "However, we should've involved them (clients) from the outset," Holub says. Benchmarking itself against other service providers also started much later than it should have. After learning the benchmarking process from Xerox, First Chicago benchmarked itself not just against banks but against other companies well known for service quality, including Spiegel and United Airlines. For example, the retail side of the bank adopted one of United's practices: sending a supervisor out to "work the line" in order to speed up processing of customer tickets. Now supervisors work the line in the bank's lobby by preapproving transactions.

10. *Let the quality ship sail.* Trying to get everyone on the quality ship before sailing off to quality land was a mistake, says Holub. If a fresh start were possible, "I'd ask, 'Who wants to get on board?' and then spend our energy on the folks who were listening." And, adds Holub, "the quest for quality is not always going to be easy, so when there is no wind, start rowing."

Performance has been affected in measurable terms, thanks to the bank's quality emphasis. The quality initiatives demonstrate in quantifiable ways the strength and scope of a carefully planned and energetically institutionalized quality measurement program. As proof of improvement, back in 1982 one of the bank's operations experienced an average of one error in every 3,000 transactions. Today, the figure is one in 10,000.

"The success of the quality process within the operating services area alone is telling proof that providing excellent products and services and containing costs can be mutually compatible efforts," says Thomas. "In fact, we've learned firsthand that an emphasis on quality is one of the most effective ways to control costs."

For example, Thomas says, it generally costs First Chicago just under $10 to perform a money transfer. But that's a transfer done right the first time. If the money goes to the wrong place or doesn't make it on schedule, the cost of fixing an error can quickly rocket to $500 or more, depending on the amount of money involved, the complexity of the case, and so on. It's no big surprise, then, that First Chicago's quality effort has saved millions of dollars.

Another reason cost savings are critical is because more and more corporate treasurers are looking at the total cost of using one bank's operating services over another. The bank with the lowest per item price might actually be more expensive to use if its error rate is high. When a bank reduces its error rate, the overall cost a customer pays is reduced. And high quality, customer satisfaction, and competitive prices also mean repeat business, referrals, and new business, which makes the quality effort even more attractive.

First Chicago also realized the importance of communicating the quality commitment to its clients. So, annually, the bank compiles a comprehensive booklet of key performance measurement charts for clients to see what the bank monitors and how it performs in those areas.

"We recognize that when we make errors, both we and our clients have to spend time and money tracking and solving problems," Holub says. "By creating a quality process based on client-sensitive issues, and backing it up with real, quantifiable measurements, we have made a genuine commitment to provide service excellence.

"Although we are proud of the recognition our quality process has received, we realize the ultimate judge of our service is the client. Because of this, we are committed to exceeding every client's expectations." ■

SOURCE: Stephen R. Stewart, Case Study 77, at the Houston-based American Productivity & Quality Center, August 1990. Reprinted in Richard B. Chase and Nicholas J. Aquilano, *Production and Operations Management*, 7th ed. (Chicago, Irwin, 1995), pp. 205–209.

CASE QUESTIONS

1. Summarize the quality journey of First National Bank of Chicago (FNBC) with its important milestones.
2. What made FNBC seek a quality leadership position in operating services?
3. How did FNBC plan to differentiate itself from the competition?
4. What are the dimensions of quality in operating services, and how did FNBC determine them?
5. Discuss the impact of FNBC's quality program on costs and customer retention.
6. Which principles of TQM did FNBC use in its quality program?
7. Evaluate the approach, deployment, and overall results of FNBC's quality program.

References

Babakus, Emin, and Gregory W. Boller, "An Empirical Assessment of the SERVQUAL Scale," *Journal of Business Research*, vol. 24 (May 1992), pp. 253–268.

Carman, James M., "Consumer Perceptions of Service Quality: An Assessment of the SERVQUAL Dimensions," *Journal of Retailing*, vol. 66 (spring 1990), pp. 33–35.

Garvin, David A., *Managing Quality* (New York, The Free Press, 1988).

Garvin, David A., "Competing on the Eight Dimensions of Quality," *Harvard Business Review* (November–December 1987), pp. 101–109.

Haksever, Cengiz, Ronald G. Cook, and Radha Chaganti, "Applicability of the Gaps Model to Service Quality in

Small Firms," *Journal of Small Business Strategy*, vol. 8, no. 1 (spring 1997), pp. 49–66.

Hart, Christopher W. L., "The Power of Unconditional Service Guarantees," *Harvard Business Review* (July–August 1988), pp. 54–62.

Hart, Christopher W. L., James L. Heskett, and W. Earl Sasser, Jr., "The Profitable Art of Service Recovery," *Harvard Business Review* (July–August 1990), pp. 148–156.

Lovelock, Christopher H., *Services Marketing*, 3rd ed. (Upper Saddle River, NJ, Prentice Hall, 1996).

Mels, Gerhard, Christo Boshoff, and Deon Nel, "The Dimensions of Service Quality: The Original European Perspective Revisited," *The Service Industries Journal*, vol. 17, no. 1 (January 1997), pp. 173–189.

Nelson, Kent C., "Quality in a Service Organization: Beyond Grand Gestures," *Executive Speeches* (August–September 1995), pp. 11–14.

Oliver, Richard L., "A Conceptual Model of Service Quality and Service Satisfaction: Compatible Goals, Different Concepts," in T. A. Swartz, D. E. Bowen, and S. W. Brown (eds.), *Advances in Services Marketing and Management: Research and Practice*, vol. 2 (Greenwich, CT, JAI Press Inc., 1993), pp. 65–85.

Port, Otis, "The Baldrige's Other Reward," *Business Week* (March 10, 1997), p. 75.

Technical Assistance Research Program Institute (TARP), *Consumer Complaint Handling in America: An Update Study*, Parts I and II (Washington, DC, TARP and U.S. Office of Consumer Affairs, April 1986).

Zeithaml, Valarie A., A. Parasuraman, and Leonard L. Berry, *Delivering Quality Service: Balancing Customer Perceptions and Expectations* (New York, The Free Press, 1990).

CHAPTER 12 SUPPLEMENT

Tools and Techniques of Total Quality Management

S12.1 INTRODUCTION

Implementing Total Quality Management (TQM) requires a long-term commitment by the management and hard work. As we indicated earlier in chapter 12, there is no recipe, or one "right way" to implement TQM. Each organization must develop its own model that responds to its needs and supports its strategy. However, there exist a variety of very effective tools and techniques one can rely on for successful implementation of TQM. In this supplement, some of the most widely used tools and techniques are reviewed.

S12.2 PLAN–DO–STUDY–ACT CYCLE

The conceptual basis for most TQM processes is what is known as the Shewhart, or plan–do–study–act (PDSA) cycle (Exhibit S12-1).

Plan. The first step of the process is to collect data and study the problem to be solved or process to be improved. This is needed to develop an in-depth understanding of the problem. Next, develop a plan for the solution of the problem or for improvement in the current situation. Then, set goals and develop criteria to measure success.

Do. Implement the plan in a laboratory setting or on a small scale (e.g., in a branch or small unit of the organization). Collect data on the results of the implementation.

Study. Evaluate the data and study the results in light of criteria to determine if the objectives have been achieved.

Act. If the implementation created the desired results, standardize the solution and implement it in the whole system. If the results do not meet the success criteria, revise the plan and repeat the process. If the plan is successful, the new improvement cycle will start at the new level, which has become the standard. The cycle is continuous.

EXHIBIT S12-1   The Shewhart (PDSA) Cycle

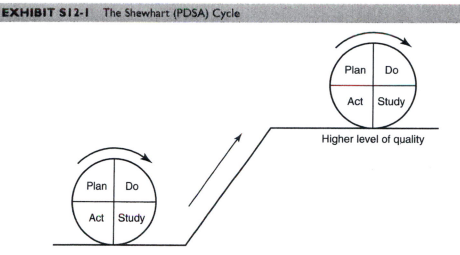

S12.3   **TOOLS OF TQM**

A number of simple but very effective graphical tools have been developed through the years for improvement of quality in manufacturing. Most of them are simple and straightforward, so practically anyone can learn and use them. They are equally effective for quality improvement efforts in services. Their simplicity and flexibility give them worldwide appeal. In this section, seven of these tools are reviewed, which are sometimes called the "magnificent seven."

Histograms   Histograms are graphical tools to represent data summaries. Large data sets can be summarized into frequency distributions for detecting patterns, central tendencies, and variability, as well as for further processing. Histograms for variables can be constructed from frequency distributions, or for attribute data, such as complaint categories, from check sheets. Exhibit S12-2 shows two histograms representing the time required by two hypothetical airlines to clean a particular aircraft and prepare it for the next flight. From the histograms, it can be seen that the variation of Company A's service is smaller than Company B's. Possible reasons are:

- A's equipment is better.
- A's employees have had more thorough training.
- A's procedures are more effective.
- A provides fewer services.
- A offers fewer routes.

Now that we have identified that Company B has a problem with service variability, we can investigate the possible causes with a cause-and-effect diagram or collect more data using check sheets.

Flowcharts   Flowcharts are diagrams consisting of pictorial symbols connected by directed line segments. Their purpose is to show the sequencing of activities, operations, tasks, materials flow, data/information flow, people movement, logic flow, or authority flow in organizations. They are very useful in designing and describing services and processes. The service blueprint, discussed in chapter 8, is just one example of flowcharts. Various types of flowcharts exist. One of the most frequently used flowcharts is the process flowchart. These charts are very useful in quality improvement

EXHIBIT S12-2 Time Required by Two Airlines to Perform Cleaning Services

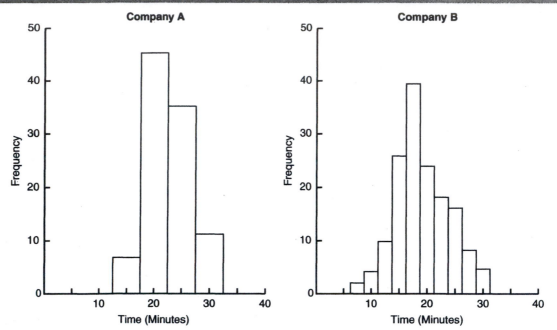

efforts because they help us develop a better understanding of the process we are trying to improve.

The flow process chart is the primary tool for developing and describing a system that converts inputs into goods and services. It provides two essential types of information about the conversion process: (1) the actions performed on materials, information, or people in providing the service; and (2) the relationships among processes. Relationships refer to the order in which actions are performed, what processes have to be performed first, which can be performed in parallel, and what has to be completed before the next step can begin.

For flow process charts, five standardized pictorial symbols are used to describe the processes: (1) operations, (2) transportation, (3) inspection, (4) storage, and (5) delay, as shown in Exhibit S12-3. The chart can track the flow of products, customers, or information. An example of a flow process chart for mortgage application and approval is given in Exhibit S12-4. In this example, the flows of information and paperwork for a particular customer are charted.

Flow process charts often include data on the distance a customer or item is moved, the time required to process a customer or item, and the time a customer or item spends waiting. This additional information helps managers to analyze the efficiency of a specified order of operations. Hopefully, tasks can be identified that should be eliminated, combined, resequenced, or simplified. Often, the flow process chart is also superimposed on a floor plan of a facility as an aid to improving facility layout and eliminating bottlenecks.

Check Sheets A check sheet is a simple tool for collecting data about problems or complaints. Check sheets are designed to make data collection and summarizing easy. Exhibit S12-5 shows a check sheet designed for collecting data on complaints about a pizza delivery service. The exhibit also contains hypothetical data for one day. A logical next step in this example may be the construction of a Pareto diagram as discussed below.

EXHIBIT S12-3   Flow Process Chart Symbols

○ *Operations*, such as performed by a lathe in a machine shop or a hair dryer in a beauty shop

⇨ *Transportation*, such as movement of materials, information, or people

▢ *Inspection*, such as moisture measurement of paper in a paper mill or a microfilm viewer in a bank for comparing signatures on checks to signatures on file; verification of an object for quality or quantity

▽ *Storage*, such as refrigeration units in manufacturing or services, vats in chemical processing, or filing cabinets in service firms

◗ *Delay*, such as papers waiting on a manager's desk to be signed or customers waiting in line at a bank

EXHIBIT S12-4   Flow Process Chart for Mortgage Application and Approval

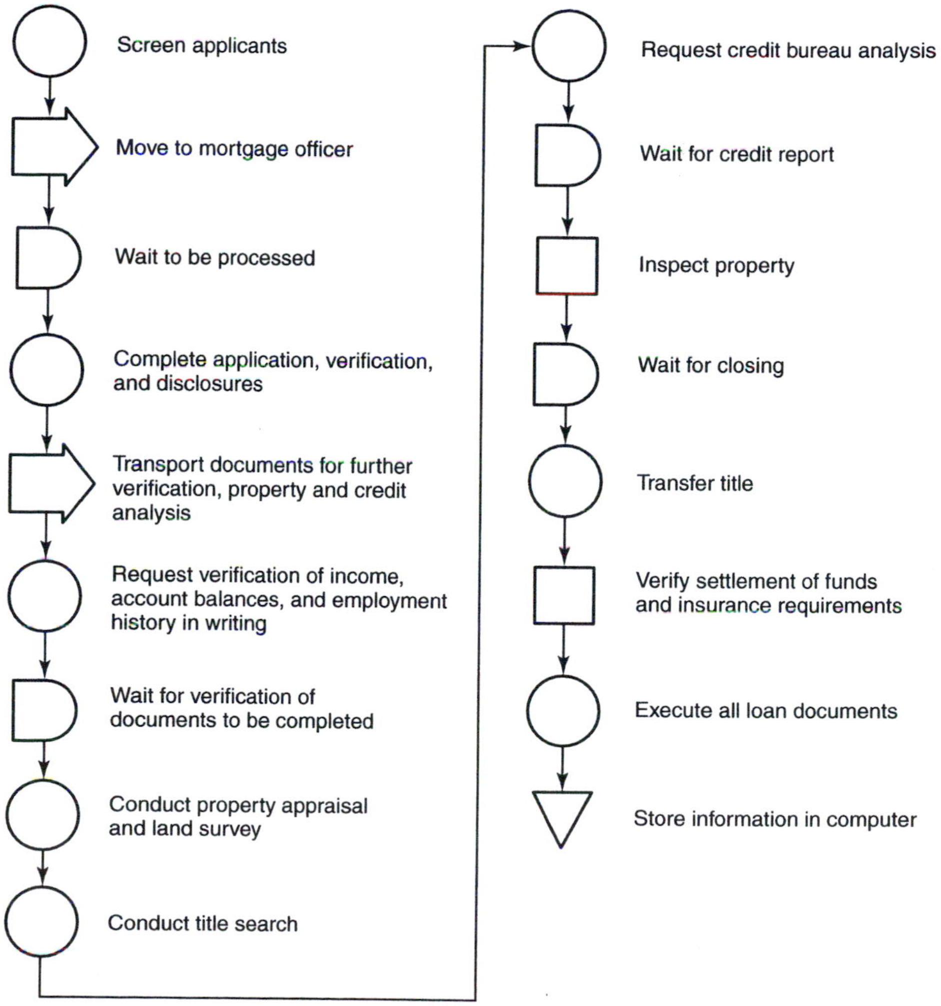

○ Screen applicants

⇨ Move to mortgage officer

◗ Wait to be processed

○ Complete application, verification, and disclosures

⇨ Transport documents for further verification, property and credit analysis

○ Request verification of income, account balances, and employment history in writing

◗ Wait for verification of documents to be completed

○ Conduct property appraisal and land survey

○ Conduct title search

○ Request credit bureau analysis

◗ Wait for credit report

▢ Inspect property

◗ Wait for closing

○ Transfer title

▢ Verify settlement of funds and insurance requirements

○ Execute all loan documents

▽ Store information in computer

EXHIBIT S12-5 Check Sheet for Complaints about a Pizza Delivery Service

DAY	TIME	Delivery Took Too Long	Cold Pizza	Wrong Topping	Wrong Size	Underbaked Pizza	Overbaked Pizza	TOTAL
				TYPE OF COMPLAINT				
M	4–5 P.M.			///	/	ℋℋ		9
	5–6	/	//	/			/	5
	6–7	ℋℋ	/	///		///		12
	7–8	//		/		//		5
	8–9			//				2
	9–10							0
	10–11 P.M.	///		//	/	ℋℋ		11
	TOTAL	11	3	12	2	15	1	44

Pareto Diagrams   A Pareto diagram is an ordered form of a histogram that attempts to isolate the few dominant factors affecting a situation from the many insignificant ones. The rectangles of the histogram are arranged from the tallest on the left to the shortest. The vertical axis may represent frequencies or relative frequencies (percentages). Exhibit S12-6 shows a Pareto diagram which continues the pizza delivery example and indicates the number of complaints in each category as obtained from column totals in Exhibit S12-5. As can be seen from the exhibit, the most frequently occurring complaint, therefore, the most serious one, is "underbaked pizza." The next most frequent two categories are "wrong topping" and "delivery time." The other three categories of complaints seem less serious compared to these three. This fact has been emphasized by the ordering of the rectangles representing the frequency of complaints. A quality improvement team would normally first focus and try to solve the most serious problem.

Scatter Diagrams   Scatter diagrams are used to provide a quick check if a relationship exists between two variables. For example, a quality improvement team may want to know if the number of underbaked pizza complaints is related to the number of orders per day. In this case, number of orders per day may be represented on the horizontal axis and the number of complaints on the vertical axis. If a scatter diagram indicates a relationship, a formal model may be developed using regression techniques. (See Exhibit S12-7.)

Cause-and-Effect Diagrams   Developed by the Japanese quality expert Kaoru Ishikawa, these diagrams are also called fishbone diagrams. They are effective tools that help quality improvement efforts to focus on finding the causes of a selected problem. The diagram has a center line, or the "spine," which leads to the "effect" or the problem, and a few major categories of possible causes connected to the spine. Causes for most quality problems can be grouped in general categories such as personnel, equipment, methods, materials, processes, and environment, or categories specific to the problem may be used. Then, usually in a brainstorming session, possible subcauses and their subcauses and so forth in each category are identified. At the end of the session, each item in the diagram is examined and eliminated if it is not a factor that contributes to the problem. The remaining causes are examined more closely, and if a link is found between them and the "effect," the quality improvement effort is directed at eliminating them. As an example, refer to Exhibit S12-8, which was developed for solving computer problems by phone.

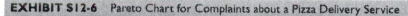

EXHIBIT S12-6   Pareto Chart for Complaints about a Pizza Delivery Service

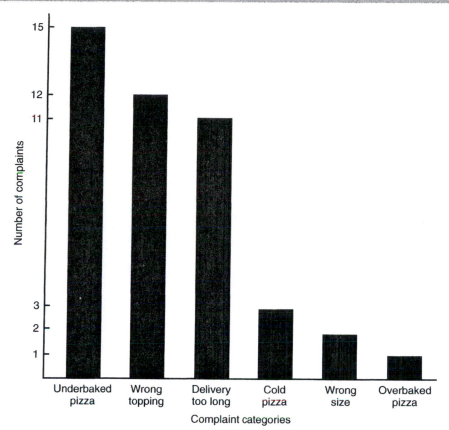

Control Charts   Control charts are statistical graphic devices that are used to monitor the performance of a manufacturing or service process over time. Because of this process focus, they are also called process control charts. A control chart has a center line and an upper and a lower limit. The center line represents the long-term process average. Control limits are determined so that any sample data point that is above the upper limit or below the lower limit is a possible indication of the process being out of control, or not performing satisfactorily. If the data point falls between the two limits,

EXHIBIT S12-7   Scatter Diagram for the Complaints about Pizza Delivery Service

EXHIBIT S12-8 Cause-and-Effect Diagram for Solving Computer Problems by Phone

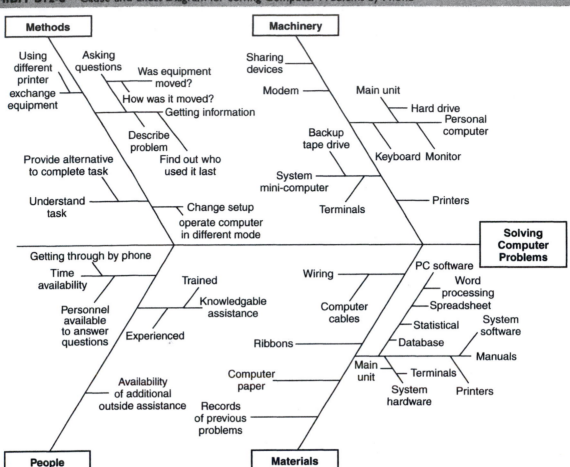

Source: D. M. Levine, P. P. Ramsey, and M. L. Berenson, *Business Statistics for Quality and Productivity* (Upper Saddle River, NJ, Prentice Hall, 1995), p. 76.

it is concluded that the process is in statistical control, or performing satisfactorily. The control chart is one of the most important tools for quality and continuous improvement efforts. For this reason we present a more detailed discussion of this tool in the next section.

S12.4 PROCESS CONTROL CHARTS

In many cases, production and consumption of a service occur simultaneously. This leaves little opportunity for the service provider to test or inspect the quality of the service before it is delivered to the customer. That is why the importance of service design and its delivery system was emphasized in many places in this book, especially in chapter 8. Also in the same chapter, and on many other occasions, the crucial role service employees play in achieving service quality and customer satisfaction was emphasized. Achieving quality and customer satisfaction in services is different; it must start with the design of the service and its delivery system in conjunction with selecting and hiring the right people. Hiring the right people is just one step—you have to give them all the necessary training and preparation and then empower them to do their best for customers.

All these advance a service organization a considerable distance on the road to quality and customer satisfaction. However, there is still much more to be done on the technical side to complement these efforts. Many services involve manufacturing-like activities and processes, such as check clearing operations in a bank, preparation and mailing of bank statements, cooking and assembling meals in a fast-food restaurant, performing tests on blood samples in a medical lab, processing insurance claims, and enplaning and deplaning passengers of an airline. Many of these processes, but not all, take place in the back room and out of sight. Regardless of where they are performed, they are an essential part of the delivery system, and without them, quality service is not possible.

Because of their manufacturing-like nature, outputs of these activities and processes can be measured, standardized, and controlled. Process control charts are very effective in such settings for monitoring conformance to standards. Output data in services may be in one of three types:

- *Measurable data*, such as time spent in a service or time spent waiting for service.
- *Percentages*, such as the percentage of goods damaged or the percentage of customers complaining.
- *Counting data*, such as the number of typos in a report or the number of mistakes in an insurance claim.

The first type is used when the output is a variable (a measurable characteristic of a service process), and the other two are used when the output is an attribute (a characteristic a service performance may or may not possess). In this section, control charts for each one of these data types are presented and discussed.

Normally, there is some degree of variation in all processes. A control chart that appears to be in control means that variations in samples of the outcome of a service process taken over time are, for the most part, random. In building control charts, averages of small service samples (often of five accounts or customers or daily averages) are used, as opposed to data on individual service encounters. Individual measurements tend to be too erratic to make trends quickly visible. The purpose of control charts is to help distinguish between natural (random) variations and variations due to assignable causes. **Random variations** affect almost every service process to some degree and are to be expected. As long as output precision remains within specified limits, this fact of life can be tolerated.

Assignable variation in a service process can usually be traced to a specific reason. Factors such as misadjusted equipment, fatigued or untrained employees, and new procedures are all common sources of assignable variations. Control charts identify when a problem is occurring and help the employee pinpoint where a problem may lie.

Control Charts for Variables

Two types of control charts, one for the sample mean ($\bar{X}$) and another for the range (R), are used to monitor processes that are measured in continuous units. For example, these control charts may monitor the time that it takes to serve a customer or the length of time that a customer waits before being served. The $\bar{X}$ chart would tell us whether significant changes have occurred in the average service time or waiting time. The R-chart values would indicate the amount of variability in service time or waiting time customers experience. The two charts go hand in hand when monitoring variables.

$\bar{X}$ Charts

The theoretical foundation for $\bar{X}$ charts is the **central limit theorem.** In general terms, this theorem states that regardless of the distribution of the population of all parts or services, the distribution of $\bar{X}$'s (each of which is a mean of a sample drawn from the population) will tend to follow a normal curve as the sample size grows large. And fortunately, even if n is fairly small (say 4 or 5), the distributions of the averages will still roughly follow a normal curve. It is also known that (1) the mean of the distribution of the $\bar{X}$'s (called $\bar{\bar{X}}$) will equal the mean of the overall population (which is called μ), and (2) the standard deviation of the sampling distribution $\sigma_{\bar{x}}$ will be the population standard deviation $\sigma_{\bar{x}}$ divided by the square root of the sample size n. In other words,

$$\bar{\bar{X}} = \mu \quad \text{and} \quad \sigma_{\bar{x}} = \frac{\sigma_x}{\sqrt{n}} \tag{S12.1}$$

Exhibit S12-9 shows three possible population distributions, each with its own mean μ and standard deviation σ_x. If a series of random samples ($\bar{X}_1, \bar{X}_2, \bar{X}_3, \bar{X}_4,$ and so on) each of size n is drawn from any of these, the resulting distribution of $\bar{X}_i$ will appear as in the bottom graph of the exhibit. Because this is a normal distribution, we can state that if the process has only random variations

1. 99.7 percent of the time the sample averages will fail within $\pm 3\sigma_{\bar{x}}$.
2. 95.5 percent of the time the sample averages will fall within $\pm 2\sigma_{\bar{x}}$.

In other words, if a point on the control chart falls outside of the $\pm 3\sigma_{\bar{x}}$ control limits, then we are 99.7 percent confident that the process has changed. Similarly, if a point on the control charts falls outside of the $\pm 2\sigma_{\bar{x}}$ control limits, we are 95.5 percent sure that the process has changed. This is the theory behind control charts.

EXHIBIT S12-9   Population and Sampling Distributions

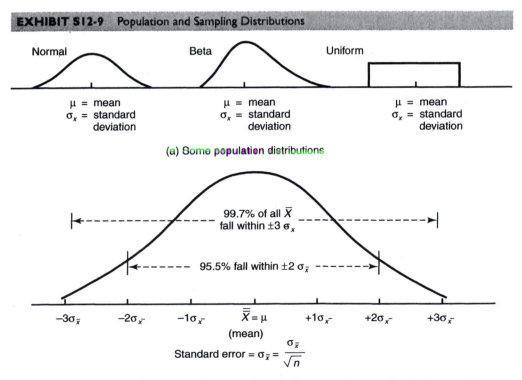

(a) Some population distributions

Standard error $= \sigma_{\bar{x}} = \dfrac{\sigma_{\bar{x}}}{\sqrt{n}}$

(b) Sampling distribution of sample means (approaches normal as sample size increases)

In practice, the standard deviation of the service process may be difficult to determine, but it can be estimated by the **range** of the service process. The range is the difference between the highest and lowest mesurement in a sample.

An $\bar{X}$ chart is simply a plot of the means of the samples taken of a process. $\bar{\bar{X}}$ is the average of the sample means. To set upper and lower control limits for the $\bar{X}$ chart, we use the following formulas:

$$\text{UCL}_{\bar{x}} = \bar{\bar{X}} + A\bar{R} \quad \text{and} \quad \text{LCL}_{\bar{x}} = \bar{\bar{X}} - A\bar{R}$$

where

$\bar{\bar{X}}$ = the average of the sample means
$\bar{R}$ = the average range of the samples
A = a factor taken from Exhibit S12-10 to establish $3\sigma_{\bar{x}}$ control limits
$\text{UCL}_{\bar{x}}$ = upper control limit for the mean
$\text{LCL}_{\bar{x}}$ = lower control limit for the mean

$\bar{R}$ Charts

In addition to being concerned with the process average, managers are interested in the process variability. Even though the process average is under control, the variability of the process may not be. The theory behind control charts for ranges is the same as for the process average. Limits are established that contain ± 3 standard deviations of the distribution for the average range $\bar{R}$. With a few simplifying assumptions, we can set the upper and lower control limits for ranges as follows:

$$\text{UCL}_R = B\bar{R} \quad \text{and} \quad \text{LCL}_R = C\bar{R}$$

where

UCL_R = upper control chart limit for the range
LCL_R = lower control chart limit for the range
B and C = values from Exhibit S12-10

EXHIBIT S12-10   Control Limit Factors (±3σ)

Same Size n	A (Mean Factor)	B (Upper-Range Factor)	C (Lower-Range Factor)
2	1.880	3.267	0
3	1.023	2.575	0
4	0.729	2.282	0
5	0.577	2.115	0
6	0.483	2.004	0
7	0.419	1.924	0.076
8	0.373	1.864	0.136
9	0.337	1.816	0.184
10	0.308	1.777	0.223
11	0.285	1.774	0.256
12	0.266	1.716	0.284
13	0.249	1.692	0.308
14	0.235	1.671	0.329
15	0.223	1.652	0.348
20	0.180	1.586	0.459
25	0.153	1.541	0.459

Mail-Order Business Example   A mail ordering business wants to measure the response time of their operators in taking customer orders over the phone. Listed below is the time recorded in minutes from five different samples of the ordering process with four customer orders per sample. We will construct 3 standard deviation $\bar{X}$ and R control charts for this process and determine if any points are out of control.

Sample	Observations				Sample Average $\bar{X}$	Sample Range R
1	5	3	6	10	24/4 = 6	10 − 3 = 7
2	7	5	3	5	20/4 = 5	7 − 3 = 4
3	1	8	3	12	24/4 = 6	12 − 1 = 11
4	7	6	2	1	16/4 = 4	7 − 1 = 6
5	3	15	6	12	36/4 = 9	15 − 3 = 12
					$\Sigma \bar{X} = 30$	$\Sigma R = 40$

$$\bar{\bar{X}} = 30/5 = 6$$
$$\bar{R} = 40/5 = 8$$
$$UCL_{\bar{x}} = 6 + 0.729(8) = 11.832$$
$$LCL_{\bar{x}} = 6 - 0.729(8) = .168$$

The $\bar{X}$ chart is shown in Exhibit S12-11.

$$UCL_R = 2.282(8) = 18.256$$
$$LCL_R = 0(8) = 0$$

The R chart is shown in Exhibit S12-12.

Examining Exhibits S12-11 and S12-12, we see that no $\bar{X}$ or R points are out of control. The operators are performing their work within reasonable time limits.

What other measures of service quality would you recommend for this process?

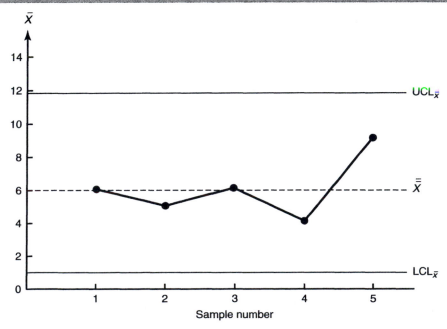

EXHIBIT S12-11 $\bar{X}$ Chart for Operator Response Time

EXHIBIT S12-12   R Chart for Operator Response Time

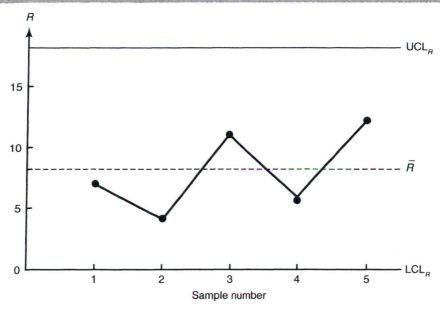

How about percentage of orders taken correctly or number of mistakes per order? For this type of quality assessment, we need two new types of control charts.

Control Charts for Attributes

Control charts for $\bar{X}$ and R do not apply when we are sampling attributes, in which items are typically classified as defective or nondefective. Measuring defects involves counting them (e.g., number of bad light bulbs in a given lot or number of data entry records typed with errors), whereas variables are usually measured for length, weight, or time. There are two kinds of attribute control charts: (1) those which measure the percent defective in a sample—called **p charts,** and (2) those which count the number of defects—called **c charts.**

p **Charts**

The principal means of controlling attributes are p charts. Although attributes that are either good or bad follow the binomial distribution, the normal distribution can be used to calculate p chart limits when sample sizes are large. The procedure resembles the $\bar{X}$ chart approach, which also was based on the central limit theorem.

The formulas for p chart upper and lower control limits are

$$\text{UCL}_p = \bar{p} + Z\sigma_p \qquad\qquad (\text{S12.2})$$
$$\text{LCL}_p = \bar{p} - Z\sigma_p \qquad\qquad (\text{S12.3})$$

where

$\bar{p}$ = mean percent defective in the samples
Z = number of standard deviates ($Z = 2$ for 95.5 percent control limits,
   $Z = 3$ for 99.7 percent control limits)
σ_p = standard deviation of the sampling distribution

σ_p is estimated by the formula

$$\sigma_p = \sqrt{\frac{\overline{p}(1 - \overline{p})}{n}} \qquad \text{(S12.4)}$$

where n = size of each sample.

***p* Chart Example**   Using a popular database software package, 20 data entry clerks at ARCO key in thousands of insurance records each day. A sample of 100 records entered by each clerk was carefully examined to make sure they contained no errors. The percent defective in each sample was then computed as shown in Exhibit S12-13.

We will develop a *p* chart that plots the percent defective and sets control limits to include 99.7 percent of the random variation in the entry process when it is in control.

$$\overline{p} = \frac{\text{total number of errors}}{\text{total number of records examined}} = \frac{80}{(100)(20)} = 0.04 \qquad \text{(S12.5)}$$

$$\sigma_p = \sqrt{\frac{(0.04)(1 - 0.04)}{(100)}} \cong 0.02$$

$\text{UCL}_p = \overline{p} + \sigma_p = 0.04 + 3(0.02) \cong 0.10$

$\text{LCL}_p = \overline{p} - Z\sigma_p = 0.04 - 3(0.02) \cong -0.02$ or 0 (since we cannot have a negative percent)

The control limits and percent defective are plotted in Exhibit S12-14. Notice that only one data entry clerk (number 17) is out of control. The firm may wish to examine that individual's work a bit more closely to see if a serious problems exists. In addition, it might be interesting to investigate the working habits of clerks 3 and 19. Do they make no errors because they work too slowly or have they developed a superior procedure?

c Charts

In the preceding example, we counted the number of defective database records entered. A defective record was one that was not exactly correct. A bad record may

EXHIBIT S12-13   Data Entry Errors

Sample Number	Records with Errors	Percent Defective	Sample Number	Records with Errors	Percent Defective
1	6	0.06	11	6	0.06
2	5	0.05	12	1	0.01
3	0	0.00	13	8	0.08
4	1	0.01	14	7	0.07
5	4	0.04	15	5	0.05
6	2	0.02	16	4	0.04
7	5	0.05	17	11	0.11
8	3	0.03	18	3	0.03
9	3	0.03	19	0	0.00
10	2	0.02	20	4	0.04
			Total	80	

n = size of each sample = 100

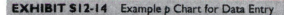

EXHIBIT S12-14   Example p Chart for Data Entry

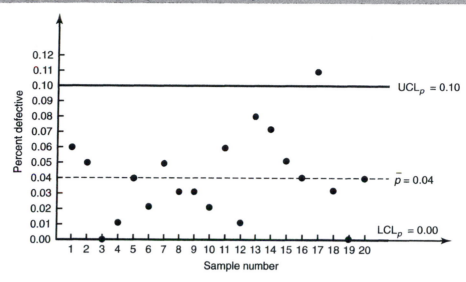

contain more than one defect, however. We use c charts to control the number of defects per unit of output (or per insurance record in the preceding case).

Control charts for defects are helpful for monitoring processes where a large number of potential errors can occur but the actual number that do occur is relatively small. Defects may be typographical errors in newspapers, blemishes on a table, or missing pickles on a fast-food hamburger.

The **Poisson probability distribution,** which has a variance equal to its mean, is the basis for c charts. Since $\bar{c}$ is the mean number of defects per unit, the standard deviation is equal to $\sqrt{\bar{c}}$. To compute 99.7 percent control limits for $\bar{c}$, we use the formula

$$\bar{c} \pm 3\sqrt{\bar{c}} \qquad \text{(S12.6)}$$

c Chart example   Red Top Cab Company receives several complaints per day about the behavior of its drivers. Over a nine-day period (where days are the units of measure), the owner received this number of calls from irate passengers: 3, 0, 8, 9, 6, 7, 4, 9, 8, for a total of 54 complaints.

To compute 99.7 percent control limits, we take

$$\bar{c} = \frac{54}{9} = 6 \text{ complaints per day}$$

Thus

$$\text{UCL}_c = \bar{c} + 3\sqrt{\bar{c}} = 6 + 3\sqrt{6} = 6 + 3(24.5) = 13.35$$
$$\text{LCL}_c = \bar{c} - 3\sqrt{\bar{c}} = 6 - 3\sqrt{6} = 6 - 3(2.45) = -1.35 \text{ or } 0$$

After plotting a control chart summarizing this data and posting it prominently in the drivers' locker room, the number of calls received dropped to an average of three per day. Can you explain why this may have occurred?

Interpretation of Control Charts

We indicated earlier that when sample data points, such as sample averages, fall within the control limits, the process is considered to be in statistical control. When they fall outside the limits, it is concluded that the process might be out of control, which requires an investigation as to the cause of the out-of-control sign. However, this is not the only case in which an investigation is warranted. Data points may fall within the limits, but if they exhibit an unusual pattern, this may be a sign of a process out of control or about to go out of control. Consequently, process control charts must be examined not only for points that fall outside the limits, but also for unusual patterns. Exhibit S12-15 provides some examples of possible patterns in control charts.

EXHIBIT S12-15   Patterns to Look for on Control Charts

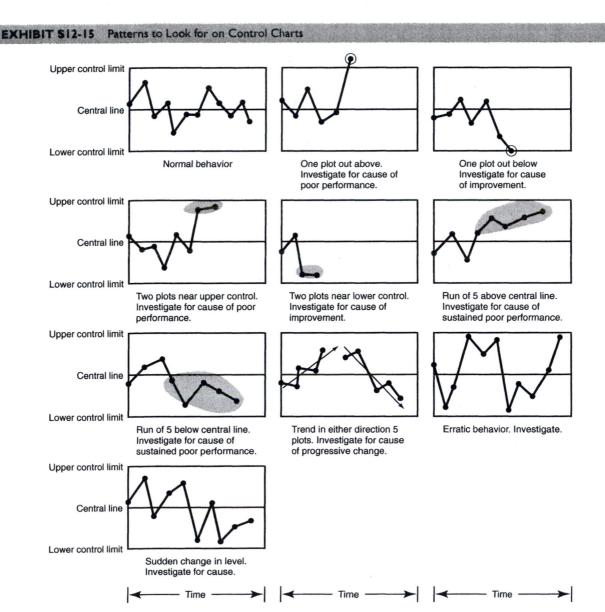

Source: Bertrand L. Hansen, *Quality Control: Theory & Applications*, © 1963, p. 65. Reprinted by permission of Prentice Hall, Inc., Upper Saddle River, New Jersey.

Using POM for Windows for SPC

POM for Windows' Quality Control module has the ability to compute and plot all the SPC control charts introduced in this supplement. Exhibit S12-16 illustrates POM for Windows output for the ARCO Data Entry Errors example. In addition to the relevant computational output for a *p* chart, POM for Windows will plot the sample points in a separate control chart as shown in the second half of Exhibit S12-16. As another example, Exhibit S12-17 contains the limits of the *c* chart and other sample information for the Red Top Cab Company problem.

EXHIBIT S12-16 POM for Windows Output of ARCO's Data Entry Errors Example

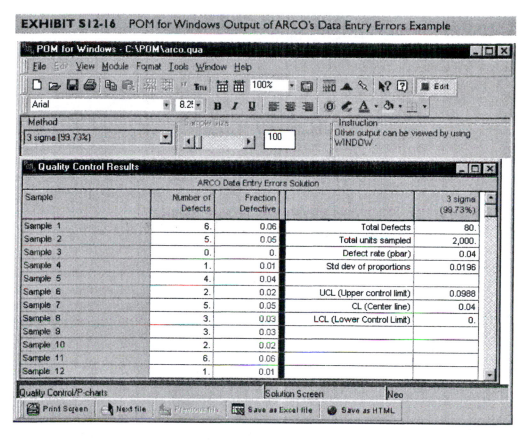

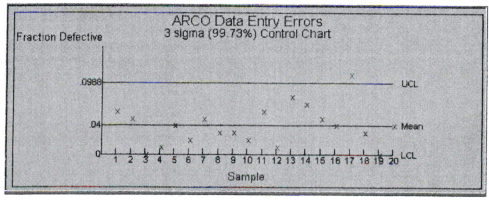

EXHIBIT S12-17 POM for Windows Output of Red Top Cab Company Example

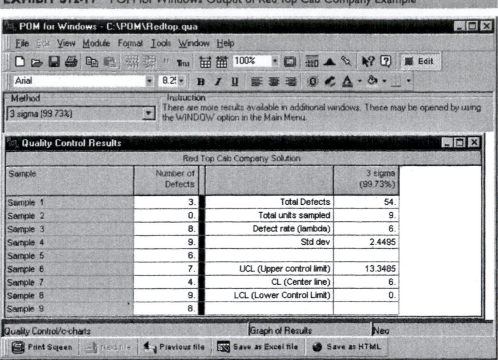

S12.5 SUMMARY

This supplement presented some of the most widely used tools and techniques of quality and continuous improvement. Most quality improvement projects can be based on the plan–do–study–act cycle. In solving quality problems and improving existing systems, one or more of the tools known as the "magnificent seven" can be used. These are simple and straightforward graphical tools that are easy to learn and use, they are also very effective in uncovering quality problems. We discussed one of these tools, the process control chart, in more detail because of its applicability in many services.

The process control chart is a quality control technique constructed to detect unacceptable levels of output variability in a process. $\bar{X}$ and R charts are used together to measure changes in the central tendency and variability of a process. The percentage defective in a sample taken from a process is measured by p charts, and c charts help monitor the number of defects.

Service employees can monitor the quality of the service they are providing by sampling their work and recording such data as the time it takes to process a customer, the number of errors made, or the percentage of customers who are satisfied. If the data recorded fall outside prespecified control limits, or an unusual pattern is observed, an investigation of the causes needs to be undertaken.

Problems

S12.1. City Council has asked the local police department to investigate the problem of slow response time to citizen calls for police service. The department randomly sampled the response time to five calls from the dispatcher's weekly logs over the past three months. Using the data provided below, develop 3σ $\bar{X}$ and R charts for police response time. Then prepare a report for city council based on your findings. Can you think of any possible problems with the data on which your report is based? What other quality control techniques might be useful for this problem?

Sample	Response Time (minutes)				
1	4	12	63	10	20
2	30	8	16	5	26
3	53	32	10	15	24
4	5	2	17	20	9
5	18	25	4	7	10
6	6	5	10	30	5
7	8	4	27	12	10
8	4	16	6	42	16
9	8	33	15	6	13
10	10	20	27	23	5
11	17	32	4	42	27
12	12	5	16	20	50

S12.2. A popular restaurant in town routinely records on customer tickets the time of each customer's arrival to the restaurant (i.e., when they asked to be seated) and the time of each customer's departure (i.e., when they paid the bill). The tickets are then placed in a large fish bowl–type container and a sample of the "time in the restaurant" for five customers is randomly drawn each night of the week. Using the data from last week provided below, develop 3σ $\bar{X}$ and R charts for customer time at the restaurant. Comment on the results. How could the restaurant use this information to control the quality of their service?

Sample	Time in Restaurant (minutes)				
1	20	35	62	43	75
2	50	38	72	92	24
3	44	36	75	54	25
4	90	48	32	71	46
5	27	52	17	68	39
6	54	39	49	35	65
7	79	53	65	72	90

S12.3. An established hospital in an urban area is trying to improve its image by providing a positive experience for its patients and their relatives. Part of the "image" program involves providing tasty, inviting patient meals that are also healthy. A questionnaire accompanies each meal served, asking the patient, among other things, whether he or she is satisfied or unsatisfied with the meal. A 100-patient sample of the survey results over the past seven days yielded the following data:

Day	No. of Unsatisfied Patients	Sample Size
1	24	100
2	22	100
3	8	100
4	15	100
5	10	100
6	26	100
7	17	100

Construct a *p* chart that plots the percentage of patients unsatisfied with their meals. Set the control limits to include 99.7 percent of the random variation in meal satisfaction. Comment on your results.

S12.4. In order to monitor the allocation of patrol cars and other police resources, the local police department collects data on the incidence of crime by city sector. The city is divided into ten sectors of 1000 residents each. The number of crime incidents reported last month in each sector is as follows:

Sector	Crime Incidence
1	6
2	25
3	5
4	11
5	20
6	17
7	10
8	22
9	7
10	33

Construct a *p* chart that plots the rate of crime by sector. Set the control limits to include 99.7 percent of the random variation in crime. Is the crime rate in any sector out of control? Do you have any suggestions for the reallocation of police resources? What other information might be helpful in your analysis?

S12.5. The school board is trying to evaluate a new math program introduced to second graders in five elementary schools across the country this year. A sample of the student scores on standardized math tests in each elementary school yielded the following data:

School	No. of Test Errors
A	52
B	27
C	35
D	44
E	55

Construct a *c* chart for test errors and set the control limits to contain 99.7 percent of the random variation in test scores. What does the chart tell you? Has the new math program been effective? Should the second graders be allowed to proceed to the next math level?

S12.6. Telephone inquiries of 100 IRS "customers" are monitored daily at random. Incidents of incorrect information or other nonconformities (such as impoliteness to customers) are recorded. The data for last week are:

Day	No. of Nonconformities
1	5
2	10
3	23
4	20
5	15

Construct a 3 standard deviation *c* chart of nonconformities. What does the control chart tell you about the IRS telephone operators?

CASE

CASE S12–1   The Morristown *Daily Tribune*

In July 1987, the Morristown *Daily Tribune* published its first newspaper in direct competition with two other newspapers—the Morristown *Daily Ledger* and the *Clarion Herald*, a weekly publication. Presently, the *Ledger* is the most widely read newspaper in the area, with a total circulation of 38,500. The *Tribune*, however, has made significant inroads into the readership market since its inception. Total circulation of the *Tribune* now exceeds 27,000.

Wilbur Sykes, editor of the *Tribune,* attributes the success of the newspaper to the accuracy of its contents, a strong editorial section, and the proper blending of local, regional, national, and international news items. In addition, the paper has been successful in getting the accounts of several major retailers who advertise extensively in the display section. Finally, experienced reporters, photographers, copy writers, typesetters, editors, and other

personnel have formed a "team" dedicated to providing the most timely and accurate reporting of news in the area.

Of critical importance to quality newspaper printing is accurate typesetting. To ensure quality in the final print, Mr. Sykes has decided to develop a procedure for monitoring the performance of typesetters over a period of time. Such a procedure involves sampling output, establishing control limits, comparing the *Tribune*'s accuracy with that of the industry, and occasionally updating the information.

First, Mr. Sykes randomly selected 30 newspapers published during the preceding 12 months. From each paper, 100 paragraphs were randomly chosen and were read for accuracy. The number of errors in each paper was recorded, and the fraction of errors in each sample was determined. Exhibit S12-18 shows the results of the sampling. ∎

EXHIBIT S12-18   Sample of Errors in Thirty Newspapers

Sample	Errors in Sample	Fraction of Errors (per 100)	Sample	Errors in Sample	Fraction of Errors (per 100)
1	2	0.02	16	2	0.02
2	4	0.04	17	3	0.03
3	10	0.10	18	7	0.07
4	4	0.04	19	3	0.03
5	1	0.01	20	2	0.02
6	1	0.01	21	3	0.03
7	13	0.13	22	7	0.07
8	9	0.09	23	4	0.04
9	11	0.11	24	3	0.03
10	0	0.00	25	2	0.02
11	3	0.03	26	2	0.02
12	4	0.04	27	0	0.00
13	2	0.02	28	1	0.01
14	2	0.02	29	3	0.03
15	8	0.08	30	4	0.04

SOURCE: Written by Professor Jerry Kinard (Francis Marion College) and Joe Iverstine (deceased).

CASE QUESTIONS

1. Plot the overall fraction of errors ($\bar{p}$) and the upper and lower control limits on a control chart using a 95.45 percent confidence level.
2. Assume the industry upper and lower control limits are 0.1000 and 0.0400, respectively. Plot them on the control chart.
3. Plot the fraction of errors in each sample. Do all fall within the firm's control limits? When one falls outside the control limits, what should be done?

CHAPTER 13

Service Productivity and Measurement of Performance

13.1   INTRODUCTION

The single greatest challenge facing managers in the developed countries of the world is to raise the productivity of knowledge and service workers. This challenge, which will dominate the management agenda for the next several decades, will ultimately determine the competitive performance of companies. Even more important, it will determine the very fabric of society and the quality of life in every industrialized nation.[1]

These were the words that began a *Harvard Business Review* article by the management philosopher Peter F. Drucker. Some researchers and management practitioners may not agree with Professor Drucker on the extent of the impact of service productivity on society. However, most, if not all, would agree that raising productivity in general, and service productivity in particular, is indeed one of the most important issues public policy makers and managers face.

This chapter focuses on the important topic of productivity, especially service productivity, and measurement of performance in service organizations. We first present a

---

[1] Peter F. Drucker, "The New Productivity Challenge," *Harvard Business Review* (November–December 1991), pp. 69–79.

377

brief background on productivity, then discuss why raising productivity is so crucial for the well being of a country as well as individual public and private organizations. We also discuss how service productivity can be raised. Finally, we present a brief discussion of data envelopment analysis as a powerful tool in measuring efficiency of service organizations.

13.2   A BRIEF BACKGROUND ON PRODUCTIVITY

Productivity represents the relationship between outputs (goods, services, or outcomes) and inputs used to produce the outputs. It is an indicator of how well an organization converts its inputs (e.g., resources) into outputs. The organization may be producing goods or services, or it may be the whole economy of a country producing all kinds of goods and services. Hence, the concept of productivity can be applied to an economy, to an industry (e.g., airline industry) or to a particular organization, or to any operation in any of these economic units.

Productivity

Productivity is defined as a ratio of output to input:

$$\text{Productivity} = \text{Output/Input}$$

The components in this ratio are in their natural physical units, such as number of 27-inch TV sets produced and number of labor hours used to produce those sets. Whether it is goods or services that are represented in the numerator, output must include only those of good quality. In other words, goods that are later found to be defective, or services that had to be repeated because they were not satisfactory the first time, should not be included in the output.

Productivity may be computed for a single output and a single input or multiple outputs and inputs. Most organizations produce more than one kind of output and use several kinds of inputs. Outputs are usually measured in different units; therefore, they must be converted to a common unit. Similarly, when there is more than one type, inputs must also be converted to a common unit, usually to dollars. In practice, both the output and input are calculated as weighted index numbers.[2]

A productivity ratio with a single input is called partial productivity, such as total output divided by number of labor hours, or capital, or number of kilowatt hours of energy, or any relevant quantity of input used. A labor productivity ratio, for example, represents units of output produced per unit of labor hour. Care should be exercised not to attribute the result entirely to labor in such ratios, because other inputs are also needed to produce a unit of a good or deliver a service.

Multifactor, or total productivity, measures are very useful when it is important to assess the outcome from the use of all the relevant inputs. Total productivity is the ratio of total output to total inputs. Clearly, total productivity index provides more information. It makes available information on trade-offs among various inputs and allows senior managers to make more informed decisions.[3] An increase in the total productivity ratio represents savings achieved in one or more of the inputs. It is im-

---

2 The Bureau of Labor Statistics of the U.S. Department of Labor publishes measures of productivity and studies on productivity change in the United States. More information on the compilation of data and computation of various productivity measures can be found in the publications of the Bureau of Labor Statistics, for example, *A BLS Reader on Productivity* (1996), or their periodical, *Monthly Labor Review*.

3 J. Jurison, "Reevaluating Productivity Measures," *Information Systems Management* (winter 1997), pp. 30–34.

portant to note that changes in the labor productivity ratio reflect not only the changes in the efficiency of labor but also the substitution effect of other inputs, such as capital, for labor. In other words, improvements in labor productivity may be due to the use of more efficient or labor-saving machines, which is substitution of capital for labor. Because total factor productivity measure includes all the inputs, all changes in inputs are represented.

Efficiency

A related concept is efficiency. Although sometimes used interchangeably, productivity and efficiency are different concepts. As mentioned earlier, productivity of an economic unit is the ratio of its output to its input used to produce that output. Efficiency, on the other hand, indicates the degree of attainment of an optimum outcome, a preselected goal, or the best practice.

Efficiency can be measured as the ratio of output obtained from a process to the maximum output that is possible for the amount of input used. Alternatively, efficiency can be measured as the ratio of the minimum input needed to produce the observed output to the actual amount of input used. It is also possible to set performance targets, such as output volume, cost, revenue, or profits, and measure the performance of an economic unit against these goals.[4] While the productivity measure can theoretically be any non-negative number, efficiency is expressed as a percentage and cannot be greater than one. Also, productivity of economic units can be compared even if they use different technologies. Efficiency comparisons, however, are meaningful only among economic units using similar technologies and inputs to produce similar outputs.

13.3   WHY PRODUCTIVITY IS IMPORTANT

Productivity ratio, as a number, is not very meaningful unless it is considered over time. In other words, productivity ratio is meaningful only when its change through regular intervals of time is considered. Clearly, the desired change is an increase in productivity. Also, it is meaningful and useful when two similar organizations are compared. In this section, the relationship between productivity and several economic and business indicators is reviewed.[5]

- *Standard of living.* At the national level, labor productivity is the most frequently used productivity measure. Output in this ratio represents all goods and services produced by the private sector of the economy. Input represents the number of hours worked in the private sector. Labor productivity is used as an index of standard of living in a country. The change in productivity through time shows if the standard of living in a country is improving.

Probably, there is nothing more important for the welfare of the citizens of a country than a steady increase in productivity in the long run. An increase in productivity means there will be more goods and services for the citizens of a country to consume. It also means that, all else being equal, the prices of these goods and services

---

[4] C. A. Knox Lovell, "Production Frontiers and Productive Efficiency," in Harold O. Fried, C. A. Knox Lovell, and Shelton S. Schmidt (eds.), *The Measurement of Productive Efficiency: Techniques and Applications* (New York, Oxford University Press, 1993), p. 4.

[5] This section has been adapted from the following two sources: Committee for Economic Development, *Productivity Policy: Key to the Nation's Economic Future* (New York, Committee for Economic Development, 1983), pp. 23–29; and W. J. Baumol, S. A. B. Blackman, and E. N. Wolff, *Productivity and American Leadership: The Long View* (Cambridge, MA, MIT Press, 1989), pp. 9–27.

will be decreasing; hence, the society will be better off in general. Although there may be a lag, an increase in productivity usually leads to a rise in wages. However, if the productivity growth falls consistently below that of other countries, it will experience a relatively (although not absolutely) lower standard of living.

The real impact of productivity increases is observed in the long run. Annual productivity increases are usually limited to a few percentage points. However, their impact becomes immense in the long run because of the effect of compounding. Examples of this effect can be seen in Exhibit 13-1, which presents estimates of productivity growth for 16 industrialized countries between 1870 and 1979.

- *Costs and competitiveness.* Productivity growth contributes to a country's competitiveness in international trade due to its cost-lowering effect. It has the same effect on a company's costs.
- *Inflation.* There is a direct relationship between productivity and inflation. An increase in productivity will help reduce the rise in the level of prices, that is, inflation.
- *Unemployment.* Productivity growth is sometimes blamed for an increase in unemployment. It is true that as productivity increases, some employees will be displaced from their regular line of employment in the short run. However, there is no evidence to indicate that productivity growth causes unemployment in the long run.
- *Social programs.* Productivity growth also makes it possible for governments to allocate resources for combating poverty, providing for the elderly, education, arts, environmental protection, or programs that in general benefit many of its citizens and contribute to a nation's well-being.
- *Resource conservation.* As an economy grows, it produces more goods and services. This may mean an increase in the use of natural resources and an increase

EXHIBIT 13-1 Growth in Productivity (GDP per capita), 1870–1979, for 16 Industrialized Countries

Country	Growth in Real GDP per Capita (%)	Growth in Real GDP per Person-Hour (%)	Growth in Volume of Exports (%)
Australia	221.0	398.0	—
United Kingdom	325.0	585.0	930.0
Switzerland	472.0	830.0	4,400.0
Belgium	411.0	887.0	6,250.0
Netherlands	423.0	910.0	8,040.0
Canada	754.0	1,050.0	9,860.0
United States	691.0	1,080.0	9,240.0
Denmark	650.0	1,090.0	6,750.0
Italy	493.0	1,220.0	6,210.0
Austria	642.0	1,260.0	4,740.0
Germany	1,396.0	1,510.0	3,730.0
Norway	872.0	1,560.0	7,740.0
France	694.0	1,590.0	4,140.0
Finland	1,016.0	1,710.0	6,240.0
Sweden	1,084.0	2,060.0	5,070.0
Japan	1,653.0	2,480.0	293,060.0

Source: William J. Baumol, Sue Anne Batey Blackman, and Edward N. Wolff, *Productivity and American Leadership: The Long View* (Cambridge, MA, MIT Press, 1989), p. 13.

in adverse impact on the environment. However, if the growth in output is achieved through productivity increases, fewer resources will be used and environmental impact will be reduced.

13.4 REVIEW OF THE SLOWDOWN OF U.S. PRODUCTIVITY GROWTH IN THE RECENT PAST

Between 1966 and 1980, the United States experienced a slowdown in the growth of its productivity. The slowdown got even worse after 1973. For example, while the average annual productivity increase between 1950 and 1973 was 2.8 percent, the rate of growth was only 0.9 percent between 1973 and 1979. Another closely related development of the period was that the rate of growth of the U.S. productivity not only slowed down, but also fell behind the rates of some other industrialized countries such as Japan, Germany, Sweden, France, and Italy. If it is persistent, such a shortfall may mean loss of competitiveness in the long run and deterioration in the standard of living. Naturally, these developments caused concern among business leaders and public policy makers. However, it was later realized that the slowdown in the productivity growth was a temporary, short-run phenomenon.[6] In other words, the long-run U.S. productivity growth rate has not fallen below its historical level. It must be emphasized, however, that the consequences of these developments, the pain and suffering they caused among the population, were real, and there is no guarantee that the United States will always maintain its historical level of productivity or its growth rate.

Major reasons for the slowdown have been identified as follows[7]:

- *A slowdown in the rate of capital formation.* The rate of capital formation in the form of plant and equipment, began to decline in 1966 and more importantly, the growth of capital per worker slowed down after 1973. American workers had less equipment to work with on the average.
- *Composition of the labor force.* Women joined the labor force in increasing numbers, and the relative share of young workers increased. These new additions were less experienced than the existing work force. However, the overall educational level of the new entrants into the labor force was higher; hence, it made a positive contribution.
- *Decline in research and development investments.* It is estimated that about 10 percent of the slowdown in productivity growth was due to a slowdown in the rate of investment in research and development (R&D) that creates cost-saving technological innovations.
- *Composition of output.* The composition of output shifted from manufacturing, whose productivity grows relatively rapidly, to services, whose productivity typically grows relatively slowly.
- *The availability and cost of energy.* Many researchers believe that the significant increase in energy prices, especially oil, that started in the early 1970s had a negative impact on the productivity growth.
- *Government regulations.* Government regulations, in general, have a negative impact on productivity because they require more paperwork, distract managers

---

[6] For example, see the discussion in Baumol, Blackman, and Wolff, *Productivity and American Leadership: The Long View*, especially chapters 1 and 4.

[7] E. N. Wolff, "The Magnitude and Causes of the Recent Productivity Slowdown in the United States: A Survey of Recent Studies," in W. J. Baumol and K. McLennan (eds.), *Productivity Growth and U.S. Competitiveness* (New York, Oxford University Press, 1985), pp. 29–57.

from their normal duties, extend the fruition period of new investment projects, and increase uncertainty about the future.

- *Cyclical factors.* Some economists believe that the slowdown in productivity growth during the period of 1966 to 1980 was due to the business cycle. They argue that productivity growth tends to decline at the tail end of an economic expansion and during recessions, but increases rapidly in the early stages of an economic expansion.

These possible causes have been supported in varying degrees by statistical evidence found by various researchers. There are, however, other causes, mostly based on general observation and judgment, that have been suggested to explain the phenomenon in question: excessive preoccupation of top business executives with the short-term results; a management reward system that encourages avoidance of risk rather than innovation, and causes a decline in the spirit of entrepreneurship; inflation, which created uncertainty, absorbing the time and effort of management, and increasing the cost of investments; growth of parochialism and protectionism in the form of rescue plans for domestic firms that were in financial trouble, both of which reduce the pressures on management to be more productive and to innovate; financing difficulties of small firms; and the role of unions, including resistance to change.[8]

13.5 RAISING PRODUCTIVITY

Productivity is influenced by many factors. First among the factors that improve productivity in the long run is technological developments that reduce labor requirement in the production of goods and services, or increase output without increasing labor input. Another factor that has both long- and short-term implications for increasing productivity is the organization and management of productive activities. However, behind these are the basic values and institutions of society that are relevant to "attitudes toward work, propensities to save and invest, willingness to innovate, take risks, and adapt to changes wrought by scientific and technological progress. . . . The important point is that the values of a people and its leaders condition the rate of technological progress and other forces directly affecting productivity."[9] For example, in a competitive private-enterprise environment, firms have strong incentives to improve productivity for survival. In such an environment, firms undertake R&D projects, innovate, and take risks in trying out new ideas and technologies, all of which may lead to improvements in productivity and profitability. Actions of central and local governments also have a significant effect on the productivity of organizations. Incentives by government for investment into R&D and new technologies usually end up increasing the productivity of private enterprises.

Naturally, productivity improvements at the firm level determine what happens at the national level. Organizations can increase productivity in the long run by introducing new technologies and innovations in existing technology. They can also achieve productivity improvements from economies of scale. As organizations grow, their productive resources, such as machines, equipment, and work force, also grow in scale and tend to specialize. Growth in capacity does not necessarily require a growth of all inputs in the same proportions. For example, when an organization increases its capacity by 25 percent, it does not necessarily need an equal expansion in the number of employees in its account-

8 Committee for Economic Development, *Productivity Policy: Key to the Nation's Economic Future* (New York, Committee for Economic Development, 1983), p. 31.

9 J. W. Kendrick, *Improving Company Productivity* (Baltimore, Johns Hopkins University Press, 1984), p. 13.

ing department. Specialization of equipment and employees also leads to an increase in productivity because of the increased output volume specialization generates.

Short-run conditions also influence productivity. Cyclical, seasonal, or erratic fluctuations in demand can influence productivity of an industry or an organization. However, organizations can achieve significant increases in efficiency in the short term by implementing better work methods and better management practices. Overall, good relationships between management and labor, common objectives adopted by both can create the right environment for productivity increases in the workplace. In general, investments into developing human resources contribute to productivity growth. Recruiting workers with the right skills and attitude, paying them competitive wages and providing attractive benefits, giving them the appropriate training and education to help them achieve their maximum potential, and motivating them to be their best are some of the most effective human resource practices to improve productivity. Teamwork and empowerment encourage participation of employees in problem solving and making suggestions for improvements in production methods. Employees are usually the best source of ideas for improvement in production processes and methods, and eliminating waste and defects.

Another factor that contributes to productivity growth in manufacturing is the development and introduction of new products. Productivity increases faster in the early stages of production of new products than in later stages due to the learning curve effect.[10]

In summary, improving productivity largely depends on good management practices. All the factors we listed above, other than cultural and environmental factors and activities of government, depend on management action. Without the right managerial approach and decisions, productivity increases will be difficult to achieve.

13.6 SERVICE PRODUCTIVITY

It is clear that raising productivity is one of the biggest challenges for public policy makers whose decisions influence the productivity performance of the economy, as well as for managers, whose decisions influence the productivity performance of their organization. Services, on the other hand present a special challenge. It is not only difficult to increase service productivity, it is also difficult to measure it and measure it accurately. In this section we first briefly review some of the reasons for the measurement problem. Then we discuss why service productivity growth is slower than manufacturing productivity. Finally, we present some suggestions for raising productivity of services.

Measurement of Service Productivity

Recall that productivity is defined as the ratio of output to input. The most common way to measure service productivity is to divide output by aggregate labor hours. Labor input is the sum of hours worked by all persons involved in producing the given output. Although by no means an easy task, measuring labor input in services is relatively straightforward. However, measurement of output presents certain challenges in some services. Difficulties emerge when we try to define the output of a service. Major problems are: (1) identifying the elements of a complex bundle of services; (2) choosing among alternative representations of an industry's output; (3) accounting for the consumer's role in the production of a service; and (4) quality differences.[11]

---

[10] Kendrick, *Improving Company Productivity*, p. 15.

[11] M. K. Sherwood, "Difficulties in the Measurement of Service Outputs," *Monthly Labor Review* (March 1994), pp. 11–19.

1. *Identifying the elements of a service.* Many services consist of a set of services which are jointly produced. It is usually difficult, if not impossible, to separate the bundle into individual services. For example, banks provide several different services when a customer opens a checking account. Safekeeping of money, record keeping, and making payments, such as bill payments, are some of the services that are jointly produced and difficult to separate.

2. *Alternative representations of service output.* The second problem arises from the nature of services. Services are performances and usually there is no physical evidence or output when a service is performed. Consequently, what to measure and how to measure becomes a thorny issue. For example, in health care a logical output measure for a hospital would be the number of patients cured, but that is not an easy output to measure and usually no such data exist. Furthermore, not everything a hospital does is directed at curing, some hospital activities are aimed at keeping patients healthy. Some hospital activities may be aimed at diagnosing problems, such as x-rays, lab tests, and computed tomography scans. Once the problem is diagnosed, the treatment may be performed by another health care provider. There are still other activities hospitals perform, such as training of interns and nurses. Because of this difficulty, output in some services may be measured indirectly by measuring relevant activities. For example, output of hospitals may be represented by the number of patient-days. In banking demand deposits are sometimes considered as part of a bank's output (safekeeping, accounting, and payment services provided to customers) and sometimes its input (they are a source of funds for the bank).

3. *Accounting for consumer's role.* Customers are involved in the creation and delivery of many services. Customer involvement creates at least three challenges in the measurement of service productivity. First, in some services, the customer supplies the labor for the delivery of service. It may be difficult to separate the contribution of the customer to the service output from that of the service organization. Normally, the labor provided by the customer is not included in the labor input, thereby causing an underestimation of labor input and overestimation of productivity. It can be argued that because the customer provides part of the labor, price of the service will be lower, thereby alleviating the estimation problem. On the other hand, inexperienced customers may adversely affect the efficiency of service delivery.[12]

   Second, service output may depend on the number of customers served. For example, the output of an airline may be measured by the number of passenger-miles. The number of passenger-miles on a particular flight, however, depends on the number of passengers on board. Similarly, if an orchestra plays to an empty concert hall, no output is produced because there are no consumers to hear it.

   Finally, demand in many services is not uniform and is difficult to predict, but the service organization must maintain its facilities and personnel must be available. For example, retail stores must remain open even if the demand is very low during certain hours of the day and tolerate its salespeople to be idle during those hours. Thus, the availability of the facility and personnel during those nonproductive periods must somehow be included in the store's output because they exist for customers' convenience. Ignoring the necessity of the idle time or excess capacity, may lead to wrong conclusions or decisions. Can you

---

[12] D. I. Riddle, *Service-Led Growth: The Role of the Service Sector in World Development* (New York, Praeger Publishers, 1986), p. 81.

imagine what would happen to a fire department's budget and personnel if its productivity is measured by the number of fires extinguished per firefighter?

4. *Quality differences.* Intangibility and nonstandard nature of service output makes the measurement of quality difficult. For example, legal services provided by lawyers are usually measured in number of hours a lawyer spends on a particular case. However, the outcome of this service, winning the case, depends on the knowledge and skills of the lawyer rather than the number of hours spent on the case. Also, the quality of some services is difficult to judge by consumers, because they do not have the specialized knowledge, as is usually the case in health care and legal services. This, together with the fact that many services require payment before delivery, may lead to an overestimation of service productivity because poor quality service becomes part of total output. Finally, quality of the output in some services may depend on the customer and her behavior. For example, a student who is not well prepared and not motivated to do the necessary work will learn very little in a course even if the teacher is competent.

Slow Rate of Service Productivity Growth

Services are known for their resistance to productivity improvement efforts. As discussed earlier in this chapter, increased share of services in gross national product (GNP) has been identified as one of the reasons for the slowdown in productivity growth. However, this generalization can be misleading; not all services are stagnant in productivity growth. Professor William J. Baumol points out that services are too heterogeneous to lend themselves to such generalizations and suggests three categories of services with respect to their amenability to productivity growth: (1) the stagnant personal services, (2) the progressive impersonal services, and (3) asymptotically stagnant impersonal services.[13]

The Stagnant Personal Services In this category are the services that are by their very nature most resistant to productivity improvement efforts. An extreme example would be the performance of a Mozart quartet, which today requires the same number of musicians and time as it did about 200 years ago. No productivity improvement effort can change those input requirements without a significant decrease in quality. Other, less extreme examples also exist. Some of the stagnant services are nonstandard and cannot be provided in mass quantities. For example, services provided by a lawyer or a physician fall in this category. Each case handled by a lawyer is different, as is each patient seen by a doctor. Usually, an increase in output or reduction in input cannot be obtained unless quality is sacrificed. The quality of most services in this category is often judged by how much time the service provider spends with the client or patient.

The Progressive Impersonal Services These are the services at the other extreme of the spectrum. They do not necessarily require the customer's involvement. It may be possible to substitute capital for labor in these services, and hence some of them can be automated. Telecommunications is an example for this category of services. Until about 50 years ago, most telephone connections were made with the aid of switchboard operators. Today, telephone calls are connected by automatic switchboards. Unless a customer requires an operator's assistance, no contact with the personnel of the telephone company is needed in making the call. The productivity in-

---

[13] The discussion in this section has been adapted from William J. Baumol, "Productivity Policy and the Service Sector," in Inman, R. P. (ed.), *Managing the Service Economy: Prospect and Problems* (New York, Cambridge University Press, 1985), pp. 301–317.

crease in this service sector is phenomenal. While the technology started with open wire transmission of calls, it moved to microwave, coaxial cable, and satellite transmission, and the costs declined steadily over the years.

Asymptotically Stagnant Impersonal Services   This category includes services whose characteristic is a mixture of the first two categories. The most important aspect of a service in this category is that it exhibits an extraordinary growth in productivity and decrease in cost during the early stages of its life cycle. The productivity growth of such a service is self-extinguishing; the greater its initial productivity growth, the more quickly it can be expected to come to an end. Computational and data processing services constitute a good example for this category. These services require two major inputs: computer hardware and software. The first component is a product of a progressive sector of the economy. As is well known, the cost of computer hardware has been declining continuously for decades mainly due to technological development and productivity growth in this industry. The other component, computer software, is a product of a stagnant sector, in which costs have been steadily increasing.

Another example is the production of television programs, such as sitcoms and soap operas. The production of these programs consists of two main components: First is the creation of the program, which involves writing, casting, rehearsals, actual performance, and taping. The second is the broadcasting of the program. The first component is the stagnant component; productivity improvements are hard to achieve in making these programs. The second component is technology driven and significant productivity and quality improvements have been achieved over many years through research and development in broadcasting technology.

Probably the most interesting aspect of these services is what happens to the costs of the two components through time. Usually, the progressive part is the expensive component at the outset. While it becomes less and less expensive because of fast productivity growth, the stagnant component experiences very little or no improvement in productivity, but becomes more and more expensive. There are two reasons for this. One is inflation, which affects most goods and services. The second is the fact that while the input quantities of the progressive component decrease due to productivity growth, the input quantities of the stagnant part do not change or decrease less; hence, the stagnant part becomes relatively more expensive. Because of this, stagnant services will become relatively more expensive even if there is no inflation.

Another interesting fact is that the productivity improvements in the progressive component may quickly become less significant in the overall cost picture. This is because of the shrinking share of the progressive component in the total cost. Eventually, the stagnant component becomes dominant and the service takes on the characteristics of that category.

Raising Productivity in Services

It is clear that not all services are resistant to efforts for improving productivity; only stagnant personal services and asymptotically stagnant services that later become stagnant provide the greatest challenges to managers. However, even those services may benefit from the outcomes of technological progress, such as computers and advanced telecommunications systems. In this section, general approaches to raising the productivity of services are discussed.

As discussed earlier in this chapter, increasing productivity depends to a large extent on managerial decisions and actions. Better organization of work, efficient work methods, better relationships between the management and employees, training, teamwork, and empowerment are only a few steps management can take to raise productivity in manufacturing as well as service organizations. A recent *Harvard Business Review* article emphasized this point by placing the blame for slow growth of service sector productivity on the ineffectiveness of many American managers and the inherent complexity of the service sector. Van Biema and Greenwald, the authors of the article, indicate that the first compelling piece of evidence for this assertion is that external competitive pressures on manufacturing managers led to significant improvements in productivity and quality.[14] The second major piece of evidence is the existence of wide and persistent differences in performance between the successful service companies and their competitors. Third, they observe that productivity growth at many companies fluctuates widely in both duration and magnitude. This much fluctuation in the short run, they argue, cannot be explained by the usually cited factors of capital, labor, and technology, but must be due to management's attention and inattention to productivity at various times. Finally, "the success of most leveraged buyout firms . . . stems from their ability to concentrate management's attention on the efficiency of basic business operations."

Then what should managers do to raise the productivity of service work? Drucker takes a macro approach to raising productivity and offers some suggestions that would help managers improve productivity in most services.[15] He observes that an important difference between services and manufacturing is that capital and labor-saving technology can be substituted for labor in manufacturing, because capital and labor are "factors of production," and they can be substitutes for each other. However, in service and knowledge work, they are "tools" of production and they may or may not be substituted for labor. How skillfully the tools are used determines if they help increase productivity in services. Therefore, we cannot depend on capital and technology investments alone to raise the productivity of service work. Instead, we must learn to "work smarter," which means working more productively without working harder or longer. Drucker recommends the following for working smarter: (1) Define the task; (2) concentrate work on the task; (3) define performance; (4) form a partnership with employees; and (5) make continuous learning part of the organization's culture.

1. *Define the task.* The first thing we must do is to question why we do what we do. In other words, ask "What is the task? What are we trying to accomplish? Why do it at all?" Frequently, we may find that the task in question can be simplified, or combined with other tasks or completely eliminated with no negative impact on the outcome, that is, customer satisfaction. Investigating these questions, one may find that the task was established for a reason in the past, but the reason had disappeared or conditions had changed long ago but managers forgot to eliminate the task.

2. *Concentrate work on the task.* Employees in many services are usually required to perform many different tasks, some of which are not essential to their main function. A common complaint heard from nurses provides a good example. Many hospitals require nurses to perform clerical duties such as completing paperwork for Medicare, Medicaid, insurers, the billing office, and for the prevention of malpractice suits. These duties are unproductive work for nurses and take considerable time and keep them from doing what they are supposed to be doing, that is, patient care. A clerk can be hired for completing paperwork and the

[14] M. van Biema and B. Greenwald, "Managing Our Way to Higher Service-Sector Productivity," *Harvard Business Review* (July–August 1997), pp. 87–95.

[15] Drucker, "The New Productivity Challenge," pp. 69–79.

nurses can concentrate on patient care. Such a simple step should improve nurses' productivity. This is a common problem for many service providers. To avoid this problem, we must ask "What do we pay for? What value is this job supposed to add?"

3. *Define performance.* Sometimes services are treated as if they are a homogeneous group. Services range from R&D, creating new knowledge and inventing new products, to flipping burgers at a fast-food restaurant. Clearly, they include a huge variety of tasks and require skills, knowledge, and training that vary widely from one job to another. Performance criteria are different in each service and we cannot expect all services to respond positively to the same productivity improvement effort. In some services, such as R&D, performance depends on the quality of the output rather than the quantity. For example, a research lab that produces a breakthrough product in a year is more valuable for an organization than a lab that produced several "me too" products. In other words, this category includes "stagnant" services. It is not clear if there is a common process that consistently creates quality results in the services of this category. Therefore, we must look into each specific area to determine "what works."

   Quantity may be the desired output in some other services. For example, the number of offices cleaned per hour may be the appropriate measure for a team of custodial service employees. These services closely resemble manufacturing tasks and therefore may benefit most from methods used for improving manufacturing productivity. Most of the services in this group can be characterized as "progressive," and capital investments may lead to significant productivity increases in these services.

   A third category consists of services for which both the quality and the quantity define performance. Most service work fall into this category and most can be characterized as "asymptotically stagnant." A bank teller's performance may be measured by the number of transactions he completes during his shift as well as the quality of his work as measured by customer satisfaction surveys. The number of transactions can be increased by investing in computers and automated systems. Customer satisfaction, on the other hand, may depend entirely on the attitude of the teller and how much time he spends with a customer.

   In these services, we must try to determine "what works" as well as apply traditional operations management and industrial engineering methods to aspects that resemble manufacturing tasks to boost productivity.

4. *Form a partnership with employees.* The days when managers did the thinking and workers implemented their commands are long gone. Before Frederick Taylor developed his scientific management, and even long after, the average worker had very little education or training; hence, managers told them what to do and closely controlled them. Today's employees, especially in industrialized countries, are much better educated and well informed through mass media. Many organizations and managers are discovering that they can be an invaluable source of good suggestions for improving quality and increasing productivity. Teamwork, employee participation, and empowerment discussed earlier in this book are all aimed at making good use of this valuable source as well as making employees happy and satisfied. The goal must be to make quality, customer satisfaction, and productivity both employees' and management's responsibility. The experience of most of the successful American manufacturers in the 1980s and 1990s indicates that employee–management partnership is the *best* way to achieve these goals. Drucker emphasizes that for knowledge and service work, it is the *only* way.

5. *Make continuous learning part of organization's culture.* Rapid pace of technological development, fast new product introductions, shortening of product life cycles, and increasing sophistication of new goods and services make continuous learning a necessity for survival for both managers and employees. Learning should include education and training, both are necessary for breakthrough as well as small continuous improvements in productivity. By their very nature, some service jobs are knowledge jobs; hence, a culture of continuous learning may come naturally to those organizations, but for others it must be developed strategically.

13.7   DATA ENVELOPMENT ANALYSIS FOR MEASUREMENT OF SERVICE EFFICIENCY

A service organization that achieves high levels of customer satisfaction is an effective organization. An efficient organization is the one that produces its output with minimum expenditure of resources. Effectiveness and efficiency must go hand-in-hand. Effectiveness without efficiency in a profit-seeking organization would eventually lead to bankruptcy, or to lower-than-normal profits, if the organization is not able to charge enough for its services to cover its costs. Conversely, efficiency without effectiveness will lead to loss of customers, and eventually the organization will go out of business. Naturally, public service organizations and some not-for-profit services are subject to different rules. Nevertheless, we can assume that efficiency and effectiveness of operations are dual goals shared by management of all service organizations.

A Brief Background on Data Envelopment Analysis

Measuring efficiency and productivity, or any aspect of performance, is an indispensable part of any productivity improvement effort, because, as the well-known adage goes, "what gets measured gets managed." As mentioned earlier, productivity and efficiency are related but different concepts. Productivity can be measured as a ratio of output to input, and a typical service organization may construct a large variety of partial and/or total productivity ratios. Tracking these ratios through time will help an organization determine its productivity improvements. However, when the purpose is to compare similar units of a service organization, such as branches of a large bank, ratios may not provide the needed information.

Sometimes, executives would like to know not only how units within their organization are performing in an absolute sense, but also relative to each other. Also, some managers would like to compare their organizations to others in the same service industry. In such cases, the use of productivity ratios may not be possible since not all organizations compute the same ratios or may be willing to share the data with others. Comparison of similar units within the same organization or comparison of similar service organizations can be accomplished through the measurement of their relative efficiencies. Data envelopment analysis (DEA) is a linear programming–based management science technique that has been developed for such purposes. This section presents a brief background on DEA as a powerful technique for measuring the relative technical efficiency of service organizations as well as a technique that may help managers identify the sources and amounts of inefficiencies in their organizations and orient them toward improvements in performance.

DEA was developed by Charnes, Cooper, and Rhodes as a response to a need to evaluate the efficiency of not-for-profit organizations where some inputs and outputs cannot be measured in monetary units, and therefore usually no "bottom line" is available for performance measurement.[16] The first application of DEA was in education,[17] but others quickly followed in both the public and private sectors.

Various efficiency concepts exist in economics such as technical efficiency, scale efficiency, and allocative efficiency. **Technical inefficiency** exists for an organization if any of its inputs or any of its outputs can be improved without worsening any other input or output. **Scale efficiency** is related to the scale of productive facilities. If the average output (i.e., output per unit input) increases as a firm increases its input quantity, the firm enjoys increasing returns to scale; however, if the average output decreases, the firm exhibits decreasing returns to scale. If the average output per unit input remains the same with increasing input, constant returns to scale exist. **Allocative efficiency** is concerned with the right mix of inputs for producing the outputs of an economic entity at minimum cost and therefore requires price data.

These entities, such as bank branches, hospitals, and school districts, responsible for converting inputs into outputs, are referred to as decision-making units (DMUs) in the DEA literature. The management of a DMU has inputs at its disposal and is responsible for deciding how to use them for producing the desired outputs. Various DEA models exist to measure each type of efficiency as well as the overall efficiency. Efficient DMUs define an empirical efficiency frontier. In some DEA models, this frontier is piecewise linear and the segments between points representing the efficient DMUs indicate alternative input–output combinations for efficient operations. Each DEA model determines a different efficiency frontier from the data of DMUs included in the analysis. Decision-making units that are not on the frontier are inefficient and those that are on the frontier may be efficient under certain conditions.

DEA is an empirical method. It uses actual data from the performance of DMUs; there is no need to convert data to a common unit (e.g., dollars) as is commonly done in productivity ratios. All inputs and outputs can be expressed in their natural units. For example, a recent study concerning the efficiency of MBA programs included Graduate Management Admission Test (GMAT) scores, tuition in dollars, percentage of students with work experience, and the number of faculty publications as input measures, and starting salaries of graduates, percentage of students who had a job by graduation, and an index of program quality as output measures.[18]

We consider a simple one-output and one-input example to introduce some of the basic ideas relevant to DEA. In this example, there are five DMUs that use different quantities of the same input to produce different quantities of the same output. (See Exhibit 13-2.) The solid line in the exhibit is the efficient frontier, which is defined by DMUs 1, 2, 4, and 5. DMUs in the exhibit are represented as points D1 through D5.

All DMUs in the data set are efficient except DMUs 3 and 5. As can be seen in the graph, DMU 5 produces the same quantity of output as DMU 4 but uses a larger quantity of input; therefore, it is not fully efficient. Hence, it is clear that being on the efficient frontier is necessary but not sufficient for being efficient. When an appropriate DEA model is solved for DMU 5, it will have a nonzero input "slack." Also, it can be seen from the graph that DMU 3 is not efficient because it is not on the efficiency frontier.

In a simple example like this, a productivity ratio may be computed by dividing output by the input quantity. However, as noted earlier, a simple ratio may be mis-

---

[16] A. Charnes, W. W. Cooper, and E. Rhodes, "Measuring the Efficiency of Decision Making Units," *European Journal of Operational Research*, vol. 2, no. 6 (1978), pp. 429–444.

[17] A. Charnes, W. W. Cooper, and E. Rhodes, "Evaluating Program and Managerial Efficiency: An Application of Data Envelopment Analysis to Program Follow Through," *Management Science*, vol. 27 (1981), pp. 668–697.

[18] C. Haksever and Y. Muragishi, "Measuring Value in MBA Programmes," *Education Economics*, vol. 6, no. 1 (1998), pp. 11–25.

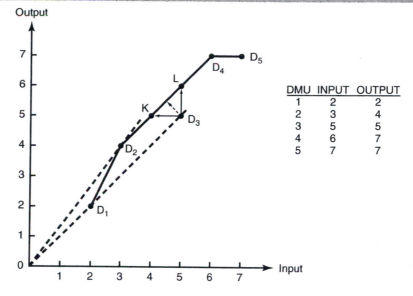

EXHIBIT 13-2   Efficiency Frontier and Evaluation in a One-Output and One-Input Example

DMU	INPUT	OUTPUT
1	2	2
2	3	4
3	5	5
4	6	7
5	7	7

leading. Notice that DMUs 1, 3, and 5 all have the same output to input ratio (i.e., productivity), but only DMU 1 is efficient. Inefficiency exhibited by DMU 3 can be eliminated if it can reduce its usage of input from five to four units without decreasing its output, and hence move to point K on the efficiency frontier, or increase its output from five to six units without increasing its input, and hence move to point L. Alternatively, DMU 3 can become efficient if it can move to any point on the frontier between K and L. Any of these moves would make DMU 3 technically efficient.

Scale efficiency can also be observed from the graph. Consider the slope of the dashed line from the origin to D1. Movement from D1 to D2 increases the slope and indicates a faster growth in average output for each additional unit of input, hence implies increasing returns to scale. Maximum returns to scale is reached at point D2 (i.e., by DMU 2). From D2 to D4, the slope of the ray decreases indicating a slower growth in average output for each additional unit of input, or decreasing returns to scale. It must be noted that returns-to-scale characterizations refer only to movement on the efficient frontier. The concept of returns-to-scale is ambiguous when applied to DMU 3, which also exhibits technical inefficiencies.[19] If DMU 3 can improve its efficiency and move to point K or point L on the efficiency frontier, or any point in between, it can become technically efficient; however, it will not be scale efficient as DMU 2.

The CCR Ratio Model of DEA

DEA is an extension and generalization of M. J. Farrell's work on measuring the efficiency of economic entities, or DMUs.[20] Farrell's work was focused on developing a summary efficiency measure from empirical data but was limited to a single-output

---

[19] R. Banker, A. Charnes, W. W. Cooper, J. Swarts, and D. A. Thomas, "An Introduction to Data Envelopment Analysis with Some of Its Models and Their Uses," *Research in Governmental and Nonprofit Accounting*, vol. 5 (1989), pp. 125–163.

[20] M. J. Farrell, "The Measurement of Productive Efficiency," *Journal of the Royal Statistical Society, Series A, Part III*, vol. 120, no. 3 (1957), pp. 253–290.

case. Charnes, Cooper, and Rhodes made the extension to multiple inputs and multiple outputs and developed the mathematical programming method to determine efficiency. The original DEA model, named the CCR ratio model after its originators, in its revised form is given below.[21] The purpose of the model is to determine weights u_r and v_i so that the DMU that is being evaluated is given the maximum possible efficiency rating, on the condition that the same weights apply to all DMUs and no DMU can have an efficiency rating greater than one.[22]

$$\text{Max } h_o = \frac{\sum_{r=1}^{s} u_r y_{ro}}{\sum_{i=1}^{m} v_i x_{i0}} \tag{13.1}$$

Subject to:

$$\frac{\sum_{r=1}^{s} u_r y_{rj}}{\sum_{i=1}^{m} v_i x_{ij}} \le 1 \qquad j = 1,...,n$$

$$\left(u_r \Big/ \sum_{i=1}^{m} v_i x_{i0} \right) \le \varepsilon \qquad r = 1,...,s$$

$$\left(v_i \Big/ \sum_{i=1}^{m} v_i x_{i0} \right) \le \varepsilon \qquad i = 1,...,m$$

where we assume that there are n DMUs in the data set, and each DMU uses various quantities of m different inputs to produce various quantities of s different outputs; y_{rj} is the rth observed output of the jth DMU, and x_{ij} is the ith observed input of the jth DMU; u_r and v_i are the weights associated with the rth output and ith input, respectively, and they are to be determined as the solution to the mathematical model. In other words, u_r and v_i are the variables in this model. The constant ε in the last two sets of constraints is an extremely small number, which assures that all observed inputs and outputs will have positive weights assigned to them. The subscript o refers to the DMU whose efficiency is being measured. The objective function represents the efficiency of DMU$_o$ and is also a part of the constraint set.

The CCR ratio model extends the engineering, or scientific, concept of efficiency to economics. This is done by generating a single "virtual" output in the numerator and a single "virtual" input in the denominator of the objective function. Also, the constraint set of the model ensures that the selection of weights does not violate the engineering principle of efficiency: that no unit can have an efficiency of more than 1.0. Because the model aims at finding u_r and v_is so that the maximum efficiency rating is assigned to DMU$_o$, DMU$_o$ is portrayed in the best possible light. The process can be repeated for any DMU in the data set. For actual computations the following transformed linear programming (LP) version may be used[23]:

---

[21] See Charnes, Cooper, and Rhodes, "Measuring the Efficiency of Decision Making Units," and A. Charnes, Z. M. Huang, J. Semple, T. Song, and D. Thomas, "Origins and Research in Data Envelopment Analysis," *The Arabian Journal for Science and Engineering*, vol. 19 (1990), pp. 617–625.

[22] It must be noted that optimization as used in DEA is not for planning purposes (e.g., production planning for optimizing profit). Optimization in DEA models is employed to assess the past performance of DMUs based on their observed inputs and outputs.

[23] See Charnes, Cooper, and Rhodes, "Measuring the Efficiency of Decision Making Units," for the details of the transformation.

$$\text{Min } h_0 = \theta_0 - \varepsilon \left(\sum_{i=1}^{m} s_i^- + \sum_{r=1}^{s} s_r^+ \right) \qquad (13.2.1)$$

Subject to:

$$\theta_0 x_{i0} - \sum_{j=1}^{n} x_{ij}\lambda_j - s_i^- = 0 \qquad i = 1,...,m \qquad (13.2.2)$$

$$\sum_{j=1}^{n} y_{rj}\lambda_j - s_r^+ = y_{r0} \qquad r = 1,2,...,s \qquad (13.2.3)$$

$$\lambda_j, s_i^-, s_r^+ \geq 0 \qquad j = 1,2,...,n \qquad (13.2.4)$$

where λ_js represent transformed variables u_r and v_is for each DMU j; s_i^-s are the slack variables for input constraints and s_r^+s are the slack variables for output constraints. DMU_o is efficient if both of the following conditions are satisfied:

1. $\theta^*_0 = 1.0$, and
2. all slacks (i.e., s_i^- and s_r^+) are zero

where * indicates an optimal value and θ^*_0 represents the relative technical efficiency of DMU_0 ($0 \leq \theta_0 \leq 1.0$). However, note that $\theta^*_0 = 1.0$ does not necessarily mean full efficiency. For a DMU to be fully efficient, both of the above conditions must be satisfied. If $\theta_0^* < 1.0$, DMU_0 is inefficient, and $\theta_0^* x_{i0} \leq \Sigma x_{ij}\lambda_j$ indicates that it is possible to form a combination of other DMUs which uses less input than DMU_0 (i.e., $\theta_0^* x_{i0} < x_{i0}$) to produce the same output; this implies excess in one or more inputs used by DMU_0. If any input slack s_i^{-*} is not zero, it implies that input i can be further reduced by an amount equal to s_i^{-*} without changing the amount of any other input or output. To determine the quantities of inputs and outputs that would make DMU_0 efficient, the following CCR projection formulas can be used: $x^*_{i0} = \theta_0^* x_{i0} - s_i^{-*}; i = 1,. . .,m$, and $y^*_{r0} = y_{r0} + s_r^{+*}; r = 1,. . .,s$, where x^*_{i0} and y^*_{r0} are the projected inputs (x_{i0}) and outputs (y_{r0}), respectively. Such projection places DMU_0 on the efficient frontier.

Example: First Bank of Gotham City has six branches around the city. Executives of the bank would like to evaluate the efficiency of these branches.[24] The purpose of the evaluation is to reward the managers and employees of the efficient branches and guide inefficient branches to efficiency. Branch managers have agreed that the number of transactions performed per month, such as checks cashed or deposited, cash withdrawals and deposits, accounts opened, accounts closed, and so forth, constitutes a reasonable representation of the output of a branch. They also agreed that the rent paid by each branch and the number of teller hours are two of the most important inputs. The rent has been selected as an input measure because it is proportional to the area of office space occupied and accurately represents the branch size and the magnitude of all resources used. Since tellers perform most of the work related to transactions it was felt that it represented the labor input into the operations of a branch.

Data from the operations of the last year have been collected as shown in Exhibit 13-3(a). Output represents the number of transactions, in thousands, performed at each branch last year. Annual rent is in thousands of dollars and number of teller hours is the sum of full time and part time teller hours, also in thousands. To help us represent the efficiency frontier graphically, we next divide the rent and the number of teller hours for each branch by the number of transactions performed.[25] This will enable us

---

[24] For large scale applications of DEA in banking see the following two sources: C. Parkan, "Measuring the Efficiency of Service Operations: An Application to Bank Branches," *Engineering Costs and Production Economics*, vol. 12 (1984), pp. 237–242; and M. Oral and R. Yolalan, "An Empirical Study on Measuring Operating Efficiency and Profitability of Bank Branches," *European Journal of Operational Research*, vol. 46 (1990), pp. 282–294.

[25] The DEA model we use in this example is units invariant. That is , if we divide, or multiply, data by a positive constant, efficiency evaluations are not affected as long as the same is done to all data of the same kind.

EXHIBIT 13-3 Annual Output and Input Quantities of the Six Branches of the First Bank of Gotham City

(a) Original data:

	Output	Inputs	
Branch (DMU)	**Number of Transactions (thousands)**	**Rent ($1000)**	**Number of Teller Hours (thousands)**
1	30	6	1.5
2	40	8	1.6
3	70	28	2.1
4	50	20	1.0
5	60	36	1.2
6	40	24	0.4

(b) Transformed data:

Branch (DMU)	**y Transactions**	**x_1 Rent (per unit output)**	**x_2 Teller Hours (per unit output)**
1	1	0.2	0.05
2	1	0.2	0.04
3	1	0.4	0.03
4	1	0.4	0.02
5	1	0.6	0.02
6	1	0.6	0.01

to express quantities of each input per unit output (transaction) and make a two-dimensional graph possible for representing the efficiencies of bank branches. The results are shown in Exhibit 13-3(b).

Exhibit 13-4 shows all six branches and the efficiency frontier. Note that each point in the graph represents a DMU using different combinations of transformed rent dollars and teller hours to produce one transaction. Branches 1, 2, 4, and 6 are on the efficiency frontier, however, only 2, 4, and 6 are efficient. Branches 1, 3, and 5 are inefficient.

We need to set up and solve a linear programming (LP) model for each branch to determine its efficiency. However, note that only a few coefficients will be different in each LP problem. Let's set up the model for DMU 3 for illustration:

$$\text{Min } h_0 = \theta_0 - \varepsilon s_1^- - \varepsilon s_2^- - \varepsilon s_3^+$$

Subject to:

$$0.4\theta_0 - 0.2\lambda_1 - 0.2\lambda_2 - 0.4\lambda_3 - 0.4\lambda_4 - 0.6\lambda_5 - 0.6\lambda_6 - s_1^- = 0$$
$$0.03\theta_0 - 0.05\lambda_1 - 0.04\lambda_2 - 0.03\lambda_3 - 0.02\lambda_4 - 0.02\lambda_5 - 0.01\lambda_6 - s_2^- = 0$$
$$\lambda_1 + \lambda_2 + \lambda_3 + \lambda_4 + \lambda_5 + \lambda_6 - s_3^+ = 1$$
$$s_1^-, s_2^-, s_3^+, \lambda_j \geq 0 \qquad j = 1, 2, ..., 6$$

The first two constraints of the above problem correspond to the constraint set (13.2.2) of the LP model. The coefficients of these constraints are x_{ij}s that are given in Exhibit 13.3(b), and the coefficients of θ_0 are the x_{ij}s of DMU 3. The third constraint corresponds to the constraint set (13.2.3) of the LP model; because DMUs generate a single output (transactions), there is only one constraint of this type. The coefficients of the third constraint (y_{rj}) are all ones as shown in Exhibit 13.3(b). The right-hand-side value of the constraint is the output quantity of DMU 3. This prob-

EXHIBIT 13-4   Efficiency Frontier and Evaluation of the Branches of First Bank of Gotham City

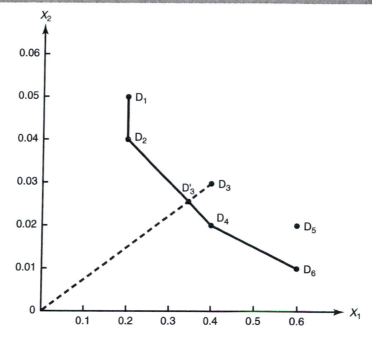

lem can be solved on any commercially available LP software to obtain the following optimal solution[26]:

$$\theta_0^* = 0.857143 \cong 0.86, \quad \lambda_2^* = 0.2857, \quad \lambda_4^* = 0.7143,$$

and all other variables equal to zero. As expected, Branch 3 is not fully efficient, but only 86 percent efficient. The optimal solution also indicates that Branches 2 and 4 form a peer group for Branch 3, because its mix of two inputs is closest to these two branches. In other words, input quantities used and the output quantities produced by Branches 2 and 4 serve as benchmarks for Branch 3 for its style of production. Consequently, Branch 3 can emulate them to become fully efficient. One way Branch 3 can become efficient is indicated by the projection formulas given earlier. Specifically, Branch 3 can become efficient if it reduces its inputs (per unit output) to the following quantities, without reducing its output:

$$x_1^* = \theta_0^* x_1 - s_1^{-*} = 0.857143\,(0.4) - 0 = 0.3428572 \cong \$0.34 \text{ per transaction}$$

or 70,000(0.3428572) = \$24,000 annual rent.

$$x_2^* = \theta_0^* x_2 - s_2^{-*} = 0.857143(0.03) - 0 = 0.02571429 \cong 0.026 \text{ hr per transaction}$$

or 70,000(0.02571429) = 1,800 hours per year.

Note that (0.34 and 0.026) are the coordinates of D'_3 in Exhibit 13-4. In other words, D'_3 represents the projection of the inefficient Branch 3 to the efficiency frontier.

---

[26] An explicit value of 10^{-6} has been used for epsilon (ε) in solving this model. This constant must be "small enough" for accurate results. However, what is "small enough" depends on the problem data. In general, the use of any explicit value in large problems carries the risk of giving inaccurate results and is not recommended. For a discussion of alternative approaches, see I. A. Ali, "Data Envelopment Analysis: Computational Issues," *Computers, Environment, and Urban Systems,* vol. 14 (1990), pp. 157–165; and I. A. Ali and L. M. Seiford, "Computational Accuracy and Infinitesimals in Data Envelopment Analysis," *INFOR,* vol. 31, no. 4 (1993), pp. 290–297.

Since the output slack is zero, the projection formula for output $y^*_{r0} = y_{r0} + s_r^{+*}$ would give us $y^*_{r0} = y_{r0}$, the same output value for DMU 3 to become efficient. Also note that the efficiency of Branch 3 can be calculated as the ratio of the distance between the origin and D'_3 on the frontier, to the distance between the origin and D_3.

$$\theta_0^* = OD'_3 / OD_3$$

The same results can be obtained if a linear combination of inputs of the branches in the peer group is formed. Specifically, if Branch 3 combines 0.2857 of the input quantities of Branch 2 and 0.7143 of the input quantities of Branch 4 as its new input quantities:

$$x^*_{13} = x_{12}\lambda^*_2 + x_{14}\lambda^*_4 = 0.2(0.2857) + 0.4(0.7143) = 0.05714 + 0.28572 = 0.34286;$$

$$x^*_{23} = x_{22}\lambda^*_2 + x_{24}\lambda^*_4 = 0.04(0.2857) + 0.02(0.7143) = 0.011428 + 0.014246 = 0.025714$$

In other words, D'_3 is a convex combination of points D_2 and D_4, which represent Branches 2 and 4.

Similar LP models can be set up and solved to determine the efficiencies of other Branches. The results are given in Exhibit 13-5. As can be seen from the exhibit, Branch 1 is not efficient. Although it has an efficiency rating of 1.0, not all slacks are zero; hence, Branch 1 does not meet all the conditions for efficiency. The slack value of 1.0 indicates that Branch 1 should reduce its usage of Input 2 (rent) by one unit to become efficient.

Lambdas with positive values in the optimal solution indicate the DMUs that comprise the peer group for each inefficient DMU. If a DMU is efficient, it serves as its own peer. Identification of a peer group is very useful in providing guidance to inefficient DMUs, because DMUs in the peer group are most like the branch being evaluated and can serve as role models for that branch.

A Review of DEA and Alternative Methods for the Measurement of Service Efficiency

DEA is not the only technique for measuring the efficiency of economic entities. As mentioned earlier, many organizations use ratios for productivity and efficiency measurement. Ratio analysis may be useful for determining if a DMU's performance deviates too much from a norm, such as an industry norm. However, when multiple outputs and multiple inputs are involved, a simple ratio of one output to one input would not be very helpful for comparative purposes. A common problem arises when a DMU may score high on some ratios and low on others. Unless some a priori weights

EXHIBIT 13-5   Efficiencies of the Branches of First Bank of Gotham City

Branch (DMU)	Variables in the Optimal Solution	θ^*	Efficient?	Peer Group If Not Fully Efficient
1	$\lambda^*_2 = 1.00$	1.00	No	Branch 2
	$s_2^{-*} = 1.00$			
2	$\lambda^*_2 = 1.00$	1.00	Yes	
3	$\lambda^*_2 = 0.2857$		No	Branch 2
	$\lambda^*_4 = 0.7143$	0.86		Branch 4
4	$\lambda^*_4 = 1.00$	1.00	Yes	
5	$\lambda^*_4 = 0.60$	0.80	No	Branch 4
	$\lambda^*_6 = 0.60$			Branch 6
6	$\lambda^*_6 = 1.00$	1.00	Yes	

are assigned to various ratios, comparison would not be possible. Selection of weights, on the other hand, is usually a troublesome task because there is usually no objective way for assignment of the weights. In other words, experts, or managers may disagree on relative weights. Another possible approach to handle multiple outputs and inputs is to aggregate various ratios into a single ratio. This approach also requires weights to reflect the relative importance of different ratios, and hence runs into the same problem.

Another common method is the regression analysis. The regression analysis can accommodate multiple outputs and inputs. However, it also has some drawbacks. First of all the least squares method used in regression finds the average relationship between an output and inputs based on data that come from both efficient and inefficient DMUs. For example, the straight line found in a simple linear regression passes through the point $\bar{X}$ and $\bar{Y}$, average values for the independent variable (e.g., input) and dependent variable (e.g., output), respectively. The average relationship is not likely to be an efficient relationship. Another shortcoming of regression is that it does not reveal much about the scale efficiency.[27]

Data envelopment analysis is an attractive alternative to ratio and regression analyses; it not only does not have the shortcomings of those two techniques, but it has additional advantages. We can summarize the advantages of DEA as follows[28]:

1. DEA accommodates multiple outputs and multiple inputs; each input or output quantity can be expressed in its natural units.
2. DEA provides a single comprehensive, defensible measure of performance.
3. If a DMU is less than fully efficient, it provides valuable information on how it can become efficient. It indicates which outputs must be increased and/or which inputs must be decreased, and by how much, for an inefficient DMU to become efficient.
4. DEA determines efficiency in a fair and equitable way. The weights in the ratio model (13.1) are determined by maximizing the objective function which is the efficiency of the DMU being evaluated. In other words, each DMU is given the highest efficiency rating possible.
5. For each inefficient DMU, DEA also provides a peer group (or best-practice group) consisting of efficient DMUs for reference purposes. In other words, DEA performs a benchmarking study at the same time as it measures efficiency. A decision maker, then, would refer only to this relatively small group of fully efficient DMUs to determine important characteristics of efficient units.
6. DEA does not assume any specific functional form of production relationship such as Cobb–Douglas production function.
7. DEA assumes all outputs and inputs have "some" value, but does not require a priori selection of weights or prices for inputs or value for outputs.
8. DEA can include external factors, such as weather, or demographic factors, in the measurement of efficiency.
9. DEA can accommodate judgment and expert opinion when needed.

---

[27] See H. D. Sherman, "Hospital Efficiency Measurement and Evaluation: Empirical Test of a New Technique," *Medical Care*, vol. 22, no. 10 (October 1984), pp. 922–938, for a discussion of the use of ratio and regression techniques in measuring the efficiency of hospitals.

[28] A. Charnes, W. W. Cooper, A. Y. Lewin, and L. M. Seiford (eds.), *Data Envelopment Analysis: Theory, Methodology, and Applications* (Boston, Kluwer Academic Publishers, 1994), pp. 7–10; and M. K. Epstein and J. C. Henderson, "Data Envelopment Analysis for Managerial Control and Diagnosis," *Decision Sciences*, vol. 20 (1989), pp. 90–119.

10. Unlike regression analysis, it focuses on individual DMUs, and it does not assume that there is only one best way for productive efficiency. It allows the possibility of being efficient with different mixes of inputs and outputs.

Like any other quantitative tool, DEA has its limitations. An important issue is the selection of output and input measures to be used in the analysis. The decision as to which input and output measures should be included in a DEA model is an important decision for at least two reasons.[29] First, efficiency ratings will not decrease when a new input or output measure is added to a DEA model; efficiency of some DMUs will remain the same while others' ratings may increase. Therefore, too many measures may diminish the discriminatory power of a model. A rule of thumb to avoid this problem is to make sure that the number of DMUs is equal to or greater than three times the sum of the number of inputs and outputs. The second reason the selection of input and output measures is important is that it is not possible to judge from results if a measure is a theoretically correct measure to use. In other words, as in regression analysis, spurious relationships may be obtained.

As one of the advantages, we mentioned that DEA allows DMUs to be efficient with different mixes of inputs and outputs. This may become a disadvantage when an unimportant input or output is included among the measures. A DMU may excel in minimizing the use of such an input or succeed in producing large quantities of that type of output and be declared as efficient. This may not agree with the objectives of the organization and may lead to behavior that takes the organization farther away from its targets.

Another potential problem is related to the same characteristic. As we indicated earlier, DEA model selects the weights for outputs and inputs so that the efficiency rating for each DMU is maximized. This may result in weights that are not congruent with the value system of the organization. However, this problem can be solved with proper limits on the weights.[30]

DEA measure of efficiency is not very robust with respect to errors in data. In other words, the accuracy of data in DEA is critical; errors in data may lead to identification of inefficient DMUs as efficient and efficient ones as inefficient, which may compromise the perceived fairness of the measure.[31]

Other DEA Models

Various DEA models have been developed since the inception of the CCR model. All DEA models aim to construct an empirical efficiency frontier that represents best practices among DMUs included in the data set. Each model tries to identify the DMUs that define this frontier. An efficiency frontier envelops all DMUs in the set and the efficiency of all units is determined relative to this frontier. The efficiency frontier may be different for different DEA models; some may be piecewise linear, piecewise loglinear, or piecewise Cobb–Douglas. Models also differ with respect to whether they assume constant or variable returns to scale. CCR model we presented in this chapter assumes constant returns to scale. Another way DEA models may differ is whether they are units invariant or not. Finally, some models may have two ver-

---

[29] See B. Golany and Y. Roll, "An Application Procedure for DEA," *Omega*, vol. 17 (1989), pp. 237–250, for a formal process for DEA applications.

[30] See, for example, R. G. Dyson, and E. Thanassoulis, "Reducing Weight Flexibility in Data Envelopment Analysis," *Journal of the Operational Research Society*, vol. 39, no. 6 (1988), pp. 563–576.

[31] See A. Charnes, W. W. Cooper, A. Y. Lewin, and L. M. Seiford (eds.), *Data Envelopment Analysis: Theory, Methodology, and Applications*, chapter 21, pp. 425–435, for a discussion of important issues involved in DEA studies, including model selection, implementation, and interpretation of results.

sions: an input oriented version and an output orientation version. For example, the model (13.2) we used in our example is the input oriented version of the CCR model. An input-oriented version focuses on reducing inputs as a way to efficient operations. Conversely, an output-oriented model focuses on output augmentation to lead inefficient DMUs to efficiency. An efficiency frontier constructed through a specific DEA model will be the same for both the input- and the output-oriented versions. The difference would be the point to which an inefficient DMU will be projected on the frontier. The output-oriented version of the CCR model is as follows.[32]

$$\text{Max } h_0 = \phi_0 + \varepsilon \left(\sum_{i=1}^{m} s_i^- + \sum_{r=1}^{s} s_r^+ \right) \tag{13.3}$$

Subject to:

$$\phi_0 y_{r0} - \sum_{j=1}^{n} y_{rj} \lambda_j - s_r^+ = 0$$

$$\sum_{j=1}^{n} x_{ij} \lambda_j - s_i^- = x_{i0}$$

$$\lambda_j, s_i^-, s_r^+ \geq 0 \qquad i = 1, 2, ..., m; r = 1, 2, ..., s; j = 1, 2, ..., n$$

and the projection formulas are given as:

$$y_{r0}^* = \phi_0^* y_{r0} + s_r^{+*} \text{ and } x_{i0}^* = x_{i0} - s_i^{-*}$$

13.8   SUMMARY

This chapter focused on productivity and efficiency of service operations. First, we discussed the basic concepts relevant to productivity and defined productivity as the ratio of output to input. Productivity may be computed for a single output and a single input or multiple outputs and inputs. Most organizations produce more than one kind of output and use several kinds of inputs. At the national level, labor productivity is the most frequently used productivity measure. Growth in labor productivity is used as an indicator of improvement in the standard of living of a country. In addition to being an indicator of standard of living, productivity growth influences other important economic variables, such as competitiveness, unemployment, inflation, social programs, and resource conservation.

Raising productivity is an important goal at both the national and organizational level. First among the factors that improve productivity in the long run is technological developments that reduce labor requirement in the production of goods and services. Another factor that has both long- and short-term implications for increasing productivity is the organization and management of productive activities. Naturally, productivity improvements at the firm level determine what happens at the national level. Organizations can increase productivity in the long run by introducing new technologies and innovations in existing technology. They can also achieve significant increases in productivity in the short term by implementing better work methods and better management practices.

Services present special challenges with respect to productivity. It is not only difficult to increase service productivity, but it is also difficult to measure it and measure it accurately. We reviewed some of the reasons for the measurement problem and dis-

---

[32] See A. Charnes, W. W. Cooper, A. Y. Lewin, and L. M. Seiford (eds.), *Data Envelopment Analysis: Theory, Methodology, and Applications,* chapter 2, pp. 23–47, for a discussion of basic DEA models. Discussion of different DEA models from a "returns to scale" perspective is presented in A. I. Ali and L. M. Seiford, "The Mathematical Programming Approach to Efficiency Analysis," in Harold O. Fried, C. A. Knox Lovell, and Shelton S. Schmidt (eds.), *The Measurement of Productive Efficiency: Techniques and Applications,* pp. 120–159.

cussed why service productivity growth is slower in some services than manufacturing productivity. Some services, called progressive, are responsive to productivity improvement efforts; however, some services are not. The main reason is that the labor requirement in the latter group usually cannot be changed without a significant deterioration in quality. These are called stagnant services. We then presented some suggestions for raising productivity of services. Raising productivity is the responsibility of management; improvements in productivity are, to a large extent, the results of management actions. Drucker proposes "working smarter" as the way to raise productivity in services. Specifically he recommends: (1) define the task; (2) concentrate work on the task; (3) define performance; (4) form a partnership with employees; and (5) make continuous learning part of organization's culture.

The last section of this chapter presented data envelopment analysis (DEA) as a powerful management science technique for measuring the efficiency of economic units that produce the same types of outputs by using the same types of inputs. One of the most frequently used models, the ratio model, was presented as a medium for the discussion of issues relevant to the application of DEA. Examples were provided for insight into the concepts and advantages of DEA.

Discussion Questions

1. What is productivity? Discuss different types of productivity.
2. Why is productivity important for a country?
3. Why is productivity important for a service organization?
4. Who is primarily responsible for productivity in a service organization?
5. What are the major factors that determine service productivity?
6. Is it true that services are not responsive to productivity improvement efforts? Explain.
7. What are progressive services? Explain with examples.
8. What are stagnant services? Explain with examples.
9. What are asymptotically stagnant services? Explain with examples.
10. What is the difference between stagnant and asymptotically stagnant services?
11. How can the productivity of service work be increased?
12. Briefly describe what data envelopment analysis (DEA) is for.
13. How can DEA be helpful to managers of service organizations?
14. Discuss the advantages of DEA.
15. What are some of the disadvantages of DEA?
16. What methods, other than DEA, can be used for measuring the efficiency of economic units? Discuss their advantages and disadvantages.

Problems

Note: The following problems require computer solution of DEA models. If you do not have access to specialized DEA software, use an appropriate LP package. Also note that the value used for epsilon (ε) will most likely influence the value of the objective function. To avoid this problem, a two-stage solution procedure is recommended. First, set the objective function coefficients of the slack variables to zero and solve the problem with only θ (or ϕ) in the objective function. Then set the value of θ (or ϕ) to that found in the first stage (e.g., you may set both the upper and lower bounds of θ to the optimal value from stage one if your software allows upper and lower bounds) and introduce the slack variables into the objective function, and solve the problem again.

13.1. Set up the **input-oriented** version of the CCR model (i.e., model 13.2) for First Bank of Gotham City using the original data. Solve the model for all DMUs.

    a. Compare your results to those given in Exhibit 13-5. Is there any difference in the results? Why?

    b. Interpret the results for Branch 3. How much should Branch 3 improve its input(s) to become efficient? Substitute the new input quantity(ies) in the problem formulation and solve the problem again. Has Branch 3 become efficient? Why?

13.2. Set up the **output-oriented** version of the CCR model (i.e., model 13.3) for First Bank of Gotham City using the original data. Solve the model for all DMUs.

    a. Interpret the results for Branch 3.

    b. How much should Branch 3 improve its output to become efficient?

    c. Substitute the new output quantity in the problem formulation and solve the problem again. Has Branch 3 become efficient? Why?

13.3. Efficiency of health care services influences health care costs for everyone and therefore is a concern for most employees and employers. Part of the health care costs is determined by the fees physicians charge. Consequently, the efficiency of physicians has an impact on the overall efficiency of healthcare providers. This problem involves the measurement of the efficiency of 12 surgeons in a single hospital over a three-month period in 1987.[33] Two input and two output measures are selected for measuring the efficiency of surgeons. One of the input measures is length of stay and the other is total dollar amount for ancillary services. The length of stay is a good indicator of the amount of inputs, or resources, used in treating patients such as admission, medical records, discharge process, meals, laundry, medical supplies, and nursing care. A variety of ancillary services with varying levels of technological sophistication exist in a hospital, they are aggregated in one input variable in this application. One measure of physician output is the number of cases, or patients treated by a physician. However, since each patient presents different challenges and requires different types and amounts of resources, it is customary to consider the case mix, or complexity, of a physician's cases when her output is evaluated. Outputs of surgeons in this problem are organized in "Low-Severity" and "High-Severity" discharges. Inputs and outputs of the 12 surgeons included in the study are shown in Exhibit 13-6.

    a. Determine the efficiency of all surgeons using the input-oriented CCR model.

    b. Consider Surgeon 4. What changes Surgeon 4 has to make in the inputs he uses to become efficient? Discuss the feasibility of these changes.

    c. Consider Surgeon 11. Identify the surgeons who are closest to Surgeon 11 in terms of input quantities used and output quantities produced? How can this identification help Surgeon 11 to become efficient. What changes she has to implement in her practice to become efficient?

13.4. Refer to Problem 13.3 and Exhibit 13-6.

    a. Determine the efficiency of all surgeons using the output-oriented CCR model.

    b. Consider Surgeon 4. What changes Surgeon 4 has to make in the outputs he uses to become efficient? Discuss the feasibility of these changes.

    c. Consider Surgeon 11. Identify the surgeons who are closest to Surgeon 11 in terms of input quantities used and output quantities produced? Is this group different from the group identified in Problem 13.3 (c)? What changes Surgeon 11 has to implement in her practice to become efficient?

---

[33] This problem has been adapted from Jon A. Chilingerian, "Exploring Why Some Physicians' Hospital Practices are More Efficient: Taking DEA Inside the Hospital," in A. Charnes, W. W. Cooper, A. Y. Lewin, and L. M. Seiford (eds.), *Data Envelopment Analysis: Theory, Methodology, and Applications* (Boston, Kluwer Academic Publishers, 1994), pp. 167–193.

EXHIBIT 13-6   Inputs Used and Outputs Produced by Surgeons

| Surgeon | Outputs | | Inputs | |
	Low-Severity Discharges	High-Severity Discharges	Total Length of Stay (days)	Total Ancillary Services ($)
S1	47	11	232	126,244
S2	36	5	264	126,971
S3	45	9	307	289,560
S4	44	13	329	238,421
S5	76	21	433	304,763
S6	22	7	148	110,228
S7	30	9	240	187,134
S8	19	11	220	185,882
S9	70	16	497	357,646
S10	88	18	691	632,603
S11	33	15	342	234,394
S12	45	21	430	290,343

Source: Jon A. Chilingerian, "Exploring Why Some Physicians' Hospital Practices are More Efficient: Taking DEA Inside the Hospital," in A. Charnes, W. W. Cooper, A. Y. Lewin, and L. M. Seiford (eds.), *Data Envelopment Analysis: Theory, Methodology, and Applications* (Boston, Kluwer Academic Publishers, 1994), pp. 167–193.

13.5   In a study of hospital efficiency, a researcher focused on the medical surgical services in seven teaching hospitals in Massachusetts.[34] The medical surgical area is important because it represented the largest single cost area separately reported on by hospitals in the state. The researcher used three input and four output measures to assess efficiencies of seven teaching hospitals as shown in Exhibit 13-7.

   a. Determine the efficiency of all seven teaching hospitals using the input-oriented CCR model and "Patient Days 65 Years of Age and Older" as out-

EXHIBIT 13-7   Input and Output Data for DEA Evaluation of Medical–Surgical Area in Seven Teaching Hospitals

Hospital	Full-Time Equivalents Nonphysicians	Supply Dollars	Bed Days Available	Patient Days 65 Years of Age or Older	Patient Days Under 65 Years of Age	Number of Nurse Students	Number of Interns and Residents in Training
A	310.0	134,600	116,000	55,310	49,520	291	47
B	278.5	114,300	106,800	37,640	55,630	156	3
C	165.6	131,300	65,520	32,910	25,770	141	26
D	250.0	316,000	94,400	33,530	41,990	160	21
E	206.4	151,200	102,100	32,480	55,300	157	82
F	384.6	217,000	153,700	48,780	81,920	285	92
G	530.4	770,800	215,000	58,410	119,700	144	89

Source: H. David Sherman, "Managing Productivity of Health Care Organizations," in R. H. Silkman (ed.), *Measuring Efficiency: An Assessment of Data Envelopment Analysis, New Directions for Program Evaluation*, no. 32 (San Francisco, Jossey-Bass, winter 1986), pp. 31–46.

---

[34] This problem has been adapted from H. David Sherman, "Managing Productivity of Health Care Organizations," in R. H. Silkman (ed.), *Measuring Efficiency: An Assessment of Data Envelopment Analysis, New Directions for Program Evaluation*, no. 32 (San Francisco, Jossey-Bass, winter 1986), pp. 31–46.

put and "Full-Time Equivalents Nonphysician" and "Bed Days" as input measures. How many of the hospitals are efficient?

b. Add "Number of Interns and Residents in Training" to the model as an output measure and determine the efficiency of all seven teaching hospitals. How many of the hospitals are efficient?

c. Add "Supply Dollars" to the model as an input measure and determine the efficiency of all seven teaching hospitals. How many of the hospitals are efficient?

d. Add "Patient Days Under 65 Years of Age" to the model as an output measure and determine the efficiency of all seven teaching hospitals. How many of the hospitals are efficient?

e. What can you conclude from the above experiments?

f. Now determine the efficiency of the seven teaching hospitals using all the input and output measures given in Exhibit 13-7. How many hospitals are efficient now? Has your conclusion from part (e) been confirmed or refuted? Explain.

CASES

CASE 13–1 Hazel

Hazel has worked for the same *Fortune* 500 company for almost 15 years. Although the company has gone through some tough times, things were starting to turn around. Customer orders were up, and quality and productivity had improved dramatically from what they had been only a few years earlier due to a company-wide quality improvement program. So it came as a real shock to Hazel and about 400 of her co-workers when they were suddenly terminated following the new CEO's decision to downsize the company.

After recovering from the initial shock, Hazel tried to find employment elsewhere. Despite her efforts, after eight months of searching she was no closer to finding a job than the day she started. Her funds were being depleted and she was getting more discouraged. There was one bright spot, though: She was able to bring in a little money by mowing lawns for her neighbors. She got involved quite by chance when she heard one neighbor remark that now that his children were on their own, nobody was around to cut the grass. Almost jokingly, Hazel asked him how much he'd be willing to pay. Soon Hazel was mowing the lawns of five neighbors. Other neighbors wanted her to work on their lawns, but she didn't feel that she could spare any more time from her job search.

However, as the rejection letters began to pile up, Hazel knew she had to make an important decision in her life. On a rainy Tuesday morning, she decided to go into business for herself—taking care of neighborhood lawns. She was relieved to give up the stress of job hunting, and she was excited about the prospects of being her own boss. But she was also fearful of being completely on her own. Nevertheless, Hazel was determined to make a go of it.

At first, business was a little slow, but once people realized Hazel was available, many asked her to take care of their lawns. Some people were simply glad to turn the work over to her; others switched from professional lawn care services. By the end of her first year in business, Hazel knew she could earn a living this way. She also performed other services such as fertilizing lawns, weeding gardens, and trimming shrubbery. Business became so good that Hazel hired two part-time workers to assist her and, even then, she believed she could expand further if she wanted to. ■

SOURCE: William J. Stevenson, *Production/Operations Management*, 5th ed. (Chicago, Irwin, 1996), pp. 35–36.

CASE QUESTIONS

1. In what ways are Hazel's customers most likely to judge the quality of her lawn care services?
2. Hazel is the operations manager of her business. Among her responsibilities are forecasting, inventory management, scheduling, quality assurance, and maintenance.
   a. What kinds of things would likely require forecasts?
   b. What inventory items does Hazel probably have? Name one inventory decision she has to make periodically.
   c. What scheduling must she do? What things might occur to disrupt schedules and cause Hazel to reschedule?
   d. How important is quality assurance to Hazel's business? Explain.
   e. What kinds of maintenance must be performed so that the productivity of operations is not adversely affected?
3. Hazel would like to increase her profits, but she doesn't believe that it would be wise to raise her prices considering the current state of the local economy. Instead, she has given some thought to increasing productivity.
   a. Explain how increased productivity could be an alternative to increased prices.
   b. What are some ways that Hazel could increase productivity?

CASE 13–2   Marriott In-Flite Services Division

It was a warm June day in Washington, D.C., and Marv Throneberry was trying to keep his mind on the problem at hand, and not on the fact that the air conditioner was malfunctioning. Marv was an MBA summer intern with the In-Flite Services Division of the Marriott Corporation. He had just completed a month-long study of Shoppe #060, an airline catering kitchen operated by the Division at Baltimore–Washington International Airport (BWI). The study was part of the Resource Management Program that had recently been instituted by upper management of In-Flite Services. Marv's boss, Jack Valenti, was the Director of the program. Mr. Valenti was expecting by the end of the week, a report from Marv on the daily operations of Shoppe #060, including any specific recommendations that Marv might have concerning increased productivity.

CORPORATE HISTORY

In Washington, D.C., in 1927, J. Willard Marriott and his wife Alice opened a nine-seat root beer stand named the Hot Shoppe. From this humble beginning, the present day Marriott Corporation evolved to include three major business units which provided 92% of the sales in 1980: Hotels, Restaurants, and the Contract Food Services of which In-Flight Services was a portion. Additionally, the firm owned and operated two amusement parks and a cruise line. In 1980, the corporation had sales of over $1.5 billion, a 21% increase over the previous year.

IN-FLITE SERVICES DIVISION

The airline catering business was begun in 1937 when J. Willard Marriott contracted with Eastern, American, and Capital Airlines to provide box lunches to their passengers departing Washington, D.C. Hot meals soon appeared which were kept warm by a heated brick and the airline catering industry was on its way. In 1980 the Marriott In-Flite Service Division was the largest independent airline food caterer in the world, servicing over 100 different airlines on four continents with 43 domestic in-flite kitchens and 20 foreign catering operations. Eastern Airlines was the largest single ac-

count for U.S. operations, with Delta and American not far behind.

Each of the 43 In-Flite kitchens in the U.S. was run as a profit center by a general manager, who ensured the correct preparation of airline menus by his catering operation. Each airline specified the type of meal or snack and its preparation in terms of quality and quantity. Specifications were maintained by each airline catering guide and updated periodically. Quality control was maintained by Marriott supervisors as well as periodic kitchen inspections by airline food service representatives. Also, passenger or flight attendant complaints concerning badly prepared food or missing meal tray items were investigated by airline food service representatives. If a departing flight was delayed due to meal catering, the airline could charge the In-Flite kitchen for lost time at the departure gate, which could amount to thousands of dollars per flight-hour.

Although individual contracts for airline food service were negotiated by a marketing department within the division, it was each general manager's responsibility to keep his kitchen's operations at the highest quality and service level possible. The importance of high quality and good service was underscored by the fact that an airline could cancel a contract for a particular location with only 30 days' notice.

Each general manager's performance was judged by comparing his annual budget with yearly financial results. The three major areas of concern for management were food and labor costs (comprising 75% of total costs), and other non-food controllable costs such as gasoline, uniforms, and utilities. The domestic catering operations were divided into seven regions with each supervised by a regional vice-president who in turn reported to the In-Flite Services Division vice-president at corporate headquarters in Washington, D.C.

RESOURCE MANAGEMENT PROGRAM

The Resource Management Program was initiated in November 1978 by the In-Flite Service Division in an effort to halt the decline in profit margins caused by rapidly inflating food and labor costs. The purpose of the program was to achieve increased productivity for each catering operation by analyzing daily work operations, identifying idle time that could be effectively utilized, and then streamlining operations with no decrease in the expected service level. Streamlining of operations could be accomplished by the elimination of work positions if an employee in another position could assume the added workload, or by an increase in productivity due to automation. As a summer intern in the Resource Management Program, Marv's efforts were focused in this area.

SHOPPE #060, BWI AIRPORT

Shoppe #060 serving the Baltimore–Washington International Airport (BWI) was typical of one of Marriott's smaller domestic airline catering operations. There were nearly 100 full-time employees at the In-Flite kitchen which operated seven days a week (part-time workers were not used). As of May 1980, the weekly total of flights catered by the kitchen was roughly 300. Weekly gross sales figures averaged $80,000 (a compilation of charges for food, beverages, and delivery of the items to the airplane). In addition, fees were charged for the cleaning of reuseable food service items (trays, etc.). In-Flite kitchen operations were divided into six activities overseen by the general manager and an assistant,

the operations manager. The six activities were: Transportation, Hot Foods, Cold Foods, Sanitation, Storeroom, and Administration/Billing. Exhibit 13-8 shows the managerial organization of the kitchen.

Due to the short time available to spend on the project at BWI, Marv chose to restrict his analysis to the Transportation and Cold Foods Departments—the two largest in terms of number of employees and opportunities for improvement. A brief description of the two departments follows.

TRANSPORTATION DEPARTMENT

The Transportation Department was responsible for the delivery and loading of meals and snacks to BWI outbound flights. Under the supervision of the transportation manager, there were seven teams composed of one food and equipment handler (FEH) and one helper. Each team worked an 8½ hour shift including a 45 minute lunch break and each worker was paid for eight hours per shift. In addition there was a dispatcher at the kitchen who ensured that the teams left for the airfield on time and with the proper number of meals requested by the airline. There were also two coordinators, one for Eastern flights and one for Delta, who supervised those airline's catering operations. Exhibit 13-9 contains an organization chart for the Transportation Department.

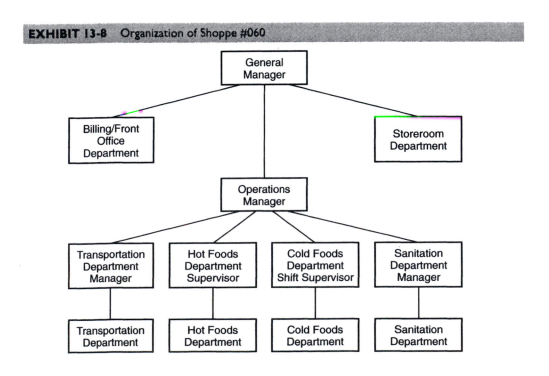

EXHIBIT 13-8 Organization of Shoppe #060

EXHIBIT 13-9   Organizational Chart Transportation Department Shoppe #060

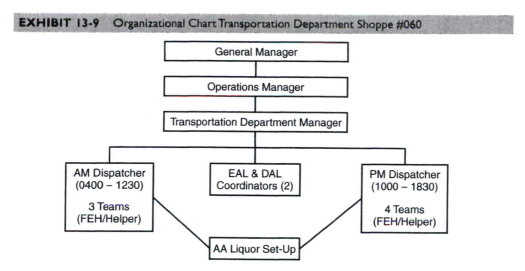

The FEH and helper positions were the highest paid in the kitchen ($7.51 average hourly wage and benefit rate), due to the heavy responsibility of maneuvering their delivery trucks alongside a multi-million dollar aircraft. (See Exhibit 13-10.) In order to service the airliner through the galley hatch, the body of the truck was hydraulically raised to hatch level and meals were transferred. Prior to departing the kitchen to cater assigned flights, each of the seven teams was required to set up these flights. This function entailed the bagging of ice cubes, assembly of specified amounts of beer and wine, coffee, milk, orange juice, and creamers, and a double check that meals were ready to be transported. Normally, this activity took no longer than 30 minutes, except in the case of wide-body jets (such as

EXHIBIT 13-10

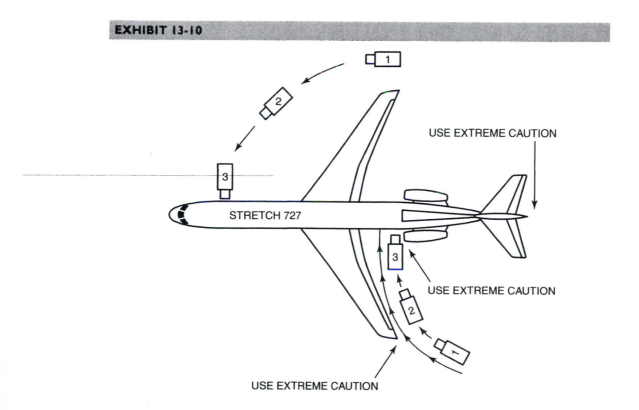

DC-10 and American 747 flights) where it could take as long as one hour. Often, the FEH and helper would set up two or more flights at one time, then transport the trays out to several planes in one trip. This resulted in batching efficiencies that reduced average setup time, and also reduced some of the travel time for driving from the kitchen to the airfield.

COLD FOODS DEPARTMENT

The Cold Foods Department was responsible for the preparation and the packing of all cold snacks, salads, fruit plates, and desserts specified by the airlines' menus. Various shifts of 8 or 8½ hours were worked in the department. Each shift included a 30-minute lunch break and another 15-minute break. Employees were paid for 7½ or 8 hours depending on the length of the shift.

Exhibit 13-11 is a bar chart of the activities performed by each worker on each shift. As shown in Exhibit 13-11, each shift contained some workers who staffed one or more packing belts. Each packing belt was a straight conveyor line at which three or four workers set-up and loaded individual meal trays with cups, silverware, salads, rolls, butter, and desserts prior to loading onto a meal carrier for transportation to the aircraft. Four belts were used for tourist-class flights, with an additional belt used exclusively for the first class trays. Each shift had a floor supervisor and a lead person who filled in wherever the need was greatest.

ANALYSIS OF SHOPPE #060 OPERATIONS

In his analysis of the Transportation Department, Marv first compiled a chart to determine how long it should take an FEH and helper to cater each of six different types of aircraft that flew into BWI (Exhibit 13-12). This chart used established time standards and was organized by different seating and galley configurations for each airline. Using the catering times and the daily team schedule (excerpt shown in Exhibit 13-13), Marv next constructed a bar chart of the daily activities of each team (Exhibit 13-14). Included on the chart when necessary were a ten-minute drive from the kitchen to the airfield, a ten-minute drive between planes, and flight set-up times. The chart accurately represented the current team schedule, but Marv knew that airlines

made minor flight schedule changes almost every month and major schedule changes quarterly, so any schedule he could devise would only be in effect for a relatively short time. Marv wanted to determine if the existing catering schedule could be accomplished with fewer than seven teams without incurring additional overtime costs or delayed flights while allowing for a flexible response to late arriving flights. Instead of immediately creating a new schedule, Marv wanted to look at each team's idle time to determine if one or more teams could be eliminated. He used the bar chart of daily activities to compile a table of idle times for each team on a daily basis (Exhibit 13-15); he thought this information would help him determine the answer to his question. Management felt that up to thirty minutes idle time per shift might be required for flexibility in responding to airline schedule variations, and present labor contracts specified that no more than eight hours of overtime could be scheduled per employee each week.

While evaluating the team workload situation, Marv knew he must consider some external factors. First, any decision he made should not lead to delayed flights. Under their service contract, which was extended on a yearly basis, any costs incurred from flight delays caused by the transportation department would be charged to Marriott. Currently the cost of a delayed flight could be as much as $5,000/hour. In addition to the threat of added costs, Marv had to consider labor issues. Shoppe #060 was a non-union shop, but he had heard that one kitchen in Boston had recently unionized.

In the Cold Foods Department, Marv was particularly interested in silverware bagging activities. As Exhibit 13-11 shows, the two silverware bagging positions on the A.M. shift bagged 1,095 and 971 sets of silverware per day. The actual time spent to bag the sets was 330 and 435 minutes, respectively. The P.M. shift position bagged 789 sets per day in 330 minutes. On this basis, the baggers' production rates appeared to be considerably less than the standard rate of 4 sets per minute. This standard had been set several years earlier by division staff personnel based on time studies and management expectations. Marv wondered what the overall labor savings would be if the standard rate could be achieved. He noted that the average hourly wage and benefit rate was $5.73 in the Cold Foods Department. He also noted that the P.M. bagger spent

EXHIBIT 13-11

AM SHIFT

Station	4	5	6	7	8	9	10	11	12	13	14	15
SILVERWARE 1	TXI - 250 SETS PLASTIC		AA-300 SETS	BRK FAST	AA CONT.	DAL - 120 FC SETS & 425 TC SETS		HELP OTHERS	B K	HELP OTHERS	THE LAST 105 MIN. OF PRODUCTIVE TIME ARE SPENT ON NONESSENTIAL ACTIVITIES		
SILVERWARE 2	EAL - 60 FC SETS	EAL - 775 TC SETS		BRK FAST	EAL - CONTINUED				B K	TWA	16 FC SETS & 120 TC SETS	
SALAD 1	EAL - 12 FC	EAL - 60 TC & SPECIALS		BRK FAST	AA - 30 FC & 250 TC		DAL 60 FC	B K	WORLD - 40 FRUIT & 354 SALADS			
SALAD 2	EAL - 125 TC	EAL - 12 FC & 80 TC		BRK FAST	DAL - 260 TC		DAL - 125 TC	B K	DAL - 125 TC	HELP WORLD		
SALAD 3	EAL - 36 FC & 450 TC			BRK FAST	EAL - CONTINUED		TXI 120	B K	TXI CONT'D	TWA - 12 FC & 125 TC		
SALAD 4					TXI - 230 COLD PLATES			B K	REP - 109 COLD PLATES	LUNCH	UPCOUNT, PREP, CLEANING	
SNACK DAL	DAL - 63 WHOLE SANDWICHES & 250 ROLL SANDWICHES			BRK FAST	DAL - 28 FC & 250 TC SNACKS			B K	HELP ON SALADS OR CHARTER			
SNACK TXI	TXI - 230 COLD PLATES			BRK FAST	TXI - 115 COLD PLATES		TWA 16 FC	B K	TWA - 127 TC COLD PLATES			
SNACK REP/DAL	REP - 115 SNACKS			BRK FAST	REP CONT'D	DAL - 123 SNACKS		B K	DAL CONT'D	DAL - 1 FC CARAPE & FT		
DESSERTS	EAL - 125	AA-30 FC & 250 TC	EAL - FC & CREW	BRK FAST	EAL - 500 TC		TXI- 125	DAL - 500	B K	TWA-12FC 125 TC	WORLD 395 CAKES	
MEAT PREP	WASH & CUT GREENS	SLICE MEATS		BRK FAST	SLICE MEAT & CHEESE			B K	SLICE & PEEL CARROTS, RADISHES & CELERY			
LEAD	FILL IN WHERE			BRK FAST	NEEDED DURING			B K	SHIFT			
BELT 1		RUN TXI BRKF FLIGHT		BRK FAST	LINE TRAYS FOR BELT PRODUCTION			AA FRUIT TRAYS & BD	CLEAN FIL D & P	B K	WRAP EAL LINEN	
BELT 2					RUN PER			B K	DAILY		LUNCH	SCHEDULE
BELT 3					RUN PER			B K	DAILY		LUNCH	SCHEDULE
BELT 4					RUN PER			B K	DAILY		LUNCH	SCHEDULE
BELT 5					RUN ALL SCHEDULED FC MEALS			B K	BREAD PREP		LUNCH	LINE WORLD TRAYS
FLOORMAN					SET UP BELT AND EQUIPMENT			B K	HELP LINE TRAYS		LUNCH	HELP WITH WORLD BELT RUN

PM SHIFT

Station	16	17	18	19	20	21	22	23	24	1
SILVERWARE 1	REF - 100 SETS	AA- 12 FC & 125 TC	PAL - 250 SETS	DIN NER	S O N ?	EAL - 36 FC & 125 TC	TWA 16FC	B K	TWA 125TC	AA - 505 KITS 9/9
PREP	PEEL CARROTS, CELERY, ETC.			DIN NER	CUT CARROTS & CELERY STICKS	SHRED CAB.	B K	SLICE RELISHES		PEEL FRUIT
FRUIT	AA 19 FC	DAL - 32 FC	TXI - 119 BOWLS		DIN NER	REP 109	TWA - 16 FC & 126 TC	B K	EAL - 12 FC & 125 TC	EAL - 125 SANDWICHES
BELT 1	EAL - 103 APPLE SNACKS		RUN BELT	DIN NER	RUN BELT PER DAILY SCHEDULE		B K	RUN CHARTERS LAST		SETUP FOR NEXT PM
BELT 2	SET UP BELT & LINE TRAYS		SAME	DIN NER	AS		B K	BELT		#1
M.D.W.	PREPARE 250 SANDWICHES			DIN NER	WRAP 270 BREAD & BUTTERS		B K	PREP FRUIT & DESSERT	BAG MEALS	HELP OTHER
LEAD	FILL IN WHERE NEEDED			DIN NER	ACT AS ASSISTANT		B K	CF MANAGER ON SHIFT		

SILVERWARE 1: EAL 4 TRAYS — THE LAST 135 MIN. ARE SPENT PERFORMING ESSENTIAL NON-BAGGING ACTIVITIES

M.D.W.: OFF FRIDAY & SATURDAY

LEAD: OFF FRIDAY & SATURDAY

EXHIBIT 13-12 Times to Strip Old Equipment and Load New Equipment on A/C Shoppe #060-BAL

	S&L	Load Only	Strip Only
DELTA			
DC-9	25 min.	15 min.	15 min.
727-S	25 min.	15 min.	15 min.
EASTERN			
DC-9	15 min.	10 min.	10 min.
727	20 min.	15 min.	15 min.
727-S	25 min.	20 min.	20 min.
AMERICAN			
707	45 min.	25 min.	25 min.
TWA			
707	40 min.	25 min.	25 min.
727-S	30 min.	20 min.	20 min.
REPUBLIC			
DC-9	20 min.	—	—
OZARK			
DC-9	20 min.	15 min.	15 min.
TEXAS INTL.			
DC-9	—	—	—
WORLD			
DC-10	50 min.	40 min.	40 min.
AIR FLORIDA			
727	25 min.	—	—
AMERICAN EAGLE			
DC-8	50 min.	—	—

EXHIBIT 13-13 Transportation Department Team Daily Schedules Shoppe #060

	Airline	FLT#	ETA	ETD	Frequency	A/C	Task/Service
TEAM #1							
0400 – DELTA	152	0215	Term	Daily		727-S	Strip
DELTA	106	Orig	0700	Daily		727-S	Load
DELTA	138	Orig	0720	Daily		727-S	Load
EASTERN	631	Orig	0800	Daily		DC-9	Load
REPUBLIC	367	0738	0820	Daily		DC-9	Strip & Load
DELTA	203	1010	1040	Daily		727-S	Strip & Load
DELTA	1717	Orig	1159	Daily		DC-9	Load
TEAM #2							
0500 – EASTERN	385	Orig	0645	Daily		727	Load
1330 EASTERN	983	0704	0735	Sat.-Only		727-S	Strip & Load
TEXAS INTL.	751	Orig	0750	Daily		DC-9	Drop Off @ TXI
EASTERN	947	Orig	00915	Daily		727-S	Load
AIR FLORIDA	Charter	0940	1020	Sat.-Only		727	Strip & Load
EASTERN	147	Orig	1036	Daily		DC-9	Load
EASTERN	291	1259	1325	Daily		DC-9	Strip & Load

EXHIBIT 13-13 (continued)

	Airline	FLT#	ETA	ETD	Frequency	A/C	Task/Service
TEAM #3							
0500 - AMERICAN	207	Orig	0745	Daily		707	Load
1330 TWA	025	Orig	0800	X-Sun		727-S	Load
WORLD	14	0735	0835	Daily		DC-10	Strip & Load
EASTERN	173	0936	1049	Daily		727-S	Strip & Load
AMERICAN EAGLE	Charter	1005	1200	Wed-Only		DC-8	Strip & Load
DELTA	130	1052	1117	Daily		727-S	Strip & Load
EASTERN	809	1159	1224	Daily		727-S	Strip & Load
TEAM #4							
1000 - AMERICAN	605	Orig	1120	Daily		707	Strip & Load
1830 OZARK	531	1345	1420	X-Sat		DC-9	Strip & Load
DELTA	337	1412	1440	Daily		727-S	Strip & Load
EASTERN	169	1505	1553	Daily		DC-9	Strip & Load
TWA	393	Orig	1630	Daily		707	Strip & Load
TEXAS INTL.	755	1622	1658	X-Sat		DC-9	Drop Off @ TXI
EASTERN	131	1709	1739	Daily		727-S	Strip & Load
EASTERN	703	1746	1841	Daily		727-S	Strip & Load
TEAM #5							
1330 – EASTERN	817	1424	1500	Sat&Mon		727	Strip & Load
2200 REPUBLIC	335	1528	1615	Daily		DC-9	Strip & Load
TEXAS INTL.	425	1525	1613	Daily		DC-9	Drop Off @ TXI
OZARK	520	1635	1705	X-Sat		DC-9	Strip
DELTA	761	Orig	1720	Daily		DC-9	Strip & Load
DELTA	237	1824	1850	Daily		727-S	Strip & Load
EASTERN	946	1953	2040	Daily		828-S	Strip & Load
EASTERN	439	2014	2120	Daily		DC-9	Strip & Load
DELTA	877	Orig	2130	Daily		DC-9	Strip & Load
TEAM #6							
1530 – AMERICAN	361	Orig	1820	Daily		707	Strip & Load
2400 AMERICAN EAGLE	Charter	1640	1710	Wed Only		DC-8	Strip & Load
REPUBLIC	305	1828	1915	Daily		DC-9	Strip & Load
TWA	843	1850	Term	Daily		707	Strip
EASTERN	172	1955	2030	Daily		727-S	Strip & Load
TWA	026	2120	Term	Daily		727-S	Strip
AMERICAN	414	2131	Term	Daily		707	Strip
EASTERN	394	2225	Term	Daily		DC-9	Strip
DELTA	834	2235	Term	Daily		717-S	Strip
EASTERN	126	2327	Term	Daily		DC-9	Strip
DELTA	560	2234	Term	Daily		727-S	Strip
TEAM #7							
1330 – DELTA	610	1644	1710	Daily		727-S	Strip & Load
2200 WORLD	33	1715	1830	Daily		DC-10	Strip & Load
EASTERN	696	1856	1925	Daily		DC-9	Strip & Load
EASTERN	982	1938	2010	Sat Only		727-S	Strip & Load
EASTERN	816	1946	2015	Mon Only		727	Strip & Load

SET UP AA 605 FOR TEAM #4

SET UP 32 EASTERN SODA KITS

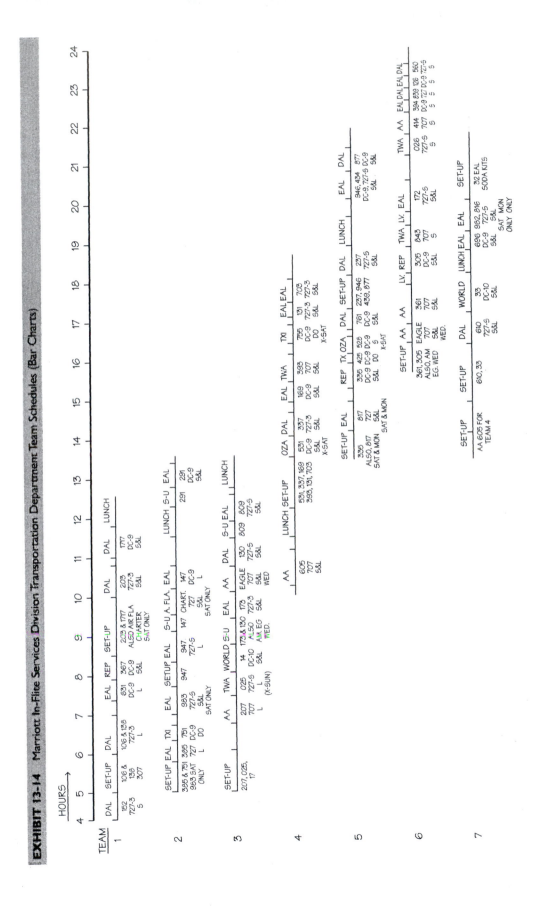

EXHIBIT 13-14 Marriott In-Flite Services Division Transportation Department Team Schedules (Bar Charts)

412

EXHIBIT 13-15   Mariott In-Flite Services Division Transportation Department—Team Idle Times

Idle Times[a]

	Sun.	Mon.	Tues.	Wed.	Thur.	Fri.	Sat.	Total
Team 1	60	60	60	60	60	60	30	390
Team 2	115	115	115	115	115	115	30	720
Team 3	100	65	65	25	65	65	65	450
Team 4	35	35	35	35	35	35	100	310
Team 5	110	45	110	110	110	110	70	665
Team 6	120	120	120	30	120	120	120	750
Team 7	0	0	0	0	0	0	0	0
Total	540	440	505	375	505	505	415	3,285

[a] Up to 30 minutes per team per day has been deducted from these figures to allow for prompt service to late-arriving planes.

135 minutes per day on essential, non-bagging activities, as indicated in Exhibit 13-11.

In addition, Marv had learned of a semi-automatic silverware bagging machine costing $6,000 that was available. Using this machine, an operator was supposed to be able to bag seven sets of silverware per minute. At this rate, based on 435 minutes of productive time on the A.M. bagger's shift, a single worker should be able to bag up to 3,045 sets per day; however, at that time, only 2,305 sets could be machine bagged since some sets had to be linen-wrapped (with the same standard applicable). With this constraint in mind, Marv wanted to determine what the annual labor savings would be if he could eliminate one or two of the silverware bagging positions. Also, since there was some question of whether

the quoted machine rate of 7 sets per minute was realistic, he wanted to determine what rate the machine would have to meet to produce a 2-year payback.

CONCLUSION

Marv had to decide what his recommendations for increasing productivity would be to Jack Valenti. He knew that the criteria for investing in capital equipment at the In-Flite Services Division included an after-tax ROI of at least 15% and a payback period of two years or less. With all these facts in mind Marv wiped the perspiration from his brow, loosened his tie and settled back in his chair to think his ideas through one more time before beginning his report. ∎

SOURCE:This case was prepared by John M. McCahon and revised by G. Steven Waters and R. D. Martin under the supervision of Professor Edward W. Davis. Copyright © 1982 by the Darden Graduate Business School Foundation, Charlottesville, Virginia. Rev. 8/86

CASE QUESTIONS

1. Can the transportation department do its work with fewer than seven teams?
2. What would the labor savings be if the silverware bagging standard (4 sets/min) could be achieved?
3. What labor savings can be achieved with the bagging machine? What production rate is required to achieve a two-year payback? Should Marv recommend purchase of the semi-automatic silverware bagging machine?

References

Ali, Iqbal A., and Lawrence M. Seiford, "The Mathematical Programming Approach to Efficiency Analysis," in Harold O. Fried, C. A. Knox Lovell, and Shelton S. Schmidt (eds.), *The Measurement of Productive Efficiency: Techniques and Applications* (New York, Oxford University Press, 1993), pp. 120–159.

Ali, Iqbal A., "Data Envelopment Analysis: Computational Issues," *Computers, Environment, and Urban Systems*, vol. 14 (1990), pp. 157–165.

Ali, Iqbal A., and Lawrence M. Seiford, "Computational Accuracy and Infinitesimals in Data Envelopment Analysis," *INFOR*, vol. 31, no. 4 (1993), pp. 290–297.

Banker, Rajiv, Abraham Charnes, William W. Cooper, John Swarts, and D. A. Thomas, "An Introduction to Data Envelopment Analysis With Some of Its Models and Their Uses," *Research in Governmental and Nonprofit Accounting*, vol. 5 (1989), pp. 125–163.

Baumol, William J., Sue Anne Batey Blackman, and Edward N. Wolff, *Productivity and American Leadership: The Long View* (Cambridge, MA, MIT Press, 1989).

Baumol, William J., and Kenneth McLennan (eds.), *Productivity Growth and U.S. Competitiveness* (New York, Oxford University Press, 1985).

Baumol, William J., "Productivity Policy and the Service Sector," in Robert P. Inman (ed.), *Managing the Service Economy: Prospect and Problems* (New York, Cambridge University Press, 1985), pp. 301–317.

Charnes, Abraham, William W. Cooper, Arie Y. Lewin, and Lawrence M. Seiford (eds.), *Data Envelopment Analysis: Theory, Methodology, and Applications* (Boston, Kluwer Academic Publishers, 1994).

Charnes, Abraham, Z. M. Huang, John Semple, T. Song, and D. Thomas, "Origins and Research in Data Envelopment Analysis," *The Arabian Journal for Science and Engineering*, vol. 19 (1990), pp. 617–625.

Charnes, Abraham, William W. Cooper, and Edwardo Rhodes, "Evaluating Program and Managerial Efficiency: An Application of Data Envelopment Analysis to Program Follow Through," *Management Science*, vol. 27 (1981), pp. 668–697.

Chilingerian, Jon A., "Exploring Why Some Physicians' Hospital Practices Are More Efficient: Taking DEA Inside the Hospital," in A. Charnes, W. W. Cooper, A. Y. Lewin, and L. M. Seiford (eds.), *Data Envelopment Analysis: Theory, Methodology, and Applications* (Boston, Kluwer Academic Publishers, 1994), pp. 167–193.

Committee for Economic Development, *Productivity Policy: Key to the Nation's Economic Future* (New York, Committee for Economic Development, 1983).

Drucker, Peter F., "The New Productivity Challenge," *Harvard Business Review* (November–December, 1991), pp. 69–79.

Epstein, Michael K., and John C. Henderson, "Data Envelopment Analysis for Managerial Control and Diagnosis," *Decision Sciences*, vol. 20 (1989), pp. 90–119.

Farrell, M. J., "The Measurement of Productive Efficiency," *Journal of the Royal Statistical Society, Series A, Part III*, vol. 120, no. 3 (1957), pp. 253–290.

Fried, Harold O., C. A. Knox Lovell, and Shelton S. Schmidt (eds.), *The Measurement of Productive Efficiency: Techniques and Applications* (New York, Oxford University Press, 1993).

Golany, Boaz, and Yaakov Roll, "An Application Procedure for DEA," *Omega*, vol. 17 (1989), pp. 237–250.

Haksever, Cengiz, and Yuki Muragishi, "Measuring Value in MBA Programmes," *Education Economics*, vol. 6, no. 1 (1998), pp. 11–25.

Jurison, Jaak, "Reevaluating Productivity Measures," *Information Systems Management* (winter 1997), pp. 30–34.

Kendrick, John W., *Improving Company Productivity* (Baltimore, Johns Hopkins University Press, 1984).

Lovell, C. A. Knox, "Production Frontiers and Productive Efficiency," in Harold O. Fried, C. A. Knox Lovell, and Shelton S. Schmidt (eds.), *The Measurement of Productive Efficiency: Techniques and Applications* (New York, Oxford University Press, 1993).

Oral, Muhittin, and Reha Yolalan, "An Empirical Study on Measuring Operating Efficiency and Profitability of Bank Branches," *European Journal of Operational Research*, vol. 46 (1990), pp. 282–294.

Parkan, Celik, "Measuring the Efficiency of Service Operations: An Application to Bank Branches," *Engineering Costs and Production Economics*, vol. 12 (1984), pp. 237–242.

Riddle, Dorothy I., *Service-Led Growth: The Role of the Service Sector in World Development* (New York, Praeger Publishers, 1986).

Sherman, H. David, "Hospital Efficiency Measurement and Evaluation: Empirical Test of a New Technique," *Medical Care*, vol. 22, no. 10 (October 1984), pp. 922–938.

Sherman, H. David, "Managing Productivity of Health Care Organizations," in Richard H. Silkman (ed.), *Measuring Efficiency: An Assessment of Data Envelopment Analysis, New Directions for Program Evaluation*, No. 32 (San Francisco, Jossey-Bass, winter 1986), pp. 31–46.

Sherwood, Mark K., "Difficulties in the Measurement of Service Outputs," *Monthly Labor Review* (March 1994), pp. 11–19.

Wolff, Edward N., "The Magnitude and Causes of the Recent Productivity Slowdown in the United States: A Survey of Recent Studies," in William J. Baumol and Kenneth McLennan (eds.), *Productivity Growth and U.S. Competitiveness* (New York, Oxford University Press, 1985), pp. 29–57.

van Biema, Michael, and Bruce Greenwald, "Managing Our Way to Higher Service-Sector Productivity," *Harvard Business Review* (July–August 1997), pp. 87–95.

CHAPTER 14

Management of Public and Private Nonprofit Service Organizations

14.1   INTRODUCTION

Americans of all ages, all stations in life, and all types of disposition are forever forming associations. There are not only commercial and industrial associations in which all take part, but others of a thousand different types— religious, moral, serious, futile, very general and very limited, immensely large and very minute. Americans combine to give fetes, found seminaries, build churches, distribute books . . . if they want to proclaim a truth or propagate some feeling by the encouragement of a great example, they form an association. In every case, at the head of any new undertaking, where in France you would find the government or in England some territorial magnate, in the United States you are sure to find an association.[1]

Alexis de Tocqueville, French social philosopher, visited the United States for nine months in 1831. The above quote is from his famous book, *Democracy in America*, which resulted from observations he made during the visit. What de Tocqueville observed more than a century and a half ago is still true today; Americans are still forming and managing associations for a wide variety of purposes, but more often than not for public service.

These organizations form what is known as the **nonprofit** sector. The variety of nonprofits is truly amazing. They range from the neighborhood church and local parent–teacher association to the National Rifle Association, the Sierra Club, and the

---

[1] Alexis de Tocqueville, *Democracy in America*, J. P. Mayer and Max Lerner (eds.), translated by George Lawrence (New York, Harper & Row, 1966), p. 485.

American Bar Association. Nonprofit organizations play such an important role in the economic and social life of the United States that it is also referred to as the **third sector,** private and public sectors being the other two.

The public sector consists of organizations that are formed and managed by the federal, state, or local governments. In the strict sense of the term, they are also nonprofit service organizations. For this reason, they are sometimes called "public nonprofits" and others are called "private nonprofits." (See Exhibit 14-1.) In this book, the term *public* is used for nonprofit organizations that are formed and managed by government at any level, and private nonprofits are referred to simply as *nonprofits.*

This chapter focuses on both types of these service organizations. The purpose is to present a synopsis of both public and nonprofit sectors and challenges their managers face. As you will discover, tasks and challenges of management in these two sectors are similar and yet they exhibit some important differences from the private sector. Organizations in both the public and nonprofit sectors need managers and managerial skills just like private firms. Although most managers in public and nonprofit organizations have their education in fields other than business, some business graduates will be working for one of these service organizations. Therefore, it is essential for service managers to understand these two important sectors of the U.S. economy.

EXHIBIT 14-1   Categories of Nonprofit Organizations

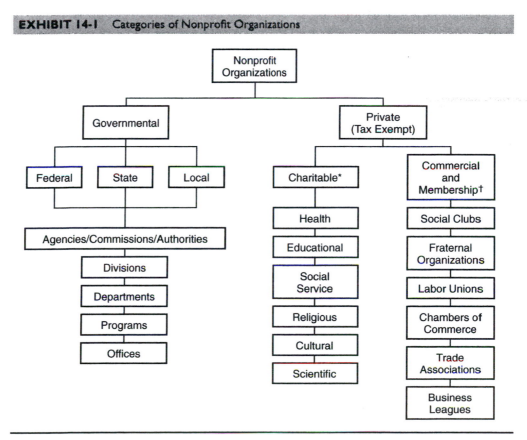

* Donor contributions are tax deductible.
† Donor contributions are not tax deductible.
Source: Robert N. Anthony and David W. Young, *Management Control in Nonprofit Organizations*, 4th ed. (Homewood, IL, Irwin, 1984).

14.2 PUBLIC AND PRIVATE NONPROFIT ORGANIZATIONS DEFINED

As indicated earlier, the public sector consists of agencies and organizations of the federal, state, and local governments. They are formed as a result of legislation at the appropriate level and are almost always financed by tax revenues and sometimes supplemented by fees. Most public organizations have a monopoly status. In other words, they usually have no competitors offering the same services. It is clear that they are not "profit-making" entities; actually no such concept exists for public organizations.[2] They may have a "surplus," but the surplus is not profit and it is usually returned to the appropriate treasury at the end of a fiscal year.

The most important characteristic of nonprofits is that they are established for purposes other than making a profit. That is why sometimes they are called "not-for-profit."[3] It may be an oversimplification, but we assume that the major objective of private sector organizations is to make a profit. Naturally, some may have additional objectives, but without profits a private company cannot survive too long. Nonprofits, on the other hand, are distinguished by the absence of the profit objective. This does not mean that they do not make a profit from their operations. They do make profits and they are allowed to keep them. Actually, some (e.g., nonprofit hospitals) at least partially depend on profits from their operations for their survival.

Perhaps the second most important characteristic that defines nonprofits is the "nondistribution" constraint. "Nondistribution" means that no part of a nonprofit's income, profits, or assets can be distributed to its members, directors or officers. Many nonprofits are exempt from federal corporate income tax and some are exempt from other federal, state, and local taxes, such as property tax, because they serve public purposes. There are 25 categories of tax-exempt organizations under the U.S. tax law. (See Exhibit 14-2.) Only one group of nonprofits, "501(c)(3) charitable institutions" receive extra privileges that contributions to them are tax deductible for individuals and corporations. In addition to the public service aim, they are specifically designated as nonprofit when they are organized, and are not allowed to distribute profits or assets to their members, officers, or directors. Nonprofits can engage in profit-making activities and keep their tax-exempt status if the activity is *related* to the tax exempt purpose or unrelated but *insubstantial*.[4]

14.3 SIGNIFICANCE OF PUBLIC AND PRIVATE NONPROFIT ORGANIZATIONS

Whether they are private or public, the essence of nonprofit organizations is service; service to the public in general, but in most cases, to a subgroup of public. There is very little, if any, manufacturing done by public sector organizations or nonprofits. Think about some of the well known agencies of the federal government, for example, the U.S. Coast Guard, U.S. Secret Service, Centers for Disease Control and Prevention, National Weather Service, Federal Aviation Administration, Forest Service, Fed-

---

[2] A few exceptions exist. For example the U.S. Postal Service and Amtrak are quasi-governmental agencies that appear to be neither profit-making nor nonprofit.

[3] Some people may see a subtle difference between the terms *nonprofit* and *not-for-profit*. Actually, the latter may describe these organizations more accurately since they are established for purposes other than making profit. The term *nonprofit* may imply an organization that is incapable of making profit. However, there seems to be no real difference between these terms as they are used in the literature.

[4] Robert N. Anthony and David W. Young, "Characteristics of Nonprofit Organizations," in David L. Gies, J. Steven Ott, and Jay M. Shafritz (eds.), *The Nonprofit Organization: Essential Readings* (Pacific Grove, CA, Brooks/Cole Publishing Company, 1990), pp. 216–235.

EXHIBIT 14-2 Tax-Exempt Organizations

Tax Code Number	Type of Tax-Exempt Organization
501(c)(1)	Corporations organized under an act of Congress
501(c)(2)	Title-holding companies
501(c)(3)	Religious, charitable, etc.[a]
501(c)(4)	Social welfare
501(c)(5)	Labor, agricultural organizations
501(c)(6)	Business leagues
501(c)(7)	Social and recreational clubs
501(c)(8)	Fraternal beneficiary societies
501(c)(9)	Voluntary employees' beneficiary societies
501(c)(10)	Domestic fraternal beneficiary societies
501(c)(11)	Teachers' retirement fund
501(c)(12)	Benevolent life insurance associations
501(c)(13)	Cemetery companies
501(c)(14)	Credit unions
501(c)(15)	Mutual insurance companies
501(c)(16)	Corporations to finance crop operation
501(c)(17)	Supplemental unemployment benefit trusts
501(c)(18)	Employee-funded pension trust
501(c)(19)	War veterans' organizations
501(c)(20)	Legal services organizations
501(c)(21)	Black lung trusts
501(c)(23)	Veterans associations founded prior to 1880
501(c)(24)	Trusts described in Section 4049 of ERISA
501(c)(25)	Holding companies for pensions, etc.
501(d)	Religious and apostolic organizations
501(e)	Cooperative hospital service organizations
501(f)	Cooperative service organizations of operating educational organizations
521	Farmers' cooperatives

[a] All Section 501(c)(3) organizations are not included, because certain organizations, such as churches, need not apply for recognition of exemption unless they desire a ruling.

Source: Internal Revenue Service, Annual Report.

eral Highway Administration, National Park Service, and the Social Security Administration. These organizations constitute only a small sample of the agencies of the U.S. government but they are all service organizations like thousands of other organizations of federal, state, and local governments. Now consider a few examples from the nonprofit sector, such as the U.S. Tennis Association, Red Cross, Salvation Army, Girl Scouts, Boy Scouts, private colleges and universities, fraternities and sororities on college campuses, professional associations, religious organizations (churches, synagogues, mosques, etc.), United Way, American Heart Association, American Cancer Society, museums, and symphony orchestras. It is clear that these private nonprofits, just like public organizations, exist to provide a variety of services. Consequently, there is no question that public and nonprofit sectors are **service** sectors.

It must be obvious that government organizations at all three levels perform vital services such as national defense, maintaining law and order, education, health care, banking (e.g., Federal Reserve, Federal Deposit Insurance Corporation), safety of air, rail, highway, and maritime transportation. Hence, no matter how much we complain about the size of government, or the quality of its services, without public organizations, social and economic life as we know it would not be possible. There are about 87,000 public organizations in the United States.[5] Their activities create a lot of business for the private sector and create many jobs for the population. The private sector is where most people work; about 84.5 million people (74 percent of the work force) are employed by the private sector. The public sector is second in terms of the number of employees. The federal government is the single biggest employer; in addition to military personnel, the federal government employs about 2.87 million civilians, which is about 2.5 percent of the workforce. State governments employ 4.56 million people and local governments employ 11.69 million. Hence, overall the public sector provides jobs to more than 19 million people, almost 17 percent of the work force.

The nonprofit sector is also a major source of employment in the United States. About 1.4 million nonprofit organizations exist, and more than 10 million people work for these organizations, which is about 9 percent of the work force. Another important fact is the significant contribution volunteers make to this sector. For example, it is estimated that volunteer labor contribution to nonprofits was the equivalent of 6 million full-time workers in 1994. Volunteers provide about 37 percent of the labor input to the operations of nonprofits. The amount of volunteer and paid labor together indicate that a total of about 16 million people work for nonprofits.

14.4 THE NATURE OF PUBLIC SECTOR ORGANIZATIONS

As indicated earlier, the U.S. economy consists of three sectors: private, public, and nonprofit. Most of the economic activity takes place in the private sector. However, as the data of the previous section demonstrated, the other two sectors are also very important to Americans not only in an economic sense, but also from political, sociological, and cultural perspectives. These two sectors also differ from the private sector in some important respects. In this section, some of the reasons that necessitate the existence of public organizations and their characteristics that make them so different from the private firms are discussed.

Why Public Organizations Exist

Four major reasons for the existence of public organizations can be identified.[6]

Providing Public Goods   Public goods are those goods and services that possess two important characteristics: (1) Their consumption by an individual does not prevent others from consuming them or diminish the benefits others receive from them; and (2) exclusion of any potential consumer from the benefits of these goods is usually not possible. Some examples include national defense, clean air, a lighthouse, parks, paved roads and highways, and radio and television broadcasts. Although economists coined the term "public goods," it is clear that most public goods are services.

Private goods are those goods that you have to pay for before you can consume them. For example, if you want to listen to music you have to buy a radio. The radio

[5] Unless otherwise mentioned, statistical data given in this chapter are from *Nonprofit Almanac, 1996–1997* (San Francisco, CA, Jossey-Bass Publishers, 1996). The latest year for which data are available is 1994. However, most statistics concerning public and nonprofit organizations do not exhibit big changes from year to year.

[6] Michael L. Vasu, Debra W. Stewart, and G. David Garson, *Organizational Behavior and Public Management*, 2nd ed. (New York, Marcel Dekker, 1990), pp. 8–11.

broadcast is a public good; your enjoyment of the broadcast does not reduce its availability for others. Also, once the broadcast is on the air, those who want to listen to it cannot be prevented from listening. The radio you purchased, however, is a private good and your use of it prevents somebody else from the benefits of a radio, at least in the short term, because resources are limited. If there is sufficient demand, an electronic appliances manufacturer will produce radios and sell them to those who are willing to pay the market price.

But who is going to pay for the broadcast? If it is a commercial radio, most likely advertisers will, but not the listeners. Listeners cannot be made to pay for the broadcast because it is available to anyone with a radio once it is produced. Hence, someone pays for it and most listeners enjoy it free. In other words, there are many "free riders" in the consumption of public goods; of course there are some radio and TV stations that receive voluntary financial support from their listeners or viewers. However, this example illustrates the basic problem with public goods; those who do not wish to pay for the service can neither be made to pay, nor can they be prevented from their use. On the other hand, there is no incentive for private companies to produce public goods if they are not getting paid for it. Most people need those goods but without someone paying for them they will not be provided by the private sector. Hence, government steps in to provide most of the public goods such as national defense, police protection, and paved streets. Governments provide these services and finance them through taxation. The fact that private companies would not produce most public goods is sometimes called "market failure," because the market mechanism that makes the production, distribution, and sale of private goods and services possible fails when it comes to providing most public goods.

Controlling Externalities   Side effects of economic activities are called externalities. Externalities are the outcomes that impact third parties. They may be negative or positive. A negative externality is called a social cost, and a positive one social benefit. Pollution is a well-understood negative externality. When a manufacturing process creates air pollution, for example, people who have nothing to do with this economic activity (i.e., those other than the owners of the firm or its employees or customers) suffer the consequences. A well-kept house on a block may be an example of a positive externality, because people who live around that house will get something positive from it even though they did not pay for the upkeep of the house. A well-kept house will provide a pleasant view, and increase the value, and hence prices, of other houses around it. Externalities are also considered a form of market failure, because the market mechanism does not necessarily extract all the costs of negative externalities from those who benefit from the activity that created it. Similarly, the mechanism cannot collect payments from those who benefit from a positive externality. An effective way to solve this problem is usually government's imposition of taxes on those who create negative externalities and subsidies to those who create positive externalities. Public organizations such as the Environmental Protection Agency and Nuclear Regulatory Commission are set up to deal with negative externalities.

Equity   Another reason for the existence of government, and therefore public organizations, is the desire for equality which is predicated on the belief that human beings must have equal rights. Various forms of inequality may result from an unlimited and uncontrolled operation of the market mechanism. For example, a private company may ignore the safety and health of its employees because taking safety precautions reduce profits. Or a company may prefer to hire only white males as employees. When there are no laws against them, some private companies may follow such practices because of their superior economic position in the transaction. This type of practice will outrage many Americans today, and they will demand government action to stop them. Clearly, this function of government originates from the value system of its citizens. The Equal Employment Opportunity Commission, for example, was established in 1964 to achieve equity in employment. Specifically, it promotes equal employment opportunities and prevents discrimination in hiring based on race, color, religion, sex, or national origin.

Providing a Framework for Law and Order and Economic Stability   An obvious function of the government is to maintain law and order and assure the safety of its citizens. Equally important is the creation and maintenance of a stable economic environment which is essential for the operation of the free market mechanism. The Constitution of the United States gives the federal government the right to print money and regulate commerce. Public organizations such as the Federal Reserve Board, Federal Trade Commission (FTC), and Securities and Exchange Commission (SEC) are some of the public organizations that contribute to the achievement of this objective. The FTC, for example, is charged with keeping business competition free and fair and preventing the dissemination of false and deceptive advertising, regulating the labeling and packaging of commodities, and enforcing antitrust laws. The SEC, on the other hand, oversees the public issuance and sale of corporate securities, and regulates the U.S. stock exchanges (New York, American, and 12 regional exchanges).

Characteristics of Public Organizations and Challenges for Their Managers

Individuals who supervise the activities of public employees and public organizations are called public managers. Some of these people are elected and some are appointed. In the federal government, the president of the United States is the highest elected official; in a state government it is the governor, and in a city government it is the mayor. Elected officials usually appoint people they know and trust to high administrative positions. They are political appointees and some of these appointments need legislative approval. Political appointees may not be reappointed if the elected official loses his position. These managers may come from the inside or outside of a public organization. Levels below them are executive managers, middle managers, and supervisors who are usually appointed from among the career employees of the organization. This chapter focuses on managers, including political appointees, but not elected officials.

Public managers face tremendous challenges because most of them have to perform duties in addition to duties private sector managers in similar positions undertake. They have to face additional challenges created by the nature and environment of public organizations that are usually not related to management. To understand these challenges, the nature of public organizations and the environment they operate in are reviewed next. The challenges public managers face are compared to those faced by managers in the private sector. Characteristics of public organizations can be understood along the following dimensions.

Reason for Existence   A private service company is created to make money for its owners. A public organization, however, is created by law passed by the appropriate legislative body. In general, a public organization tries to fulfill one or more of the four purposes of government discussed in the previous section by providing one or more services to the public. In other words, its mission is determined by the legislative body and is ultimately accountable to the public or to the legislative body that created it.

Source of Funds   A private company is established with capital provided by its owners. Additional funds for investments or operating expenses may be obtained through loans from financial institutions. Also, revenues from the sale of goods and/or services constitute a very important source of funds for a private company. For a public company the capital (e.g., buildings, furniture, equipment) and operating funds and salaries paid to employees are provided by the government from tax revenues. Most public organizations have no revenue to speak of. Some may collect fees, but fees usually do not constitute a major source of income for public organizations. Remaining funds at the end of a fiscal year cannot be kept for the following year, they must be returned to the appropriate treasury.

Environment   A private company pursues its profit goal, and other goals, in a market environment and must follow the rules of the market. Market mechanism determines the answers to three basic economic questions: what combination of goods and services to produce, how to produce them, and for whom they are produced. Market mechanism works when buyers and sellers of a good or service interact to determine its price and quantity. Public organizations are not part of this environment; they do not seek profit and therefore they are not subject to most of the rules and forces of the market. They do not need prices to determine what services to produce and for whom. All these decisions are made by legislators. In short, public organizations are part of the government and the political system, but not the market system. They have to follow the rules of the political system, not the market system. The political system includes the laws and regulations, as well as the wishes of elected officials and legislators.

Goals[7]   The profit goal of a private organization is very clear and easily understandable. Because of this clear goal, it is also relatively easy to measure efficiency in the private sector. Efficiency of operations is a significant contributor to the achievement of profitability. Consequently, efficiency, in addition to effectiveness, is an important goal for private organizations. Efficiency and effectiveness are also important for public organizations, but they have other important goals, such as responsiveness to the general public, responsiveness to the affected clientele, and political rewards for the legislature and executive. Often, there is conflict among these goals. It is easy to imagine the difficult time a public manager has trying to balance these conflicting goals and satisfy demands from various stakeholders.

Public Pressure   Public organizations often operate under intense public pressure due to controversial issues they sometimes have to deal with. Private companies may also come under pressure from public, politicians, and the news media. However, what public organizations face is usually much more complicated and intense. Some public managers feel like they live in a "fish bowl." They are under constant public scrutiny because these organizations belong to the public and they are supposed to serve the public interest.

Internal Organization   Public organizations have formal hierarchical structures. However, their managers operate under a fragmented authority structure. This is mainly because there is a division of authority in federal and state governments among executive, legislative, and judicial branches. In the private sector, a manager usually has only one boss. In the public sector, managers have many bosses; their di-

---

[7] This and the next four dimensions have been adapted from James E. Swiss, *Public Management Systems: Monitoring and Managing Government Performance* (Upper Saddle River, NJ, Prentice Hall, 1991), pp. 6–8.

rect supervisor, their supporting interest groups, and the members of the legislative overseeing committee.

Background of Public Managers   Public managers usually are not professional managers. In other words, their education is usually in a field other than business administration. Hence, it is not surprising to see lawyers running legal agencies, doctors running health-related agencies, and professional politicians heading a variety of other organizations. The lack of professional management training puts public managers at a disadvantage in dealing with some of the routine managerial tasks their counterparts face in the private sector.

Legal Restrictions   Public organizations are bound by many legal restrictions in their external actions. They can do only what the laws and regulations allow them to do; going outside these boundaries for higher efficiency or effectiveness is usually not permitted. Internal operations of a public organization are also bound by extensive procedures and formal specifications and controls designed to insure accountability to the taxpayer and conformance to laws and regulations. Consequently, public managers also have far more restrictions on their internal operations than managers in the private sector. Private sector managers hire, fire, promote, and demote employees with relative ease. They can add another shift to increase output or eliminate a shift to reduce output. Normally, these options are not available to public managers. They are generally bound by "merit" systems that put severe restrictions on how they manage employees. Some actions may require approval from the top authority of the administration or even from the legislative body. In short, public managers have much less flexibility and authority in decision making.

14.5   THE NATURE OF PRIVATE NONPROFIT ORGANIZATIONS

In this section, the nature of the third sector of the U.S. economy is reviewed: private nonprofits. First, the question of how to classify nonprofits is considered. Then, the economic reasons for the emergence of this sector are discussed. Finally, some important characteristics of nonprofits that separate them from private companies and public organizations are summarized. As these characteristics are discussed, the challenges they create for managers in this sector will also be pointed out.

Types of Nonprofit Organizations

Nonprofits exhibit great variety in terms of their purposes, causes they serve, sources of funding, services they provide, use of volunteers, and size and nature of their customers. Understanding why these organizations have so much diversity may be aided if they can be categorized into meaningful groups. However, this is not an easy task, simply because on every dimension of categorization, these organizations form a continuum, rather than clearly separated groups. The U.S. government classifies nonprofits for tax purposes, as shown in Exhibit 14-2. Another attempt for classification is along two dimensions: (1) source of income and (2) the way in which they are controlled.[8] Two groups of nonprofits can be identified with respect to source of income: donative and commercial (Exhibit 14-3). "Donative" nonprofits receive a substantial portion of their income in the form of donations, and "commercial" nonprofits receive their income primarily or exclusively from sales of goods and services. With respect to the control dimension, two groups exist: "mutual" and "entrepreneurial." If the ulti-

[8] Henry Hansmann, "Economic Theories of Nonprofit Organization," in Walter W. Powell, (ed.), *The Nonprofit Sector: A Research Handbook* (New Haven, CT, Yale University Press, 1987), pp. 27–42.

EXHIBIT 14-3   A Four-Way Categorization of Nonprofit Firms

	Mutual	**Entrepreneurial**
Donative	Common cause National Audubon Society Political clubs	CARE March of Dimes Art museums
Commercial	American Automobile Association Consumers Union[a] Country clubs	National Geographic Society[b] Educational Testing Service Hospitals Nursing homes

[a] Publisher of *Consumer Reports*.

[b] Publisher of *National Geographic*.

Source: Henry Hansmann, "The Role of Nonprofit Enterprise," *Yale Law Journal*, vol. 89 (1980), pp. 835–901.

mate control of the organization is in the hands of its patrons (i.e., donors, members, or customers), they fall into the first group. Nonprofits whose boards are self-perpetuating are in the second group. Of course, the four groups are not clearly separated from each other; organizations exist between the two groups along each dimension. For example, many private universities depend heavily on both donations and tuition, and some university boards of trustees include members elected by the alumni and members who are self-perpetuating.

Another useful way to categorize nonprofits is along the following four dimensions: nature of the product, nature of the market, mission focus on clients, and use of volunteers. This approach to categorization is given in Exhibit 14-4 with examples.

Why Nonprofits Exist

The four major reasons discussed in the previous section are generally accepted as explanation for the existence of public organizations. When the same question is asked for private nonprofits, however, the answer is not unique. Economists have been debating the issue for some time and have advanced various theories, which can be grouped under four titles.[9]

The Public Goods Theory   The first of these theories attributes the existence of nonprofits to the failure of both the market and government in providing public goods.[10] As discussed earlier, the private sector does not produce public goods when it does not get paid for its efforts; hence, the government steps in to provide some of those services and taxes people for the cost of provision. However, the government faces some limitations as the provider of these services, the most important one being a limited budget. Consequently, it has to choose carefully the kinds and quantities of public services to provide. In a democratic country, a government will normally

---

[9] See the followng sources for a detailed discussion of these theories: Henry Hansmann, "Economic Theories of Nonprofit Organization"; Estelle James and Susan Rose-Ackerman, *The Nonprofit Enterprise in Market Economics* (London, Harwood Academic Publishers, 1986); and Lester M. Salamon, *Partners in Public Service: Government-Nonprofit Relations in the Modern Welfare State* (Baltimore, Johns Hopkins University Press, 1995).

[10] Burton Weisbrod, "Toward a Theory of the Voluntary Nonprofit Sector in a Three-Sector Economy," in Burton Weisbrod (ed.), *The Voluntary Nonprofit Sector* (Lexington, MA, D.C. Heath, 1977), pp. 51–76.

EXHIBIT 14-4   Classification Schema for Nonprofit Organizations

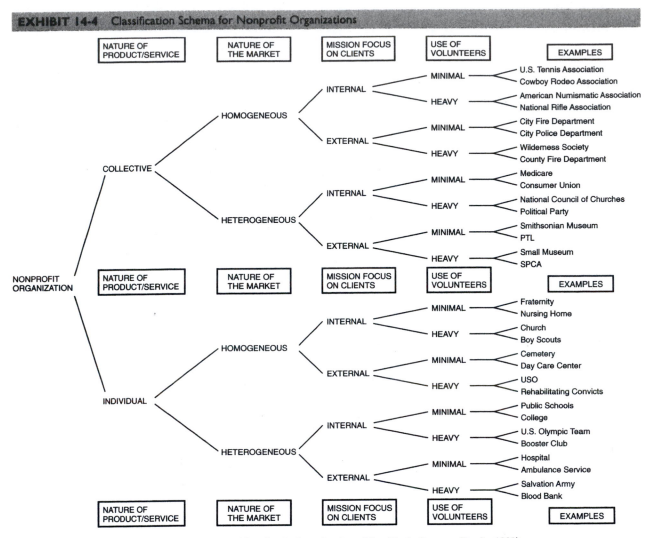

Source: Robert D. Hay, *Strategic Management in Non-Profit Organizations* (New York, Quorum Books, 1990).

choose those services that would command majority support. This implies that there will be services some segment of the public demands but cannot garner majority support for their provision. According to the theory, private nonprofit organizations are formed to meet the demand for such services.

The Contract Failure Theory   Consumers have difficulty in evaluating the quality of some services, especially those that require technical knowledge and special skills and services provided by professionals. These services are said to be high in **credence qualities.**[11] The quality and the quantity of some services are even harder to evaluate when the recipient of the service is different from the purchaser. Some examples include health care, care for the aged, and day care services. Economists describe the situation as a case of **asymmetric information** between the service provider and the consumer. In other words, the service provider has more information about the qual-

---

[11] See chapter 3 for a discussion of credence qualities as well as search and experience qualities.

ity and the quantity of the service than does the consumer. Consequently, when these services are provided by a profit-seeking private firm, there is an incentive to cheat. The theory predicts that the nondistribution characteristic of the nonprofit organizations, together with the fact that they are not primarily seeking profit, makes these organizations more trustworthy in the eyes of consumers. For similar reasons, donors give money and/or their time to nonprofits because these organizations are more likely to use donations for the intended purposes.

The Consumer Control Theory   Some nonprofits, such as mutual benefit organizations that provide services exclusively to their members or supporters, such as a country club, do not seem to result from the contract failure.[12] These organizations are formed, according to the theory, to provide more control to its members over the quality and cost of the services provided. Such control helps avoid monopolistic exploitation of members by the owners of a private company. The major reason for joining exclusive clubs is the opportunity to meet and associate with people who have qualities and connections that make them attractive companions. Consequently, a private owner of such an exclusive club would charge membership fees that cover not only the operating costs, but also the value to each member of associating with other members.[13] The theory also explains why nonprofit form is preferred when quality rather than cost is the dominant concern in some social services or when donors are also consumers. For example, most people who serve on the boards of directors of opera companies, symphonies, and museums are also consumers of the services and they serve to monitor the quality of the output.[14]

The Subsidy Theory   Governments at three levels contribute about 31 percent of the income of nonprofits. Contributions may be in the form of grants or contracts for the provision of services for which government has accepted some responsibility. Other forms of government contribution are loans and loan guarantees. In addition to these, the tax-exempt status of most nonprofits is an implicit government subsidy. Hence, subsidies constitute a major source of funding for nonprofits. It has been suggested that these subsidies encourage the establishment of nonprofits, especially in those industries in which nonprofits compete with private profit seeking companies.[15] An important question is: Why doesn't the government provide these services but delegate the production task to nonprofits? According to one view, the major reason is that nonprofits can charge fees for these services, so that the government's share of total cost is reduced. A second important reason is that nonprofits may have lower costs than public organizations, especially for labor. Another relevant question is why nonprofits are preferred for the provision of the needed services while many equally capable private companies exist. Of course, sometimes the government uses the private sector for some services. For example, large defense contracts are given to private firms, and some private companies now provide prison services. In other cases, nonprofits may be the only alternative, or the government may prefer to use nonprofits if costs can be lowered. For example, a nonprofit organization may come up with matching donations for the desired service.[16]

---

[12] Henry Hansmann, "The Role of Nonprofit Enterprise," *Yale Law Journal*, vol. 89 (1980), pp. 835–901.

[13] Hansmann, "Economic Theories of Nonprofit Organization."

[14] James and Rose-Ackerman, *The Nonprofit Enterprise in Market Economics*, p. 23.

[15] See, for example, Eugene Fama and Michael Jensen, "Agency Problems and Residual Claims," *Journal of Law and Economics*, vol. 26 (June 1983), pp. 327–350.

[16] James and Rose-Ackerman, *The Nonprofit Enterprise in Market Economics*, p. 30.

These theories present an economic perspective of nonprofits. There is, however, another very important noneconomic reason for the existence of nonprofits. As the quote from de Tocqueville at the beginning of the chapter hinted, in addition to economic reasons, Americans form nonprofit organizations to express their religious, political, social, or artistic views or promote a cause that may or may not be popular. In other words, through nonprofit organizations Americans can exercise their First Amendment freedoms. Nonprofits also limit the political impact of America's remarkable religious, ethnic, and ideological diversity and help reduce tensions that may originate from this diversity.[17]

Characteristics of Nonprofits and Challenges for Their Managers

Private nonprofit organizations not only constitute the third sector of the U.S. economy, but they also assume a role and a set of characteristics that fall somewhere between the private and public sectors. In some respects, they have characteristics similar to the private sector, because they are established and run by private citizens and are subject to most of the rules and forces of the market. In other respects, they are similar to the public sector because their mission is public service. In this section, some of these characteristics and the challenges they create for their managers are reviewed.

Purpose/Mission   Two of the most important characteristics of nonprofit organizations are that profit is not the main purpose and there is a nondistribution constraint on their assets; they cannot distribute any part of their income, profits, or assets to their members, directors, or officers. These organizations must be specifically designated as "nonprofit" in their charters when they are established.[18] Nonprofits may provide a wide variety of services which can be grouped in six major categories: health care, education and research, social services, arts and culture, community development, and religion. A nonprofit organization tends to accumulate multiple purposes or missions for various reasons. Additional purposes may be added to increase the utilization of the existing fundraising and service delivery systems; with a few modifications to the existing systems, additional needs may be met.[19] Multiplicity of purposes may make management's task harder, especially if the purposes are incongruent.

Ideology   Ideology may be a major reason for the establishment of many nonprofits. Many organizations have been founded by people who have a set of strongly held beliefs. These people are motivated by their ideals, and spend their time and money to promote their ideals. Ideology may stem from religious faiths or from secular thoughts, political beliefs, different artistic approaches, or from subscription to a particular theory in any field, such as education, science, or child development.[20]

Ownership   Nonprofits do not have owners. Private companies belong to their shareholders, public organizations belong to the government, or the public at large, but nonprofits do not have owners. This is because ownership implies a claim on assets which clearly contradicts the nondistribution constraint. If a nonprofit organiza-

[17] David C. Hammack and Dennis R. Young, "Perspectives on Nonprofits in the Marketplace," in David C. Hammack and Dennis R. Young (eds.), *Nonprofit Organizations in a Market Economy* (San Francisco, Jossey-Bass Publishers, 1993), 1–19.

[18] L. Howard Oleck, *Nonprofit Corporations, Organizations, and Associations*, 5th ed. (Upper Saddle River, NJ, Prentice Hall, 1988), p. 5.

[19] David E. Mason, *Voluntary Nonprofit Enterprise Management* (New York, Plenum Press, 1984), p. 128.

[20] James and Rose-Ackerman, *The Nonprofit Enterprise in Market Economics*, p. 51.

tion is dissolved, its assets are transferred to another nonprofit organization or to the state or municipality in which it operates, but never to private individuals.[21]

Source of Funds/Capital   Owners, or shareholders, provide the capital and operating funds for a private company, and for this reason they have claims on the company's assets and profits. Since nonprofits cannot have owners, the capital, and possibly some portion of operating funds, must be donated. Fundraising is a vital function for many nonprofits. However, donors are not the only source of funds for nonprofits; they may charge a fee for some of their services. Even if they are not sufficient to cover all the costs, fees may be a significant source of revenue for a nonprofit organization. For example, a nonprofit hospital may rely on revenues from its patients as well as donations. Similarly, a private university may mainly depend on tuition it receives from students for survival. Government grants and service contracts constitute the third important source of funds for nonprofits. As mentioned earlier, the tax-exempt status of most nonprofits can be considered as an implicit government subsidy to these organizations.

Management Structure   A private corporation is governed by its board of directors which represents the interests of its shareholders. A nonprofit organization is governed by a board of trustees, but since there are no owners, the board's main responsibility is to see that the mission of the organization is accomplished. Other responsibilities of the board include determining the mission and purpose, setting policies, making long-range plans, designing fiscal policy and plans, appointing a chief executive officer, and developing the bylaws of the organization.[22] Most trustees of a nonprofit do not receive any compensation for their services; in addition, many are also donors. They may be chosen for political or financial reasons rather than for their managerial talent or knowledge of the organization.

Volunteers   Volunteers provide about 37 percent of the labor input of nonprofits, and therefore constitute a significant resource. Because of this, they also create a challenge for managers. Since volunteers do not receive any compensation, they are not financially dependent on the organization. Some may even be major donors, and hence they may be difficult to manage and control. A nonprofit organization may also have paid employees. The existence of two types of employees multiplies the complexity of the tasks of management.

Internal Organization   The formal hierarchical structure of public organizations or clear lines of authority in private companies may not be found in nonprofits. Especially large nonprofit organizations have a more complex and less rigid internal structure. Large nonprofits such as universities, hospitals, opera companies, and social welfare agencies lack clear lines of hierarchy.[23] For example, a university may have a hierarchical structure such as a board of trustees, president, provost, deans, and department chairs; but individual faculty members, especially tenured faculty, have considerable freedom of action and cannot be managed or controlled like employees in a private company. Another unique feature of most nonprofit organizations is that they consist of two distinct systems. One system is for the development of resources and the other is for the provision of services (Exhibit 14-5). In a private company, there is only one system for both.[24] For example, consider a nonprofit organization that runs a

[21] Anthony and Young, "Characteristics of Nonprofit Organizations."

[22] Thomas Wolf, *Managing a Nonprofit Organization* (New York, Fireside, Simon and Schuster, 1990), p. 29.

[23] James and Rose-Ackerman, *The Nonprofit Enterprise in Market Economics*, p. 75.

[24] Mason, *Voluntary Nonprofit Enterprise Management*, p. 63.

EXHIBIT 14-5   Internal Systems of Private and Nonprofit Enterprises

The Single System of a Private Firm

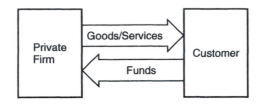

The Dual System of a Nonprofit Firm

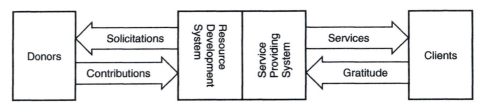

Source: Adapted from David E. Mason, *Voluntary Nonprofit Enterprise Management* (New York, Plenum Press, 1984), p. 65.

needle exchange program for the prevention of the spread of AIDS. While the funds for this mission may be raised by one branch of the organization, another branch may be in charge of the distribution of clean needles to drug addicts. The main reason for this dual system is increased efficiency from specialization. It is clear that a nonprofit with such a structure has two categories of external customers: (1) those who provide the funds, such as individuals, private companies, or government; and (2) those who receive the services. This feature of some nonprofits also increases organizational complexity and makes the job of managers harder.

Goals   Organizational goals in nonprofits are usually numerous, vague, and sometimes contradictory. One reason for this is the fact that some nonprofits pursue multiple purposes as discussed earlier. Multiple purposes lead to multiple, and possibly, contradictory goals. For example, a nonprofit whose mission is to help victims of an incurable disease may face conflicting goals of allocating resources to the care of victims of the disease and contributing funds to ongoing research to find a cure. The existence of multiple goals may lead to a diffusion of management attention and energy, and less than ideal outcomes. Vagueness of goals, on the other hand, contributes to measurement problems as discussed in the next paragraph.

Measurement Problems   Performance of a private company or its management can be assessed relatively easily by looking at the bottom line. In other words, profit is a reliable overall indicator of both effectiveness and efficiency in the private sector. Profit as a measure serves several purposes in private companies. For example, it can be used for evaluating proposed courses of action in a quantitative analysis of alternatives; as a measure of managerial performance; and as a common measure for comparing the performance of dissimilar units.[25] Such a reliable measure does not usually exist for nonprofit organizations; therefore, it is difficult to develop an effective measurement and control system in these organizations. Since goals are not usually ex-

---

[25] Anthony and Young, "Characteristics of Nonprofit Organizations."

pressed in monetary terms, assessment of organizational or managerial performance is very difficult. These difficulties are in addition to measurement difficulties inherent in the provision of services, because nonprofits are almost never manufacturing organizations.

Complexity   Complexity is the main source of challenges for the management of a nonprofit and therefore deserves special emphasis. We have mentioned that many nonprofits may consist of dual internal systems, may have two groups of employees and two groups of customers. In addition, nonprofits typically have multiple purposes; their goals are abstract, and sometimes contradictory. Each of these multiply the complexity of internal and external relationships of a nonprofit organization and implies a variable to control or manage. Add to these the difficulties of measuring outcomes or performance, and the constant struggle to generate enough funds to survive, and it becomes clear that managers of nonprofits face tremendous challenges.

14.6   SUMMARY

The economy of the United States consists of three sectors: private, public, and nonprofit. This chapter reviewed the nature of public and private nonprofit organizations and challenges their managers face. Private sector is clearly the most important sector because it employs the majority of the working population and produces most of the goods and services of the economy. However, the other two sectors are also important, not only for economic reasons but also for sociological and political reasons. For example, without public organizations there may not be any national defense, safe neighborhoods, safe air travel, paved streets, public education, state universities and colleges, national parks, clean environment, warning and protection systems against natural disasters, such as hurricanes and flood, protection against epidemics and other health hazards, and many other services we take for granted. Also, without private nonprofits, many museums, symphony orchestras or other classical music groups, private universities and colleges, research organizations, religious organizations, charities, fraternal organizations, professional societies, and organizations that fight incurable diseases may not exist. In short, without public and private nonprofits the society we live in would be very different and probably not as convenient or pleasant.

Organizations in public and nonprofit sectors have some characteristics in common: They have purposes other than profit making, they serve the public in general or a subgroup of it, and they are all service organizations. Public organizations are created by law and may be federal, state, or local government organizations. Their main purposes are to provide public goods, control externalities, ensure equality and equal treatment of its citizens, and provide a framework for law and order and economic stability. Public organizations are funded by tax revenues collected by the appropriate level of government. They operate in a political environment, they are subject to many internal and external restrictions brought upon by laws and regulations, and they are under public scrutiny most of the time. These characteristics create unique challenges for the managers of public organizations. Top-level public managers are usually elected; others who serve under them are usually appointed from within the organization. Most managers in public organizations have their training in fields other than business, which complicates the already difficult task they face.

Nonprofit sector is placed somewhere between the public and private sectors. Nonprofits are not created by government; therefore, they are not public organizations. However, their purpose, in general, is to serve the public. They not only provide a wide variety of services, but they also form an outlet for the expression of a variety of beliefs and ideologies. Nonprofits are established by private citizens, but they have no owners. They can and do make a profit from their operations, but cannot distribute their profits or assets to their officers, members, or directors. Main sources of funds for nonprofits are donations, fees they collect for their services, and government grants and contracts for services. Many nonprofits have dual internal systems, one for the acquisition of resources and the other for producing service. They also have two groups of external customers, donors and those who are the consumers of the nonprofit's service. Furthermore, many nonprofits have two types of employees: volunteers and paid employees. These characteristics multiply the complexity of internal and external relationships of a nonprofit organization. Nonprofits usually pursue multiple goals that are abstract and sometimes contradictory. These characteristics make measurement of individual or organizational performance very difficult. Finally, most nonprofits constantly struggle to generate funds for survival. It is clear that managers of nonprofits face tremendous challenges.

Discussion Questions

1. Explain what is meant by "nonprofit organization."
2. Explain "nondistribution" constraint. Does it apply to public organizations?
3. Compare and contrast private and public sector organizations.
4. Compare and contrast private and nonprofit sector organizations.
5. What are the most important similarities between the public and private nonprofits?
6. What are the most important differences between the public and private nonprofits?
7. Why do public organizations exist?
8. What is a "public good"? Explain, with examples.
9. What is "externality"? Explain, with examples.
10. Briefly explain the theories that explain the emergence of nonprofits.
11. Do we really need public organizations? Explain.
12. Do we really need nonprofits? Explain.
13. Discuss the most important challenges managers of public organizations face.
14. Discuss the most important challenges managers of nonprofits face.

CASES

CASE 14–1   Presque Isle State Park*
(Is This Place for the Birds?)

Harry Leslie was a legendary windsor knot tier, but tonight he was not having much luck. As he struggled in front of the bedroom mirror his wife called from the kitchen to remind him of his 7:00 P.M. meeting. "Better hurry it up Harry, it's almost 6:15 and you said that you were going to get there early!" "OK, OK," he muttered, "I'm almost ready." As she kissed him on his way out, neither acknowledged the tension that Harry felt. He hadn't mentioned it often as the fateful evening approached, but tonight's community information meeting had the unsettling potential to threaten his job. And this was, indeed, Harry's dream job: Chief Superintendent of Presque Isle State Park.

Harry closed the door carefully as he stepped out of the lighthouse that was home to his family (see Exhibit 14-6). The structure was old (1892) and a gust of November wind could easily rip the massive door from its hinges. It was a cold, clear night and the surf was pounding the beach near the lighthouse. As he bent his 220-pound frame into his car, Harry savored his family's living quarters. They lived in a working lighthouse on the north beach of a beautiful state park. His children had a magical existence with a beach at the back door and woods near the front entrance.

While he was driving the seven miles of deserted beach road toward the park gates and the city, a park police cruiser pulled next to him, waved, and motioned to the two-way radio. "Good luck boss, you're going to need it," chuckled officer Brandon. "Thanks, but I don't think it will be all that bad," replied Harry. "People are basically reasonable when it counts!"

As he left the park and headed toward the university where the public forum was to be held, Harry hoped that these had not been empty words. His predecessor had caused himself political difficulties by making what he had considered "reasonable" changes at the park. Ultimately, however, community turmoil over those changes had helped to initiate his transfer to the political offices of Pennsylvania's Department of Environmental Resources (DER) in Harrisburg, a

fate which didn't interest Harry. He was an outdoor person, not a bureaucrat or politician, and loved living in the park, being involved in day-to-day problems and using a hands-on approach. If a tree fell in a windstorm, Harry might be first at the scene, setting up warning signs and cutting away branches with his chain saw. He was less political and more practical than the previous park chief, and the park staff loved that about him.

The public meeting had been announced four weeks ago and was to be an information session. Harry and his staff had worked hard to develop a park management plan, an attempt to balance the diverse interests of the park and its constituency groups. The dilemma concerned how to juggle the various needs of the community and fit them into a strategic plan that would be acceptable to the various stakeholders who had concerns about how the park was to be used "for the public good."[1] He was also aware of the political "noise" that any of these factions could make if they didn't get their own way. But his plan was a reasonable one. It split the difference between commercial interests in the park and the concerns of the environmentally oriented groups.[2]

---

* This case is intended for classroom discussion only, not to depict effective or ineffective handling of administrative situations. All rights reserved to the author(s). When ordering this case from the Prentice Hall Custom Case Program, please use ISBN 0-13-079953-X.

[1] Presque Isle State Park operates under the Pennsylvania Bureau of State Parks. This division of the Department of Environmental Resources sets forth strategic management direction for all the Commonwealth's park areas. Management at Presque Isle incorporated this framework into its 1993 Strategic Management Publication. Agency goals must be developed within the context of these planning documents.

[2] The mission of Presque Isle State Park is to conserve the park's natural and historic resources for current and future generations and to provide educational and recreational activities. Presque Isle's goals are set up to achieve the overall mission of the park. These goals are to manage park attendance while maintaining the fragile ecosystem and preserving the natural historical resources.

The *Resource Management Plan* compiled and published by park management details key activities and strategically critical tasks that provide a foundation for the organization's structure and direction.

EXHIBIT 14-6 Presque Isle State Park

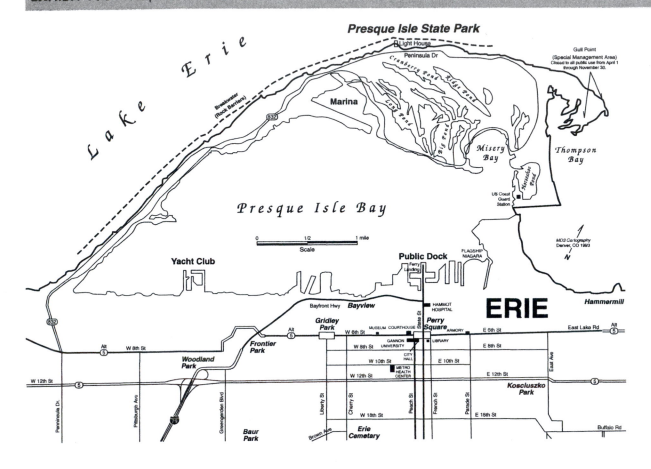

Harry's hope for the meeting was that there would be a group of understanding individuals in attendance and that he could orchestrate a compromise. He believed that somehow all of the involved individuals and groups would have an important common interest: the well-being of Presque Isle.

It was 6:35 as Harry steered his car onto university grounds and threaded his way between people walking along the narrow campus road. He was amazed at the congestion. There were hundreds of people walking the narrow road to the parking lot, and cars were illegally parked on the lawn. Approaching the parking area, Harry's heart almost stopped as he realized what was actually happening. The parking lot was full and the crowd was streaming toward the lecture hall and *his* meeting!

Suddenly someone in the crowd recognized Harry's state vehicle, and a voice from the crowd yelled, "There's Leslie, the guy who's trying to ruin our park!" "Great," he thought to himself, "my ca-reer is ruined and I get a parking ticket all in the same evening."

PRESQUE ISLE STATE PARK[3]

Presque Isle State Park (see Exhibit 14-6) is a sand spit peninsula which extends seven miles into Lake Erie. The peninsula joins the mainland just west of Erie, Pennsylvania, creating a sheltering arm that forms a beautiful natural harbor. The city of Erie is located near the center of Lake Erie's southern shore, and the peninsula has historically been critical to the development of the area. The population of Erie itself has stabilized at approximately 115,000, but the sur-

---

[3] The Pennsylvania Legislature formed the Pennsylvania State Park and Harbor Commission in 1921 under Act 436. This Commission was given authority to acquire, develop, and operate Presque Isle State Park, which was formerly known as the Pennsylvania State Park at Erie.

rounding suburbs have been growing steadily. Combined, the areas have reached a population of 250,000.

The peninsula is one of central Lake Erie's two major sand spits, and is a unique geological and biological preserve. Presque Isle, along with its mirror image twin Long Point across the lake on the north shore, create a hydrodynamic lake effect which is said to be critical to the health of the entire lake. The eastward flowing waters pass between the points over a relatively deep water trench and increase in depth and velocity as they flow into Lake Erie's eastern basin. At the line which connects the tips of the two peninsulas, the average width of Lake Erie changes from forty-five to twenty-seven miles.

Presque Isle is a biologist's dream, and a classic example of secession forestation. The secession process, which is essential to the continued health and structural integrity of the peninsula, is activated at its eastern tip, an area called Gull Point. Secession is driven by a combination of natural forces. In late summer, water levels drop and winds calm. Sand, carried by westerly winds, comes to rest along the peninsula's north beaches just east of Gull Point, causing a series of sculpted sand bars. In the fall there are always several strong storms from the northeast (nor'easters). The winds tend to push the sandbars back (southwesterly) toward Gull Point creating parallel beach lines some thirty or forty feet east of the orginal beach.

Over the winter, water levels fall again. The effect on the beach looks as though nature is creating a double water's edge (two beaches). In the spring, cottonwood trees, common along freshwater beaches and the quintessential species on Presque Isle, pollinate by releasing fluffy air-driven seed balls. As spring winds freshen and water levels rise, these cottonwood balls are blown into the water. The cottonwood seeds float back onto Gull Point, and become lodged on the previous year's newly formed sand ridge. Over the summer the seeds root along the outer sand bar, forming a structure covered with scrub brush near the newly developing beach.

Assuming that this new ridge survives the next year's storms and water level shifts (which it does approximately thirty percent of the time), Presque Isle will have grown to the east by the width of the new parallel beach line. This (secession) is the process which has systematically driven Presque Isle eastward. A helicopter view of Presque Isle's eastern tip shows a series of arch-shaped rows of cottonwood trees. From the water's edge moving westward, rows grow further apart and the trees get

taller. As the cottonwoods mature, organic materials build up near their bases and the curved rows of trees develop ridge lines to go with them. The older the secession line, the higher the ridge. Between the easternmost ridges, which are tiny compared to their westerly cousins, there are ponds formed by the water which is trapped between the parallel ridges.

As the ridge lines mature and grow taller (moving east to west), the pond structures between them also change. The eastern ponds are bottom-water fed, clearwater repositories with fish (trapped by secession) and limited plant growth. The second tier of ponds (to the west) usually develops a variety of marine algae and other plant life. As the ponds along Gull Point age, they change to marshy areas and finally rich soil which separates and nourishes the organic materials between the mature ridge lines.

From an ecological perspective, Presque Isle represents a rare environment where climax forest secession can be studied in a compact area. As a further bonus, the variety of structures provided by the secession environment makes a productive home for a vast array of birds and mammals. Presque Isle and Long Point create an important bird flyway. The area is registered as a National Natural Landmark, and the process of plant and animal succession is a source of both research and educational interest. Researchers, college professors, and students from across the U.S. and Canada have been engaged in the study of birds at both Presque Isle and Long Point for decades.

BUSINESS AND LOCAL INTERESTS

To the local recreational and business communities, the easterly growth of the peninsula and the scientific interests of academics are more of a threat than a benefit. The regional economy has always been fueled by tourism rather than science.[4] Since the park

---

[4] Tourism now brings in approximately $80 million per year to the Erie area; this is mainly a function of visitor attraction to Presque Isle State Park. This industry has historically been viewed as a renewable, resource-based industry, and under this perspective tourists are perceived to *view* area attractions, but do not *consume* them. However, an increased recognition of the fragility surrounding the environment and its natural resources has now begun to change this perception, and for Presque Isle, tourism is perceived as competing for scarce resources and capital. The perception is based on an increasing awareness that a different type of tourist-consumption is occurring in the form of deleterious effects on the ecosystem.

was established in 1921 and a roadway built to its popular bathing beaches and picnic groves, millions of people have flocked to Erie and Presque Isle.

Since the demise of the local industrial base in the 1970s, tourism has taken on even more importance to the regional economy.[5] By 1990, economic data suggested that tourism, anchored by visits to Presque Isle, was the number two component of the regional economy. Attendance at Presque Isle has consistently been greater than that of Yellowstone National Park. By 1990, a wall of motels, restaurants, fishing tackle shops, bike rental centers, and other amusements had built up near the park entrance. Regional chambers of commerce estimate that the summer population of the Erie area is 160% of its winter totals.

For the tourist-based economy, any threat to the use of the peninsula is a potential business crisis, and there have been many threats over the years. In the 1950s, there was concern that the narrow western arm of the peninsula might wash away due to erosion. The continuous eastward motion of wind and water tends to wash sand from the western beaches toward Gull Point. Thus the natural process which causes secession threatens the peninsula's narrow western arm, beaches, and park entrance.

Since before the 1950s it was common for storm waters to break through the western arm, making the peninsula into an island. As a result, it was not unusual for visitors to be unable to exit the park. This problem was tackled by the U.S. Army Corps of Engineers which launched a rebuilding program in the late 1950s, adding dredged beach sand to the western arm of the peninsula. At the same time, an improved roadway system was built, solving the problem of weekend traffic congestion.

The Corps of Engineers has long suggested that, if left to its own devices, Presque Isle would ulti-

mately separate from the mainland, becoming an island and continuing its relentless eastward migration away from Erie. Since the major rebuilding of the western arm, the Corps has continuously trucked sand to the peninsula to protect the bathing beaches.

This ongoing renewal plan had a multimillion-dollar price tag, so to save money, the Corps made a decision in the early 1980s to replenish the beaches with sand from quarrys south of Erie. Quarry sand is much coarser and less aesthetically pleasing than the dredged sand used in the early days of beach nourishment. But the coarser sand is less expensive, and it has been therefore argued that its heavier consistency will help hold the beaches in place.

During the middle 1980s, high water levels in combination with several severe fall storms did significant damage to the beaches. As in the 1950s, lake waters overflowed the peninsula, closing roads and reminding the public of the fragile nature of Presque Isle. Therefore, in a "final" move to stabilize the peninsula, the Army Corps announced a new program using parallel rock mound barrier reefs which were to run parallel to the north beach at a distance of approximately 500 yards from shore.

Theoretically the rock mound reefs would attenuate wave action from either prevailing southwesterlies or the fall/spring nor'easters. The movement of sand from west to east would have to be added to beach fronts to ensure stabilization. The final project was completed at a cost of more than twenty-three million dollars over a three and one half-year period.

As the last of an immense flow of federal and state tax dollars was spent for this project, a low water cycle began on the lake and it was beginning to appear that the threat of the loss of Presque Isle, or its roadways, had subsided and that the Army Corps had overreacted. Investment in tourism at the entrance to the park accelerated once more with two new bars, a restaurant, a windsurfing/rollerblading center, condominiums, and a scuba diving shop.

PARK ADMINISTRATION

Erie's first settlers were attracted to the natural harbor formed by Presque Isle. They generally came via water, arriving by schooner or bateaux in the late 1700s. They settled on the creek inlets which

[5] The demise of Erie's industrial base during the late 1970s and early 1980s had a great impact on Presque Isle and the tourist economy. Massive layoffs and plant closings had resulted from revolutionary changes in the steelmaking and shipping industries which were the area's primary economic base. In a short time, tourism was a strong component of the local economy.

An *analysis of* Presque Isle State Park attendance records suggests that during periods of economic downturn, people are more inclined to take comparatively inexpensive trips to a local state park. Travel is dependent on the course of the U.S. economy and visits to the park may be viewed as an alternative to longer, more expensive trips. Since competition for discretionary spending becomes intense in a sluggish economy, park visitation and tourism take on additional importance for the financial health of the local community.

emptied into the sheltered bay. As the town developed in the 1800s, the peninsula became a harbor barrier and a wilderness area utilized by citizens for hunting, fishing, and recreation. The federal government (whose needs decreased after hostilities with Canada and the War of 1812 ended) and the City of Erie both saw the land mass as an important strategic acquisition.

In 1921, while city and federal governments quibbled over ownership, the state of Pennsylvania negotiated a complex political deal in which the federal government could use an area for a Coast Guard station, but the State owned the peninsula. Meanwhile, the city was assured that a park would be developed for the well-being of the local population, and the city's water supply infrastructure (on the peninsula) would remain under the jurisdiction of the city of Erie.

Thus began a long history of state administration and the controversies which were to arise in later years. In the first and possibly most significant of all developments, it was determined that a roadway system would span the length of the park. In prior years a crude road ran from the mainland for the first few miles along the north beaches. Governor Fisher's proposed roadway was to loop around the eastern end of Presque Isle and encourage "motoring." Citizens could tour with automobiles to view flora, fauna, and wildlife.

Between 1938 and 1994, however, the volume of traffic grew at rates beyond the imagination of early park architects. Weekend totals reached astronomical numbers and the extension of park driving hours during summer months resulted in a constant stream of automobiles circling Presque Isle's fourteen-mile roadway system.

Over the first decades of development several personnel additions were needed in park administration, which now reports to Pennsylvania's Department of Environmental Resources. By 1982, the staff consisted of the superintendent, administrative staff, maintenance, a police department, the marina staff, and a lifeguard organization. (Later review of the Park personnel revealed the lack of a full-time naturalist position. An on-site individual was needed to continuously assess and monitor park preservation activities.) A number of superintendents were involved in the development of Presque Isle, but the greatest growth occurred between 1956 and 1986 under the direction of long-time Superintendent Michael Wargo. During the Wargo

regime the park matured, a 473-boat marina was constructed, tourism grew, and the Corps of Engineers initiated and completed major renovations.

Upon Wargo's retirement, the state, which was beginning to sense the potential for both growth and political controversy, appointed Eugene Giza to the post. Giza was young and ambitious and understood the park's growth potential. He was also politically astute and sensed that there might be a linkage between park use and funding. The budget had undergone cuts in the early 1980's, and Giza developed activities which would encourage visitation and rationalize more funding. Unfortunately, budget cuts continued.[6]

Under the Giza administration the following developments occurred:

1. Old-fashioned "hole in the ground" outhouses were replaced with modern lavatory facilities. These featured an above-ground sand mound leach bed (similar to a septic system) and did not have to be emptied on a regular basis.
2. An all-purpose black top trail was built along the south (bayside) edge of the park. This encouraged hiking, running, biking, and rollerblading.
3. Winter activities such as festivals and carnivals were initiated.
4. A cross-country ski trail system was developed and an entrepreneur was given concession rights.
5. Running and bike races were encouraged in the park.
6. A Citizen's Advisory Committee was formed to shepherd the park.

THE ENVIRONMENTAL BACKLASH

As early as the Wargo administration, an environmentalist reaction against peninsula policies began to build. Local groups such as the Audubon Society and the Birdwatchers began raising objections to park projects. The most significant blow to the continuity of tourist-related developments came when Presque Isle's own Citizen's Advisory Group began to lean toward environmental issues.

---

[6] Presque Isle's status as a state-controlled entity makes if vulnerable to threats not shared with the private sector. Its operating budget is solely funded by the Department of Environmental Resources, which must allocate a shrinking budget to over 100 parks. Presque Isle is not permitted to spend all the revenue it generates, as those funds are turned over to the state for allocation among all the state parks.

In summary, the environmental position was that too many park decisions were designed simply to increase use. This subsequently threatened the delicate environment, plants, animals, and water quality. An example was the early decision to place a roadway around the park and encourage motoring. Environmentalists argued that the delicate sand spit could not tolerate this volume of carbon-spewing gasoline engines. From an environmental posture it would have been preferable to make park visitors leave their automobiles at the park gates and hike or bicycle to the eastern portions of the park, or to operate an electric tram service to the eastern beaches and picnic areas.

Using this early decision as an example, business and tourist interests argued that the accessibility of park roads kept a constant stream of people (sightseers, swimmers, picnickers, hikers, and fishermen) traveling to the park. Any constraint to free access represented a threat to business. The increasingly vocal environmentalists cited examples of abuses of the park by motorists who crowded the roads. They polluted the air, parked cars in unauthorized areas, and disturbed plant life. This posed a threat to animals such as deer and foxes by changing their natural patterns of behavior, frightening them during late evening drives, and even hitting them with automobiles.

Some more reasonable environmental voices understood that old practices, like allowing automobile access, were not likely to be reversed. These ongoing threats to the park's environment, it was argued, created a special responsibility for park administration to be careful of the environmental implications of new decisions. As the Giza administration began its efforts to increase usage (and hopefully the budget allocation from Harrisburg), seeds of the final conflict were firmly sown.

Superintendent Giza explained to the environmental groups that his usage-driven decisions would ultimately be in the best interests of the park. Increased funding, he argued, could be used to safeguard the park's fragile geology and ecology. With more funding he could hire a full-time naturalist and initiate programs of public environmental awareness. And many of his ideas—for example, 10K races and biking—would be easy on the environment. But as defects in decisions began to emerge, various groups began to lose patience and take public stands against new programs.

While a number of these new plans which were perceived as a threat to the park were not actually the inventions of Giza, he began to take the administrative heat for them. During the final years of his administration the following issues came to the attention of the public:

1. **The Presque Isle Marina** opened in 1962, grew to 473 slips, and added underground fuel tanks as well as sewage treatment facilities.
2. **The lagoon system** was connected to the marina lake, and a continuous navigable loop was created. This action joined two previously separate wetland and pond areas, and allowed plant life from the two areas to invade each other.
3. **Parking lot and pavilion construction** continued through the 1980s, taking a toll on mature trees.
4. **The all-purpose trail** was built in 1984 to allow hikers and bikers access to the south waterfront, but wetlands had been violated and endangered plant species were compromised.
5. **Lyme disease** was reported in the park and linked to mismanagement (oversupply) of the whitetail deer herd.
6. **Sand mound toilets,** constructed along the entire length of the park, had replaced the older pit toilet outhouses. The new design, viable in other (primarily mountainous) regions, proved to be inappropriate for a sand spit peninsula.
7. **Beach replenishment** shifted from the use of dredged Lake Erie sand to quarry sand in order to save money.
8. **Rock mound barrier reefs** were constructed between 1989 and 1992 to solve the problem of sand replenishment by slowing erosion. It was argued that these structures were not aesthetic and would lead to water pollution in the stagnant areas behind them.
9. **Beach closings** occurred due to fecal coliform and other contaminants. Closings were beginning to occur at the same general time the sand mound toilets and the barrier reefs were installed.

While most of the environmental issues fell on deaf ears with respect to the business community and the general public, the beach closings were another matter. What would a closed beach, or even the rumor of a closed beach, do to tourism, business, and the public view of the park? This dilemma quickly raised a previously altruistic issue to the level of a real problem.

THE GULL POINT CONTROVERSY

The "mother of all controversies" however, was the Gull Point issue. Gull Point, the 319-acre eastern tip of the peninsula had become a popular summer congregating point for local boaters. The natural curves of the point provide protection from prevailing southwesterly winds. The pristine beach, located miles away from public beaches and roadways, creates a sanctuary for boaters. Generations of persons had grown accustomed to anchoring, picnicking, and swimming at the tip of the point.

Boating season in Erie begins in early May and lasts through October, although there are a few hearty souls who push both extremes of the season. As the summer months progress, an increasing number of boaters is attracted to the Gull Point anchorage. The waters to the east of Gull Point and its sand spits offers protection from all but easterly winds. The many odd-shaped inlets of the developing sand spit tip, as well as the secession sand ponds, serve as an additional attraction, especially to boaters in shallow draft vessels. By early July a typical weekend finds hundreds of sail and power boats anchored at Gull Point. Sooner or later, boaters would find their way onto the fragile tip of the point where they participate in a variety of seemingly innocent activities: picnicking, sunbathing, hiking, exploring, and Frisbee.

Boaters knew that this area of Presque Isle was officially declared a bird sanctuary in 1957, and most Gull Point visitors perceived themselves as being careful about their usage of the area. They would yell at their children for throwing rocks at birds and go out of their way not to put a beach blanket on a nest. They thought they were being good citizens.

In the early days of the bird sanctuary, park police were unlikely to enforce the issue of the bird sanctuary. After all, many boaters reasoned, Gull Point is 319 acres and we are simply using the edge of the beach! What harm could that possibly do?

By the end of the 1980s, however, a storm of protests arose from environmental groups. They pointed to the huge list of endangered bird species which needed to make use of the peninsula. They further noted the critical nature of the water's edge to many of these migratory birds. A number of species reach the safe haven of Gull Point in a weakened condition, desperately needing respite at the water's edge to gather food and regain strength so they can continue their migration. Even episodic (weekend) disturbances by boaters could spell doom for these birds.[7] Other species used Gull Point for the express purpose of raising young, and episodic boat traffic could threaten the breeding process. The environmental groups were demanding that boaters, as well as hikers, stay away from Gull Point.

In and around Erie, the piping plover became the symbolic "poster child" of the Gull Point movement. This diminutive shore bird had become rare on Gull Point, almost in synchrony with the increase in the recreational boating industry. By the early 1990s, environmental groups were pointing to the fact that the endangered creature was no longer able to nest on Gull Point and asked if this might be the first of a long series of birds that would cease to exist as a result of lenience granted to suit the whims of boaters.

GUNFIGHT AT THE OK CORRAL

As Harry stepped through the doorway of the lecture hall, the crowd grew quiet in anticipation. This was clearly a revisitation of Wyatt Earp, badge and all, trying to settle things between the forces of good and the forces of evil. "Folks," he began, "my name is Harry Leslie and the important thing is that we do what is right for future generations and for Presque Isle!" As he presented the main points of the park's new management plan, Harry began to realize that the question period might not go as smoothly as he had hoped. His plan included a variety of objectives: increasing park visitor capacity, limiting the number of approved duck blind locations, and prohibiting access to Gull Point from April 1 to November 30. It also included an additional 200 pages of meticulous detail: history, definitions, lists, and more. This was clearly the finest piece of systematic work ever produced in the name of planning for Presque Isle.

But the members of the audience wanted specific assurances. "Do you mean to tell me that I can't take my family to Gull Point in my boat any more?" "Who appointed you the king of the penin-

---

[7] In 1937 the Park and Harbor Commission was supported by special legislation which gave the Commission jurisdiction over the waters up to 500 feet off the shores of Presque Isle, including the waters of Misery Bay. This was done to prevent encroachment by moored houseboats; today this code enables the park to prohibit water-skiing within the 500 feet of coastal waters surrounding the Park.

sula?" commented a second. "Are you going to refund the money that I spent for my boat?" asked a third. "What do you mean increased visitor capacity?" questioned a birdwatcher. "There are already too many people in the park!" "How come boaters can't disturb seagulls, but hunters can shoot ducks?" asked an irate sailor. "Typical liberal commie type," retorted a row of duck hunters who owned grandfathered rights to duck blinds within the Gull Point bird sanctuary.

As the session with the overflow crowd grew more agitated and ugly, Harry's stomach began to hurt. Many of these folks were the wealthy, the influential and elite forces of the community, and they acted like the fans at a professional wrestling match. As he struggled to answer questions, maintain order, and explain his environmental management plan, his thoughts turned to his children, sleeping in their lighthouse home. Would he really be able to maintain the lifestyle that had become such an important part of their family life? Or was his dream rapidly disintegrating into a nightmare? ■

SOURCE: P. Wright, M. J. Kroll, and J. Parnell, *Strategic Management: Concepts and Cases*, 4th ed. (Upper Saddle River, NJ, Prentice Hall, 1998).

CASE QUESTIONS

1. Who are the primary stakeholders in this case? Based on their demands, what should be the foremost goals for Presque Isle State Park?

2. Discuss the efficiency and effectiveness with which Presque Isle State Park has been managed under the Giza administration.

3. Given that strategic evaluation should increase understanding of activities and lead to improvements that produce financial savings, how would you evaluate the current situation in which Harry Leslie finds himself?

4. Explain the difference between policy and strategy as it relates to management of Presque Isle State Park.

5. What is the overall organizational strategy under which Presque Isle operates? What business-level strategy?

6. What are the pros and cons of government regulation for Presque Isle State Park?

CASE 14–2   Vancouver Public Aquarium

Richard Knight, public relations director for the Vancouver Public Aquarium, reread the memo he had just received from Elizabeth Dewey, the aquarium's educational programs coordinator. Ms. Dewey had proposed that, starting the following fall, the aquarium restrict weekday admissions to only school tours during the hours from 10:00 A.M. to 3:00 P.M. and exclude the general public during those hours.

During the school year, the Vancouver Public Aquarium (VPA) offered five formal educational programs for students from kindergarten to grade 12. Further, the aquarium's trained guides (docents) gave children guided tours which included various performances offered to the general public. Though these tours were successful, there was evidence that both individual visitors and the schools felt that the aquarium could be better utilizing their facilities. For instance, some members of the general paying public found it irritating to browse through the galleries with "all the screaming kids around." Also, the teachers felt that the feeding performances, one of the highlights of the aquarium, could be geared more to the predominantly younger weekday market. Because the school market was important to the aquarium and weekday attendance by the general paying public was low, Mr. Knight felt that he must examine the proposal fully before giving Ms. Dewey a response.

BACKGROUND

The VPA opened its doors on June 3, 1956, in Vancouver's Stanley Park, a popular recreational area adjacent to downtown Vancouver. Accessible by bus or car, the park was centrally located within the Greater Vancouver Regional District (GVRD), an association of Vancouver and its surrounding communities (Burnaby, North Vancouver, Richmond, West Vancouver, and others). Most of the GVRD's population of 1.3 million people lived within ten miles of Stanley Park.

The aquarium's facilities had undergone numerous renovations in the 30 years following its opening. In 1967, the B.C. Telephone Pool was constructed to hold dolphins, but the aquarium acquired a killer whale (orca) instead. It quickly became evident that the pool was unsuitable for such a large mammal, and so in 1972, the killer whale pool was opened. In conjunction with these outdoor "gallery" changes, the aquarium continued to improve its indoor exhibits. Perhaps the most significant indoor change was the addition of the Amazon Gallery, which recreated the environment of an Amazon River valley. Opened in 1983 by Queen Elizabeth II, the Amazon Gallery, with its 2,200 specimens, was the only indoor exhibit of its kind in the world. Funds for it were donated by government, VPA members, and private donations. In May 1986, the Max Bell Marine Mammal Centre was opened, incorporating the first Killer Whale Habitat in the world. Designed and constructed to house only killer whales, this exhibit set what many experts viewed as the world standard in both exhibit philosophy and animal husbandry.

With Expo '86, Vancouver's 100th birthday, and the aquarium's 30th birthday, 1986 was a record year for attendance with 876,825 visitors (Exhibit 14-7). Increasing attendance beyond that level was a challenge that faced Mr. Knight.

Current Offerings

In 1987, the aquarium housed some 7,100 specimens (669 species) of marine and aquatic life. Its sea otter breeding program was most successful and had helped to preserve this once endangered species; five pups had been born at the aquarium. The aquarium saw itself on the leading edge of both marine research and display of mammals and Northern Pacific marine species.

The main product offered to visitors by the aquarium was the opportunity to see its collection of aquatic life. Related species were housed in "galleries," usually be geographic region. In addition, the aquarium offered whale shows, films, tours, and special showings (such as "Fishes of China"), all included in the admission price. There were no restaurants or food services on the aquarium's grounds, although a number of food stands were located nearby in Stanley Park.

The aquarium also offered several secondary products. It had rented its facilities for social functions; companies could have staff parties, meetings, and dinner/dances in the various galleries; for children, birthday parties, complete with cake, were available. The aquarium also offered special lectures and school programs on aquatic life. Members could take advantage of whale watching tours, beach walks, and special previews. These programs had been very successful.

The aquarium also ran a retail operation, the Clam Shell Gift Shop, which sold aquarium-related books, animal prints, nature calendars, and numerous aquarium souvenirs.

MISSION

The VPA stated its mission as follows:

> The Vancouver Aquarium is dedicated to the perservation and enhancement of aquatic life through education, recreation, and research. It is a private, nonprofit society, and is completely self-supporting.

This mission statement was the driving force behind the aquarium. Every program had to fit into one of the three categories in the statement; all staff were required to follow its guidelines. As expressed by VPA staff and literature, the aquarium's main business was to educate the public about aquatic life. The aquarium accomplished this through such activities as demonstrations and interpretive programs. In particular, the VPA offered numerous programs—such as lectures, tours, and beach walks—to educate school children, teens, and adults.

MARKETS

During the past two years, the aquarium's average weekday attendance in winter had been 550 patrons per day. Weekends were busier, with Saturdays aver-

EXHIBIT 14-7 Annual Attendance, 1982–1986

Attendance	1982	1983	1984	1985	1986
Paid					
Adults	216,161	257,400	237,312	248,742	329,334
Youths and senior citizens	76,123	84,276	70,713	79,285	—
Groups	43,465	45,665	46,605	34,983	55,280
Education programs	10,580	6,226	8,983	14,638	—
Family rate	166,696	181,107	166,736	120,409	196,481
Children and seniors	—	—	—	—	86,186
Youths	—	—	—	—	22,784
	513,025	574,674	530,349	498,057	690,065
Other attendance					
Members	54,783	91,891	73,064	66,963	73,148
Other	70,399	89,003	99,614	87,162	113,612
Total	638,207	755,568	703,567	652,182	876,825
Single admission, per person					
Adults	$ 4.25	$ 4.50	$ 4.50	$ 5.00	$ 5.25
Senior citizens	$ 2.00	$ 2.25	$ 2.25	$ 2.50	$ 2.75
Youths (5–18 years)	$ 2.00	$ 2.25	$ 2.25	—	—
Youths (12–18 years)	—	—	—	$ 3.75	—
Youths	—	—	—	—	$ 4.00
Children	—	—	—	$ 2.50	$ 2.75
Group admission					
Family	$10.00	$11.00	$11.00	$13.00	$13.25
Adults, 10–34 persons	$ 3.00	$ 3.25	$ 3.25	—	—
35 or more	$ 2.50	$ 2.75	$ 2.75	—	—
Adults, 10 or more	—	—	—	$ 3.75	$ 4.00
Youths, 10 or more	$ 1.25	$ 1.50	$ 1.50	$ 2.00	$ 2.25

aging 1,300 patrons and Sundays averaging 2,100. Mr. Knight felt that Saturday's attendance could be higher, possibly reaching Sunday's levels.

During this summer, there was still a difference between weekdays and weekends but general attendance levels were higher. In fact, the weekday levels were more than double those of the winter months.

The aquarium had at least six significant markets; schools, members, general admissions, donors, volunteers, and scientists. Mr. Knight felt that the first five markets would be affected by any decision relating to school tour admissions.

Members

By the end of 1986, the Vancouver Public Aquarium Association had 39,360 members, based on the sale of 15,077 memberships (up from 11,850 in 1985) to individuals, couples, and families. Members accounted for 73,148 of the aquarium's total attendance of 876,825.

Diverse programs were offered to this group, whic ranged from special educational programs to free admission to the aquarium; educational programs included whale watching in Johnstone Strait, previews of special displays, Galiano Island beach walks, and behind-the-scenes tours. Members received a 10 percent discount on gift shop purchases and an informative newsletter, called the *Sea Pen,* about once a month.

Mr. Knight realized that the membership was vital to the aquarium's finances and philosophy. He wondered how the members would react to not being allowed to use "their" aquarium on demand.

General Admissions

The general admissions category accounted for 61 percent of revenues. A recent study of summer visitors found that 97 percent of those surveyed felt they had received good value for their entertain-

EXHIBIT 14-8   Selected Results from January, 1987, Questionnaire

Quesiton	Response	No. of Responses[a]	
		Weekday	Weekend
1. Are you a resident of the Greater Vancouver Regional District?	Yes	71	60
	No	51	20
2. Are you currently a member of the Vancouver Aquarium?	Yes	26	34
	No	96	46
3. Is this you first visit to the Aquarium?	Yes	47	23
	No	75	57
4. Was your last visit to the Aquarium within the last two years?	Yes	23	46
	No	52	11
5. On average, how much time did you spend on this visit?	Less than ½ hour	0	0
	½–1 hour	44	30
	1–3 hours	72	50
	Over 3 hours	6	0
6. Are you alone or are you visiting with others?	Alone	9	4
	Others	113	76
7. How did you first learn about the Aquarium?	Friend/relative	29	15
	TV	9	0
	Radio	2	0
	Tourist magazine	2	0
	Brochure	8	4
	Newspaper	0	1
	Magazine article	2	0
	Billboard	0	0
	"Discovered"	14	0
	"Just knew"	40	40
	Other	16	10
8. Do you feel that you have received your entertainment dollar value at the Aquarium?	Yes	122	78
	No	0	2
9. Sex:	Male	85	47
	Female	37	33
10. What is your age group?	18–25	22	4
	26–30	34	18
	31–35	14	18
	36–40	22	14
	41–50	10	10
	51–60	12	8
	Over 61	8	8

[a] Total respondents: Weekdays: 122; weekends: 80.

Source: Based on a survey conducted during two weeks in January 1987. Interviewers were stationed near the exit and asked visitors, as they were leaving, to answer a brief questionnaire.

ment dollar. The aquarium offered various programs to educate and entertain this public: There were feeding shows, interpretive talks, films and volunteers to answer exhibit inquiries. In addition, the aquarium was open for extended hours during the summer.

The VPA's primary market was the Greater Vancouver Regional District. This area accounted for 28 percent of summer admissions and for 65 percent of off-season visitors (see Exhibit 14-8). A second market was the province of British Columbia, outside Greater Vancouver.

Other areas served included the Pacific Northwest of the United States to the south and the province of Alberta to the east. Though no programs were designed for these markets, visitors from these areas did patronize the aquarium during the summer months.

During the summer months, visitor parking, although free, could be a problem. Unfortunately, the VPA could do little to alleviate this problem because adjacent land in Stanley Park could not be appropriated for extra parking.

Donors

The donor market was seen as very important for the aquarium. Without donor support, many capital projects could not have been completed. For instance, some 17,000 individuals, 130 corporations, 4 foundations, and the federal government contributed more than $4.3 million to build the Max Bell Marine Mammal Centre. The aquarium recognized donors in various ways, including plaques, exhibit names (like the H. R. MacMillan Tropical Gallery), and publication of donors' names in VPA publications.

Volunteers

The 180 VPA volunteers, made up of Aquarium Association members and their families, volunteered 13,000 hours to the aquarium in 1986. They supervised educational tours, and worked in the Clam Shell Gift Shop. Management believed that the main attractions for volunteers were their sense of pride in the aquarium and genuine concern for its success.

Schools

Over 7,500 students took part in the following VPA educational programs in the most recent year:

Water Wonders	Kindergarten, Grades 1 and 2
Secrets of Survival	Grades 3 and 4
Mysterious Marine Mammals	Grades 5, 6, 7
Spineless Wonders (a laboratory program)	Grades 5, 6, 7
B.C.'s Marine Invertebrates (a laboratory program)	Grades 11 and 12
Royaume Aquatique	French-speaking groups
Travelling Teacher	Outreach program— an aquarium teacher visiting schools

In addition to these formal programs, tours of the aquarium, films, and interpretive workshops were offered to school groups. To accommodate French Immersion classes, the aquarium offered French language tours. There was also a "travelling teacher," employed by the aquarium, who toured the province teaching students in out-of-town schools about aquatic life and the work being done by the aquarium.

To make teachers aware of the aquarium's programs, each school in the Vancouver area received a descriptive brochure at the beginning of the school year. During the third week of September, the VPA offered an "Open House for Educators" that gave teachers the opportunity to participate in workshops, preview the programs offered, and pick up various resource materials. Afterward, teachers could book their classes into the programs and tours.

These programs were very popular. Usually most available spaces for the formal programs were filled by the second week in October. During the school year, the aquarium averaged five school tours per day. At present, the aquarium could handle no more than six tours a day. Though school groups were given special group rates and a volunteer was provided to guide the tours, no other special accommodations were offered by the aquarium.

Ms. Dewey's proposal would required the VPA to alter its presentations (such as the killer whale feedings) to better suit a school-age audience and to restrict the VPA's galleries to school children until 3 P.M. on weekdays. Closing the galleries to the general public on school days would have two effects on the VPA's operaton. First, the "conflict" between the general public and school tours would be eliminated; the public would not be fighting the crowds of school children. However, the frustrations of aquarium members and the general admission market might shift from annoyance with the school children to anger at not being allowed admission at all. Second, the Clam Shell Gift Shop's hours of operation could be reduced; the shop would not need to be open during the hours of school tours. Currently, the aquarium used two full-time salaried employees and one part-time staff member, in addition to volunteers, to handle admissions and run the gift shop during weekdays. If the proposal were adopted, the aquarium's staffing needs could be reduced by at least one paid position during the school tour periods.

Mr. Knight sat down to do a preliminary study to see if the proposal was economically feasible. During the winter months, an average of 550 people per day visited the aquarium on weekdays. Of these 550, roughly 70 percent were "General Admission" (385 persons). A "typical" weekday group consisted to two adults ($5.50 each) and one child ($3). Mr Knight felt that for the school proposal to be implemented, revenues from the school programs would have to be increased to cover at least part of the $1,700 loss of general admissions revenues. Of course, some proportion of the weekday visitors would come another time. There was also the possibility of opening the aquarium to general admission after 3 P.M., but currently few winter visitors came at that time.

School admissions were priced at $2.50 per student and the average school group's size was 34 students. Mr. Knight wondered if the aquarium, particularly the volunteer guides, could handle a significant increase in school tours. If not, could the aquarium attract new volunteer docents? He was relatively confident that the aquarium would not have to hire more paid staff.

PRICING AND PROMOTIONS

VPA's prices were to be increased by an average of 10 percent on April 1, 1987 (see Exhibit 14-9). Adult admission would then cost $5.50, a price that

included both the killer whale and beluga whale shows, tours, seal feedings, films, and entrance to all galleries.

Pricing policy was ultimately determined by the Vancouver Public Aquarium Association membership through its Board of Governors. Though the board had the final say, most pricing changes were initiated by VPA staff. The pricing policy was cost-oriented. The aquarium budgeted its expenditures for the coming year and then set ticket prices, membership fees, etc., to balance these expenses. Discounting practices were usually reserved for the aquarium's membership and groups of ten people or more.

The aquarium had two short-term promotional pricing programs. Both were offered in December and were marketed as the aquarium's gift to the city. During the first week in December, general admission was free. In 1986, 6,906 people took advantage of this opportunity. There were occasional other free days. For example, on March 9, 1987, the aquarium had a free day to thank Vancouver for its generous support of the Tropical Fish Gallery restocking. An astounding 12,000 people visited the aquarium.

The second promotion was the Christmas train program, which the aquarium participated in for the first time in 1986. In conjunction with Vancouver's Stanley Park Zoo, the aquarium had special nightly openings during one week of the Christmas holiday period. Patrons purchased a train ticket, entitling them to ride on a specially decorated miniature train. The train ride ran through a portion of Stanley Park as a tourist and family attraction. For

EXHIBIT 14-9   The Vancouver Public Aquarium's Price List

General Admission	Price	Membership Fee	Price
Individuals			
Adult	$ 5.50	Adult	$20.00
Youth or Senior	4.25	Special[a]	15.00
Child	3.00	Couple[b]	30.00
Family	14.00	Family	35.00
Groups (10+)			
Adult	4.25		
Child	2.50		
School	2.50		

[a] This group included students, out-of-province residents, and seniors.
[b] A senior couple could purchase a membership for $15.00.
Source: Vancouver Public Aquarium's Annual Report.

most of the year, the train was run only during daylight hours. After the ride, the VPA offered admission to the aquarium and special performances of killer whale shows at a reduced price. The program helped increase awareness of the aquarium, but rain during four of the five nights kept attendance down to only 860 people.

Communication

The aquarium's communication objective was to increase awareness of VPA programs. The membership was kept informed through special direct mail communication and regular quarterly editions of *Sea Pen* magazine. The local, nonmember segments were exposed to PSA advertisements on both radio and television. In addition, newspaper advertising was used to promote special events/exhibits. Aquarium brochures were available at Tourist Information Centers, Grayline Tour Booths, and at the Vancouver Travel Infocentre. During the summer months, billboard advertising was used.

Advertising budgets were set in December for the following year, with few changes in the mix from year to year.

Relations with the media were very good—so good that sometimes things got a little hectic. Along with regular coverage of aquarium events by local news media, major promotions generated wider coverage. The opening of the new Killer Whale Habitat, the appearance of the killer whales in the Vancouver Bach Choir/Vancouver Symphony Orchestra's "In Celebration of Whales" concert, the birth of two sea otters, and the major "Fishes of China" display all received national coverage in 1986. When an act of vandalism wiped out almost the entire tropical marine collection in late 1986, media around the world picked up the story. In addition to news coverage, TV programs like "Midday," "Sesame Street," and "The Nature of Things" featured segments on the Vancouver Public Aquarium. "Danger Bay," the CBC/Disney series, was filmed at the aquarium for a third season in 1986, continuing the adventures of Grant Roberts and his family.

The aquarium had recently started to track its visitors and ask how they found out about the aquarium. For instance, in a summer 1986 survey, 24 percent of people surveyed stated that they had seen an aquarium brochure. However, 54 percent stated that they hadn't seen any advertising. Selected results from a January 1987 survey are shown in Exhibit 14-8. With a budget of $120,000. Mr. Knight wondered how he could be more effective in increasing awareness.

Operating Hours

The aquarium had three distinct sets of operating hours. During the summer, the aquarium was open from 9:00 A.M. to 9:00 P.M., seven days per week. VPA managers felt that the extended summer hours increased attendance and also took advantage of the longer daylight hours. However, a 1982 study found that only 28 percent of visitors were aware of the extended summer hours. During the spring and fall, the aquarium was open from 10:00 A.M. to 6:00 P.M. Management felt that the public would not patronze the aquarium during winter evenings, so for winter months, the hours were further reduced to 10:00 A.M. to 5:00 P.M. To increase revenues, the aquarium offered evening and restricted daytime rentals of the facilities from September to May. The typical fee ranged from $100 for a luncheon meeting using a small room in the aquarium to $1,700 for use of the entire facility during an evening. (Food was provided by outside caterers.) In 1986, the VPA received more than $200,000 in rental revenue.

Though the aquarium had used these opening hours in the past, Mr. Knight had heard of other nonprofit groups who had altered their hours to "fit" the working public. In essence, these institutions would not be open in the mornings or early afternoons but would keep their facilities open during the evening to accommodate the working public.

Weekend hours could be kept the same or extended into the evening. This might allow the aquarium to keep its present weekend customers, and if the public knew that the aquarium was open until the same hour every night, awareness of the later hours would increase. If management were to set the same operating hours for the whole year, much of the confusion caused by the changing hours might be alleviated.

THE DECISION

At February's board meeting, various alternatives for more effective use of aquarium facilities had been raised. Board approval would be required prior to implementation of any recommendation to change opening hours significantly. Also, all programs had to be compatible with the aquarium's mission statement. Though the VPA had been successful in the past, Mr. Knight felt that a new approach to marketing could improve usage of the aquarium.

He recognized that Ms. Dewey's proposal had merits and that the survey results might help the aquarium better target its winter markets.

As Mr. Knight drove home, he wondered, "Can I solve these problems?" ■

SOURCE: Christopher H. Lovelock, *Services Marketing*, 3rd ed. (Upper Saddle River, NJ, Prentice Hall, 1996). Copyright © 1988 by Charles B. Weinberg.

CASE QUESTIONS

1. What are the objectives of Vancouver Public Aquarium? How well are these being fulfilled?
2. What are the major problems facing Mr. Knight?
3. Define the major customers and publics of the Vancouver Public Aquarium and indicate how they would be affected by the proposal.
4. What are the major advantages and disadvantages of the proposal?
5. What should Mr. Knight do?

References

Anthony, Robert N., and David W. Young, "Characteristics of Nonprofit Organizations," in David L. Gies, J. Steven Ott, and Jay M. Shafritz (eds.), *The Nonprofit Organization: Essential Readings* (Pacific Grove, CA, Brooks/Cole Publishing Company, 1990), pp. 216–235.

Fama, Eugene, and Michael Jensen, "Agency Problems and Residual Claims," *Journal of Law and Economics*, vol. 26 (June 1983), pp. 327–350.

Graham, Cole Blease, and Steven M. Hays, *Managing the Public Organization* (Washington, DC, Congressional Quarterly, Inc., 1986).

Hammack, David C., and Dennis R. Young, "Perspectives on Nonprofits in the Marketplace," in David C. Hammack and Dennis R. Young (eds.), *Nonprofit Organizations in a Market Economy* (San Francisco, Jossey-Bass Publishers, 1993), pp. 1–19.

Hansmann, Henry, "The Role of Nonprofit Enterprise," *Yale Law Journal*, vol. 89 (1980), pp. 835–901.

Hansmann, Henry, "Economic Theories of Nonprofit Organization," in Walter W. Powell (ed.), *The Nonprofit Sector: A Research Handbook* (New Haven, CT, Yale University Press, 1987), pp. 27–42.

James, Estelle, and Susan Rose-Ackerman, *The Nonprofit Enterprise in Market Economics* (London, Harwood Academic Publishers, 1986).

Mason, David E., *Voluntary Nonprofit Enterprise Management* (New York, Plenum Press, 1984).

Oleck, L. Howard, *Nonprofit Corporations, Organizations, and Associations*, 5th ed. (Upper Saddle River, NJ, Prentice Hall, 1988).

Salamon, Lester M., *Partners in Public Service: Government-Nonprofit Relations in the Modern Welfare State* (Baltimore, Johns Hopkins University Press, 1995).

Swiss, James E., *Public Management Systems: Monitoring and Managing Government Performance* (Upper Saddle River, NJ, Prentice Hall, 1991).

Tocqueville, Alexis de, *Democracy in America*, J. P. Mayer and Max Lerner (eds.), translated by George Lawrence (New York, Harper & Row, 1966).

Vasu, Michael L., Debra W. Stewart, and G. David Garson, *Organizational Behavior and Public Management*, 2nd ed. (New York, Marcel Dekker, 1990).

Wolf, Thomas, *Managing a Nonprofit Organization* (New York, Fireside, Simon and Schuster, 1990).

CHAPTER 15

Forecasting Demand for Services

15.1   INTRODUCTION

Every day, managers make decisions without knowing what will happen in the future. Making good estimates is the main purpose of forecasting. This chapter explains why forecasting is so important to service operations, what types of service outputs are forecast, and the factors that affect our choice of forecasting methods. A variety of forecasting models are also presented, such as exponential smoothing, moving averages, time series extrapolation, and linear regression.

Good forecasts are an essential input to all types of productive systems because they form the basis for planning. There are many types of services, however, that would be chaotic without careful forecasting of demand. A few situations that differ widely from manufacturing companies are described briefly below.

Fixed Capacity with Widely Fluctuating Demand

If a service organization has a relatively limited range of capacity and widely fluctuating demand for its services, it must establish policies to prevent idle facilities when demand is normally low. It also must seek means for treating customers when demand exceeds capacities. As an example, tennis clubs in South Florida usually have very little activity during the summer, so that courts may be utilized only 25 percent of the time. Policies may establish lower-priced summer memberships, tennis "camps," party-tournaments, corporate tournaments, and short clinics to keep the courts in use. On the other hand, in the winter, when demand usually exceeds court time, policies may include higher prices to reduce demand. In addition, activities such as parties, tours, and matches with clubs that have available court capacity may be arranged to shift the demand to other facilities and avoid losing members.

Service Systems That Cannot Carry Inventories

One of the features of manufacturing that allows adjustments for fluctuations to be made more easily is the ability to carry inventory for extended periods of time. Although many "embedded" service outputs such as videotapes, books, maps, and blood for transfusions can be carried in inventory, most services are intangible and are consumed during production. In the case of intangible outputs of services, capacity must be very closely matched to demand. Delays in supplying the service may lead to lost sales or ill will.

Sharing Capacity

A recent innovation in the service industries is **sharing capacity.** This has long been done by the electric utility industry with plants connected in major interstate grids in the United States. As another example, Service Corporation International of Houston, owner of a chain of funeral homes and cemeteries, has been clustering funeral homes in specific cities so that they can share personnel and automobiles. Their competitors have since developed similar but informal arrangements to do the same.[1] Obviously, realistic forecasting by each funeral home is essential to plan the correct total capacity for the group.

15.2 THE DEMAND FORECAST AS THE BASIS FOR OPERATIONS PLANNING

The **demand forecast** is the starting point for all planning. If the good or service is new for the organization, it must estimate whether it should produce such a product. It is not necessary to design the product for the preliminary demand forecast. The organization needs to determine initially if there is a latent demand for a new product or what share of an established industry it can reasonably obtain. Therefore, only the product concept is needed for this forecast. Once the good or service has been designed in detail, the demand forecast may be revised based on design superiorities or differences from competitors' offerings.

The demand forecast provides estimates of the number of units of services that could be sold by the organization, as bounded by the demand for the services and the potential capacity of the organization. The number of units that are forecasted to be sold must be based on an approximate price. Therefore, the **total annual revenue** results from the demand forecast. The forecast of revenue is important for making the decision as to whether the service should be marketed. It permits an annual budget and a breakdown analysis.

The preliminary annual budget is primarily based on volume of production and marketing plans. Exhibit 15-1 shows income and expense items as components of profit plans for (a) a manufacturing company and (b) a service firm—an airline.

15.3 WHAT TYPES OF SERVICE OUTPUTS ARE FORECAST?

In manufactured products, the forecast is clearly in terms of units of product. In the manufacture of intermediate goods, the demand forecast may be in tons (steel), pounds (chemicals), square feet (textiles, wallboard), or other similar physical units, as well as product units (motors, gears, etc.). All these goods are clearly defined "countables."

---

[1] Jo Ellen Davis, "Bob Waltrip Is Making Big Noises in a Quiet Industry," *Business Week* (August 25, 1986).

EXHIBIT 15-1   The Sales Forecast as the Basis for Operations Planning

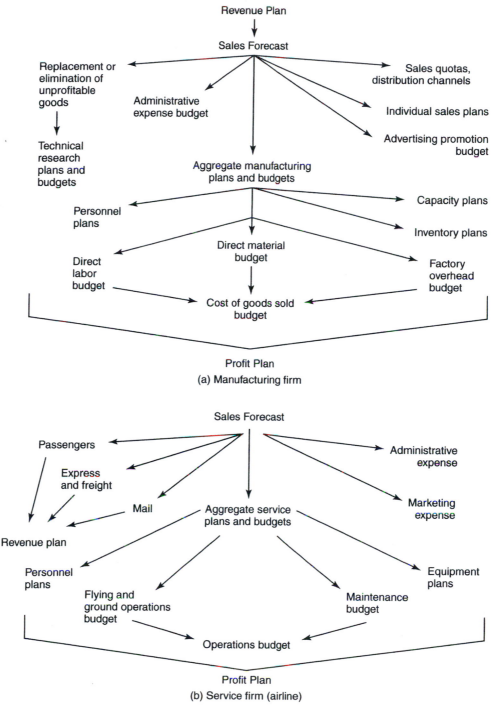

(a) Manufacturing firm

(b) Service firm (airline)

But what of services? The hospital may count emergency operations of accident victims, but these may vary considerably in nature and length of time. The consulting firm may wish to forecast demand for services, but projects may vary in time and complexity. Although the service manager may forecast the number of customers fairly accurately, the mix of services and the nature of services may vary tremendously. The units of services forecasted therefore are:

- Number of customers
- Number of hours of service supplied
- Variety of services supplied and number of each (meals, surgical operations, tailoring, real estate transactions, bank services, financial projects, repair jobs, etc.)
- Units of product supplied (gallons of gasoline, number of dial-a-song calls, number of newspapers sold)

One interesting difference between manufacturing and services forecasting is that net demand in manufacturing involves sales minus returns of goods. In most services (except retail and wholesale sales), the service has disappeared or been used up, so that the only "two-way" transaction is when a customer refuses to pay for unsatisfactory services.

15.4 FACTORS THAT AFFECT THE CHOICE OF FORECASTING METHOD

The choice of forecasting method, like most operating decisions, is an economic one. Therefore, each method should be reviewed from a cost–benefit perspective. The factors that should be taken into consideration in forecasting are:

1. Time
   a. Span of the forecast
   b. Urgency with which the forecast is needed
   c. Frequency that updates must be made

2. Resource requirements
   a. Mathematical sophistication available to the company
   b. Computer resources
   c. Financial resources

3. Input characteristics
   a. Antecendent data availability
   b. Variability or fluctuation range and frequency
   c. External stability

4. Output characteristics required
   a. Detail or degree of disaggregation
   b. Accuracy

Choosing a Forecasting Method

The output of many services fluctuates widely according to hour of the day, day of the week, week of the month, and month of the year. Other random factors peculiar to demand for services are the weather, special news, items on sale, the economy, some famous personality, the results of a medical study, or changes in interpretations of the law, such as, for example, tax accounting services. Holidays and days before and after holidays also produce surprises many times.

Service forecasting requires, in many cases, forecasts of hour-by-hour and day-to-day activities as well as aggregate forecasts, whereas in manufacturing, weekly, monthly, and aggregate forecasts are more common. This means that in services, very short-range forecasts must be made very frequently.

Basically, all forecasting techniques can be classified under these four groups:

- Judgment
- Counting
- Time series
- Association or causal

Forecasting with **judgment methods,** the manager uses experience, mental estimates of the market, intuition, personal value systems, guesses, and expert opinion to arrive at a forecast.

Counting means just that—counting the number of people who will buy or who *say* they will buy. A *census* is a count of the entire population that is being investigated. A *probability sample* is the counting of a portion of the population in order to estimate some characteristic of the whole population. With such surveys, forecasts may be in error because people change their minds after the survey or did not or could not answer the survey truthfully.

Time series are quantitative models that predict based on the assumption that the future of a data set is a function of the past of that data set. In other words, these models look at what has happened over a period of time and use a series of past data to make a forecast. One weakness of this method is that new factors in the future can throw off the results.

Association or **causal methods,** such as linear regression, are also mathematical models. They incorporate the variables or factors that might influence demand. A causal model for lawn mower sales might include factors such as new housing starts, advertising budget, and competitors' prices.

While many quantitative or mathematical forecasts include some subjectivity, some researchers believe that forecasters should rely more heavily on the output of a quantitative forecast than on their own judgment. Ashton and Ashton have concluded that even simple quantitative techniques outperform the unstructured intuitive assessments of experts in many cases. In addition, using judgment to adjust the values of a quantitatively derived forecast can reduce its accuracy.[2] This is so because judgment methods are susceptible to bias and managers are limited in their ability to process information and also to maintain consistent relationships among variables.[3]

While each forecasting technique has strengths and weaknesses, every forecasting situation is limited by such constraints as time, funds, competencies, or data. Balancing the advantages and disadvantages of techniques with regard to a situation's limitations and requirements is an important, but tough managerial task.

In choosing a forecasting method many forecasters use a technique driven approach which follows the Problem → Technique → Application → Result (PTAR) sequence. Murdick and Georgoff suggest a results driven approach which follows the Problem → Result → Technique → Application (PRTA) sequence.[4] In this sequence, the desired results define the method rather than having the method define the results.

---

[2] For survey articles that address this issue, see Essam Mahmoud, "Accuracy in Forecasting: A Survey," *Journal of Forecasting*, vol. 3, no. 2 (April–June 1984), p. 139; Robin M. Hogarth and Spyros Makridakis, "Forecasting and Planning: An Evaluation," *Management Science*, vol. 27, no. 2 (February 1981), p. 115; and A. H. Ashton and R. H. Ashton, "Aggregating Subjective Forecasts," *Management Science*, vol. 31, no. 12 (December 1985), pp. 1499–1508.

[3] Lennard Sjoberg, "Aided and Unaided Decision Making Improved Intuitive Judgment," *Journal of Forecasting*, vol. 1, no. 4 (October–December 1982), p. 349.

[4] Robert G. Murdick and David M. Georgoff, "Forecasting: A Systems Approach," *Technological Forecasting and Social Change*, vol. 44 (1993), pp. 1–16.

15.5   TIME SERIES FORECASTING MODELS

A **time series** is based on a sequence of evenly spaced (hourly, daily, weekly, monthly, and so on) data points. Examples include weekly sales of IBM PCs, quarterly revenue passenger miles on TWA, monthly admissions to General Hospital, and daily ridership on the Washington, D.C. subway. Forecasting time series data implies that future values are predicted *only* from past values and that other variables are incorporated into the past behavior of the time series.

Decomposition of a Time Series

Analyzing time series means breaking down past data into components and then projecting them forward. A time series typically has four components: trend, seasonality, cycles, and random variation.

1. **Trend** is the gradual upward or downward movement of the data over time. (See Exhibit 15-2.)
2. **Seasonality** is a pattern of demand fluctuation above or below the trend line that occurs every year.
3. **Cycles** are patterns in the data that occur every several years; they are usually tied into the business cycle.
4. **Random variations** are "blips" in the data caused by chance and unusual situations; they follow no discernible pattern.

In *most* models, forecasters assume that the random variations are averaged out over time. They then concentrate on only the seasonal component and a component that is a combination of trend and cyclical factors.

EXHIBIT 15-2   Demand for Services Charted over Four Years with Trend and Seasonality Indicated

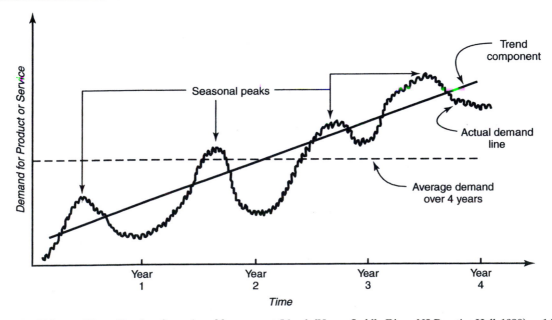

Source: Jay Heizer and Barry Render, *Operations Management*, 5th ed. (Upper Saddle River, NJ, Prentice Hall, 1999), p. 148.

Moving Averages

Moving averages are useful if we can assume that demand for services will stay fairly steady over time. A four-month moving average is found by simply summing the demand during the past four months and dividing by 4. With each passing month, the most recent month's data are added to the sum of the previous three months' data, and the earliest month is dropped. This tends to smooth out short-term irregularities in the data series.

Mathematically, the simple moving average (which serves as an estimate of the next period's demand) is expressed as

$$\text{Moving average} = \frac{\Sigma \text{ demand in previous } n \text{ periods}}{n} \qquad (15.1)$$

where n is the number of periods in the moving average—for example, four, five, or six months, respectively, for a four-, five-, or six-period moving average.

For example, customer demand at Donna's Garden Supply is shown in the following table. A three-month moving average forecast appears on the right.

Month	Actual Shed Sales	3-Month Moving Average
January	10	
February	12	
March	13	
April	16	(10 + 12 + 13)/3 = 11⅔
May	19	(12 + 13 + 16)/3 = 13⅔
June	23	(13 + 16 + 19)/3 = 16
July	26	(16 + 19 + 23)/3 = 19⅓
August	30	(19 + 23 + 26)/3 = 22⅔
September	28	(23 + 26 + 30)/3 = 26⅓
October	18	(26 + 30 + 28)/3 = 28
November	16	(30 + 28 + 18)/3 = 25⅓
December	14	(28 + 18 + 16)/3 = 20⅔

Weighted Moving Averages

When there is a trend or pattern, weights can be used to place more emphasis on recent values. This makes the techniques more responsive to changes, because more recent periods may be more heavily weighted. Deciding which weights to use requires some experience and a bit of luck. Choice of weights is somewhat arbitrary, because there is no set formula to determine them. If the latest month or period is weighted too heavily, the forecast might reflect a large unusual change in the demand or sales pattern too quickly. A weighted moving average may be expressed mathematically as

$$\frac{\text{Weighted moving}}{\text{average}} = \frac{\Sigma (\text{weight for period } i)(\text{demand for period } i)}{\Sigma \text{ weights}} \qquad (15.2)$$

For example, using the demand shown above, Donna's Garden Supply decides to forecast demand for services by weighting the past three months as follows.

Weights Applied	Period
3	Last month
2	2 months ago
1	3 months ago

The results of this weighted average forecast are shown in the following table.

Month	Actual Shed Sales	Three-Month Weighted Moving Average
January	10	
February	12	
March	13	
April	16	$[(3 \times 13) + (2 \times 12) + (10)]/6 = 12\frac{1}{6}$
May	19	$[(3 \times 16) + (2 \times 13) + (12)]/6 = 14\frac{1}{3}$
June	23	$[(3 \times 19) + (2 \times 16) + (13)]/6 = 17$
July	26	$[(3 \times 23) + (2 \times 19) + (16)]/6 = 20\frac{1}{2}$
August	30	$[(3 \times 26) + (2 \times 23) + (19)]/6 = 23\frac{5}{6}$
September	28	$[(3 \times 30) + (2 \times 26) + (23)]/6 = 27\frac{1}{2}$
October	18	$[(3 \times 28) + (2 \times 30) + (26)]/6 = 28\frac{1}{3}$
November	16	$[(3 \times 18) + (2 \times 28) + (30)]/6 = 23\frac{1}{3}$
December	14	$[(3 \times 16) + (2 \times 18) + (28)]/6 = 18\frac{2}{3}$

In this particular forecasting situation, weighting the latest month more heavily provides a slightly more accurate projection.

Both simple and weighted moving averages are effective in smoothing out sudden fluctuations in the demand pattern in order to provide stable estimates. Moving averages are not without problems, however. Increasing the size of *n* (the number of periods averaged) does smooth out fluctuations better, but it makes the method less sensitive to *real* changes in the data. In addition, simple moving averages cannot pick up trends very well. Since they are averages, they will always stay within past levels and will not predict a change to either a higher or lower level.

Exhibit 15-3, a plot of the data in the preceding examples, illustrates the lag effect of the moving average models.

Exponential Smoothing

Exponential smoothing is a moving-average forecasting method that is easy to use and efficiently handled by computers. The basic exponential smoothing formula can be shown as follows:

New forecast = last period's forecast
$$+ \alpha \text{ (last period's actual demand – last period's forecast)} \qquad (15.3)$$

where α is a weight, or **smoothing constant,** that has a value of 0 and 1, inclusive. Equation 15.3 also can be written mathematically as

$$F_t = F_{t-1} + \alpha(A_{t-1} - F_{t-1}) \qquad (15.4)$$

where

F_t = the new forecast
F_{t-1} = the previous forecast
α = smoothing constant $(0 \le \alpha \le 1)$
A_{t-1} = previous period's actual demand

The concept is not complex. The latest estimate of demand is equal to the old forecast adjusted by some percentage of forecast error. This error is the difference between the last period's actual demand and the old estimate.

EXHIBIT 15-3   Actual Demand versus Moving Average and Weighted Moving Average Methods for Donna's Garden Supply

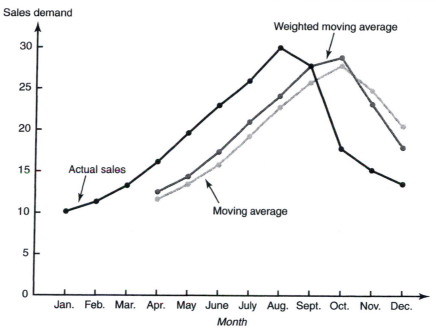

Source: Jay Heizer and Barry Render, *Operations Management*, 5th ed. (Upper Saddle River, NJ, Prentice Hall, 1999), p. 151.

Here is an example. In January, a car dealer predicted a February demand for 142 Ford Tauruses. Actual February demand was 153 autos. Using a smoothing constant of $\alpha = 0.20$, we can forecast the March demand using the exponential smoothing model. Substituting into the formula, we obtain

New forecast (for March demand) $= 142 + 0.2(153 - 142) = 144.2$

Thus, the demand forecast for Ford Tauruses in March is rounded to 144.

The smoothing constant α can be changed to give more weight to recent data (when it is high) or more weight to past data (when it is low). The closer α is to 0, the closer the forecast will fall to last period's forecast of this period. This contrasts to a regular moving average, in which all data are given equal weight in computing the next period's forecast.

Selecting the Smoothing Constant   The exponential smoothing approach is easy to use, and it has been successfully applied by numerous services industries. The appropriate value of the smoothing constant α, however, can make the difference between an accurate forecast and an inaccurate forecast. In picking a value for the smoothing constant, the objective is to obtain the most accurate forecast. The overall accuracy of a forecasting model can be determined by comparing the forecasted values with the actual or observed values.

The **forecast error** is defined as

Forecast error = demand − forecast   **(15.5)**

One measure of the overall forecast error for the model is the **mean absolute deviation** (MAD). This is computed by taking the sum of the absolute values of the individual forecast errors and dividing by the number of periods of data (n).

$$\text{MAD} = \frac{\Sigma|\text{forecast error}|}{n} \qquad (15.6)$$

Let us now apply this concept with a trial-and-error testing of two values of α.

The Port of Baltimore has unloaded large quantities of a grain from ships during the past eight quarters. The port's operations manager wants to test the use of exponential smoothing to see how well the technique works in predicting tonnage unloaded. He assumes that the forecast of grain unloaded in the first quarter was 175 tons. Two values of α are examined, $\alpha = 0.10$ and $\alpha = 0.50$. Exhibit 15-4 shows actual tonnage, forecasts for both $\alpha = 0.10$ and $\alpha = 0.50$ (each rounded to the nearest ton), and absolute deviations for both forecasts.

Based on this analysis, a smoothing constant of $\alpha = 0.10$ is preferred to $\alpha = 0.50$ because its MAD is smaller. As a matter of fact, values for α typically lie in the range of 0.10 to 0.30. A simple computer program can help evaluate potential smoothing constants and find the best value of α.

Besides the MAD, there are three other measures of the accuracy of historical errors in forecasting that are sometimes used. The first, **mean squared error** (MSE), is the average of the squared differences between the forecasted and the observed values. The second, **mean absolute percent error** (MAPE), is the average of the absolute difference between the forecasted and observed values expressed as a percentage of the observed values. The third, the **bias,** tells whether the forecast is too high or too low, and by how much. In effect, bias provides the average total error and its direction.

Time Series Extrapolation and Seasonal Adjustments

Time series extrapolation is a technique that fits a trend line to a series of historical data points and then projects the line into the future for medium- to long-range forecasts. In this section we will look at *linear* (straight-line) trends only.

EXHIBIT 15-4 Exponential Smoothing MAD Calculations for the Port of Baltimore

Quarter	Actual Tonnage Unloaded	Rounded Forecast with $\alpha = 0.10$	Absolute Deviations for $\alpha = 0.10$	Rounded Forecast with $\alpha = 0.50$	Absolute Deviation for $\alpha = 0.50$
1	180	175	5	175	5
2	168	176	8	178	10
3	159	175	16	173	14
4	175	173	2	166	9
5	190	173	17	170	20
6	205	175	30	180	25
7	180	178	2	193	13
8	182	178	4	186	4
		Sum of absolute deviations	84		100

$$\text{MAD} = \frac{\Sigma|\text{deviations}|}{n} = 10.05 \qquad \text{MAD} = 12.50$$

Source: Jay Heizer and Barry Render, *Operations Management*, 5th ed. (Upper Saddle River, NJ, Prentice Hall, 1999), pp. 153–154.

If we decide to develop a linear trend line by a precise statistical method, we can apply the **least-squares method.** This approach, described in detail in every introductory statistics textbook, results in a straight line that minimizes the sum of the squares of the vertical differences from the line to each of the actual observations. We can express the line with the following equation.

$$\hat{y} = a + bx \qquad (15.7)$$

where $\hat{y}$ = computed value of the demand for services to be predicted (called the **dependent variable**)

a = y-axis intercept

b = slope of the regression line (or the rate of change in y for given changes in x)

x = the independent variable (which is *time* in this case)

The slope b is found by

$$b = \frac{\Sigma xy - n\bar{x}\bar{y}}{\Sigma x^2 - n\bar{x}^2} \qquad (15.8)$$

The y intercept, a, is computed as follows:

$$a = \bar{y} - b\bar{x} \qquad (15.9)$$

The following example shows how to apply these concepts. Shown below are data on the demand for copies of the software program Lotus 1-2-3 from a Midwestern software retailer over the period 1992 to 1998. Let us fit a straight-line trend to these data and forecast 1999 demand.

Year	Copies of Lotus 1-2-3 Sold
1992	74
1993	79
1994	80
1995	90
1996	105
1997	142
1998	122

With a series of data over time, we can minimize the computations by transforming the values of x (time) to simpler numbers. Thus, in this case, 1992 can be designated as year 1, 1993 as year 2, and so on.

Year	Time Period	Lotus 1-2-3 Demand	x^2	xy
1992	1	74	1	74
1993	2	79	4	158
1994	3	80	9	240
1995	4	90	16	360
1996	5	105	25	525
1997	6	142	36	852
1998	7	122	49	854
	$\Sigma x = 28$	$\Sigma y = 692$	$\Sigma x^2 = 140$	$\Sigma xy = 3{,}063$

$$\bar{x} = \frac{\Sigma x}{n} = \frac{28}{7} = 4 \qquad \bar{y} = \frac{\Sigma y}{n} = \frac{692}{7} = 98.86$$

$$b = \frac{\Sigma xy - n\bar{x}\bar{y}}{\Sigma x^2 - n\bar{x}^2} = \frac{3,063 - (7)(4)(98.86)}{140 - (7)(4^2)} = \frac{295}{28} = 10.54$$

$$a = \bar{y} - b\bar{x} = 98.86 - 10.54(4) = 56.70$$

Hence, the least-squares trend equation is $\hat{y} = 56.70 + 10.54\,x$. To project demand in 1999, we first denote the year 1999 in our new coding system as $x = 8$:

Sales (in 1999) = 56.70 + 10.54(8)
= 141.02, or 141 copies of the program

We can estimate demand for 2000 by inserting $x = 9$ in the same equation:

Sales (in 2000) = 56.70 + 10.54(9)
= 151.56, or 152 copies of the program

To check the validity of the model, we plot historical demand and the trend line in Exhibit 15-5. In this case, we may wish to be cautious and try to understand the 1997–1998 swings in demand.

Time series forecasting such as that in the preceding example involves looking at the *trend* of data over a series of time observations. Sometimes, however, recurring variations at certain seasons of the year make a *seasonal* adjustment in the trend-line

EXHIBIT 15-5 Demand for Lotus 1-2-3 and the Computed Trend Line

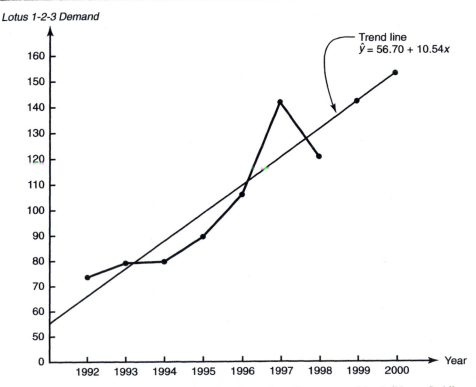

Source: Adapted from Jay Heizer and Barry Render, *Operations Management*, 5th ed. (Upper Saddle River, NJ, Prentice Hall, 1999), p. 160.

forecast necessary. Demand for coal and fuel oil, for example, usually peaks during cold winter months. Demand for golf clubs or suntan lotion may be highest in summer. Analyzing data in monthly or quarterly terms usually makes it easy to spot seasonal patterns. Seasonal indices can then be developed by several common methods. The next example illustrates one way to compute seasonal factors from historical data.

Monthly sales of one brand of telephone answering machine at Plane Supplies are shown in Exhibit 15-6 for 1998–1999. Using these seasonal indices, if we expected the 2000 annual demand for answering machines to be 1,200 units, we would forecast the monthly demand as follows:

Jan $\frac{1,200}{12} \times 0.957 = 96$ Jul $\frac{1,200}{12} \times 1.117 = 112$

Feb $\frac{1,200}{12} \times 0.851 = 85$ Aug $\frac{1,200}{12} \times 1.064 = 106$

Mar $\frac{1,200}{12} \times 0.904 = 90$ Sep $\frac{1,200}{12} \times 0.957 = 96$

Apr $\frac{1,200}{12} \times 1.064 = 106$ Oct $\frac{1,200}{12} \times 0.851 = 85$

May $\frac{1,200}{12} \times 1.309 = 131$ Nov $\frac{1,200}{12} \times 0.851 = 85$

Jun $\frac{1,200}{12} \times 1.223 = 122$ Dec $\frac{1,200}{12} \times 0.851 = 85$

For simplicity, trend calculations were ignored in the preceding example. The following example illustrates how indices that have already been prepared can be applied to adjust trend line forecasts.

EXHIBIT 15-6   Monthly Sales of Answering Machines for a Two-Year Period

Month	Sales Demand 1998	1999	Average 1998–1999 Demand	Average Monthly Demand[a]	Seasonal Index[b]
Jan	80	100	90	94	0.957
Feb	75	85	80	94	0.851
Mar	80	90	85	94	0.904
Apr	90	110	100	94	1.064
May	115	131	123	94	1.309
Jun	110	120	115	94	1.223
Jul	100	110	105	94	1.117
Aug	90	110	100	94	1.064
Sep	85	95	90	94	0.957
Oct	75	85	80	94	0.851
Nov	75	85	80	94	0.851
Dec	80	80	80	94	0.851

Total average demand = 1,128

[a] Average monthly demand $= \frac{1,128}{12 \text{ months}} = 94$

[b] Seasonal index $= \frac{\text{Average 1998–99 demand}}{\text{Average monthly demand}}$

Hospital Forecasting Example   As another example of an estimated trend line and seasonality adjustments, we borrow data from a San Diego hospital that used 66 months of adult inpatient hospital days to reach the following equation[5]:

$$\hat{y} = 8,091 + 21.5x$$

where $\hat{y}$ = patient-days

   x = time, in months

Based on this model, the hospital forecasts patient-days for the next month (period 67) to be

$$\text{Patient-days} = 8,091 + 21.5(67) = 9,532$$

As well as this model recognized the slight upward trend in the demand for inpatient services, it ignored the seasonality that the administration knew to be present. Exhibit 15-7 provides seasonal indices for inpatient days that are typical of hospitals across the nation. Note that January, March, July, and August seem to exhibit significantly higher patient-days on average, while February, September, November, and December reveal lower patient-days.

To correct the time series extrapolation for seasonality, the hospital should multiply the monthly forecast by the appropriate seasonal index. Thus, for period 67, which was a January,

$$\text{Patient-days} = (9,532)(1.04) = 9,913 \text{ (trend and seasonal)}$$

Using this method, patient days can be forecasted for January through June (periods 67 through 72) as 9,913, 9,266, 9,766, 9,596, 9,618, and 9,639. Taking seasonal effect into consideration will lead to better patient-day forecasts, as well as more accurate budgets.

15.6   CAUSAL FORECASTING: REGRESSION ANALYSIS

Causal forecasting models usually consider several variables that are related to the variable being predicted. Once these related variables have been found, a statistical model is built and used to forecast the variable of interest.

EXHIBIT 15-7   Typical Seasonal Indices for Inpatient Days at Hospitals

Month	Seasonal Index
Jan	1.04
Feb	0.97
Mar	1.02
Apr	1.00
May	1.00
Jun	1.00
Jul	1.03
Aug	1.04
Sep	0.96
Oct	1.00
Nov	0.96
Dec	0.98

[5] The source of the data for this hospital example is W. E. Sterk and E. G. Shryock, "Modern Methods Improve Hospital Forecasting," *Healthcare Financial Management*, vol. 41, no. 3 (March 1987), pp. 96–98.

Many factors can be considered in a causal analysis. For example, the sales of a product might be related to the firm's advertising budget, the price charged, competitors' prices and promotional strategies, or even the economy and unemployment rates. In this case, sales would be called the **dependent variable** and the other variables would be called **independent variables.** The manager's job is to develop the best statistical relationship between sales and the set of independent variables. The most common quantitative causal forecasting model is **linear regression analysis.**

We can use the same mathematical model we employed in the least-squares method of time series extrapolation to perform a simple linear regression analysis. The dependent variable that we want to forecast will still be $\hat{y}$. But now the independent variable x need no longer be time.[6]

$$\hat{y} = a + bx$$

where $\hat{y}$ = value of the dependent variable, sales in this case
$\quad\quad a$ = y-axis intercept
$\quad\quad b$ = slope of the regression line
$\quad\quad x$ = the independent variable

To illustrate, we consider the case of the Schatz Construction Company, which renovates old homes in Winter Park, Florida. Over time, the company has found that its dollar volume of renovation work is dependent on the Winter Park area payroll. The following table lists Schatz's revenues and the amount of money earned by wage earners in Winter Park during the past six years.

Schatz's Sales *($000,000)* *y*	*Local Payroll* *($000,000,000)* *x*
2.0	1
3.0	3
2.5	4
2.0	2
2.0	1
3.5	7

Using the least-squares regression approach, we find that

$$\hat{y} = 1.75 + 0.25x$$

or

$$\text{Sales} = 1.75 + 0.25 \text{ payroll}$$

If the local chamber of commerce predicts that the Winter Park area payroll will be $600 million next year, we can estimate sales for Schatz with the regression equation.

$$\text{Sales (in \$000,000)} = 1.75 + 0.25(6) = 1.75 + 1.50 = 3.25$$

or

$$\text{Sales} = \$3,250,000$$

---

[6] If there were more than one independent variable introduced, the general form of this *multiple* regression would be

$$\hat{y} = a + b_1 x_1 + b_2 x_2 + b_3 x_3 + \cdots + b_n x_n$$

where the b_i values represent slope coefficients for the respective x-independent variables.

The final part of this example illustrates a central weakness of causal forecasting methods such as regression. Even when we have computed a regression equation, it is necessary to provide a forecast of the independent variable x—in this case payroll—before estimating the dependent variable y for the next time period. Although not a problem for all forecasts, you can imagine the difficulty in determining future values of *some* common independent variables (such as unemployment rates, gross national product, price indices, and so on).

15.7 GENERAL APPROACHES TO FORECASTING

There are three general approaches to forecasting demand for services that employ the various methods just discussed.

Fundamental System-to-Subsystem Approach

The fundamental method of demand forecasting may employ combinations of techniques described in this chapter. It consists of forecasting the economy, then forecasting industry sales (which are dependent on the economy), and finally forecasting company sales (which are dependent on industry sales).

Economic forecast → Industry demand forecast → Company demand forecast

For example, if the industry demand forecast for next year is $1,222,000 and the company's market share is estimated at 2 percent, the demand forecast is $24,000.

Most companies cannot afford a staff of economists, so their marketing departments either buy economic and industry forecasts when needed or use forecasts of the economy and industry found in *Business Week*, the *Wall Street Journal*, *Forbes*, government publications, or forecasting service publications.

Industry demand forecasts may be made by using the past year's demand and adjusting this figure up or down according to predictions about the economy for next year. Industry demand forecasts may be found in *U.S. Industrial Outlook*, published annually by the U.S. Department of Commerce, or in trade publications. In addition, most industries have a trade association (see *Encyclopedia of Associations*, published by Gale Research Co.) that may forecast industry demand. Individual studies of industries are prepared by Predicasts, Inc., in Cleveland, Ohio.

For a new firm, a demand forecast is determined by estimating the market share the company will obtain in its first year of business. This depends on considerations of the value-in-use of the product or service, the degree of differentiation of its product or service, the competitive edge of the new firm, and the marketing program of the new firm. Usually, the initial share of an established market will be very small, and a conservative estimate should be made.

Aggregate-to-Component Forecasts

A restaurant manager may forecast total customers and then estimate the number of dinners, luncheons, and breakfasts. An auto repair shop may estimate the total number of jobs per year and then forecast the number of each type of job. A painting firm may estimate the aggregate of jobs for next month and then forecast the number of residential and the number of commercial jobs. If the total or aggregate number of services can be forecasted, the forecast provides a general bound for the sum of the components and makes component forecasting easier.

Disaggregation into components may be on the following bases:

1. Service disaggregation
   a. Services by classes or types
   b. Services by time of day or week they are supplied
2. Market disaggregation
   a. Geographic disaggregation
   b. Industry, government, and consumer sectors
   c. Industry sectors within the total market
3. Performer disaggregation—a forecast for each person or shop that performs the services

Component-to-Aggregate Forecasts

When an aggregate forecast is desired, it may be more accurate if a forecast of each component of the aggregate is made and then these forecasts added. The preceding section has given the components that make up aggregates.

Using POM for Windows in Forecasting

The Forecasting module of POM for Windows can handle all the forecasting techniques we have discussed in this chapter. Exhibit 15-8 shows the weighted moving average forecast and relevant statistics for Donna's Garden Supply example. Exhibit 15-9 has the detailed information on errors and forecasts. Exhibits 15-10 and 15-11 illustrate the time series trend line output from POM for Windows for the Lotus Software example with all the relevant statistics.

EXHIBIT 15-8   POM for Windows Solution of Donna's Garden Supply Example

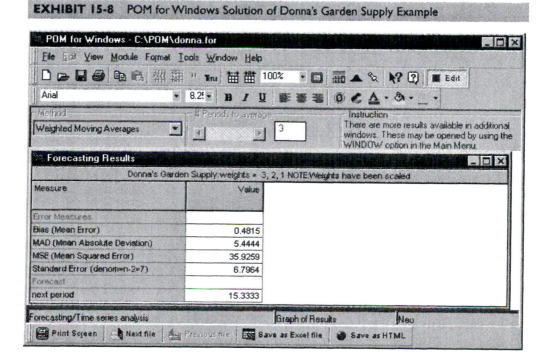

EXHIBIT 15-9 Details of Weighted Moving Average Forecast for Donna's Garden Supply Example

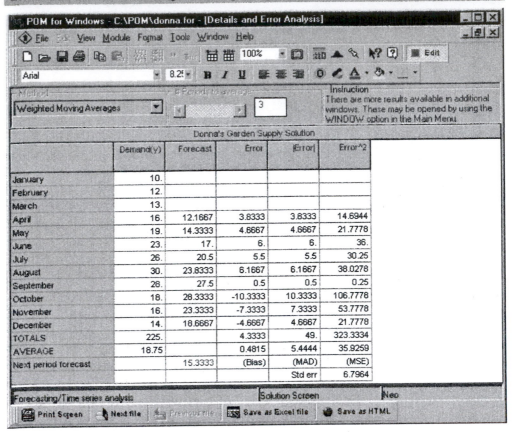

EXHIBIT 15-10 POM for Windows Solution of Lotus Software Example

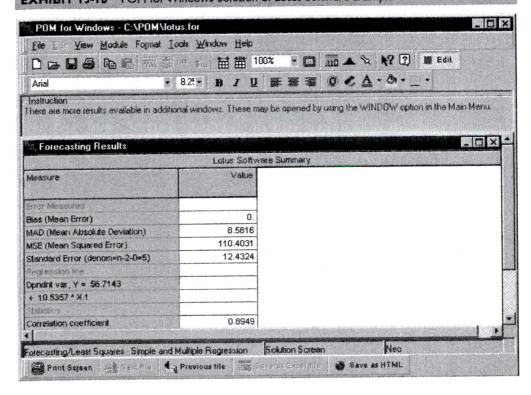

EXHIBIT 15-11 Details of Time Series Trend Calculation for Lotus Software Example

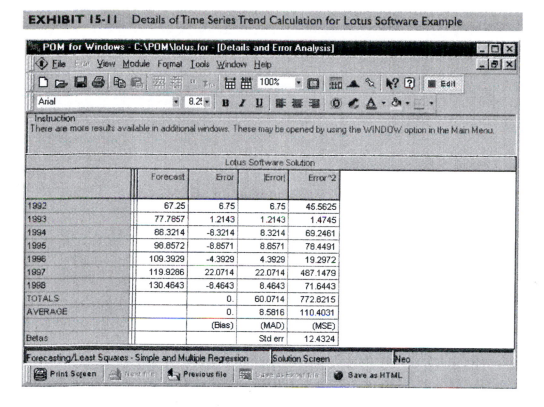

15.8 SUMMARY

Forecasting demand for services is very important in most services because fluctuations in demand cannot usually be taken care of by building inventory. When the service is "embedded" in a physical product, forecasting and meeting demand fluctuations are analogous to the manufacturing situation. In either case, the demand forecast is the basis for all planning.

In manufacturing, demand is forecasted in terms of units of physical product. In services, it is not always clear *what* to forecast and what *can be* forecasted. That is, the outputs of some service firms are of almost infinite variety. Basically, however, service demand is in terms of (1) number of customers and (2) number of services and a number of each anticipated service to be desired.

The selection of a forecasting method depends on four basic factors:

1. Time requirements
2. Resource requirements
3. Input characteristics available or required
4. Output characteristics required

There are four basic methods of forecasting:

1. Judgment
2. Counting
3. Time series
4. Association or causal

Within these categories there are numerous methods with variations of each. The strategic approaches to forecasting utilize combinations of these methods. These approaches are:

- Economic system to industry system to company system
- Aggregate forecast to component forecast
- Component forecast to aggregate forecast

The technical aspects of actually making a forecast are complex, and a number of books and journals are available that deal with this subject. No forecasting method, as we learned in this chapter, is perfect under all conditions. And even once management has found a satisfactory approach, it must still monitor and control its forecasts to make sure errors do not get out of hand. Forecasting can often be a very challenging, but rewarding, part of managing.

Discussion Questions

1. What is a time series extrapolation model? Explain why this model is so widely used in service organizations. Name some services in which time series would be the best forecasting model.
2. What is the difference between a causal model and a time-series model?
3. What is a judgmental forecasting model? Give some service-organization examples where judgmental forecasts are appropriate.
4. What is the meaning of least squares in a regression model? What are some independent variables that might be used in service examples?
5. What are some of the problems and drawbacks of the moving-average forecasting model?
6. What effect does the value of the smoothing constant have on the weight given to the past forecast and the past observed value?
7. What is MAD, and why is it important in the selection and use of forecasting models?
8. Why is forecast accuracy so important in service organizations?

Problems

15.1. Judy Smith has developed the following forecasting model:

$$\hat{y} = 36 + 4.3x$$

where $\hat{y}$ = demand for K10 air conditioners
    x = the outside temperature (°F)

a. Forecast demand for K10 when the temperature is 70°F.
b. What is it for a temperature of 80°F?
c. What is demand for a temperature of 90°F?

15.2. Data collected on the yearly demand for 50-lb bags of fertilizer at Rhonda's Garden Supply are shown in the following table. Develop a three-year moving average to forecast sales. Then estimate demand again with a weighted moving average in which sales in the most recent year are given a weight of 2 and sales in the other two years are each given a weight of 1. Which method do you think is best?

Year	Demand for Fertilizer (thousands of bags)
1	4
2	6
3	4
4	5
5	10
6	8
7	7
8	9
9	12
10	14
11	15

15.3. Develop a two- and a four-year moving average for the demand for fertilizer in Problem 15.2.

15.4. In Problems 15.2 and 15.3, four different forecasts were developed for the demand for fertilizer. These four forecasts are a 2-year moving average, a 3-year moving average, a weighted moving average, and a 4-year moving average. Which one would you use? Explain your answer.

15.5. Use exponential smoothing with a smoothing constant of 0.3 to forecast the demand for fertilizer given in Problem 15.2. Assume that last period's forecast for year 1 is 5,000 bags to begin the procedure. Would you prefer to use the exponential smoothing model or the weighted-average model developed in Problem 15.2? Explain your answer.

15.6. Sales of Cool-Man air conditioners have grown steadily during the past five years (see table). The sales manager had predicted in 1994 that 1995 sales would be 410 air conditioners. Using exponential smoothing with a weight of $\alpha = 0.30$, develop forecasts for 1996 through 2000.

Year	Sales	Forecast
1995	450	410
1996	495	
1997	518	
1998	563	
1999	584	
2000	?	

15.7. Demand for patient surgery at Washington General Hospital has increased steadily in the past few years, as seen in the following table.

Year	Outpatient Surgeries Performed
1	450
2	495
3	518
4	563
5	584
6	?

The director of medical services predicted 6 years ago that demand in year 1 would be for 410 surgeries.

a. Use exponential smoothing, first with a smoothing constant of 0.6 and then with one of 0.9, to develop forecasts for years 2 through 6.

b. Use a 3-year moving average to forecast demand in years 4, 5, and 6.

    c. Use the extrapolation method to forecast demand in years 1 through 6.

    d. With MAD as the criterion, which of the preceding four forecasting approaches is best?

15.8. Sales of industrial vacuum cleaners at R. Lowenthal Supply Co. over the past 13 months are shown in the following table.

Sales (thousands)	Month
11	Jan
14	Feb
16	Mar
10	Apr
15	May
17	June
11	July
14	Aug
17	Sept
12	Oct
14	Nov
16	Dec
11	Jan

    a. Using a moving average with three periods, determine the demand for vacuum cleaners for next February.

    b. Using a weighted moving average with three periods, determine the demand for vacuum cleaners for February. Use 3, 2, and 1 for the weights of the most recent, second most recent, and third most recent periods, respectively. For example, if you were forecasting the demand for February, November would have a weight of 1, December would have a weight of 2, and January would have a weight of 3.

    c. Evaluate the accuracy of each of these methods.

    d. What other factors might R. Lowenthal consider in forecasting sales?

15.9. Room registrations in the Toronto Towers Plaza Hotel have been recorded for the past 9 years. Management would like to determine the mathematical trend of guest registration in order to project future occupancy. This estimate would help the hotel determine whether a future expansion will be needed. Given the following time-series data, develop a least-squares equation relating registrations to time. Then forecast 2002 registrations. Room registrations are in thousands:

1992: 17	1995: 21	1998: 23
1993: 16	1996: 20	1999: 25
1994: 16	1997: 20	2000: 24

15.10. Quarterly demand for Jaguar XJ6s at a New York auto dealer are forecast with the equation:

$$\hat{y} = 10 + 3x$$

where x = quarters—Quarter I of 2000 = 0
                          Quarter II of 2000 = 1
                          Quarter III of 2000 = 2
                          Quarter IV of 2000 = 3
                          Quarter I of 2001 = 4
                          and so on
       $\hat{y}$ = quarterly demand

The demand for sports sedans is seasonal and the indices for Quarters I, II, III, and IV are 0.80, 1.00, 1.30, and 0.90, respectively. Forecast demand for each quarter of 2002. Then seasonalize each forecast to adjust for quarterly variations.

15.11. The operations manager of a musical instrument distributor feels that demand for bass drums may be related to the number of television appearances by the popular rock group Green Shades during the previous month. The manager has collected the data shown in the following table.

Demand for Bass Drums	Green Shades TV Appearances
3	3
6	4
7	7
5	6
10	8
8	5

a. Graph these data to see whether a linear equation might describe the relationship between the group's television shows and bass drum sales.
b. Use the least squares regression method to derive a forecasting equation.
c. What is your estimate for bass drum sales if the Green Shades performed on TV nine times last month?

15.12. Dr. Jerilyn Ross, a New York City psychologist, specializes in treating patients who are phobic and afraid to leave their homes. The following table indicates how many patients Dr. Ross has seen each year for the past 10 years. It also indicates what the robbery rate was in New York City during the same year.

Year	Number of Patients	Crime Rate (robberies per 1,000 population)
1991	36	58.3
1992	33	61.1
1993	40	73.4
1994	41	75.7
1995	40	81.1
1996	55	89.0
1997	60	101.1
1998	54	94.8
1999	58	103.3
2000	61	116.2

Using trend analysis, how many patients do you think Dr. Ross will see in 2001, 2002, and 2003? How well does the model fit the data?

15.13. Using the data in Problem 15.12, apply linear regression to study the relationship between the crime rate and Dr. Ross's patient load. If the robbery rate increases to 131.2 in 2001, how many phobic patients will Dr. Ross treat? If the crime rate drops to 90.6, what is the patient projection?

15.14. Management of Davis's Department Store has used time series extrapolation to forecast retail sales for the next four quarters. The sales estimates are $100,000, $120,000, $140,000, and $160,000 for the respective quarters. Seasonal indices for the four quarters have been found to be 1.30, 0.90, 0.70, and 1.15, respectively. Compute a seasonalized or adjusted sales forecast.

15.15. Passenger miles flown on Northeast Airlines, a commuter firm serving the Boston hub, are shown for the past 12 weeks below.

Week	Actual Passenger Miles (in thousands)
1	17
2	21
3	19
4	23
5	18
6	16
7	20
8	18
9	22
10	20
11	15
12	22

a. Assuming an initial forecast for week 1 of 17,000 miles, use exponential smoothing to compute miles for weeks 2 through 12. Use $\alpha = 0.2$.

b. What is the MAD for this model?

15.16. Bus and subway ridership in Washington, D.C. during the summer months is believed to be heavily tied to the number of tourists visiting that city. During the past 12 years, the following data have been obtained.

Year	No. of Tourists (millions)	Ridership (100,000's)
1989	7	15
1990	2	10
1991	6	13
1992	4	15
1993	14	25
1994	15	27
1995	16	24
1996	12	20
1997	14	27
1998	20	44
1999	15	34
2000	7	17

a. Plot these data and decide if a linear model is reasonable.

b. Develop a regression relationship.

c. What is expected ridership if 10 million tourists visit the city?

d. If there are no tourists of all, explain the predicted ridership.

15.17. Emergency calls to Winter Park, Florida's 911 system for the past 24 weeks are shown below.

Week	Calls	Week	Calls
1	50	13	55
2	35	14	35
3	25	15	25
4	40	16	55
5	45	17	55
6	35	18	40
7	20	19	35
8	30	20	60
9	35	21	75
10	20	22	50
11	15	23	40
12	40	24	65

a. Compute the exponentially smoothed forecast of calls for each week. Assume an initial forecast of 50 calls in the first week and use $\alpha = 0.1$. What is the forecast for the twenty-fifth week?
b. Reforecast each period using an $\alpha = 0.6$.
c. Actual calls during the twenty-fifth week were 85. Which smoothing constant provides a superior forecast? Explain and justify the measure of error used.

CASE

CASE 15–1   The North–South Airline

In 1997, Northern Airlines[1] merged with Southeast Airlines to create the fourth largest U.S. carrier. The new North–South Airline inherited both an aging fleet of Boeing 737-200 aircraft and Stephen Ruth. Ruth was a tough former Secretary of the Navy who stepped in as new President and Chairman of the Board.

Ruth's first concern in creating a financially solid company was maintenance costs. It was commonly surmised in the airline industry that maintenance costs rise with the age of the aircraft. He quickly noticed that historically there had been a significant difference in the reported B737-200 maintenance costs (from ATA Form 41s) both in the airframe and engine areas between Northern Airlines and Southeast Airlines, with Southeast having the newer fleet.

On November 12, 1997, Peg Young, Vice President for Operations and Maintenance, was called into Ruth's office and asked to study the issue. Specifically, Ruth wanted to know (1) whether the average fleet age was correlated to direct airframe maintenace costs, and (2) whether there was a relationship between average fleet age and direct engine

maintenance costs. Young was to report back with the answer, along with quantitative and graphical descriptions of the relationship, by November 26.

Young's first step was to have her staff construct the average age of Northern and Southeast B737-200 fleets, by quarter, since the introduction of that aircraft to service by each airline in late 1988 and early 1989. The average age of each fleet was calculated by first multiplying the total number of calendar days each aircraft had been in service at the pertinent point in time by the average daily utilization of the respective fleet of total fleet hours flown. The total fleet hours flown was then divided by the number of aircraft in service at that time, giving the age of the "average" aircraft in the fleet.

The average utilization was found by taking the actual total fleet hours flown at September 30, 1996, from Northern and Southeast data, and dividing by total days in service for all aircraft at that time. The average utilization for Southeast was 8.3 hours per day, and the average utilization for Northern was 8.7 hours per day. Since the available cost data were calculated for each yearly period ending at the end of the first quarter, average fleet age was calculated at the same points in time.

The fleet data are shown in Exhibit 15-12. Airframe cost data and engine cost data are both shown paired with fleet average age in that table. ∎

---

[1] Dates and names of airlines and individuals have been changed in this case to maintain confidentiality. The data and issues described here are actual.

EXHIBIT 15-12   North–South Airline Data for Boeing 737-200 Jets

Year	Northern Airline Data			Southeast Airline Data		
------	Airframe Cost per Aircraft	Engine Cost per Aircraft	Average Age (hrs)	Airframe Cost per Aircraft	Engine Cost per Aircraft	Average Age (hrs)
1990	$51.80	$43.49	6,512	$13.29	$18.86	5,107
1991	54.92	38.58	8,404	25.15	34.55	8,145
1992	69.70	51.48	11,077	32.18	40.43	7,360
1993	68.90	58.72	11,717	31.78	22.10	5,773
1994	63.72	45.47	13,275	25.34	19.69	7,150
1995	84.73	50.26	15,215	32.78	32.58	9,364
1996	78.74	79.60	18,390	35.56	38.07	8,259

SOURCE: Jay Heizer and Barry Render, *Operations Management*, 5th ed. (Upper Saddle River, NJ, Prentice Hall, 1999), p. 188.

CASE QUESTION

Prepare Peg Young's response to Stephen Ruth.

References

Ashley, R., and J. Guerard, "Applications of Time Series Analysis to Texas Financial Forecasting," *Interfaces*, vol. 13, no. 4 (August 1983), pp. 46–55.

Ashton, A. H., and R. H. Ashton, "Aggregating Subjective Forecasts," *Management Science*, vol. 31, no. 12 (December 1985), pp. 1499–1508.

Becker, B. C., and A. Sapienza, "Forecasting Hospital Reimbursement," *Hospital and Health Services Administration*, vol. 32 (November 1987), pp. 521–530.

Box, G. E. P., and G. Jenkins, *Time Series Analysis: Forecasting and Control* (San Francisco, Holden Day, 1970).

Brown, R. G., *Statistical Forecasting for Inventory Control* (New York, McGraw-Hill, 1959).

Brozovich, J. P., and D. Loftus, "Physician–Administrator Decision Making for High-Technology Purchases," *Health Care Management Review*, vol. 6, no. 3 (summer 1981), pp. 63–73.

Bunn, D. W., and J. P. Seigal, "Forecasting the Effects of Television Programming upon Electricity Loads," *Journal of the Operational Research Society*, vol. 34 (January 1983), pp. 17–25.

Chambers, J. C., C. Satinder, S. K. Mullick, and D. D. Smith, "How to Choose the Right Forecasting Technique," *Harvard Business Review*, vol. 49, no. 4 (July–August 1971), pp. 45–74.

Claycombe, W. W., and W. G. Sullivan, "Current Forecasting Techniques," *Journal of System Management* (September 1978), pp. 18–20.

Gardner, E. S., "Exponential Smoothing: The State of the Art," *Journal of Forecasting*, vol. 4, no. 1 (March 1985).

Georgoff, D. M., and R. G. Murdick, "Managers Guide to Forecasting," *Harvard Business Review*, vol. 64, no. 1 (January–February 1986), pp. 110–120.

Gips, J., and B. Sullivan, "Sales Forecasting—Replacing Magic with Logic," *Production and Inventory Management Review*, vol. 2, no. 2 (February 1982).

Heizer, J., and B. Render, *Production and Operations Management*, 5th ed. (Upper Saddle River, NJ, Prentice Hall, 1999).

Holz, B. W., and J. M. Wroth, "Improving Strength Forecasts: Support for Army Manpower Management," *Interfaces*, vol. 10, no. 6 (December 1980), pp. 31–52.

Lane, D., et al., "Forecasting Demand for Long Term Care Services," *Health Services Research*, vol. 20, no. 4 (October 1985), pp. 435–459.

Lee, D. R., "A Forecast of Lodging Supply and Demand," *The Cornell HRA Quarterly*, vol. 25, no. 2 (August 1984), pp. 27–40.

Mabert, V. A., and R. L. Stocco, "Managing and Monitoring a Forecasting System: The Chemical Bank Experience," *Journal of Bank Research*, vol. 13, no. 3 (autumn 1982), pp. 195–201.

MacStravic, R. S., "An Early Warning Technique," *Hospital and Health Services Administration*, vol. 31, no. 1 (January–February 1986), pp. 86–98.

Mahmoud, E., "Accuracy in Forecasting: A Summary," *Journal of Forecasting*, vol. 3, no. 2 (April–June 1984).

Makridakis, S., S. C. Wheelright, and V. E. McGee, *Forecasting Methods and Applications*, 2nd ed. (New York, Wiley, 1983).

Murdick, R. G., and D. M. Georgoff, "Forecasting: A Systems Approach," *Technological Forecasting and Social Change*, vol. 44 (1993), pp. 1–16.

Nandola, K., M. Koshal, and R. K. Koshal, "Forecasting Restaurant Food Sales," *The Cornell HRA Quarterly*, vol. 23, no. 2 (August 1982), pp. 92–96.

Parker, G. C., and E. L. Segura, "How to Get a Better Forecast," *Harvard Business Review*, vol. 49, no. 2 (March–April 1971), pp. 99–109.

Plossl, G. W., and O. W. Wight, *Production and Inventory Control* (Upper Saddle River, NJ, Prentice Hall, 1967).

Rao, P. S., "Forecasting the Demand for Railway Freight Services," *Journal of Transportation Economics and Policy*, vol. 12, no. 1 (January 1978), pp. 7–22.

Render, B., and R. M. Stair, *Quantitative Analysis for Management*, 7th ed. (Upper Saddle River, NJ, Prentice Hall, 2000).

Schnaars, S. P., and R. J. Bavuso, "Extrapolation Models on Very Short-Term Forecasts," *Journal of Business Research*, vol. 14 (1986), pp. 27–36.

Young, M. A., "Sources of Competitive Data for the Management Strategist," *Strategic Management Journal*, vol. 10, no. 4 (July–August 1989), pp. 285–293.

CHAPTER 16

Vehicle Routing and Scheduling

16.1   INTRODUCTION

The scheduling of customer service and the routing of service vehicles are at the heart of many service operations. For some services, such as school buses, public health nursing, and many installation or repair businesses, service delivery is critical to the performance of the service. For other services, such as mass transit, taxis, trucking firms, and the U.S. Postal Service, timely delivery *is* the service. In either case, the routing and scheduling of service vehicles has a major impact on the *quality* of the service provided.

This chapter introduces some routing and scheduling terminology, classifies different types of routing and scheduling problems, and presents various solution methodologies. Although every effort has been made to present the topic of vehicle routing and scheduling as simply and as straightforward as possible, it should be noted that this is a technical subject and one of the more mathematical topics in this text. The chapter begins with an example of service delivery to illustrate some of the practical issues in vehicle routing and scheduling.

A Service Delivery Example: Meals-for-ME

A private, nonprofit meal delivery program for the elderly called Meals-for-ME has been operating in the state of Maine since the mid-1970s.[1] The program offers home delivery of hot meals, Monday through Friday, to "home-bound" individuals who are over 60 years of age. For those individuals who are eligible (and able), the program also supports a "congregate" program that provides daily transportation to group-meal sites. On a typical day within a single county, hundreds of individuals receive

---

[1] Gail Ward of Meals-for-ME provided the information contained in this section.

476

this service. In addition, individuals may be referred for short-term service because of a temporary illness or recuperation. Thus, on any given day, the demand for the service may be highly unpredictable. Scheduling of volunteer delivery personnel and vehicles as well as construction of routes is done on a weekly to monthly basis by regional site managers. It is the task of these individuals to coordinate the preparation of meals and to determine the sequence in which customers are to be visited. In addition, site managers must arrange for rides to the "group meals" for participating individuals.

Although these tasks may seem straightforward, there are many practical problems in routing and scheduling meal delivery. First, the delivery vehicles (and pickup vehicles) are driven by volunteers, many of whom are students who are not available during some high-demand periods (Christmas, for example). Thus, the variability in available personnel requires that delivery routes be changed frequently. Second, because the program delivers hot meals, a typical route must be less than 90 minutes. Generally, 20 to 25 meals are delivered on a route, depending on the proximity of customers. Third, all must be delivered within a limited time period, between 11:30 A.M. and 1:00 P.M. daily. Similar difficulties exist for personnel who pick up individuals served by the congregate program. Given the existence of these very real problems, the solution no longer seems as simple. It is obvious that solution approaches and techniques are needed that allow the decision maker to consider a multitude of variables and adapt to changes quickly and efficiently.

16.2   OBJECTIVES OF ROUTING AND SCHEDULING PROBLEMS

The objective of most routing and scheduling problems is to minimize the toal cost of providing the service. This includes vehicle capital costs, mileage, and personnel costs. But other objectives also may come into play, particularly in the public sector. For example, in school bus routing and scheduling, a typical objective is to minimize the total number of student-minutes on the bus. This criterion is highly correlated with safety and with parents' approval of the school system.[2] For dial-a-ride services for the handicapped or elderly, an important objective is to minimize the inconvenience for all customers. For the Meals-for-ME program, the meals must be delivered at certain times of the day. For emergency services, such as ambulance, police, and fire, minimizing response time to an incident is of primary importance. Some companies promise package delivery by 10:30 A.M. the next morning. Thus, in the case of both public and private services, an appropriate objective function should consider more than the dollar cost of delivering a service. The "subjective" costs associated with failing to provide adequate service to the customer must be considered as well.

16.3   CHARACTERISTICS OF ROUTING AND SCHEDULING PROBLEMS

Routing and scheduling problems are often presented as graphical **networks.** The use of networks to describe these problems has the advantage of allowing the decision maker to visualize the problem under consideration. As an example, refer to Exhibit 16-1. The figure consists of five circles called **nodes.** Four of the nodes (nodes 2 through 5) represent pickup and/or delivery points, and a fifth (node 1) represents a **depot node,** from which the vehicle's trip originates and ends. The depot node is the "home base" for the vehicle or provider.

---

[2] See Lawrence Bodin, Bruce Golden, Arjang Assad, and Michael Ball, "Routing and Scheduling of Vehicles and Crews: The State of the Art," *Computers and Operations Research*, vol. 10, no. 2 (1983), pp. 70–71.

EXHIBIT 16-1 Routing Network Example

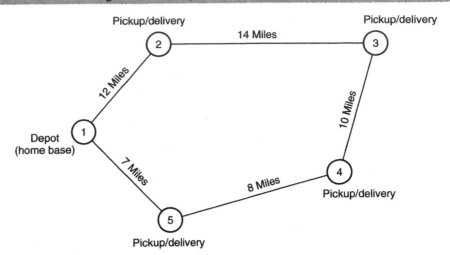

Connecting these nodes are line segments referred to as **arcs.** Arcs describe the time, cost, or distance required to travel from one node to another. The numbers along the arcs in Exhibit 16-1 are distances in miles. Given an average speed of travel or a distribution of travel times, distance can be easily converted to time. However, this conversion ignores physical barriers, such as mountains, lack of access, or traffic congestion. If minimizing time is the primary goal in a routing and scheduling problem, then historical data on travel times are preferable to calculations based on distances.

Arcs may be directed or undirected. **Undirected arcs** are represented by simple line segments. **Directed arcs** are indicated by arrows. These arrows represent the direction of travel in the case of routing problems (e.g., one-way streets) or precedence relationships in the case of scheduling problems (where one pickup or delivery task must precede another).

The small network in Exhibit 16-1 can be viewed as a route for a single vehicle. The route for the vehicle, also called a **tour,** is $1 \rightarrow 2 \rightarrow 3 \rightarrow 4 \rightarrow 5 \rightarrow 1$ or, because the arcs are undirected, $1 \rightarrow 5 \rightarrow 4 \rightarrow 3 \rightarrow 2 \rightarrow 1$. The total distance for either tour is 51 miles.

The tour described in Exhibit 16-1 is a solution to a simple routing problem where the objective is to find the route that minimizes cost or any other criterion that may be appropriate (such as distance or travel time). The minimum-cost solution, however, is subject to the tour being **feasible.** Feasibility depends on the type of problem, but, in general, implies that:

1. A tour must include all nodes.
2. A node must be visited only once.
3. A tour must begin and end at a depot.

The output of all routing and scheduling systems is essentially the same. That is, for each vehicle or provider, a route and/or a schedule is provided. Generally, the **route** specifies the sequence in which the nodes (or arcs) are to be visited, and a **schedule** identifies when each node is to be visited.

Classifying Routing and Scheduling Problems

The classification of routing and scheduling problems depends on certain characteristics of the service delivery system, such as size of the delivery fleet, where the fleet is housed, capacities of the vehicles, and routing and scheduling objectives. In the simplest case, we begin with a set of nodes to be visited by a single vehicle. The nodes may be visited in any order, there are no precedence relationships, the travel costs between two nodes are the same regardless of the direction traveled, and there are no delivery-time restrictions. In addition, vehicle capacity is not considered. The output for the single-vehicle problem is a route or a tour where each node is visited only once and the route begins and ends at the depot node (see Exhibit 16-1, for example). The tour is formed with the goal of minimizing the total tour cost. This simplest case is referred to as a **traveling salesman problem** (TSP).

An extension of the traveling salesman problem, referred to as the **multiple traveling salesman problem** (MTSP), occurs when a fleet of vehicles must be routed from a single depot. The goal is to generate a set of routes, one for each vehicle in the fleet. The characteristics of this problem are that a node may be assigned to only one vehicle, but a vehicle will have more than one node assigned to it. There are no restrictions on the size of the load or number of passengers a vehicle may carry. The solution to this problem will give the order in which each vehicle is to visit its assigned nodes. As in the single-vehicle case, the objective is to develop the set of minimum-cost routes, where "cost" may be represented by a dollar amount, distance, or travel time.

If we now restrict the capacity of the multiple vehicles and couple with it the possibility of having varying demands at each node, the problem is classified as a **vehicle routing problem** (VRP).

Alternatively, if the demand for the service occurs on the arcs, rather than at the nodes, or if demand is so high that individual demand nodes become too numerous to specify, we have a **Chinese postman problem** (CPP). Examples of these types of problems include street sweeping, snow removal, refuse collection, postal delivery, and paper delivery. The Chinese postman problem is very difficult to solve, and the solution procedures are beyond the scope of this text.[3] Exhibit 16-2 summarizes the characteristics of these four types of routing problems.

Finally, let us distinguish between **routing** problems and **scheduling** problems. If the customers being serviced have no time restrictions and no precedence relationships exist, then the problem is a pure routing problem. If there is a specified time for the service to take place, then a scheduling problem exists. Otherwise, we are dealing with a combined routing and scheduling problem.

EXHIBIT 16-2 Characteristics of Four Routing Problems

Type	Demand	Arcs	No. of Depots	No. of Vehicles	Vehicle Capacity
Traveling salesman problem (TSP)	At the nodes	Directed or undirected	1	= 1	Unlimited
Multiple traveling salesman problem (MTSP)	At the nodes	Directed or undirected	1	>1	Unlimited
Vehicle routing problem (VRP)	At the nodes	Directed or undirected	1	>1	Limited
Chinese postman problem (CPP)	On the arcs	Directed or undirected	1	≥1	Limited or unlimited

---

[3] For more information on the Chinese postman problem, see Lawrence Bodin et al., "Routing and Scheduling of Vehicles and Crews: The State of the Art," *Computers and Operations Research*, vol. 10, no. 2 (1983), pp. 111–112. The problem name derives from the fact the original paper was published in the *Chinese Journal of Operations Research*.

Solving Routing and Scheduling Problems

Another important issue in routing and scheduling involves the practical aspects of solving these types of problems. Consider, for example, the delivery of bundles of newspapers from a printing site to dropoff points in a geographic area. These dropoff points supply papers to newspaper carriers for local deliveries. The dropoff points have different demands, and the vehicles have different capacities. Each vehicle is assigned a route beginning and ending at the printing site (the depot). For a newspaper with only ten dropoff points there are 2^{10} or 1,024 possible routings. For 50 dropoff points, there are 2^{50} or over 1 trillion possible routings. Realistic problems of this type may have over 1,000 drop points! It is evident that problems of any size quickly become too expensive to solve optimally even with supercomputers. Fortunately, some very elegant heuristics or "rule of thumb" solution techniques have been developed that yield "good," if not optimal, solutions to these problems. Some of the more well known of these heuristic approaches are presented in this chapter.

16.4 ROUTING SERVICE VEHICLES

The Traveling Salesman Problem

The traveling salesman problem (TSP) is one of the most studied problems in management science. Optimal approaches to solving traveling salesman problems are based on mathematical programming (see chapter 18). But in reality, most TSP problems are not solved optimally. When the problem is so large that an optimal solution is impossible to obtain, or when approximate solutions are good enough, heuristics are applied. Two commonly used heuristics for the traveling salesman problem are the **nearest neighbor procedure** and the **Clark and Wright savings heuristic.**

The Nearest Neighbor Procedure   The nearest neighbor procedure (NNP) builds a tour based only on the cost or distance of traveling from the last-visited node to the closest node in the network. As such, the heuristic is simple, but it has the disadvantage of being rather shortsighted, as we shall see in an example. The heuristic does, however, generate an "approximately" optimal solution from a distance matrix. The procedure is outlined as follows:

1. Start with a node at the beginning of the tour (the depot node).
2. Find the node closest to the last node added to the tour.
3. Go back to step 2 until all nodes have been added.
4. Connect the first and the last nodes to form a complete tour.[4]

Example of the Nearest Neighbor Procedure   We begin the nearest neighbor procedure with data on the distance or cost of traveling from every node in the network to every other node in the network. In the case where the arcs are undirected, the distance from i to j will be the same as the distance from j to i. Such a network with undirected arcs is said to be **symmetrical.** Exhibit 16-3 gives the complete distance matrix for the symmetrical six-node network shown in Exhibit 16-4.

Referring to Exhibit 16-5, the solution is determined as follows:

1. Start with the depot node (node 1). Examine the distances between node 1 and every other node. The closest node to node 1 is node 3, so designate the **partial**

---

[4] The outline of the nearest neighbor procedure is taken from Lawrence Bodin et al., "Routing and Scheduling of Vehicles and Crews: The State of the Art," p. 87.

EXHIBIT 16-3   Symmetric Distance Matrix

From Node	To Node (distances in miles)					
	1	**2**	**3**	**4**	**5**	**6**
1	—	5.4	2.8	10.5	8.2	4.1
2	5.4	—	5.0	9.5	5.0	8.5
3	2.8	5.0	—	7.8	6.0	3.6
4	10.5	9.5	7.8	—	5.0	9.5
5	8.2	5.0	6.0	5.0	—	9.2
6	4.1	8.5	3.6	9.5	9.2	—

tour or **path** as $1 \rightarrow 3$. [See Exhibit 16-5(a). Note that the $\rightarrow$ means that the nodes are connected, not that the arc is directed.]

2. Find the closest node to the last node added (node 3) that is not currently in the path. Node 6 is 3.6 miles from node 3, so connect it to the path. The result is the three-node path $1 \rightarrow 3 \rightarrow 6$. [See Exhibit 16-5(b).]

3. Find the node closest to node 6 that has not yet been connected. This is node 2, which is 8.5 miles from node 6. Connect it to yield $1 \rightarrow 3 \rightarrow 6 \rightarrow 2$. [See Exhibit 16-5(c).]

4. The node closest to node 2 is node 5. The partial tour is now $1 \rightarrow 3 \rightarrow 6 \rightarrow 2 \rightarrow 5$. [See Exhibit 16-5(d).]

5. Connect the last node (node 4) to the path and complete the tour by connecting node 4 to the depot. The complete tour formed is $1 \rightarrow 3 \rightarrow 6 \rightarrow 2 \rightarrow 5 \rightarrow 4 \rightarrow 1$. The length of the tour is 35.4 miles. [See Exhibit 16-5(e).]

But is this the best-possible route? Examine the network again and try to come up with a better tour. How about $1 \rightarrow 2 \rightarrow 5 \rightarrow 4 \rightarrow 3 \rightarrow 6 \rightarrow 1$? The total distance of this tour is 30.9 miles versus 34.5 miles for the nearest neighbor–constructed tour. This result points to the limitation of heuristics; they cannot guarantee optimality. For this small a network, it would be possible to enumerate every possible tour. However, for large problems with 100 to 200 nodes, enumerating every combination would be impossible.

Before leaving the nearest neighbor heuristic, it should be noted that, in practice, the heuristic is applied repeatedly by assigning every node to be the depot node, re-solving the problem, and then selecting the lowest-cost tour as the final solution. For

EXHIBIT 16-4   Traveling Salesman Problem

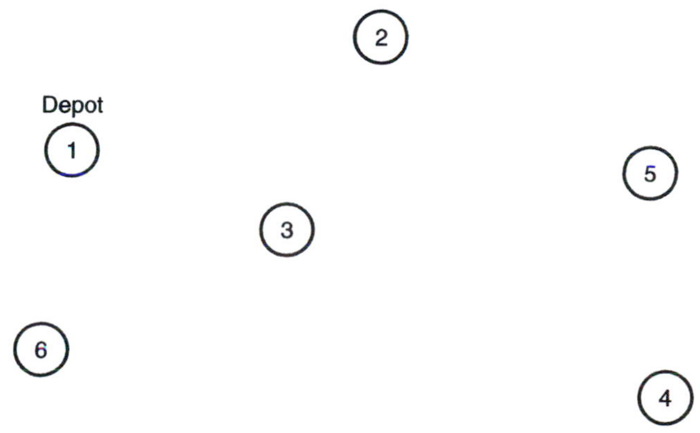

EXHIBIT 16-5 Nearest Neighbor Procedure

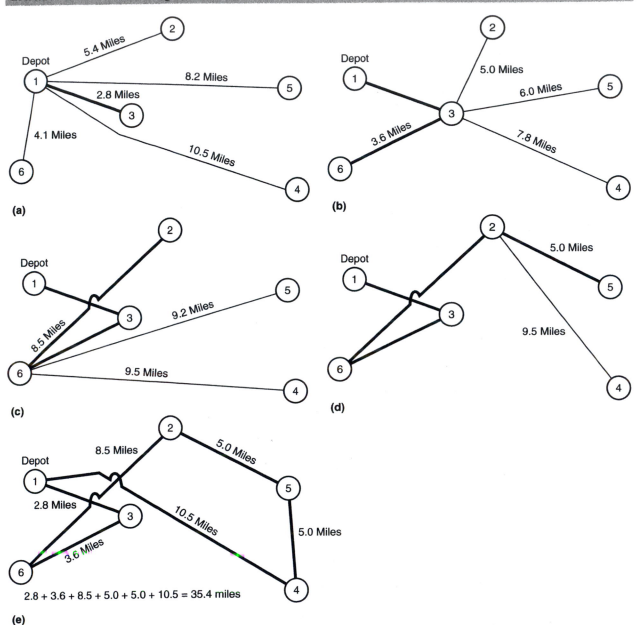

example, if we repeat the procedure using node 6 as the depot node, the tour that results is $6 \rightarrow 3 \rightarrow 1 \rightarrow 2 \rightarrow 5 \rightarrow 4 \rightarrow 6$ with a total length of 31.3 miles.

Clark and Wright Savings Heuristic The Clark and Wright savings heuristic (C&W) is one of the most well-known techniques for solving traveling salesman problems. The heuristic begins by selecting a node as the depot node and labeling it node 1. We then assume, for the moment, that there are $n - 1$ vehicles available, where n is the number of nodes. In other words, if we have six nodes in the network, then there are five vehicles available. Each vehicle travels from the depot directly to a node and returns to the depot. Exhibit 16-6 shows this for a three-node network where the miles are shown on the arcs and the arcs are undirected. The distance from node 2 to node 3 is 5 miles. The total distance covered by the two vehicles in Exhibit 16-6 is 36 miles: 20 miles for the trip from the depot to node 2 and return, and 16 miles for the trip from the depot to node 3 and return.

But this is not a feasible solution because the objective of a traveling salesman problem is to find a tour in which all nodes are visited by *one* vehicle, rather than by two vehicles, as shown in Exhibit 16-6. To reduce the number of vehicles needed, we now need to combine the $n - 1$ tours originally specified.

The key to the C&W heuristic is the computation of savings. **Savings** is a measure of how much the trip length or cost can be reduced by "hooking up" a pair of nodes (in the case of Exhibit 16-6, nodes 2 and 3) and creating the tour $1 \rightarrow 2 \rightarrow 3 \rightarrow 1$, which can then be assigned to a single vehicle. The savings is computed as follows. By linking nodes 2 and 3, we *add* 5 miles (the distance from node 2 to node 3), but we *save* 10 miles for the trip from node 2 to node 1 and 8 miles for the trip from 3 to 1. The total tour length for the complete tour, $1 \rightarrow 2 \rightarrow 3 \rightarrow 1$, is 23 miles. The savings obtained, over the configuration shown in Exhibit 16-6, is 13 miles. For a network with n nodes, we compute the savings for every possible pair of nodes, rank the savings gains from largest to smallest, and construct a tour by linking pairs of nodes until a complete route is obtained.

A statement of the C&W savings heuristic is as follows:

1. Select any node as the depot node (node 1).
2. Compute the savings, S_{ij}, for linking nodes i and j:

$$S_{ij} = c_{1i} + c_{1j} - c_{ij} \text{ for } i \text{ and } j = \text{nodes } 2, 3, \ldots, n \qquad \textbf{(16.1)}$$

where
c_{ij} = the cost of traveling from node i to node j.

3. Rank the savings from largest to smallest.
4. Starting at the top of the list, form larger **subtours** by linking appropriate nodes i and j. Stop when a complete tour is formed.[5]

EXHIBIT 16-6   Initial C&W Network Configuration: Three-Node Problem

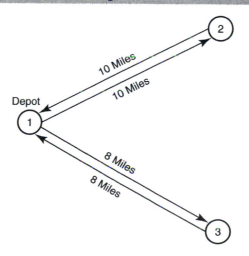

---

[5] The outline of the Clark and Wright savings heuristic is taken from Lawrence Bodin et al., "Routing and Scheduling of Vehicles and Crews: The State of the Art," p. 87.

Example Using the C&W Savings Heuristic   To demonstrate how the C&W heuristic is used to solve a TSP problem, consider the network shown in Exhibit 16-7. Here, as in Exhibit 16-6, we assume that there is one vehicle for every node (excluding the depot) in the network. The solid lines show arcs that are in use as we begin the C&W procedure. The dashed lines show arcs that *may* be used but are not in use currently. Distances, in miles, are shown on the arcs. The savings obtained from linking nodes 2 and 3 is 13 miles. This is computed as (10 miles + 8 miles) − (5 miles). The 10- and 8-mile distances are the lengths of the return trip from nodes 2 and 3, respectively, to the depot; 5 miles is the distance from node 2 to node 3. Similarly, the savings of linking nodes 2 and 4 is 12 miles: (5 miles + 10 miles) − (3 miles). The last pair of nodes to be considered for linking is [4, 3], which yields a savings of 6 miles: (5 miles + 8 miles) − (7 miles).

We next rank the savings for every pair of nodes not yet linked. In order of savings, the pairs are [2, 3], [2, 4], and [3, 4]. The first step in specifying a tour is to link the nodes with the highest savings, nodes 2 and 3. The resulting path is shown in Exhibit 16-8(a). Proceeding to the next highest savings, nodes 2 and 4 are linked as shown in Exhibit 16-8(b). The tour is now complete—the last pair, nodes 3 and 4, cannot be linked without "breaking" the tour. The complete tour is $1 \rightarrow 4 \rightarrow 2 \rightarrow 3 \rightarrow 1$, which has a total tour length of 21 miles. The total savings obtained over the "one vehicle per node" configuration shown in Exhibit 16-7 is 25 miles.

In general, because C&W considers cost when constructing a tour, it yields better-quality solutions than the nearest neighbor procedure. Both the Clark and Wright savings heuristic and the nearest neighbor procedure can be easily adjusted to accomodate problems with directed arcs.

Multiple Traveling Salesman Problem

The MTSP is a generalization of the traveling salesman problem where there are multiple vehicles and a single depot. In this problem, instead of determining a route for a single vehicle, we wish to construct tours for all M vehicles. The characteristics of the tours are that they begin and end at the depot node. Solution procedures begin by "copying" the depot node M times. The problem is thus reduced to M single-vehicle TSPs, and it can be solved using either the nearest neighbor or Clark and Wright heuristics.

EXHIBIT 16-7   Initial C&W Network: Four-Node Problem

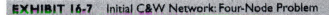
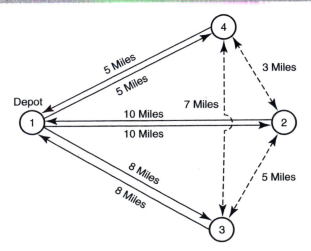

EXHIBIT 16-8   First and Second Node Hookups: C&W Heuristic

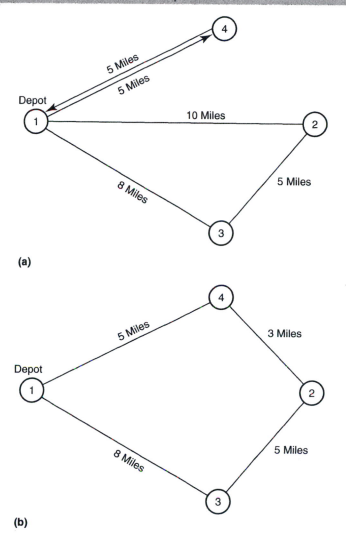

(a)

(b)

The Vehicle Routing Problem

The classic VRP expands the multiple traveling salesman problem to include different service requirements at each node and different capacities for vehicles in the fleet. The objective of these problems is to minimize total cost or distance across all routes. Examples of services that show the characteristics of vehicle routing problems include United Parcel Service deliveries, public transportation "pickups" for the handicapped, and the newspaper delivery problem described earlier.

The vehicle routing problem cannot be fully solved with the same procedures as the multiple traveling salesman problem. Consider the simple example illustrated in Exhibit 16-9. Suppose we have a single depot and two buses, 1 and 2. Vehicle 1 has a capacity of 20 people and vehicle 2 a capacity of 10. There are three nodes where travelers are to be picked up. The number of travelers to be picked up is shown in brackets beside each node.

Ignoring for the moment the capacity of the buses and the demand at each node, the Clark and Wright heuristic would construct a tour for each vehicle as follows:

EXHIBIT 16-9 Four-Node Vehicle Routing Problem

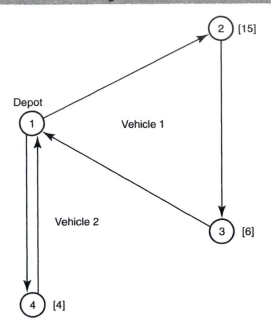

- Bus 1's tour: $1 \rightarrow 2 \rightarrow 3 \rightarrow 1$
- Bus 2's tour: $1 \rightarrow 4 \rightarrow 1$

This assignment, however, sends 21 passengers on bus 1, which violates the capacity constraints of bus 1. Thus, this type of problem cannot be solved as a multiple traveling salesman problem. The characteristics of the vehicle routing problem also make it a difficult problem to solve optimally. However, a good heuristic solution can be obtain with the cluster first, route second approach.[6]

Cluster First, Route Second Approach

The **cluster first, route second approach** is best illustrated by an example. Exhibit 16-10 shows a 12-node problem in which two vehicles must deliver cargo to 11 stations and return to the depot. Cargo demand is bracketed at each node, and distances, in miles, are shown on the arcs. The 12 nodes have been clustered initially into two groups, one for each vehicle. Nodes 2 through 6 are assigned to vehicle 1 and nodes 7 through 12 to vehicle 2. Node 1 is the depot node. In practice, clustering takes into account physical barriers such as rivers, mountains, or interstate highways, as well as geographic areas such as towns and cities that form a natural cluster. Capacity restrictions are also taken into account when developing the clusters. For this example, the capacities of vehicles 1 and 2 are 45 and 35 tons, respectively.

From the initial clustering, vehicle 1 must carry 40 tons and vehicle 2 must carry

---

[6] The cluster first, route second approach is most appropriate for situations characterized by isolated "clumps" of demand points. However, there is another heuristic called the **route first, cluster second approach** that is more appropriate for areas in which demand points are evenly dispersed across a region. The procedure begins by constructing a large single tour using, for example, the Clark and Wright heuristic, but this first tour is infeasible because all the vehicles are not in use. The next step is to partition the single tour into smaller feasible tours such that all vehicles are used and the tours are constructed from nodes that are grouped in some natural fashion, if possible. A description of these approaches is given in Lawrence Bodin et al., "Routing and Scheduling of Vehicles and Crews: The State of the Art," p. 98.

EXHIBIT 16-10   Vehicle Routing Problem: Initial Solution

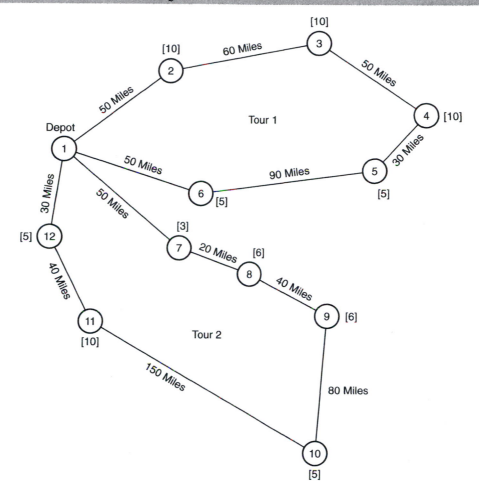

34 tons. Both assignments are feasible (i.e., the demands do not exceed either vehicle's capacity). Using the C&W heuristic, a tour is constructed for vehicle 1 (tour 1), $1 \rightarrow 2 \rightarrow 3 \rightarrow 4 \rightarrow 5 \rightarrow 6 \rightarrow 1$, with a total tour length of 330 miles. Vehicle 2's tour (tour 2) is $1 \rightarrow 7 \rightarrow 8 \rightarrow 9 \rightarrow 10 \rightarrow 11 \rightarrow 12 \rightarrow 1$. Its length is 410 miles.

The next phase of the procedure is to determine whether a node or nodes can be switched from the longest tour (tour 2) to tour 1 such that the capacity of vehicle 1 is not exceeded and the sum of the two tour lengths is reduced. This step is referred to as **tour improvement.** We first identify the nodes in tour 2 that are closest to tour 1. These are nodes 7 and 8. Node 8 has a demand of 6 tons and cannot be switched to tour 1 without exceeding vehicle 1's capacity. Node 7, however, has a demand of 3 tons and is eligible to switch. Given that we wish to consider a switch of node 7, how can we evaluate where the node should be inserted into tour 1 and whether it will reduce the distance traveled? Both these questions can be answered by means of the **minimum cost of insertion technique.**

The minimum cost of insertion is calculated in the same way as the Clark and Wright heuristic. If all distances are symmetrical, then the cost of insertion, I_{ij}, can be calculated as follows:

$$I_{ij} = c_{i,k} + c_{j,k} - c_{ij} \quad \text{for all } i \text{ and } j, i \neq j \tag{16.2}$$

where c_{ij} = the cost of traveling from node i to node j. Nodes i and j are already in the tour, and node k is the node we are trying to insert. Referring to Exhibit 16-10, node 7 is a candidate for insertion because it is near tour 1. Node 7 could be inserted between nodes 6 and 1 or between nodes 5 and 6. Both alternatives will be evaluated. In order to calculate the cost of inserting node 7 into tour 1, we require the additional distance information provided in the following table. In practice, this information would be available for all pairs of nodes.

From Node	To Node	Distance
1	7	50 miles
6	7	30 miles
5	7	60 miles
1	5	130 miles
1	8	60 miles

The cost of inserting node 7 between nodes 1 and 6 is 30 miles: $(30 + 50 - 50)$. The cost of inserting the node between nodes 5 and 6 is 0: $(60 + 30 - 90)$. The lowest cost is found by inserting node 7 between nodes 5 and 6, resulting in a completed tour for vehicle 1 of $1 \rightarrow 2 \rightarrow 3 \rightarrow 4 \rightarrow 5 \rightarrow 7 \rightarrow 6 \rightarrow 1$. Exhibit 16-11 shows the revised solution.

EXHIBIT 16-11 Vehicle Routing Problem: Revised Solution

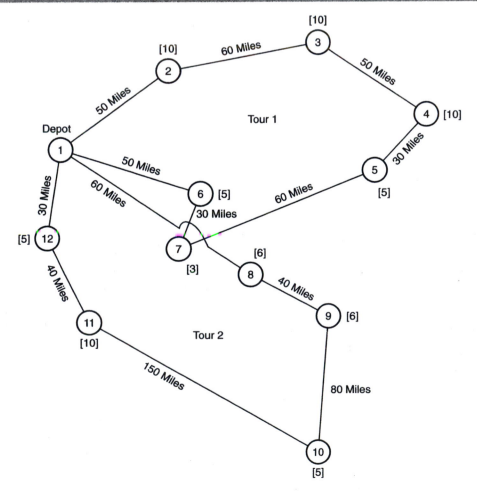

The total length of tour 1 is now 330 miles, and the length of tour 2 is 400 miles. The distance traveled by the two vehicles has decreased from 410 to 400 miles.

16.5   SCHEDULING SERVICE VEHICLES

Scheduling problems are characterized by delivery-time restrictions. The starting and ending times for a service may be specified in advance. Subway schedules fall into this category in that the arrival times at each stop are known in advance and the train must meet the schedule. Time windows bracket the service time to within a specified interval. Recall that in the Meals-for-ME program described earlier, meals had to be delivered between 11:30 A.M. and 1:00 P.M. This is an example of a **two-sided window.** A **one-sided time window** either specifies that a service precede a given time or follow a given time. For example, most newspapers attempt to have papers delivered before 7:00 A.M. Furniture delivery is usually scheduled after 9:00 A.M. or before 4:30 P.M. Other characteristics that further complicate these problems include multiple deliveries to the same customer during a week's schedule.

The general input for a scheduling problem consists of a set of tasks, each with a starting and ending time, and a set of directed arcs, each with a starting and ending location. The set of vehicles may be housed at one or more depots.

The network in Exhibit 16-12 shows a five-task scheduling problem with a single depot. The nodes identify the tasks. Each task has a start and an end time associated with it. The directed arcs mean that two tasks are assigned to the same vehicle. The dashed arcs show other feasible connections that were not used in the schedule. An

EXHIBIT 16-12   Schedule for a Five-Task Network (S = Start Time, E = End Time)

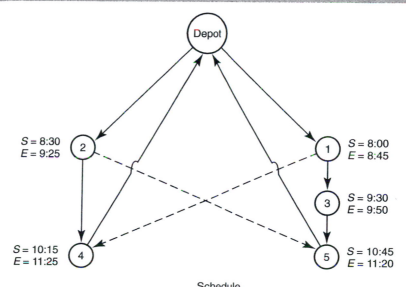

	Schedule	
	Task	Start Time
Vehicle 1	1	8:00
	3	9:30
	5	10:45
Vehicle 2	2	8:30
	4	10:15

arc may join node i to node j if the start time of task j is greater than the end time of task i. An additional restriction is that the start time of task j must include a user-specified period of time longer than the end time of task i. In this example, the time is 45 minutes. This is referred to as **deadhead time** and is the nonproductive time required for the vehicle to travel from one task location to another or return to the depot empty. Also, the paths are not restricted in length. Finally, each vehicle must start and end at the depot.

To solve this problem, the nodes in the network must be partitioned into a set of paths and a vehicle assigned to each path. If we can identify the minimum number of paths, we can minimize the number of vehicles required and thus the vehicle capital costs. Next, if we can associate a weight to each arc that is proportional or equal to the travel time for each arc (i.e., the deadhead time), we can minimize personnel and vehicle operating costs as well as time.

The Concurrent Scheduler Approach

This problem may be formulated as a special type of network problem called a **minimal-cost-flow problem.**[7] Alternatively, a heuristic approach may be used. One that is simple to use is the **concurrent scheduler approach.** The concurrent scheduler proceeds as follows:

1. Order all tasks by starting times. Assign the first task to vehicle 1.
2. For the remaining number of tasks, do the following. If it is feasible to assign the next task to an existing vehicle, assign it to the vehicle that has the minimum deadhead time to that task. Otherwise, create a new vehicle and assign the task to the new vehicle.[8]

Exhibit 16-13 presents start and end times for 12 tasks. The deadhead time is 15 minutes. The problem is solved using the concurrent scheduler approach. Initially, vehicle 1 is assigned to task 1. Because task 2 begins before vehicle 1 is available, a second vehicle is assigned to this task. Vehicle 2 finishes task 2 in time to take care of task 3 also. In the meantime, vehicle 1 completes task 1 and is available for task 4. A third vehicle is not required until task 5, when vehicles 1 and 2 are busy with tasks 4 and 3, respectively. Continuing in a similar fashion, the schedule for vehicle 1 is $1 \rightarrow 4 \rightarrow 7 \rightarrow 10 \rightarrow 12$, for vehicle 2 the schedule is $2 \rightarrow 3 \rightarrow 6 \rightarrow 9$, and for vehicle 3 the schedule is $5 \rightarrow 8 \rightarrow 11$.

16.6   OTHER ROUTING AND SCHEDULING PROBLEMS

Scheduling workers is often concerned with staffing desired vehicle movements. The two are of necessity related in that vehicle schedules restrict staffing options, and vice versa. In general, vehicle scheduling is done first, followed by staff scheduling. This ap-

---

[7] The minimal-cost-flow problem is a special type of network problem that consists of a depot node, a set of intermediate nodes, and a set of demand nodes. The depot node has a supply of materials to be delivered to the demand nodes, each of which has a known demand. The intermediate nodes do not have demand. For example, an intermediate node could be a train stop where material is not removed from the cars. The network also consists of a set of arcs that may or may not have a limited capacity. For example, an arc may be able to "carry" between 0 and 20 tons of material. In addition, the per-unit cost of transporting material over an arc is known. The objective of the problem is to find the least expensive means (routing) of transporting materials from the depot to the demand nodes. A description of this problem may be found in S. P. Bradley, A. C. Hax, and T. L. Magnanti, *Applied Mathematical Programming* (Reading, MA, Addison-Wesley, 1977).

[8] This outline of the concurrent scheduler approach is taken from Lawrence Bodin et al., "Routing and Scheduling of Vehicles and Crews: The State of the Art," p. 133.

EXHIBIT 16-13   Task Times and Schedule for the Concurrent Scheduler Example

Task	Start	End	Assign to Vehicle
1	8:10 A.M.	9:30 A.M.	1
2	8:15 A.M.	9:15 A.M.	2
3	9:30 A.M.	10:40 A.M.	2
4	9:45 A.M.	10:45 A.M.	1
5	10:00 A.M.	11:30 A.M.	3
6	11:00 A.M.	11:45 A.M.	2
7	1:00 P.M.	1:45 P.M.	1
8	1:15 P.M.	2:45 P.M.	3
9	1:45 P.M.	3:00 P.M.	2
10	2:00 P.M.	2:45 P.M.	1
11	3:00 P.M.	3:40 P.M.	3
12	3:30 P.M.	4:00 P.M.	1

	Schedule	
	Task	Start Time
Vehicle 1	1	8:10 A.M.
	4	9:45 A.M.
	7	1:00 P.M.
Vehicle 2	2	8:15 A.M.
	3	9:30 A.M.
	6	11:00 A.M.
Vehicle 3	5	10:00 A.M.
	8	1:15 P.M.

proach is appropriate for services such as airlines, where the cost of personnel is small in comparison to the cost of operating an airplane. It is less appropriate, however, for services such as mass transit systems, where personnel costs may account for up to 80 percent of operating costs. For such systems it is more appropriate to either schedule personnel first, then schedule vehicles, or to do both at the same time.

Problems that have elements of both routing and scheduling are numerous. Examples include school bus routing and scheduling, dial-a-ride services, municipal bus transportation, and the Meals-for-ME program and other meals-on-wheels programs. Certain routing problems also may take on the characteristics of a combined problem. For example, snow plows must clear busier streets prior to clearing less-traveled streets. In addition, there are usually repeated visits depending on the rate of snowfall. These components introduce a scheduling aspect to the routing problem. Considering the fact that there may be literally thousands of variables involved in the formulation of such problems, it becomes apparent that an optimal solution is impossible to obtain. In order to solve real-world problems of this type, management scientists have developed some elegant solution procedures. With rare exception, the procedures use heuristic approaches to obtain "good" but not optimal routes and schedules.

The delivery of emergency services, such as ambulance, police, and fire, is not usually considered a routing or scheduling problem.[9] Rather, emergency services are

---

[9] For a complete discussion of emergency service delivery, see R. C. Larson and A. R. Odoni, *Urban Operations Research* (Upper Saddle River, NJ, Prentice Hall, 1981).

more concerned with resource allocation (how many units are needed) and facility location (where the units should be located).

16.7 SUMMARY

Effective routing and scheduling of service vehicles are two important and difficult problems for managers of services. The consequences of poor planning are costly, and a decision maker must frequently fine-tune the system to ensure that the needs of the customer are being met in a timely and cost-effective fashion. The criterion used to measure the effectiveness of service delivery depends on the type of service. Although minimizing total cost is an important criterion, for some services, criteria such as minimizing customer inconvenience and minimizing response time may be equally if not more important.

Solution of routing and scheduling problems begins with a careful description of the characteristics of the service under study. Characteristics, such as whether demand occurs on the nodes or the arcs, whether there are delivery-time constraints, and whether the capacity of the service vehicles is a concern, determine the type of problem being considered. The type of problem then determines the solution techniques available to the decision maker.

This chapter discussed the characteristics of routing problems, scheduling problems, and combined routing and scheduling problems. Optimal solution techniques for these types of problems are generally based on mathematical programming. However, in practice, a good but perhaps nonoptimal solution is usually sufficient. To obtain a good solution, several heuristic solution approaches have been developed. Two well-known heuristics for solving the traveling salesman problem were presented, the nearest neighbor procedure and the Clark and Wright savings heuristic. Also presented was the minimum cost of insertion technique for use in solving the vehicle routing problem.

Discussion Questions

1. Compare the characteristics of the following types of problems:
   a. Routing problems
   b. Scheduling problems
   c. Combined routing and scheduling problems
2. Describe the differences between and give an example of:
   a. A traveling salesman problem
   b. The Chinese postman problem
   c. A vehicle routing problem
3. A mail carrier delivers mail to 300 houses in Blacksburg. The carrier also must pick up mail from five drop boxes along the route. Mail boxes have specified pickup times of 10:00 A.M., 12:00 noon, 1:00 P.M., 1:30 P.M., and 3:00 P.M. daily. Describe the characteristics of this problem using the information provided in Exhibit 16-1. What types of service-time restrictions apply?
4. Define each of the following:
   a. Deadhead time
   b. Depot node
   c. Undirected arc
5. Describe what is meant by
   a. A feasible tour for a vehicle routing problem
   b. A feasible tour for a traveling salesman problem

     c. A two-sided time window
     d. A node precedence relationship
6. Discuss the differences between the nearest neighbor procedure and the Clark and Wright savings heuristic procedure for constructing a tour.
7. Discuss under what circumstances a distance or cost matrix in a routing problem would be asymmetrical.
8. What are some objectives that might be used to evaluate routes and schedules developed for
     a. School buses
     b. Furniture delivery trucks
     c. Ambulances
9. What are some practical problems that might affect the routing and scheduling of
     a. A city's mass transit system
     b. A national trucking fleet
     c. Snow plows
10. What is the "savings" in the Clark and Wright savings heuristic?

Problems

16.1. Use the Clark and Wright savings heuristic procedure, and the data that follow, to compute the savings obtained by connecting
     a. 2 with 3
     b. 3 with 4
     c. 2 with 5

	To Node (distances in miles)			
From Node	2	3	4	5
1	10	14	12	16
2	—	5	—	18
3	5	—	6	—

16.2. Assume that a tour $1 \rightarrow 3 \rightarrow 5 \rightarrow 1$ exists and has a total length of 23 miles. Given the distance information that follows and using the minimum cost of insertion technique, determine where node 2 should be inserted.

From Node	To Node	Distance
1	3	6
1	5	9
3	5	8
1	2	5
2	3	7
2	6	5
2	5	8

EXHIBIT 16-14

From Node	Distance to Node (in miles)							
	1	2	3	4	5	6	7	8
1	—	2.2	5.8	4.0	5.0	8.5	3.6	3.6
2	2.2	—	4.1	3.6	5.8	9.4	5.0	5.8
3	5.8	4.1	—	3.2	6.1	9.0	6.7	9.2
4	4.0	3.6	3.2	—	3.0	6.3	3.6	6.7
5	5.0	5.8	6.1	3.0	—	3.6	2.0	6.0
6	8.5	9.4	9.0	6.3	3.6	—	3.6	8.5
7	3.6	5.0	6.7	3.6	2.0	3.6	—	4.0
8	3.6	5.8	9.2	6.7	6.0	8.5	4.0	—

16.3. A vehicle routing problem has twenty nodes and two vehicles. How many different routes could be constructed for this problem?

16.4. Given the distance matrix for a traveling salesman problem shown in Exhibit 16-14,
   a. Assume node 1 is the depot node, and construct a tour using the nearest neighbor procedure.
   b. Assume the depot is node 4, and construct a tour using the nearest neighbor procedure.

16.5. Using the Clark and Wright savings heuristic, construct a tour for the data given in the distance matrix for Problem 16.4. Assume node 1 is the depot node.

16.6. You have been asked to route two vehicles through a ten-node network. Node 1 is the depot node; nodes 2 through 5 have been assigned to vehicle 1 and nodes 6 through 10 to vehicle 2. The cost matrix for the network is given in Exhibit 16-15.
   a. Construct the two tours using the nearest neighbor procedure and state the total cost of the tour.
   b. Construct the two tours using the Clark and Wright savings heuristic and state the total cost of the tour.

16.7. Referring to Problem 16.6, assume vehicle 1 has a capacity of 35 passengers and vehicle 2 a capacity of 55 passengers. The number of passengers to be picked up at each node is

EXHIBIT 16-15

From Node	Cost to Node ($)									
	1	2	3	4	5	6	7	8	9	10
1	—	22	22	32	32	14	45	56	51	35
2	22	—	32	22	54	36	67	78	67	41
3	22	32	—	22	36	41	42	67	70	64
4	32	22	22	—	56	51	71	86	83	63
5	32	54	36	56	—	32	10	32	45	54
6	14	36	41	51	32	—	40	45	32	32
7	45	67	42	71	10	40	—	20	42	71
8	56	78	67	86	32	45	20	—	32	71
9	51	67	70	83	45	32	42	32	—	45
10	35	41	64	63	54	32	71	71	45	—

Node	Number of Passengers
2	10
3	10
4	5
5	5
6	5
7	5
8	20
9	10
10	5

Using the tours constructed in Problem 16.6, attempt to improve the total cost of the two tours using the minimum cost of insertion technique.

16.8. Convert the distance matrix given in Problem 16.4 to a cost matrix using the following information. The cost of routing a vehicle from any node i to any node j is $100. This is a fixed cost of including a link in a tour. The variable cost of using a link (or arc) is $3.30 per mile for the first 5 miles and $2.00 for the remainder of the arc distance. After computing the cost matrix, resolve the problem using the Clark and Wright savings heuristic.

16.9. Using the task times provided below, determine the number of vehicles required and the task sequence for each vehicle using the concurrent scheduler approach. The deadhead time is 30 minutes.

Task	Start	End
1	8:00 A.M.	8:30 A.M.
2	8:15 A.M.	9:15 A.M.
3	9:00 A.M.	9:30 A.M.
4	9:40 A.M.	10:20 A.M.
5	10:10 A.M.	11:00 A.M.
6	10:45 A.M.	11:30 A.M.
7	12:15 P.M.	12:40 P.M.
8	1:30 P.M.	1:50 P.M.
9	2:00 P.M.	2:40 P.M.
10	2:15 P.M.	3:30 P.M.

CASE

CASE 16–1 Routing and Scheduling of Phlebotomists

Phlebotomists are clinical laboratory technicians who are responsible for drawing blood specimens from patients in the hospital. Their routine responsibilities include drawing samples for laboratory tests ordered that are to be completed on that day by the day crew. A 500-bed medical center usually employs five to seven technicians in this capacity. The morning pickups are made between 6:30 A.M. and 8:00 A.M. On a given morning there may be requests to draw blood samples from 120 to 150 patients. The time required to draw the blood necessary to complete a physician's order varies depending on age, physical condition, and the number of different types of tests required of a patient. For example, a single phlebotomist may be able to draw samples for twenty maternity patients in 90 minutes, since most of these women are healthy and do not require "unusual" types of blood work. However, that same phlebotomist may only be able to draw blood from eight critically ill patients, who usually require more varied tests and may, because of their physical condition, require more time. The same limitation is true for infants and small children who require special collection techniques due to their size.

In addition to their routine pickups, which must be completed within the 90-minute preshift interval, there are routine specimens that must be drawn at a specified time. These timed specimens include fasting specimens (such as blood glucose tests), which must be collected before the patient eats, and blood gases, which are collected 30 minutes after a patient has received a respiratory treatment. With either of these tests, there is a margin for "error" of 15 minutes. Generally, more routine tests are also collected along with the timed specimens.

The medical center has five floors, each of which specializes in a particular type of patient. For example, one floor may handle surgical patients and another orthopedic patients. In addition, there are special sections, including the nursery, the pediatric floor, and the intensive care unit. Because of the location of the respiratory equipment and monitors, all patients requiring daily blood gases are located in intensive care.

It is the task of the chief phlebotomist to estimate the number of phlebotomists needed on a given day and to assign patients to technicians such that all deliveries are made before the start of the day shift and timed specimens are collected within a 15-minute window of the specified time. ■

CASE QUESTIONS

1. What characteristics of routing and scheduling are exhibited in this problem?
2. What type of data would you need to collect in order to most effectively schedule technicians?
3. Does a deadhead time exist in this situation? If so, where?
4. If you were to view this as a cluster first, route second situation, based on what criteria would you form clusters?
5. Suggest how you would solve the problem if the timed specimens and routine pickups were considered separately.

References

Baker, J. R., M. A. McKnew, T. R. Gulledge, and J. R. Ringuest, "An Application of MAUT to the Planning Emergency Medical Services," *Socio-Economic Planning Sciences*, vol. 18, no. 4 (1984), pp. 273–280.

Baker, J. R., and R. T. Sumichrast, "A DSS for Ambulance Allocation and Scheduling," in *Proceedings of the Decision Sciences Institute* (Las Vegas, Decision Sciences Institute, November 1988), pp. 157–158.

Bodin, Lawrence, Bruce Golden, Arjang Assad, and Michael Ball, "Routing and Scheduling of Vehicles and Crews: The State of the Art," *Computers and Operations Research*, vol. 10, no. 2 (1983), pp. 63–211.

Bradley, S. P., A. C. Hax, and T. L. Magnanti, *Applied Mathematical Programming* (Reading, MA, Addison-Wesley, 1977).

"Emergency Medical Service Systems Act," *Federal Register*, vol. 39, no. 62, part 3 (March 29, 1974), pp. 11758–11766.

Fitzpatrick, K. E., "Predicting Demand for Emergency Transportation Services in South Carolina," in R. G. Flood (ed.), *Proceedings of the Southeast Decision Sciences Institute* (Williamsburg, VA, 1984), pp. 207–209.

Fitzsimmons, J. A., and R. S. Sullivan, "Service Vehicle Scheduling and Routing," in *Service Operations Management* (New York, McGraw-Hill, 1982), pp. 312–336.

Larson, R. C., and A. R. Odini, *Urban Operations Research* (Upper Saddle River, NJ, Prentice Hall, 1981).

Russell, R., and R. Morrel, "Routing Special Education School Buses," *Interfaces*, vol. 16 (September–October 1986), pp. 56–64.

CHAPTER 17

Project Management

17.1 INTRODUCTION

Most service organizations have to take on large, complex projects at one point or another. For example, an airline opening new routes or pulling a jumbo jet out of service for major maintenance faces large expenses if these tasks are delayed for any reason. A department store chain installing a new inventory control system can suffer lost sales and painful ordering costs if timetables are unmet. A government agency installing and debugging an expensive computer spends months preparing details for a smooth conversion to new hardware. The National Aeronautics and Space Administration (NASA) completes thousands of individual activities in its extensive overhaul of a space shuttle after each flight. A hospital modernizing its operating rooms can endure not only inconvenience, but a loss of life if the many technical steps involved are not properly controlled.

Large, often one-time projects are difficult challenges to service managers. The stakes are high. Millions of dollars in cost overruns have been wasted due to poor planning on projects. Unnecessary delays have occurred due to poor scheduling. And companies have gone bankrupt due to poor controls.

Special projects that take months or years to complete are usually developed outside the normal operations system. Project organizations within the firm are set up to handle such jobs and are often disbanded when the project is complete. The management of large projects involves three phases (see Exhibit 17-1):

- Planning
- Scheduling
- Controlling

This chapter will begin with a brief overview of these functions. Two popular techniques to allow managers to plan, schedule, and control—program evaluation and re-

EXHIBIT 17-1   Project Planning, Scheduling, and Controlling

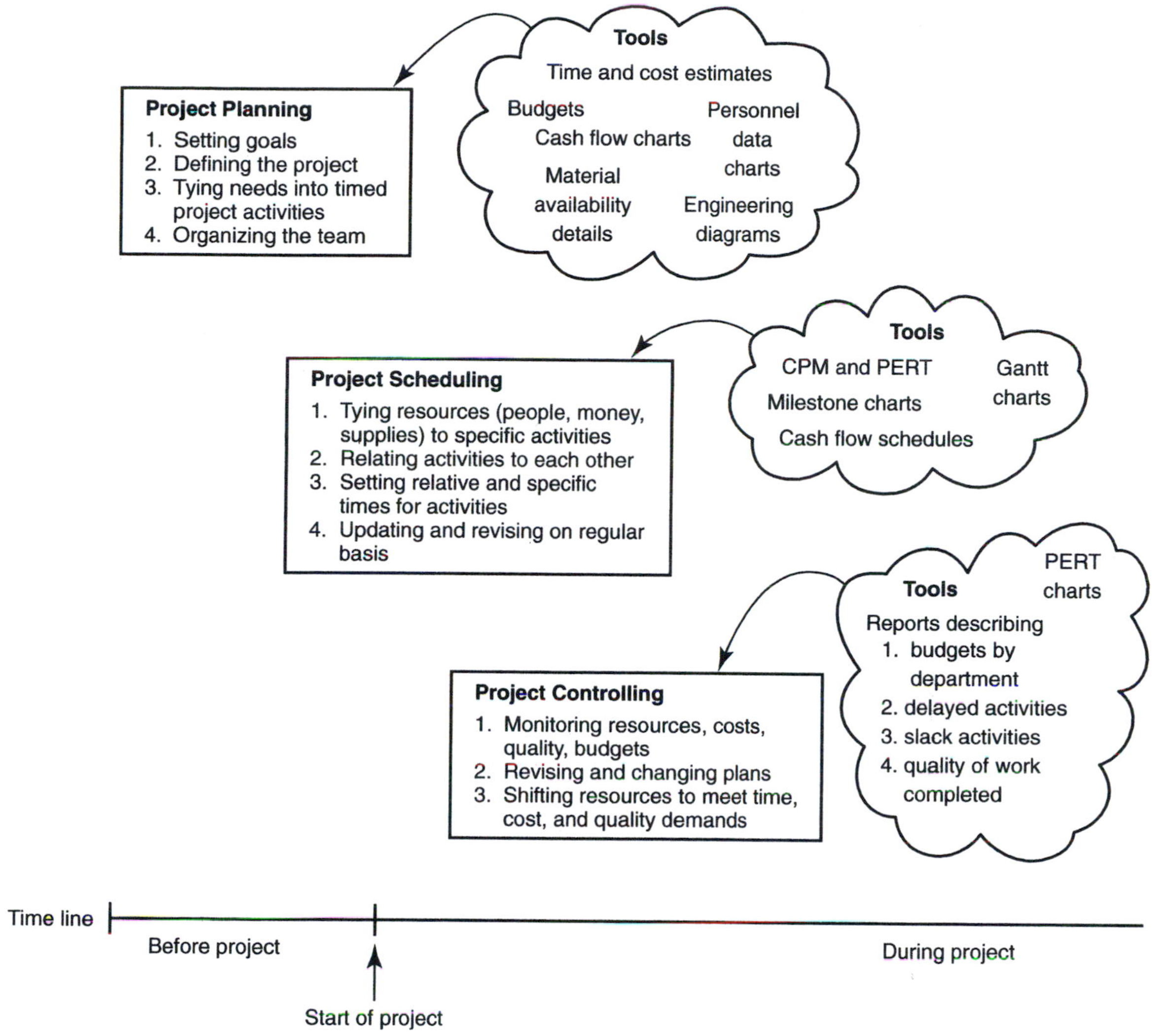

Tools

Time and cost estimates

Project Planning

1. Setting goals
2. Defining the project
3. Tying needs into timed project activities
4. Organizing the team

Budgets

Cash flow charts

Material availability details

Personnel data charts

Engineering diagrams

Tools

CPM and PERT

Milestone charts

Cash flow schedules

Gantt charts

Project Scheduling

1. Tying resources (people, money, supplies) to specific activities
2. Relating activities to each other
3. Setting relative and specific times for activities
4. Updating and revising on regular basis

Tools

PERT charts

Reports describing

1. budgets by department
2. delayed activities
3. slack activities
4. quality of work completed

Project Controlling

1. Monitoring resources, costs, quality, budgets
2. Revising and changing plans
3. Shifting resources to meet time, cost, and quality demands

Time line

Before project

Start of project

During project

view technique (PERT) and critical path method (CPM)—will then be described in some detail.

17.2   PROJECT PLANNING

Projects can usually be defined as a series of related tasks directed toward a major output. A new organization form, developed to make sure existing programs continue to run smoothly on a day-to-day basis while new projects are successfully completed, is called **project organization.**

A project organization is an effective way of pooling the people and physical resources needed for a limited time to complete a specific project or goal. It is basically a temporary organizational structure designed to achieve results by using specialists from throughout the firm. For many years, NASA successfully used the project approach to reach its goals. You may recall Project Gemini and Project Apollo. These terms were used to describe teams NASA organized to reach space exploration objectives.

The project organization works best when:

1. Work can be defined with a specific goal and deadline.
2. The job is somewhat unique or unfamiliar to the existing organization.
3. The work contains complex interrelated tasks requiring specialized skills.
4. The project is temporary but critical to the organization.

When a project organization takes on a more permanent form, it is usually called a **matrix organization.** This structure can be used when it is critical for the firm to be highly responsive to external pressures. The firm might find that a matrix structure allows quicker responses to the environment while maintaining continuity and competence in the functional area. Some industries employing matrix project management include chemical, banking, and electronics.

The project management team begins its task well in advance of the project, so that a plan can be developed. One of its first steps is to set carefully the project's objectives, then define the project and break it down into a set of activities and related costs. Gross requirements for people, supplies, and equipment are also estimated in the planning phase.

17.3 PROJECT SCHEDULING

Project scheduling is determining the project's activities in the time sequence in which they have to be performed. Materials and people needed at each stage of production are computed in this phase, and the time each activity will take is also set.

One popular project scheduling approach is the Gantt chart (named after Henry Gantt). As seen in Exhibit 17-2, **Gantt charts** reflect time estimates and can be easily understood. The horizontal bars are drawn for each project activity along a time line. The letters to the left of each bar tell the planner which other activities have to be completed before that one can begin.

Gantt charts are low-cost means of helping managers make sure that (1) all activ-

EXHIBIT 17-2 Sample Gantt Chart

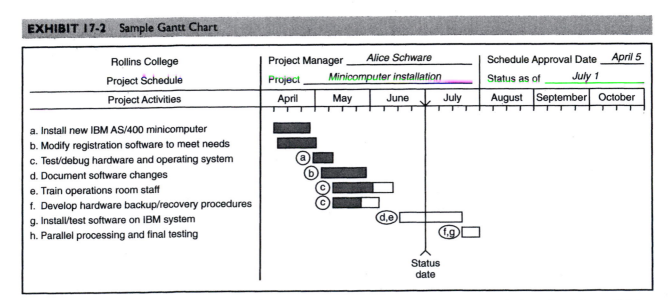

Circled items represent precedence relationships (for example, activity c, test/debug hardware, may not begin until activity a, which is circled, is completed).

ities are planned for, (2) their order of performance is accounted for, (3) the activity time estimates are recorded, and (4) the overall project time is developed.

Activity progress is noted, once the actual project is underway, by shading the horizontal bars as an activity is partially or fully completed. For examle, as seen in Exhibit 17-2, activities *a*, *b*, *c*, and *d* are on schedule because their bars have been shaded up to the vertical status date line. The date line, July 1 in this case, is a status-reporting period that lets participants see which tasks are on time, which are ahead of time, and which have fallen behind schedule. Activities *e*, *f*, and *g* are all behind schedule; their bars are not shaded in their entirety or up to the status date line.

Scheduling charts such as this one can be used alone on simple projects. They permit managers to observe the progress of each activity and to spot and tackle problem areas. Gantt charts are not easily updated, though. And more importantly, they don't adequately illustrate the interrelationships between the activities and the resources.

A second example of a Gantt chart is shown in Exhibit 17-3. This illustration of a routine servicing of a Boeing 747 airplane during a 50-minute layover shows that Gantt charts also can be used for scheduling repetitive operations. In this case, the chart helps point out potential delays.

PERT and CPM, the two widely used network techniques that will be discussed shortly, *do* have the ability to consider precedence relationships and interdependency of activities. On complex projects, the scheduling of which is almost always computerized, PERT and CPM thus hold an edge on the simpler Gantt charts. Even on huge projects, though, Gantt charts can be used as a summary of project status and may complement the other network approaches.

To summarize, whatever the approach taken by a project manager, project scheduling serves several purposes:

1. It shows the relationship of each activity to others and to the whole project.
2. It identifies the precedence relationships among activities.
3. It encourages the setting of realistic time and cost estimates for each activity.
4. It helps make better use of people, money, and material resources by identifying critical bottlenecks in the project.

17.4   PROJECT CONTROLLING

The control of large projects, like the control of any management system, involves close monitoring of resources, costs, quality, and budgets. It also usually means using a feedback loop to revise and update the project plan and schedule and having the ability to shift resources to where they are needed most. Computerized PERT/CPM reports and charts are widely available today on mainframes and personal computers (PCs).

There are a wide variety of reports that can be generated for control purposes by project management software. Here is a summary and brief description of eight that are commonly available in PC software.

1. Detailed cost breakdown for each task
2. Total program manpower curves showing each department's resource contribution
3. Cost distribution table listing yearly or quarterly costs by task (it resembles a project cash flow summary for each activity)
4. Functional cost and hour summary of how manhours and dollars will be spent by each department
5. Raw material and expenditure forecast showing a cash flow based on vendor lead times, payment schedules, and commitments

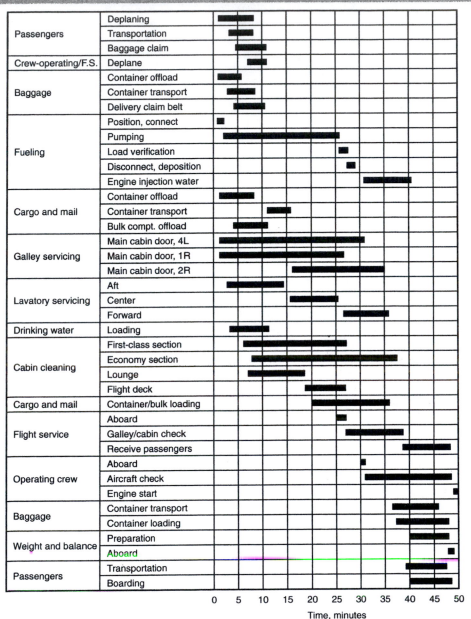

EXHIBIT 17-3   Service Activities for a Boeing 747 Jumbo Jet

6. Variance report using a percent complete figure for each activity, including planned versus actual costs to date, estimated costs to date, total cost at completion, earned value of work in progress, and a cost performance index
7. Time analysis reports related to PERT/CPM schedules, giving estimated completion times, slack and float time, project calendars
8. Work status report giving weekly task analyses for submission to the project manager for aggregation

17.5 PROJECT MANAGEMENT TECHNIQUES: PERT AND CPM

Program evaluation and review technique (PERT) and the **critical path method** (CPM) were both developed in the 1950s to help managers schedule, monitor, and control large and complex projects. CPM arrived first, in 1957, as a tool developed by J. E. Kelly of Remington Rand and M. R. Walker of DuPont to assist in the building and maintenance of chemical plants at DuPont. Independently, the Special Projects Office of the U.S. Navy, working with Booz, Allen, and Hamilton, developed PERT in 1958 to plan and control the Polaris missile program. That project involved the coordination of thousands of contractors, and PERT was credited with cutting 18 months off the project length. Today, PERT is still required in many government contract schedules. If a person were to walk into the offices of a project manager working on a defense department contract, it would not be unusual these days to find a wall covered with a 20-foot-long PERT printout.

The Framework of PERT and CPM

There are six steps common to both PERT and CPM. The procedure is as follows:

1. Define the project and all its significant activities or tasks.
2. Develop the relationships among the activities. Decide which activities must precede and which must follow others.
3. Draw the network connecting all the activities.
4. Assign time and/or cost estimates to each activity.
5. Compute the longest time path through the network; this is called the **critical path.**
6. Use the network to help plan, schedule, monitor, and control the project.

Step 5, finding the critical path, is a major part of controlling a project. The activities on the critical path represent tasks that will delay the entire project if they are delayed. Managers derive flexibility by identifying noncritical activities and replanning, rescheduling, and reallocating resources such as manpower and finances.

Although PERT and CPM differ to some extent in terminology and in the construction of the network, their objectives are the same. Furthermore, the analysis used in both techniques is very similar. The major difference is that PERT employs three time estimates for each activity. Each estimate has an associated probability of occurrence, which, in turn, is used in computing expected values and standard deviations for the activity times. CPM makes the assumption that activity times are known with certainty, and hence only one time estimate is given for each activity.

For purposes of illustration, this section concentrates on a discussion of PERT and PERT/Cost. **PERT/Cost** is a technique that combines the benefits of both PERT and CPM. Most of the comments and procedures described, however, apply just as well to CPM.

PERT, PERT/Cost, and CPM are important because they can help answer questions such as the following about projects with thousands of activities.

- When will the entire project be completed?
- What are the critical activities or tasks in the project, that is, the ones that will delay the entire project if they are late?
- Which are the noncritical activities, that is, the ones that can run late without delaying the whole project's completion?
- What is the probability that the project will be completed by a specific date?
- At any particular date, is the project on schedule, behind schedule, or ahead of schedule?

- On any given date, is the money spent equal to, less than, or greater than the budgeted amount?
- Are there enough resources available to finish the project on time?
- If the project is to be finished in a shorter amount of time, what is the best way to accomplish this at the least cost?

Activities, Events, and Networks

The first step in PERT is to divide the entire project into events and activities. An **event** marks the start or completion of a particular task or activity. An **activity,** on the other hand, is a task or subproject that occurs between two events. Exhibit 17-4 restates these definitions and shows the symbols used to represent events and activities.

Any project that can be described by activities and events may be analyzed by a PERT **network.** Given the following information, for example, the network shown below can be developed.

Activity	Immediate Predecessors
A	—
B	—
C	A
D	B

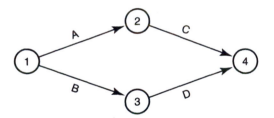

Note that each event was assigned a number. As will be seen later, it is possible to identify each activity with a beginning and an ending event or node. For example, activity *A* above is the activity that starts with event 1 and ends at node, or event, 2. In general, nodes are numbered from left to right. The beginning node, or event, of the entire project is number 1, while the last node, or event, in the entire project bears the largest number. The last node shows the number 4.

Networks can also be specified by events and the activities that occur between events. The following example shows how to develop a network based on this type of specification scheme. Given the following table, the newtork illustrated below can be developed.

EXHIBIT 17-4 Events and Activities

Name	Symbol	Description
Event	○ (node)	A point in time, usually a completion date or a starting date
Activity	→ (arrow)	A flow over time, usually a task or subproject

Beginning Event	Ending Event	Activity
1	2	1–2
1	3	1–3
2	4	2–4
3	4	3–4
3	5	3–5
4	6	4–6
5	6	5–6

Instead of using a letter to signify activities and their predecessor activities, activities can be specified by their starting event and their ending event. Beginning with the activity that starts at event 1 and ends at event 2, the following network can be constructed.

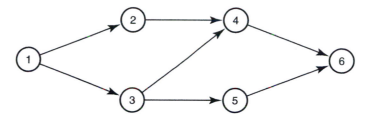

All that is required to construct a network is the starting and ending event for each activity.

Dummy Activities and Events

A network may be encountered that has two activities with identical starting and ending events. **Dummy activities** and **events** can be inserted into the network to deal with this problem. The use of dummy activities and events is especially important when computer programs are to be employed in determining the critical path, project completion time, project variance, and so on. Dummy activities and events also can ensure that the network properly reflects the project under consideration. To illustrate, a network is developed based on the following information.

Activity	Immediate Predecessors	Activity	Immediate Predecessors
A	—	E	C,D
B	—	F	D
C	A	G	E
D	B	H	F

Given these data, the following network might result.

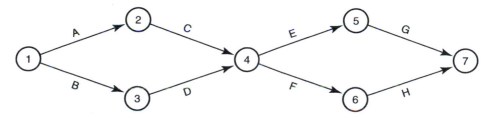

Look at activity *F*. According to the *network*, both activities *C* and *D* must be completed before we can start *F*, but in reality, only activity *D* must be completed (see the table). Thus, the network is not correct. The addition of a dummy activity and a dummy event can overcome this problem, as shown below.

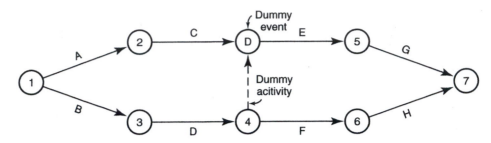

Now the network embodies all the proper relationships and can be analyzed as usual. A dummy activity should have completion time *t* of zero.

PERT and Activity Time Estimates

As mentioned earlier, one distinguishing difference between PERT and CPM is the use of three **activity time estimates** for each activity in the PERT technique. Only one time factor is given for each activity in CPM.

For each activity in PERT, an **optimistic time,** a **most probable** (or most likely) **time,** and a **pessimistic time** estimate must be specified. These three time estimates are then used to calculate an expected completion time and variance for each activity. If we assume, as many researchers do, that activity times follow a **beta probability distribution,** we can use the formulas[1]

$$t = \frac{a + 4m + b}{6} \quad \text{and} \quad v = \left(\frac{b-a}{6}\right)^2 \tag{17.1}$$

where
a = optimistic time for activity completion
b = pessimistic time for activity completion
m = most likely time for activity completion
t = expected time of activity completion
v = variance of activity completion time

In PERT, after the network has been developed, expected times and variances for each activity are computed. For example, consider the following time estimates:

Activity	a	m	b
1–2	3	4	5
1–3	1	3	5
2–4	5	6	7
3–4	6	7	8

---

[1] Although the beta distribution has been widely used in PERT analysis for many years, its applicability has been called into question in a recent article. See M. W. Sasieni, "A Note on PERT Times," *Management Science*, vol. 32, no. 12 (December 1986), pp. 1662–1663.

In the table below, expected times and variances of completion for each activity above are computed.

Activity	a + 4m + b	t	$\dfrac{b - a}{6}$	v
1–2	24	4	$\dfrac{2}{6}$	$\dfrac{4}{36}$
1–3	18	3	$\dfrac{4}{6}$	$\dfrac{16}{36}$
2–4	36	6	$\dfrac{2}{6}$	$\dfrac{4}{36}$
3–4	42	7	$\dfrac{2}{6}$	$\dfrac{4}{36}$

Critical Path Analysis

The objective of **critical path analysis** is to determine the following quantities for each activity:

ES = earliest activity start time. All *predecessor* activities must be completed before an activity can be started. This is the earliest time an activity can be started.

LS = latest activity start time. All *following* activities must be completed without delaying the entire project. This is the latest time an activity can be started without delaying the entire project.

EF = earliest activity finish time.

LF = latest activity finish time.

S = activity slack time, which is equal to (LS – ES) or (LF – EF).

For any activity, if ES and LS can be calculated, the other three quantities can be found as follows:

$$EF = ES + t \tag{17.2}$$

$$LF = LS + t \tag{17.3}$$

$$S = LS - ES \qquad \text{or} \qquad S = LF - EF \tag{17.4}$$

Once these quantities are known for every activity, the overall project can be analyzed. Typically, this analysis includes:

1. The **critical path**—the group of activities in the project that have a slack time of zero. This path is *critical* because a delay in any activity along this path would delay the entire project.

2. *T*—the total project completion time, which is calculated by adding the expected time t values of those activities on the critical path.

3. *V*—variance of the critical path, which is computed by adding the variance v of those individual activities on the critical path.

Critical path analysis normally starts with the determination of ES and EF. The following example illustrates the procedure.

Sample Calculations Given the following illustration, ES and EF will be determined for each activity.

Activity	t
1–2	2
1–3	7
2–3	4
2–4	3
3–4	2

ES is found by moving from the starting activities of the project to the ending activities of the project. For the starting activities, ES is either zero or the actual starting date, say, August 1. For activities 1–2 and 1–3, ES is zero. (By convention, all projects start at time zero.)

There is one basic rule. Before an activity can be started, *all* of its predecessor activities must be completed. In other words, search for the *longest* path leading to an activity in determining ES. For activity 2–3, ES is 2. Its only predecessor activity is 1–2, for which $t = 2$. By the same reasoning, ES for activity 2–4 also is 2. For activity 3–4, however, ES is 7. It has two predecessor paths: activity 1–3 with $t = 7$ and activities 1–2 and 2–3 with a total expected time of 6 (or 2 + 4). Thus, ES for activity 3–4 is 7 because activity 1–3 must be completed before activity 3–4 can be started. EF is computed next by adding t to ES for each activity. See the following table.

Activity	ES	EF
1–2	0	2
1–3	0	7
2–3	2	6
2–4	2	5
3–4	7	9

The next step is to calculate LS, the latest activity starting time for each activity. Start with the last activities and work backward to the first activities. The procedure is to work backward from the last activities to determine the latest possible starting time (LS) without increasing the earliest finishing time (EF). This task sounds more difficult than it really is.

To illustrate, determine LS, LF, and S (the slack) for each activity based on the following data:

Activity	t	ES	EF
1–2	2	0	2
1–3	7	0	7
2–3	4	2	6
2–4	3	2	5
3–4	2	7	9

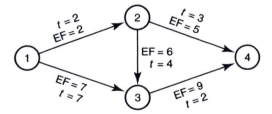

The earliest time by which the entire project can be finished is 9 because activities 2–4 (EF = 5) and 3–4 (EF = 9) *both* must be completed. Using 9 as a basis, work backward by subtracting the appropriate values of t from 9.

The latest time activity 3–4 can be started is at time 7 (or 9 – 2) in order still to complete the project by time period 9. Thus, LS for activity 3–4 is 7. Using the same reasoning, LS for activity 2–4 is 6 (or 9 – 3). If activity 2–4 is started at 6 and it takes 3 time units to complete the activity, it can still be finished in 9 time units. The latest activity 2–3 can be started is 3 (or 9 – 2 – 4). If activity 2–3 is started at 3 and it takes 2 and 4 time units for activities 2–3 and 3–4, respectively, it can still be finished on time. Thus, LS for activity 2–3 is 3. Using the same reasoning, LS for activity 1–3 is zero (or 9 – 2 – 7). Analyzing activity 1–2 is more difficult because there are two paths. Both must be completed in 9 time units.

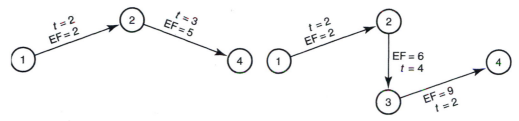

Because both the preceding paths must be completed, LS activity 1–2 is computed from the most binding, or slowest, path. Thus, LS for activity 1–2 *is 1* (or 9 – 2 – 4 – 2) and *not 4* (or 9 – 3 – 2). Noting the following relationships, we can construct a table summarizing the results.

$$LF = LS + t$$
$$S = LF - EF \qquad \text{or} \qquad S = LS - ES$$

Activity	ES	EF	LS	LF	S
1–2	0	2	1	3	1
1–3	0	7	0	7	0
2–3	2	6	3	7	1
2–4	2	5	6	9	4
3–4	7	9	7	9	0

Once ES, EF, LS, LF, and S have been computed, the entire project can be analyzed. Analysis includes determining the critical path, project completion time, and project variance. Consider the following example.

Project Analysis   We wish to find the critical path, total completion time T, and project variance V, of the following network.

Activity	t	v	ES	EF	LS	LF	S
1–2	2	$\frac{2}{6}$	0	2	1	3	1
1–3	7	$\frac{3}{6}$	0	7	0	7	0
2–3	4	$\frac{1}{6}$	2	6	3	7	1
2–4	3	$\frac{2}{6}$	2	5	6	9	4
3–4	2	$\frac{4}{6}$	7	9	7	9	0

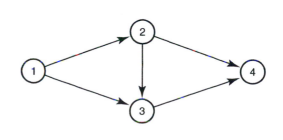

The critical path consists of those activities with zero slack. These are activities 1–3 and 3–4.

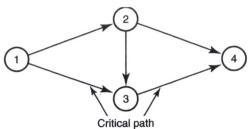

Critical path

The total project completion time is 9 (or 7 + 2). The project variance is the sum of the *activity variances* along the *critical path*, which is 7/6 (or 3/6 + 4/6).

Knowing a network and values for activity times and variances (*t* and *v*) makes it possible to perform a complete critical path analysis, including the determination of ES, EF, LS, LF, and S for each activity as well as the critical path, *T*, and *V* for the entire project.

The Probability of Project Completion

Having computed the expected completion time *T* and completion variance *V*, we can determine the probability that the project will be completed at a specified date. If we make the assumption that the distribution of completion dates follow a normal curve, we can calculate the probability of completion as in the following example.

Let us say that the expected project completion time *T* is 20 weeks and the project variance *V* is 100. What is the probability that the project will be finished on or before week 25?

$T = 20$
$V = 100$
$\sigma = \text{standard deviation} = \sqrt{\text{project variance}} = \sqrt{V}$
   $= \sqrt{100} = 10$
$C = \text{desired completion date}$
   $= 25 \text{ weeks}$

The normal curve would appear as follows:

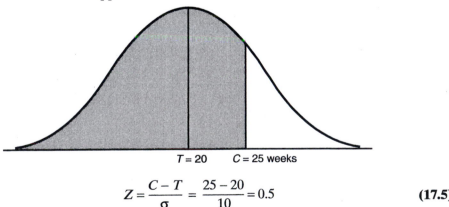

$T = 20$ $C = 25$ weeks

$$Z = \frac{C - T}{\sigma} = \frac{25 - 20}{10} = 0.5 \qquad \textbf{(17.5)}$$

where *Z* equals the number of standard deviations from the mean. The area under the curve, for *Z* = 0.5, is 0.6915. (See the normal curve table in the Appendix.) Thus, the probability of completing the project in 25 weeks is approximately 0.69, or 69 percent.

17.6   PERT/COST

Until now, we have assumed that it is not possible to reudce activity times. This is usually not the case, however. Perhaps additional resources can reduce activity times for certain activities within the project. These resources might be additional labor, more equipment, and so on. Although it can be expensive to shorten activity times, doing so might be worthwhile. If a company faces costly penalties for being late with a project, it might be economical to use additional resources to complete the project on time. There may be fixed costs every day the project is in process. Thus, it might be profitable to use additional resources to shorten the project time and save some of the daily fixed costs. But which activities should be shortened? How much will this action cost? Will a reduction in the activity time in turn reduce the time needed to complete the entire project? Ideally, we would like to find the least expensive method of shortening the entire project. This is the purpose of PERT/Cost.

In addition to time, the service manager is normally concerned with the cost of the project. Usually it is possible to shorten activity times by committing additional resources to the project. Exhibit 17-5 shows cost–time curves for two activities. For activity 5–6, it costs $300 to complete the activity in eight weeks, $400 for seven weeks, and $600 for six weeks. Activity 2–4 requires $3,000 of additional resources for completion in 12 weeks and $1,000 for 14 weeks. Similar cost–time curves or relationships can usually be developed for all activities in the network.

The objective of PERT/Cost is to reduce the entire project completion time by a certain amount at the least cost. Although there are several good computer programs that perform PERT/Cost, it is useful to understand how to complete this process by hand. To accomplish this objective, a few more variables must be introduced. For each activity, there will exist a reduction in activity time and the cost incurred for that time reduction. Let

M_i = maximum reduction of time for activity i
C_i = additional cost associated with reducing activity time for activity i
K_i = cost of reducing activity time by one unit for activity i
$K_i = C_i/M_i$

With this information, it is possible to determine the least cost of reducing the project completion date.

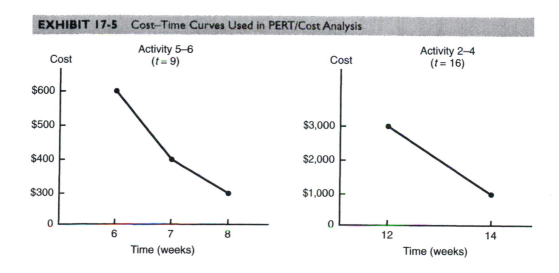

EXHIBIT 17-5   Cost–Time Curves Used in PERT/Cost Analysis

Reducing Completion Time Example   As an illustration, the following information is used to determine the least cost of reducing the project completion time by one week.

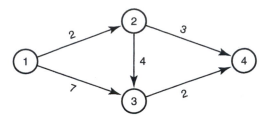

Activity	t (weeks)	M (weeks)	C	Activity	ES	EF	LS	LF	S
1–2	2	1	$ 300	1–2	0	2	1	3	1
1–3	7	4	2000	1–3	0	7	0	7	0
2–3	4	2	2000	2–3	2	6	3	7	1
2–4	3	2	4000	2–4	2	5	6	9	4
3–4	2	1	2000	3–4	7	9	7	9	0

The first step is to compute K for each activity.

Activity	M	C	K	Critical Path
1–2	1	$ 300	$ 300	No
1–3	4	2000	500	Yes
2–3	2	2000	1000	No
2–4	2	4000	2000	No
3–4	1	2000	2000	Yes

The second step is to locate that activity on the critical path with the smallest value of K_i. The critical path consists of activities 1–3 and 3–4. Because activity 1–3 has a lower value of K_i, the project completion time can be reduced by one week, to eight weeks, by incurring an additional cost of $500.

We must be very careful in using this procedure. Any further reduction in activity time along the critical path would cause the critical path also to include activities 1–2, 2–3, and 3–4. In other words, there would be two critical paths and activities on both would need to be "crashed" to reduce project completion time.

17.7   OTHER SERVICE APPLICATIONS OF PERT

To further illustrate the potential for project management techniques in services, this section provides two larger illustrations. The first deals with the relocation of a hospital, and the second with the planning and control of an audit by a CPA firm.

Relocating a Hospital with Project Networks

When St. Vincent's Hospital and Medical Center moved from a 373-bed facility in Portland, Oregon, to a new 403-bed building in the suburbs five miles away, a large variety of planning considerations had to be taken into account. Army vehicles and private ambulances had to be used to move patients; police escorts would be needed; local stores would be affected by the move, among many other concerns. To coordinate all the activities, a project network was developed and used as a basic planning tool eight months before the move. Although the actual network contained dozens of activities, a portion of it is provided in Exhibit 17-6 to illustrate how valuable project management tools can be in planning and carrying out a complex project.

Audit Planning and Control with PERT

As a second example, we turn to the use of PERT in an audit application. These tools have proven to be of practical value to auditors in scheduling audit work, in allocating personnel resources, in predicting engagement completion time, in anticipating work bottlenecks, and in guiding audit acceleration. Exhibit 17-7 shows an engagement network for one firm. Because auditors are usually familiar with the conditions of a client's book, internal controls, and problem areas and have actual work times from previous audits, reasonably good time estimates are usually available for each activity. In an audit case, completion deadlines are often imposed by clients or regulators. If the probability of finishing the audit after the deadline is too high, the firm may decide to add more personnel to shorten the critical path's duration.

17.8 A CRITIQUE OF PERT AND CPM

It has been more than four decades since PERT and CPM were first introduced as project management tools. This is just enough time to step back and examine their strengths and limitations objectively—a process that helps us understand the role of critical path scheduling today.

Because the Department of Defense (DOD) overwhelmingly adopted PERT and made its use a requirement for all defense contractors, PERT's first 10 years were its zenith. Many managers, professors, computer professionals, and magazine and journal editors became converts (and "experts"). With enthusiasm and interest strong, PERT even became a verb, and all good projects were "perted out." This sometimes meant wall-to-wall computer-generated and updated charts and a tendecy to trust PERT as a solution to solve all project management problems.

As was probably inevitable, PERT's fashionability dropped off during the 1970s. As some converts became critics, others who had long resented the forced burdens of the PERT and CPM approach became vocal in their scorn of the tool.[2]

Now critical path analysis appears to be leveling out and even increasing once again in popularity. Project managers are more knowledgeable about the pluses and minuses of PERT use and are aided by the spread of powerful but easy-to-use microcomputer-based software packages. As a summary of our discussions of PERT, here are some of its features about which operations managers need to be aware.

ADVANTAGES

1. PERT is useful at several stages of project management, especially in the scheduling and control of large projects.
2. It is straightforward in concept and not mathematically complex. Although projects with hundreds or thousands of activities are usually computerized, smaller ones can be tackled easily by hand.
3. The graphical displays using networks help to perceive quickly relationships among project activities.

[2] Two articles describing these new attitudes both candidly and humorously are M. Krakowski, "PERT and Parkinson's Law," *Interfaces*, vol. 5, no. 1 (November 1974); and A. Vazsonyi, "L'Historie de la grandeur et de la decadence de la methode PERT," *Management Science*, vol. 16, no. 8 (April 1970). Both articles make interesting reading (and are both written in English).

EXHIBIT 17-6 A Portion of St. Vincent's Hospital Project Network: Critical Activities

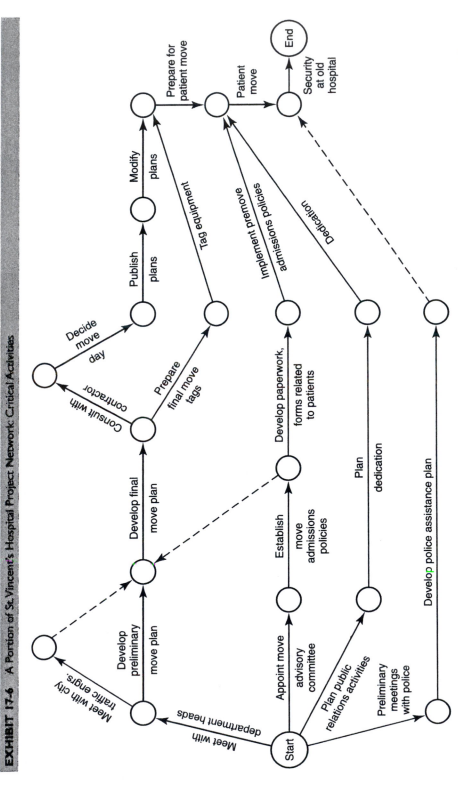

Source: Adapted from R. S. Hanson, "Moving the Hospital to a New Location," *Industrial Engineering* (November 1982). Copyright Institute of Industrial Engineers, 25 Technology Park/Atlanta, Norcross, GA 30092.

EXHIBIT 17-7 Engagement for a Sample Audit

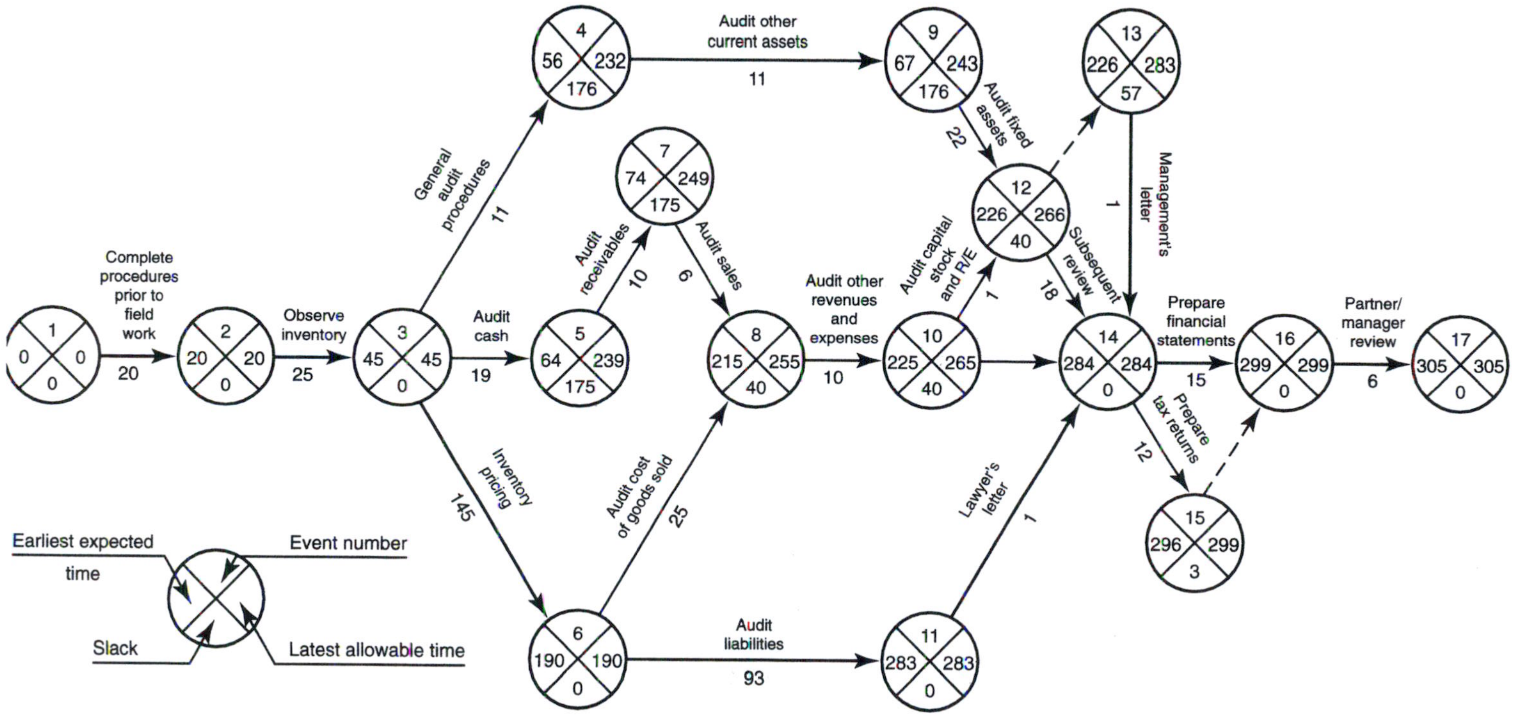

Source: J. L. Krogstad, G. Grudnitski, and D. W. Bryant, "PERT and PERT/Cost for Audit Planning and Control," *Journal of Accounting*, vol. 144, no. 5 (1977), pp. 82–91. Reprinted with permission from The Journal of Accountancy, copyright © 1977 by the American Institute of CPAs. Opinions of the authors are their own and do not necessarily reflect policies of the AICPA.

4. Critical path and slack time analyses help pinpoint activities that need to be closely watched. This provides opportunity for resource reallocation when the project needs to be shortened ("crashed").
5. The networks generated provide valuable project documentation and graphically point out who is responsible for various activities.
6. PERT is applicable to a wide variety of service projects and industries.
7. It is useful in monitoring not only schedules, but costs as well. This helps avoid cost overrun penalties and facilitates "early finish" bonuses.

LIMITATIONS

1. Project activities have to be clearly defined, independent, and stable in their relationships. In spite of our focus on the techniques of project management, this step is typically the most difficult.
2. Precedence relationships must be specified and networked together. Sometimes precedences are hard to clarify and are not shown correctly.
3. Time activities in PERT are assumed to follow the beta probability distribution. It is difficult for users to verify whether or not this really holds true for each activity. There is now some question about the validity of this assumption.
4. Time estimates tend to be subjective and are subject to fudging by managers who fear the dangers of being overly optimistic or not pessimistic enough.
5. There is the inherent danger of too much emphasis being placed on the longest, or critical, path. Near-critical paths need to be monitored closely as well.

Using POM for Windows for Project Management

POM for Windows Project Scheduling module can be used to determine expected project completion time for a CPM or PERT network with either one or three time estimates. In addition, the software calculates earliest start, earliest finish, latest start, and latest finish times, as well as slack for each activity. Exhibit 17-8 shows the output from POM for Windows solution of the Audit Planning example.

17.9 SUMMARY

PERT, CPM, and other scheduling techniques have proven to be valuable tools in controlling large and comlex projects. With these tools, managers understand the status of each activity and know which activities are critical and which have slack; in addition, they know where crashing makes the most sense. Projects are segmented into discrete activities, precedence relationships among them are determined, and specific resources are identified. This allows project managers to respond to the challenges of managing large and complex projects. Effective project management also allows firms to create products and services for global markets. A wide variety of software packages to help managers handle network modeling problems are available.

PERT and CPM do not, however, solve all the project scheduling and management problems of service organizations. Good management practices, clear responsibilities for tasks, and straightforward and timely reporting systems are also needed. It is important to remember that the models described in this chapter are only tools to help managers make better decisions.

EXHIBIT 17-8   POM for Windows Solution of Audit Planning Example

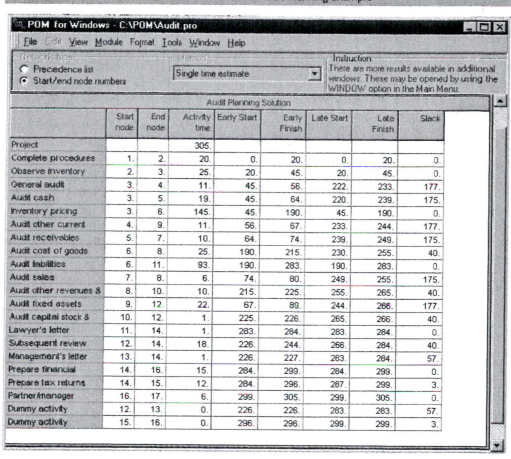

	Start node	End node	Activity time	Early Start	Early Finish	Late Start	Late Finish	Slack
Project			305.					
Complete procedures	1.	2.	20.	0.	20.	0.	20.	0.
Observe inventory	2.	3.	25.	20.	45.	20.	45.	0.
General audit	3.	4.	11.	45.	56.	222.	233.	177.
Audit cash	3.	5.	19.	45.	64.	220.	239.	175.
Inventory pricing	3.	6.	145.	45.	190.	45.	190.	0.
Audit other current	4.	9.	11.	56.	67.	233.	244.	177.
Audit receivables	5.	7.	10.	64.	74.	239.	249.	175.
Audit cost of goods	6.	8.	25.	190.	215.	230.	255.	40.
Audit liabilities	6.	11.	93.	190.	283.	190.	283.	0.
Audit sales	7.	8.	6.	74.	80.	249.	255.	175.
Audit other revenues &	8.	10.	10.	215.	225.	255.	265.	40.
Audit fixed assets	9.	12.	22.	67.	89.	244.	266.	177.
Audit capital stock &	10.	12.	1.	225.	226.	265.	266.	40.
Lawyer's letter	11.	14.	1.	283.	284.	283.	284.	0.
Subsequent review	12.	14.	18.	226.	244.	266.	284.	40.
Management's letter	13.	14.	1.	226.	227.	283.	284.	57.
Prepare financial	14.	16.	15.	284.	299.	284.	299.	0.
Prepare tax returns	14.	15.	12.	284.	296.	287.	299.	3.
Partner/manager	16.	17.	6.	299.	305.	299.	305.	0.
Dummy activity	12.	13.	0.	226.	226.	283.	283.	57.
Dummy activity	15.	16.	0.	296.	296.	299.	299.	3.

Discussion Questions

1. What are some of the questions that can be answered with PERT and CPM?
2. What is an activity? What is an event? What is an immediate predecessor?
3. Describe how expected activity times and variances can be computed in a PERT network.
4. Briefly discuss what is meant by critical path analysis. What are critical path activities and why are they important?
5. What are the earliest activity start time and latest activity start time and how are they computed?
6. Describe the meaning of slack and discuss how it can be determined.
7. How can we determine the probability that a project will be completed by a certain date? What assumptions are made in this computation?
8. Briefly describe PERT/Cost and how it is used.
9. What is crashing and how is it done by hand?
10. Select a service industry with which you are familiar and describe how a Gantt or PERT chart could be used to improve the operation.

Problems

17.1. Sally Rider is the personnel director of Babson and Willcount, a company that specializes in consulting and research. One of the training programs that Sally is considering for the middle-level managers of Babson and Willcount is leadership training. Sally has listed a number of activities that must be completed before a training program of this nature could be conducted. The activities and immediate predecessors appear in the accompanying table. Develop a network for this problem.

Activity	Immediate Predecessor	Activity	Immediate Predecessor
A	—	E	A,D
B	—	F	C
C	—	G	E,F
D	B		

17.2. Sally Rider was able to determine the activity times for the leadership training program. She would like to determine the total project completion time and the critical path. The activity times appear in the accompanying table. (See Problem 17.1.)

Activity	Time (days)
A	2
B	5
C	1
D	10
E	3
F	6
G	8
Total	35 days

17.3. Insert dummy activities and events to correct the following network:

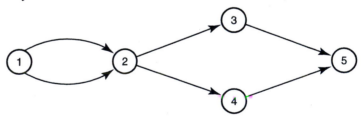

17.4. Calculate the critical path, project completion time T, and project variance V based on the following information.

Activity	t	v
1–2	2	2/6
1–3	3	2/6
2–4	2	4/6
3–5	4	4/6
4–5	4	2/6
4–6	3	1/6
5–6	5	1/6

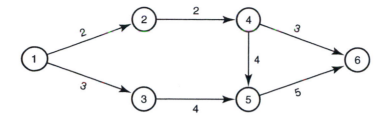

17.5. Given the following information, perform a critical path analysis.

Activity	t	v	Activity	t	v
1–2	2	$\frac{1}{6}$	4–5	4	$\frac{4}{6}$
1–3	2	$\frac{1}{6}$	4–6	3	$\frac{2}{6}$
2–4	1	$\frac{2}{6}$	5–7	5	$\frac{1}{6}$
3–4	3	$\frac{2}{6}$	6–7	2	$\frac{2}{6}$

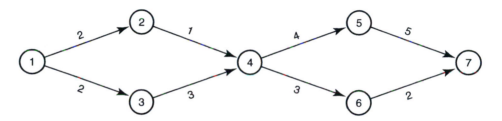

17.6. Zuckerman Computing provides computer services to business and government. The company is bidding on the replacement of a mainframe system and has identified the following activities and time estimates (in hours) for the activities that will make up the project. Determine the expected completion time and variance for each activity.

Activity	a	m	b	Immediate Predecessors
A	3	6	8	
B	2	4	4	
C	1	2	3	
D	6	7	8	C
E	2	4	6	B,D
F	6	10	14	A,E
G	1	2	4	A,E
H	3	6	9	F
I	10	11	12	G
J	14	16	20	C
K	2	8	10	H,I

17.7. Jane Zuckerman would like to determine the total project completion time and the critical path for replacing the old computer system. See Problem 17.6 for details. In addition, determine ES, EF, LS, LF, and slack for each activity.

17.8. What is the probability that Zuckerman will finish the project described in Problems 17.6 and 17.7 in 40 hours or less?

17.9. Using PERT, Jan Ross was able to determine that the expected project completion time for the overhaul of a pleasure yacht is 21 weeks, and the project variance is 4 weeks.
   a. What is the probability that the project will be completed in 17 weeks?
   b. What is the probability that the project will be completed in 20 weeks?
   c. What is the probability that the project will be completed in 23 weeks?
   d. What is the probability that the project will be completed in 25 weeks?

17.10. The following information has been computed from a project:

$$T = 62 \text{ weeks}$$
$$V = 81$$

What is the probability that the project will be completed 18 weeks *before* its expected completion date?

17.11. Determine the least cost of reducing the project completion date by three months based on the following information:

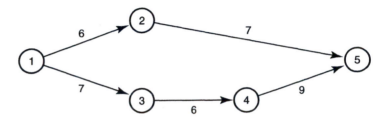

Activity	t (months)	M (months)	C
1–2	6	2	$400
1–3	7	2	$500
2–5	7	1	$300
3–4	6	2	$600
4–5	9	1	$200

17.12. Getting a degree from a college or university can be a long and difficult task. Certain courses must be completed before other courses may be taken. Develop a network diagram, where every activity is a particular course that must be taken for a given degree program. The immediate predecessors will be course prerequisites. Don't forget to include all university, college, and departmental course requirements. Then try to group these courses into semesters or quarters for your particular school. How long do you think it will take you to graduate? Which courses, if not taken in the proper sequence, could delay your graduation?

17.13. The Bender Construction Company is involved with constructing municipal buildings and other structures that are used primarily by city and state municipalities. This requires developing legal documents, drafting feasibility studies, obtaining bond ratings, and so forth. Recently, Bender was given a request to submit a proposal for the construction of a municipal building. The first step is to develop legal documents and to perform all necessary steps before the construction contract is signed. This requires approximately 20 separate activities that must be completed. These activities, their immediate predecessors, and time requirements are given in Exhibit 17-9. As you can see, optimistic (*a*), most likely (*m*), and pessimistic (*b*) time estimates have been given for all of the activities described in the above table. Using these data, determine the total project completion time for this preliminary step, the critical path, and slack time for all activities involved.

EXHIBIT 17-9   Developing Documents for Bender Construction

Activity	Time Required (weeks)			Description	Immediate Predecessor(s)
	a	m	b		
1	1	4	5	Drafting legal documents	—
2	2	3	4	Preparation of financial statements	—
3	3	4	5	Draft of history	—
4	7	8	9	Draft demand portion of feasibility study	—
5	4	4	5	Review and approval of legal documents	1
6	1	2	4	Review and approval of history	3
7	4	5	6	Review feasibility study	4
8	1	2	4	Draft final financial portion of feasibility study	7
9	3	4	4	Draft facts relevant to the bond transaction	5
10	1	1	2	Review and approval of financial statements	2
11	18	20	26	Firm price received of project	—
12	1	2	3	Review and completion of financial portion of feasibility study	8
13	1	1	2	Draft statement completed	6, 9, 10, 11
14	0.10	0.14	0.16	All material sent to bond rating services	13
15	0.2	0.3	0.4	Statement printed and distributed to all interested parties	14
16	1	1	2	Presentation to bond rating services	14
17	1	2	3	Bond rating received	16
18	3	5	7	Marketing of bonds	15, 17
19	0.1	0.9	0.2	Purchase contract executed	16
20	0.1	0.14	0.16	Final statement authorized and completed	19
21	2	3	6	Purchase contract	19
22	0.1	0.1	0.2	Bond proceeds available	20
23	0.0	0.2	0.2	Sign construction contract	21, 22

CASE

CASE 17–1 Bay Community Hospital

The staff of the Bay Community Hospital had committed itself to introduce a new diagnostic procedure in the clinic. This procedure required the acquisition, installation, and introduction of a new medical instrument. Dr. Ed Windsor was assigned the responsibility for assuring that the introduction be performed as quickly and smoothly as possible.

Dr. Windsor created a list of activities that would have to be completed before the new service could begin. Initially, three individual steps had to be taken: (1) write instructions and procedures, (2) select techniques to operate the equipment, and (3) procure the equipment. The instructions and selection of the operators had to be completed before training could commence. Dr. Windsor also believed it was necessary to choose the operators and evaluate their qualifications before formally announcing the new service to the local medical community. Upon arrival and installation of the equipment and completion of the operators' training, Edward Windsor wanted to spend a period checking out the procedures, operators, and equipment before declaring the project was successfully completed. The activities and times are listed in Exhibit 17-10.

Jack Worth, a member of the Bay Community Hospital staff, reported that it would be possible to save time on the project by paying some premiums to complete certain activities faster than the normal schedule listed in Exhibit 17-10. Specifically, if the equipment were shipped by express truck, one week could be saved. Air freight would save two weeks. However, a premium of $200 would be paid for the express truck shipment and $750 would be paid for air shipment. The operator training period could also be reduced by one week if the trainees worked overtime. However, this would cost the hospital an additional $600. The time required to complete the instructions could be reduced by one week with the additional expenditure of $400. However, $300 could be saved if this activity was allowed to take three weeks. ■

SOURCE: From W. Earl Sasser, Jr., R. Paul Olsen, and D. Daryl Wyckoff, *Management Service Operations*, pp. 97–98. Copyright © 1978 by Allyn and Bacon. Reprinted with permission.

CASE QUESTIONS

1. What is the shortest time period in which the project can be completed using the expected times listed in Exhibit 17-10?
2. What is the shortest time in which the project can be completed?
3. What is the lowest cost schedule for this shortest time?

EXHIBIT 17-10 Bay Community Hospital Activities Required to Introduce a New Diagnostic Procedure

Activity	Duration (weeks)	Immediately Preceding Activities	Immediately Following Activities
A. Write instructions	2	Start	C
B. Select operators	4	Start	C,D
C. Train operators	3	A,B	F
D. Announce new service	4	B	End
E. Purchase, ship, and receive equipment	8	Start	F
F. Test new operators on equipment	2	C,E	End

References

Ameiss, A. P., and W. A. Thompson, "PERT for Monthly Financial Closing," *Management Advisor* (January–February 1974).

Clayton, E. R., and L. J. Moore, "PERT vs. GERT," *Journal of Systems Management*, vol. 23 (February 1972), pp. 11–19.

Cleland, D. I., and W. R. King, *Project Management Handbook* (New York, Von Nostrand Reinhold, 1984).

Dusenbury, W., "CPM for New Product Introductions," *Harvard Business Review*, vol. 45, no. 4 (July–August 1967).

Heizer, J., and B. Render, *Operations Management*, 5th ed. (Upper Saddle River, NJ, Prentice Hall, 1999).

Kefalas, A. G., "PERT Applied to Environmental Impact Statements," *Industrial Engineering*, vol. 8, no. 10 (October 1976), pp. 38–42.

Kerzner, H., and H. Thamhain, *Project Management for Small and Medium Size Business* (New York, Van Nostrand Reinhold, 1984).

Krogstad, J. L., G. Grudnitski, and D. W. Bryand, "PERT and PERT/Cost for Audit Planning and Control," *The Journal of Accountancy* (November 1977).

Levy, F., A. Thompson, and J. Weist, "The ABC's of Critical Path Method," *Harvard Business Review*, vol. 41, no. 5 (September–October 1963), pp. 98–108.

Moder, J., and C. Phillips, *Project Management with CPM and PERT* (New York, Van Nostrand Reinhold, 1970).

Render, B., and R. M. Stair, *Quantitative Analysis for Management*, 7th ed. (Upper Saddle River, NJ, Prentice Hall, 2000).

Ryan, W. G., "Management Practice and Research—Poles Apart," *Business Horizons* (June 1977).

CHAPTER 18

Linear and Goal Programming Applications for Services

18.1 INTRODUCTION

Many service operations management decisions involve trying to make the most effective use of an organization's resources. Resources typically include labor, money, storage space/capacity, or materials. These resources may be used to produce services such as schedules for shipping and production, advertising policies, investment decisions, or hospital meal plans. **Linear programming** (LP) and **goal programming** (GP) are widely used mathematical techniques designed to help operations managers in planning and decision making relative to the tradeoffs necessary to allocate resources.

Examples of problems in which LP and GP have been applied successfully in service management include the following:

- Improving bank scheduling operations at Banc Ohio[1]
- Allocating police patrol units to high-crime areas[2]
- Developing long-range manpower planning in the U.S. Army[3]
- Scheduling school buses in New Haven, Connecticut[4]

---

[1] V. A. Mabert and J. P. McKenzie, "Improving Bank Operations: A Case Study at Banc Ohio/Ohio National Bank," *Omega*, vol. 8, no. 3 (1980), pp. 345–354.

[2] K. Chelst, "An Algorithm for Deploying a Crime Directed Patrol Force," *Management Science*, vol. 24, no. 12 (August 1978), pp. 1314–1327.

[3] S. Gass et al., "The Army Manpower Long-Range Planning System," *Operations Research*, vol. 36, no. 1 (January–February 1988), pp. 5–17.

[4] A. J. Swersey and W. Ballard, "Scheduling School Buses," *Management Science*, vol. 30, no. 7 (July 1984), pp. 844–853.

- Controlling the fleet of 3,300 trucks at North American Van Lines[5]
- Planning the repairs of boxcars at Chesapeake and Ohio rail yards[6]

This chapter stresses the importance of *formulating* linear programming problems; it leaves the mathematical details of solving such problems to management science texts.[7] Because computer programs are readily available to conduct the mechanics of LP (and are illustrated in this chapter), most operations managers can avoid the complex manual algorithms associated with LP and GP. Most of the chapter looks at the more common linear programming formulation, in which a service organization has but one objective to be attained (such as minimizing labor costs). Later, the chapter concludes with an extension of LP known as **goal programming** (GP). GP is capable of handling decision problems having multiple goals, some of which may be contradictory.

18.2 OVERVIEW OF LINEAR PROGRAMMING

All LP problems have four properties in common.

1. All problems seek to *maximize* or *minimize* some quantity (usually profit or cost). We refer to this property as the **objective function** of an LP problem. The major objective of a typical firm is to maximize dollar profits in the long run. In the case of a trucking or airline distribution system, the objective might be to minimize shipping costs.
2. The presence of restrictions, or **constraints,** limits the degree to which we can pursue our objective. For example, deciding how many units of each product in a firm's warehouse should be stocked in one retail outlet is restricted by space, available labor, and budgets. We want, therefore, to maximize or minimize a quantity (the objective function) subject to limited resources (the constraints).
3. There must be *alternative courses of action* to choose from. For example, if a store stocks three different products, management may use LP to decide how to allocate among them its limited display space and advertising budget. If there were no alternatives to select from, we would not need LP.
4. The objective and constraints in linear programming problems must be expressed in terms of *linear* equations or inequalities.

The best way to illustrate these properties and how to formulate an LP problem is through an example. Let's consider the case of a small furniture retailer.

Dixon Furniture Store

Dixon Furniture is planning for its Labor Day weekend special sale. The two items that have been selected for promotion, because of the time of year, are folding tables and chairs; both are ideal for backyard parties. The store has only 100 square feet of space available for displaying and stocking these items. Each table has a wholesale cost of $4, takes up 2 square feet of space, and will retail for $11. The wholesale price of a chair is $3; each requires 1 square foot to stock and will sell for $8. The manager believes that no more than 60 chairs can possibly be sold, but that the demand for the

[5] D. Avramovich et al., "A Decision Support System for Fleet Management," *Interfaces,* vol. 12, no. 3 (June 1984), pp. 1–6.

[6] L. C. Brosch et al., "Boxcars, Linear Programming, and the Sleeping Kitten," *Interfaces,* vol. 10, no. 6 (December 1980), pp. 53–61.

[7] See B. Render and R. M. Stair, *Quantitative Analysis for Management,* 7th ed. (Upper Saddle River, NJ, Prentice Hall, 2000).

$11 tables is almost unlimited. Finally, Dixon's budget for procuring the tables and chairs is $240. The question facing the store manager is to decide how many tables and chairs to stock so as to maximize profit.

We begin to formulate this situation as an LP problem by introducing some simple notations for use in the objective function and constraints. Let

$$X_1 = \text{number of tables in stock}$$
$$X_2 = \text{number of chairs in stock}$$

Now we can create the LP objective function in terms of X_1 and X_2:

$$\text{Maximize net profit} = \text{retail price} - \text{wholesale cost} = (\$11X_1 + \$8X_2) - (\$4X_1 + \$3X_2)$$
$$= \$7X_1 + \$5X_2$$

The next step is to develop mathematical relationships to describe the three constraints in this problem. One general relationship is that the amount of a resource *used* is to be less than or equal to the amount of resource *available*.

First constraint: Budget used ≤ budget available

$$4X_1 + 3X_2 \leq 240 \text{ dollars available for purchases}$$

Second constraint: Space used ≤ space available

$$2X_1 + X_2 \leq 100 \text{ square feet of floor space}$$

Third constraint: Chairs ordered ≤ anticipated chair demand

$$X_2 \leq 60 \text{ chairs that can be sold}$$

All three of these constraints represent stocking restrictions and, of course, affect the total profit. For example, Dixon Furniture cannot order 70 tables for the sale because if $X_1 = 70$, the first two constraints will be violated. It also cannot order $X_1 = 50$ tables and $X_2 = 10$ chairs. Hence, we note one more important aspect of linear programming. That is, certain interactions will exist between variables. The more units of one product that the store orders, the less it can order of other products.

18.3 GRAPHICAL SOLUTION TO A LINEAR PROGRAMMING PROBLEM

The easiest way to solve a small LP problem such as that of the Dixon Furniture Store is the graphical solution approach. The graphical procedure is useful only when there are two decision variables (such as number of tables to order, X_1, and number of chairs to order, X_2) in the problem. Where there are more than two variables, it is *not* possible to plot the solution on a two-dimensional graph, and we must turn to more complex approaches or to the use of a computer (which we shall do shortly). But the graphical method is invaluable in providing us with insights into how other approaches work.

Graphic Representation of Constraints

In order to find the optimal solution to a linear programming problem, we must first identify a set, or **region,** of feasible solutions. The first step in doing so is to plot each of the problem's constraints on a graph.

The variable X_1 (tables, in our example) is usually plotted as the horizontal axis of the graph, and the variable X_2 (chairs) is plotted as the vertical axis. The complete problem may be restated as

$$\text{Maximize profit} = \$7X_1 + \$5X_2$$

subject to the constraints:

$$4X_1 + 3X_2 \leq 240 \text{ (budget constraint)}$$
$$2X_1 + X_2 \leq 100 \text{ (space constraint)}$$
$$X_2 \leq 60 \text{ (chair demand constraint)}$$
$$X_1 \geq 0 \text{ (number of tables ordered is greater than or equal to 0)}$$
$$X_2 \geq 0 \text{ (number of chairs ordered is greater than or equal to 0)}$$

To represent graphically the constraints of this problem, the first step is to convert the constraint *inequalities* into *equalities* (or equations); that is,

Constraint 1:	$4X_1 + 3X_2 = 240$
Constraint 2:	$2X_1 + X_2 = 100$
Constraint 3:	$X_2 = 60$

The equation for constraint 1 is plotted in Exhibit 18-1.

To plot the line in Exhibit 18-1, find the points at which the line $4X_1 + 3X_2 = 240$ intersects the X_1 and X_2 axes. When $X_1 = 0$ (the location where the line touches the X_2 axis), it implies that $3X_2 = 240$ or that $X_2 = 80$. Likewise, when $X_2 = 0$, we see that $4X_1 = 240$ and that $X_1 = 60$. Thus, constraint 1 is bounded by the line running from ($X_1 = 0$, $X_2 = 80$) to ($X_1 = 60$, $X_2 = 0$). The shaded area represents all points that satisfy the original *inequality*.

Constraints 2 and 3 are handled similarly. Exhibit 18-2 shows all three constraints together. Note that the third constraint is just a straight line, which does not depend on the values of X_1.

The shaded region in Exhibit 18-2 is the part that satisfies all three restrictions. This region is called the area of feasible solutions, or simply the **feasible region.** This region must satisfy *all* conditions specified by the program's constraints and thus is

EXHIBIT 18-1   Plotting the Budget Constraint for Dixon

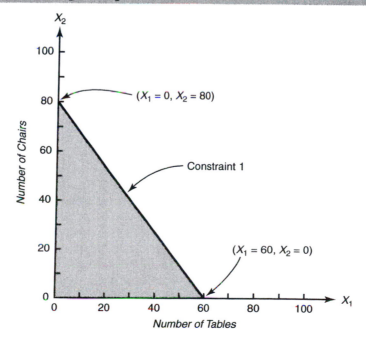

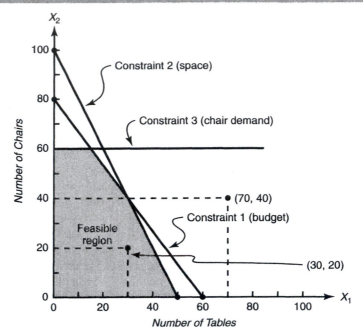

EXHIBIT 18-2 All Constraints Plotted to Produce the Feasible Region for Dixon

the region where all constraints overlap. Any point in the region would be a **feasible solution** to the Dixon Furniture Store problem. Any point outside the shaded area would represent an **infeasible solution.** Hence, it would be feasible to order thirty tables and twenty chairs ($X_1 = 30$, $X_2 = 20$), but it would violate the constraints to order 70 tables and 40 chairs. This can be seen by plotting these points on the graph of Exhibit 18-2.

Iso-Profit Line Solution Method

Now that the feasible region has been graphed, we may proceed to find the optimal solution to the problem. The mathematical theory behind linear programming states that an optimal solution to any problem (i.e., the values of X_1, X_2 that yield the maximum profit) will lie at a *corner point*, or *extreme point*, of the feasible region. The optimal solution is then the corner point lying in the feasible region that produces the highest profit.

There are several approaches that can be taken in solving for the optimal solution once the feasible region has been established graphically. The speediest one to apply is called the **iso-profit line method.**

We start by letting profits equal some arbitrary, but small, dollar amount. For the Dixon Furniture problem, we may choose a profit of $210. This is a profit level that can easily be obtained without violating any of the three constraints. The objective function can be written as $210 = 7X_1 + 5X_2$.

This expression is just the equation of a line; we call it an **iso-profit line.** It represents all combinations of (X_1, X_2) that would yield a total profit of $210. To plot the profit line, we proceed exactly as we did to plot a constraint line. First, let $X_1 = 0$ and solve for the point at which the line crosses the X_2 axis.

$$210 = \$7(0) + \$5X_2$$
$$X_2 = 42 \text{ chairs}$$

Then let $X_2 = 0$ and solve for X_1.

$$\$210 = \$7X_1 + \$5(0)$$
$$X_1 = 30 \text{ tables}$$

These two points can now be connected with a straight line. This profit line is illustrated in Exhibit 18-3. All points on the line represent feasible solutions that produce a profit of $210.

Now, obviously, the iso-profit line for $210 does not produce the highest possible profit to Dixon. In Exhibit 18-4, we try graphing a new line, one yielding a higher profit. Note that the further we move from the origin, the higher the profit will be. Another important point to note is that these iso-profit lines are parallel. There are now two clues as to how to find the optimal solution to the original problem. A series of parallel profit lines can be drawn (by carefully moving the ruler away from the origin parallel to the first profit line). The highest profit line that still touches some point of the feasible region will pinpoint the optimal solution.

The highest possible iso-profit line touches the tip of the feasible region of Exhibit 18-4 at the corner point $(X_1 = 30, X_2 = 40)$ and yields a profit of $410.

18.4   COMPUTER SOLUTION TO A LINEAR PROGRAMMING PROBLEM

As mentioned earlier, it is not possible to solve any linear programming problem graphically that has more than two variables. Fortunately, many linear programming software packages are available for larger problems. This section demonstrates how to interpret the output of POM for Windows software. POM for Windows, as well as many other commercial LP software operate by using an algebraic technique known as the **simplex algorithm.**

EXHIBIT 18-3   A Profit Line of $210 Plotted for Dixon

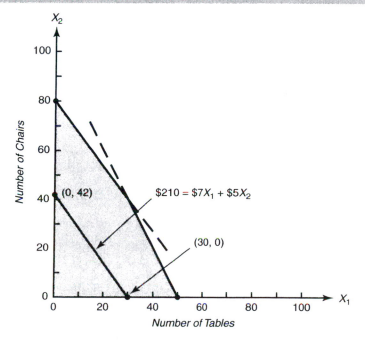

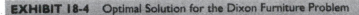

EXHIBIT 18-4 Optimal Solution for the Dixon Furniture Problem

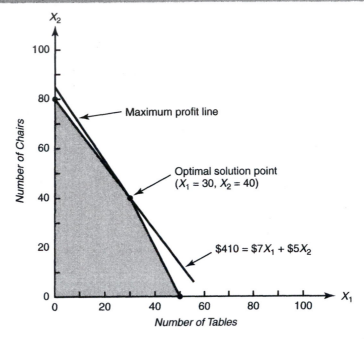

The simplex method systematically examines corner points of the feasible region, always searching for the corner point that yields a better value for the objective function. It not only provides the optimal solution to any LP problem, but also provides information in the form of **shadow prices** and **sensitivity analysis** that may be very valuable to managers in their decision-making process. One of the early steps of the simplex method is the conversion of inequality constraints into equalities. It does this by adding a **slack variable** to the left-hand side of each less than or equal to (≤) constraint, and subtracting a slack (or surplus) variable from the left-hand side of each greater than or equal to (≥) constraint. Slack and surplus variables represent the difference between the right-hand and left-hand sides of constraints. After this conversion, the constraints of the Dixon Furniture problem would be:

$$4X_1 + 3X_2 + S_1 = 240 \text{ (budget constraint)}$$
$$2X_1 + X_2 + S_2 = 100 \text{ (floor space constraint)}$$
$$X_2 + S_3 = 60 \quad \text{(chair demand constraint)}$$

For a resource constraint, such as the budget constraint in the Dixon Furniture problem, slack variable (S_1) represents the **unused** portion of that resource (i.e., budget). The slack variable for the floor space constraint S_2 represents unused floor space, and the slack for the third constraint S_3 is the unsatisfied portion of chair demand.

Exhibit 18-5 shows the solution to the Dixon Furniture problem. This is only one of several outputs you can obtain from POM for Windows for linear programming problems. If the problem has two variables, the graphical solution is also available (Exhibit 18-6). The optimal solution in Exhibit 18-5 indicates that slack variables S_1 and S_2 are both zero. This means that both budget and floor space resources will be utilized to the fullest extent if the optimal solution is implemented, that is if 30 tables and 40 chairs are produced. Slack variable $S_3 = 20$ indicates that the chair demand will not be fully satisfied.

EXHIBIT 18-5   POM for Windows Solution of Dixon Furniture Problem

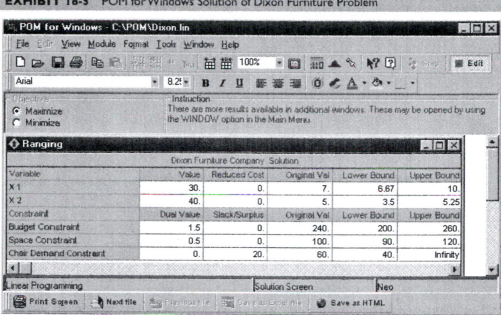

Shadow Prices

Output shown in Exhibit 18-5 also leads us to the important subject of shadow prices. Shadow prices are indicated as **dual values** in the computer output. **Shadow price** (or dual value) represents the **change** in the objective function value (i.e., profit for Dixon Furniture) for one unit **increase** in the right-hand side of a constraint. For example, how much should Dixon Furniture be willing to pay to obtain an additional unit of each resource (i.e., increase the number on the right-hand side of each constraint by one)? Is renting one more square foot of floor space worth $1 or $5 or 25 cents to

EXHIBIT 18-6   POM for Windows Graphical Solution of Dixon Furniture Problem

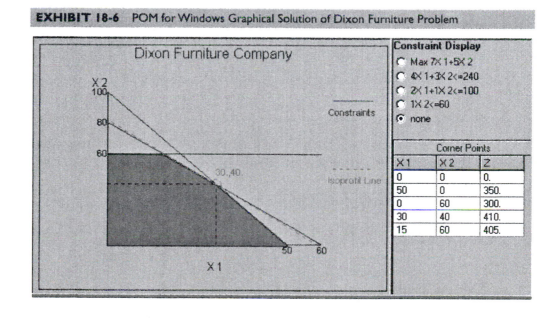

Dixon? Will an extra dollar added to the budget increase profit by more than $1, or will it not be worthwhile to seek additional funding for the sale? Will an advertising campaign to increase the demand for chairs be a worthwhile effort?

Exhibit 18-5 shows that each additional unit of the first resource (i.e., budget dollars) will increase Dixon's overall profit by $1.50. This **shadow price** is valuable information for management. Furthermore, each additional square foot of display area (above the 100 square feet currently fully utilized) would increase the current $410 profit by $0.50. There is clearly no value to an increase in chair demand. Increasing the demand for chairs from 60 to 61 will not increase profit at all; this is indicated by a zero shadow price. This is so because the optimal solution does not recommend stocking enough chairs to satisfy the chair demand for 60 chairs; there is no point in increasing a demand we are not currently meeting. Slack variable $S_3 = 20$ indicates that the optimal plan is 20 units short of satisfying the chair demand. A shadow price will always be zero if its constraint's corresponding slack variable is not zero.

Sensitivity Analysis

Shadow pricing is actually one form of **sensitivity analysis,** that is, the study of how sensitive the optimal solution would be to errors or changes in inputs to the LP problem. For example, if the store manager at Dixon Furniture had been off by 10 percent in setting the net profit per table at $7, would that drastically alter the decision to order 30 tables and 40 chairs? What would be the impact of a budget of $265 instead of $240?

Exhibit 18-5 has information available to help a decision maker know whether or not a solution is relatively insensitive to reasonable changes in one or more of the parameters of the problem. First, let us consider changes to the right-hand side of a constraint. In doing so, we assume changes are made in only one constraint at a time; the other two remain fixed at their original values. **Lower bound** and **upper bound** values tell us over what range of right-hand side values the shadow prices (dual values) for that constraint will remain valid. In the Dixon example, the $1.50 shadow price for the budget constraint will apply even if the current budget of $240 drops as low as $200 or increases as high as $260.

This concept that the right-hand side range limits the shadow price is important in sensitivity analysis. Suppose Dixon Furniture could obtain additional funding at a cost less than the shadow price. The question of how much to obtain is answered by the upper bound, that is, secure $20 more than the original value $240.

Now let us look at changes in one of the objective function coefficients (unit profits for chairs and tables in the Dixon problem). Sensitivity analysis provides, for each decision variable in the solution, the range of objective function coefficients over which the answer will be the same. For example, the net profit of $7 per table ($X_1$) in the objective function could range from $6.67 to $10.00 without the optimal solution of $X_1 = 30$, $X_2 = 40$ changing. Of course, if a profit coefficient changed at all, the total profit of $410 would change, even if the optimal quantities of X_1 and X_2 do not.

18.5 FORMULATING LINEAR PROGRAMMING MODELS

The purpose of this section is to show how a large number of real-life problems can be tackled using LP. We do this by presenting applications in the areas of ingredient blending, transportation/shipping, employee scheduling, labor planning, and media planning. Although some of these problems are relatively small numerically, the principles developed here are definitely applicable to larger problems.

Ingredient Blending Applications: The Diet Problem

The **diet problem,** one of the earliest applications of linear programming, was originally used by hospitals to determine the most economical diet for patients. Known in agricultural applications as the **feed mix problem,** the diet problem involves specifying a food or feed ingredient combination that satisfies stated nutritional requirements at a minimum cost level.

The Whole Food Nutrition Center uses three bulk grains to blend a natural cereal that sells by the pound. The store advertises that each 2-ounce serving of the cereal, when taken with one-half cup of whole milk, meets an average adult's minimum daily requirement for protein, riboflavin, phosphorus, and magnesium. The cost of each bulk grain and the protein, riboflavin, phosphorus, and magnesium units per pound of each are shown in Exhibit 18-7.

The minimum adult daily requirement (called the *U.S. Recommended Daily Allowance,* or *USRDA*) for protein is 3 units; for riboflavin, 2 units; for phosphorus, 1 unit; and for magnesium, 0.425 units. Whole Food wants to select the blend of grains that will meet the USRDA at a minimum cost.

We let

X_A = pounds of grain A in one 2-ounce serving of cereal
X_B = pounds of grain B in one 2-ounce serving of cereal
X_C = pounds of grain C in one 2-ounce serving of cereal

Objective function:

Minimize total cost of mixing a 2-ounce serving = $\$0.33X_A + \$0.47X_B + \$0.38X_C$

Constraints:

$$22X_A + 28X_B + 21X_C \geq 3 \quad \text{(protein units)}$$
$$16X_A + 14X_B + 25X_C \geq 2 \quad \text{(riboflavin units)}$$
$$8X_A + 7X_B + 9X_C \geq 1 \quad \text{(phosphorus units)}$$
$$5X_A + 0X_B + 6X_C \geq 0.425 \quad \text{(magnesium units)}$$
$$X_A + X_B + X_C = \tfrac{1}{8} \quad \text{(total mix is 2 ounces or } \tfrac{1}{8} \text{ pound)}$$
$$X_A, X_B, X_C \geq 0$$

The solution to this problem requires mixing together 0.025 pounds of grain A, 0.050 pounds of grain B, and 0.050 pounds of grain C. Another way of stating the solution is in terms of the proportion of the 2-ounce serving of each grain, namely, ⅖ ounces of grain A, ⅘ ounces of grain B, and ⅘ ounces of grain C in each serving. The cost per serving is \$0.05075, a little over \$0.05 per serving.

EXHIBIT 18-7   Whole Food's Natural Cereal Requirements

Grain	Cost per Pound	Protein (units/lb)	Riboflavin (units/lb)	Phosphorus (units/lb)	Magnesium (units/lb)
A	33¢	22	16	8	5
B	47¢	28	14	7	0
C	38¢	21	25	9	6

Transportation Applications: The Shipping Problem

The **transportation** or **shipping problem** involves determining the amount of goods or items to be transported from a number of origins to a number of destinations. The objective is usually to minimize total shipping costs or distances. Constraints in this type of problem deal with capacities at each origin and requirements at each destination. The transportation problem is a very specific case of linear programming.

The Top Speed Bicycle Company markets a line of 10-speed bicycles nationwide. The firm has warehouses in two cities, New Orleans and Omaha. Its three retail outlets are located near the large market areas of New York, Chicago, and Los Angeles.

The sales requirements for the next year at the New York store are 10,000 bicycles, at the Chicago store 8,000 bicycles, and at the Los Angeles store 15,000 bicycles. The capacity at each warehouse is limited. New Orleans can store and ship 20,000 bicycles, while the Omaha site can warehouse 15,000 bicycles per year.

The cost of shipping one bicycle from each warehouse to each retail outlet differs, and these unit shipping costs are

	To		
From	*New York*	*Chicago*	*Los Angeles*
New Orleans	$2	$3	$5
Omaha	$3	$1	$4

The company wishes to determine a shipping schedule that will minimize its total annual transportation costs.

To formulate this problem using LP, we employ the concept of double-subscripted variables. For example, we can let X_{11} = number of bicycles shipped from New Orleans to New York. We let the first subscript represent the origin (warehouse) and the second subscript the destination (retail outlet). Thus, in general, X_{ij} refers to the number of bicycles shipped from origin i to destination j. We could instead denote X_6 as the variable for origin 2 to destination 3, but we think you will find the double subscripts more descriptive and easier to use. So we also let

X_{12} = number of bicycles shipped from New Orleans to Chicago
X_{13} = number of bicycles shipped from New Orleans to Los Angeles
X_{21} = number of bicycles shipped from Omaha to New York
X_{22} = number of bicycles shipped from Omaha to Chicago
X_{23} = number of bicycles shipped from Omaha to Los Angeles

The objective function and constraints then become

Minimize total shipping costs = $2X_{11} + 3X_{12} + 5X_{13} + 3X_{21} + 1X_{22} + 4X_{23}$

Subject to:

$X_{11} + X_{21} = 10,000$ (New York demand)
$X_{12} + X_{22} = 8,000$ (Chicago demand)
$X_{13} + X_{23} = 15,000$ (Los Angeles demand)
$X_{11} + X_{12} + X_{13} \le 20,000$ (New Orleans warehouse supply)
$X_{21} + X_{22} + X_{23} \le 15,000$ (Omaha warehouse supply)

Why are transportation problems a special class of linear programming problems? The answer is that every coefficient in front of a variable in the constraint equations is always equal to 1. This special trait is also seen in another special category of LP problems, the assignment problem.

The computer-generated solution to Top Speed's problem is shown below. The total shipping cost is $9,600.

From	To		
	New York	**Chicago**	**Los Angeles**
New Orleans	10,000	0	8,000
Omaha	0	8,000	7,000

Employee Scheduling Applications: An Assignment Problem

Assignment problems involve determining the most efficient assignment of people to jobs, machines to tasks, police cars to city sectors, salespeople to territories, and so on. The objective might be to minimize travel times or costs, or to maximize assignment effectiveness. Assignment problems are unique because they not only have a coefficient of 1 associated with each variable in the LP constraints, but also because the right-hand side of each constraint is always equal to 1 also. The use of LP in solving this type of problem yields solutions of either 0 or 1 for each variable in the formulation. The following is an example situation.

The law firm of Ivan and Ivan maintains a large staff of young attorneys who hold the title of junior partner. Ivan, concerned with the effective utilization of his manpower resources, seeks some objective means of making lawyer-to-client assignments.

On March 1, four new clients seeking legal assistance come to Ivan. While the current staff is overloaded, Ivan would like to accomodate the new clients. He reviews current case loads and identifies four junior partners who, although busy, could possibly be assigned to the cases. Each young lawyer can handle at most one new client. Furthermore, each lawyer differs in skills and specialty interests.

Seeking to maximize the overall effectiveness of the new client assignments, Ivan draws up the following table in which he rates the estimated effectiveness (on a 1-to-9 scale) of each lawyer on each new case.

Lawyer	Client's Case			
	Divorce	**Corporate Merger**	**Embezzlement**	**Insider Trading**
Adams	6	2	8	5
Brooks	9	3	5	8
Carter	4	8	3	4
Darwin	6	7	6	4

To solve using LP, we again employ double-scripted variables.

$$\text{Let } X_{ij} = \begin{cases} 1 & \text{if attorney } i \text{ is assigned to case } j \\ 0 & \text{otherwise} \end{cases}$$

where $i = 1, 2, 3, 4$ stands for Adams, Brooks, Carter, and Darwin, respectively

$j = 1, 2, 3, 4$ stands for divorce, merger, embezzlement, and insider trading, respectively

The LP formulation follows.

$$\begin{aligned} \text{Maximize effectiveness} = {} & 6X_{11} + 2X_{12} + 8X_{13} + 5X_{14} \\ & + 9X_{21} + 3X_{22} + 5X_{23} + 8X_{24} \\ & + 4X_{31} + 8X_{32} + 3X_{33} + 4X_{34} \\ & + 6X_{41} + 7X_{42} + 6X_{43} + 4X_{44} \end{aligned}$$

Subject to:

$$X_{11} + X_{21} + X_{31} + X_{41} = 1 \quad \text{(divorce case)}$$
$$X_{12} + X_{22} + X_{32} + X_{42} = 1 \quad \text{(merger)}$$
$$X_{13} + X_{23} + X_{33} + X_{43} = 1 \quad \text{(embezzlement)}$$
$$X_{14} + X_{24} + X_{34} + X_{44} = 1 \quad \text{(insider trading)}$$
$$X_{11} + X_{12} + X_{13} + X_{14} = 1 \quad \text{(cases assigned to Adams)}$$
$$X_{21} + X_{22} + X_{23} + X_{24} = 1 \quad \text{(cases assigned to Brooks)}$$
$$X_{31} + X_{32} + X_{33} + X_{34} = 1 \quad \text{(cases assigned to Carter)}$$
$$X_{41} + X_{42} + X_{43} + X_{44} = 1 \quad \text{(cases assigned to Darwin)}$$

The law firm's problem is solved with a total effectiveness rating of 30 by letting $X_{13} = 1$, $X_{24} = 1$, $X_{32} = 1$, and $X_{41} = 1$. All other variables are therefore equal to 0.

Labor Planning

Labor planning problems address staffing needs over a specific time period. They are especially useful when managers have some flexibility in assigning workers to jobs that require overlapping or interchangeable talents. Large banks frequently use LP to tackle their labor scheduling.

Arlington Bank of Commerce and Industry is a busy bank that has requirements for between 10 and 18 tellers depending on the time of day. The lunch time, from noon to 2 P.M., is usually heaviest. Exhibit 18-8 indicates the workers needed at various hours that the bank is open.

The bank now employs 12 full-time tellers, but many women are on its roster of available part-time employees. A part-time employee must put in exactly four hours per day, but can start anytime between 9 A.M. and 1 P.M. Part-timers are a fairly inexpensive labor pool, since no retirement or lunch benefits are provided to them. Full-timers, on the other hand, work from 9 A.M. to 5 P.M. but are allowed one hour for lunch. (Half the full-timers eat at 11 A.M., the other half at noon.) Full-timers thus provide 35 hours per week of productive labor time.

By corporate policy, the bank limits part-time hours to a maximum of 50 percent of the day's total requirement.

Part-timers earn $4 per hour (or $16 per day) on average, while full-timers earn $50 per day in salary and benefits on average. The bank would like to set a schedule that would minimize its total manpower costs. It will release one or more of its full-time tellers if it is profitable to do so.

EXHIBIT 18-8 Arlington Bank of Commerce and Industry

Time Period	Number of Tellers Required
9 A.M.–10 A.M.	10
10 A.M.–11 A.M.	12
11 A.M.–Noon	14
Noon–1 P.M.	16
1 P.M.–2 P.M.	18
2 P.M.–3 P.M.	17
3 P.M.–4 P.M.	15
4 P.M.–5 P.M.	10

We can let

F = number of full-time tellers
P_1 = number of part-timers starting at 9 A.M. (leaving at 1 P.M.)
P_2 = number of part-timers starting at 10 A.M. (leaving at 2 P.M.)
P_3 = number of part-timers starting at 11 A.M. (leaving at 3 P.M.)
P_4 = number of part-timers starting at noon (leaving at 4 P.M.)
P_5 = number of part-timers starting at 1 P.M. (leaving at 5 P.M.)

Objective function:

Minimize total daily manpower cost = $\$50F + \$16(P_1 + P_2 + P_3 + P_4 + P_5)$

Constraints: For each hour, the available man-hours must be at least equal to the required man-hours.

$$
\begin{aligned}
F + P_1 &\geq 10 \text{ (9 A.M. to 10 A.M. needs)} \\
F + P_1 + P_2 &\geq 12 \text{ (10 A.M. to 11 A.M. needs)} \\
\tfrac{1}{2}F + P_1 + P_2 + P_3 &\geq 14 \text{ (11 A.M. to noon needs)} \\
\tfrac{1}{2}F + P_1 + P_2 + P_3 + P_4 &\geq 16 \text{ (noon to 1 P.M. needs)} \\
F + P_2 + P_3 + P_4 + P_5 &\geq 18 \text{ (1 P.M. to 2 P.M. needs)} \\
F + P_3 + P_4 + P_5 &\geq 17 \text{ (2 P.M. to 3 P.M. needs)} \\
F + P_4 + P_5 &\geq 15 \text{ (3 P.M. to 4 P.M. needs)} \\
F + P_5 &\geq 10 \text{ (4 P.M. to 5 P.M. needs)}
\end{aligned}
$$

Only 12 full-time tellers are available, so

$$F \leq 12$$

Part-time worker hours cannot exceed 50 percent of total hours required each day, which is the sum of the tellers needed each hour.

$$4(P_1 + P_2 + P_3 + P_4 + P_5) \leq 0.50(10 + 12 + 14 + 16 + 18 + 17 + 15 + 10)$$

or

$$4P_1 + 4P_2 + 4P_3 + 4P_4 + 4P_5 \leq 0.50(112)$$
$$F, P_1, P_2, P_3, P_4, P_5 \geq 0$$

There are two alternative optimal schedules that Arlington Bank can follow. The first is to employ only 10 full-time tellers ($F = 10$) and to start two part-timers at 10 A.M. ($P_2 = 2$), seven part-timers at 11 A.M. ($P_3 = 7$), and five part-timers at noon ($P_4 = 5$). No part-timers would begin at 9 A.M. or 1 P.M.

The second solution also employs 10 full-time tellers, but starts six part-timers at 9 A.M. ($P_1 = 6$), on part-timer at 10 A.M. ($P_2 = 1$), two part-timers at 11 A.M. and noon ($P_3 = 2$ and $P_4 = 2$), and three part-timers at 1 P.M. ($P_5 = 3$). The cost of either of these two policies is $724 per day.

Marketing Applications: Media Selection

Linear programming models have been used in the advertising field as a decision aid in selecting an effective media mix. Sometimes the technique is employed in allocating a fixed or limited budget across various media, which might include radio or television commercials, newspaper ads, direct mailings, magazine ads, and so on. In other applications, the objective is taken to be the maximization of audience exposure. Restrictions on the allowable media mix might arise through contract requirements, limited media availability, or company policy. An example follows.

The Win Big Gambling Club promotes gambling junkets from a large midwestern city to casinos in the Bahamas. The club has budgeted up to $8,000 per week for local advertising, the money to be allocated among four promotional media: TV spots, newpaper ads, and two types of radio advertisements. Win Big's goal is to reach the largest possible high-potential audience through the various media. The following table presents the number of potential gamblers reached by making use of an advertisement in each of the four media. It also provides figures regarding the cost per advertisement placed, and the maximum number of ads that can be purchased per week.

Medium	Audience Reached per Ad	Cost per Ad	Maximum Ads per Week
TV spot (1 minute)	5,000	$800	12
Daily newspaper (full-page ad)	8,500	$925	5
Radio spot (½ minute, prime time)	2,400	$290	25
Radio spot (1 minute, afternoon)	2,800	$380	20

Win Big's contractual arrangements require that at least five radio spots be placed each week. To ensure a broad-scoped promotional campaign, management also insists that no more than $1,800 be spent on all radio advertising every week.

The problem can now be stated mathematically as follows. Let

X_1 = number of 1-minute TV spots taken each week
X_2 = number of full-page daily newspaper ads taken each week
X_3 = number of 30-second prime-time radio spots taken each week
X_4 = number of 1-minute afternoon radio spots taken each week

Objective function:

$$\text{Maximize audience coverage} = 5{,}000X_1 + 8{,}500X_2 + 2{,}400X_3 + 2{,}800X_4$$

Subject to:

$$X_1 \leq 12 \quad \text{(maximum TV spots per week)}$$
$$X_2 \leq 5 \quad \text{(maximum newspaper ads per week)}$$
$$X_3 \leq 25 \quad \text{(maximum 30-second radio spots per week)}$$
$$X_4 \leq 20 \quad \text{(maximum one-minute radio spots per week)}$$
$$800X_1 + 925X_2 + 290X_3 + 380X_4 \leq 8{,}000 \quad \text{(weekly advertising budget)}$$
$$X_3 + X_4 \geq 5 \quad \text{(minimum radio spots contracted)}$$
$$290X_3 + 380X_4 \leq 1{,}800 \quad \text{(maximum \$ spent on radio)}$$

The solution to this LP formulation, using our microcomputer software package, was found to be

$$X_1 = 1.9 \quad \text{TV spots}$$
$$X_2 = 5 \quad \text{newspaper ads}$$
$$X_3 = 6.2 \quad \text{30-second radio spots}$$
$$X_4 = 0 \quad \text{1-minute radio spots}$$

This produces an audience exposure of 67,240 contacts. Because X_1 and X_3 are fractional, Win Big would probably round them to 2 and 6, respectively. Problems that demand all-integer solutions are discussed in detail in most management science textbooks.

18.6   GOAL PROGRAMMING

In today's business environment, profit maximization or cost minimization are not always the only objectives that a service organization sets forth. Often, maximizing total profit is just one of several goals, including such contradictory objectives as maximizing market share, maintaining full employment, providing quality ecologic management, minimizing noise level in the neighborhood, and meeting numerous other noneconomic goals.

Linear programming has the shortcoming that its objective function is measured in one dimension only. It is not possible for linear programming to have *multiple goals* unless they are all measured in the same units (such as dollars), a highly unusual situation. An important technique that has been developed to supplement linear programming is called **goal programming.**

In typical decision-making situations, the goals set by management can be achieved only at the expense of other goals. It is necessary to establish a hierarchy of importance among these goals so that lower-priority goals are tackled only after higher-priority ones are satisfied. Since it is not always possible to achieve every goal to the extent the decision maker desires, goal programming attempts to reach a satisfactory level of multiple objectives. This, of course, differs from linear programming, which tries to find the best possible outcome for a *single* objective.

How, specifically, does goal programming differ from linear programming? The objective function is the main difference. Instead of trying to maximize or minimize the objective function directly, with goal programming we try to minimize **deviations** between set goals and what we can actually achieve within the given constraints. In the LP simplex approach, such deviations are called **slack variables,** and they are used only as dummy variables. In goal programming, these slack terms are either positive or negative, and not only are they real variables, but they are also the only terms in the objective function. The objective is to minimize these deviational variables.

Once the goal programming model is formulated, the computational algorithm is almost the same as for an LP problem solved by the simplex method.

Goal Programming Example: Dixon Furniture Revisited

To illustrate the formulation of a GP problem, let's look back at the Dixon Furniture Store case, presented earlier in this chapter as an LP problem. That formulation, you recall, was

$$\text{Maximize net profit} = \$7X_1 + \$5X_2$$

Subject to:

$$4X_1 + 3X_2 \leq 240 \qquad (\$ \text{ of budget constraint})$$
$$2X_2 + 1X_2 \leq 100 \qquad (\text{space constraint})$$
$$X_2 \leq 60 \qquad (\text{chair demand constraint})$$
$$X_1, X_2 \geq 0$$

where

X_1 = number of tables ordered
X_2 = number of chairs ordered

We saw that if Dixon management had a single goal, say profit, linear programming could be used to find the optimal solution. But let's assume that the store is breaking in a whole new staff of sales clerks on the Labor Day weekend and feels that maximizing profit is not a realistic goal. The store manager sets a profit level, which would be satisfactory during the training period, of $380. We now have a goal programming problem in which we want to find the mix of tables and chairs that achieves the goal as closely as possible, given the budgetary and space constraints. This simple case will provide a good starting point for handling more complicated goal programs.

We first define two deviational variables:

$$d_1^- = \text{the underachievement of the profit target}$$
$$d_1^+ = \text{the overachievement of the profit target}$$

Now we can state the Dixon Furniture problem as a *single-goal* programming model.

$$\text{Minimize under- or overachievement of target profit} = d_1^- + d_1^+$$

Subject to:

$$7X_1 + 5X_2 + d_1^- - d_1^+ = 380 \qquad \text{(profit goal constraint)}$$
$$4X_1 + 3X_2 \leq 240 \qquad \text{(budget constraint)}$$
$$2X_1 + 1X_2 \leq 100 \qquad \text{(space constraint)}$$
$$X_2 \leq 60 \qquad \text{(chair demand constraint)}$$
$$X_1, X_2, d_1^-, d_1^+ \leq 0$$

Note that the first constraint states that the profit made, $\$7X_1 + \$5X_2$, plus any underachievement of profit minus any overachievement of profit has to equal the target of $380. For example, if $X_1 = 10$ tables and $X_2 = 60$ chairs, then $370 profit has been made. This misses the $380 target by $10, so d_1^- must be equal to 10. Since the profit goal was *underachieved*, Dixon did not overachieve and d_1^+ will clearly be equal to 0. This problem is now ready for solution by a goal programming algorithm.

If the target profit of $380 is exactly achieved, we see that both d_1^+ and d_1^- are equal to zero. The objective function will be minimized at 0. If Dixon's manager was only concerned with *underachievement* of the target goal, how would the objective function change? It would be

$$\text{Minimize underachievement} = d_1^-$$

This is also a reasonable goal, since the store would probably not be upset with an overachievement of its profit target.

In general, once all goals and constraints are identified in a problem, management should analyze each goal to see if under- or overachievement of that goal is an acceptable situation. If overachievement is acceptable, the appropriate d^+ variable can be eliminated from the objective function. If underachievement is okay, the d^- variable should be dropped. If management seeks to attain a goal exactly, both d^- and d^+ must appear in the objective function.

An Extension to Equally Important Multiple Goals

Let's now look at the situation in which Dixon's manager wants to achieve several goals, each equal in priority.

Goal 1: To produce as much profit above $380 as possible during Labor Day sale
Goal 2: To fully utilize the available budge to $240
Goal 3: To avoid using more than the allotted floor space
Goal 4: To avoid overstocking chairs

The deviational variables can be defined as follows:

$d_1^- =$ underachievement of the profit target
$d_1^+ =$ overachievement of the profit target

d_2^- = underspending of the allotted budget (underutilization)
d_2^+ = overspending of the allotted budget (overutilization)
d_3^- = underuse of the floor space allotted (underutilization)
d_3^+ = overuse of the floor space allotted (overutilization)
d_4^- = underachievement of the chair goal
d_4^+ = overachievement of the chair goal

Dixon is unconcerned about whether there is overachievement of the profit goal, overspending of the allotted budget, underuse of the floor space, or whether less than 60 chairs are ordered; hence, d_1^+, d_2^+, d_3^-, and d_4^- may be omitted from the objective function. The new objective function and constraints are

$$\text{Minimize total deviation} = d_1^- + d_2^- + d_3^+ + d_4^+$$

Subject to:

$$7X_1 + 5X_2 + d_1^- - d_1^+ = 380 \qquad \text{(profit constraint)}$$
$$4X_1 + 3X_2 + d_2^- - d_2^+ = 240 \qquad \text{(budget constraint)}$$
$$2X_1 + 1X_2 + d_3^- - d_3^+ = 100 \qquad \text{(space constraint)}$$
$$X_2 + d_4^- - d_4^+ = 60 \qquad \text{(chair constraint)}$$
$$\text{All } X_i, d_i \text{ variables} \geq 0$$

The setup and solution of this goal programming problem is shown in Exhibit 18-9 and sensitivity analysis output is given in Exhibit 18-10. According to the optimal solution 15 tables and 60 chairs will be stocked. This solution will help Dixon Furniture exceed the minimum profit goal by $d_1^+ = \$25$, and achieve an underutilization of

EXHIBIT 18-9   Setup and Solution of Dixon Furniture Multiple Goals Problem by POM for Windows

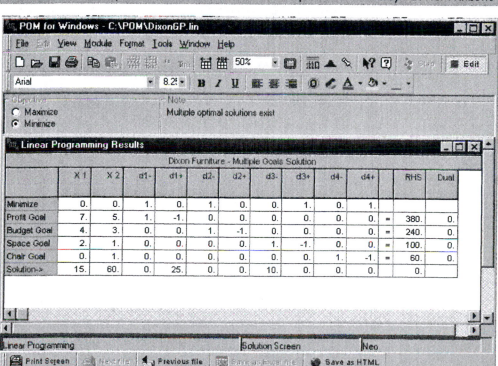

EXHIBIT 18-10 Sensitivity Analysis Output for Dixon Furniture Multiple Goals Problem from POM for Windows

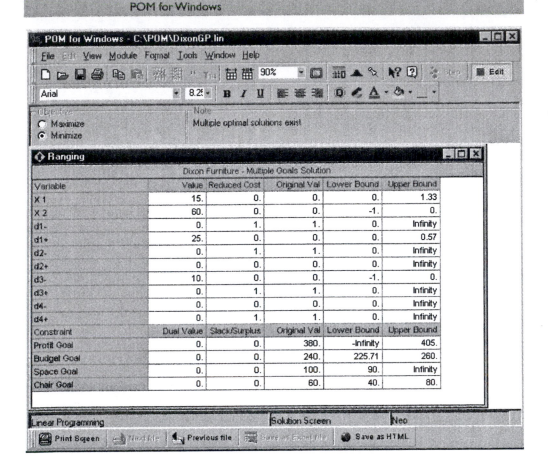

floor space of $d_3^- = 10$ square feet. The other two goals will be achieved exactly ($d_2^+ = d_2^- = d_4^+ = d_4^- = 0$).

Ranking Goals   In most goal programming problems, one goal will be more important than another, which in turn will be more important than a third. The idea is that goals can be ranked with respect to their importance in management's eyes. Lower-order goals are considered only after higher-order goals are met. Priorities (P_i's) are assigned to each deviational variable—with the ranking that P_1 is the most important goal, P_2 the next important, then P_3, and so on.

Let's say Dixon Furniture sets the priorities shown in the accompanying table.

Goal	*Priority*
Reach a profit as much above $380 as possible	P_1
Fully use budget available	P_2
Avoid using more space than available	P_3
Ordering less than 60 chairs	P_4

This means, in effect, that the priority of meeting the profit goal (P_1) is infinitely more important than the budget goal (P_2), which is, in turn, infinitely more important than the space goal (P_3), which is infinitely more important than ordering no more than 60 chairs (P_4).

With ranking of goals considered, the new objective function becomes

$$\text{Minimize total deviation} = P_1 d_1^- + P_2 d_2^- + P_3 d_3^+ + P_4 d_4^+$$

The constraints remain identical to the previous ones.

18.7   SUMMARY

Linear programming has proven to be a popular tool that can handle a wide variety of service operations management problems. Although a graphical method can be used to actually solve small problems, most organizations have access to LP software that runs on either microcomputers or larger systems and uses a solution procedure known as the **simplex algorithm.** LP not only finds optimal solutions to problems that can be formulated mathematically, but it also provides valuable management information in the form of shadow pricing and sensitivity analysis.

In this chapter we saw how to formulate LP problems with marketing, shipping, labor scheduling, assignment, ingredient blending, and retail ordering applications. Many of the problems at the end of the chapter involve extending the skills you have developed so far and tackling yet more complex service problems.

The final section introduced an extension of LP known as goal programming. GP helps the service manager who is faced with multiple goals. It tries to satisfy goals in priority order rather than maximize or minimize a single objective. The simplex method of LP can be manipulated to also solve goal programming problems, but special software is available specifically for the GP technique.

Discussion Questions

1. It has been said that each linear programming problem that has a feasible region has an infinite number of solutions. Explain.
2. Is sensitivity analysis a concept applied to linear programming only, or could it also be used when analyzing other techniques? Provide examples to prove your point.
3. What is a shadow price?
4. The mathematical relationships that follow were formulated by an operations research analyst at the Smith–Lawton Chemical Company. Which ones are invalid for use in a linear programming problem, and why?

$$\text{Maximize profit} = 4X_1 + 3X_1 X_2 + 8X_2 + 5X_3$$

Subject to:

$$2X_1 + X_2 + 2X_3 \leq 50$$
$$8X_1 - 4X_2 \geq 6$$
$$1.5X_1 + 6X_2 + 3X_2 \geq 21$$
$$19X_2 - \tfrac{1}{3}X_3 = 17$$
$$5X_1 + 4X_2 + 3\sqrt{X_3} \leq 80$$
$$-X_1 - X_2 + X_3 = 5$$

5. What is the value of the computer in solving linear programming problems today?
6. Compare the similarities and difference between linear and goal programming.
7. What are deviational variables? How do they differ from decision variables in traditional linear programming problems?
8. If you were the president of the college you are attending and were employing goal programming to assist in decision making, what might your goals be? What kinds of constraints would you include in your model?
9. What does it mean to rank goals in goal programming? How does this affect the problem's solution?

Problems

18.1. Solve the following linear programming problem using the graphical method.

$$\text{Maximize profit} = 4X_1 + 4X_2$$

Subject to:

$$3X_1 + 5X_2 \leq 150$$
$$X_1 - 2X_2 \leq 10$$
$$5X_1 + 3X_2 \leq 150$$
$$X_1, X_2 \geq 0$$

18.2. Consider the following linear programming formulation:

$$\text{Minimize cost} = \$1X_1 + \$2X_2$$

Subject to:

$$X_1 + 3X_2 \geq 90$$
$$8X_1 + 2X_2 \geq 160$$
$$3X_1 + 2X_2 \geq 120$$
$$X_2 \leq 70$$

Graphically illustrate the feasible region. Indicate which corner point produces the optimal solution. What is the cost of this solution?

18.3. The famous Y. S. Chang Restaurant is open 24 hours a day. Waiters and busboys report for duty at 3 A.M., 7 A.M., 11 A.M., 3 P.M., 7 P.M., or 11 P.M., and each works an eight-hour shift. The following table shows the minimium number of workers needed during the six periods into which the day is divided.

Period	Time	Number of Waiters and Busboys Required
1	3 A.M.–7 A.M.	3
2	7 A.M.–11 A.M.	12
3	11 A.M.–3 P.M.	16
4	3 P.M.–7 P.M.	9
5	7 P.M.–11 P.M.	11
6	11 P.M.–3 A.M.	4

Chang's scheduling problem is to determine how many waiters and busboys should report for work at the start of each time period in order to minimize the total staff required for one day's operation. (*Hint*: Let X_1 equal the number of waiters and busboys beginning work in time period i, where $i = 1, 2, 3, 4, 5, 6$.)

18.4. The advertising director for Diversey Paint and Supply, a chain of four retail stores on Chicago's North Side, is considering two media possibilities. One plan is for a series of half-page ads in the Sunday *Chicago Tribune* newspaper, and the other is for advertising time on Chicago TV. The stores are expanding their line of do-it-yourself tools, and the advertising director is interested in an exposure level of at least 40 percent within the city's neighborhoods and 60 percent in northwest suburban areas.

The TV viewing time under consideration has an exposure rating per spot of 5 percent in city homes and 3 percent in the northwest suburbs. The Sunday newspaper has corresponding exposure rates of 4 percent and 3 percent per ad. The cost of a half-page *Tribune* advertisement is $925; a television spot costs $2,000.

Diversey Paint would like to select the least costly advertising strategy that would meet desired exposure levels. Formulate this using LP.

18.5. The Krampf Lines Railway Company specializes in coal handling. On Friday, April 13, Krampf had empty cars at the following towns in the quantities indicated.

Town	Supply of Cars
Morgantown	35
Youngstown	60
Pittsburgh	25

By Monday, April 16, the following towns will need coal cars.

Town	Demand for Cars
Coal Valley	30
Coaltown	45
Coal Junction	25
Coalsburg	20

Using a railway city-to-city distance chart, the dispatcher constructs a mileage table for the preceding towns. The result is shown in Exhibit 18-11.
a. Formulate as a linear programming problem to minimize total miles over which cars are moved to new locations.
b. Compute the best shipment of coal cars using a linear programming computer program.

18.6. The state of Missouri has three major power-generating companies (A, B, and C). During the months of peak demand, the Missouri Power Authority authorizes these companies to pool their excess supply and to distribute it to smaller independent power companies that do not have generators large enough to handle the demand.

Excess supply is distributed on the basis of cost per kilowatt-hour transmitted. Exhibit 18-12 shows the demand and supply in millions of kilowatt hours and the costs per kilowatt hour of transmitting electric power to four small companies in cities W, X, Y, and Z.
a. Formulate an LP model for this problem.
b. Find the least cost distribution system using an LP computer program.

18.7. The hospital administrator at St. Charles General must appoint head nurses to four newly established departments: urology, cardiology, orthopedics, and obstetrics. In anticipation of this staffing problem, he had hired four nurses: Hawkins, Condriac, Bardot, and Hoolihan. Believeing in the quantitative analysis approach to problem solving, the administrator has interviewed each nurse, considered her background, personality, and talents, and developed a cost scale ranging from 0 to 100 to be used in the assignment. A 0 for Nurse Bardot being assigned to the cardiology unit implies that she would be perfectly suited to that task. A value close to 100, on the other hand, would imply that she is not at all suited to head that unit. Exhibit 18-13 gives the complete set of cost figures that the hospital administrator felt represented all possible assignments. Which nurse should be assigned to which unit?

EXHIBIT 18-11

	To			
From	Coal Valley	Coaltown	Coal Junction	Coalsburg
Morgantown	50	30	60	70
Youngstown	20	80	10	90
Pittsburgh	100	40	80	30

EXHIBIT 18-12

From	To				Excess Supply
	W	**X**	**Y**	**Z**	
A	12¢	4¢	9¢	5¢	55
B	8¢	1¢	6¢	6¢	45
C	1¢	12¢	4¢	7¢	30
Unfilled power demand	40	20	50	20	

18.8. The Gleaming Company has just developed a new dishwashing liquid and is preparing for a national television promotional campaign. The firm has decided to schedule a series of one-minute commercials during the peak housewife audience viewing hours of 1 to 5 P.M. To reach the widest possible audience, Gleaming wants to schedule one commercial on each of four networks and to have one commercial appear during each of the four one-hour time blocks. The exposure ratings for each hour, which represent the number of viewers per $1,000 spent, are presented in the following table. Which network should be scheduled each hour in order to provide the maximum audience exposure?

	Networks			
	A	**B**	**C**	**Independent**
1–2 P.M.	27.1	18.1	11.3	9.5
2–3 P.M.	18.9	15.5	17.1	10.6
3–4 P.M.	19.2	18.5	9.9	7.7
4–5 P.M.	11.5	21.4	16.8	12.8

18.9. The Arden County, Maryland, superintendent of education is responsible for assigning students to the three high schools in his county. He recognizes the need to bus a certain number of students, for several sectors of the county are beyond walking distance to a school. The superintendent partitions the county into five geographic sectors as he attempts to establish a plan that will minimize the total number of student miles traveled by bus. He also recognizes that if a student happens to live in a certain sector and is assigned to the high school in that sector, there is no need to bus him since he can walk from home to school. The three schools are located in sectors B, C, and E.

Exhibit 18-14 reflects the number of high-school-age students living in each sector and the distance in miles from each sector to each school.

Each high school has a capacity of 900 students. Set up the objective function and constraints of this problem using linear programming so that the total number of student miles traveled by bus is minimized.

EXHIBIT 18-13

Nurse	Department			
	Urology	**Cardiology**	**Orthopedics**	**Obstetrics**
Hawkins	28	18	15	75
Condriac	32	48	23	38
Bardot	51	36	24	36
Hoolihan	25	38	55	12

EXHIBIT 18-14

Sector	Distance to School			No. of Students
	School in Sector B	School in Sector C	School in Sector E	
A	5	8	6	700
B	0	4	12	500
C	4	0	7	100
D	7	2	5	800
E	12	7	0	400
			Total	2,500

18.10. Harris Segal, marketing director for North-Central Power and Light, is about to begin an advertising campaign promoting energy conservation. In trying to budget between television and newspaper advertisements, he sets the following goals in order of importance:
1. The total advertising budget of $120,000 should not be exceeded.
2. There should be a mix of TV and newspaper ads, with at least 10 TV spots (costing $5,000 each) and at least 20 ads (costing $2,000 each).
3. The total number of people to read or hear the advertisements should be at least 9 million.

Each television spot reaches approximately 300,000 people. A newspaper advertisement is read by about 150,000 persons. Formulate Segal's goal programming problem to find out how many of each type of ad to place.

18.11. Major Bill Bligh, director of the Army War College's new six-month attaché training program, is concerned about how the 20 officers taking the course spend their precious time while in his charge. Major Bligh recognizes that there are 168 hours per week and thinks his students have been using them rather inefficiently. Bligh lets

X_1 = number of hours of sleep needed per week
X_2 = number of personal hours (eating, personal hygiene, handling laundry, etc.)
X_3 = number of hours of class and studying
X_4 = number of hours of social time off-base (dating, sports, family visits, etc.)

He thinks that 30 hours per week should be enough study/class time for students to absorb the material and that this is his most important goal. Bligh feels that students need at most seven hours sleep per night on average and that this goal is number 2. He believes that goal number 3 is to provide at least 20 hours per week of social time. Formulate this as a goal programming problem.

18.12. New Orlean's Mt. Sinai Hospital is a large, private, 600-bed facility complete with laboratories, operating rooms, and x-ray equipment. In seeking to increase revenues, Mt. Sinai's administration has decided to make a 90-bed addition on a portion of adjacent land currently used for staff parking. The administrators feel that the labs, operating rooms, and x-ray department are not being fully utilized at present and do not need to be expanded to handle additional patients. The addition of 90 beds, however, involves deciding how many beds should be allocated to the medical staff (for medical patients) and how many to the surgical staff (for surgical patients).

The hospital's accounting and medical records departments have provided the following pertinent information. The average hospital stay for a medical patient is eight days, and the average medical patient generates $2,280 in revenues. The average surgical patient is in the hospital five days and receives a

$1,515 bill. The laboratory is capable of handling 15,000 tests per year more than it *was* handling. The average medical patient requires 3.1 lab tests and the average surgical patient takes 2.6 lab tests. Furthermore, the average medical patient uses one x-ray, while the average surgical patient requires two x-rays. If the hospital were expanded by 90 beds, the x-ray department could handle up to 7,000 x-rays without significant additional cost. Finally, the administration estmates that up to 2,800 additional operations could be performed in existing operating room facilities. Medical patients, of course, require no surgery, while each surgical patient generally has one surgery performed.

Formulate this problem so as to determine how many medical beds and how many surgical beds should be added in order to maximize revenues. Assume that the hospital is open 365 days per year.

18.13. South Central Utilities has just announced the August 1 opening of its second nuclear generator at its Baton Rouge, Louisiana, nuclear power plant. Its personnel department has been directed to determine how many nuclear technicians need to be hired and trained over the remainder of the year.

The plant currently employs 350 fully trained technicians and projects the following manpower needs:

Month	*Manpower Needed (in hours)*
August	40,000
September	45,000
October	35,000
November	50,000
December	45,000

By Louisiana law, a reactor employee can actually work no more than 130 hours per month. (Slightly over one hour per day is used for check-in and checkout record keeping and for daily radiation health scans.) Policy at South Central Utilities also dictates that layoffs are not acceptable in those months when the nuclear plant is overstaffed. So, if more trained employees are available than are needed in any month, each worker is still fully paid, even though he or she is not required to work the 130 hours. Training new employees is an important and costly procedure. It takes one month of one-on-one classroom instruction before a new technician is permitted to work alone in the reactor facility. Therefore, South Central must hire trainees one month before they are actually needed. Each trainee teams up with a skilled nuclear technician and requires 90 hours of that employee's time, meaning that 90 hours less of the technician's time are available that month for actual reactor work.

Personnel department records indicate a turnover rate of trained technicians at 5 percent per month. In other words, about 5 percent of the skilled employees at the start of any month resign by the end of that month.

A trained technician earns an average monthly salary of $2,000 (regardless of the number of hours worked, as noted earlier). Trainees are paid $900 during their one month of instruction.

a. Formulate this staffing problem using LP.

b. Solve the problem. How many trainees must begin each month?

CASES

CASE 18–1   Northwest General Hospital

Northwest General, a large hospital in Providence, Rhode Island, has initiated a new procedure to ensure that patients receive their meals while the food is still as hot as possible. The hospital will continue to prepare the food in the kitchen, but will now deliver it in bulk (not individual servings) to one of three new serving stations in the building. From there, the food will be reheated, meals will be placed on individual trays, loaded onto a cart, and distributed to the various floors and wings of the hospital.

The three new serving stations are as efficiently located as possible to reach the various hallways in the hospital. The number of trays that each station can serve are as follows:

Location	Capacity (meals)
Station 5A	200
Station 3G	225
Station 1S	275

There are six wings to Northwest General that must be served. The number of patients in each follows:

Wing	Patients
1	80
2	120
3	150
4	210
5	60
6	80

The purpose of the new procedure is to increase the temperature of the hot meals that the patient receives. Therefore, the amount of time needed to deliver a tray from a serving station will determine the proper distribution of food from serving station to wing. Exhibit 18-15 summarizes the distribution time (in minutes) associated with each possible distribution channel. ■

EXHIBIT 18-15

From	To					
	Wing 1	Wing 2	Wing 3	Wing 4	Wing 5	Wing 6
Station 5A	12	11	8	9	6	6
Station 3G	6	12	7	7	5	8
Station 1S	8	9	6	6	7	9

SOURCE: From Barry Render and Ralph M. Stair, *Quantitative Analysis for Management*, 7th ed. (Upper Saddle River, NJ, Prentice Hall, 2000). Reprinted with permission.

CASE QUESTION

What is your recommendation for handling the distribution of trays from the three serving stations?

CASE 18–2   Schank Marketing Research

Schank Marketing Research has just signed contracts to conduct studies for four clients. At present, three project managers are free for assignment to the tasks. Although all are capable of handling each assignment, the times and costs to complete the studies depend on the experience and knowledge of each manager. Using his judgment, John Schank, the president, has been able to establish a cost for each possible assignment. These costs, which are really the salaries each manager would draw on each task, are summarized as follows:

| Project Manager | Client | | | |
	Hines Corp.	NASA	General Foundry	CBT Television
Gardener	$3,200	$3,000	$2,800	$2,900
Ruth	2,700	3,200	3,000	3,100
Hardgraves	1,900	2,100	3,300	2,100

Schank is very hesitant about neglecting NASA, which has been an important customer in the past. (NASA has employed the firm to study the public's attitude toward the Space Shuttle and proposed Space Station.) In addition, Schank has promised to try to provide Ruth a salary of at least $3000 on his next assignment. From previous contracts, Schank also knows that Gardener does not get along well with the management at CBT Television, so he hopes to avoid assigning her to CBT. Finally, as Hines Corporation is also an old and valued client, Schank feels it is twice as important to immediately assign a project manager to Hines' task as it is to provide one to General Foundry, a brand new client. Schank wants to minimize the total costs of all projects while considering each of these goals. He feels that all these goals are important, but if he had to rank them, he would put his concern about NASA first, his worry about Gardener second, his need to keep Hines Corporation happy third, his promise to Ruth fourth, and his concern about minimizing all costs last.

Each project manager can handle, at most, one new client. ■

SOURCE: From Barry Render and Ralph M. Stair, *Quantitative Analysis for Management*, 7th ed. (Upper Saddle River, NJ, Prentice Hall, 2000). Reprinted with permission.

CASE QUESTIONS

1. If Schank were not concerned about noncost goals, how would he formulate this problem so that it could be solved quantitatively?

2. Develop a formulation that will incorporate all five objectives.

References

Anderson, A. M., and Earle, M. D., "Diet Planning in the Third World by Linear and Goal Programming," *Journal of Operations Research Society*, vol. 34 (1983), pp. 9–16.

Balbirer, Sheldon D., and David Shaw, "An Application of Linear Programming to Bank Financial Planning," *Interfaces*, vol. 11, no. 5 (October 1981), pp. 77–82.

Bres, E. S., D. Burns, A. Charnes, and W. W. Cooper, "A Goal Programming Model for Planning Officer Accessions," *Management Science*, vol. 26, no. 8 (August 1980), pp. 773–781.

Brosch, Lee C., Richard J. Buck, William H. Sparrow, and James R. White, "Boxcars, Linear Programming and the Sleeping Kitten," *Interfaces*, vol. 10, no. 6 (December 1980), pp. 53–61.

Buffa, Frank P., and Wade M. Jackson, "A Goal Programming Model for Purchasing Planning," *Journal of Purchasing and Material Management* (fall 1983), pp. 27–34.

DeKluyver, Cornelis A., and Herbert Moskowitz, "Assessing Scenario Probabilities Via Interactive Goal Programming," *Management Science*, vol. 30, no. 3 (March 1984), pp. 273–278.

Holloran, Thomas, and Judson Byrn, "United Airlines Stationed Manpower Planning System," *Interfaces*, vol. 16, no. 1 (January–February 1986), pp. 39–50.

Ignizio, J. P., *Goal Programming and Extensions*. Lexington, MA, D. C. Heath, 1976.

Jackson, Bruce L., and John M. Brown, "Using LP for Crude Oil Sales at Elk Hills," *Interfaces*, vol. 10, no. 3 (June 1980), pp. 65–70.

Jones, Lawrence, and N. K. Kwak, "A Goal Programming Model for Allocation of Human Resources for the Good Laboratory Practice Regulations," *Decision Sciences*, vol. 13, no. 1 (1982), pp. 156–166.

Lee, S. M., *Good Programming for Decision Analysis* (Philadelphia, Auerbach Publishers, 1972).

Lee, Sang M., and Marc J. Schniederjans, "A Multicriterial Assignment Problem: A Goal Programming Approach," *Interfaces*, vol. 13, no. 4 (August 1983), pp. 75–79.

Leff, H. Stephen, Maqbool Dada, and Stephen C. Graves, "An LP Planning Model for a Mental Health Community Support System," *Management Science*, vol. 32, no. 2 (February 1986), pp. 139–155.

Marsten, Roy E., and Michael R. Muller, "A Mixed Integer Programming Approach to Air Cargo Fleet Planning," *Management Science*, vol. 26, no. 11 (November 1980), pp. 1096–1107.

Render, Barry, and Ralph M. Stair, *Quantitative Analysis for Mangement*, 7th ed. (Upper Saddle River, NJ, Prentice Hall, 2000).

Ruth, R. Jean, "A Mixed Integer Programming Model for Regional Planning of a Hospital Inpatient Service," *Management Science*, vol. 27, no. 5 (May 1981), pp. 521–533.

Schniederjans, Marc J., N. K. Kwak, and Mark C. Helmer, "An Application of Goal Programming to Resolve a Site Location Problem," *Interfaces*, vol. 12, no. 3 (June 1982), pp. 65–72.

Taylor, B. W., et al., "An Integer Nonlinear Goal Programming Model for the Development of State Highway Patrol Units," *Management Science*, vol. 31, no. 11 (November 1985), pp. 1335–1347.

Tingley, Kim M., and Judith S. Liebmen, "A Goal Programming Example in Public Health Resource Allocation," *Management Science*, vol. 30, no. 3 (March 1984), pp. 279–289.

CHAPTER 19

Service Inventory Systems

19.1   INTRODUCTION

To date, operations managers, both practitioners and academicians, have focused on developing the theory and planning of inventory control systems for manufacturing operations. In this chapter we extend this theory to the area of service inventory management.

If a service is a deed, performance, or effort, as some writers have defined it, why are we concerned with inventory problems? There are several reasons for giving considerable consideration to inventories in service businesses.

First, practically all services utilize some sort of input materials that are kept in inventory. Second, many services supply an output product in addition to some sort of performance. Third, adequate service levels usually mean that performance of service cannot be permitted to be delayed for lack of materials or related products.

Input inventory for services is required for matching service to demand. It is also an operating cost of the system, as in manufacturing. However, the cost of running out of inventory is usually much higher for services because of customer expectations of prompt service. In manufacturing, inventories separate production from customers. In contrast, in services, input materials in inventory are used on customers, provided for customers during the performance of the service, or used up to generate the service.

Many services fall in a classification called the **knowledge industry.** These services usually provide stored rather than oral information. The storage device (book, disk, tape, or report) that contains the information is the unit that is sold. The service is embedded in a low-value container that may be stored. Other services, such as retail, wholesale, and restaurants, must usually retain some output goods in inventory. In Exhibit 19-1 we show examples of input materials and output goods for services.

EXHIBIT 19-1   Input Materials and Output Goods in Services

Type of Service	Input Materials (What Is Processed)	Output Goods (What Is Sold)
Retailers, wholesalers	Consumer goods, repair parts	Consumer goods, repair parts
Restaurant	Raw food, cooked food, beverages	Prepared food, beverages
Publisher	Paper, ink	Books, magazines, newspapers
Bank	Currency, gold	Currency, gold, coins, legal documents
Consulting and advisory	Forms, paper, ink or ribbons	Reports
Legal firm	Forms, paper	Legal documents, reports
Airline, bus, rail line	Gasoline or oil, food and beverages, tickets	Tickets, food and beverages
Movie theater	Tickets, snack foods	Tickets, food
Real estate	Forms, real estate	Legal documents, reports, real estate

19.2   CHARACTERISTICS OF SERVICE INVENTORIES

Input and Output Materials

Manufacturing is concerned with changing the form of input materials. In many services, however, the form of input materials remains unchanged. Retailing and wholesaling, for example, usually involve no change in the form of goods. Real estate services usually accept property as the owner supplies it to sell. Even restaurants serve some foods in exactly the form in which they buy it. Banks, of course, deal in currency, so that input and output are identical.

In services, input materials are often a trivial cost of doing business. That is, many services use only blank paper or forms as process input materials. Inventories of these are usually a very small cost of operations.

Output materials may be used on the customer directly, as in the cases of proprietory cosmetics, surgical thread, anesthetics, and prepared food. The customer cannot store such output materials for use at such time as she needs them again. In manufacturing, the customer can always store the goods he needs and continue uninterrupted production. If the service supplier runs out of raw materials, however, the service cannot be performed and customers may be lost.

Perishability

Style goods of retailers, input and output food items of restaurants, and newspapers are examples of perishable inventory items of services. Exhibit 19-2 shows examples of input and output goods with different degrees of **perishability.**

Sometimes an item in input inventory may have a long life while the same item in output inventory may have a short life. For example, newspapers keep files on notable

EXHIBIT 19-2   Perishables in Service Inventories

Life of Items	Items
Very short	Certain transplant organs, tickets for same-day event
Short	Fresh fruit, certain transplant organs, retail items for a commemorative occasion
Medium	Certain retail goods, hospital drugs, seasonal style goods in retailing, credit cards
Long	Postage stamps, books, certain retail and wholesale goods

EXHIBIT 19-3   Lumpiness of Input Materials in Services

Lumpiness	Examples
Smooth	Provision of gas for cooking/heating applications by gas service firms
Minor lumpiness	Office supplies, paint, food supplies, and other locally available items
Moderate lumpiness	Office forms, mail order supplies, textile materials, or lumber cut to order
Major lumpiness	Office forms, clothing, cosmetics, and chemicals requiring months of lead time

living people. Such data are kept for long periods. However, when data from the files are used in a newspaper article, the resale output item (newspaper) has a very short inventory life. Conversely, the input information represented by actors playing in a movie is very short, but the finished film has a very long inventory life.

These examples of perishability are indications that in services the inventory problem varies tremendously and is often quite different from that of manufacturing. In many services, the amount of inventory purchased is heavily weighted by perishability factors. This implies that the cost of holding perishable items beyond a certain period is very high.

Lumpiness of Input Materials

Lumpiness refers to the need to buy in quantities, or "lumps," because of the nature of the input materials, the lead time, and the difficulty or high cost of obtaining small shipments from vendors. It is common in services to have a low degree of lumpiness and a smoother flow of input materials than in manufacturing. Many small services simply pick up input materials locally as needed. Exhibit 19-3 gives examples of materials for various levels of lumpiness. This aspect of services means that holding costs for input inventory tend to be negligible.

19.3   THE INPUT MATERIAL DECISION PROBLEM

There is a close relationship between the timing of inventory orders and the size of an order. The greater the frequency of orders, the smaller is the order size.

There is also a decision to be made as to whether orders of variable size are to be placed at regular intervals, whether constant-size orders will be placed at irregular intervals, or whether it is possible to place consistant-size orders at regular periods.

Because of random variations in demand for services and in lead time for delivery of input materials, the two variables of order size and timing of purchases may be difficult to specify. The adverse effects of errors in quantity or timing are indicated in Exhibit 19-4. They include excessive carrying costs, poor customer service, and excessive order processing or purchase costs.

The input material decision problem must often take into account a series of inventories through which materials move. In Exhibit 19-5 we see that the service maintains its own inventory. For replenishment, the service calls on its vendor or supplier. The vendor calls on the factory warehouse, which, in turn, calls on manufacturing for replenishment. If any link in the chain runs short, replenishment of the service firm's inventory may be additionally delayed. Such a system, with information loops, has been simulated by distribution requirements planning models.[1]

---

[1] For a complete treatment of distribution requirements planning (DRP), see Andre Martin, *DRP: Distribution Resource Planning* (Essex Junction, VT, Oliver Wight Limited Publications, 1983).

EXHIBIT 19-4   Adverse Effects of Wrong Timing and Quantity

| | PLANNING PRODUCTION AND PURCHASE ORDERS | | | |
| | *Wrong Timing* | | *Wrong Quantity* | |
Effects	*Order Is Late*	*Order Is Early*	*Too Large*	*Too Small*
Customer service	Poor	—	—	Poor
Inventory carrying cost	—	Excessive	Excessive	—
Order-processing cost	Excessive	—	—	Excessive
Capacity control	Poor	—	Poor	Poor

Source: Richard J. Schonberger, *Operations Management* (Homewood, IL, BPI/Irwin, 1981), p. 166. Used with permission.

19.4   SERVICE INVENTORY CONTROL SYSTEMS

Managers of service operations can establish control systems for managing inventory. The first step in such a system is to classify inventory items by the ABC method of classification.

ABC analysis divides on-hand inventory into three classifications based on annual dollar volume. ABC analysis is an inventory application of what is known as the **Pareto principle.** The Pareto principle states that there are a critical few and trivial many.[2] The idea is to focus resources on the critical few and not the trivial many.

To determine annual dollar volume for ABC analysis, we measure the *annual* demand of each inventory item times the *cost per unit.* Class A items are those on which the annual dollar volume is high. Such items may represent only about 15 percent of total inventory items, but they represent 70 to 80 percent of the total inventory cost. Class B items are those inventory items of medium annual dollar volume. These items may represent about 30 percent of the items and 15 percent of the value. Those with low annual dollar volume are class C, which may represent only 5 percent of the annual dollar volume but about 55 percent of the total items.

Graphically, the inventory of many organizations would appear as presented in Exhibit 19-6.

EXHIBIT 19-5   Storage Points for Alternative Channels for Materials Supply

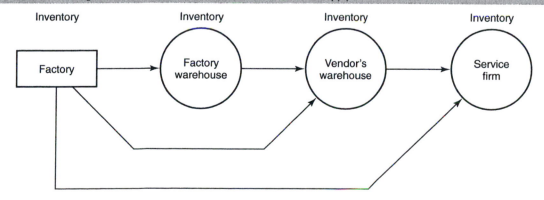

---

[2] Villefredo Pareto, eighteenth-century Italian economist.

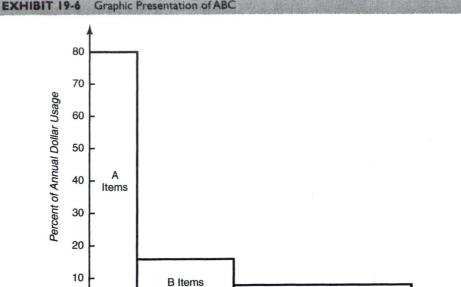

EXHIBIT 19-6 Graphic Presentation of ABC

19.5 INVENTORY CONTROL SYSTEMS FOR INDEPENDENT DEMAND ITEMS

The inventory models discussed in this section are based on the assumption that demand for a service/service item is *independent* of the demand for another service/service item. These services (or service items) are directly demanded by the customer, usually as a completed service (or service item), which is also known as an **end service** or **end item.** For example, the demand for the services of a dentist may be independent of the demand for the services of a heart surgeon. The demand at your drugstore for a *USA Today* newspaper may be independent of the demand for a copy of the *PC World* magazine. This section is concerned with the application of classical inventory models and systems to an independent service demand situation. Section 19.7 will discuss models dealing with dependent service demand situations, where the demand for one service will *depend* on the demand for another. This means that the demand for this service is directly related to or derived from the demand for other end services.

As services subject to independent demand are directly demanded by the customers, they are exposed to demand uncertainty and therefore need to be forecast. Hence, it becomes necessary to forecast the number of patients who will require the services of a dentist, as well as the number of daily newspapers that are to be ordered by a newsstand.

An inventory control system has a set of procedures that indicate the quantity of material that should be added to inventory and the time to do so. Control systems for independent demand service inventory can be broadly divided into two classes: fixed-quantity and fixed-period (i.e., periodic) systems.

Fixed-Quantity Systems

A **fixed-quantity system** adds the same amount to the inventory of an item each time it is reordered. Orders are placed when the inventory on hand is reduced to an amount known as the **reorder point.** Hence, it is event-triggered, with the event of reaching a reorder point occurring any time, depending on the demand for the specific inventory item. Each time the inventory balance is depleted by a sale, the amount of inventory on hand is compared with the reorder point. If the on-hand balance has dropped to this point, a new order (of a prespecified quantity) is placed. If not, no action is taken by the inventory system until the next sale. (See Exhibit 19-7.)

The advantage of a fixed-quantity system is that sometimes a fixed order size is desirable, as in the case of quantity discounts being offered for an order that exceeds a certain size. This method is also appropriate when an order is constrained by certain physical limitations. For example, one may have to order by the truckload and the capacity of a truck will define the size of the order.

An additional advantage of the fixed-quantity system is that it has lower safety stocks when compared to a fixed-period system. This is because it has to guard against demand uncertainty only during the period between placement of a new order and the receipt of that order.

Fixed-Period Systems

In a **fixed-period system,** the inventory level is checked at uniform time intervals. It is time-triggered, with the replenishment of inventory occurring by the passage of a given amount of time. Therefore, there is no tally of the on-hand balance of an item when a withdrawal takes place. The stock on hand is counted only when the ordering date occurs. The quantity ordered is the amount necessary to bring the inventory level up to a prespecified target level. Exhibit 19-8 illustrates this concept.

The advantage of the fixed-period system is that there is no physical count of inventory items after an item is withdrawn—this occurs only when the time for the next review comes up. This procedure is also convenient administratively, especially if inventory control is one of several duties of an employee.

This type of inventory control system and the placement of orders on a periodic basis are appropriate when vendors make routine (i.e., at a fixed time interval) visits to customers to take fresh orders or when purchasers want to combine orders to save ordering and transportation costs (therefore, they will have the same review period for similar inventory items).

The disadvantage of this system is that since there is no tally of inventory during the review period, there is the possibility of a stockout during this time. This scenario is possible if a large order draws the inventory level down to zero right after an order

EXHIBIT 19-7   Inventory Level in a Fixed-Quantity System

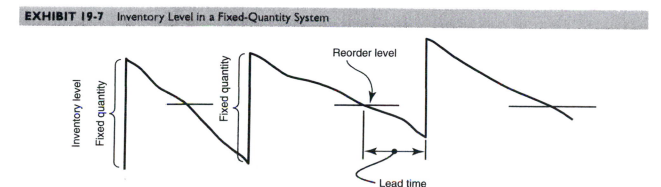

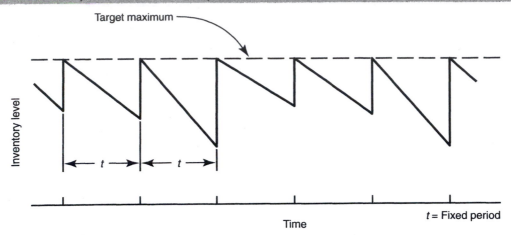

EXHIBIT 19-8 Inventory Level in a Fixed-Period System

is placed. Therefore, a higher level of safety stock (as compared to a fixed-quantity system) needs to be maintained to provide protection against stockout both during the review period and during the time required for a fresh order to come in.

19.6 INVENTORY PLANNING

Economic Order Quantity (EOQ) Model

Services may buy and store such items as printed forms, various office supplies, cosmetics (in beauty parlors), medical supplies, consumer goods (in retail and wholesale firms), food (in restaurants), and sporting goods (in resort shops). The service firm's inventory control objective will be to minimize the cost of input inventories.

We will develop a fixed-quantity model in which the **economic order quantity** is used to maintain an inventory of business forms. Such forms may be purchased loose, in pads, or in cartons. It is important to specify the unit whenever calculations are made. In our example, we will assume that the forms come in a box of 24 pads.

The inventory cost system is made up of two components: holding costs and procurement costs. **Holding costs** are the costs of holding one box for one year.

These costs consist of such items as rent for space, insurance, obsolescence, utilities, and opportunity cost of money tied up in inventory. (The time period is arbitrary and could be days, weeks, or months, for example.) **Procurement costs** are the costs involved in placing a single purchase order, receiving the goods, moving the goods to storage, and processing payment.

In order to develop the inventory model, we let

Q = number of units purchased at one time
D = demand (usage) rate for the printed forms for one year
LT = lead time, that is, the time between placing and receiving an order
ROP = reorder point

The first part of our model is shown in Exhibit 19-9. An order of size Q is used up at rate D. When the inventory reaches zero, a new order arrives. This is so because we placed an order when the inventory reached the ROP to allow for the lead time (LT) that it takes to obtain the goods.

EXHIBIT 19-9   Inventory Usage Over Time

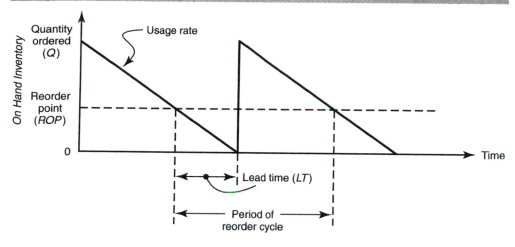

The second part of the model shows the cost side. In selecting the order size, we note that the larger the order that is placed, the larger is the average inventory for the year. Hence total inventory cost for a year is larger for a large order size Q than for a small order quantity. On the other hand, as Q is increased, fewer orders need to be placed during the year. Therefore, procurement costs decrease as the order size is increased.

Let

H = holding cost for one box of forms for one year
S = cost of placing a single order

Then

$Q/2$ = average inventory (assuming constant demand)
D/Q = the number of purchase cycles per year

The total system cost TC is then

$$TC = S\left(\frac{D}{Q}\right) + H\left(\frac{Q}{2}\right) \qquad (19.1)$$

In Exhibit 19-10, the component costs and total cost are sketched. The economic order size Q^* occurs when the component costs are equal.

$$S\left(\frac{D}{Q}\right) = H\left(\frac{Q}{2}\right)$$

and therefore,

$$Q^* = \sqrt{\frac{2DS}{H}} \qquad (19.2)$$

As an example, suppose that the cost of placing an order for business forms is $S =$ $20, the cost of holding one box in inventory for one year is $H = \$3.6$ per year, and the demand for the forms is $D = 36$ boxes per year. Then,

$$Q^* = \sqrt{\frac{2 \times \$20 \times 36}{\$3.6}} = 20 \text{ boxes}$$

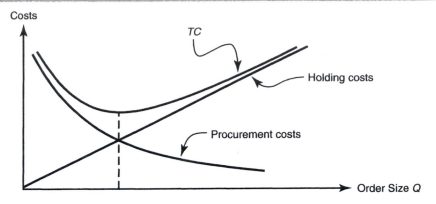

EXHIBIT 19-10 Cost Components

If it takes two months from the time that an order is placed until the forms arrive in the stock room, then the reorder level is

$$ROP = (\text{monthly demand} \times \text{lead time}) = 3 \times 2 = 6 \text{ boxes} \qquad \textbf{(19.3)}$$

As a safety precaution, a **buffer stock** of two or three extra boxes may be kept in reserve so that if the shipment is delayed, a stockout may be avoided.

Perishable Goods Model

A simple example will illustrate a model for ordering perishable goods. Suppose that a student club has obtained rights to sell brochures for a high school football game. These brochures describe the players of both teams, personalities of the school, and photos of interest. Some local advertising helps pay the publication cost.

The brochures sell for $3 and may be ordered from a local printer for a cost of $1 each. The club faces the problem of how many brochures to order from the printer because those which are not sold are worthless. The cost of the unsold brochures must be deducted from the profits of those that are sold.

As a start, the students

- Estimate alternative possible demands for the brochure
- Estimate a probability that each demand will occur
- Compute the conditional profit for stocking an amount equal to each potential demand

Exhibit 19.11 shows these data. To illustrate the computations, we consider a demand of 2,100 brochures and an inventory of 2,300 brochures. Then we earn $2 × 2,100 but

EXHIBIT 19-11 Conditional Profit for Different Combinations of Demand and Order Quantity

		Order Quantity			
Alternative Demands	*Probability*	*2,000*	*2,100*	*2,200*	*2,300*
2,000	0.10	$4,000	$3,900	$3,800	$3,700
2,100	0.30	$4,000	$4,200	$4,100	$4,000[a]
2,200	0.40	$4,000	$4,200	$4,400	$4,300
2,300	0.20	$4,000	$4,200	$4,400	$4,600

[a] [$2 × 2,100] − [$1 × (2,300 − 2,100)] = $4,000

EXHIBIT 19-12   Expected Values for Ordering Different Quantities

Alternative Demands	Order Quantity			
	2,000	2,100	2,200	2,300
2,000	$ 400	$ 390	$ 380	$ 370
2,100	$1,200	$1,260	$1,230	$1,200
2,200	$1,600	$1,680	$1,760	$1,720
2,300	$ 800	$ 840	$ 880	$ 920
Expected profit	$4,000	$4,170	$4,225	$4,210

have an additional cost of $1 on each of the 200 unsold brochures. Our net profit of $4,000 is shown in the right column, second row.

Exhibit 19-12 shows the computations of expected values for each alternative amount to be ordered. The expected value (or profit) of a particular order quantity is calculated by multiplying each demand probability in Exhibit 19-11 by its respective conditional profit, then summing over all possible levels of demand. Exhibit 19-12 shows that ordering 2,200 brochures gives us the highest expected profit, $4,225. Therefore, the club should order and, hopefully, sell 2,200 copies.

19.7   REQUIREMENTS PLANNING FOR DEPENDENT DEMAND

The demand for many serivces or service items may be classified as dependent demand, which requires a different type of inventory control system than previously discussed. Service demand is considered **dependent** when it is directly related to or derived from the demand for other services (known as end services or end items). For example, in a restaurant where bread and vegetables are included in every meal ordered, the demand for bread and vegetables is *dependent* on the demand for meals. The demand for meals may be forecasted. The demand for bread and vegetables is calculated or *derived* from the demand for meals. The meal is an *end* item. The bread and vegetables are *component* items.

A **bill of materials** (BOM) may be created for end items or services, such as a meal, that *lists* the materials and quantity of materials needed to provide the final service in the *order* they are needed. Exhibit 19-13 shows a bill of materials and accompanying product structure tree for veal picante, a top-selling entree in a New Orleans restaurant. Notice that the various components of veal picante (that is, veal, sauce, and linguini) are prepared by different kitchen personnel (a chef, assistant chef, and helpers). These preparations also require different amounts of time to complete. Exhibit 19-14 shows a **bill of labor** (BOL) for veal picante. It lists the operations to be performed, the order of operations, and the labor requirements for each operation (type of labor and labor hours).

Basically, a **requirements planning system** takes a schedule or forecast of end items or services and, using the bill of materials and bill of labor, determines what component items or services are required and when they are required. It also specifies when an operation should be started or item purchased so that it will be completed or arrive when it is required. Thus, a requirements planning system is both an inventory control system (it decides when to order materials and how much to order) and a scheduling system (it decides when an operation should begin).

Requirements planning systems in manufacturing firms initially were called MRP for material requirements planning. As the name implies, these systems were used to plan for

EXHIBIT 19-13 Product Structure Tree and Bill of Materials for Veal Picante

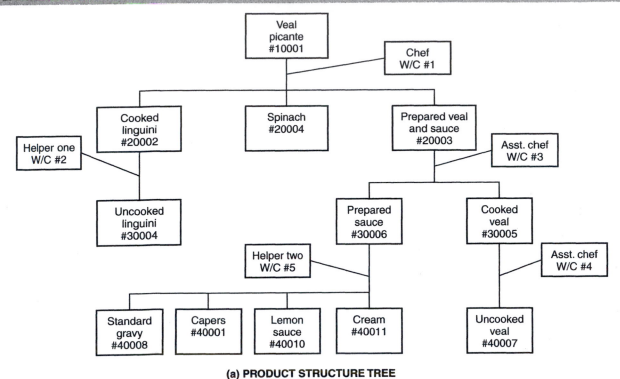

(a) PRODUCT STRUCTURE TREE

Part Number	Description	Quantity	Unit of Measure	Unit Cost
10001	Veal picante	1	Serving	—
20002	Cooked linguini	1	Serving	—
20003	Prepared veal and sauce	1	Serving	—
20004	Spinach	0.1	Bag	0.94
30004	Uncooked linguini	0.5	Pound	—
30005	Cooked veal	1	Serving	—
30006	Prepared sauce	1	Serving	—
40007	Uncooked veal	0.25	Pound	2.15
40008	Standard gravy	1	Serving	0.42
40009	Capers	0.20	Carton	0.80
40010	Lemon sauce	0.050	Bottle	1.15
40011	Cream	0.066	Pint	1.30

(b) BILL OF MATERIALS

Source: John G. Wacker, "Effective Planning and Cost Control for Restaurants," *Production and Inventory Management Journal* (first quarter 1985), pp. 55–69. Reprinted with permission, APICS—The Educational Society for Resource Management.

the availability of *materials* as required to manufacture a product. Later, as the systems evolved to include the planning and control of resources other than materials, such as labor hours, machine hours, tooling, and cash, they became known as MRP-II systems for manufacturing resource planning. Exhibit 19-15 defines some terms common to MRP systems. As you can see, many of these terms can be used in services as well as manufacturing. The next section describes in more detail the use of MRP-II systems in services.

EXHIBIT 19-14   Bill of Labor for Veal Picante

Workcenter	Operation	Labor Type	Labor Hours Set-Up Time	Run Time
1	Assemble dish	Chef	.0069	.0041
2	Cook linguini	Helper one	.0005	.0022
3	Cook veal and sauce	Assistant chef	.0125	.0500
4	Cook veal	Assistant chef	.0125	.0833
5	Prepare sauce	Helper two	.0166	.0833

Source: Adapted from John G. Wacker, "Effective Planning and Cost Control for Restaurants," *Production and Inventory Management Journal* (first quarter 1985), p. 60. Reprinted with permission, APICS—The Educational Society for Resource Management.

MRP-II in the Service Context

Exhibit 19-16 shows how MRP-II logic can be applied to service planning.[3] Referring to the exhibit, the blocks represent plans or schedules at varying levels of detail. The diamonds represent capacity checks to ensure that the resources are available to exe-

EXHIBIT 19-15   Definitions of Terms Used in an MRP Context

Aggregate Production Planning   The planning function of setting the overall level of manufacturing output. Usually stated in broad terms (e.g., product groupings, families of products), its main aim is to establish production rates that will achieve management's objectives (in terms of inventory levels, backlogs, work-force levels, etc.).

Bill of Labor (BOL) or Bill of Resources   A statement of the key resources required to produce an item or service. This can be used to predict the impact of the service (or item) scheduled in the master service (or production) schedule.

Bill of Material (BOM)   A listing of all the parts, components, and raw materials and the quantities required of each that go into an end item or parent assembly.

Dependent Demand   The demand for an item or service when it is directly related to or derived from the demand for other items or services. Dependent demand is calculated from the production plans for parent items.

End Item   An item sold as a completed item (i.e., finished product) or repair part. Any item that is subject to a customer order or sales forecast is an end item.

End Service   A service that is subject to customer orders or sales forecasts. Often, the service that is directly offered to the customer.

Independent Demand   The demand for an item or service when such demand is not related to the demand for other items or services. Independent demand is generated directly by the customers and needs to be forecast.

MRP (Material Requirements Planning)   A set of techniques that uses bills of material, inventory data, and the master production schedule to calculate requirements for materials. It is used to efficiently order and schedule the production of dependent demand inventory items.

MRP-II (Manufacturing Resource Planning)   A set of techniques for the effective planning of all the resources (and capacities) of a manufacturing company. It includes and links a variety of functions: business planning, aggregate production planning, master production scheduling, materials requirements planning (MRP), capacity requirements planning, shop-floor and production activity control, and so on. Output from MRP-II systems can be integrated with financial reports, shipping budgets, and inventory projection in dollars.

Master Production Schedule (MPS)   A statement of what the firm expects to manufacture of end items and service parts. It provides the specific quantities to be produced and dates for producing them.

---

[3] This section is adapted from B. M. Khumawala, C. Hixon, and J. S. Law, "MRP II in the Service Industries," *Production and Inventory Management Journal* (third quarter 1986), pp. 57–63.

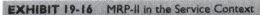

EXHIBIT 19-16 MRP-II in the Service Context

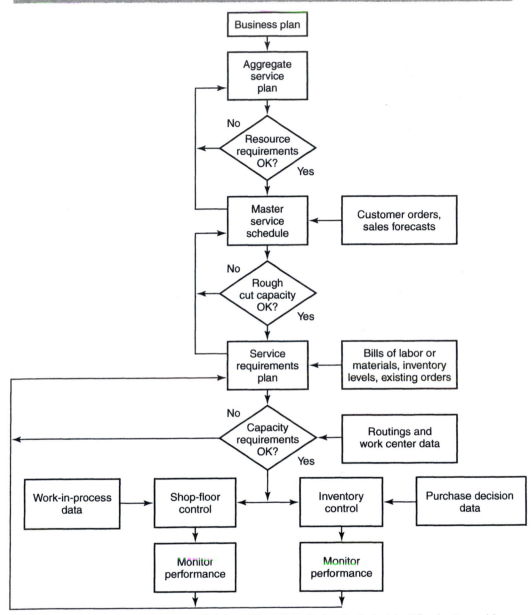

Source: B. M. Khumawala, C. Hixon, and J. S. Law, "MRP-II in the Service Industries," *Production and Inventory Management Journal* (third quarter 1986), pp. 57–63. Reprinted with permission, APICS—The Educational Society for Resource Management.

cute each plan or schedule. Service firms will vary (as do manufacturing firms) in the amount and level of planning for their requirements. Nevertheless, we will discuss all of the planning levels presented in Exhibit 19-16 for completeness.

Business Planning Both long-term resources (e.g., equipment requirements) and short-term resources (e.g., working capital requirements, inventory costs, wages) are considered at this level, together with their corresponding budgets. Units of service are converted to dollars to keep the business plan up-to-date and are integrated with

EXHIBIT 19-17   Alternatives for Absorbing Variations in Demand

To Modify Demand	*To Control Supply*
Vary price—seasonal prices	Specialize tasks during peak demand periods
Vary services offered during peaks and troughs	Vary customer participation
Develop alternative services to shift peaks	Vary available work force
Smooth demand via reservations	Under/overtime
	Hire/fire
	Subcontract

financial reports. Marketing strategies such as industry variables, competitors' actions, and service mix are also considered in developing the business plan.

Aggregate Service Planning   The aggregate service plan is a general plan on how the service organization expects to respond to forecasted demand. It is an overall contract between finance, marketing, and operations, answering questions of what services to provide, how much to provide, and when to provide them. This function should be performed monthly or quarterly and should consider current business conditions along with immediate past company performance. It consists of identifying resources and service rates required to support the business plan in a manner consistent with the overall objectives of the company. These overall objectives include how demand variations are to be absorbed. Exhibit 19-17 shows some alternatives for handling demand variations by modifying demand and/or controlling supply.

Resource Requirements Planning   Resource requirements planning involves establishing long-term overall levels of capacity. Its purpose is to evaluate the aggregate service plan prior to its implementation. To check its impact on key resources, the aggregate service plan is converted to standard cost dollars, man-hours, and/or equipment hours by using service load profiles and bills of resources. Capacity levels or limits are established, measured, and adjusted so that they are consistent with the aggregate service plan.

Master Service Scheduling   The master service schedule (MSS) is a realistic, detailed statement of what the service firm expects to accomplish in terms of services delivered to the customer: what, when, and how many. It is more detailed than the aggregate service plan in terms of timing (hours or days) and the type of service (specifically what the customer has requested).

The master service schedule can vary considerably depending on the type of service. The master schedule is based on *customer orders* if the service can be prepared in advance. However, if demand for the service is immediate, it must be *forecast* for inclusion in the master schedule. For example, a physician uses an appointment calendar as a master schedule. This master schedule includes a number of customer orders (appointments made in advance, such as routine check-ups or nonemergency calls), as well as forecast demand (blocks of time reserved for walk-ins and emergency calls). The master schedule for a beautician would also take the form of an appointment calendar. The master schedule for restaurants may be derived solely from customer orders (when reservations are required), solely from forecast demand (when no reservations are taken), or a combination of the two.

Rough-Cut Capacity Planning   Rough-cut capacity planning (RCCP) involves short-term capacity considerations that are affected by irregularities in demand. It establishes benchmarks for the proper use of personnel, machines, and shifts.

Bills of capacity and bills of labor for *critical* services or resources are the primary inputs to determine rough-cut capacity. From these bills, the capacity requirements for critical work centers are itemized and evaluated. Any work center that cannot produce the desired output within a given time frame because of capacity limitations is highlighted for adjustment. Such adjustments may include increasing capacity, reassigning services to other work centers if possible, and/or rescheduling planned services. If the RCCP shows that the capacity is available, then the numbers in the master service schedule become the set of planning numbers that "drive" the service requirements plan.

Service Requirements Planning   Service requirements planning (SRP) determines the relative importance of services: which services should be performed and when. It uses bills of labor, bills of material, and data on existing orders to convert the master service schedule into requirements for component services. As in MRP, it makes recommendations for service releases and for rescheduling when due dates cannot be met. Specifically, the service requirements plan uses the bill of materials to decide how much of what material is needed to meet the demand contained in the master schedule, and the bill of labor to determine how much of what type of labor is needed to meet the master schedule demand. The SRP will take into account when material is needed and how long it takes to receive the material and generate purchase orders. It will examine when an operation must be completed and how long it takes to complete the operation and generate work schedules for particular service operations.

Capacity Requirements Planning   The SRP generates purchase orders and work schedules sufficient to meet master schedule demand, but it does not consider whether the firm has enough capacity (e.g., workers, space, money) to execute the schedules. The capacity requirements plan (CRP) determines whether labor and other resources exist to accomplish the service requirements plan. Levels of capacity that are consistent with the service plan are established, measured, and adjusted. For services that use appointment calendars to schedule their work, capacity is predefined as the number of "slots" on the calendar and no overloads are typically allowed. Emergency cases can be handled with overtime or by rescheduling existing orders.

Lead times play a major role in CRP. Of the five basic elements of lead time in services (preparation, setup, processing, movement, and queue times), it is queue times that are subject to wide variations. Services are typically more sensitive to lengthy queues than are manufacturing concerns. Thus, most services establish a maximum queue length beyond which they perceive queue time to be excessive. Flexible capacity, such as multiskilled workers, allows resources to be shifted and queues reduced.

Shop-Floor Control   This maintains, evaluates, and communicates data such as work-in-process and actual versus planned service requirements. The foundation for good shop-floor control is realistic planning at higher levels (e.g., the master service schedule).

The basis for shop-floor control is a work-in-process file. This file is created when a planned service commences. It states the plan for all existing service orders, operation by operation, as the customer passes through each service. The scheduled completion time is derived from the service requirements planning process. The *appointment calendar* often serves as a dispatch list, showing customer, service(s) to be performed, required setup times, service times, priorities, and expected completion times. Unsatisfactory services can require rework (i.e., reservicing). This can create additional capacity problems if rework time has not been considered during the planning process.

Uncertainty and MRP-II

Services must often deal with indefinite lead times and uncertain bills of materials. Although some services can be based on a time standard (such as an hourly rate), the completion time of many services is difficult to predict. One reason is that a service may involve an undefined parent service. The customer describes the symptoms, from which the service provider determines the problem that needs service (i.e., the end item). If the symptoms described are incomplete or inaccurate, or if the service provider is not aware of all the possible alternative solutions to the problem, then the wrong bill of labor may be derived and the wrong service performed without the desired end results. For example, if an incorrect diagnosis has been made for a patient or until a diagnosis can be correctly made, the bill of material or labor necessary to support the patient's therapy will be uncertain. In case the patient develops other complications, the BOM/BOL has to change accordingly.

One way to alleviate this problem is to split the desired service into common and optional services. The common services will include those services that are always present in the final service configuration. These can be exploded through the requirements planning process without difficulty. The optional services will vary with the customer needs and must be forecast. For example, an automobile repair shop will offer a tune-up as a service. All the basic tune-up procedures will form the common service. The replacement of faulty parts (parts and labor) discovered during the tune-up will be an optional service because it is not possible to know beforehand what parts will need to be replaced.

Applications of MRP-II

Regardless of how unstructured a service is, planning for the service requirements enhances efficiency and accountability. Requirements planning systems are being used increasingly in many service industries. The list now includes health care, educational, and food services.[4]

Using POM for Windows to Solve Inventory Problems

POM for Windows inventory module can solve the ABC and economic order quantity models discussed in this chapter as well as some others that were not discussed. Exhibit 19-18 illustrates the application of this software to the business forms example that was discussed.

19.8 SUMMARY

Inventory often plays a small role in services because:

1. There may be no finished goods inventory.
2. Input inventory such as office supplies may be minimal.
3. Input materials may be immediately obtained from local suppliers so that lead time is very short (e.g., auto repair parts, food, gasoline).

In other cases, major input inventories may be required.

Service systems utilize input and output inventories to meet predetermined service levels. These inventories represent a cost system that must be managed and con-

[4] See J. G. Wacker, "Effective Planning and Cost Control for Restaurants: Making Resource Requirements Planning Work," *Production and Inventory Management Journal* (first quarter 1985), pp. 55–69; and M. J. Showalter, M. S. Froseth, and M. J. Maxwell, "Production-Inventory Systems Design for Hospital Food Service Operations," *Production and Inventory Management Journal* (second quarter 1984), pp. 67–81.

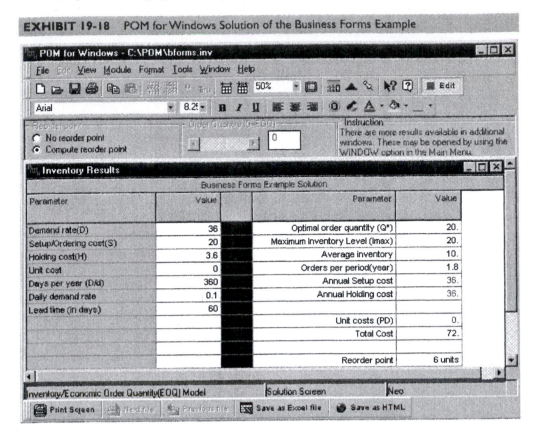

EXHIBIT 19-18 POM for Windows Solution of the Business Forms Example

Business Forms Example Solution

Parameter	Value		Parameter	Value
Demand rate(D)	36		Optimal order quantity (Q*)	20.
Setup/Ordering cost(S)	20		Maximum Inventory Level (Imax)	20.
Holding cost(H)	3.6		Average inventory	10.
Unit cost	0		Orders per period(year)	1.8
Days per year (D/d)	360		Annual Setup cost	36.
Daily demand rate	0.1		Annual Holding cost	36.
Lead time (in days)	60			
			Unit costs (PD)	0.
			Total Cost	72.
			Reorder point	6 units

trolled. Service inventory control systems are classified into two types: independent demand and dependent demand inventory control systems.

Two independent demand inventory control systems have been discussed: they are the fixed-period and the fixed-quantity systems. Other topics addressed include ABC analysis, the EOQ model, and the perishable goods model.

Control of dependent demand inventory items is especially difficult in a service environment, which is characterized by demand variability, on-site production, intermittent processing, low volume requirements, indefinite lead times, and uncertain bills of labor. Concepts derived from manufacturing resource planning (MRP-II) systems, used for similar situations in manufacturing, can be used to control dependent demand inventory items. Effective implementation of MRP-II logic to service industries can contribute to reduced inventory and improved customer service.

Discussion Questions

1. With the advent of low-cost computing, do you see options for the ABC classification method for service inventory items?
2. What are the main reasons for a service organization to have inventory?
3. What is the difference between independent and dependent demand?
4. Describe the costs associated with ordering and maintaining inventory.
5. How can MRP-II be applied to service inventory management?
6. What are the various functions of the master service schedule?
7. What are the problems associated with inventory planning in a service environment?

Problems

19.1. Develop the equation for the optimal number of orders per year. Use the symbols developed in this chapter. You should use the following steps.
   a. Determine the annual carrying cost.
   b. Determine the annual ordering cost.
   c. Set the annual ordering cost equal to the annual carrying cost.
   d. Solve for the optimal number of orders per year.

19.2. Develop the equation for the optimal number of days between orders. Use the same variables that are used in this chapter and the following steps.
   a. Determine the annual carrying cost.
   b. Determine the annual ordering cost.
   c. Set the annual carrying cost equal to the annual ordering cost.
   d. Solve for the optimal number of days between orders.

19.3. Lila Battle has determined that the annual demand for number 6 screws is 100,000 screws. Lila, who works in her brother's hardware store, is in charge of purchasing. She estimates that it costs $10 every time an order is placed. This cost includes her wages, the cost of the forms used in placing the order, and so on. Furthermore, it is estimated that the cost of carrying one screw in inventory for a year is one-half of one cent. How many number 6 screws should Lila order at a time?

19.4. It takes approximately two weeks for an order of number 6 screws to arrive once the order has been placed. (Refer to Problem 19.3) The demand for number 6 screws is fairly constant, and on the average, Lila has observed that her brother's hardware store sells 500 of these screws each day. Since the demand is fairly constant, Lila believes that she can avoid stockouts completely if she only orders the number 6 screws at the correct time. What is the reorder point?

19.5. Lila's brother believes that she places too many orders for screws per year. He believes that an order should be placed only twice per year. If Lila follows her brother's policy, how much more would this cost every year over the ordering policy that she developed in Problem 19.3? If only two orders were placed each year, what effect would this have on the reorder point (ROP)?

19.6. In Problem 19.3 you helped Lila Battle determine the optimal order quantity for number 6 screws. She had estimated that the ordering cost was $10 per order. At this time, though, she believes that this estimate was too low. Although she does not know the exact ordering cost, she believes that it could be as high as $40 per order. How would the optimal order quantity change if the ordering cost were $20, $30, and $40?

19.7. Shoe Shine is a local retail shoe store located on the north side of Centerville. Annual demand for a popular sandal is 500 sandals, and John Dirk, the owner of Shoe Shine, has been in the habit of ordering 100 sandals at a time. John estimates that the ordering cost is $10 per order. The cost of the sandal is $5. For John's ordering policy to be correct, what would the carrying cost as a percentage of the unit cost have to be? If the carrying cost were 10 percent of the cost, what would the optimal order quantity be?

19.8. Pampered Pet, Inc., is a large pet store located in Eastwood Mall. Although the store specializes in dogs, it also sells fish, turtle, and bird supplies. Everlast Leader, which is a leather lead for dogs, costs Pampered Pet $7 each. There is an annual demand for 6,000 Everlast Leaders. The manager of Pampered Pet has determined that the ordering cost is $10 per order, and the carrying cost as a percent of the unit cost is 15 percent. Pampered Pet is now considering a new supplier of Everlast Leaders. Each lead would cost only $6.65, but in order to get this discount, Pampered Pet would have to buy shipments of 3,000 Everlast Leaders at a time. Should Pampered Pet use the new supplier and take this discount for quantity buying?

19.9. Annual demand for the notebook binders at Eck's Stationery Shop is 10,000 units. Mary Eck operates her business 300 days per year and finds that deliveries from her supplier generally take five working days. Calculate the reorder point for the notebook binders that she stocks.

19.10. Your service firm uses a fixed-quantity system where the inventory position of each item is updated after every transaction. The firm operates 52 weeks per year. One of the items has the following characteristics:

Demand D = 19,500 units/year
Ordering cost S = $25/order
Holding cost H = $4/unit/year
Lead time L = 2 weeks

a. Calculate the EOQ for this item.
b. For these policies, what are the annual costs of holding the cycle inventory? Placing the orders?

19.11. Suppose instead that your service firm uses a fixed-period system, but otherwise the data are the same as in Problem 19.10. Calculate the period that gives approximately the same number of orders per year as the EOQ. Round your answer to the nearest week.

19.12. Blank Brothers Funeral Home maintains five models of caskets in its basement warehouse area. The item number or stock keeping unit (called the SKU), annual demand, and cost of each casket is as follows:

SKU	Annual Demand	Cost
234	50	$200
179	10	$200
222	100	$800
410	50	$100
160	15	$200

The funeral director, Alfred Blank, asks his son Reid, who just completed his MBA degree, to complete an ABC analysis. What should Reid report back to his father?

19.13. McKenzie Services is considering using ABC analysis to focus attention on its most critical inventory items. A random sample of twenty items has been taken and the dollar usages have already been calculated as shown below. Rank the items and assign them to an A, B, or C class. On the basis of this sample, does it appear that ABC analysis will help management identify the significant few items?

Item	Dollar Usage	Item	Dollar Usage
1	$ 9,200	11	$ 300
2	400	12	10,400
3	33,400	13	70,800
4	8,100	14	6,800
5	1,100	15	57,900
6	600	16	3,900
7	44,000	17	700
8	900	18	4,800
9	100	19	19,000
10	700	20	15,500

CASES

CASE 19–1   Western Ranchman Outfitters

Western Ranchman Outfitters (WRO) is a family owned and operated mail order and retail store business in Cheyenne, Wyoming. It bills itself as "The Nation's Finest Western Store" and carries high-quality western apparel and riding supplies. Its catalog is mailed all over the world; the store and its president, John Veta, have appeared in a short article in *Fortune* magazine; and clothes from WRO were featured in the August 1980 *Mademoiselle*.

One of WRO's most staple items is the button front, shrink-to-fit blue jean made by Levi Strauss (model no. 501). This is the original riveted denim pant that cowboys shrunk by sitting in a tub of hot water. It is the epitome of durability and fit and is still a popular jean. When Mr. Veta was asked his stockout philosophy for this item, he answered, "Would you expect a drugstore to have aspirin?" Further, Mr. Veta has had a pleasant relationship with Levi Strauss for all the years of his business career.

Don Randell, director of merchandising, takes a physical inventory of this item once a month. His records show annual usage, amount on hand, quantity ordered, and quantity received (which has been averaging 185 pairs per month, except in January–March when it averages 150 pairs per month), all dated by the month. The store attempts to keep a safety stock adequate for 60 days for two reasons: production problems of the supplier and a hedge against unusually large orders.

Mr. Randell described the problems of ordering. "The rag business," as it is known, "is made up of the most disorganzied group of people I've ever had the opportunity to be associated with," according to Randell. The problems he cited include not specifying a delivery date, unexplained late deliveries, a general lack of productivity, and lead times of up to six months.

Randell contrasted this situation with his experience in the flexible packaging industry, where reliability was a hallmark, and a delay of a single day warranted notification to the customer.

The most recent eight-month period is used to illustrate WRO's ordering difficulties. While the sample figures in Exhibit 19-19 may seem peculiar, they reflect WRO's philosophy of offering a full range of sizes and Mr. Randell's attempts to predict Levi Strauss' delivery pattern so that the store is close to obtaining the stock it needs. For example, in the last eight months, no one bought a pair sized 27 × 36. Nevertheless six were ordered and received so that should such a customer appear, he would be able to satisfy his needs. For size 27 × 34, 33 were ordered, but only 21 were received, which is very close to the 18 sold in the eight months of the previous year. The 27-inch and 28-inch waist sizes shown in the exhibit are but two of the many available waist sizes, of course—waist sizes up to 60 inches are produced and sold.

Randell places an order for Levi blue jeans every month, doing his best to ensure an adequate supply for the business. Normally, WRO customers are not disappointed when requesting the Levi 501. However, in the past two months, the Wyoming Game and Fish department has been requiring extra pairs of this jean, and WRO has not always had this exact jean in stock. Since there are at least four styles that satisfy the state requirements, the problem is usually overcome with other styles or brands.

Annual demand at WRO for the Levi 501 is 2,000 pair. The cost of placing an order is about $10, the carrying cost is 12 percent, and the cost of the Levi to WRO is $10.05 per pair. ∎

SOURCE: Sharon Veta Synder, in Barry Render and Ralph M. Stair, *Cases and Readings in Management Science*, 2nd ed. (Boston: Allyn and Bacon, 1990). Used with permission.

CASE QUESTION

Evaluate Randell's ordering policy. How does it compare with formal mathematical approaches?

Size (in inches), Waist × Length	Usage	Number Ordered	Number Received
27 × 28	11	—	—
27 × 29	1	—	—
27 × 30	6	—	—
27 × 31	0	—	—
27 × 32	4	—	—
27 × 33	—	—	—
27 × 34	18	33	21
27 × 36	—	6	6
28 × 28	—	—	—
28 × 29	—	—	—
28 × 30	—	—	—
28 × 31	—	3	3
28 × 32	4	—	—
28 × 33	7	—	—
28 × 34	8	21	12
28 × 36	27	30	18
	86	93	60[a]

EXHIBIT 19-19 Usage and Ordering of the Levi 501 for Selected Sizes

[a] Approximately 65 percent of the number ordered were received.

CASE 19–2   Touro Infirmary

Touro Infirmary is a medium-sized teaching hospital located in New Orleans. The department of dietetics must meet the varying needs for the feeding of patients, staff, and visitors of the facility. The nutritional requirements of the patients are diverse, necessitating a complex menu structure. Diet options include sodium-restricted, bland, calorie-restricted, and numerous other regimes.

The bed capacity for the institution is 500, indicating a maximum of approximately 1,500 meals daily. Since Touro has a large number of Jewish patients, a unique demand is the frequent serving of kosher food. Kosher food must be prepared and served in accordance with strict religious rules. For example, the food must be blessed by a rabbi and prepared with equipment that is used exclusively for kosher products. Additionally, there are restrictions placed upon the food combinations that can be offered in a kosher meal and certain types of meats and fishes may not be served.

Approximately 1,825 kosher meals are served to Touro patients over a one-year period. Because the hospital cannot prepare these meals in its kitchens, all kosher meals are ordered from Schreiber Foods in New York, and are shipped by air mail. The cost per dinner is $3.50. If more than 150 dinners are ordered at once, the price is reduced to $3.25 per dinner. The order is placed by telephone and shipment can be expected to be received in three working days. The cost of placing an order is $10. It is estimated that carrying costs are 25 percent of the meal cost; the many additional requirements of religious laws, including special silverware, are part of the reason for this high cost.

A problem arises when a patient orders a kosher meal and the hospital has run out of stock. An alternative source is available in New Orleans but at a premium of $10. Another unusual problem is storage. A separate freezer must be used to store the kosher food. The present freezer has a capacity of 75 dinners. Patton Industries offers a commercial freezer that has a capacity of 225 dinners. The cost of the freezer is $1,800 and it has a useful life of ten years.

The head of the dietary department, Mrs. Kathy Fedorko, has requested an inventory analysis to determine a method for inventory control that will minimize costs. ∎

SOURCE: John J. Fedorko, in Barry Render and Ralph M. Stair, *Cases and Readings in Management Science*, 2nd ed. (Boston: Allyn and Bacon, 1990). Used with permission.

CASE QUESTIONS

1. What is the optimal amount to be ordered and how often? At what point should the hospital reorder?
2. Besides quantitative methods to determine proper inventory control, what other considerations should be taken into account? Is there an alternative method that will minimize costs?
3. Should the hospital purchase the larger freezer?

References

Aft, L. S., *Production and Inventory Control* (Orlando, FL, Harcourt, 1987).

Chase, R. B., N. J. Aquilano, and F. R. Jacobs, *Production and Operations Management*, 8th ed. (Irwin McGraw Hill, 1998).

Fogarty, D. W., and T. R. Hoffman, *Production and Inventory Management* (West Chicago, South Western Publishing Company, 1983).

Heizer, J., and B. Render, *Operations Management*, 5th ed. (Upper Saddle River, NJ, Prentice Hall, 1999).

Khumawala, B. M., C. Hixon, and J. S. Law, "MRP-II in the Service Industries," *Production and Inventory Management* (third quarter 1986), pp. 57–63.

Krajewski, L. J., and L. P. Ritzman, *Operations Management: Strategy and Analysis*, 5th ed. (Reading, MA, Addison-Wesley, 1999).

Orlicky, J., *Material Requirements Planning* (New York, McGraw-Hill, 1975).

Showalter, M. J., M. S. Froseth, and M. J. Maxwell, "Production-Inventory Systems Design for Hospital Food Service Operations," *Production and Inventory Management* (second quarter 1984), pp. 67–81.

Steinberg, E., B. Khumawala, and R. Scamell, "Requirements Planning Systems in the Health Care Environment," *Journal of Operations Management*, vol. 2, no. 4 (August 1982), pp. 251–259.

Vollmann, T. E., W. L. Berry, and D. C. Whybark, *Manufacturing Planning and Control Systems* (Homewood, IL, Irwin, 1988).

Wacker, J. G., "Effective Planning and Cost Control for Restaurants: Making Resource Requirements Planning Work," *Production and Inventory Management* (first quarter 1985), pp. 55–69.

Wallace, T. V. (ed.), *APICS Dictionary,* 5th ed. (Falls Church, VA, American Production and Inventory Control Society, 1986).

APPENDIX

Areas under the Standard Normal Curve

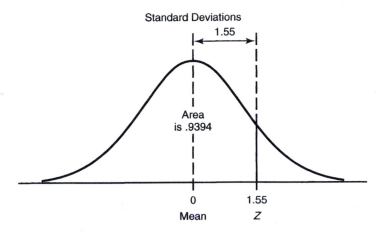

Example of a One-Tail Test. To find the area under the normal curve, you must know how many standard deviations that point is to the right of the mean. Then the area under the normal curve can be read directly from the normal table. For example, the total area under the normal curve for a point that is 1.55 standard deviations to the right of the mean is 0.9394.

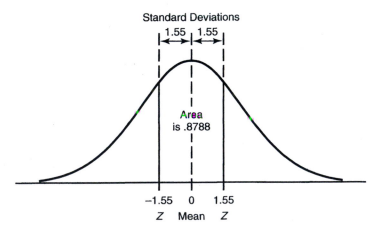

Example of a Two-Tail Test. For some problems, you may want to find the area under the normal curve between two tails (e.g., when the problem states ± a certain number of standard deviations). Then, additional calculations are required. For example, the total area under the normal curve for a point that is 1.55 standard deviations to the right of the mean *and* − 1.55 standard deviations to the left of the mean is

$$1.0 - [(1.0 - .9394) \times 2] = .8788$$

z	.00	.01	.02	.03	.04	.05	.06	.07	.08	.09
.0	.5000	.5040	.5080	.5120	.5160	.5199	.5239	.5279	.5319	.5359
.1	.5398	.5438	.5478	.5517	.5557	.5596	.5636	.5675	.5714	.5753
.2	.5793	.5832	.5871	.5910	.5948	.5987	.6026	.6064	.6103	.6141
.3	.6179	.6217	.6255	.6293	.6331	.6368	.6406	.6443	.6480	.6517
.4	.6554	.6591	.6628	.6664	.6700	.6736	.6772	.6808	.6844	.6879
.5	.6915	.6950	.6985	.7019	.7054	.7088	.7123	.7157	.7190	.7224
.6	.7257	.7291	.7324	.7357	.7389	.7422	.7454	.7486	.7517	.7549
.7	.7580	.7611	.7642	.7673	.7704	.7734	.7764	.7794	.7823	.7852
.8	.7881	.7910	.7939	.7967	.7995	.8023	.8051	.8078	.8106	.8133
.9	.8159	.8186	.8212	.8238	.8264	.8289	.8315	.8340	.8365	.8389
1.0	.8413	.8438	.8461	.8485	.8508	.8531	.8554	.8577	.8599	.8621
1.1	.8643	.8665	.8686	.8708	.8729	.8749	.8770	.8790	.8810	.8830
1.2	.8849	.8869	.8888	.8907	.8925	.8944	.8962	.8980	.8997	.9015
1.3	.9032	.9049	.9066	.9082	.9099	.9115	.9131	.9147	.9162	.9177
1.4	.9192	.9207	.9222	.9236	.9251	.9265	.9279	.9292	.9306	.9319
1.5	.9332	.9345	.9357	.9370	.9382	.9394	.9406	.9418	.9429	.9441
1.6	.9452	.9463	.9474	.9484	.9495	.9505	.9515	.9525	.9535	.9545
1.7	.9554	.9564	.9573	.9582	.9591	.9599	.9608	.9616	.9625	.9633
1.8	.9641	.9649	.9656	.9664	.9671	.9678	.9686	.9693	.9699	.9706
1.9	.9713	.9719	.9726	.9732	.9738	.9744	.9750	.9756	.9761	.9767
2.0	.9772	.9778	.9783	.9788	.9793	.9798	.9803	.9808	.9812	.9817
2.1	.9821	.9826	.9830	.9834	.9838	.9842	9846	.9850	.9854	.9857
2.2	.9861	.9864	.9868	.9871	.9875	.9878	.9881	.9884	.9887	.9890
2.3	.9893	.9896	.9898	.9901	.9904	.9906	.9909	.9911	.9913	.9916
2.4	.9918	.9920	.9922	.9925	.9927	.9929	.9931	.9932	.9934	.9936
2.5	.9938	.9940	.9941	.9943	.9945	.9946	.9948	.9949	.9951	.9952
2.6	.9953	.9955	.9956	.9957	.9959	.9960	.9961	.9962	.9963	.9964
2.7	.9965	.9966	.9967	.9968	.9969	.9970	.9971	.9972	.9973	.9974
2.8	.9974	.9975	.9976	.9977	.9977	.9978	.9979	.9979	.9980	.9981
2.9	.9981	.9982	.9982	.9983	.9984	.9984	.9985	.9985	.9986	.9986
3.0	.9987	.9987	.9987	.9988	.9988	.9989	.9989	.9989	.9990	.9990
3.1	.9990	.9991	.9991	.9991	.9992	.9992	.9992	.9992	.9993	.9993
3.2	.9993	.9993	.9994	.9994	.9994	.9994	.9994	.9995	.9995	.9995
3.3	.9995	.9995	.9995	.9996	.9996	.9996	.9996	.9996	.9996	.9997
3.4	.9997	.9997	.9997	.9997	.9997	.9997	.9997	.9997	.9997	.9998

Source: Adapted from John Neter, William Wasserman, and G. A. Whitmore, *Applied Statistics*, 3rd ed. Copyright © 1988 by Allyn and Bacon.

Index

Note: Numbers in *italic* indicate material in exhibits.